A Frequency Dictionary of Persian

A Frequency Dictionary of Persian is an invaluable tool for all learners of Persian, providing a list of the 5,000 most frequently used words in the language.

Based on a 150 million word corpus of written and spoken Persian texts from the Iranian world, the *Dictionary* provides the user with a detailed frequency-based list, plus alphabetical and part-of-speech indices. All entries feature the English equivalent, and an example of use in context. The *Dictionary* also features thematically-based lists of frequently used words on a variety of topics. Also featured are some grammatically-oriented lists, such as simple verbs and light verb constructions, and comparisons of different ways of expressing the months of the year.

The *Dictionary* provides a rich resource for language teaching and curriculum design, while a separate CD version provides the full text in a tab-delimited format ideally suited for use by corpus and computational linguists.

A Frequency Dictionary of Persian enables students of all levels to build on their study of Persian in an efficient and engaging way.

Corey Miller is a Lead Computational Linguist at MITRE Corporation, Virginia, USA.

Karineh Aghajanian-Stewart is a Senior Faculty Research Specialist at the Center for Advanced Study of Language, University of Maryland, USA.

Routledge Frequency Dictionaries

General Editors

Paul Rayson, *Lancaster University, UK*

Mark Davies, *Brigham Young University, USA*

Editorial Board

Michael Barlow, *University of Auckland, New Zealand*

Geoffrey Leech, *Lancaster University, UK*

Barbara Lewandowska-Tomaszczyk, *University of Lodz, Poland*

Josef Schmied, *Chemnitz University of Technology, Germany*

Andrew Wilson, *Lancaster University, UK*

Adam Kilgarriff, *Lexicography MasterClass Ltd and University of Sussex, UK*

Hongying Tao, *University of California at Los Angeles*

Chris Tribble, *King's College London, UK*

Other books in the series

A Frequency Dictionary of Arabic

A Frequency Dictionary of Czech

A Frequency Dictionary of Contemporary American English

A Frequency Dictionary of Dutch

A Frequency Dictionary of German

A Frequency Dictionary of French

A Frequency Dictionary of German

A Frequency Dictionary of Japanese

A Frequency Dictionary of Korean

A Frequency Dictionary of Mandarin Chinese

A Frequency Dictionary of Persian

A Frequency Dictionary of Portuguese

A Frequency Dictionary of Russian

A Frequency Dictionary of Spanish

A Frequency Dictionary
of Persian

Core Vocabulary for Learners

Corey Miller and Karineh Aghajanian-Stewart

With the assistance of

Aric Bills
Ryan Corbett
Jack Diaz
Ewa Golonka
Evan Jones
Jace Livingston
Shahla Mostafavi
Peter Osthus
Joseph Ritch
Dustin Stewart
Rachel Strong
Thomas Triebwasser
Mark Vinson
David Zajic

Routledge
Taylor & Francis Group

LONDON AND NEW YORK

First published 2018
by Routledge
2 Park Square, Milton Park, Abingdon, Oxon OX14 4RN

and by Routledge
711 Third Avenue, New York, NY 10017

Routledge is an imprint of the Taylor & Francis Group, an informa business

British Library Cataloguing-in-Publication Data
A catalogue record for this book is available from the British Library

Library of Congress Cataloging-in-Publication Data
Names: Miller, Corey (Corey Andrew) author. I Aghajanian-Stewart, Karineh author.
Title: A frequency dictionary of Persian : core vocabulary for learners / Corey Miller
    and Karineh Aghajanian-Stewart with the assistance of [fourteen others].
Description: Milton Park, Abingdon, Oxon ; New York, NY : Routledge, 2017. I
    Series: Routledge frequency dictionaries I Includes bibliographical references
    and indexes.
Identifiers: LCCN 2016049336I ISBN 9781138833234 (hardback : alk. paper) I
    ISBN 9781138833241 (pbk. : alk. paper) I ISBN 9781138833258 (cd-rom) I
    ISBN 9781315735511 (ebook)
Subjects: LCSH: Persian language—Word frequency—Dictionaries.
Classification: LCC PK6385 .M35 2017 I DDC 491/.553—dc23
LC record available at https://lccn.loc.gov/2016049336

ISBN: 978-1-138-83323-4 (hbk)
ISBN: 978-1-138-83324-1 (pbk)
ISBN: 978-1-138-83325-8 (CD)
ISBN: 978-1-315-73551-1 (ebk)

Typeset in TradeGothicLTStd
by Swales & Willis Ltd, Exeter, Devon, UK

Contents

Thematic vocabulary lists

Series preface

Frequency information has a central role to play in learning a language. Nation (1990) showed that the 4,000–5,000 most frequent words account for up to 95% of a written text and the 1,000 most frequent words account for 85% of speech. Although Nation's results were only for English, they do provide clear evidence that, when employing frequency as a general guide for vocabulary learning, it is possible to acquire a lexicon which will serve a learner well most of the time. There are two caveats to bear in mind here. First, counting words is not as straightforward as it might seem. Gardner (2007) highlights the problems that multiple word meanings, the presence of multiword items, and grouping words into families or lemmas have on counting and analyzing words. Second, frequency data contained in frequency dictionaries should never act as the only information source to guide a learner. Frequency information is nonetheless a very good starting point, and one which may produce rapid benefits. It therefore seems rational to prioritize learning the words that you are likely to hear and read most often. That is the philosophy behind this series of dictionaries.

Lists of words and their frequencies have long been available for teachers and learners of language. For example, Thorndike (1921, 1932) and Thorndike and Lorge (1944) produced word-frequency books with counts of word occurrences in texts used in the education of American children. Michael West's *A General Service List of English Words* (1953) was primarily aimed at foreign learners of English. More recently, with the aid of efficient computer software and very large bodies of language data (called corpora), researchers have been able to provide more sophisticated frequency counts from both written text and transcribed speech. One important feature of the resulting frequencies presented in this series is that they are derived from recently collected language data. The earlier lists for English included samples from, for example, Austen's *Pride and Prejudice* and Defoe's *Robinson Crusoe*, thus they could no longer represent present-day language in any sense.

Frequency data derived from a large representative corpus of a language brings students closer to language as it is used in real life as opposed to textbook language (which often distorts the frequencies of features in a language, see Ljung, 1990). The information in these dictionaries is presented in a number of formats to allow users to access the data in different ways. So, for example, if you would prefer not to simply drill down through the word frequency list, but would rather focus on verbs, the part of speech index will allow you to focus on just the most frequent verbs. Given that verbs typically account for 20% of all words in a language, this may be a good strategy. Also, a focus on function words may be equally rewarding – 60% of speech in English is composed of a mere 50 function words. The series also provides information of use to the language teacher. The idea that frequency information may have a role to play in syllabus design is not new (see, for example, Sinclair and Renouf, 1988). However, to date it has been difficult for those teaching languages other than English to use frequency information in syllabus design because of a lack of data.

Frequency information should not be studied to the exclusion of other contextual and situational knowledge about language use and we may even doubt the validity of frequency information derived from large corpora. It is interesting to note that Alderson (2008) found that corpus frequencies may not match a native speaker's intuition about estimates of word frequency and that a set of estimates of word frequencies collected from language experts varied widely. Thus corpus-derived frequencies are still the best current estimate of a word's importance that a learner will come across. Around the time of the construction of the first machine-readable corpora, Halliday (1971: 344) stated that 'a rough indication of frequencies is often just what is needed'. Our aim in this series is to provide as accurate as possible estimates of word frequencies.

Paul Rayson and Mark Davies
Lancaster and Provo, 2008

References

Alderson, J. C. (2008). 'Judging the frequency of English words.' *Applied Linguistics*, 28 (3): 383–409.

Gardner, D. (2007). 'Validating the construct of Word in applied corpus-based vocabulary research: a critical survey.' *Applied Linguistics*, 28: 241–65.

Halliday, M. A. K. (1971). 'Linguistic functions and literary style.' In S. Chatman (ed.) *Style: A Symposium*. Oxford University Press, pp. 330–65.

Ljung, M. (1990). *A Study of TEFL Vocabulary*. Almqvist & Wiksell International, Stockholm.

Nation, I. S. P. (1990). *Teaching and Learning Vocabulary*. Heinle & Heinle, Boston.

Sinclair, J. M. and Renouf, A. (1988). 'A lexical syllabus for language learning.' In R. Carter and M. McCarthy (eds.) *Vocabulary and Language Teaching*. Longman, London, pp. 140–58.

Thorndike, E. (1921). *Teacher's Word Book*. Columbia Teachers College, New York.

Thorndike, E. (1932). *A Teacher's Word Book of 20,000 Words*. Columbia University Press, New York.

Thorndike, E. and Lorge, I. (1944). *The Teacher's Word Book of 30,000 Words*. Columbia University Press, New York.

West, M. (1953). *A General Service List of English Words*. Longman, London.

Acknowledgments

This dictionary would not exist but for Tim Buckwalter's gracious introduction to the series editors and publisher, all of whom we thank for their encouragement and patience. Ewa Golonka's leadership on the original Lexical Learning project at the University of Maryland Center for Advanced Study of Language (CASL) provided the initial impetus for this project. It is hard to characterize the complexity of this enterprise, and we are so grateful to all of those who had a hand in it. Jay Ritch built the software architecture that lasted the test of time and enabled us to ensure accurate counting. Jack Diaz, whom Jay introduced to us, carried the software forward in Jay's absence. Aric Bills kindly pitched in after the original developers had moved on. Pete Osthus built us a concordancer that lasted for years and enabled us to find well-formed and concise sentences peskily buried in our corpus. Ryan Corbett kept us on our toes by ensuring that our statistical interpretations were sound. David Zajic managed an intense effort to make the best use of our spoken corpora. A crackerjack team of Persian experts persevered through seemingly endless stemming overrides and sentence explorations: Evan Jones introduced the pronunciation /ˈkɑnkə-ˌdænsɪŋ/ which helped keep the rest of the core linguistic team, Rachel Strong, Jace Livingston, Mark Vinson and Shahla Mostafavi, motivated and focused on the end goal. Dustin Stewart provided invaluable linguistic support as we neared the finish line. Corey Miller would like to thank Carole Miller for her endless encouragement and ideas for him to make the most of his life and Lixin Yang, for his companionship and the convenience of having to study for the CPA exam during the final summer. He would also like to thank Dan Loehr for his thorough reading of the manuscript and kind supervision. Karineh Aghajanian-Stewart would like to extend her gratitude to her parents Satenick Davidian and Yeprem Aghajanian for their never-ending love, and to her husband Dustin Stewart for his support and encouragement, despite all of the hours she spent away from him on this journey.

The views and opinions expressed in this work are those of the authors and not necessarily those of their employers, MITRE Corporation and the University of Maryland.

Introduction

Purpose

This dictionary is another contribution following the lines established by the volumes of the Routledge Frequency Dictionary series already published, representing one of the less covered, as well as typologically different, languages. It is the first Persian frequency dictionary, based on a balanced selection of both written and spoken language, providing a reliable core vocabulary for learners and all other students of Persian. Note that the Persian language is also known as: Farsi, generally referring to the variety spoken in Iran; Dari, referring to the variety spoken in Afghanistan; and Tajik, referring to the variety spoken in the former Soviet republic of Tajikistan (Spooner 2012). Since Tajik is generally written in the Cyrillic alphabet and shows substantial Russian and Uzbek influence (Perry 2005), it seems problematic to merge its vocabulary with the Iranian and Afghan varieties, and is not treated in this work.

While many excellent grammars, textbooks and dictionaries of Persian exist, there is at present no study in English treating its vocabulary according to frequency. Farhang Moaser's *Kimia* (Emami 2009) is an excellent Persian-English bilingual dictionary containing most of the words frequently encountered, but it is arranged alphabetically and provides no guidance on frequency. Two dictionaries designed for foreign learners organize the vocabulary according to semantic themes: *A Thematic Dictionary of Modern Persian* (Turner 2004) and *Le Persan par les mots et les textes* (Kianvach-Kechavarzi and Simon-Hamidi 2002) in French. Neither provides any guidance as to the relative importance of the included words. Finally, there is a tradition of concordances of literary works, such as Wolff (1935) and Utas (1978), from which frequency can be inferred, but these are necessarily limited to the works they cover.

At present, the Persian language is characterized by somewhat more orthographic variation than is common in the major European languages (Hashabeiky 2005).

Most of this variation revolves around spacing; for example, whether morphemes or words should be space-separated. This naturally puts the onus on the creators of a frequency dictionary to clearly establish the notion of words and to develop reliable methods for tokenizing them in a consistent fashion when deriving vocabularies from corpora.

Corpora

Table I.1 indicates the corpora we have used. They represent a balance between text and speech and cover a variety of genres. We sought to represent both text and speech because Persian exhibits a notably wider gulf (arguably diglossic) between the the language traditionally used in writing ('standard') and that used in speech ('colloquial'), even among educated speakers, than one might encounter in the main varieties of English (Jeremias 1984, Perry 2003). As a kind of bridge between the text sources and the speech sources, we developed an online corpus of blogs. Online material can be referred to as Computer Mediated Communication (CMC), and has been found to represent a kind of middle ground between traditional text and speech (Warschauer 2006).

The Hamshahri Corpus (AleAhmad et al. 2009) covers 11 years of the *Hamshahri* newspaper, published in Tehran. Articles are tagged with 1 of 35 subject categories. The Bijankhan corpus (Oroumchian et al. 2006) is derived from news and common texts, and each article is assigned 1 or more of 168 subject categories. The fiction corpus was built at the University of Maryland and contains over 120 pieces of literature, including contemporary novels, plays and short stories from more than 80 authors, including prominent figures such as Jalal Al-e Ahmad, Houshang Golshiri and Samad Behrangi. The Dari corpus was built at the University of Maryland and contains news, government reports, announcements and speeches as well as books and articles on a variety of academic subjects from Afghan sources. The Blogs corpus was built at the University of Maryland

Table I.1 Persian Corpora

Corpus	Tokens	Types	Modality	Comments
Hamshahri	148,438,042	1,066,204	Text	subject-labeled
Bijankhan	2,409,535	76,540	Text	POS-tagged, subject-labeled
Fiction	1,001,754	61,692	Text	novels, plays and short stories
Dari	1,099,752	65,705	Text	news, government reports, academic articles
Blogs	561,482	63,142	CMC	blogs
LDC CALLFRIEND Farsi	198,098	11,182	Speech	telephone conversations
Raytheon BBN Broadcast Monitoring System (IRINN)	2,783,424	50,712	Speech	speech recognition of television broadcasts
Top 10k				

and contains excerpts from a variety of online blogs covering a range of topics.

The LDC CALLFRIEND corpus (Canavan, Zipperlen & Graff 2014) consists of 60 telephone conversations between native speakers of Persian. Each conversation lasts between 5 and 30 minutes, and was transcribed into Persian orthography by LDC. The Raytheon BBN Broadcast Monitoring System Corpus contains the output of a speech recognition system running over 1 year of Iranian television broadcasts covering a wide variety of topics. It features 2 channels, IRIB (Islamic Republic of Iran Broadcasting) and IRINN (Islamic Republic of Iran News Network). The word error rate for a transcribed portion of the IRINN set ranged between 5–15% per passage, which was substantially better than for IRIB, which has a wider range of programming. We restricted ourselves to the top 10K highest accuracy passages from the IRINN dataset. While the broadcast corpus is based on audio, it covers a range of styles from formal, i.e. more similar to writing, to informal. Further details on the processing of the audio corpus are provided in Miller et al. (2013).

Data Processing

Spelling normalization/Tokenization
There are two main ways in which Persian spelling tends to vary: with respect to spacing of words and morphemes, and with respect to the representation of colloquial speech. Hashabeiky (2005) provides a summary of the issues regarding spacing, which of course impact tokenization. For example, the plural and progressive morphemes can be separated from the stem by space, zero-width non-joiner (ZWNJ) or nothing. For example, the word for 'books', comprised

of the stem كتاب /ketɑb/ and the plural morpheme ها /hɑ/ can be written with space: كتاب ها; with ZWNJ: كتابها; or nothing in between the morphemes: كتابها. To the extent possible, we have normalized these variants using ZWNJ so that space could remain as a true word delimiter. Other spelling variants, for example those involving substitution of a *hamze* seated on *yeh* followed by a *yeh* with two *yehs*, are discussed in Miller (2016). The representation of colloquial speech tends to vary along a continuum of using normal written forms, to using Persian characters to provide a phonetic approximation. For example, the colloquial form of میرود /mirævæd/ 'he goes' is pronounced /mire/ and could be written using the standard form, میرود, or a phonetic approximation, میره. To the extent possible, we have grouped the colloquial forms in the same word families (see next section) as their associated written forms.

Persian uses a modified version of the Arabic alphabet, which does not distinguish between upper- and lowercase, and therefore does not provide an obvious way to identify proper nouns, as in languages using the Roman alphabet. This, in combination with the fact that, as in English, many proper nouns employ the same letters as common nouns, has led us to include proper nouns in our counts just as any other member of the vocabulary. While proper nouns have long been avoided in many standard and frequency dictionaries, perhaps due to their perceived ephemerality or open-endedness, it is our belief that in a dictionary designed for learners of a language such as Persian, it is crucial to include them. Many learners stumble over proper names, even those that are renditions of English places and figures, simply due to the sometimes unexpected modifications that they undergo in transfer to the Persian writing system. For this reason, we hope that their inclusion here will lead to more fluent reading and understanding of Persian on the part of learners.

Multiword expressions

In some cases, space can legitimately delimit words, but the space-separated words may be considered a single lexical unit, as in English *ice cream*. As is the case with many languages, there are a substantial number of such multiword expressions in Persian that can be considered lexicalized and thus warrant counting in a frequency dictionary. In fact, many Persian verbs are expressed by light verb constructions (LVCs) which consist of a verb and a noun or adjective, such as گوش دادن 'to listen', literally 'to give ear'. In many cases, the elements of an LVC are not contiguous, due to the intervention of various possible suffixes and arguments. We have endeavored to include a sample of the most common lexicalized multiword expressions in our counts. To give an English example, in addition to including *ice* and *cream*, we have included *ice cream*. *Ice* and *cream* would only be counted as such when not included in the multiword expression *ice cream*.

We identified the multiword expressions to include by the following procedure. Initially, a list of common multiword expressions was derived from online sources. The corpus was assessed using five collocation metrics: Chi-squared, Pointwise-Mutual Information, Log-likelihood, raw frequency, and the Student-*t* test. The most highly-ranked bigram pairs for each of these methods were analyzed as potential multiword expressions based on their compositionality, presence in monolingual and bilingual dictionaries, and usage in context. The multiword expressions that we chose to count were those that were essentially non-compositional, lexicalized in a dictionary, or used as proper nouns or in LVCs in the encountered contexts.

Word family grouping

We employed the notion of word families for grouping and counting words. This notion has been widely employed in corpus studies of vocabulary (Schmitt, Jiang and Grabe 2011, Nation 2006) and in some studies has been ascribed psychological reality (Nagy et al. 1989). According to Bauer and Nation (2003), 'a word family consists of a base word and all its derived and inflected forms that can be understood by a learner without having to learn each form separately'.

They proceed to elaborate 7 levels of word family relationships using English examples, each one including all lower levels, where at Level 1 each word form is a separate word (types), at Level 2 word forms of a given lexeme/lemma are considered together, and at Level 3 word forms with 'the most frequent and regular derivational affixes' are included (e.g. *-able, -er, -ish, -less, -ly, -ness*). The higher levels include affixes of either diminishing regularity or frequency, culminating in Level 7, which groups together words sharing 'classical roots and affixes', for which in the Persian context words sharing Arabic roots could be considered an analogue.

We had initially planned to include in one entry word families consisting of Levels 1–3, including both standard and transparently related colloquial variants, as well as other spelling variants, of any of the word forms comprising a word family (Miller 2016). This, of course, casts a wider net than the lemma, usually understood to include inflected forms alone (Bauer and Nation's Level 2), which has generally been used in the other Routledge Frequency Dictionaries. While this procedure would have allowed us to avoid difficult disambiguation of certain homographs, to be described below, we ultimately found that it inhibited our ability to gain counts of important words. Therefore, we returned to a traditional lemmatic grouping, including spelling variants and cliticized forms, with the addition of grouping standard and colloquial forms together.

For example, the following words are considered within the word family for رفتن /ræftæn/ 'to go': می‌رود /mirævæd/ 'he/she/it goes' (ZWNJ spelling); میرود /mirævæd/ 'he/she/it goes' (connected spelling); میره /mire/ 'he/she/it goes (colloquial); رفت /ræft/ 'he/she/it went', بروم /berævæm/ 'I go' (subjunctive); برم /beræm/ 'I go' (subjunctive, colloquial); رفتنش /ræftæneʃ/ 'his going' (cliticized); etc.

As an example of the homograph problem, the ی /ye/ suffix in Persian has multiple uses: it can turn a noun into an adjective; it can turn a concrete noun into an abstract noun; it can essentially case-mark a noun or adjective as a member of an *ezafe* construction; it can signal the antecedent of a relative clause; or it can make a noun indefinite. For example, from the noun مرد /mærd/ 'man', we can form the word مردی /mærdi/, which could mean 'a man' or 'manliness', and from the noun کتاب /ketab/ 'book', we can form the word کتابی /ketabi/, which could mean 'a book' or 'bookish'. In such cases, we had originally felt it would be more useful to the dictionary-user to include مردی /mærdi/ and کتابی /ketabi/ in the counts for the same entry as مرد /mærd/ and کتاب /ketab/, respectively, rather than to try and disambiguate between the inflected and derived forms, since the meanings of the derived forms are straightforward. However, such a procedure would have prevented us from counting words like ماهی /mahi/ 'fish' or صورتی /suræti/ 'pink', since they would have been part of the ماه /mah/ 'month' and صورت /suræt/ 'face' word families, respectively. While we feel it is useful to the learner to be aware of such words, one disadvantage of our approach is the potentially artificial boosting in frequency of certain homographs. For example, کرد /kord/ 'Kurd' shares an orthographic form with کرد /kærd/ 'he/she/it did' which would normally be part of the کردن /kærdæn/ 'do' word family. So we gain by having کرد /kord/ 'Kurd' in our dictionary, but we suffer from its inflated frequency, likely due to the presence of /kærd/ 'he/she/it did'. While the kind of word sense disambiguation that would be required to distinguish such senses has been explored for Persian (Rezapour et al. 2014), it was deemed to be beyond the scope of our project.

In order to perform word family grouping, we employed a pipeline consisting of an override file, a Persian morphological analyzer developed at the University of Maryland, and a Persian stemmer, *Perstem*, developed by Jon Dehdari (described in Jadidinejad et al. 2010), which was modified for our purposes. Words that had been found to be misanalyzed by the analyzer and stemmer were handled in the override file. While the analyzer had good accuracy, its use was limited by the requirement that it could only analyze words in its lexicon. The stemmer was useful for the remaining words, but would on occasion mistake beginning and ending letters of a word as morphological prefixes and suffixes. This process is described in more detail in Miller (2016).

The word form used to represent each word family follows traditional conventions for citation forms in Persian dictionaries; for example, singular nouns and infinitive (*masdar*) verbs. In cases where multiple spelling variants, and possibly standard and colloquial forms, were counted together, we chose the spelling of the standard form preferred by Sadeghi and Moghaddam (2013).

Frequency calculations

We followed the procedure outlined in Londsdale and Le Bras (2009) in Routledge's *A Frequency Dictionary of French*. In order to address the problems with raw frequency discussed by Gries (2008), we employed the DP ('deviation of proportions') metric to assess the dispersion of words across corpora. The result is a measure between 0 and 1, where 0 means the word is evenly distributed and 1 means it is narrowly restricted. In our case, we combined all the members of a given word family for calculating raw frequency and DP. In order to rank words by frequency, taking their dispersion thus calculated into account, we divided the raw frequency of each word family by its DP, in what we will call a 'dispersion-adjusted frequency'. In order to provide a sense of the range of word families within the corpus, the DP has been converted into a dispersion or range code, by using the following exponential function: $100*exp^{-DP}$. This has resulted in a set of integers between 38 and 97, where values approaching 100 were evenly distributed throughout the corpus, and values below 70 were limited to narrower portions of the corpus.

Developing associated information

Alongside the headword for each entry, representing its word family, we also provide the pronunciation of the headword in the International Phonetic Alphabet (IPA), reflecting the common Iranian pronunciation of the word. Due to the fact that the Persian alphabet does not represent short vowels, and that even long vowels such as و may be pronounced /ow/ or /u/, we felt it crucial to provide learners with a pronunciation guide. An alternative for indicating pronunciation, the use of the Arabic vowel diacritics, was rejected, due to its inherent ambiguity when representing Persian pronunciation. The pronunciation has been created by consulting sources such as *Kimia* (Emami 2009) and Deyhim (2008), a pronunciation dictionary based on a survey of educated speakers. As in any language, Persian is subject to both dialectal and sociolinguistic variation with respect to pronunciation, especially in the rendering of diphthongs, glottal stop, and some vowels and consonants. For this reason, the pronunciation provided should be considered as a general guideline, and learners should seek out and follow native speaker models as appropriate in both refining their own pronunciation and their ability to understand the variation associated with particular words.

Each headword is also associated with the set of parts of speech represented by the members of its word family as indicated in the Bijankhan corpus (Oroumchian et al. 2006), which was hand-tagged for part of speech. In the case of word families unrepresented in Bijankhan, and multiword expressions, identified by the procedure described above, part of speech information was provided by hand.

One or more glosses for each headword was provided by hand, by consulting a set of common Persian-English bilingual dictionaries. The glosses are not meant to be exhaustive, and an attempt was simply made to provide a general guide. Learners are advised to consult standard print and online dictionaries and encyclopedic information (such as *Wikipedia*) in order to get a fuller picture of individual words.

An example sentence of the use of a member of each headword's word family is provided for each headword. Such sentences were pulled from the corpus by means of a concordancer specially developed for the project. These sentences are intended to provide the user with one example of how the given word family may be used. Each of these sentences has been translated into idiomatic English. For this reason, users should not be surprised if there is not an exact match between a given gloss and the representation of the headword in the English sentence translation.

A set of thematic word lists was constructed along the lines established in the Routledge frequency dictionary series. Membership of a given word family in such thematic lists was assigned by hand, by consulting other dictionaries in the series, as well as intuition and Turner (2004). Note that a larger frequency list, including the 20,000 most frequent words as established by our counting methods, was consulted for the creation of the thematic lists.

The main frequency index

This is the main portion of the book and includes the 5,000 most frequently occurring Persian words in the corpus, in descending dispersion-adjusted frequency order. Each entry consists of the following information:

Ranked score (1, 2, 3 . . .), headword, pronunciation, gloss, part of speech, sample context, English translation of sample context, dispersion value, raw frequency total.

For example, here is the entry for the word رفتن /ræftæn/ 'go':

---

128 رفتن ræftæn *go* adj,n,v
- با آن پسر رفت بيرون چند مرتبه — She went out with that guy several times
71 | 20988

This indicates that this word family is the 128th most frequent of the 5,000 families in the book. Since it is a verb, it is given in the infinitive (*masdar*) form, and the pronunciation of that form is given in IPA. The set of parts of speech included in the word family is given in alphabetical order: adj for adjective; n for noun; and v for verb (full set of part of speech abbreviations is provided below). One may reasonably ask why adjective and noun are listed for this word family. Note that the past participle, رفته /ræfte/ '(having) gone' is part of the word family and may serve as an adjective. The so-called infinitive can function as a gerund, or noun, as in رفتنش /ræftæneʃ/ 'his going'. Next comes the dispersion code, described above, whose value of 71 in this case indicates that the word is well-distributed throughout the corpus. Finally, the raw frequency value, 20988, indicates the number of total word family members associated with this headword that were counted in the corpus.

When a given headword has more than one major sense all pronounced the same, the senses are provided in the gloss field separated by comma, for example شير /ʃir/ 'milk, lion'. When a headword has more than one pronunciation, and a single sense associated with each pronunciation, both the pronunciations and glosses are separated by an equal number of commas, for example نه /næ, noh/ 'no, nine', which means that the first pronunciation, /næ/, is associated with the first gloss, 'no', and the second pronunciation, /noh/, is associated with the second gloss, 'nine'. When there is more than one pronunciation, and a larger number of glosses, the slash (/) is used to separate glosses having the same pronunciation, resulting in an equal number of commas separating both pronunciations and glosses.

For example, گل /gol, gel/ 'flower/goal, mud' means that 'flower' and 'goal' share the first pronunciation /gol/, and 'mud' is associated with the second pronunciation, /gel/.

The full set of part of speech abbreviations are as follows:

Abbreviation	Part of speech
adj	adjective
adv	adverb
conj	conjunction
n	noun
prep	preposition
pron	pronoun
pn	proper noun
q	quantifier
v	verb

Callout boxes

Interspersed throughout the main frequency index there are a set of callout boxes containing thematic groups of words, constructed as described above. These cover a set of semantic and linguistic groupings. Note that glosses and pronunciations in callout boxes may differ from those in the main list, in order to highlight the relevant senses.

Alphabetic and part of speech indices

The alphabetic index lists headwords in alphabetical order. For each word, the headword is accompanied by its pronunciation, gloss, part of speech, and rank in the main frequency index. The part of speech index lists each part of speech followed by the word families containing that part of speech in decreasing frequency rank order. Each entry in the part of speech index contains its rank, headword, pronunciation and gloss. Note that glosses and pronunciations in indices may differ from those in the main list, in order to highlight the relevant senses for the given parts of speech.

References

AleAhmad, Abolfazl, Amiri, Hadi, Rahgozar, Masoud, and Oroumchian, Farhad (2009) 'Hamshahri: A standard Persian text collection', *Journal of Knowledge-Based Systems*, 22 (5), 382–387.

Bauer, Laurie and Nation, Paul (1993) 'Word families', *International Journal of Lexicography* 6(4): 253–279.

Buckwalter, Tim, and Parkinson, Dilworth (2011) *A Frequency Dictionary of Arabic*. London: Routledge.

Canavan, Alexandra, Zipperlen, George and Graff, David (2014) *CALLFRIEND Farsi Second Edition Speech*. Philadelphia: Linguistic Data Consortium.

Deyhim, Guiti (2008) *Persian Pronunciation Dictionary*. Tehran: Fahrang Moaser Publishers.

Emami, Karim (2009) *Kimia Persian-English Dictionary*. Tehran: Farhang Moaser Publishers.

Gries, Stefan Th. (2008) 'Dispersions and Adjusted Frequencies in Corpora', *International Journal of Corpus Linguistics*, 13(4): 403–437.

Hashabeiky, Forogh (2005) *Persian Orthography*. Uppsala: Uppsala University.

Jadidinejad, Amir H., Mahmoudi, Fariborz, and Dehdari, Jon (2010) 'Evaluation of Perstem: A simple and efficient stemming algorithm for Persian', *Multilingual Information Access Evaluation I Text Retrieval Experiments: Lecture Notes in Computer Science* 6241: 98–101.

Jeremias, Eva (1984) 'Persian Diglossia', *Acta Linguistica Academiae Scientiarum Hungaricae* 34: 271–287.

Kianvach-Kechavarzi, Monireh and Simon-Hamidi, Brigitte (2002) *Le Persan par les mots et les textes*. Paris: L'Asiathèque.

Lonsdale, Deryle, and Le Bras, Yvon (2009) *A Frequency Dictionary of French*. London: Routledge.

Miller, Corey, Brugman, Claudia, Corbett, Ryan, Golonka, Ewa, Livingston, Jace, Ritch, Joseph, Strong, Rachel and Zajic, David (2012) 'Methodology for selecting words for instructional use: High-frequency and topic-specific vocabulary list of Persian-Farsi', Technical Report, University of Maryland Center for Advanced Study of Language.

Miller, Corey, Corbett, Ryan, Diaz, Jack, Livingston, Jace, Ritch, Joseph, Strong, Rachel and Zajic, David (2013) 'Construction of a Persian Corpus from Spoken Material', Technical Report, University of Maryland Center for Advanced Study of Language.

Miller, Corey (2016) 'Theoretical Issues in Counting Persian Words', *Cahiers de Studia Iranica* 58: 113–133.

Nagy, William, Anderson, Richard C., Schommer, Marlene, Scott, Judith Ann and Stallman, Anne C. (1989) 'Morphological Families in the Internal Lexicon', *Reading Research Quarterly* (24)3: 262–282.

Nation, I.S.P. (2006) 'How Large a Vocabulary is Needed for Reading and Listening?', *The Canadian Modern Language Review* (63)1: 59–82.

Oroumchian, Farhad, Tasharofi, Samira, Amiri, Hadi, Hojjat, Hossein and Raja, Fahimeh (2006) 'Creating a feasible corpus for Persian POS tagging', Technical Report, no. TR 3/2006, University of Wollongong in Dubai.

Perry, John R. (2003) 'Persian as a Homoglossic Language', *Cahiers de Studia Iranica* 27: 11–28.

Perry, John R. (2005) *A Tajik Persian Reference Grammar*. Leiden: Brill.

Pilevar, Mohammad T., Faili, Heshaam, Pilevar, Abdol H. (2011) 'TEP: Tehran English-Persian Parallel Corpus', *Computational Linguistics and Intelligent Text Processing: Lecture Notes in Computer Science* 6609: 68–79.

Rezapour, Abdoreza, Fakhrahmad, Seyed Mostafa, Sadreddini, Mohammad Hadi and Jahromi, Mansoor Zolghadri (2014) 'An Accurate Word Sense Disambiguation System based on Weighted Lexical Features', Literary & Linguistic Computing 29(1): 74–88.

Sadeghi, Ali Ashraf and Moghaddam, Zahra Zandi (2013) *A Dictionary of Persian Orthography and Spelling*. Tehran: Academy of Persian Language and Literature.

Schmitt, Norbert, Jiang, Xiangying, and Grabe, William (2011) 'The Percentage of Words Known in a Text and Reading Comprehension', *The Modern Language Journal* (95)i: 26–43.

Spooner, Brian (2012) 'Persian, Farsi, Dari, Tajiki: Language Names and Language Policies', in Schiffman, H. (ed.) *Language Policy and Language Conflict in Afghanistan and its Neighbors*. Leiden: Brill.

Turner, Colin (2004) *A Thematic Dictionary of Modern Persian*. London: RoutledgeCurzon.

Utas, Bo (1978) *A Persian Sufi poem: vocabulary and terminology*. London: Curzon Press.

Wolff, Fritz (1935) *Glossar zu Firdosis Schahname*. Berlin: Deutsche Morgenländische Gesellschaft.

Warschauer, Mark (2006) *Laptops and Literacy: Learning in the Wireless Classroom*. New York: Teachers College Press.

Frequency index

1 و vav, væ *and* conj
- این پسر بچه با پدرش تنها زندگی می‌کرد و رابطه ویژه ای بین آن دو وجود داشت. — This boy lived alone with his father and a special relationship existed between the two.
96 | 533712

2 بودن budæn *be* v
- پیمان خسته است. — Payman is tired.
97 | 322841

3 از æz *from* prep
- از بچه ها نگهداری میکنند. — They look after the children.
97 | 258065

4 به be *to* prep
- به من دروغ نگو. — Don't lie to me.
97 | 306826

5 که ke *which, that* conj
- بنظر می آید که شلوغتر از جاهای دیگه است. — It seems that it's more crowded than other places.
95 | 225140

6 این in *this, it* pron
- این شماره تلفن عوض شده. — This telephone number has been changed.
96 | 198860

7 در dær *in* prep
- چند روز در هفته ورزش میکنی؟ — How many days in a week do you exercise?
89 | 301087

8 با ba *with* prep
- میخواهم با مریم صحبت کنم. — I want to speak with Maryam.
95 | 131450

9 شدن ʃodæn *become* adj,v
- سرد شده اینجا. — It has become cold here.
95 | 137218

10 برای bærɑje *for* prep
- دنیا اسباب بازی هایش را برای بچه ها گذاشته است. — Donya has set out her toys for the children.
96 | 65058

11 خود xod *self* pron
- از خود خانم بپرس. — Ask the woman herself.
96 | 54218

12 یک jek *one* n,pron
- یک هفته بیمارستان بودی؟ — You were in the hospital for a week?
94 | 75302

13 آن ɑn *that, Anne* n,pron,pn
- چند شعبه مختلف آن نیز در لس‌آنجلس و شیکاگو قرار دارد. — Some of its different branches are located in Los Angeles and Chicago, too.
92 | 71442

14 خواستن xɑstæn *want* v
- دلش نمی خواست برود. — He didn't want to go.
96 | 35170

15 تا ta *until* prep
- صبرکن تا آخرین لحظه. — Wait until the last moment.
95 | 38737

16 داشتن dɑʃtæn *have* v
- دوتا خواهر دارد. — He has two sisters.
93 | 58525

17 کردن kærdæn *do* adj,n,v
- هر روز از خودم می پرسیدم چه کار کردم که جوابم کرده اند! — Everyday I would ask myself what I did to make them fire me.
92 | 65925

18 کرد kærd, kord *did, Kurd* v
- بسیاری از کردهای ترکیه به استانبول مهاجرت کرده‌اند. — Many of Turkey's Kurds have immigrated to Istanbul.
93 | 40656

19 بایستن bɑjestæn *must* v
- تک تک اینان می بایست اجرا میشد. — Each one of them should have been implemented.
95 | 24037

20 اول ævvæl *first* adj,n
- مرد اول از خدا خانه، لباس و غذای بیشتری خواست. — The first man asked God for more clothing, food, and housing.
97 | 13438

21 بر bær *on, fruit, side* n,prep
- ایزاک نیوتن با افتادن سیبی بر سرش جاذبه را کشف کرد. — Isaac Newton discovered gravity by an apple dropping on his head.

22 سال sɑl *year* n
- بیش از پنج سال اینجا اقامت دارند. — They have more than five years' residency here.
93 | 36047

23 توانستن tævanestæn *be able* n,v
- افراد معمولی هم میتوانند برند. — Regular people can also go.
92 | 27589

24 رسیدن residæn *arrive* adj,n,v
- رسید به سیصد تومن. — It reached three hundred toman.
94 | 19901

25 پس pæs *so, then* adj,conj,n
- پس خودت الان گرسنه ات نیست. — So, you are not hungry now.
96 | 14957

26 هر hær *each* q
- هر جای دنیا هم که باشی این به درد میخورد. — Wherever you may be in the world, this will help you.
93 | 22251

27 کار kɑr *work* n
- کار پیدا کردی؟ — Did you find work?
94 | 18832

28 بیش biʃ *more* adj,adv,q
- معمولا تو از من خیلی بیشتر انگلیسی حرف میزنی. — Usually you speak far more English than I do.
93 | 20504

29 دیگر digær *other, again* adj,adv,conj,pron
- دو نفر دیگر هم استخدام کردند. — They also hired two other people.
89 | 34518

30 روز ruz *day* n
- سه روز دیگه برمیگردند. — They will return in three days.
93 | 20471

31 اما æmma *but* conj
- پول خوبی در میآورند میگوید اما زندگی اهمیت ندارد. — He says they make good money, but life has no importance.
92 | 22938

32 ما mɑ *we* pron
- ما تو فرودگاه همراهش بودیم. — We were with him in the airport.
90 | 30277

33 کشور keʃvær *country* n
- تو هم توی سفارت این کشور نشستی. — You also sat in this country's embassy.
82 | 52853

34 گرفتن gereftæn *take* adj,n,v
- اینرا هم از کتابخانه گرفته بودم. — I had also gotten this from the library.
90 | 24303

35 پیش piʃ *before, forward, by* adj,n
- مربی با یک تلگرام پیش او آمد. — The coach came up to him with a telegram.
95 | 10976

36 هم hæm *both, also* conj,pron
- من هم بهایی هستم. — I am also Baha'i.
80 | 46392

37 گفتن goftæn *say* v
- بابا هم گفت عیب ندارد. — Dad also said it's not a problem.
78 | 50426

38 بزرگ bozorg *large* adj
- نادرشاه رهبران بزرگ شیعه و سنّی را گرد هم آورد. — Nader Shah brought the great Shia and Sunni leaders together.
95 | 9719

39 دو do, dow *two, running* n
- جمعاً ۷۸ آسانسور در این دو ساختمان فعال هستند. — A total of 78 elevators are in use in these two buildings.
87 | 28637

40 شهر ʃæhr *city* n
- با عجله به طرف شهر حرکت کرد. — She hurriedly moved in the direction of the city.
93 | 13281

41 یا jɑ *or* conj
- حدود 40 یا 45 ساله به نظر می رسید. — He seems to be approximately 40 to 45 years old.
90 | 21597

42 دادن dɑdæn *give* n,v
- شماره به من داد. — He gave me a number.
89 | 22600

43 ایران irɑn *Iran* pn
- هر زمان و مکانی که باشید موبایل شما راهنمایتان خواهد بود. — Whenever and wherever you are in Iran, your mobile phone will be your guide.
82 | 36695

44 نیز niz *also* conj
- پیرمرد کمی نوشابه خورد و همسرش نیز از همان لیوان کمی نوشید. — The old man drank a little of the beverage and his wife also drank some from the same glass.
87 | 24057

45 میان miɑn *between* n,prep
- از میان آن کتابها یکی را که به عبارت ساده تر و کلمات و اصطلاحات فنی در آن نسبتاً کمتر بود اختیار کردم. — From among those books I selected one with simpler terms and less technical words and phrases.
95 | 9232

46 صورت suræt *face* n
- دود سیگارش را توی صورت او فوت کرد. — She blew cigarette smoke in his face.
93 12689

47 راه rɑh *way, road* n
- این کشور دارای راه آبی به دریاهای آزاد نیست. — This country does not have a waterway to open waters.
95 | 8208

48 داشته dɑʃte *had, possession* adj,v

• ما می‌توانیم لیست بلند بالایی از داشته‌هامون تهیه کنیم. — We can provide a long list of our possessions.
94 | 10240

49 کند konæd, kond *does, slow* v

• خرس‌های کوالا یکی از کندترین حیوانات جهان هستند. — Koala bears are one of the world's slowest animals.
89 | 17679

50 داده dɑde *given, datum* adj,v

• این داده‌ها را در یک محل واحد جمع کردند. — They collected these data in a single place.
95 | 8564

51 بسیار besjɑr *very* adj,adv,q

• حرف‌های بسیاری هست که باید گفته شود. — There are a lot of words that must be said.
91 | 14140

52 قبل qæbl *before* adj,n

• پدرش را سال‌ها قبل از دست داده بود. — He had lost his father years ago.
96 | 5373

53 مدت moddæt *term, period* n

• در این مدت که همدیگر را ندیده ایم چه کتابی خوانده ای؟ — In this period of time that we haven't seen each other what books have you read?
96 | 5595

54 او u *he, she* pron

• او در سال ۱۸۸۸ پسری به دنیا آورد. — She gave birth to a son in the year 1888.
86 | 22462

55 نظر næzær *opinion* n

• نظر شما در این مورد چیست؟ — What is your opinion on this?
90 | 14467

56 مردم mærdom *people* n

• خیلی از مردم دنباله کار اند. — Many people are looking for work.
86 | 21520

57 تنها tænhɑ *only, lonely* adj,adv

• تنها در داخل دره‌ها امکان سکونت و کشاورزی وجود دارد. — Habitation and agriculture are possible only within the valleys.
95 | 7421

58 همه hæme *every* pron,q

• متأسفانه همه چیز روسی نوشته‌شده. — Unfortunately, everything has been written in Russian.
88 | 15907

59 مهم mohem *important* adj,n

• پاکی از همه چیز مهم‌تر است ! — Purity is the most important thing!
93 | 8903

60 کم kæm *low, little* adj,adv,n,q

• به طور معمول بارندگی در این کشور کم است. — Typically, there is little rainfall in this country.
93 | 9593

61 نزدیک næzdik *close* adj,n

• میز‌ها بسیار بهم نزدیک بودند. — The tables were very close to each other.
97 | 3825

62 عنوان onvɑn *title* n

• می خواستم عرض کنم بهتر نبود عنوان این برنامه را برعکس می کردید. — I wanted to suggest, would it not be better if you switched the title of this program?
89 | 13484

63 مورد mowred *case* n

• این موردش فرق می کند، به شماها ربطی ندارد! — This case is different, it has nothing to do with you.
85 | 18709

64 بین bejn *between* n,prep

• هیچ چیز غیر عادی بین ما رد و بدل نشد. — Nothing out of the ordinary was exchanged between us.
93 | 8405

65 تمام tæmɑm *whole, all* adj,q

• با تمام وجود خوشحال بود. — With all of her being she was happy.
93 | 8119

66 دست dæst *hand* n

• دست خالی به خانه باز نمی گشت. — He wouldn't return home empty-handed.
86 | 17032

67 چند ʧænd *several* n

• طی این سال‌ها فقط چند باری توانسته بود برایشان نامه بنویسد. — In these years he had only been able to write them a few letters.
92 | 9282

68 قرار qærɑr *agreement* n

• قرار شد نامه هایی که برای شما می نویسم به او نشان بدم تا یک نگاهی بکند. — It was decided that I would show him the letters I write for you so that he could take a look.
97 | 3222

69 همین hæmin *the same, this very* pron

• شاید اولین نفری که شهر رو ترک کرد همین گوینده بود. — Perhaps the first person who left the city was this very same speaker.
89 | 12030

70 گروه goruh *group* adj,n,q

• رهبر این گروه موسیقی در زندگی‌نامه خود در این مورد هم صحبت کرده است. — The leader of this musical group has also discussed this in his biography.
88 | 12890

71 برنامه bærnɑme *program, plan* n

• چه برنامه ایی برای آینده داری ؟ — What is your future plan?
89 | 11453

72 بخش bæxʃ *section, part* n,q

● بخش عظیمی از این کهکشان از دیدمان پنهان است. — A large part of this galaxy is hidden from our view.

87 | 13393

73 وجود vodʒud *existence* n

● قبلاً از وجودشان بی‌خبر بودیم. — We were unaware of their existence before.

93 | 7151

74 مسئله mæsʔæle *problem* n,pn

● این مسئله همیشه باعث دردسر می شه. — This issue always causes headaches.

90 | 9970

75 توجه tævædʒdʒoh *attention* n

● توجه دکتر را به خود جلب کرده بود. — He had attracted the doctor's attention to himself.

90 | 9681

76 امر æmr *affair, order* n

● این یک امر عادی است. — This is an ordinary affair.

90 | 10056

77 اگر ægær *if* conj

● اگر زن نبودم و یک «مرد معمولی» بودم، در این جهان «موفق» تر بودم. — If I weren't a woman and were an "ordinary man," I would be more "successful" in this world.

85 | 15182

78 گذشته gozæʃte *past* adj,n

● لیبریا از گذشته‌های دور اهمیت زیادی برای ایالات متحدۀ آمریکا دارد. — Liberia has had great importance to the United States of America since long ago.

90 | 9160

79 ماه mɑh *month, moon* n

● سه روز از آخر ماه می گذرد و هنوز لیست حقوق کارمندان را امضا نکرده است. — It's three days past the end of the month and he still hasn't signed the workers' payroll.

91 | 8815

80 طور towr *manner, way* n

● دولت حل معضل آب را بطور جدی پیگیری می‌کند. — The government is searching for a solution to the water problem in a serious manner.

92 | 7820

81 بدون bedune *without* prep

● بدون مادر نمی توانم زندگی کنم. — I cannot live without mother.

94 | 5390

82 رو ru *on, face* n,prep

● وقتی بسته را باز کرد مامان اولین کسی بود که رو به پدرم جیغ زد. — When she opened the package, Mom was the first person who yelled at Dad.

77 | 23851

83 زمان zæman *time* n

● در زمان‌های قدیم، پادشاهی سه پسر داشت. — In ancient times, a king had three sons.

92 | 7080

84 هیچ hiʧ *none* q

● نیمی از حمله‌های قلبی هیچ علامتی ندارند. — Half of heart attacks have no warning signs.

90 | 8976

85 مشکل moʃkel *problem* adj,n

● او به زودی با مشکل روبرو خواهد شد. — She will soon face problems.

90 | 8907

86 اسلامی eslami *Islamic* adj

● افغانستان یک کشور اسلامی است. — Afghanistan is an Islamic country.

84 | 14627

87 دانستن danestæn *know* v

● با نگرانی منتظر دانستن علت احضارش پابه پا می‌شد. — He paced around, anxiously awaiting to know the reason for his summons.

85 | 14379

88 رئیس ræʔis *head* n

● رئیس موزه لوور به تهران می‌آید. — The Louvre Museum director visits Tehran.

85 | 14200

89 بهتر behtær *better* adj,adv

● بهتر است من بمانم توی خانه، پهلوی بچه‌ها. — It's better for me to stay in the house by the children.

94 | 5683

90 دولت dowlæt *government* n

● این جایزه از طرف دولت اعطا می‌شود. — This award is granted by the government.

82 | 16275

91 جمله dʒomle *sentence, total* n

● یک بار دیگر همین جمله را گفته بود. — He had said this very sentence earlier.

94 | 5402

92 نتیجه nætidʒe *result* n

● برای حصول نتیجه بهتر ممکن است یک روش و یا ترکیبی از روشها بکار گرفته شود. — In order to achieve better results a method or a combination of methods may be used.

91 | 7210

93 آمدن amædæn *come* adj,v

● پسر تازه از ایران آمده بود. — The boy had recently come from Iran.

78 | 18443

94 سو su *side* n

● مسئولان نظامی ناتو از یک سو اعتراف کردند که شهر کبیسه را بمباران کردند ولی از سوی دیگر مدعی اند که ... — NATO military authorities on one hand admitted that they bombed Kabisa, but on the other hand, they claim that . . .

90 | 7781

95 یعنی jæ?ni *namely, meaning* adv,conj

• گفتم: یعنی چه؟ — I said, "What's that mean?".
91 | 7301

96 بار bar *load, turn, time* adv,n

• دختر برای اولین بار مستقیم در چشمان او نگاه کرد. — For the first time the girl looked directly into his eyes.
89 | 8752

97 منطقه mæntæɣe *region* n

• وجود راه آهن در این منطقه باعث خسارتهای جانی و مالی بسیار شده است. — The existence of a railway in this region has been the cause of a lot of fatalities and financial damages.
83 | 13488

98 نفر næfær *person* n

• چند نفر دیگر هم حمله کردند. — A few other people also attacked.
87 | 10157

99 یافتن jaftæn *find* n,v

• می خواستند برای یافتن شغل به شهر بروند. — They wanted to go to the city to find jobs.
88 | 9520

100 مختلف moxtælef *different* adj

• سوزاندن جسد در بین ادیان و فرق مختلف رایج است. — Cremation is popular in various religions and sects.
90 | 7557

101 بالا bala *top, high* adj,adv,n,prep

• همسایه طبقه بالا را در آسانسور دیدم. — I saw the neighbor from the floor above in the elevator.
93 | 5606

102 من mæn *I* pron

• با من بیایید. — Come with me.
67 | 29019

103 سیاسی sijasi *political* adj

• مدیریت شهری نباید سیاسی باشد. — The city management must not be political.
86 | 11199

104 جهان dʒæhan *world* n

• یکی از فرماندهان برجسته امریکایی در جنگ جهانی دوم بود. — He was one of the prominent American commanders in the Second World War.
87 | 10138

105 رابطه rabete *relation* n

• منابع نوشتاری کمی در این رابطه وجود دارند. — There are few written sources in this regard.
91 | 6697

106 شرط ʃært *condition* n

• شرط صادرات طلای خام اعلام شد. — The condition for exporting raw gold was announced.
91 | 6885

107 امریکا amrika *America* pn

• میلیاردر ایرانی مقیم امریکا، چندی پیش درگذشت. — The billionaire Iranian living in America recently passed away.
75 | 19625

108 جدید dʒædid *new* adj

• شماره تلفن جدید آقای فلانی را دارید؟ — Do you have so and so's new telephone number?
87 | 9861

109 علی æli *Ali* pn

• او شاگرد حضرت علی علیه السلام بوده‌است — He has been a disciple of Imam Ali.
93 | 4715

110 چه tʃe *what* adv,conj,n,pron,v

• تو نمیدانی چه صبحانه شیک و واقعاً مجللی دادند. — You have no idea what a chic and truly luxurious breakfast they served.
74 | 20233

111 اساس æsas *basis* n

• اعتدال بنای اندیشه اسلامی و اساس پیشرفت کشور است. — Moderation is the foundation of Islamic thought and the basis of the country's progress.
90 | 7273

112 آوردن aværdæn *bring* adj,n,v

• برای ما چای آوردند. — They brought tea for us.
86 | 9805

113 حال hal *condition, state* n

• حال شما چه طوره؟ — How are you?
89 | 7419

114 وارد vared *enter* adj,n,prep

• مسعود بدون موجودیت یک حکومت دلخواه و مورد قبول مردم بار دیگر نمی خواست وارد کابل شود. — Masoud did not want to enter Kabul again without the existence of a desirable government accepted by the people.
95 | 3565

115 نشان دادن neʃan dadæn *show* v

• با دست فروشگاه بزرگی را از آن طرف خیابان نشان داد و گفت: «فروشگاه بسته است، برای ناهار!» — He pointed to a supermarket on the other side of the street and said, "The supermarket is closed for lunch!"
92 | 5118

116 وی vej *he, she* pron

• وی در مصاحبه‌های تلویزیونی و رادیویی بسیاری حضور داشته اشت. — She has been on a lot of television and radio interviews.
78 | 16246

117 زمینه zæmine *background, field* n
- زمینه‌های گسترش روابط اقتصادی با هند فراهم شده است. — The grounds for expanding economic relationships with India have been provided.
89 | 7314

118 بعد bæʔd *then, after* adj,conj,n
- دفعه بعد هم باید بیای. — You have to come next time, too.
81 | 13927

119 سازمان sazman *organization* n
- مدیر یک سازمان کوچک دولتی. — the director of a small government organization.
83 | 12463

120 فرد færd *individual* n
- با فرد مورد نظر صحبت کنید. — Speak with the intended individual.
87 | 8892

121 تیم tim *team* n
- یکی از بهترین دروازه بانان فوتبال جهان دروازه بان تیم ملی اسپانیا «ایکر کاسیاس» است. — One of the best soccer goalies in the world is Iker Casillas, the goalie for Spain's national team.
79 | 14850

122 جوان dʒævan *young* adj,n
- پسر جوان آرام تلگرام را خواند و سکوت کرد. — The young boy read the telegram quietly then fell silent.
92 | 5627

123 ملی melli *national* adj
- صندوق توسعه ملی از این پس می‌تواند به شریک داخلی اعتبار لازم را بدهد. — From now on the National Development Fund can give the requisite credit to domestic companies.
84 | 11425

124 شورا ʃura *council* n
- این سند توسط شورای سیاستگذاری صنعت خودرو و یا کمیته‌های تخصصی این شورا مورد بازنگری قرار می‌گیرد. — This document will be revised by either the Policymaking Council for the auto industry or specialized committees of that Council.
87 | 8911

125 البته ælbætte *of course* adv,conj
- البته این تلاش ها بی ثمر نماند. — Of course these efforts were not fruitless.
92 | 5042

126 دوم dovvom *second* adj,n
- کلاس دوم بودم که یه روز از مدرسه فرار کردم. — I was in the second grade when one day I escaped from school.
86 | 9425

127 دلیل dælil *reason* n
- آنها می‌گویند دلیلی برای ترس وجود ندارد. — They say that there's no reason to be afraid.
89 | 7334

128 رفتن ræftæn *go* adj,n,v
- با آن پسر بیرون رفت چند مرتبه. — She went out with that guy several times.
71 | 20988

129 نقش næxʃ *role* n
- نقش ایران در عراق مفید بوده است. — Iran's role in Iraq has been beneficial.
92 | 5114

130 نام nam *name* adj,n
- نام کاربری خود را وارد کنید. — Enter your username.
88 | 8105

131 ولی væli *but* conj
- ولی مرد دوم هنوز هیچ نداشت. — But the second man still didn't have anything.
86 | 9619

132 دوره dowre *period* n
- دوره سختی‌ها گذشته است. — The period of troubles has passed.
90 | 6613

133 وزیر væzir *minister* n
- با شاه و وزیر چه کار داری؟ — What business do you have with the Shah and minister?
88 | 7631

134 استفاده estefade *use* n
- استفاده از طعمه‌های مسموم و خطرناک — The use of poisonous and dangerous bait.
90 | 6197

135 آقا aɣa *mister, gentleman* n,pn
- آن آقا، می پرسد چطور در فقط برای تو باز بود؟ — The gentleman is asking how come the door was open just for you.
85 | 10023

136 حرکت hærekæt *motion, movement* adj,n
- سنگ را برداشت و با عجله به طرف شهر حرکت کرد. — He picked up the stone and moved hastily towards the city.
94 | 3660

137 قرار گرفتن qærar gereftæn *be located* v
- فرودگاه جدید بوشهر در مرکز شش شهر قرار گرفته‌است. — The new Bushehr airport is situated at the center of six cities.
88 | 7707

138 شرکت ʃerkæt *company* n
- امروزه شرکت‌های زیادی هستند که هواپیمای مسافربری تولید می‌کنند. — Nowadays there are many companies that manufacture passenger aircraft.
83 | 10790

139 طرح *tærh design* n
- این طرح ها چه طورند؟ — How are these designs?
- 84 | 10266

140 تهران tehran *Tehran* pn
- پس از چند ساعتی با هواپیمای کوچکتری، تهران را به مقصد شیراز ترک کرد. — After a few hours he left Tehran on a smaller plan headed for Shiraz.
- 78 | 14116

141 برخی *bærxi some* pron,q
- قیمت زمین در برخی نقاط شهر تهران جزء گرانترینهاست در کل جهان میباشد. — The price of land in some parts of Tehran is among the most expensive in the whole world.
- 89 | 6772

142 سه *se three* n
- لازم نیست سه هفته تمام تو بیمارستان بماند. — It's not necessary for him to stay three whole weeks in the hospital.
- 80 | 12627

143 درحال *dærhal in the process of* conj
- شکل دشمنیها علیه ایران در حال تغییر است. — The form of animosities against Iran is in the process of changing.
- 84 | 10186

144 حدود *hodud limits, range, approximately* n,q
- میانگین بارش سالیانه در حدود 300 میلیمتر است. — Average annual precipitation is about 300 mm.
- 90 | 6292

145 ایجاد *idʒad creation* n
- تصویر مثبتی از پول وموفقیت در ذهنتان ایجاد کنید. — Create a positive image of money and success in your mind.
- 89 | 6735

146 کس *kæs person* n
- ۴۰ نفر از کسانی که در ورود به ساختمان سفارت سعودی نقش داشتند، دستگیر شدهاند. — 40 of the people who had a role in entering the Saudi Embassy building have been arrested.
- 86 | 8759

147 بردن *bordæn take* n,v
- بالا بردن کیفیت آموزشی دانشگاهها و مراکز آموزش عالی کشور — Increasing quality of education at the universities and higher education centers in the country.
- 88 | 7131

148 شما *ʃoma you* pron
- بعد شما کاری ندارید. — You don't have anything to do after.
- 80 | 12659

149 اقتصادی *eɣtesadi economic* adj
- شرایط اقتصادی بر وزن کودکان اثر میگذارد. — Economic conditions have an effect on childrens' weight.
- 82 | 11122

150 هزار *hezar thousand* n
- بیست هزار دلار دارد. — He has twenty thousand dollars.
- 71 | 19285

151 حضور *hozur presence* n
- دکتر در شیراز حضور داشت. — The doctor was present in Shiraz.
- 84 | 9680

152 نیرو *niru power, force* n
- فرمانده به پیروزی نیروهایش اطمینان داشت. — The commander was confident of the victory of his forces.
- 84 | 9937

153 عضو *ozv member* n
- من حالا عضو این مجتمع هستم. — Now I'm a member of this complex.
- 89 | 6193

154 فعالیت *fæʔalijæt activity* n
- فصل پاییز در واقع فصل آغاز فعالیتهای بیرون از منزل است. — The fall season is actually the season of the beginning of activities outside the house.
- 89 | 6000

155 تن *tæn, ton body, ton* n
- تن مردهها را نمیلرزانیم. — We will not shake the bodies of the dead.
- 91 | 5010

156 اشاره *eʃare indication, hint* n
- بعد اشاره کرد به پشت سرش. — Then he pointed behind his head.
- 89 | 6340

157 چون *ʧun like, because* adv,conj
- پشیمون نیستم چون دوستش داشتم. — I do not have any regrets, because I loved her.
- 88 | 6603

158 حاضر *hazer present, ready* adj
- حاضرم شرط ببندم. — I am ready to make a bet.
- 92 | 4647

159 درصد *dærsæd percent* adj,n
- هفتاد درصد عطر رز در بازارهای بینالمللی از بلغارستان میآید. — Seventy percent of rose perfume in international markets comes from Bulgaria.
- 82 | 10146

160 حتی *hætta even* adv,conj
- روزها حتی باید چراغ روشن کرد، هم چراغ اتاق را و هم چراغ راهرو را. — The lights have to be turned on even during the days, both the room light and the hall light.
- 89 | 6274

1 Animals

Rank	Headword	Pronunciation	Gloss	Rank	Headword	Pronunciation	Gloss
351	ماده	made	female	6993	مورچه	murtʃe	ant
1434	ماهی	mahi	fish	6999	نر	nær	male
1593	شیر	ʃir	lion	7124	پشه	pæʃe	mosquito
1675	کره	korre	foal	7770	نهنگ	næhæng	whale
1927	حیوان	hejvan	animal	8091	خزنده	xæzænde	reptile
1952	پرنده	pærænde	bird	8120	روباه	rubah	fox
2761	اسب	æsb	horse	8209	کبوتر	kæbutær	pigeon
3050	پروانه	pærvane	butterfly	8421	بید	bid	moth
3405	سگ	sæg	dog	9254	خرگوش	xærguʃ	rabbit
3670	موش	muʃ	mouse, rat	9405	پرستو	pæræstu	swallow
3877	پیشی	piʃi	cat, kitten	9548	پستاندار	pestandar	mammal
4238	گاو	gav	cow, bull, ox	9605	یوزپلنگ	juzpælæng	cheetah
4490	مار	mar	snake	9808	دلفین	dolfin	dolphin
4548	گوسفند	gusfænd	sheep	10124	خفاش	xoffaʃ	bat
4858	جانور	dʒanevær	animal	10240	مگس	mægæs	fly
4888	گربه	gorbe	cat	10496	گوساله	gusale	calf
5012	وال	val	whale	10830	گوزن	gævæzn	deer
5061	کرم	kerm	worm	11326	توله	tule	pup, cub
5126	ببر	bæbr	tiger	11817	کرگدن	kærgædæn	rhinoceros
5135	گرگ	gorg	wolf	11866	گورخر	gurexær	wild ass
5235	خر	xær	donkey	11950	مرغابی	morɣabi	duck
5470	شتر	ʃotor	camel	12260	سوسک	susk	beetle
5537	میمون	mejmun	monkey, ape	13049	قاطر	ɣater	mule
6049	اردک	ordæk	duck	13484	شغال	ʃoɣal	jackal
6126	جوجه	dʒudʒe	chick	14181	مادیان	madijan	mare
6140	قوچ	quʃ	ram	14785	تمساح	temsah	crocodile
6190	فیل	fil	elephant	14806	حلزون	hælæzun	snail
6678	پلنگ	pælæng	leopard	14897	غزال	ɣæzal	gazelle
6687	خرس	xers	bear	14974	شامپانزه	ʃampanze	chimpanzee
6696	آهو	ahu	deer	15094	گراز	goraz	boar
6778	خوک	xuk	pig	15989	کفتر	kæftær	pigeon
6898	قورباغه	ɣurbaɣe	frog	17691	زالو	zalu	leech

161 محمد mohæmmæd *Mohammad* pn
- چهره پیامبر در فیلم حضرت محمد (ص) به نمایش درنمی‌آید. — The Prophet's face is not shown in the film Muhammad (PBUH).
92 | 4213

162 وجودداشتن vodʒud daʃtæn *exist* v
- نوشته های قرآنی مشهوری وجود دارد که به قرن هفتم میلادی بازمی گردد. — There are well-known Koranic writings which date to the 7th century A.D.
89 | 5886

163 پایان pajan *end* n
- یکصد دوربین جدید کنترل سرعت تا پایان تابستان در جاده‌ها ● نصب می‌شود. — 100 new traffic cameras will be installed on the roads by the end of the summer.
87 | 7055

164 همچنین hæmtʃenin *so, also* conj
- پاکزاد همچنین به عنوان یک شخص عاشق ماشین شناخته ● شد. — Pakzad was also recognized as a lover of cars.
85 | 8318

165 قانون ɣanun *law* n
- این هم قانون این بازی است. — This is the rule of ● this game.
85 | 8313

166 جا dʒa *place* n
- جایی که کسی پیر نمی‌شود. — A place where ● nobody gets old.
83 | 9229

167 ممکن momken *possible* adj
- اگر ممکن است یک تخفیفی هم قائل بشوید. — If ● possible could you discount it a bit?
93 | 3646

168 هدف hædæf *goal, target* n
- فقط هدف را می بینم. — I only see the goal. ●
86 | 7402

169 انجام دادن ændʒam dadæn *accomplish* v
- ما میخواستیم کاری انجام دهیم و پیرمرد را دستگیری کنیم. ● — We wanted to do something and support the old man.
94 | 2846

170 بزرگی bozorgi *magnitude* adj,n
- بزرگی‌هایی که از فرصت های کوچک می‌رویید! ● — Greatnesses which grow from small opportunities!
97 | 1391

171 جامعه dʒameʔe *society* n
- چگونه تو رهبانیت و دوری از جامعه را انتخاب کرده‌ای؟ ● — How have you chosen monasticism and isolation from society?
85 | 8255

172 حق hæɣ *right* n
- حق دارند که بکشند. — They have the right to kill. ●
93 | 3576

173 اثر æsær *mark, effect* n
- اثری از دود نبود. — There was no sign of ● smoke.
84 | 8726

174 بحث bæhs *discussion* n
- بعد از یک بحث طولانی، جوانترین لاک پشت برای آوردن ● نمک از خانه انتخاب شد. — After a long debate, the youngest turtle was selected to bring salt from the house.
91 | 4285

175 ارزش ærzeʃ *value* adj,n
- این سنگ چقدر ارزش دارد؟ — How valuable is this ● stone?
92 | 4133

176 موضوع mowzuʔ *subject, topic* n
- فهمیدم موضوع جدی است. — I realized it is a ● serious issue.
88 | 6246

177 طرف tæræf *side* n
- پس از یک دعوای حقوقی بی‌حاصل، دو طرف با یکدیگر ● به توافق رسیدند. — After an unproductive legal suit, the two sides came to an agreement together.
86 | 6901

178 نه næ, noh *no/not/neither/nor, nine* adv, conj,n
- در ظرف نه ماه — In the span of nine months. ●
77 | 12482

179 آب ɑb *water* n,pn
- با یک لیوان آب به اتاق برگشت. — She returned to ● the room with a glass of water.
88 | 6192

180 آینده ajænde *future* adj,n
- آیا آینده ، ریشه ای درگذشته ندارد؟ — Does the future ● not have its roots in the past?
87 | 6368

181 نوع nowʔ *type* n
- این نوع فراموشی مرا غافلگیر نکرده بود. — This kind ● of forgetfulness had not surprised me.
86 | 7011

182 مقام mæɣam *rank, official* n
- ما به مقامات عالی گزارش می‌دهیم. — We report to ● the senior officials.
86 | 7110

183 زیادی zijadi *excessive* adj
- زنجبیل هم زیادی‌اش خوب نیست. — Even excessive ● ginger is not healthy.
91 | 4512

184 جهت dʒæhæt *direction, reason* n,prep
- از این جهت دیگر شبهه ای در من باقی نماند که زن ● فرانسوی راست می گوید. — For this reason, I had no doubt that the French woman is telling the truth.
89 | 5161

185 اجرا edʒra *implementation* n
- پلیس، اجرای طرح تغییرات ترافیکی منطقه ۱۲ را لغو کرد. ● — Police canceled the implementation of the plan for District 12 traffic changes.
86 | 6701

186 اصلی æsli *main* adj
- از پشت درخت‌ها به خیابان اصلی آمد. — He came from ● behind the trees to the main road.
90 | 4628

187 مجلس **mædʒles** *parliament* n

در مجلسی که به افتخار او برپا شده بود، یکی از چهره‌های فرهنگی سخنرانی کرد. — One of the cultural figures gave a speech in an assembly that had been held in her honor.

83 | 8493

188 آخر **axær** *final* adj,adv,conj,n

آخرین کتلت رو از روی ماهیتابه برمی‌دارم. — I'll take the last cutlet from the frying pan.

87 | 6257

189 عمل **æmæl** *action, operation* n

مومن، یعنی کسانی‌که هم ایمان دارند و هم اعمالشان صالح است. — "Faithful" means those who both have faith and righteous deeds.

89 | 5002

190 زندگی **zendegi** *life* n

این پسر بچه با پدرش تنها زندگی می‌کرد — This boy used to live alone with his father.

88 | 5647

191 چنین **ʧenin** *such* adv,pron

اگر واقعاً او چنین اظهاری درباره این جوان کرده باشد تردیدی باقی نمی ماند. — If he had really made such a statement about this young man, then there would remain no doubt.

88 | 5532

192 رساندن **resandæn** *deliver* adj,n,v

سلام رساند و گفت به پادشاه بگو خیلی ممنون. — He sent his regards and said, "Tell the king, thank you very much."

93 | 3347

193 نظام **nezam** *system* n

هدف اصلی دشمنان نظام توقف انقلاب است. — The main goal of the enemies of the system is stopping the revolution.

87 | 6229

194 گذاشتن **gozaʃtæn** *put, leave* adj,v

هرگز جرأت نکرده ام که دست روی شانه اش بگذارم و بگویم: چطوری مرد؟ — I've never dared to put my hand on his shoulder and say, "How are you, man?"

82 | 8881

195 شکل **ʃekl** *shape* adj,n

او به شکل صورت سگ مجسم شده است. — He has been sculpted into the shape of a dog's face.

90 | 4541

196 نسبت **nesbæt** *relation* n

نسبت‌های خانوادگی بر سه گونه‌اند. — Family relations come in three types.

87 | 6012

197 دنیا **donja** *world* n

درسراسر دنیا آدم‌ها جیغ کشیده‌اند. — People have cried out all over the world.

90 | 4750

198 خارجی **xaredʒi** *foreign* adj

تعدادی از خارجیان را اخراج نمودند. — They expelled a number of foreigners.

87 | 5901

199 همراه **hæmrah** *together, along* adj,n

آنها رفتند و رفتند تا همه نان و آبی که همراه داشتند ته کشید. — They walked and walked until all the bread and water that they had with them ran out.

90 | 4528

200 کتاب **ketab** *book* n

صاحب کتاب گفته بود اشیاء هم جان دارند. — The owner of the book had said that objects have life too.

87 | 6092

201 امروز **emruz** *today* adv

لطفا اجازه بدهید من امروز بازی کنم. — Please allow me to play today.

85 | 7167

202 دیدن **didæn** *see* n,v

تو کنسرت هم من را دید. — He also saw me at the concert.

74 | 12834

203 جهانی **dʒæhani** *global* adj

بدون اقدامی جهانی و یکپارچه نمی‌توان بر ترور غلبه کرد. — Without a unified and global action we cannot defeat terror.

83 | 7886

204 توسعه **towseʔe** *expansion, development* n

کم کم کارش توسعه پیدا کرد. — Slowly her work expanded.

85 | 6750

205 ویژه **viʒe** *special* adj,adv,conj

در این هنگام اعتماد به نفس ویژه وی برگشته بود. — By then, his special self-confidence had returned.

87 | 5829

206 انجام **ændʒam** *performance* n

این کار را انجام دهد — To accomplish this task.

91 | 4149

207 مرکز **mærkæz** *center* n

پارک ساحلی مرجان یکی از زیباترین مراکز دیدنی کیش است. — Coral Beach Park is one of the most beautiful attractions of Kish.

87 | 5810

208 اعلام **eʔlam** *announcement* n

با اعلام نقاط مثبت کاری تان، فروش کالایتان را بیشتر کنید. — Increase the sale of your products by announcing the good points of your work.

82 | 8076

209 اطلاع **ettelaʔ** *information* adj,n

ممنون میشم اطلاعات بیشتری در اختیارم بگذاری. — I would be grateful if you'd provide me more information.

86 | 6206

210 داخل daxel *inside* n,prep
- برنج مانند جریان آب به داخل سطل می ریزد. — The
  rice pours into the bucket like a current of
  water.
  94 | 2773

211 پرداختن pærdaxtæn *pay, engage in* adj,n,v
- به انتقاد از یکدیگر پرداختند. — They started
  criticizing each other.
  90 | 4332

212 کاملاً kamelæn *completely* adv
- اما اکنون قلمرو علم و دین کاملاً از یکدیگر جدا شده است.
  — But now the domains of science and
  religion are completely separated from each
  other.
  95 | 2177

213 گفته gofte *saying* adj,n
- جان کری گفته‌های اخیر آیت‌الله خامنه‌ای را نگران‌کننده و
  مشکل‌ساز توصیف کرد. — John Kerry described
  Ayatollah Khamenei's recent statements as
  concerning and problematic.
  88 | 5026

214 زن zæn *woman, wife* adj,n
- برای ما حیاتی است که حقوق زنان را مورد توجه قرار
  بدهیم. — It is crucial for us to consider
  women's rights.
  79 | 9394

215 گزارش gozaref *report* n
- به گزارش زنده‌ای که هم‌اکنون از بغداد رسیده توجه
  بفرمایید. — Please pay attention to this live
  report which has just arrived from Baghdad.
  80 | 8904

216 سر sær, serr *head, secret* n
- به آرامی سر برداشت. — She slowly lifted her
  head.
  76 | 11075

217 دست دادن dæst dadæn *shake hands, lose* v
- لحظه‌ای که انسان و روبات با هم دست دادند. — The
  moment when humans and robots shook
  hands.
  96 | 1438

218 هنوز hænuz *still, yet* adv
- مادر هنوز هم اصرار داشت که به چیزی نیاز ندارند.
  — Mother still insisted that she didn't need
  anything.
  88 | 4969

219 جمهوری dʒomhuri *republic* n
- ا — تلفن می‌زنم به سفارت جمهوری اسلامی در پاریس.
  will call the embassy of the Islamic Republic
  in Paris.
  83 | 7626

220 تغییر tæɣjir *change* n
- حتی لباس اش نیز تغییری نکرده بود. — Even his
  clothes didn't change.
  89 | 4592

221 تعداد teʔdad *number* n,q
- ما یک خانواده نبودیم فقط تعدادی افراد بودیم که با هم
  زندگی می‌کردیم. — We weren't a family, we were
  just a number of individuals who lived together.
  88 | 4870

222 میلیون miljun *million* n
- میلیون ها ستاره می بینم. — I see millions of stars.
  83 | 7312

223 سیاست sijasæt *policy, politics* n
- اتخاذ سیاست‌های مالی و پولی مناسب — The adoption
  of appropriate fiscal and monetary policies.
  87 | 5611

224 بررسی bærresi *check* n
- قبل از امضاء و یا قبول هر موضوعی، تحقیق و بررسی
  لازم است. — Before signing or accepting any
  matter, research and investigation is required.
  87 | 5661

225 اقدام eɣdam *action* n
- استانهایی که فاقد روزنامه بوده و یا یک روزنامه بیشتر
  ندارند باید اقدام به انتشار روزنامه کنند. — Provinces
  that lack a newspaper or do not have more
  than one newspaper should act to publish
  newspapers.
  84 | 6743

226 افزایش æfzajef *increase* n
- کاری کنید که اختیارشان را افزایش دهند. — Do
  something that will increase their authority.
  81 | 8153

227 برابر bærabær *equal, opposite* adj,n
- در تهران که بودم حتی آدم های آهنی هم در برابر من نرم
  می شدند. — When I was in Tehran, even iron
  men would turn soft in front of me.
  88 | 4702

228 درباره dærbare *about* prep
- این داستان درباره پسر بچه لاغر اندامی است که عاشق
  فوتبال بود. — This story is about a scrawny boy
  who loved soccer.
  86 | 5839

229 گونه gune *type, species, cheek* n
- باغ‌وحش تارونگا در سیدنی از تولد یکی از نادرترین
  گونه‌های میمون در جهان خبر داد. — The Taronga
  Zoo in Sydney reported the birth of one of
  the rarest species of monkey in the world.
  88 | 4915

230 سوم sevvom *third* adj,n
- سامسونگ به عنوان سومین کمپانی ارزشمند در جهان شناخته
  شد. — Samsung was recognized as the third
  most valuable company in the world.
  87 | 5359

231 خدمت xedmæt *service* adj,n
- دیشب از مشهد حرکت کردیم و حالا هم در خدمت
  شماییم! — We departed from Mashhad last
  night and now we are at your service!
  87 | 5393

232 خبر xæbær *news* n
- بوگو ببینم چه خبر چی کار میکنی. — Tell me, what's up, what are you up to?
- 81 | 7772

233 ایرانی irɑni *Iranian* adj,n
- آیا سوفیا اسم اصیل ایرانی است؟ — Is Sophia an authentic Iranian name?
- 84 | 6453

234 کامل kɑmel *complete* adj
- مدیر مدرسه تسلط کاملی به زبان انگلیسی نداشت. — The principal didn't have complete command of the English language.
- 92 | 2981

235 آزاد ɑzad *free* adj
- استفاده از مطالب سایت صدای روسیه با ذکر مرجع آزاد است. — Use of content from the Voice of Russia website is free with a reference.
- 93 | 2641

236 منبع mænbæʔ *source* n
- روستاها می‌توانند منبع تولید تخم‌مرغ و مرغ باشند. — The villages can be a source of egg and poultry production.
- 89 | 4428

237 خط xætt *line* adj,n
- زیرش خط کشید. — He underlined it.
- 91 | 3660

238 قدرت γodræt *power* n
- من از بازی قدرت بیزارم. — I am sick of the power game.
- 86 | 5426

239 نیاز niɑz *need* n
- کارکنان نیاز به نظارت دائمی ندارند. — Workers don't have a need for constant supervision.
- 89 | 4326

240 مسئول mæsʔul *responsible* adj,n
- بالاخره او مسئول بود. — Finally he was responsible.
- 87 | 5181

241 نماینده næmɑjænde *representative* n
- بد نیست که نماینده در پاسخ به درخواست های اقتصادی مردم بگوید دولت نوپا و مجلس نوآموز است و باید صبر کرد. — It's not bad for a representative to say in response to the economic requests of the people that the government is a fledgling and the parliament is newly-recruited, and one must be patient.
- 86 | 5373

242 ساعت saʔæt *hour, time* n
- نیم ساعت مانده به زنگ. — It's half an hour till the break
- 85 | 5942

243 زمین zæmin *ground, earth* n,pn
- جون خرسش را به زمین انداخت و گریه کرد. — Jun dropped her bear on the ground and cried.
- 88 | 4715

244 ملت mellæt *nation* n
- سلام به ملت نجیب ایران. — Greetings to the noble nation of Iran.
- 78 | 9039

245 میزان mizan *rate* n
- به میزان زیادی تولید می کرد. — He was producing at a high rate.
- 87 | 4781

246 تحت tæht *under* n,prep
- احساس می کنم تحت فشار زیادی قرار گرفته‌ام. — I feel like I've come under a great deal of pressure.
- 90 | 3712

247 اختیار extijɑr *authority* n
- توانایی فرد برای کسب اختیار بیشتر. — One's ability to gain more authority.
- 92 | 3071

248 نخست noxost *first* adj,adv,n
- تو نخستین کسی هستی که به نام من «آقای» افزوده است. — You're the first person to add the word "mister" to my name.
- 87 | 5036

249 ارائه erɑʔe *presentation* n
- به هنگام ارائه کمک های اولیه ارزیابی مصدوم یکی از مهمترین مهارت هاست. — While offering first aid, assessing the injured is one of the most important skills.
- 87 | 4644

250 باعث bɑʔes *cause* n
- آنقدر رابطه ی عاشقانه دربین آنها بود که هر گاه در جایی تنها می شدند ، یکدگر را در آغوش می کشیدند و این باعث شده بود که فرصتی برای کار دیگری برایشان نگذارد. — There was such a loving relationship between them that any time they got to a place alone they would pull one another into an embrace and this caused them not to have the opportunity to do anything else.
- 93 | 2678

251 رشد roʃd *growth* n
- پدر و مادر و برادران و خواهرانش همه چهره و اندام عادی داشتند و اثری از رشد بی‌اندازه استخوان‌ها در آنها دیده نمی‌شد. — His father, mother, brothers and sisters had normal faces and statures, and there was no sign of extreme bone growth in them.
- 89 | 3908

252 دنبال dombal *follow* n
- دنبال کلید می‌گردد. — He is looking for the key.
- 92 | 2976

253 انتخاب entexɑb *selection, choice* adj,n
- آدمی با انتخابهایش تعریف می شود. — A human being is defined by her choices.
- 90 | 3694

254 گفتوگو goftogu *conversation* n
- به نظر من باید با هم گفت‌وگو کنیم. — In my opinion, we should have a discussion with each other.
- 87 | 4635

255 موفق *movæffæɣ successful* adj
- شرکت سبحان دارو یکی از موفقترین شرکتهای دارویی ایران است. — Sobhan Darou is one of Iran's most successful pharmaceutical companies.
93 | 2648

256 روزنامه *ruznɑme newspaper* n
- یک تکه کاغذ روزنامه به دیوار سنجاق شده بود. — A piece of newspaper had been pinned to the wall.
85 | 5764

257 گذشتن *gozæʃtæn pass* n,v
- سالها گذشتند. — Many years passed.
91 | 3303

258 طی *tej during* n,prep
- در طی این سالها چون چرایی در اصول نکرده — During all these years he never questioned the principles.
88 | 4430

259 خاطر *xɑter mind, sake* n
- اما به هر حال این اتفاق افتاده است و درست به همین خاطر امروز صبح شما را به اتاق خود خواندم! — But at any rate, the event has occurred, and for that very reason I called you to my room this morning!
92 | 3003

260 سمت *sæmt, semæt side, position* n
- داشتم میرفتم به سمت تهران. — I was going toward Tehran.
93 | 2522

261 عامل *ɑmel agent, factor* adj,n
- مهمترین عاملی که ماهیّت ایرانی را رقم زده است، جغرافیای اوست. — The most important factor that has marked the Iranian character is geography.
88 | 4357

262 تأثیر *tæʔsir impression, effect* n
- تحت تأثیر چه عاملی این داستان را نوشتید؟ — Under what influence did you write this story?
91 | 3256

263 جنگ *dʒæng war* n
- چرا آن پادشاه در تمام جنگها شکست میخوردد؟ — Why is that king defeated in every war?
84 | 5741

264 ساخت *sɑxt construction, structure, built* n,v
- برخی اصطلاحات و یا ساختها در فارسی زنانهاست. — Some terms or structures in Persian are feminine.
89 | 4044

265 طریق *tæriɣ way* n
- ذخیرهسازی یک روی زیبا از طریق چشم. — Memorizing a beautiful face through the eyes.
89 | 4066

266 کاهش *kɑheʃ decrease* n
- فروش او ناگهان شدیدا کاهش یافت. — His sales suddenly decreased drastically.
82 | 6670

267 اخیر *æxir recent* adj
- در 4 سال اخیر واردات 20 درصد افزایش یافت که این مسئله ناشی از وجود تحریم است. — In the last four years, imports increased 20 percent and this issue resulted from the presence of sanctions.
88 | 4230

268 خارج *xɑredʒ outside, abroad* n
- در خارج زندگی می کند. — She lives abroad.
91 | 3125

269 هفته *hæfte week* n
- پس از گذشت یک هفته بازی تمام شد. — After one week the game was finished.
83 | 6201

270 آغاز *ɑɣɑz beginning* n
- بازگشت مصدق به ایران با آغاز جنگ جهانی اول مصادف بود. — Mossadegh's return to Iran coincided with the start of World War One.
89 | 3639

271 مرحله *mærhæle stage* n
- با حمایت ما به این مرحله رسیده است. — With our support she has reached this stage.
85 | 5387

272 همان *hæmɑn that very* pron
- برای مردم همان را بخواه که برای خود میخواهی. — Desire the very same thing for people that you desire for yourself.
81 | 6749

273 صنعت *sæn?æt industry* n
- صادرات صنایع دستی باید به یک میلیارد دلار برسد. — The exports of the handicraft industry must reach one billion dollars.
84 | 5632

274 تشکیل *tæʃkil formation* n
- این سوره از ۷ آیه تشکیل شده. — This Surah consists of 7 verses.
89 | 3692

275 همکاری *hæmkɑri collaboration* n
- همکاری دو شرکت همچنان ادامه خواهد یافت. — The collaboration between the two companies will still continue.
85 | 5392

276 اسلام *eslɑm Islam* n
- رحم از فرایض اسلام است. — Mercy is one of the practices of Islam.
86 | 4907

277 افزودن *æfzudæn add* v
- مبلغ ۲۵۰۰ تومان، بلافاصله به حساب شما افزوده خواهد شد. — The amount of 2,500 toman will be immediately added to your account.
79 | 7585

278 حسن *hæsæn, hosn Hasan, virtue* n,pn
- حسن صادقلو دارای مدرک دکترای تاریخ است. — Hasan Sadeghlu holds a Ph.D degree in history.
95 | 1772

279 یافته jafte *found, finding* adj,v

- یافته‌هایشان را در یک شماره از مجله «ساینس» منتشر کردند. — They published their findings in an issue of the journal *Science*.

90 | 3391

280 خواندن xandæn *read* adj,n,v

- کتاب شاه نعمت الله مرحوم را می خواندند. — They were reading the book of the late Shah Nemattollah.

86 | 4689

281 غیر yejr *other, non-, un-* n

- این غیر ممکن است. — This is impossible.

89 | 3791

282 خانواده xanevade *family* n

- مهمترین تصمیمات را در خانواده، او می گیرد. — She makes the most important decisions in the family.

89 | 3633

283 دور dowr, dur *period, far* adj,n

- اخترشناسان توانستند قدیمی‌ترین و دورترین کهکشان جهان را کشف کنند. — Astronomers were able to discover the world's most ancient and distant galaxy.

85 | 5097

284 نقطه noɣte *point* n

- صرف بودجه هنگفت در یک نقطه از شهر اقدامی نامناسب و تبعیض‌آمیز است. — Spending a huge amount of budget in one part of the city is an inappropriate and discriminatory act.

91 | 2817

285 بازی bazi *game, play* n

- در مسابقه ای بازی کند — For her to play in a tournament.

79 | 7531

286 تولید towlid *production* n

- کمبود بودجه روند تولیدات سینمایی را کند کرد. — The lack of budget slowed down the cinema production process.

81 | 6471

287 برگزار bærgozar *held* adj

- مسابقات محلی در شهر برگزار میشود. — The local tournaments will be held in the city.

81 | 6517

288 پیدا کردن pejda kærdæn *find* v

- آمریکایی‌ها از پیدا کردن شغل ناامید شدند. — Americans have lost hope in finding jobs.

91 | 3056

289 وزارت vezaræt *ministry* n

- چهاردهم ماه جاری وزارت امور خارجه سوریه عضویت در کنوانسیون بین المللی منع سلاح های شیمیایی را پذیرفت و صد و نودمین کشور عضو در این کنوانسیون شناخته شد. — On the fourteenth of this month, the Syrian Ministry of Foreign Affairs accepted membership into the International Convention for the Prevention of Chemical Weapons and was recognized as the 190th member-state of this convention.

81 | 6443

290 دیده dide *eye, seen* adj,n

- به دور از دیدگان مردم در شهر مهاباد به دار آویخته شد. — He was hanged in the city of Mahabad, away from the public eyes.

92 | 2580

291 بلکه bælke *but* conj

- این نه یک توافق بلکه یک توافق خوب است. — This is not just an agreement but a good one.

89 | 3707

292 اصل æsl *principle* n

- رعایت بهداشت مهم تر ین اصل است. — Practicing good hygiene is the most important principle.

89 | 3663

293 کمک komæk *help* n

- یک کارگر هم برای کمک به آنها آمد. — A laborer also came to help them.

87 | 4302

294 قابل ɣabel *capable* adj

- بگذارید فرزندتان احساس نماید که فردی با لیاقت و قابل است. — Let your child feel that he is someone capable and worthy.

87 | 4155

295 توسط tævæssot *by* prep

- این کتاب بارها توسط ناشران مختلف در ایران ترجمه و چاپ شده است. — This book has been translated and printed by various publishers in Iran many times.

83 | 5639

296 زیر zir *under* adj,n,prep

- زیر سایه‌ی درخت نارگیلی شاید می‌ایستاده. — Perhaps she stood under the shade of a coconut tree.

83 | 5611

297 مانند manænd *like* adv,n

- شما مانندِ گنجشکِ پُرگویی مرتب حرف می زدید. — Like a talkative sparrow, you are constantly talking.

89 | 3484

298 اکنون æknun *now* adv

- اکنون زندگی را چگونه می بینی. — How do you see life now?

89 | 3686

299 اهمیت ahæmmijjæt *importance* n

- در ایام ماه مبارک رمضان از اهمیت ویژه‌ای برخوردار است. — During the holy month of Ramadan, it has special importance.

91 | 2683

300 اندیشه ændiʃe *thought* n
- خداوند متعال فکر و اندیشه انسان را به این حقیقت بزرگ رهنمون می شود که اونمی تواند بیرون از سنتهای الهی زندگی کند. — God the great guides our thought toward this big truth that we cannot live outside of God's divine traditions.

93 | 2155

301 استان ostan *province* n
- استان یزد نیز جدای از سایر استان ها نیست. — The province of Yazd is also not separate from other provinces.

79 | 7158

302 دفاع defaʔ *defense* n
- تو آلان برای چی داری ازش دفاع میکنی؟ — Now, why are you defending him?

89 | 3400

303 نامه name *letter* n
- می خواهی برای آن دنیا نامه بنویسی. — Do you want to write a letter for the other world?

91 | 2655

304 انسان ensan *human* n
- تمایلات همه انسانها به یکدیگر شبیه نیست. — Not all human tendencies are similar to each other.

86 | 4497

305 نمودن nemudæn *show, do* adj,n,v
- اگرچه حجم کلی آب‌های موجود برروی زمین نسبتاً زیاد می‌نماید اما متجاوز از ۹۷٪ این آبها در دریاها و اقیانوسها متمرکز هستند. — Although the total volume of water available on earth appears to be relatively large, more than 97% of the water is concentrated in seas and oceans.

72 | 9755

306 عمومی omumi *public* adj
- گوشی تلفن عمومی شکسته بود و سیمش را بریده بودند. — The handset of the public phone was broken, and they had cut the cord.

85 | 4881

307 جدی dʒeddi *serious* adj
- می‌تونم یه لحظه جدی باشم؟ — May I be serious for a moment?

91 | 2918

308 دیدار didar *visit* n
- به دیدار همسایه رفت که از خویشان نزدیک بود. — She went to go visit her neighbor who was a close relative.

80 | 6608

309 سایر sajer *other* n
- همینک چندین روزنامه در کابل و سایر ولایات افغانستان فعالیت میکنند. — Right now, several newspapers are operating in Kabul and other provinces of Afghanistan.

90 | 3241

310 زدن zædæn *strike, beat* adj,n,prep,v
- زدن حریف خطا محسوب می‌شود. — Striking the opponent is considered a penalty.

72 | 9745

311 فرصت forsæt *opportunity* n
- ملک ابراهیم فرصت نداد یک کلمه دیگر از دهان دیو بیرون بیاید. — King Ebrahim didn't give the opportunity for another word to come out of the demon's mouth.

91 | 2734

312 دانشگاه daneʃgah *university* n
- خانم صادقی در دانشگاه هم درس می‌داد. — Ms. Sadeghi also used to teach at the university.

82 | 5665

313 قراردادن ɣærar dadæn *put, place* v
- این فضا جای مناسبی برای قرار دادن کتاب و وسایل اضافه است. — This area is a reasonable place for placing books and extra materials.

88 | 3752

314 تأکید tæʔkid *emphasis* n
- بر رعایت حجاب و عفاف در سازمان های دولتی و عمومی تأکید کرده است. — He has emphasized the observance of modesty and the hijab in public and government organizations.

86 | 4424

315 نوشتن neveʃtæn *write* adj,n,v
- نمی‌خواهم گلایه کنم، می‌دانی که نوشتن را دوست دارم. — I don't want to complain; you know that I like writing.

85 | 4552

316 ساختن saxtæn *build* n,v
- از آن در ساختن طناب و مواد دیگر استفاده می کردند. — They used to use it to make rope and other materials.

85 | 4754

317 ترتیب tærtib *order* n
- مرحوم علامه امینی در کتاب الغدیر خود نام راویان حدیث غدیر را به ترتیب زمان زندگی ذکر کرده است. — The late Allameh Amini in his book "Alghadir" has mentioned the name of the narrators of Hadith of Ghadir in the order of the time of their living.

92 | 2520

318 فقط fæɣæt *only* adv
- من فقط چند ماهی در شیراز می مانم. — I will only stay in Shiraz for a few months.

83 | 5462

319 علت ellæt *reason* n
- دیدم زیاد کسل و پکر است و علت را پرسیدم. — I found him so weary and despondent, and I asked what the reason was.

86 | 4144

2 Body

Rank	Headword	Pronunciation	Gloss	Rank	Headword	Pronunciation	Gloss
46	صورت	suræt	face	3639	شانه	ʃane	shoulder
66	دست	dæst	hand	3946	زانو	zanu	knee
82	رو	ru	face	4140	کمر	kæmær	waist
216	سر	sær	head	4160	مشت	moʃt	fist
229	گونه	gune	cheek	4190	رحم	ræhem	womb
383	زبان	zæban	tongue	4365	شکم	ʃekæm	stomach
531	رخ	rox	face	4585	بازو	bazu	arm
566	خون	xun	blood	5122	کله	kælle	head
587	چهره	tʃehre	face	5345	معده	meʔde	stomach
590	چشم	tʃeʃm	eye	5511	روده	rude	intestine
628	پا	pa	foot, leg	5611	عضله	æzole	muscle
660	عین	ejn	eye	5643	گلو	gælu	throat
740	شش	ʃoʃ	lung	5700	ابرو	æbru	eyebrow
910	دل	del	heart	5739	پیشانی	piʃani	forehead
958	پشت	poʃt	back	5912	ساعد	saʔed	forearm
1083	کلیه	kolje	kidney	6387	ریه	rije	lung
1341	قلب	γælb	heart	6606	قیافه	γijafe	face
1650	مغز	mæγz	brain	7395	جگر	dʒegær	liver
1715	گوش	guʃ	ear	7484	ماهیچه	mahiʃe	muscle
1766	رأس	ræʔs	head	7857	اسکلت	eskelet	skeleton
1872	سینه	sine	breast	7889	چانه	tʃane	chin
2059	پوست	pust	skin	8101	شریان	ʃæræjan	artery
2525	بینی	bini	nose	8189	کبد	kæbed	liver
2544	گردن	gærdæn	neck	8361	دماغ	dæmaγ	nose
2581	مو	mu	hair	8665	ناخن	naxon	nail
2635	دهان	dæhan	mouth	8918	مچ	motʃ	wrist, ankle
2816	کف	kæf	palm	9650	پاشنه	paʃne	heel
2891	دندان	dændan	tooth	10709	مژه	moʒe	eyelash
2991	استخوان	ostoxan	bone	12001	مخ	mox	cerebrum
3114	لب	læb	lip	12588	پستان	pestan	breast
3162	انگشت	ængoʃt	finger	16065	لپ	lop	cheek
3207	عصب	æsæb	nerve	16877	آرواره	arvare	jaw

320 داخلی dɑxeli *internal* adj
• در سال تولد آیزاک نیوتن، جنگ‌های داخلی انگلستان آغاز شد. — The year Isaac Newton was born, the English Civil War began.
87 | 3995

321 آزادی ɑzadi *freedom* n
• سزار، بسیار عزیز است، اما آزادی از او عزیزتر است. — Caesar is very dear, but freedom is dearer.
88 | 3642

322 وضعیت væzʔijjæt *situation* n
• این وضعیت تا سال ۱۳۴۷ ادامه داشت. This situation continued until 1347.
88 | 3602

323 آیا ɑja *whether* adv,conj
• آیا می‌دانستید او نابینا بود؟ — Did you know that she was blind?
87 | 3758

324 جریان dʒæræjɑn *flow* n
- گل سرخ همراه جریان آب می رفت. — The rose was going along with the water's current.
87 | 3957

325 تلاش tælɑʃ *effort* n
- این تلاش، مقدس است. — This is a holy effort.
83 | 4976

326 لازم lɑzem *necessary* adj
- حتی برای آخرین بازی در روز شنبه هم لازم نیست بیایی. — You do not even need to come for the last game on Saturday.
87 | 3899

327 حمایت hemɑjæt *protection* n
- فقط از کارهای ایرانی حمایت مالی می شه. — Only Iranian work is financially supported.
82 | 5553

328 چیز tʃiz *thing* n
- از دیدگاه انسان مدرن، افسانه و تاریخ دو چیز متمایز و کاملاً متفاوت اند. — From the perspective of modern humans, myth and history are two distinct and totally different things.
71 | 9392

329 ادامه edɑme *continuation* n
- حاضر به ادامه کار نیست. — She is not ready to continue working.
78 | 6835

330 دلار dolɑr *dollar* n
- پسرم هم پول می خواهد، دلار، فقط دلار، نقد. — My son also wants money, dollars, only dollars, cash.
84 | 4616

331 قرار داشتن qærɑr dɑʃtæn *be located* v
- امروزه داخل مرز های آذربایجان، ارمنستان و گرجستان قرار دارد. — Nowadays it is located within the borders of Azerbaijan, Armenia, and Georgia.
89 | 3019

332 تاریخ tɑrix *history* n
- مدتها از این تاریخ گذشت تا اینکه مادر دوباره به جنگل بازگشت. — A long period of time passed from that date until the mother returned to the forest.
83 | 4864

333 علمی elmi *scientific* adj
- بعضی آن را بزرگ ترین کتاب علمی تاریخ دانسته اند. — Some consider it history's greatest scientific book.
86 | 3890

334 سطح sæth *level* n
- ا — از سطح دریا محاسبه می کردم نه از سر سلطان! — I would calculate from the sea level not the Sultan's head!
84 | 4601

335 اجتماعی edʒtemɑʔi *social* adj
- از مهمترین مسائل اجتماعی شهر مشهد مسئله طلاق است. — The issue of divorce is among the most important social issues of Mashhad.
79 | 6196

336 استاد ostɑd *professor* n
- هیئتی مسئول و مرجع رسیدگی به شکایت های دانشجویان و اساتید تشکیل می شود. — A responsible delegation and a commission for addressing the complaints of the students and professors will be formed.
89 | 3070

337 انتخابات entexɑbɑt *elections* n
- حتی اگر یک نفر مخالف باشد انتخابات باید باطل شود. — If even one person is opposed, the election should be invalidated.
79 | 6089

338 مرکزی mærkæzi *central* adj
- طرح بانک مرکزی برای جلوگیری از نوسانات ارز — The Central Bank's plan for preventing currency fluctuations.
86 | 3875

339 تصویر tæsvir *image* n
- تصویر مثبتی از پول و موفقیت در ذهنتان ایجاد کنید. — Create a positive image of money and success in your mind.
92 | 2210

340 مطرح mætræh *talked about, much discussed* adj
- مدیران موزه های مطرح دنیا بر اساس چه سابقه فرهنگی انتخاب می شوند؟ — Based on what cultural background are the world's top museum directors selected?
90 | 2650

341 انسانی ensɑni *human* adj,n
- History — یکی از رشته های علوم انسانی، تاریخ است. is one of the humanities.
92 | 2232

342 خاص xɑss *specific* adj,n
- He does — کارهای خاص را برای او انجام می دهد. specific work for him.
86 | 3784

343 مقابل moɣɑbel *opposite, against* adj,n,prep
- هر دو در مقابل یکدیگر و چشم در چشم هم قرار گرفتند. — Both of them stood opposite each other, eye to eye.
84 | 4513

344 سفر sæfær *travel* n
- Of — البته این سفر زودتر از اینها باید به آخر می رسید. course this trip should have wrapped up earlier than it did.
86 | 3781

345 مشخص moʃæxxæs *specified* adj
- برنامه مشخصی برای رئال دارید یا به تست کردن ادامه می دهید؟ — Do you have any specific plan for Real Madrid, or you are going to keep testing?
89 | 2992

346 فرهنگ færhæng *culture* n
- What kind — این چه فرهنگی است که ما پیدا کردیم؟ of culture is this that we have adopted?
83 | 4851

347 استفاده کردن estefɑde kærdæn *use* v
- چرا باید از عینک آفتابی استفاده کرد؟ — Why should one use sunglasses?
92 | 2263

348 انقلاب enɢelɑb *revolution* n
- چند سالی از انقلاب مکزیک گذشته بود. — A few years had passed since the Mexican Revolution.
78 | 6351

349 جمع dʒæmʔ *total, addition, plural* n
- در ادبیات فارسی معاصر واژۀ «عراب» را به عنوان جمع «عرب» به کار می‌برند. — In contemporary Persian literature, the word "a'raab" is used as the plural of "Arab."
92 | 2150

350 پیشنهاد piʃnehɑd *proposal* n
- هرگز به اولین پیشنهاد پاسخ مثبت ندهید. — Never respond positively to the first proposal.
92 | 2178

351 ماده mɑde, mɑdde *female, matter* n
- یك شب خواب دیدم به شکل ماده آهویی در آمده ام و در بیابان می‌گردم و می‌چرم. — One night I had a dream that I turned into a female deer who was grazing and moving around in the desert.
81 | 5404

352 معنا mæʔnɑ *meaning* adj,n
- موضوع آن مرد برایش کاملا بی معنا شده بود. — The man's topic had become completely meaningless for her.
86 | 3671

353 کنار kenɑr *edge, beside* n,prep
- تا آخرین لحظه در کنار مردم خواهم ماند. — I will stay until the last moment beside the people.
86 | 3663

354 رأی ræʔj *vote* n
- به نظر من تعداد رأیی که هر کاندیدا می‌آره هم باید تعیین‌کننده باشه. — In my opinion the number of votes that each candidate receives should also be decisive.
88 | 3249

355 کلی kolli *total, general* adj
- چارچوبی کلی برای گروه خود تنظیم کنید. — Set a general framework for your group.
92 | 2086

356 حقیقت hæɣiɣæt *truth* n,pn
- حقیقت چیست؟ — What is the truth?
93 | 1926

357 تأمین tæʔmin *securing* n
- به منظور تأمین انرژی مورد نیاز برای فعالیت‌های زیستی. — In order to provide the required energy for biological activities.
86 | 3869

358 خانه xɑne *house* n
- روز آخر را تماماً به خرید و انباشتن آذوقه در خانه گذراند. — She spent the entire last day buying and storing provisions in the house.
76 | 6864

359 جمعیت dʒæmʔijjæt *population* adj,n
- رئیس «یکی از سازمان‌های پرجمعیت» به سوال خوبی اشاره کرد و پرسید: . . . — The head of "one of the most populous organizations" pointed to a good question and asked: . . .
89 | 2886

360 دین din *religion* n
- متافیزیک هیچ ربطی به دین ندارد. — Metaphysics has nothing to do with religion.
90 | 2527

361 امکان emkɑn *possibility* n
- بهره برداری از امکان سرمایه گذاری مستقیم خارجی. — Tapping the potential of direct foreign investment.
85 | 3992

362 علم elm *science* n
- تو خودت از هر کس می دانی که الان هشت نه سال است شب و روزم صرف ریاضیات و علم اعداد شده است. — You know better than anyone that for 8 or 9 years now my days and nights have been spent on mathematics and numerical science.
84 | 4159

363 انتظار entezɑr *waiting, expectation* n
- و برای شروع کار، حقوق مورد انتظار شما چیست؟ — To start working, what is your expected salary?
92 | 2021

364 کوتاه kutɑh *short* adj
- پیراهن آستین کوتاه پوشیده بود، اما یک چیزی مثل شال روی شکمش بسته بود. — He was wearing a short sleeve shirt, but he had something like a scarf around his belly.
92 | 2023

365 بازار bɑzɑr *market* n
- صدای خنده بازار را پر کرد. — The sounds of laughter filled the market.
78 | 5934

366 کل kol *whole, total* n,q
- کل مسیر از مشهد تا نیشابور حدودا ۱۱۰ کیلو متر می باشد. — The entire route from Mashhad to Nishapur is about 110 km.
85 | 4001

367 میدان mejdɑn *plaza, square, field* n
- به میدان رسیدم. — I reached the square.
89 | 2935

368 فرهنگی færhæŋgi *cultural, educational* adj
- این واقعه با واکنش فرهنگیان و نویسندگان افغانستانی مواجه شد. — This event was met with the reaction of Afghan academics and writers.
78 | 6006

369 خارج شدن xɑredʒ ʃodæn *leave* v
- بریتانیا از اتحادیه اروپا خارج می‌شود. — Britain is withdrawing from the European Union.
96 | 970

370 شدت ʃeddæt *intensity* adv,n
- در راه به مسافری برخورد که از شدت گرسنگی به حالت ضعف افتاده بود. — On the way, he encountered a traveler who had fallen into a state of weakness due to the severity of his hunger.
- 92 | 2050

371 حقوق hoɣuɣ *rights, salary* n
- دولت نمی‌تواند نسبت به حقوق زنان بی‌تفاوت باشد. — The government can't be indifferent to women's rights.
- 87 | 3416

372 گل gol, gel *flower/goal, mud* n
- من گل می خواهم که بزنم به موی سرم. — I want a flower to put in my hair.
- 87 | 3377

373 رشته reʃte *field, noodle* n
- برخی رشته هاي دانشگاهي رشد و پيشرفت خود را مديون صنعت خودرو هستند. — Some of the academic disciplines owe their growth and advancement to the auto industry.
- 90 | 2420

374 جلسه dʒælæse *meeting* n
- او با دوستانش جلسه دارد و شب دیر می‌آید. — She has a meeting with her friends and she'll be coming late tonight.
- 86 | 3430

375 دکتر doktor *doctor* n
- دکتر لبخندی زد. —The doctor smiled.
- 80 | 5121

376 سؤال soʔal *question* n
- مرد سؤالش را تکرار کرد. — The man repeated his question.
- 88 | 3038

377 فضا fæza *space* n
- این ترفند، فضایی برای مذاکره در اختیارتان قرار می‌دهد. — This trick will give you room for negotiation.
- 88 | 2992

378 فیلم film *film* n
- فکر کردم این یک فیلم وسترن یا یک فیلم پلیسی است. — I thought that this was a Western or a cop film.
- 76 | 6475

379 منظور mænzur *intention, purpose* n
- منظورم این است سه تا پسر داشتم ، حالا دو تا دارم. — I mean that I had three sons and now I have two.
- 88 | 2978

380 دفتر dæftær *office* n
- انجمن کلیمیان ایران پیام شفاهی را به مناسبت سال نو عبری از دفتر ریاست جمهوری ایران دریافت کرده اند. — Iran's Jewish association received a verbal message from the president's office on the occasion of the Jewish New Year.
- 91 | 2293

381 تو to, tu *you, in* n,prep,pron
- تو چکار میکنی. — What do you do?
- 53 | 14651

382 هیئت hejʔæt *board* n
- تمام هیئت‌های کشورهای اروپایی در صف ملاقات با رئیس جمهور بودند. — All the delegates from European countries were in line to meet the president.
- 85 | 3736

383 زبان zæban *language, tongue* n
- در حال حاضر کتاب‌ها و مجلاتی به ۶۱ زبان دنیا منتشر می‌شود. — Right now magazines and books are being published in 61 of the world's languages.
- 81 | 4946

384 مسابقه mosabeɣe *competition* n
- در این مسابقه شرکت کنندگان باید با لباس‌های سنتی حاضر شوند. — In this competition, the participants must show up in traditional dress.
- 78 | 5796

385 حوزه howze *district, domain* n
- دارند حوزه ی اسلام را ضعیف می کنند. — They are weakening the domain of Islam.
- 85 | 3797

386 چرا ʧera, ʧæra *why, grazing* adv
- چرا یک بار دیگر برایش نامه نمی نویسید؟ — Why don't you write him a letter again?
- 80 | 5212

387 خیلی xejli *very* adv,q
- خیلی جالب بود. — It was very interesting.
- 70 | 8331

388 دقیقه dæɣiɣe *minute* n
- چند دقیقه بعد صدای عرعر خری را شنیدیم. — A few minutes later I heard the sound of a donkey braying.
- 89 | 2684

389 فرانسه færanse *France, French* pn
- فرانسه شخصیت‌های بزرگ و برجسته‌ای مانند مالرو دارد. — France has great and prominent figures like Malraux.
- 82 | 4417

390 بیان bæjan *expression* n
- به بیانات ایشان توجه کنید. — Pay attention to their statements.
- 87 | 3312

391 واحد vahed *unit* adj,n
- واحدهای تجاری غیر رقابتی را کنار بگذارید. — Give up uncompetitive trade units.
- 81 | 4730

392 کاری kɑri *active, working* adj,n
- سالانه ۲۷۰میلیون حادثه در محیط‌های کاری رخ می‌دهد. — 270 million workplace accidents occur each year.

85 | 3625

393 مرگ mærg *death* n
- بیشترین علت مرگ و میر چیست؟ — What is the most common cause of death?

90 | 2286

394 سخن soxæn *speech* n
- رئیس دفتر رئیس جمهور در ادامه سخنان خود بر ضرورت مهار هرچه بیشتر تورم و توجه به توسعه اقتصاد کشور تأکید کرد. — The head of the office of the President in his speech emphasized the need for reining in inflation and developing the country's economy.

88 | 2868

395 ادامه دادن edame dadæn *continue* v
- مادام کوری پس از مرگ شوهرش به مطالعات خود ادامه داد. — Madame Curie continued her research after the death of her husband.

92 | 1969

396 زمانی zæmɑni *chronological* adj,n
- ما با امریکا ۱۲ساعت اختلاف زمانی داریم. — We have a 12-hour time difference with America.

87 | 3042

397 ارتباط ertebɑt *connection, contact* n
- اگر کسی می‌توانست با خورشید، پادشاه ستارگان، ارتباط برقرار کند . . . — If one could make a connection with the Sun, the king of stars . . .

85 | 3563

398 موافق movɑfeɣ *agreeable* adj,n,v
- با نظر شما کاملاً موافقم. — I completely agree with your point of view.

97 | 657

399 شهید ʃæhid *martyr* adj,n
- به او خبر دادند که در حادثه کربلا هر چهار پسر تو شهید شدند. — They told him that all of your four sons were martyred in the Karbala incident.

90 | 2460

400 شاهد ʃɑhed *witness* adj,n
- جریان‌های ورودی و خروجی سرمایه را شاهد خواهیم بود. — We will witness inflow and outflow of capital.

91 | 2182

401 حد hædd *limit* n
- البته با تلاش‌هایی که انجام شده است میزان رشد تورم تا حد قابل ملاحظه‌ای کاهش یافته است. — Of course, with the efforts that have been carried out, inflation growth rate has decreased to a noticeable extent.

89 | 2653

402 امید omid *hope* n
- به جامعه نشاط و امید بدهید. — Give hope and joy to society.

92 | 1779

403 روش ræveʃ *method* n
- در گزارش های قبلی یک روش ساده و کاربردی هم ارائه گردیده بود. — In the previous reports, a simple and practical method was also provided.

85 | 3685

404 امنیت æmnijæt *security* n
- همین خوب است، لااقل امنیت داریم. — This is good, at least we have security.

81 | 4666

405 قرار بودن ɣærɑr budæn *be supposed to* v
- قرار بود قسمت دوم این فیلم در سال بعد ساخته شود. — The second part of this film was supposed to be made next year.

89 | 2556

406 نفت næft *oil* n
- بوی نفت انسان را گیج می کرد. — The smell of oil was confusing people.

79 | 5203

407 دوران dowran, dæværan *period, circulation* n
- فرهنگ ایران در دوران انتقال از عصر ساسانی به عصر اسلامی — Iranian culture in the period of transition from the Sasanian to the Islamic Era.

88 | 2786

408 چاپ ʧɑp *print* n
- اولین کتابش که چاپ شد یک نسخه به من هدیه داد. — She gave me a copy of her first book when it was printed.

86 | 3307

409 شبکه ʃæbæke *network* n
- مسائل مطرح در شبکه های حسگر بی سیم — Issues raised by wireless sensor networks.

76 | 5885

410 وقت væɣt *time* n
- وقت اضافی نیز به پایان رسید. — The extra time has also ended.

79 | 5074

411 وقتی væɣti *when* conj,n
- وقتی اینشتین پنج ساله بود، پدرش به او یک قطب‌نمای جیبی نشان داد. — When Einstein was five years old, his father showed him a pocket compass.

77 | 5750

412 حزب hezb *party* n
- عضو سازمان جوانان حزب توده بوده ام. — I have been a member of the youth wing of the Tudeh Party.

82 | 4227

413 مانع mane? *obstacle* adj,n
- ایران با تکیه بر مردم خویش از همه‌مراحل و موانع خواهد گذشت. — Iran will overcome all phases and obstacles by relying on its people.
- 92 | 1707

414 فصل fæsl *season, chapter* n
- این کتاب از دو فصل «علیه تهران» و «اعتراف» تشکیل می‌شود. — This book consists of two chapters, "Against Tehran" and "Confession."
- 90 | 2192

415 نشان neʃan *sign* n
- نشان‌های راهنمایی و رانندگی در ایران به سه دسته تقسیم می‌شوند. — The roadsigns in Iran are divided into three categories.
- 93 | 1669

416 مناسب monaseb *appropriate* adj
- چه زمانی برای راه اندازی آن مناسب است؟ — What would be the right time to launch it?
- 87 | 3091

417 شب ʃæb *night* n
- شب قبل آمده بودند. — They had come the night before.
- 81 | 4558

418 روند rævænd *process* n
- روند تأمین گاز مورد نیاز — The process of supplying the required gas.
- 86 | 3166

419 مدرسه mædrese *school* n
- اولین مدرسه در تاریخ مدرن ایران، مدرسه دارالفنون بود. — The first school in modern Iranian history was Dar ol-Fonun.
- 86 | 3122

420 حاکم hakem *ruler* adj,n
- خوب، همین برادر حاتم طایی‌تان چطور حاکم شد؟ — Well, how did your brother Hatim Tai became a governor?
- 89 | 2429

421 آماده amade *ready* adj
- اروپا آماده است. — Europe is ready.
- 90 | 2150

422 پول pul *money* n
- بیشتر از همیشه پول گرفتیم. — We got more money than ever before.
- 86 | 3096

423 پاسخ pasox *reply* n
- ندا پاسخ داد: از من خواست که تمام خواسته های تو را اجابت کنم. — The voice replied: he asked me to comply with all your requests.
- 88 | 2606

424 ایشان iʃan *they* pron
- از ایشان شماره تلفن آقای صالحی را گرفتم. — I got Mr. Salehi's number from them.
- 86 | 3124

425 میلیارد miljard *billion* n
- تعداد کهکشان های کشف شده تا به امروز بیش از 120 هزار میلیارد است. — The number of galaxies discovered to date is more than 120 trillion.
- 79 | 4817

426 مسیر mæsir *route* n
- در مسیر خوبی حرکت می‌کنید. — You're going down a good path.
- 87 | 2837

427 واقعیت vaʁe?ijjæt *reality* n
- این داستان به احتمال زیاد واقعیت ندارد. — This story most probably doesn't have much truth to it.
- 91 | 2063

428 موجود mowdʒud *available, creature* adj
- به علت نواقص موجود در اجرای خصوصی سازی براساس اصل 44 قانون اساسی — Because of the existing shortcomings in the implementation of privatization according to Article 44 of the constitution.
- 85 | 3296

429 فشار feʃar *pressure* n
- فشار خون مرا گرفت. — He took my blood pressure.
- 87 | 2969

430 دستور dæstur *order, instruction* n
- از دستورات مرسی اطاعت کنید. — Obey Morsi's orders.
- 91 | 1910

431 اصلاح eslah *correction* n
- میان دولت و مجلس قرار شد که این مسئله اصلاح شود. — This issue was supposed to be rectified between the government and the parliament.
- 83 | 3802

432 کوچک kuʧæk *small* adj
- میرزا گفت: «فقط یک اشکال کوچک، خیلی کوچک هست» — Mirza said "There is only a minor, very minor, problem."
- 88 | 2531

433 افغانستان æfɣanestan *Afghanistan* pn
- نخستین نیروگاه برق در افغانستان در زمان پادشاهی امیر حبیب الله خان در کابل ساخته شد. — The first electric power plant in Afghanistan was built in Kabul during the reign of Emir Habibullah Khan.
- 53 | 13169

434 پیدا pejda *find* adj,v
- من شماره تلفن شما را به سختی پیدا کردم. — I found your telephone number with difficulty.
- 89 | 2341

435 طولانی tulani *long* adj
- طولانی‌ترین پل دریایی جهان ساخته شد. — The longest sea bridge in the world was built.
- 95 | 1159

436 سعی sæʔj *try* n

- سعی کن زیاد نخوری سبک باشی شب هم همین طور
  بخور سبک — . — Try not to eat too much
  to be light, eat light in the evening
  as well.
  95 | 1118

437 شروع ʃoruʔ *start* n

- بازی ما شروع شد — . — Our game began.
  92 | 1730

438 چهار tʃæhar *four* n

- چهار سال بیشتر نداشت که پدرش مُرد — . — He
  was no older than four when his
  father died.
  71 | 6995

439 پرداخت pærdaxt *payment, paid* n,v

- پرداخت حقوق‌های بالا در جامعه نگرانی ایجاد کرده است.
  — Paying high salaries has caused concerns
  in the community.
  86 | 2959

440 طول tul *length* n

- کاهش کالری‌های مصرفی می‌تواند طول عمر را افزایش
  دهد. — Decreasing calorie intake can
  increase the length of life.
  86 | 3072

441 معتقد moʔtæɣed *believing* adj,v

- معتقد بود این دو ارتباطی نزدیک با هم دارند — . — He
  believed that these two had a very close
  relation to each other.
  88 | 2628

442 حفظ hefz *preservation* n

- باید دلایل حذف یا حفظ آن اعلام شود — . — The reasons
  for removing or keeping it should be
  announced.
  89 | 2380

443 چهارم tʃæharom *fourth* adj,n

- المپیاس چهارمین همسر فیلیپ بود — . — Olympias was
  Philip's fourth wife.
  89 | 2444

444 مشترک moʃtæræk, moʃtærek *common, subscriber*
adj

- جلسه مشترک شورای اسلامی شهرمهربان با
  فرماندارسراب. — Joint meeting of Islamic
  council of Mehraban city with the governor
  of Sarab.
  88 | 2653

445 خوبی xubi *goodness* adj,adv,n

- رودکی شاعر خوبی‌ها و عدالت بود — . — Rudaki was
  the poet of goodness and justice.
  85 | 3274

446 زیاد zijad *many, a lot* adj,adv

- عیبی ندارد، زیاد خطرناک نیست — . — It's no problem,
  it's not very dangerous.
  87 | 2701

447 حادثه hadese *accident, incident* n

- سپس فرمود: مگر چه حادثه ای برای تو رخ داده است که
  این سؤال را می کنی؟ — Then he said: what
  happened to you that you are asking this
  question?
  85 | 3109

448 محل mæhæl *location* n

- مسیر برگشت من از محل کار به سمت منزل از محدوده
  میدان صادقیه تا میدان پونک است. — My return
  route from work to home is from Sadeghiyeh
  Square to Punak Square.
  85 | 3244

449 مستقیم mostæɣim *direct* adj

- در حقیقت در فقدان زیرساخت های صنعت ملی، پروژه
  کاملاً از بالا و به صورت متمرکز و دستوری با تکیه بر
  انتقال مستقیم سرمایه و تکنولوژی از یک کشور خارجی،
  مدیریت گردید. — In fact, in the absence of a
  national infrastructure, the project was
  managed in a focused and orderly way,
  dependent on direct transfer of capital and
  technology from a foreign country.
  92 | 1559

450 اروپا orupa *Europe* pn

- این ارقام در امریکا و اروپا نسبت تقریباً مشابهی دارند.
  — These figures in America and Europe
  have approximately similar proportions.
  76 | 5493

451 عرصه ærse *area* n

- نمی توانند در این عرصه حرفی برای گفتن داشته باشند.
  — In this arena, they cannot have a say.
  88 | 2450

452 آمریکایی amrikaji *American* adj

- آمریکایی‌ها هم هستند — . — There are also
  Americans.
  77 | 5132

453 مالی mali *financial* adj

- هنوز مشکلات مالی و فن آوری این طرح حل نشده است.
  — The financial and technological problems
  of this plan still haven't been solved.
  82 | 3855

454 جز dʒoz *except* conj

- دلیل هم این که هیچ کدام از نوه هایش به جز خوبیلو به
  زبان مایایی صحبت نمی کردند. — The reason is
  that none of his grandchildren except
  Khubilu spoke the Mayan language.
  91 | 1730

455 تازه taze *fresh* adj,adv

- خانم آن همکارمان که تازه زندانی شده بود، دم در داشت
  خداحافظی می‌کرد. — The wife of that
  coworker of ours who was recently
  imprisoned was at the door saying
  goodbye.
  85 | 3256

456 ساخته saxte *manufactured* adj,n

- ظرفهای «سفالی»، شاید یکی از قدیمیترین ساختههای آدمی
است. — Earthenware pots are perhaps one of
the oldest human artifacts.
87 | 2778

457 مقاله mæɣale *article* n

- تحت تاثیر مقالهای که یکی از جامعهشناسان در یکی از
روزنامهها چاپ کرده، قرار گرفتهام. — I am
impressed by an article that a sociologist
published in one of the newspapers.
91 | 1844

458 چین ʧin *China* pn

- نمایندگان ژاپن و چین به زودی به ایران خواهند آمد.
— The representatives of Japan and China
will soon come to Iran.
81 | 4171

459 مرد mærd *man* n

- فقط دو مرد توانستند به سوی جزیره کوچک بی آب و علفی
شنا کنند. — Only two men were able to swim to
the small barren island.
77 | 5055

460 امام emam *imam* n,pn

- آنهایی هم که منتظر امام زمانند، همین را می گویند.
— Those who are awaiting the Imam of the
Age say the same thing.
79 | 4416

461 واقعی vaɣeʔi *real* adj

- یک نمونه ی واقعی از انحطاط اخلاقی و رفتاری یک ایل.
— One real example of moral and behavioral
deterioration of a tribe.
92 | 1612

462 انجام شدن ændʒam ʃodæn *be done* v

- بر اساس اطلاعات جدیدی که سازمان سیا منتشر کرده
آزمایش برخی هواپیماهای سری آمریکا از جمله هواپیماهای
جاسوسی مشهور U-2، هواپیمای F-117، SR-71 و..در
این مرکز انجام شده است. — According to new
information that the CIA published, the
testing of some secret American planes,
including the well-known U-2, F-117, and
SR-71 spy planes, took place at this site.
86 | 2827

463 وضع væzʔ *situation, condition* n

- وضع جسمی شما در حال حاضر چطور است؟ — How is
your current physical condition?
83 | 3479

464 دستگاه dæstgah *machine, system* n

- زمین لرزه ها توسط دستگاه زلزله سنج یا لرزه نگار ثبت
میشوند. — Earthquakes recorded by the
seismometer or seismograph devices.
83 | 3532

465 سیستم sistem *system* n

- سیستم مدیریت اقتصادی کشور — Economic
management system of the country.
86 | 2940

466 دینی dini *religious* adj

- این کتاب معتبرترین متن دینی نزد مسلمانان است. — This
book is the most reliable religious text among
Muslims.
90 | 1935

467 کودک kudæk *child* n

- چگونه می توان کودک را طوری تربیت کرد تا در منزل و
اجتماع برخورد خوبی داشته باشد؟ — How to train a
child so that he will behave nicely at home
and in the society?
80 | 4184

468 ابتدا ebteda *beginning, at first* adv,n

- ابتدا جلسه با بیانات مختصر ریاست بیمارستان آغاز شد.
— First, the session began with brief
statements by the head of the hospital.
88 | 2304

469 خواست xast *wish, wanted* n,v

- هیچگاه امکان برآورده ساختن خواستهای همگان میسر
نمیگشت. — The opportunity of making
everyone's wish come true was never
possible.
90 | 2057

470 دولتی dowlæti *governmental* adj,n

- پدر وی حسابدار دولتی بود. — His father was a
government accountant.
84 | 3365

471 رسمی ræsmi *official* adj

- شکلگیری آرایش نظامی در منطقه غرب آسیا و شمال آفریقا
و همچنین بیانیههای رسمی ارتش ایالات متحده همگی خبر
از آغاز قریبالوقوع این جنگ جدید در منطقه میدادند.
— The formation of the deployment in West
Asia and North Africa, as well as official
statements by the United States Army were
all indications of the start of an imminent
new war in the region.
89 | 2107

472 هزینه hæzine *cost* n

- لیست هزینه ها رو بده. — Give me the list of
expenditures.
82 | 3679

473 بانک bank *bank* n

- رئیس بانک مرد محترم و در عین حال پرحرفی بود.
— The head of the bank was respectful and
verbose at the same time.
79 | 4395

474 هوا hæva *air* n

- حال و هوای آشپزخانه به شدت متشنج بود. — The
atmosphere of the kitchen was extremely
tense.
86 | 2708

475 فکر fekr *thought* n

- برو یک فکری برای خودت بکن. — Go find a
solution to your own problem!
83 | 3469

3 Clothing

Rank	Headword	Pronunciation	Gloss	Rank	Headword	Pronunciation	Gloss
1508	لباس	lebas	*clothing*	10061	جوراب	dʒurab	*socks*
2692	پوتین	putin	*boots*	10255	یقه	jæɣe	*collar*
3463	جامه	dʒame	*clothes*	11059	پالتو	paltow	*overcoat*
3539	پیراهن	pirahæn	*shirt*	11894	عبا	æba	*sleeveless outer garment*
3678	کیف	kif	*bag*				
3844	کفش	kæfʃ	*shoe*	12564	مانتو	manto	*loose female outer garment*
3955	دامن	damæn	*skirt*				
3998	جیب	dʒejb, dʒib	*collar, pocket*	12820	روپوش	rupuʃ	*loose female outer garment, uniform*
4140	کمر	kæmær	*belt*				
4256	کلاه	kolah	*hat*	13000	ردا	ræda	*outer garment*
4290	کمربند	kæmærbænd	*belt*	13033	کراوات	kravat	*tie*
4682	چادر	tʃador	*chador*	13902	آستر	astær	*lining*
4691	تل	tel	*headband*	14384	پاچه	patʃe	*trouser leg*
4838	پوشاک	puʃak	*clothing*	14612	چارقد	tʃarɣæd	*scarf*
5106	بارانی	barani	*raincoat*	14935	جلیقه	dʒeliɣe	*vest*
6378	شلوار	ʃælvar	*pants*	15472	روبان	ruban	*ribbon*
6532	کت	kot	*coat*	16070	گیوه	give	*cotton sandals*
7376	روسری	rusæri	*headscarf*	16169	مایو	majo	*swimsuit*
7490	عصا	æsa	*cane*	16174	زیرپوش	zirpuʃ	*underwear*
7531	دستمال	dæstmal	*handkerchief*	17267	تنبان	tomban	*underpants*
7539	شال	ʃal	*shawl*	17576	مقنعه	mæɣnæʔe	*head covering*
7594	چکمه	tʃækme	*boots*	17723	کاپشن	kapʃen	*parka*
7617	آستین	astin	*sleeve*	17906	دگمه	dogme	*button*
7680	رخت	ræxt	*clothes*	17991	شورت	ʃort	*underwear*
8344	دکمه	dokme	*button*	18630	عرقچین	æræɣtʃin	*skullcap*
9645	دستکش	dæstkeʃ	*glove*	19806	ژاکت	ʒakæt	*cardigan*
9650	پاشنه	paʃne	*heel*				

476 شنبه ʃæmbe *Saturday* n
- ملاقات های بعدی شنبه ها خواهدبود. — The next meetings will happen on Saturdays.
89 | 2088

477 انتقال enteɣal *transfer* n
- انتقال این فرهنگ چه کاربردی دارد؟ — What is the use of transferring this culture?
88 | 2269

478 انگلیسی engelisi *English* adj,n,pn
- او داشت برای پدر به انگلیسی حرف می‌زد. — She was speaking in English for her father.
90 | 1883

479 تحقیق tæhɣiɣ *research* n
- تحقیقات علمی و موفقیت‌های بین‌المللی در زمینه گل‌ها و گیاهان. — Scientific research and international achievements in the field of plants and flowers.
81 | 3782

480 پی pej *foundation, tendon* n
- در قسمت غربی برج آثاری از پی ساختمان قابل رویت است. — Traces of the building's foundation are visible on the western part of the tower.
84 | 3057

481 ده dæh, deh *ten, village* n
- قاسم بیشتر از ده دقیقه با فوزی حرف زد. — Ghasem talked to Fowzi for more than ten minutes.
79 | 4309

482 موجب mudʒeb *cause, reason* n
- دعاي فرج اگر موجب فرج عمومي نشود براي دعا كننده
موجب فرج خواهد بود. — If the Faraj prayer does
not cause relief for the public, it will cause a
relief for those who pray.
85 | 2845

483 سنگين sæŋgin *heavy* adj
- خانلرخان از بس سنگين بود به سختي مي توانست تكان
بخورد. — Khanlar Khan was so heavy that he
could barely move.
94 | 1196

484 اداره edare *office* n
- اداره راهنمايي و رانندگي اين كشور از چند ماه پيش رسما
اعلام كرد. — The Department of Motor
Vehicles of this country was formally
announced a few months ago.
84 | 3242

485 خطر xætær *risk* n
- امنيت جاني او در خطر مي باشد. — His safety is at
risk.
89 | 2169

486 نظامي nezami *military, Nezami* adj,n,pn
- به جناب سرهنگ سلام نظامي مي داد. — He was
giving a military salute to the general.
69 | 6754

487 نقل næɣl, noɣl *conveyance/narration, comfit* n
- وظيفه آن نقل مشكلات مردم شهر قزوين بوده‌است.
— Its task was to relay the people of
Qazvin city's problems.
88 | 2292

488 شديد ʃædid *severe* adj
- در روزهاي آلودگي شديد هوا چرا دولت فقط مدارس را
تعطيل مي‌كند؟ — On days with severe air
pollution why does the government only
close schools?
88 | 2315

489 مربوط mærbut *related* adj
- استرس مي‌تواند احتمال نقصان فكري مربوط به آلزايمر
را افزايش دهد. — Stress can increase the risk
of neurological disorders related to
Alzheimer's.
83 | 3330

490 فوتبال futbal *soccer* n
- در فوتبال مردان تعداد بازيكنان بالاي ۲۳ سال در هر تيم
نبايد بيشتر از ۳ نفر باشد. — In men's soccer, the
number of players over 23 years old must
not be over 3 on each team.
79 | 4125

491 واقع vaɣe? *located* adj
- مزار بسياري از چهره‌هاي سياسي و مذهبي در اين گورستان
واقع است. — The tombs of many political and
religious figures are located in this cemetery.
79 | 4250

492 كافي kafi *sufficient* adj
- از نظر يونگ فرصت مناسب براي توسعه شخصيت انسان
كافي نيست. — In Jung's view, a good
opportunity for human personality
development is not enough.
91 | 1619

493 آموزش amuzeʃ *teaching* n
- مركز آموزش فني و حرفه اي و مركز تحقيقات كشاورزي
بهبهان آغاز به كار كردند. — The Behbahan
Technical and Vocational Education Center
and Agriculture Research Center opened for
business.
77 | 4660

494 شايستن ʃajæstæn *be possible* adv
- براي كريستين شايد مهم بود. — It was probably
important for Christian.
80 | 3864

495 كنترل kontrol *control* n
- هنگامي كه خشم از كنترل خارج شده و تبديل به خشونت
مي‌گردد . . . — When anger is out of control
and turns to violence . . .
88 | 2302

496 دوست dust *friend* n
- مربي و بازيكنان از ديدن دوست وفادارشان حيرت زده
شدند. — The trainer and players were
astonished at seeing their loyal friend.
85 | 2826

497 تاكنون taknun *yet* adv
- قلب او به راستي زيباترين قلبي است كه تاكنون ديده اند.
— His heart is the most beautiful heart they
have seen so far.
85 | 2771

498 انتخاب كردن entexab kærdæn *elect, choose* v
- بيا، خودت انتخاب كن. — Come on, choose for
yourself.
96 | 771

499 دهه dæhe *decade* n
- وارد دهه تازه اي از عمرم مي شوم و به چهل سالگي سلام
مي گويم! — I start a new decade in my life,
and I say hello to forty!
88 | 2311

500 صاحب saheb *master* n
- اگر مردم آنچه را مي يابند برندارند، صاحبش مي آيد و آن
را برمي دارد. — If people do not take
everything they find, the owner will come and
pick it up.
89 | 2062

501 نشست neʃæst *sitting, meeting, subsiding, sat* n,v
- حضور در نشست‌هاي مجلس براي عموم آزاد است.
— Attending parliamentary meetings is open
to the public.
79 | 4117

502 نگاه negah *look* n

- بیرون آمدم تا دوباره پیراهن های توی ویترین را نگاه کنم. — I came outside to look at the shirts in the window again.

82 | 3524

503 معاون moʔaven *assistant* n

- امروز من در شهر کاری را باید انجام دهم ولی معاون من اینجا می ماند. — Today, I have something to do in town, but my assistant will be here.

85 | 2824

504 خصوص xosus *concern, regard* n

- دولت در خصوص خروج از کشور مقرراتی معین کرده که حتماً باید مراعات شود. — The government has set some rules regarding exiting the country which must certainly be followed.

80 | 3907

505 ماندن mandæn *stay* n,v

- درباره احتمال رفتن یا ماندن وی پرسید. — He asked about the possibility of his leaving or staying.

83 | 3312

506 برق bærɣ *electricity, lightning* n

- هرجا برق وارد شد زندگی نیز سنگین شد. — Wherever electricity went, life became heavy.

91 | 1666

507 مبارزه mobareze *struggle* n

- ازدواج یک مبارزه است. — Marriage is a struggle.

84 | 3032

508 مؤسسه moʔæssese *foundation, establishment* n

- مامانم یک مؤسسه گردشگری داره که تور مسافرتی به خارج از کشور و داخل ایران رو سازماندهی می‌کنه. — My mom has a tourism establishment that arranges tours abroad and within Iran.

88 | 2131

509 نمونه nemune *sample* adj,n

- چند نمونه از ماشین خریدنهای عجیب دیگر در ژاپن به شرح زیرند — Some examples of other strange vending machines in Japan are as follows.

90 | 1907

510 خوب xub *good* adj,adv

- انگلیسیش هم خوب نبود. —His English also wasn't good.

63 | 8010

511 عصر æsr *afternoon, age* n

- عصرها به محض ورود دکتر، نوشیدنی خنکی به دستش می داد و بعد هم چند نوبت چای خوش رنگی در مقابلش می گذاشت. — In the afternoons, upon the doctor's arrival, she would give him a cold drink and put fresh tea in front of him several times.

91 | 1665

512 پنج pændʒ *five* adj,n

- فقط پنج مرد و زن در اتاق مانده بود. — There were only five men and two women left in the room.

65 | 7352

513 همیشه hæmiʃe *always* adv

- عکسی که توی هالی‌فاکس یا لندن انداخته بودند همیشه روی میز پدر هست. — The photo that they took in London or Halifax was always on father's desk.

84 | 3013

514 باز baz *open, again* adj,adv

- فردا مدارس شهر تهران باز هستند. — The schools in Tehran will be open tomorrow.

75 | 4884

515 موفقیت movæffæɣijæt *success* n

- این مهمترین پایه و اساس موفقیت است. — This is the most important foundation and basis for success.

90 | 1728

516 آنچه anʧe *that which* pron

- نمی‌توانستند آنچه را که می‌دیدند باور کنند. — They couldn't believe what they saw.

84 | 2977

517 مصرف mæsræf *consumption* n

- وی با تأکید بر اینکه یارانه‌ها باید به جای مصرف غیر هدفمند به سمت تولید برود، تصریح کرد: — By emphasizing that subsidies should be directed toward production rather than untargeted consumption he clarified that:

86 | 2655

518 عراق eraɣ *Iraq* pn

- خلیل زاد از سال ۱۹۸۵ میلادی تا ۱۹۸۹ میلادی مشاور وزارت امور خارجه این کشور در امور جنگ ایران و عراق و همچنین اشغال افغانستان توسط ارتش سرخ شوروی سابق بود. — From 1985 to 1989, Khalilzad was the advisor to the State Department on Iran-Iraq War affairs and also the occupation of Afghanistan by the former Soviet Red Army.

71 | 5775

519 کسب kæsb *acquisition, business* n

- اینک تیمهای فرانسه و هلند و پرتغال نیز با کسب شش امتیاز به این مرحله راه یافته اند. — Now the teams of France, Holland, and Portugal having earned 6 points have also headed to this round.

83 | 3087

520 آمار amar *statistics* adj,n

- وزارت دادگستری عربستان در آخرین آمار خود میانگین طلاق را 21 درصد اعلام کرده است. — Saudi Arabia's Ministry of Justice has announced the average divorce rate as 21% in its latest statistics.

87 | 2391

521 دانشجو daneʃʤu *student* n

- صبح روز بعد، نخستین سمپوزیوم علمی دکتر ملک در حضور شماری از اساتید و دانشجویان پزشکی برگزار شد. — The next morning, Dr. Malek's first symposium was held in the presence of a number of professors and medical students.

86 | 2652

522 نوشته neveʃte *writing* adj,n
- مورّخان غالباً به اهمیت نوشته‌های تاریخی اشاره می‌کنند. — Historians often refer to the importance of historical writings.
84 | 2956

523 ریاست rijɑsæt *presidency* n
- کلینتون نامزد نهایی حزب دمکرات در انتخابات ریاست جمهوری شد. — Clinton became the final Democratic party nominee in the presidential elections.
83 | 3228

524 رهبر ræhbær *leader* n
- رهبران فرانسه و آلمان خواستار تحویل هر چه سریع‌تر قدرت به عراقی‌ها شده‌اند. — The leaders of France and Germany asked for power to be handed over to the Iraqis as soon as possible.
83 | 3155

525 دارا dɑrɑ *having* adj
- در این مطلب به معرفی تعدادی از مواد غذایی دارای کربوهیدرات پرداخته‌ایم. — In this article we have introduced a number of foods containing carbohydrates.
79 | 4081

526 تصمیم tæsmim *decision* n
- تصمیم گرفت زیر درخت مدتی استراحت کند. — He decided to rest a while beneath a tree.
88 | 2190

527 فرزند færzænd *child* n
- تنها فرزندم را از مرگ نجات دادی. — You saved my only child from death.
89 | 1922

528 تجربه tædʒrobe *experience* n
- این تجربه را هرگز نباید فراموش کرد. — One must never forget this experience.
87 | 2318

529 آسیا ɑsijɑ *Asia* n,pn
- پیروزی انقلاب اسلامی به معنای ظهور قدرتی جدید در منطقه غرب آسیا است. — The triumph of the Islamic Revolution signifies the appearance of a new power in western Asia.
82 | 3257

530 قیمت ɣejmæt *price* n
- قیمت مهم نیست. — The price is not important.
77 | 4401

531 رخ rox *face* n
- از خودم می‌پرسیدم چه جنایتی در مطب من رخ داد. I was asking myself what crime was committed in my clinic.
94 | 1087

532 تحول tæhævvol *evolution, development* n
- یک تحول جدی برای گسترش روابط اقتصادی — A serious development for the expansion of economic relations.
85 | 2640

533 رقابت reɣɑbæt *competition* n
- تختی در رقابتهای قهرمانی کشور طی سالهای ۱۳۲۹ تا ۱۳۳۸ هشت بار قهرمان کشور شد. — Takhti was champion in the national competitions eight times between 1329 and 1338.
74 | 4931

534 حمله hæmle *attack* n
- علایم این سندرم مشابه علایم حمله قلبی است. The symptoms of this syndrome are similar to the symptoms of a heart attack.
77 | 4265

535 شمار ʃomar *number* n,q
- شمار کشته‌های انفجار‌های تروریستی بغداد به ۲۶ نفر رسید. — The number of those killed in terrorist bombing in Baghdad reached 26.
83 | 3155

536 فاصله fasele *distance* n
- به فاصله کمی از آنها ۳ متهم که در نگاهشان شرارت موج می‌زد، — In a short distance from them three suspects who had a wave of viciousness in their eyes . . .
91 | 1649

537 اقتصاد eɣtesad *economy* n
- صادرات نفت از گذشته نقش اصلی را در اقتصاد عراق بر عهده داشته. — Oil exports have played a major role in the economy of Iraq since long ago.
81 | 3597

538 حکومت hokumæt *government* n
- حکومت ما سلطنتی نیست. — Our government is not monarchical.
76 | 4499

539 نقشه næɣʃe *map, plan* n
- دریانوران پرتغالی راه‌های دریایی گوناگونی را کشف و بر روی نقشه ثبت کردند. — Portuguese sailors discovered a variety of maritime routes and recorded then on maps.
95 | 880

540 همواره hæmvɑre *always* adv
- به همین دلیل همواره این صنعت در سایه حمایت همه جانبه دولت قرار داشته است. — That's why this industry has always had comprehensive support from the government.
90 | 1683

541 غرب ɣærb *west* n,pn
- آقای روحانی تنها کاری که درنیویورک در رابطه با آمریکا و کشور‌های غربی انجام دادند این بود که با ایشان با زبان ادب و احترام صحبت کردند. — The only thing that Mr. Rowhani did in New York regarding America and the Western nations was speak to them in the voice of courtesy and respect.
80 | 3794

542 گسترش gostæreʃ *spread* n

- کلینتون بر گسترش روابط دوجانبه امنیتی تاکید کرده است. — Clinton has emphasized the expansion of bilateral security relations.

83 | 3065

543 حل hæll *solution* n

- مشکل حل خواهد شد. — The problem will be solved.

85 | 2660

544 روشن rowʃæn *bright, turned on* adj

- سماوري كه مادر از قبل روشن کرده بود به جوش بود. — The samovar that mother turned on previously was boiling.

87 | 2374

545 گام gɑm *step* n

- او گام بلند دیگری برداشت. — He took another big step.

91 | 1492

546 خدا xodɑ *God* n,pn

- لعنت خدا بر دل سیاه شیطان! — God damn Satan's black heart!

77 | 4353

547 احساس ehsɑs *feeling* adj,n

- در وجودش لرزشی احساس کرده بود. — She had felt a tremble in her being.

88 | 2195

548 ساله sɑle *years-old* n

- پانزده ساله بودم که او را نیز از دست دادم. — I was fifteen years old when I lost her too.

86 | 2504

549 قرارداد yærɑrdɑd *contract* adj,n

- در این قرارداد یک قیمت به عنوان قیمت علی‌الحساب ذکر می‌شود. — In this contract one price is mentioned as a partial payment.

89 | 1896

550 مرز mærz *border* n

- این رودخانه، مرز مشترک ایران و عراق محسوب شد. — This river was considered the common border between Iran and Iraq.

88 | 2091

551 خاک xɑk *soil, dust* n

- خارجی‌ترین بخش زمین از خاک تشکیل شده است. — The outermost part of Earth is composed of soil.

89 | 1970

552 جمعه dʒomʔe *Friday* n

- آره همین جمعه میرووم. — Yes, I will go this Friday.

88 | 2061

553 عملیات æmælijɑt *campaign, operation* n

- مرحله اول عملیات موصل بیش از دو ماه پیش آغاز شد. — The first phase of the Mosul operation began two months ago.

87 | 2190

554 سرانجام særɑndʒɑm *finally* adv,conj,n

- فیفا، سرانجام اصلاحات را پذیرفت. — FIFA ultimately accepted the reforms.

95 | 790

555 معرفی moærrefi *introduction* n

- قصدم از معرفی ایشان تبلیغ نیست. — My intention for introducing them is not an advertisement.

92 | 1330

556 سبب sæbæb *cause* n

- نه تنها سبب شادی و سرور او نشد، بلکه او را به سرحد مرگ خشمگین و سوگوار کرد. — Not only did it not cause him happiness and joy, but up to death, it also made him angry and grieving.

91 | 1607

557 عهده ohde *responsibility* n,prep

- کاری که عامل برای اداره سرمایه و معامله ی با آن بر عهده می گیرد. — A task for which the agent takes responsibility for capital management and trade.

88 | 2122

558 زیرا zirɑ *because* conj

- برخی حیوانات که گروهی زندگی می کردند دور هم جمع شده بودند زیرا با این روش می توانستند بهتر خود را گرم کنند. — Some animals that lived in groups gathered together since this way, they could keep warm better.

84 | 2727

559 ضمن zemn *inside, while* n,prep

- کم کم در ضمن دیدنهائی که از او می کردم با چهار نفر مریض دیگر که در آن منزل داشتند سلام علیك و آشنائی پیدا کردم. — Gradually while I was visiting him, I started getting to know and communicate with four other patients who lived in the rooms of the house.

86 | 2497

560 صحنه sæhne *stage, scene* n

- برای انتخاب استاندار یزد، خاتمی و عارف وارد صحنه می شوند!؟ — For electing governor of Yazd, do Khatami and Aref enter the scene?

88 | 2083

561 خارجه xɑredʒe *foreign* adj

- بوریس جانسون وزیر خارجه بریتانیا شد. — Boris Johnson became the Foreign Minister of Britain.

82 | 3120

562 صدا sedɑ *sound, voice* n

- چند قدم مانده به جمعیت، صدای انفجار شوکه اش کرد. — A few steps away from the crowd, he was startled by the sound of an explosion.

73 | 5173

563 بعضی bæʔzi *some* n,pron,q

- چرا بعضی‌ها در خواب راه میروند؟ — Why do some people walk in their sleep?

86 | 2427

564 مراسم mærɑsem *ceremony* n

- وجود موسیقی برای مراسم مذهبی پرستش خداوند، بسیار ضروری بوده‌است. — The presence of music has been most essential for the religious ceremony of worshiping God.

84 | 2779

565 دریافت dærjaft *receipt, perception* n

- دریافت‌های افراد از زیبایی دیگران با یکدیگر متفاوت است. — Individuals' perceptions of others' beauty are different from each other.

88 | 2025

566 خون xun *blood* n

- برای افراد مبتلا به پرفشاری خون بخصوص کسانی که از داروهای کاهنده فشار خون استفاده می کنند، محدودیت مصرف دارد. — For people who are suffering from high blood pressure, especially those who use antihypertensive drugs, its consumption should be limited.

89 | 1873

567 مقدمه moɣæddæme *introduction* adj,n

- علی‌اکبر فیاض آمد و از او خواست که برای دیوانش مقدمه‌ای بنویسد. — Ali Akbar Fayyaz came and requested that he write an introduction for his divan.

92 | 1247

568 روسیه rusije *Russia* pn

- اقتصادی سیاسی ما اول به انگلیس، بعد به روسیه و امروز به ایالات متحده آمریکا و جامعه جهانی وابسته می باشد. — Our political economy was first dependent on England, then Russia, and today it is dependent on the United States of America and global society.

72 | 5119

569 استقلال esteɣlal *independence, Esteghlal* n,pn

- طبق اصول مافیایی، پدرخوانده نمی‌تواند اجازه استقلال و مقاومت موفقیت‌آمیز را بدهد، بنابراین ایران باید برای این کارش تنبیه می‌شد. — According to the principles of the mafia, the godfather cannot give permission for independence and successful resistance; therefore, Iran should have been punished for what it did.

88 | 1972

570 مثل mesl, mæsæl *like, proverb* adv,n

- فردی مثل من می‌تواند امروز کاری انجام دهد و فردا کار دیگری. — A person like me can do one thing today, and another thing tomorrow.

73 | 5017

571 سخت sæxt *hard* adj,adv

- خودتان که می‌دانید برای ماها خیلی سخت است. — You know yourself that it is very difficult for us.

90 | 1656

572 برگزاری bærgozari *holding* n

- منتظر اعلام نظر شورای نگهبان درباره زمان برگزاری انتخابات هستیم. — We are waiting for the Guardian Council's announcement regarding when the elections will be held.

82 | 3178

573 دسته dæste *bunch* n

- پل‌ها به سه دسته تقسیم می‌شوند. — Bridges are divided into three categories.

90 | 1724

574 آتش ɑtæʃ *fire* n

- فقط دریا می تواند آتش درونم را سرد کند. — Only the ocean can quell the fire inside me.

90 | 1623

575 سرعت sorʔæt *speed* adj,n

- درصد تخلفات سرعت غیرمجاز در استان مرکزی ۱۸ درصد است. — The percentage of illegal speed infractions in Markazi province is 18%.

90 | 1608

576 بین‌المللی bejnolmelæli *international* adj

- صندوق بین‌المللی پول — International Monetary Fund.

70 | 5598

577 مشارکت moʃarekæt *participation, partnership* n

- با مشارکت نهادها و سازمان های غیردولتی و تمام امضاکنندگان «اعلامیه جهانی حقوق زبانی» در همایشی که در تاریخ ششم تا نهم ژوئنیه ۱۹۹۶ (۱۳۷۵) در شهر بارسلون اسپانیا برگزار شد. — A conference was held in Barcelona, Spain on July 6th–9th 1996 (1375), with the participation of foundations, non-governmental organizations, and all the signatories of the "Universal Declaration of Linguistic Rights."

85 | 2567

578 وظیفه væzife *duty* n

- ما فقط وظیفه داریم اینجا مراقب باشیم که دزدی انجام نشود. — Our duty is only being careful that robbery doesn't happen here.

85 | 2602

579 فعال fæʔal *active* adj,n

- پایانه مرزی خسروی از فعال‌ترین پایانه های مرزی کشور است. — Khosravi border terminal is one of the most active border terminals in the country.

85 | 2422

580 رقم ræɣæm *digit, number* adj,n,pn

- جاعلان حرفه‌ای با تغییر ارقام چک، حساب‌ها را خالی می‌کردند. — Professional counterfeiters would empty the bank accounts by changing the check figures.

89 | 1768

581 نیمه nime *half, middle* n

- وی در نیمه‌های سال ۶۰۷ در یزد زاده شد. — He was born in Yazd in the middle of the year 607.

89 | 1745

582 شمال ʃomal *north* n

- از شمال به جنوب وارد تهران می شوند. — They enter Tehran from the north to the south.

83 | 2851

583 یاد jad *memory* n

- این جایزه هر سال برای گرامیداشت یاد مارتین آنالز اهدا می‌شود. — Every year this award is bestowed to commemorate the memory of Martin Ennals.

83 | 2757

584 بهار bæhar *spring* n,pn

- مرد کور هیچوقت ندانست که او چه نوشته است ولی روی تابلو خوانده می‌شد: امروز بهار است، ولی من نمی‌توانم آن

را ببینم. — The blind man never found out what he had written, but the sign said: It's spring today, but I can't see it.

93 | 1079

585 برداشتن bærdɑʃtæn *pick up, remove* adj,n,v
- چند قدم به طرف وانت برداشتم. — I took some steps towards the pickup truck.

84 | 2576

586 سریع særiʔ *fast* adj,adv
- با شروع طرح اصلاحات اقتصادی دنگ ژیائوپینگ، توسعه سریع اقتصادی و به تبع آن تغییر ساختار اجتماعی در دستور کار دولت قرار گرفت. — With the start of Deng Xiaoping's economic reform plan, rapid economic development and as a consequence change in social structure was put on the government's agenda.

91 | 1350

587 چهره ʧehre *face* n
- نگاهی به چهره مادرم انداختم. — I glanced at my mother's face.

90 | 1514

588 محصول mæhsul *product* n
- کمتر تولیدکننده ای در این شرایط به کیفیت در محصولات خود توجه دارد. — Fewer manufacturers in this situation pay attention to the quality of their products.

85 | 2399

589 تاریخی tɑrixi *historical* adj
- این بنای تاریخی در زمان جنگ های داخلی افغانستان به شدت آسیب دید. — This historical monument was seriously damaged during the civil war in Afghanistan.

83 | 2823

590 چشم ʧeʃm, ʧæʃm *eye, yessir* n
- چشمها برای دیدن این آثار کافی نیستند. — Eyes are not enough for viewing these artifacts.

72 | 4778

591 بند bænd *string, paragraph* n
- بندهایی از قطعنامه 598 اجرا نشده است. — Some articles of Resolution 598 have not been executed.

85 | 2446

592 مخالف moxɑlef *opposed* adj,n
- من از همون اول با ازدواجتون مخالف بودم. — I was against your marriage from the very beginning.

81 | 3072

593 بیست bist *twenty* n
- هیچ کس نفهمید و بیست سال گذشت. — No one realized and twenty years passed.

57 | 8232

594 آلمان ɑlmɑn *Germany* pn
- رئیس جمهور آلمان برای دور دوم کاندیدا نخواهد شد. — The president of Germany will not run for a second term.

82 | 2980

595 تقویت tæɣvijæt *reinforcement* n
- امام جمعه مهربان با تاکید بر تقویت دستگاه دیپلماسی کشورمان گفت: — Mehraban's Friday imam with an emphasis on strengthening our country's diplomatic system said:

89 | 1693

596 احتمال ehtemɑl *probability* n
- احتمال پیروزی شما را افزایش خواهد داد. — It will increase the probability of your success.

91 | 1425

597 تعیین tæʔjin *determination* n
- همچنین عوامل غیراقتصادی در تعیین نرخ ارز لحاظ می‌شود. — Non-economic factors are also considered in determining the currency exchange rate.

86 | 2221

598 پلیس polis *police* n
- ۳ پلیس دیگر در آمریکا کشته شدند. — 3 more police officers were killed in America.

82 | 2816

599 فروش foruʃ *sale* n
- او می دانست که این سنگ آن قدر قیمتی است که با فروش آن می تواند تا آخر عمر در رفاه زندگی کند. — She knew that this stone was so precious that by selling it she could live the rest of her life in prosperity.

83 | 2700

600 رسانه resɑne *medium* n
- عکس های زیر که توسط زائران خانه خدا عکاسی شده و در رسانه های خارجی و داخلی منتشر شده اند به خاطر آماتور بودن عکاس با کیفیت پائینی در نمایش در می‌آید. — The pictures below that were photographed by visitors of the Kaaba and published in foreign and domestic media came out low quality because the photographer was an amateur.

82 | 2908

601 جنوب dʒonub *south* n
- از دور که می بینم که از طرف جنوب به سمت ما می آید. — I can see from far off that she is approaching us from the south.

83 | 2711

602 تهیه tæhijje *preparation* n
- هیزم شکن بسیار قوی بود و می توانست در کمتر از یک هفته یکصد تنه تراشیده درخت قطور را تهیه و تحویل دهد. — The woodcutter was very strong and he could prepare and deliver one hundred thick carved tree trunks in less than a week.

86 | 2208

603 بیماری bimɑri *illness* n
- دوپامین یک ماده شیمیایی است که کمبود آن به بیماری پارکینسون می‌انجامد. — Dopamine is a chemical whose deficiency leads to Parkinson's disease.

80 | 3151

604 گردیدن gærdidæn *turn, become* adj,v
- باعث صحنههای وحشتناک و خشونت آمیز گردیدند. — They caused horrifying and violent scenes.
70 | 5078

605 صرف særf, serf *spending/consuming, pure* adj,n
- بعد از صرف ناهار هیزم شکن با شادی و خوشحالی برخاست. — After eating lunch, the woodcutter got up with joy and happiness.
92 | 1273

606 مجموعه mædʒmuʔe *collection* n
- نخستین مجموعه آثار شکسپیر کشف شد. — The first collection of Shakespeare's works was discovered.
81 | 3027

607 نمایش næmajeʃ *exhibiting, display* adj,n
- نقشه ها و عکسهای پیوستی وضعیت موجود شهر را به نمایش می گذارد. — The attached pictures and maps portray the existing situation of the city.
79 | 3395

608 اساسی æsasi *basic, fundamental* adj
- پیچیدگیها وقتی به وجود میآید که افراد از داشتن اطلاعات اساسی و حیاتی محروم شوند. — Complexity occurs when people are deprived from having fundamental and vital information.
78 | 3644

609 قبلی γæbli *previous* adj
- از دور به زندگی قبلی خود نگاه کنید. — Look at your previous life from afar.
93 | 1037

610 پایه paje *base* adj,n
- این مهمترین پایه و اساس موفقیت است باید بیاموزید مسئولیت صد درصد زندگی خود را به عهده بگیرید. — This is the most important foundation and basis for success; you should learn to take one hundred percent of the responsibility for your life.
89 | 1701

611 انگلیس engelis *England, Britain* pn
- انگلیس مخفیانه کلاهک جدید هستهای میسازد. — Britain is secretly building a new nuclear warhead.
78 | 3538

612 موقعیت mowγeʔijjæt *situation, position* n
- سعی کنید برای هر موقعیت طرحی با جزئیات کامل داشته باشید. — Try to have a completely detailed plan for each situation.
88 | 1765

613 مهر mehr, mohr *sun/Mehr/affection, seal* n
- صبح فردا، پیرزن بلند شد. چند تا مهر و تسبیح برداشت. — The next morning the old woman woke up and picked up some prayer beads and *mohr*.
90 | 1468

614 عمل کردن æmæl kærdæn *act, perform* v
- بی درنگ عمل کردن — To act immediately.
92 | 1139

615 جایگاه dʒajgah *position* n
- اسکیبازان ایران در جایگاههای دوازدهم و پانزدهم مارپیچ بزرگ قهرمانی جهان قرار گرفتند. — Iranian skiers won twelfth and fifteenth place in the world giant slalom championship.
86 | 2091

616 اعتقاد eʔteγad *belief* adj,n
- شما به زندگی پس از مرگ اعتقاد دارید؟ — Do you believe in life after death?
89 | 1630

617 شعر ʃeʔr *poetry* adj,n
- هر بیت شعر حافظ به طور مستقل قابل تفسیر است. — Each couplet of Hafez's poetry may be interpreted independently.
80 | 3171

618 نو now *new* adj
- چادر خالدار بود، اما نو بود و مشکی، نه سرمه ای. — The chador was speckled, but it was new and black, not navy.
92 | 1193

619 احترام ehteram *respect* n
- من به فاطمه احترام میگذارم. — I respect Fatima.
92 | 1099

620 متر metr *meter* n
- یک لیتر مازوت پنج برابر قیمت یک متر مکعب گاز است. — A litre of *mazut* equals the price of five cubic meters of gas.
87 | 1943

621 ترکیه torkije *Turkey* pn
- فکر کنم میشد یه ماه دیگه هم ترکیه بمونی. — I think it would work for you to stay yet another month in Turkey.
79 | 3399

622 پیروزی piruzi *victory, Piroozi (F.C.)* n,pn
- ما از پیروزی هایمان لذت میبریم. — We enjoy our victories.
80 | 3216

623 اختلاف extelaf *difference* n
- مسئله سر اختلاف نژاد بود. — The issue was over the racial diference.
86 | 2096

624 محسوب mæhsub *considered* adj
- شهر مرزی از نظر موقعیت استراتژیکی ، یک پایگاه مهم محسوب می شد و از نظر آذوقه و تدارکات خیلی به آن می رسیدند. — A border city in terms of strategic location, it was considered a major base, and it was very well supported regarding food and supplies.
91 | 1385

625 دریا dærja *sea* n
- انتقال آب خزر به سمنان باعث نابودی حیات این دریا
می‌شود. — The transfer of Caspian water to Semnan is causing the destruction of the sea's life.

86 | 2190

626 حضرت hæzræt *holiness* n
- حضرت محمد(ص) بهترین الگوی فکری و عملی اسلام است. — His holiness Mohammad (PBUH) is the best model for Islamic thought and action.

83 | 2643

627 بنا bæna, bænna *building, bricklayer* n
- در دخمه‌های اطراف هرم مدفون گشتند تا آرامگاه ابدی فرعون بنا شود. — They were buried in the crypt of the pyramid to build the final resting place of Pharaoh.

81 | 2919

628 پا pa *foot, leg* n
- به در ورودی زنانه که رسیدم، یادم افتاد جوراب به پا ندارم. — Upon reaching the women's entrance, I remembered that I didn't have stockings on my legs.

76 | 3853

629 خبرنگار xæbærnegar *reporter* n
- مریم سجادپور متخصص تغذیه در گفتگو با باشگاه خبرنگاران گفت: — Maryam Sadjadpour, nutritionist, in an interview with the reporters' club said:

80 | 3119

630 غربی yærbi *western* adj
- الرطبه، غربی‌ترین شهر الانبار آزاد شد. — Rutbah, the westernmost city of Anbar province, was freed.

78 | 3456

631 چندین ʧændin *several* n
- چندین سال پیش بود. — It was a several years ago.

91 | 1229

632 ورود vorud *entry, arrival* n
- پس از ورود اش به رم، پاپ او را امپراتور روم لقب داد. — After his arrival in Rome, the pope gave him the title "Roman Emperor."

86 | 2032

633 جان dʒan *life* n,pn
- جان خود را از دست دادند. — They lost their lives.

77 | 3672

634 پرواز pærvaz *flight* adj,n,pn
- در هفته 3 پرواز از تهران به دوشنبه و بالعکس و یک پرواز از مشهد به تهران و بالعکس صورت می‌گیرد. — Every week there are three flights from Tehran to Dushanbe and back, and one flight from Mashhad to Tehran and back.

93 | 1010

635 علیه ælejh *against* n,prep
- تحریم های اتحادیه اروپا علیه ایران تصویب شد. — The European Union sanctions against Iran were approved.

74 | 4181

636 پیشرفت piʃræft *progress* n
- بچه ها زیر سایه شما خوب پیشرفت می کنند. — Under your auspices the children make good progress.

85 | 2286

637 ابراز ebraz *expression* n
- بعضی از مسؤولان از افزایش مصرف داروهای نشاط‌آور در کشور ابراز نگرانی کرده‌اند. — Some officials expressed concern over the increase in consumption of stimulants.

90 | 1394

638 توان tævan *ability* n
- توان پریدن ندارند. — It does not have the ability to fly.

79 | 3225

639 حالت halæt *condition* n,pn
- وضع بغداد به حالت عادی بازگشت. — The Baghdad situation returned to normal conditions.

88 | 1824

640 فراهم færahæm *available* n
- شرایط بسیار خوب تفریحی در این استان فراهم است. — Very good conditions for recreation are available in this province.

86 | 2002

641 برخورد bærxord *collision* n
- دست کم ۲۰ تن در برخوردهای شب گذشته در «خارطوم» کشته شدند. — At least 20 people were killed in last night's confrontation in Khartoum.

87 | 1978

642 رفتار ræftar *behavior* n
- رفتار آنها قابل پیش‌بینی و تحلیل است. — Their behavior can be predicted and analyzed.

86 | 2090

643 نکته nokte *point* n
- این نکته بر کسی پوشیده نیست که اولویت اصلی در روابط دیپلماتیک باید معطوف به کشورهای همجوار باشد. — The point does not escape anybody that the first priority in diplomatic relations should be given to the neighboring countries.

83 | 2553

644 جلوگیری dʒelowgiri *prevention* n
- برای جلوگیری از مهاجرت‌ها به حمایت اروپا نیازمندیم. — We are in need of Europe's support to prevent immigration.

88 | 1727

4 Colors

Rank	Headword	Pronunciation	Gloss	Rank	Headword	Pronunciation	Gloss
720	صورتی	suræti	pink	5528	سیاهی	sijahi	blackness
951	رنگ	ræng	color	5676	زیتونی	zejtuni	olive-green
1403	سبز	sæbz	green	5956	رنگارنگ	rængaræng	colorful
1595	سیاه	sijah	black	8118	مشکی	mejki	black
1597	سفید	sefid	white	8518	قهوه‌ای	yæhve?i	brown
1968	قرمز	yermez	red	8904	سفیدی	sefidi	whiteness
2011	طلایی	tælaji	golden	9151	نیلی	nili	indigo
2092	آبی	abi	blue	9221	کبود	kæbud	dark blue
2223	سرخ	sorx	red	9363	بنفش	bænæʃ	violet
2720	رنگی	rængi	colored	10507	فیروزه‌ای	firuze?i	turquoise
2912	کمرنگ	kæmræng	pale, light	11193	نقره‌ای	noyre?i	silver
3061	زرد	zærd	yellow	11816	سرخی	sorxi	redness
4289	رنگین	rængin	colored	11861	ارغوانی	æryævani	purple
4596	پررنگ	porræng	vividly colored, dark	12024	قرمزی	yermezi	redness
				12996	زردی	zærdi	yellowness
5014	طوسی	tusi	gray	14724	همرنگ	hæmræng	same color
5020	خاکستری	xakestæri	gray	15545	بی‌رنگ	biræng	colorless
5467	نارنجی	narendʒi	orange	16118	کبودی	kæbudi	blueness
				16359	خرمایی	xormgji	chestnut brown

645 سابق sabey *former* adj
- The — مدیر عامل ورشکسته، منشی سابقش را ربود. bankrupt managing director kidnapped his former secretary.
- 88 | 1666

646 گویا guja *talking, clear, seems* adj,adv
- گویا سهم کودکان و نوجوانان روزه دار نادیده گرفته شده است. — Apparently, the proportion of children and adolescents fasting has been ignored.
- 96 | 604

647 متهم mottæhæm *accused* adj,n
- فهمیدم چادر سرمه ای برای زنان متهم یا زندانی است. — I realized that the navy blue veil is for accused or imprisoned women.
- 87 | 1888

648 تأسیس tæ?sis *establishing, foundation* n
- شاید سایر دوستانی که در تأسیس این مرکز همکاری دارند از وجود خانه کودکان افغانستان بی اطلاع باشند. — Most likely the other friends who are helping establish this center are unaware of the existence of the Afghanistan Children's Home.
- 90 | 1462

649 سال بودن sal budæn *be years since* v
- شش سال است که از دیدار خانواده‌ام محروم بوده‌ام. — It's six years now that I've been deprived of the sight of my family.
- 91 | 1275

650 تحقق tæhæyyoy *realization* n
- پیش نیازها و بسترهای لازم برای تحقق اهداف — Prerequisites and conditions for achieving the goals.
- 90 | 1459

651 قانونی yanuni *legal* adj,n
- این نمایندگان اطلاعی از وظایف قانونی خود ندارند. — These representatives are not aware of their legal duties.
- 85 | 2219

652 ادعا edde?a *claim* adj,n
- تکرار ادعاهای بی‌اساس، تأثیری بر تمامیت ارضی ایران ندارد. — Repeating unfounded claims has no effect on the territorial integrity of Iran.
- 92 | 1086

653 دیدگاه didgah *point of view* n
- معیار هایی را به وجود آورید که با دیدگاه کلی شرکت هماهنگ باشد. — Develop values that match the general vision of the company.
- 88 | 1687

654 مکان mækan *place* n
- امشب به حرمسرا نقل مکان می کنند. — Tonight, they move to the harem.
- 88 | 1708

655 مطلب mætlæb *subject* n
- گفتند باید مطلب را به تو تحویل دهم. — They said I must deliver the matter to you.
- 82 | 2573

656 امسال emsal *this year* adv
- پارسال برایش ساعت طلا خریده بودی، چرا امسال کتاب لغت خریده‌ای؟ — Last year you bought her a gold watch; why have you bought her a dictionary this year?
- 80 | 3014

657 درآمد dæramæd *income* n,v
- بیشتر درآمد ندارم. — I don't have more income.
- 83 | 2435

658 گشتن gæʃtæn *turn, search, become* n,v
- ما همه‌جا را دنبالش‌گشتیم. — We looked for him everywhere.
- 77 | 3518

659 همچون hæmtʃun *like* adv
- در حقیقت طرحی جدید در شبکه های اجتماعی همچون توئیتر و فیس بوک راه افتاد. — In fact, a new plan has been launched by social media like Twitter and Facebook.
- 90 | 1421

660 عین ejn *same, original, eye* n
- عین این مورد قبلاً هم رخ داده. — The same thing happened before too.
- 90 | 1348

661 کارشناس karʃenas *expert* n
- وی کارشناس و مترجم رسمی انستیتوی زبانشناسی لندن است. — She is an expert and official translator in the London Institute of Linguistics.
- 78 | 3196

662 هنر honær *art* n
- منظور از هنرهای زیبا هنرهایی است که تنها به دلیل زیبا بودنشان خلق شده‌اند. — By fine art we mean the type of art that has been created only because of being beautiful.
- 84 | 2319

663 همچنان hæmtʃenan *thus, still* adv
- ما همچنان علاقمندیم که درخصوص موضوعات مختلف با اروپاییها مذاکره کنیم. — We are still interested in negotiations with the Europeans about different subjects.
- 79 | 3155

664 شامل ʃamel *included* adj
- آیا این قاعده شامل قصاص هم می شود؟ — Does this rule include retaliation?
- 81 | 2755

665 روستا rusta *village* n
- از پریشب تلاش داشتند که این روستا را اشغال کنند. — Since the night before last, they have been trying to occupy this village.
- 90 | 1336

666 رهبری ræhbæri *leadership* n
- بیانات مقام معظم رهبری درمورد شرکت در انتخابات — His eminence the supreme leader's statements about participation in the elections.
- 83 | 2452

667 ظرفیت zærfijæt *capacity* n
- رویکرد اصلی دولت این است که بخش خصوصی با حداکثر ظرفیت احساس کند که میدان عمل دارد. — The main approach of the government is to let the private sector feel to the maximum capacity that it has ground for action.
- 87 | 1803

668 نظارت nezaræt *supervision* adj,n
- در این شرایط بانک مرکزی طبق قانون وظیفه نظارت بر بازار ارز را دارد. — In these conditions, the central bank has a lawful duty to supervise the currency market.
- 86 | 2013

669 طبیعی tæbiʔi *natural* adj
- این حق طبیعی ملت ایران است. — This is the natural right of the Iranian nation.
- 82 | 2537

670 آغاز شدن aɣaz ʃodæn *begin* v
- راهپیمایی روز قدس آغاز شد. — The Ghods Day rally started.
- 83 | 2396

671 صنعتی sænʔæti *industrial* adj
- استان مرکزی از جمله استان‌های صنعتی کشور است. — Markazi province is among the industrial provinces of the country.
- 83 | 2343

672 هنگام hengam *time* n
- خانم صراحت به هنگام مرگ 46 سال داشت. — At her time of death, Mrs. Sarahat was 46 years old.
- 81 | 2720

673 مثبت mosbæt *positive* adj
- با ارائه پیشنهادی مثبت، کاری کنید که اختیارشان را افزایش دهند. — By offering a positive proposal, do something to increase their power.
- 89 | 1492

674 یکدیگر jekdigær *each other* pron
- در کنار یکدیگر زندگی می کنند. — They live alongside each other.
- 87 | 1733

675 پروژه poroʒe *project* n
- این پروژه در دو مرحله انجام خواهد شد. — The project will be carried out in two stages.
87 | 1792

676 خلاف xælɑf *contrary* adj,conj,n
- بر خلاف چند سال پیش خوب بود. — Unlike a few years ago, it was good.
90 | 1402

677 شیخ ʃejx *sheikh* n,pn
- شیخ صدوق یکی از فقها و دانشمندان شیعه است. — Sheikh Saduq is one of the Shiite jurists and scholars.
92 | 1130

678 سن senn *age* n
- یک زن سن و سال دار مذهبی — An aged religious woman.
89 | 1464

679 حکم hokm *order, sentence* adj,n
- این حکم را به امضاء رسانده بودم. — I had signed this order.
84 | 2273

680 تصویب tæsvib *approval* n
- در حال حاضر کلیات اصلاحیه تصویب شده و کمیسیون‌های بودجه و اقتصادی در حال بررسی هستند. — At present, the general amendment is approved and the budget and economic commissions are investigating.
81 | 2644

681 شخصیت ʃæxsijjæt *personality* adj,n
- در معرفی شخصیت و احساس درونی او نقش بسیار مهمی دارند. — They have a very important role in introducing his character and internal emotion.
85 | 1996

682 کدام kodɑm *which* n
- تحکیم روابط زوجین به رعایت کدام عوامل بستگی دارد؟ — Strengthening couples' relations depends on observing which factors?
84 | 2137

683 سرزمین særzæmin *land, country* n
- دانش و اندیشه ، پایه های نیرو و توان یک سرزمین است. — Knowledge and thinking are foundations of power and strength in a country.
86 | 1961

684 مسلمان mosælmɑn *Muslim* adj,n
- طرح جامعه شناسی مستقل از سوی اندیشمندان مسلمان. — Independent sociology plan from Muslim scholars.
83 | 2340

685 ساز sɑz *instrument* adj,n,v
- از طرف دیگر صدای ساز و آواز به گوش می رسید. — From the other side, the sound of instruments and song was being heard.
78 | 3135

686 خوردن xordæn *eat* adj,n,v
- مرد دوم چیزی برای خوردن نداشت. — The second man didn't have anything to eat.
69 | 4755

687 مسئولیت mæsʔulijjæt *responsibility* n
- البته مردم لر و بختیاری انتظاراتی فراتر از مسئولیتهای ایشان داشته اند. — Of course, Luri and Bakhtiari people have had expectations which are beyond his responsibilities.
86 | 1964

688 جام dʒɑm *cup* n
- بده آن جام شراب. — Give me that goblet of wine.
81 | 2688

689 پذیرفتن pæziroftæn *accept* v
- اصول پذیرفته شده حسابداری — Accepted accounting principles.
85 | 2051

690 عبور obur *passing* n
- از ذهن دکتر عبور کرد. — It crossed the doctor's mind.
92 | 1073

691 سید sejjed *descendant of prophet, Seyyed* n
- سیدحسن خمینی نامزد انتخابات نمی‌شود. — Seyyed Hassan Khomeini will not be a candidate for elections.
87 | 1789

692 پیام pæjɑm *message* n
- ژاپن پیام‌های هشدار بر روی پاکت سیگار را افزایش می‌دهد. — Japan has added warning messages to cigarette packs.
86 | 1867

693 خصوصی xosusi *private* adj
- آموزش زبان عربی و انگلیسی در مدارس دولتی و خصوصی اجباری است. — Teaching the Arabic and English languages is mandatory in public and private schools.
84 | 2235

694 حداقل hæddeæɣæl *at least, minimum* adv,n,q
- تاکنون قانونی برای «تعیین حداقل سن ازدواج» در عربستان سعودی وضع نشده است. — So far, no law for the "minimum marriage age" in Saudi Arabia has been established.
87 | 1660

695 هرچه hærtʃe *whatever* adv
- درخت هرچه ستبرتر و درازتر باشد، سن بیشتری دارد. — The thicker and taller a tree is, the older it is.
90 | 1295

696 وابسته vɑbæste *dependent, attached* adj,n
- دلم به هیچ کسی وابسته نبود. — Emotionally, I was not attached to anybody.
90 | 1255

697 دعوت dæʔvæt *invitation* n

● مرا باید زودتر از همه دعوت می کردید — You should have invited me before everyone else.

85 | 2074

698 ترک tærk, tork *leave, Turk* adj,n

● در حالی که از ترس فریاد می کشید اتاق را ترک کرد. — While screaming from fear, he left the room.

91 | 1094

699 کنفرانس konferans *conference* n

● در سپتامبر ۱۹۶۵ کنفرانس یونسکو در تهران برگزار شد. — The UNESCO conference was held in Tehran in September of 1965.

88 | 1599

700 نمایشگاه næmajeʃgah *exhibition* n

● حتی اگر رییس جمهور از این نمایشگاه دیدار کند بسیار خوب است. — Even if the president visits the fair, it would be very good.

80 | 2794

701 تکرار tekrar *repeating* n

● دیگر این اسم رمز را تکرار نکنید. — Don't repeat this password again.

94 | 817

702 بسته bæste *package* adj,n

● یک بسته را از دور به ما نشان می داد. — She was showing us a package from far off.

86 | 1814

703 عملکرد æmælkærd *operation* n

● گزارشی از عملکرد عمرانی شهرداری مهربان در سال جاری — A report on the development operation of the Mehraban town council in the current year.

87 | 1691

704 ریشه riʃe *root* n

● تنها وقتی واقعا احساس خوشبختی می‌کنیم که منشاء رویدادهای خوب و خوشایند از درون هر یک از ما ریشه بگیرد. — We only feel happiness when the origin of good and pleasant events are rooted from the inside of each one of us.

91 | 1138

705 شناختن ʃenaxtæn *know, recognize* adj,n,v

● هیچ قانونی را نمی شناختند. — They didn't recognize any laws.

82 | 2337

706 سرمایه særmaje *capital* n

● منابع و سرمایه‌ها را در اختیار دارند. — They have resources and capital at their disposal.

84 | 2102

707 گاه gah *time, sometimes* adv,n

● واژه تمدن زمانی به شکل جمع و گاهی به شکل مفرد مورد استفاده قرار می‌گیرد. — The word civilization is sometimes used in plural form and sometimes in singular form.

81 | 2538

708 مدیر modir *manager, director* adj,n

● میزان سقف حقوق برای مدیران ارشد اعلام شد. — The salary ceiling for senior executives was announced.

75 | 3468

709 سهم sæhm *share, lot* n

● تحصیل سهم من نیست، حق من است. — Education is not my lot, it is my right.

77 | 3199

710 سرنوشت særneveʃt *fate* n

● شما ریخته گر و شکل دهنده سرنوشت خود خواهید شد. — You will become the founder and shaper of your own destiny.

93 | 912

711 کمیته komite *committee* n

● در سال ۱۸۹۷ او یکی از اعضای کمیته بین‌المللی المپیک شد. — In 1897 he became a member of the International Olympic Committee.

85 | 1919

712 هند hend *India* pn

● این رشد به خصوص در کشور هند که مردم زیادی برای اولین بار وارد بازار خودرو می شوند، بسیار چشمگیر و قابل توجه خواهد بود. — This growth, especially in India where many people for the first time enter the automotive market, is very eye-catching and considerable.

83 | 2188

713 اعلام کردن eʔlam kærdæn *announce* v

● آنها نتایج بررسی‌های خود را اعلام کردند. — They announced the results of their reviews.

80 | 2659

714 بخشیدن bæxʃidæn *forgive, give* adj,n,v

● پسرجان چند وقت پیش من آمدم، یک روزنامه به من بخشیدی. — Dear son, I came some time ago, and you gave me a newspaper.

87 | 1706

715 مدیریت modirijjæt *management* adj,n

● کتاب مدیریت بازاریابی، اصول و مبانی منتشر شد. — The book 'Marketing Management, Principles and Basics' has been published.

79 | 2886

716 عده edde *number* n,q

● عده‌ای دیگر هنوز بر نیمکت‌ها منتظر نشسته بودند. — A number of other people were still sitting on benches, waiting.

89 | 1385

717 متاسفانه moteʔæssefane *unfortunately* adv

● متاسفانه آمریکا، عراق را به ایران تسلیم کرد. — Unfortunately, America surrendered Iraq to Iran.

88 | 1516

718 حساب hesab *account* n

● در بانک‌های سوئیس چندین حساب بانکی مخفی داشت. — He had several secret bank accounts in Swiss banks.

87 | 1663

719 فکر کردن fekr kærdæn *think* v
- فکر می‌کردند واقعا مرده‌ام. — They thought that I had actually died.
- 75 | 3485

720 صورتی suræti *pink, a form* adj,n
- صورتی رنگ شادی و نشاط است. — Pink is the color of happiness and exhilaration.
- 91 | 1077

721 کالا kala *goods* n
- کیف، کفش و پوشاک، اصلی‌ترین کالاهایی هستند که در آن به فروش می‌رسند. — Bags, shoes and clothing are the main goods sold in there.
- 81 | 2452

722 طبق teby, tæbæy *according to, tray* n
- به جای ترنج قالی وسط اتاق هم یک طبق بود با هفت رنگ غذا از ترشی هفت‌سبزی گرفته تا تمجین گوشت بره که هنوز بخار ازش بلند می‌شد. — Instead of a carpet medallion in the middle of the room, there was an elaborate food tray including seven kinds of vegetable pickle and lamb tahchin which was still steaming.
- 86 | 1781

723 ملاحظه molaheze *observation* n
- بله قربان هم اکنون آنرا ملاحظه کردم. — Yes sir, I just saw that.
- 94 | 724

724 فراوان færavan *abundant* adj,adv
- روز تعطیل بود و ما نیاز فراوان به پول داشتیم. — It was a holiday and we had a deep need for money.
- 92 | 976

725 پیچیده pitʃide *complex* adj
- کارهای ساده را به راحتی می توان پیچیده کرد. — Simple tasks can easily be made complicated.
- 93 | 800

726 اظهار ezhar *statement* n
- کریمی با اشاره به اظهارات اخیر رییس‌کل بانک مرکزی در مورد قیمت ارز و بازار و انعکاس آن در رسانه‌ها، گفت: — Karimi, pointing to the recent statements of the Central Bank's president about the price of foreign currency and the market and its reflection in the media, said:
- 85 | 1896

727 نجات nedʒat *rescue* n
- تو جانم را نجات داده ای و من مدیون تو هستم. — You have saved my life and I am indebted to you.
- 91 | 1075

728 گاز gaz *gas* n
- مشکلات و وابستگی‌ها در زمینه صنعت نفت و گاز — The problems and dependencies regarding the gas and oil industry.
- 81 | 2427

729 شیوه ʃive *method* n
- یک روزنامه آمریکایی در تحلیلی در شیوه دموکراتها در تبلیغات خود نوشت — One American newspaper in an analysis of the methods Democrats use in advertising wrote:
- 86 | 1840

730 عباس æbbas *Abbas* pn
- عباس نظری دیروز در گفتگو با خبرنگاران گفت — In an interview with reporters Abbas Nazari said yesterday.
- 92 | 990

731 عالی ɑli *high* adj
- از نظر اجتماعی توریسم تاثیری عالی بر جوامع میزبان دارد. — From a social perspective, tourism has a great impact on host communities.
- 73 | 3727

732 بعدی bæʔdi *next* adj,n
- امیدوارم استقلال بازی بعدی‌اش را هم ببرد. — I hope Esteghlal will win its next game too.
- 87 | 1570

733 زندان zendan *prison* n
- برای قاتلش فقط چندین سال حکم زندانی اعلام میکنن. — For his murderer they are only announcing a prison sentence of several years.
- 86 | 1754

734 مشاهده moʃahede *observation* n
- در روش علمی برای فرمول‌بندی و مطرح‌کردن فرضیه‌ها به مشاهده طبیعت نیاز است. — In the scientific method, the formulation and proposal of hypotheses requires the observation of nature.
- 88 | 1450

735 دادگاه dadgah *court* n
- دادگاه کیفری استان تهران، محمود احمدی نژاد رئیس جمهوری اسلامی ایران را به دادگاه احضار کرد. — Tehran criminal court summoned Mahmoud Ahmadinejad, President of the Islamic Republic of Iran.
- 83 | 2161

736 معرفی کردن moʔærrefi kærdæn *introduce* v
- یکی از دوستهای ما آمد خودش رو معرفی کرد. — One of our friends came and introduced himself.
- 95 | 623

737 نرخ nerx *rate* n
- نرخ ارز متغیر بسیار مهمی به ویژه برای بانک‌های مرکزی است. — Currency exchange rate is an important variable especially for central banks.
- 84 | 2053

738 کننده konænde *doer* n
- کمتر تولیدکننده ای در این شرایط به کیفیت در محصولات خود توجه دارد. — Fewer manufacturers in this situation pay attention to the quality of their products.
- 77 | 3033

739 ضرورت zæruræt *necessity* n
- تحقیق مورد نظر از ضرورت خاصی برخوردار است. — The research under discussion is of special necessity.
- 88 | 1536

740 شش ʃeʃ, ʃoʃ *six, lung* n
- امروز دقیقاً شش سال و چهار ماه می‌شد که کشورش را ترک کرده بود. — Today made exactly six years and four months since she had left her country.
- 66 | 4875

741 مجبور mædʒbur *forced* adj
- آن قدر اصرار کردم تا مجبور شدند نامه مربوط به ملاقات را آوردند و نشان دادند. — I kept insisting until they were forced to bring and show the letter about the meeting.
- 90 | 1185

742 عکس æks *picture* adj,n
- حالا میخواهم یه عکس بگیرم برایتان. — Now, I want to take a picture for you.
- 84 | 2012

743 تردید tærdid *hesitation,* doubt n
- در این مورد جای هیچ گونه تردیدی نیست. — In this case there is no room for any sort of doubt.
- 92 | 913

744 خبری xæbæri *news* adj,n
- آژانس خبری مراکش در سال ۱۹۵۸ توسط محمد پنجم گشایش یافت. — The Morocco News Agency was founded in 1958 by Mohammed V.
- 81 | 2371

745 بهبود behbud *improvement* n
- روابط تا حدودی بهبود پیدا کرد. — To some extent, the relations improved.
- 89 | 1358

746 نشانه neʃane *sign* n
- نشانه های تعجب و پرسش معمولاً در داخل گیومه قرار می گیرد. — Exclamation and question marks are usually placed inside quotation marks.
- 90 | 1251

747 رژیم reʒim *regime* n
- کمک رژیم صهیونیستی برای خلع سلاح شیمیایی سوریه. — The Zionist regime's aid for Syria's chemical disarmament.
- 59 | 6107

748 اوج owdʒ *altitude, highest point* n
- کم کم صدایش اوج گرفت. — Her voice slowly reached a crescendo.
- 95 | 638

749 منفعت mænfæʔæt *profit, gain* n
- همین موضوع منفعت کارفرما و کارگر را به هم گره می‌زند. — This issue ties the benefit of employers and employees together.
- 85 | 1924

750 منجر mondʒær *leading to* adj
- دولت قبل غیر واقعی بود و منجر به بدهکاری دولت می‌شد. — The previous government was unrealistic and was leading to government debt.
- 89 | 1308

751 نهاد næhad *institution, placed* n,v
- قانون اساسی آلمان هرگونه دخالت نهادهای مذهبی در حکومت را منع می‌کند. — The German constitution forbids any religious institutions' interference in government.
- 79 | 2634

752 کشاندن keʃandæn *drag, pull* adj,n,v
- گردشگران را از نقاط مختلف دنیا به این منطقه می‌کشاند. — It attracts tourists from around the world to this region.
- 94 | 667

753 سابقه sabeʝe *precedent* n
- دبیرکل حزب وحدت مردمی با بن علی به رقابت می پردازند و این رقابت در تاریخ سیاسی تونس پس از استقلال سابقه نداشته است. — The Secretary-General of the People's Unity Party competes with Ben Ali and this rivalry has been unprecedented in the political history of post-revolution Tunisia.
- 90 | 1159

754 سپس sepæs *then* conj
- سپس سیب زمینی ها را به دقت شمرد و تقسیم کرد. — Then she carefully counted and divided the potatoes.
- 86 | 1726

755 نیم nim *half* n,q
- نیم ساعتی به ظهر مانده بود. — A half hour remained till noon.
- 85 | 1863

756 درخواست dærxast *request* n
- چرا از قاضی درخواست ملاقات حضوری نکرده بودم. — Why did I not ask the judge for a face to face meeting?
- 89 | 1284

757 رد rædd *refusal, trail* adj,n
- میخوام که ردش رو دنبالش کنی. — I want you to follow his trail.
- 91 | 1084

758 منزل mænzel *house* n
- منزل به منزل رفتند تا رسیدند به نزدیک شهر خودشان. — They went from house to house until they arrived close to their own city.
- 91 | 1102

759 پرونده pærvænde *file* n
- چنانچه دولت هم‌اکنون بخواهد این پرونده‌ها را مجدد بازنگری و بررسی کند تولیدکننده باید اسناد و مدارک لازم را ارائه دهد. — If the government now wants to re-review and examine the files, producers must provide the required documents.
- 82 | 2263

760 حالا hala *now* adv
- حالا فهمیدید از چه کسی خواستگاری کرده اید؟ — Now do you understand who you have proposed to?
- 61 | 5506

761 کنونی konuni *present* adj
- از آنها پرسیده است چگونه به جایگاه کنونی‌شان رسیده‌اند. — He asked them how they had reached their current position.
- 86 | 1725

762 وزن væzn *weight* n
- قد تامبلینا ۴۳ سانتی‌متر و وزنش ۲۶ کیلوگرم است. — Thumbelina's height is 43 cm and her weight is 26 kg.
- 87 | 1509

763 تومان tuman *toman* n
- بله عرض کردم آن یکی را اگر بخواهید هزار و چهارصد تومان است. — Yes, I told you that if you want that one, it is one thousand four hundred toman.
- 73 | 3478

764 عدم ædæm *lack* n
- او عدم انگیزه اش را نشان داد. — She showed her lack of motivation.
- 79 | 2662

765 اتفاق افتادن ettefaɣ oftadæn *happen* v
- تجربه کودکی فقط یک بار اتفاق می‌افتد! — Childhood experience only happens once!
- 92 | 887

766 بودجه buddʒe *budget* n
- همه پروژه‌های بزرگ با کمبود شدید بودجه مواجه هستند. — All major projects are facing a severe shortage of funds.
- 77 | 2848

767 اختصاص extesas *allocation* n
- 70 درصد تسهیلات بانک به بخش صنعت اختصاص یافته. — Seventy percent of the bank's credit is allocated to the industrial sector.
- 85 | 1818

768 متعدد motæʔædded *numerous* adj
- حملات متعدد دزدان دریایی به کشتی‌های ایرانی ناکام ماند. — Numerous pirate attack on Iranian ships have been frustrated.
- 90 | 1163

769 سی si *thirty* n,pn
- زن جوان سی و چند ساله ای رو روبروی دیدم. — I saw a young, thirty-something year old woman in front of me.
- 64 | 5039

770 اهل æhl *native* n
- پیرزن جواب سلام شاهزاده ابراهیم را داد و گفت «ای جوان! اهل کجایی؟» — The old woman responded to Prince Ebrahim's greeting and said, "Young man! Where are you from?"
- 86 | 1628

771 هدایت hedajæt *guidance* n,pn
- دو کلمه به هدایت علی نوشتم. — I wrote two words to Hedayat Ali.
- 93 | 846

772 سند sænæd *document* n,pn
- این طور که برمی‌آید در کار تنظیم سند مشکلاتی پیش آمده. — It seems that there are some difficulties in arranging the document.
- 86 | 1633

773 صد sæd *hundred* n
- سه اسکناس صد تومانی جدا کرد. — She separated three one hundred toman bills.
- 66 | 4562

774 نشستن neʃæstæn *sit* adj,n,v
- او را به نشستن دعوت کرد. — She invited him to sit.
- 74 | 3314

775 آنجا andʒa *there* adv,n
- خیلی ها آنجا هستند. — There are a lot of them there.
- 75 | 3114

776 تسلیم tæslim *surrender* n
- من تسلیم تو هستم. — I am surrendering to you.
- 95 | 602

777 تقریباً tæɣribæn *approximately* adv
- تقریباً ۹۹ درصد آمریکاییان دارای حداقل سواد پایه هستند. — Nearly 99 percent of Americans have at least a basic education.
- 89 | 1305

778 وارد شدن vared ʃodæn *enter* v
- کالسکه از انتهای کوچه وارد می شود. — The carriage enters from the end of the alley.
- 92 | 949

779 طراحی tærrahi *design* n
- از جمله آنها طراحی لباس‌های رنگی تنیس علاوه بر لباس‌های ساده سفید بود. — Among them was the design of colorful tennis outfits in addition to the plain white ones.
- 88 | 1400

780 دانش daneʃ *knowledge* n
- دانش‌های پایه، زیربنای اصلی سایر دانش‌ها به شمار می‌آیند. — Foundational knowledge is the basic infrastructure of other forms of knowledge.
- 84 | 1851

781 علاوه ælave *addition* n
- علاوه بر آن به سایر بازیکنان روحیه می‌داد. — In addition, he was encouraging other players.
- 81 | 2301

782 راهی rahi *bound for, a path* adj,n
- روحانی چهارشنبه راهی استانبول می‌شود. — Rowhani is going to Istanbul on Wednesday.
- 90 | 1105

783 انرژی enerʒi *energy* n
- تنها جایی که انرژی مثبت به بدن برمیگردانید مسح پا میباشد. — The only place that you bring positive energy back to the body is wiping the feet.
- 79 | 2509

784 قالب ɣaleb *model, bar* n
- یک قالب صابون مراغه برداشت و آورد. He got a bar of Maragheh soap and brought it.
- 89 | 1270

785 جمهور dʒomhur *republic* n
- همسر رئیس جمهور بود. — She was the president's spouse.
- 64 | 4778

786 کشیدن keʃidæn *pull, draw* conj,n,v
- هدف محدود کردن و خط کشیدن دور خود نیست. — The goal is not to limit and draw a line around oneself.
- 74 | 3233

787 باور bavær *belief* n,v
- من نمی‌توانم باور کنم. — I cannot believe it.
- 86 | 1579

788 مسجد mæsdʒed *mosque* n
- در راه مسجد، مرد زمین خورد و لباس‌هایش کثیف شد. — On the way to the mosque the man fell and his clothes got dirty.
- 85 | 1775

789 دشمن doʃmæn *enemy* n
- از این به بعد می دانم چطور زندگی کنم و دوست و دشمن را از هم بشناسم. — From now on, I know how to live and differentiate a friend from an enemy.
- 83 | 1981

790 پایین pajin *bottom, down* adj,adv,n
- جوون سه چار پله پایین‌تر می‌نشست. — The young guy was living three or four steps down.
- 82 | 2141

791 ناشی naʃi *resulting* adj
- ناشی از عوامل غیراقتصادی و اقتصادی. — Because of non-economic and economic factors.
- 83 | 1935

792 روبرو ruberu *opposite* adj,adv,n,prep,v
- مؤدب روی صندلی روبروی جناب رئیس نشستم. — Politely, I sat on the chair in front of the boss.
- 92 | 918

793 دقیق dæɣiɣ *exact* adj,pn
- در فاصله ی بین انقلاب و جنگ یا دقیق تر بگوییم، در فاصله ی بین سنگ و تفنگ، قلم به دست گرفتیم. — In between the time of revolution and the war, or saying it more precisely, between rock and gun time, we put pen in hand.
- 87 | 1492

794 پخش pæxʃ *distribution, broadcasting* n
- ناصر می توانست آنچه را که روی میز پخش شده بود، به راحتی ببیند. — Naser could easily see whatever was scattered on the table.
- 87 | 1524

795 محمود mæhmud *Mahmoud* pn
- در دستگاه میرزا محمود هم پیدا نشد. — It was not found In Mirza Mahmoud's system either.
- 89 | 1186

796 خیابان xijaban *street, avenue* n
- اولین خیابان‌های تهران کی ساخته شدند؟ — When were the first avenues of Tehran built?
- 80 | 2310

797 ساختمان saxteman *building* n
- ضلع غربی کوچه، دیوار ساختمانی است که دفتر اداره اطلاعات زندان اوین در آن قرار دارد، همان دفتر صدور اجازه ملاقات. — On the west side of the street is a wall of a building containing the information office of Evin prison, the office that issues permission for visits.
- 83 | 1960

798 محقق mohæɣɣeɣ, mohæɣɣæɣ *scholar, ascertained* adj,n,pn
- اگر این هدف محقق شود نخبگان و متخصصان خارج و داخل کشور، شوق بیشتری برای حضور در ایران و فعالیت بیشتر در روند پیشرفت علمی بدست خواهند آورد. — If this goal is reached, elites and experts outside and inside the country will be more motivated to be in Iran and to be active in the process of scientific progress.
- 88 | 1414

799 ساکن saken *resident* adj,n
- او ساکن کربلا بود. — He was a resident of Karbala.
- 90 | 1124

800 شخص ʃæxs *person* n
- دیشب شخص ناشناسی تلفن زد. — Last night an unknown person called.
- 85 | 1721

801 کمیسیون komisijon *commission* n
- رییس کمیسیون بهداشت مجلس آلودگی برنج‌های وارداتی را تأیید کرد. — The Parliamentary Health Committee chairman confirmed contamination of the imported rice.
- 80 | 2426

802 خواسته xaste *demand* adj,adv,n
- شرکت نفت هنوز حاضر به پذیرش خواسته‌های اعتصابیون نبود. — The Oil Company was still not willing to accept the strikers' demands.
- 85 | 1771

803 تبدیل tæbdil *conversion* n
- با گذشت زمان تبدیل به فردی قدرتمند و موفق شود. — As time passed, she changed into a powerful and successful individual.
- 89 | 1209

804 امتیاز emtijaz *point, privilege* adj,n
- اگر به خود و دارندگی‌ها و امتیازات خود اعتقاد نداشته باشید، دیگران هم به شما و دارندگی‌هایتان اعتقاد نخواهند داشت. — If you do not believe in yourself, what you have, and your privileges, others also will not believe in what you have.
- 79 | 2456

5 Countries

Rank	Headword	Pronunciation	Gloss	Rank	Headword	Pronunciation	Gloss
43	ایران	iran	Iran	2712	بریتانیا	beritanja	Britain
107	آمریکا	amrika	America	2759	مکزیک	mekzik	Mexico
389	فرانسه	færanse	France	2768	ارمنستان	ærmænestan	Armenia
433	افغانستان	æfɣanestan	Afghanistan	2794	مغرب	mæɣreb	Morocco
458	چین	ʧin	China	2870	بلژیک	belʒik	Belgium
518	عراق	eraɣ	Iraq	3104	اندونزی	ændonezi	Indonesia
568	روسیه	rusije	Russia	3135	آرژانتین	arʒantin	Argentina
594	آلمان	alman	Germany	3237	اوکراین	okrajn	Ukraine
611	انگلیس	engelis	England, Britain	3242	الجزایر	ældʒæzajer	Algeria
621	ترکیه	torkije	Turkey	3278	پرتغال	porteɣal	Portugal
712	هند	hend	India	3309	تونس	tunes	Tunisia
845	پاکستان	pakestan	Pakistan	3404	لهستان	læhestan	Poland
856	سوریه	surije	Syria	3407	کلمبیا	kolombija	Colombia
867	ژاپن	ʒapon	Japan	3429	عمان	omman	Oman
913	اسرائیل	esraʔil	Israel	3437	گرجستان	gordʒestan	Georgia
1000	ایتالیا	italija	Italy	3444	فیلیپین	filipin	Philippines
1119	مصر	mesr	Egypt	3524	کوبا	kuba	Cuba
1125	لبنان	lobnan	Lebanon	3552	سودان	sudan	Sudan
1130	انگلستان	engelestan	England	3905	اتریش	otriʃ	Austria
1135	فلسطین	felestin	Palestine	3924	مجارستان	mædʒarestan	Hungary
1364	قطر	ɣætær	Qatar	4032	دانمارک	danmark	Denmark
1430	اسپانیا	espanja	Spain	4096	بوسنی	bosni	Bosnia
1497	استرالیا	ostralija	Australia	4121	رومانی	romani	Romania
1614	یونان	junan	Greece	4230	کره جنوبی	korejedʒonubi	South Korea
1801	کانادا	kanada	Canada	4282	ایرلند	irlænd	Ireland
1957	برزیل	berezil	Brazil	4331	سنگاپور	sængapur	Singapore
1967	کویت	kovejt	Kuwait	4386	غنا	ɣæna	Ghana
2001	ترکمنستان	torkæmænestan	Turkmenistan	4431	سومالی	somali	Somalia
2108	اردن	ordon	Jordan	4600	نیجریه	nidʒerije	Nigeria
2331	تاجیکستان	tadʒikestan	Tajikistan	4612	بلغارستان	bolɣarestan	Bulgaria
2460	هلند	holænd	Holland	4619	قرقیزستان	ɣerɣizestan	Kyrgyzstan
2481	تایلند	tajlænd	Thailand	5044	قبرس	ɣebres	Cyprus
2495	لیبی	libi	Libya	5052	کرواسی	keroasi	Croatia
2529	مالزی	malezi	Malaysia	5172	صربستان	serbestan	Serbia
2555	بحرین	bæhrejn	Bahrain	5323	شیلی	ʃili	Chile
2621	قزاقستان	ɣæzaɣestan	Kazakhstan	5525	نروژ	norveʒ	Norway
2623	یمن	jæmæn	Yemen	5552	فنلاند	fænland	Finland
2699	چک	ʧek	Czech	5790	سریلانکا	serilanka	Sri Lanka
				5981	بنگلادش	bængladeʃ	Bangladesh

Rank	Headword	Pronunciation	Gloss	Rank	Headword	Pronunciation	Gloss
6424	اکوادور	ekvador	*Ecuador*	7204	مراکش	mærakeʃ	*Morocco*
6482	اتیوپی	etijopi	*Ethiopia*	7869	کامرون	kameron	*Cameroon*
6733	بلاروس	belarus	*Belarus*	8448	کامبوج	kambodʒ	*Cambodia*
6846	میانمار	mijanmar	*Myanmar*	9571	سوئیس	suʔis	*Switzerland*
7146	سوئد	suʔed	*Sweden*	11726	آنگولا	angola	*Angola*

805 لحاظ læhaz *perspective* n

- صادقلو از لحاظ گرایش سیاسی اصلاح طلب بوده و علاوه بر زبان فارسی، به ترکی قزلباش و ترکمنی نیز تسلط دارد. — Sadeghloo's political affiliation was reformist, and in addition to Farsi, he had dominance over Qizilbash Turkish and Turkmen.
  84 | 1803

806 شرق ʃærɣ *east* n

- این دریا حلقه اتصال بین شرق و غرب را تشکیل می‌دهد. — This sea forms the link between east and west.
  82 | 2046

807 وسیله væsile *means, instrument* n

- وسایل الکترونیک کهنه را چکار می‌کنید؟ — What do you do with old electronic devices?
  80 | 2284

808 نسل næsl *generation* n

- به این ترتیب دوران نخستین نسل سپری شد. — The first generation passed in this manner.
  87 | 1439

809 قسمت ɣesmæt *section* n

- در واقع فرم مسواک به منظور تمیز کردن همه‌ی قسمت‌های دندان ساخته می‌شود. — Indeed the form of the brush has been constructed to clean all parts of the teeth.
  80 | 2348

810 سراسر særasær *throughout* n,q

- دلم می خواهد از آنها که زندگی را سراسر رنج می دانند بپرسم خیلی خب ، چه باید کرد؟ — I would like to ask of those who think life is all suffering, well, what should be done?
  85 | 1671

811 اعتبار eʔtebar *credit, validity* n

- این فرمان به اعتبار خودش باقی است. — This command remains valid.
  84 | 1820

812 گسترده gostærde *widespread* adj

- این عکس تا کجا گسترده شده. — How far has this picture spread?
  79 | 2432

813 دوباره dobare *again* adj,adv

- تو دوباره تلفن زدی. — You called again.
  82 | 2069

814 جاده dʒadde *road* n

- یکصد دوربین جدید کنترل سرعت تا پایان تابستان در جاده‌ها نصب می‌شود. — One hundred new traffic cameras will be installed on the streets by the end of summer.
  90 | 1040

815 فارس fars *Fars* pn

- جمعیت فارس‌ها حدود ۷۳ تا ۷۵ درصد جمعیت ایران است. — The Fars population is around 73–75% of the population of Iran.
  85 | 1717

816 سالگی salegi *years old* n

- سر آیزاک نیوتن در سن ۸۴ سالگی در لندن درگذشت. — Sir Isaac Newton died in London at age 84.
  94 | 597

817 اشتباه eʃtebah *mistake* adj,adv,n

- البته که نه ولی شما با پیدا کردن یک مقصر و سرزنش آن فقط می خواهید اشتباهات خود را منطقی جلوه دهید. — Of course not, but with finding a guilty person and punishing him, you just want to show that your mistakes are logical.
  90 | 1041

818 چگونه tʃegune *how* adv

- به من یاد بده که چگونه می توانم مثل تو باشم! — Teach me how I can be like you!
  84 | 1797

819 کشته koʃte, keʃte *killed, cultivated* adj,n

- تعداد کشته‌ها به ۷۳ نفر رسید. — The death toll rose to 73.
  77 | 2647

820 متفاوت motæfavet *different* adj

- هر فردی که بر روی این کره خاکی زندگی می کند، یک دنیای متفاوت در ذهن خود دارد. — Any person who lives on this earthy planet has a different world in his mind.
  85 | 1701

821 اینجا indʒa *here* adv,n
- چرا اینجا نشسته‌ای؟ — Why are you sitting here?
- 70 | 3635

822 برخوردار بودن bærxordar budæn *be in possession* v
- پیروی از یک برنامه غذایی صحیح در ایام ماه مبارک رمضان از اهمیت ویژه‌ای برخوردار است. — Special importance is attached to following the correct dietary program during the holy month of Ramadan.
- 87 | 1438

823 کشتی، کشتی keʃti, koʃti *ship, wrestling* n
- تیم ایران قهرمان رقابت‌های کشتی فرنگی شد. — Iran's team won Greco-Roman wrestling competitions.
- 84 | 1742

824 جنوبی dʒonubi *southern* adj
- در سال ۱۹۲۷ برای انجام مأموریت دیگری به آمریکای جنوبی رفت. — In 1927, he went on another mission to South America.
- 82 | 2045

825 بروز boruz *appearance* n
- این تغییرات منشاء بروز بسیاری از بیماری‌های جسمی و روانی‌تنی خواهند بود. — These changes will be the origin of many physical and psychological diseases.
- 86 | 1583

826 کشاورزی keʃaværzi *agriculture* adj,n
- پردرآمدترین محصول کشاورزی قم پسته است. — Pistachios are the most profitable agricultural product of Qom.
- 81 | 2098

827 انتقاد enteɣad *criticism* n
- این بیانات اعتراض ایرانیان را بر انگیخت و از سوی مردم مورد انتقادهای شدید قرار گرفت. — These expressions resulted in Iranian objections, and it was strongly criticized by the people.
- 86 | 1571

828 شناخته ʃenaxte *known* adj
- پاریس از شناخته‌ترین مقصدهای گردشگران جهان است. — Paris is one of the most well known tourist destinations in the world.
- 90 | 1030

829 تعریف tæʔrif *definition, description* n
- رزا برایم تعریف کرد. —Rosa explained it to me.
- 86 | 1489

830 بازیکن bazikon *player* n
- اسامی بازیکنان تیم ملی بسکتبال بزرگسالان اعلام شد. — The names of the adult national basketball team players was announced.
- 79 | 2344

831 پست post *post, position* adj,n
- پس از مدتها وقتش رسید که این پست رو عمومی کنم. — After a long period of time, it is time to make this position public.
- 88 | 1256

832 زندگی کردن zendegi kærdæn *live* v
- تنها ۱۱ درصد جمعیت کشور در تهران زندگی می‌کنند. — Only 11 percent of the country's population lives in Tehran.
- 87 | 1379

833 باقی baɣi *remaining* adj,n,pn
- رازی بین ما باقی ماند. — A secret remained between us.
- 90 | 1045

834 حسین hosejn *Hossein* pn
- امام حسین (ع) می‌فرمایند :همنشینی با خردمندان از نشانه های خوشبختی است. — Imam Hussein (AS) said: company of wise men is a sign of prosperity.
- 81 | 2166

835 جمعی dʒæmʔi *collective* adj,n,q
- سایر رسانه های جمعی شکل می گیرند. — The rest of the mass media are taking shape.
- 89 | 1214

836 مقایسه moɣajese *comparison* n
- در ایران هر کدام از شخصیت های برجسته امروز را مقایسه کنیم کدامیک چنین توانایی های دارد. — If we compare any of the prominent figures in Iran, which one has these capabilities?
- 88 | 1329

837 زمینی zæmini *land, earthling* adj,n
- زمینی‌ها مهیای مهاجرت به مریخ می‌شوند. — The earthlings are preparing to emigrate to Mars.
- 94 | 637

838 اجازه دادن edʒaze dadæn *permit* v
- اگر اجازه دهید همین چند ماه را در خدمتتان باشم. — If you'll allow me I'd like to serve you in these few months.
- 92 | 794

839 پذیرش pæzireʃ *reception, admission* n
- مثلاً پذیرش دانشجو برای دوره کاردانی ادبیات فارسی دانشگاه آزاد در نسبت به تعداد داوطلبان بسیار زیاد است. — For example, the admission rate for associate degree in Persian Literature at Azad University is much higher than the number of applicants.
- 90 | 1052

840 درمان dærman *treatment* n
- آیا ورزش در درمان اعتیاد مؤثر است؟ — Is exercise effective in the treatment of addiction?
- 83 | 1811

841 کار کردن kar kærdæn *work* v
- نزدیک به یک میلیون از جمعیت ۶ میلیونی قرقیزستان در روسیه کار می‌کنند. — Nearly one million of the 6 million population of Kyrgyzstan works in Russia.
- 81 | 2127

842 جلب dʒælb *attraction* n

- Her — توجه اش به روزنامه ی روی میز جلب می شود. attention is drawn to the newspaper on the table.

90 | 1071

843 محروم mæhrum *deprived, banned* adj,n

- ۴۳۳ میلیارد سرمایه گذاری در مناطق محروم کشور شده است. — 433 billion has been invested in deprived regions of the country.

94 | 650

844 صادرات saderat *exports* n

- نرخ را به سمتی خواهد برد که هم ارزش پول ملی حفظ شود و هم به صادرات و تامین مواد اولیه تولید و ماشین‌آلات کمک شود. — It takes the rate in the direction that keeps our national currency rate up, helps exports and the supply of production raw materials and machinery.

81 | 2037

845 پاکستان pakestan *Pakistan* pn

- The — تاثیر فرهنگ ترک بر تمدن و فرهنگ پاکستان. effect of Turkish culture on Pakistani civilization and culture.

67 | 3996

846 قضایی ɣæzaji *judiciary* adj

- ملکشاهی رئیس کمیسیون قضایی مجلس شد. — Malekshahi became chairman of the House Judiciary Committee.

84 | 1669

847 پزشکی pezeʃki *medical* adj,n

- مخارج بالای پزشکی در چین بیماران را مقروض می‌کند. — High medical expenses in China put patients in debt.

82 | 1942

848 عالم alem, alæm *learned, world* n

- از آثار این عالم فرزانه است. — It is one of the works of this wise scientist.

82 | 1932

849 آموزشی amuzeʃi *educational* adj

- ده درصد بودجه سالانه افغانستان به امور آموزشی اختصاص دارد. — Ten percent of Afghanistan's annual budget is devoted to education.

78 | 2391

850 افتادن oftadæn *fall* adj,v

- روی میز افتادند. — They fell on the table.

71 | 3361

851 برداشت bærdaʃt *harvest, withdrawal, understanding, removed* n,v

- برداشت‌های متفاوت از مفهوم اوتانازی، وجود دارد. — There are different takes on the concept of euthanasia.

88 | 1264

852 نویسنده nevisænde *writer* n

- نویسنده اش را نمی شناختم. — I didn't recognize its author.

82 | 1955

853 هفت hæft *seven* n

- او تقریبا هفت هکتار زمین پسته داشت. — He had approximately seven hectares of pistachio land.

67 | 3885

854 تجارت tedʒaræt *trade* n

- رییس هیات مدیره شورای مرکزی خانه‌های صنعت، معدن و تجارت ایران — Head of the board of directors of the Central Council of Industry, Mine and Trade of Iran.

86 | 1513

855 خرید xærid *purchase, bought* n,v

- تقریباً تمام خریدهای نظامی ایران از آمریکا لغو شد. — Nearly all of Iran's military purchases from America were canceled.

80 | 2182

856 سوریه surije *Syria* pn

- سوریه همسایه عراق است. — Syria is Iraq's neighbor.

57 | 5438

857 دچار dotʃar *afflicted with* adj

- مبتلایان به میگرن دچار کمبود ویتامین هستند. — Those suffering from migraines have a vitamin deficiency.

83 | 1848

858 فردی færdi *individual* adj,n

- انتقال اطلاعات فردی از اروپا به آمریکا ممنوع است. — Transferring personal information from Europe to America is prohibited.

86 | 1409

859 دختر doxtær *girl, daughter* adj,n

- دختران در بسیاری از مهارت‌ها از پسرها جلوتر هستند. — Girls are ahead of boys in many skills.

69 | 3559

860 نهایی næhaji *final* adj

- البته آمار ۱۲ ماهه هم محاسبه شده و در مرحله بررسی نهایی است. — Indeed, the 12-month statistics have been calculated, and it is at the final stage for reviewing.

86 | 1469

861 کمک کردن komæk kærdæn *help* v

- ما تجهیزات و پوشاکی را ارائه می‌دهیم که به آنها کمک می‌کند. — We will offer equipment and clothing that will help them.

89 | 1081

862 احمد æhmæd *Ahmad* pn

- خلاصه احمد بچه با ادبی است! — In short, Ahmad is a polite kid!

84 | 1623

863 ارسال ersal *sending* n

- بینندگان رضوان نیوز می توانند با ارسال یادداشت خود، مطلب ذیل را تایید یا نقد کنند. — The viewers of Rezvan News by sending a note can confirm or reject this subject.

88 | 1241

864 ابزار **æbzar** *tool* adj,n
- ابزار گردآوری اطلاعات. — Information gathering tools.
- 88 | 1217

865 هرچند **hærtʃænd** *however* adv,conj
- به مدیران خود بیاموزید کمتر (در امور زیردستان خود) دخالت کنند هرچند ممکن است برای دخالت بیشتر تعلیم دیده باشند. — Teach your supervisors to interfere less (in the affairs of their subordinates) even though they might have been trained to intervene more.
- 92 | 799

866 بنابراین **bænabærin** *therefore* conj
- بنابراین دست به دعا برداشتند. — So they lifted their hands in prayer.
- 80 | 2085

867 ژاپن **ʒapon** *Japan* pn
- اوباما راهی ویتنام و ژاپن شد. — Obama was bound for Vietnam and Japan.
- 80 | 2179

868 حرف **hærf** *letter, talk* n
- کی از ازدواج حرف زد؟ — Who talked about marriage?
- 71 | 3287

869 داستان **dastan** *story* n
- هیچوقت داستان را تمام نکرد. — He never finished the story.
- 81 | 2036

870 خانم **xanom** *lady, Mrs.* N
- خانم ها، آقایان! — Ladies and gentlemen!
- 75 | 2674

871 قربانی **ɣorbani** *victim, sacrifice* adj,n,pn
- تعداد قربانیان انفجار خوی به ۵ نفر رسید. — The number of victims of the explosion in Khoy reached 5.
- 90 | 1040

872 معدن **mæʔdæn** *mine* n
- این معدن و این همه چیز باید در خدمت تو باشد. — This mine and all of these things should be at your service.
- 88 | 1205

873 مسافر **mosafer** *traveler, passenger* n
- خوشبختانه مسافر اتاقها را می پسندد و اجاره می کند. — Luckily, the traveler likes the rooms and will rent them.
- 91 | 898

874 قوه **ɣovve** *strength, branch* n
- لیست اموال خود را علاوه بر قوه قضایی به طور علنی به مردم هم اعلام کرد. — Beyond the judicial branch, he also openly announced his list of property to the people.
- 77 | 2467

875 زیبا **ziba** *beautiful* adj
- زیباترین سنگ عقیق جهان در معادن جنوب کشور استرالیا کشف شد. — The prettiest agate stone in the world was discovered in Australia's southern mines.
- 86 | 1425

876 مشغول **mæʃɣul** *busy* adj
- تو را دیدم که با کس دیگری مشغول صحبت بودی. — I saw you were busy talking to someone else.
- 89 | 1105

877 حاصل **hasel** *result* adj,n
- برخی از این اتفاقات حاصل تغییر نرخ ارز از 1226 تومان به 2226 تومان است. — Some of these events are the results of currency price change from 1226 toman to 2226 toman.
- 84 | 1629

878 اتفاق **ettefaɣ** *event* n
- این هیجان انگیزترین اتفاقی بود که می توانست برایمان بیفتد. — This is the most exciting thing that could have happened to us.
- 86 | 1391

879 اندازه **ændaze** *size* n
- دو طرف خیابان اصلی بوته‌های سبز شمشادهای یک قد و اندازه بود. — The green boxwoods on both sides of the main street were the same height and size.
- 85 | 1516

880 ورزشی **værzeʃi** *athletic* adj
- فدراسیون‌های ورزشی استفاده از داروهای نیروزا را منع کردند. — Sports federations banned the use of performance-enhancing drugs.
- 80 | 2129

881 باعث شدن **baes ʃodæn** *cause* v
- آنان در همه این نبردها خرابی‌های زیادی را باعث شدند. — They caused a lot of destruction in all of these battles.
- 85 | 1545

882 اجازه **edʒaze** *permit* n
- بهم اجازه میدهند که آن امتحان را بدهم. — They let me take that exam.
- 88 | 1154

883 پدر **pedær** *father* n
- پدرم به عنوان تماشاچی در تمام مسابقه‌ها شرکت می‌کرد. — My father was a bystander in all competitions.
- 71 | 3175

884 بازگشت **bazgæʃt** *return, returned* n,v
- میخواهد مانع بازگشت مردم به این مناطق شود. — He wants to prevent the return of people to the region.
- 88 | 1172

885 پر pær, por *feather, full* adj,n
- تهران پر از کازینوهای خانگی است. — Tehran is full of home casinos.
79 | 2237

886 مطالعه motaleʔe *study* adj,n
- من بحران‌های اقتصادی زیادی را مطالعه و مشاهده کرده‌ام. — I have studied and observed many economic crises.
79 | 2182

887 ارتش ærteʃ *army* n
- این در ارتش بی سابقه است. — This is unprecedented in the army.
76 | 2537

888 ضعف zæʔf *weakness* n
- این ضعف اراده‌پایدار و مستحکم‌شده است و برطرف کردن آن بسیار دشوار است. — This weakness has become an enduring and powerful resolve and setting it aside is very difficult.
91 | 915

889 افتخار eftexar *honor* n
- میتونین بهش افتخار کنین. — You can be proud of her.
92 | 816

890 آمادگی amadegi *readiness, preschool* n
- فکر می کنی چقدر آمادگی داری؟ — How prepared do you think you are?
87 | 1273

891 نامزد namzæd *candidate* n
- نامزد حزب جمهوری‌خواه پیشی گرفته است. — The Republican presidential candidate has taken the lead.
89 | 1119

892 ویژگی viʒegi *characteristic* n
- یک همسفر خوب چه ویژگی‌هایی باید داشته باشد؟ — What qualities should a good travel companion have?
85 | 1557

893 تلویزیون televizijon *television* n
- الان همه تلویزیون دارند و تحت تاثیر رسانه‌ها هستند. — Now everybody has television and is under the influence of media.
85 | 1549

894 شیعه ʃiʔe *Shiite* adj,n
- این قضیه مال ده سال پیش بود که جنگ شیعه و سنی تازه آغاز شده بود. — This affair is from ten years ago when the war between Sunnis and Shias had just begun.
91 | 916

895 خواستار xastar *applicant, desirous* n
- همه ی ما خواستار زندگی توام با آرامش هستیم. — All of us are desirous of a tranquil life together.
84 | 1646

896 مذهبی mæzhæbi *religious* adj
- تو که می‌گفتی پدرت مذهبی است. — But you used to say that your father is very religious.
88 | 1153

897 میلادی miladi *A.D.* adj
- نوروز در تقویم میلادی با ۲۰، ۲۱ یا ۲۲ مارس مطابقت دارد. — Nowruz corresponds with the 20th, 21st, or 22nd of March in the Gregorian calendar.
73 | 2851

898 مناسبت monasebæt *suitability, relevance to occasion* n
- به مناسبت ماه مبارک رمضان. — On the occasion of the holy month of Ramadan.
86 | 1423

899 محترم mohtæræm *honorable* adj
- مصاحبه با کمک راهنمای محترم شعبه آقای حجت الله انتظامی. — Interview with the help of honorable guide of the branch, Mr. Hojatollah Entezami.
82 | 1776

900 کارخانه karxane *factory* n
- شهرستان قائمشهر حدود ۲ تا ۳ کارخانه تولیدی مبلمان بزرگ دارد. — Ghaemshahr County has about 2–3 giant furniture production plants.
87 | 1321

901 موافقت movafeyæt *agreement* n
- او موافقت خود را اعلام داشت. — He announced his agreement.
91 | 866

902 مجموع mædʒmu? *total* n
- نتوانستم از مجموع آنها چیزی بفهمم. — I could not understand anything from the whole package.
88 | 1214

903 کشتن koʃtæn *kill* n,v
- آنانی که شمشیر به روی امام حسین کشیدند و او را کشتند. — Those who drew their swords against Imam Hossein and killed him.
81 | 1913

904 محلی mæhælli *local* adj,n
- از بحرینی ها و محلی ها مروارید می خریدم . . . — I was buying pearls from the Bahrainis and locals . . .
85 | 1514

905 عادی adi *normal* adj
- آمدنش به اینجا عادی نیست. — Her coming here is not ordinary.
91 | 912

906 اتحادیه ettehadije *union* n
- شورای اتحادیه اروپا با تحریم‌های ژانویه 2012 علیه بانک مرکزی و بخش انرژی ایران این قوانین را تکمیل کردند. — The Council of the European Union supplemented these laws with the January 2012 sanctions against Iran's central bank and energy sector.
70 | 3295

907 قدیمی yædimi *old, old-fashioned* adj

- میرزا عبدالحمید از دوستان قدیمی پدر مرحومم بود.
  — Mirza Abdolhamid was one of my dearly
  departed father's old friends.

87 | 1302

908 وحدت væhdæt *unity* n

- He — معتقد بود که شاه فقط باید نمادی برای وحدت باشد.
  believed that the king should be only a
  symbol for unity.

87 | 1321

909 بحران bohran *crisis* n

- The — بحران اقتصادی بر روی تجارت آن تاثیر نداشت.
  economic crisis did not have an effect on its
  trade.

67 | 3690

910 دل del *heart* n

- گاهی در ادبیات عرفانی آینه به دل شخص مؤمن اشاره دارد.
  — Sometimes in mystical literature, "mirror"
  refers to the heart of a believer.

66 | 3833

911 فرمانده færmande *commander* n

- فرمانده به پیروزی نیروهایش اطمینان داشت ولی سربازان
  The commander was certain of — دو دل بودند.
  his troops' victory, but the soldiers were
  vacillating.

88 | 1179

912 سنت sonnæt *tradition* n

- هر کشوری سنت‌های خاص خود را دارد که خیلی جالب و
  Every country has its own — دیدنی هستند.
  special traditions which are very interesting
  and noteworthy.

89 | 1083

913 اسرائیل esraʔil *Israel* pn

- اسرائیل می‌تواند در مقابل صلح بخش‌هایی از کرانه
  In return for — باختری را به فلسطینی‌ها بدهد.
  peace, Israel can return some parts of the
  West Bank to Palestinians.

81 | 1892

914 اروپایی orupaji *European* adj

- The line for — دست چپ صف اتباع اروپایی‌ست.
  European citizens is to the left.

77 | 2320

915 مانده mande *stale, leftover, balance, remained* adj,v

- Leftover — نان مانده فطیر از تازه آن خوشمزه تر است.
  unleavened bread is tastier than the fresh
  version.

84 | 1596

916 عدالت edalæt *justice* adj,n

- Justice — عدالت از درون آزادی سر بر می‌آورد.
  arises out of freedom.

87 | 1248

917 سرمایه‌گذاری særmajegozari *investment* n

- Why — چرا شرکت‌های سرمایه‌گذاری به ایران نمی‌روند؟
  don't investment companies go to Iran?

78 | 2249

918 صبح sobh *morning* n

- She's been — از صبح منتظر ملاقات پسرش است.
  waiting to visit her son since morning.

78 | 2186

919 سخنرانی soxænrani *speech* n

- داعش با سخنرانی‌های منحرف جوانان مسلمان را فریب
  ISIS deceives Muslim youth with — می‌دهد.
  perverted speeches.

89 | 1074

920 باشگاه baʃgah *club* n

- استاد پذیرفت و به پدر کودک قول داد که یک سال بعد
  می تواند فرزندش را در مقام قهرمانی کل باشگاه‌ها
  The master agreed and promised — ببیند.
  the child's father that within a year he
  would see his son as champion of
  all the clubs.

80 | 1960

921 کشف kæʃf *discovery* n

- فکر می کرد در حال کشف یک توطعه و فساد بزرگ است.
  — She thought that she was discovering a
  great conspiracy and corruption.

83 | 1699

922 تبدیل شدن tæbdil ʃodæn *convert* v

- TV shows — سریال‌ها به آگهی‌ بازرگانی تبدیل شده‌اند.
  have changed into commercial
  advertisements.

87 | 1229

923 قهرمانی yæhremani *heroism, championship* adj,n

- برنده این بازی فقط شانس قهرمانی‌اش بالاتر می‌رود.
  — The winner of this game will only
  increase his chance of obtaining the
  championship.

76 | 2457

924 جشنواره dʒæʃnvare *festival* n

- He was — او کاندیدای جایزه جشنواره فجر گردید.
  nominated for a Fajr festival award.

74 | 2673

925 سود sud *profit* n

- و عده‌ای ناخواسته با زیان‌های هنگفت یا سودهای هنگفت
  And some unintentionally — مواجه شوند.
  encounter huge losses or profits.

82 | 1738

926 شمالی ʃomali *northern* adj

- امروز طولانی‌ترین روز در نیمکره شمالی است.
  — Today is the longest day in the northern
  hemisphere.

86 | 1392

927 تهدید tæhdid *threat* n
- همین مسئله می‌تواند یک تهدید جدی برای سیستم مدیریت اقتصادی کشور باشد. — This issue can be a serious threat to the country's economic management system.

78 | 2185

928 ساده sade *simple* adj
- موضوع ساده ای به نظر می آید، اما در واقع خیلی پیچیده است. — It seems like a simple subject, but in reality it's very complicated.

87 | 1279

929 قادر yader *able* adj
- این زن قادر به راه رفتن نیست. — This woman is not able to walk.

89 | 1064

930 مادر madær *mother* n
- هر مادر این احساس را به بچه‌هاش دارد. — Every mother has this feeling towards her children.

71 | 3086

931 فرار færar *escape* n
- از تهران فرار کردم. — I ran away from Tehran.

93 | 605

932 زنده zende *live* adj
- اگر من را زنده بخوری، می‌زنم شکمت را پاره می‌کنم و می‌آیم بیرون. — If you eat me alive, I'll strike and rip your stomach, and get out.

84 | 1574

933 قتل yætl *killing, murder* n
- او به قتل رسید. — He was killed.

84 | 1569

934 سالم salem *healthy* adj
- قلب تو سالم به نظر می‌رسد اما من هرگز قلبم را با قلب تو عوض نمی‌کنم. — Your heart seems healthy, but I'd never trade my heart for yours.

89 | 1013

935 ثبت sæbt *registration* n
- شناسنامه ات را بده اسمت را ثبت کنیم. — Give me your birth certificate to have your name registered.

85 | 1457

936 شهروند fæhrvænd *citizen* n
- آگاهی از نقش یک شهروند مسئول. — Being aware of the role of a responsible citizen.

79 | 2029

937 صلح solh *peace* n
- البته بعدها وي نظر خود راجع به صلح با فلسطيني ها را تغيير داد و هرگونه طرح صلح با فلسطيني‌ها را رد نمود. — But later he changed his opinion about the peace with Palestinians and rejected any kind of plan for peace with Palestinians.

70 | 3161

938 طلا tæla *gold* adj,n
- شکست کودتای ترکیه قیمت طلا را کاهش داد. — The failed coup in Turkey decreased the price of gold.

80 | 1947

939 هوایی hævaji *aerial* adj
- سرکرده داعش در حمله هوایی کشته شد. — ISIS leader was killed in an air strike.

84 | 1577

940 دیروز diruz *yesterday* adv
- از فردا نمی ترسم چراکه دیروز را دیده ام و امروز را دوست دارم. — I am not afraid of tomorrow because I have seen yesterday, and I love today.

73 | 2803

941 سعیکردن sæ?j kærdæn *try* v
- سعی کردم بهترین‌ها را دعوت کنم. — I tried to invite the best.

89 | 1050

942 عرب æræb *Arab* adj,n,pn
- اعراب از اقدامات ایران نگران هستند. — The Arabs are concerned about Iran's actions.

80 | 1978

943 جاری dʒari *flowing, current, sister-in-law* adj
- اشک از چشمان دخترک جاری شد. — Tears began to flow from the little girl's eyes.

77 | 2304

944 هویت hovijjæt *identity* n
- انسان هویت خود را از چه می‌گیرد؟ — Where do humans get their identity from?

90 | 882

945 بدن bædæn *body* n
- با نوشیدن یک فنجان قهوه در روز می‌توان بدن خود را در مقابل بعضی از سرطان‌ها مصون کرد. — By drinking one cup of coffee per day, one can protect the body against some cancers.

84 | 1557

946 سلاح selah *weapon* n
- افزایش صادرات سلاح به کشور های خاورمیانه. — Increasing arms exports to the middle eastern countries.

80 | 1988

947 دانشمند danefmænd *scientist* adj,n
- فعاليت دانشمندان دانماركی در معرفی فرهنگ ایرانی قابل تقدير است. — Danish scholars' work in introducing Iranian culture is admirable.

85 | 1392

948 بدین bedin *to this* adv
- بدین ترتیب احتمال بروز جنگ جهانی سوم وجود دارد. — In this way, there is a possibility of the third world war.

87 | 1180

949 منفی mænfi *negative* adj
- بلغارستان بیشترین رشد منفی جمعیت را در جهان دارد. — Bulgaria has the highest negative population growth in the world.
88 | 1152

950 درون dærun *inside* n,prep
- سنگ زیبایی درون چشمه دید، آن را برداشت و در خورجینش گذاشت و به راهش ادامه داد. — He saw a beautiful stone in the spring, fished it out, placed it in his sack, and went on his way.
86 | 1342

951 رنگ ræng *color* n
- کارتی آبی رنگ به من دادند. — They gave me a blue card.
79 | 2042

952 فرانسوی færansævi *French* adj,n
- زبان فرانسوی به عنوان زبان دوم در مدارس آموزش داده می‌شود. — French is studied as a second language in the schools.
89 | 1051

953 کیفیت kejfijjæt *quality* n
- همه روزه غذای گرم را با کیفیت خوب و بسیار ارزان ارایه می‌دهند. — Every day they offer hot food with good quality and low price.
85 | 1446

954 اجرایی edȝraji *executive* adj
- ایران عضو شورای اجرایی یونسکو شد. — Iran became a member of UNESCO's executive council.
81 | 1794

955 خشونت xoʃunæt *violence* n
- اما اصولاً چرا خشونت و درگیری رخ می‌دهد؟ — But basically why do violence and conflicts occur?
85 | 1444

956 مبنی mæbni *based* adj
- با توجه به تعطیلی یک هفته‌ای دولت آمریکا که موجب افزایش نگرانی‌هایی مبنی‌بر احتمال چالش کنگره برای افزایش به موقع سقف بدهی این کشور شده است. — With regard to the one week closing of the US government which has increased concerns for the possible challenge of congress in raising the country's debt ceiling on time.
87 | 1222

957 شماره ʃomare *number* n
- این بار هیچ شماره تلفنی روی صفحه تلفن ما نیفتاد. — This time no phone number appeared on our phone's screen.
80 | 1911

958 پشت poʃt *back* n,prep
- نگاهی به پشت پرده چاپ و انتشار مجموعه‌های شعر در ایران. — A behind the scenes glance at printing and publishing poetry collections in Iran.
72 | 2856

959 عملی æmæli *practical* adj,n
- چه کسی بهشما گفت که این‌کار عملی نیست. — Who told you that this wasn't practical?
86 | 1292

960 مذاکرات mozakerat *negotiations* n
- مذاکرات صلح یمن به تعویق افتاد. — The Yemen peace negotiations were postponed.
82 | 1698

961 ورزش værzeʃ *sport* n
- یک معلم ورزش هم داشتیم. — We also had a sports teacher.
82 | 1732

962 جالب dȝaleb *interesting, attractive* adj
- در زمان سفر اولم اتفاق جالبی در تفکرم رخ داد. — During my first trip an interesting thing happened in my thought.
88 | 1125

963 موضع mowze? *position* n
- اکنون موضع وی تغییر کرده است. — Now she has changed her stance.
84 | 1476

964 اضافه ezafe *addition* adj
- شما می‌توانید صفاتی را به آن اضافه کنید. — You can add adjectives to that.
82 | 1725

965 دستگیر dæstgir *arrested* adj
- حتما هم دستگیر شد. — Certainly she was detained.
90 | 890

966 متوجه motevædȝdȝeh *conscious* adj,n
- می‌فهمم، متوجه‌ام، و حق با توست. — I understand, I realize, and you are right.
92 | 671

967 فرمودن færmudæn *order* v
- بله ارباب، من غلام حلقه‌بگوش جنابعالی هستم، تا احضارم فرمودید خدمت رسیدم. — Yes Lord, I am your servant sir, and as soon as you called me, I arrived.
78 | 2063

968 عبارت ebaræt *phrase, expression* n,v
- به عبارت بهتر زندگی اخلاقی خود پاداش خود است. — To put it better, the moral life is its own reward.
77 | 2223

969 ارزیابی ærzjabi *assessment* n
- هر فردی خود را ارزیابی می کند. — Each individual assesses himself.
85 | 1361

6 Electronics

Rank	Headword	Pronunciation	Gloss	Rank	Headword	Pronunciation	Gloss
71	برنامه	bærname	program	3360	گوشی	guʃi	receiver, headphones, phone
409	شبکه	ʃæbæke	network				
759	پرونده	pærvænde	file	3372	رایانه‌ای	rajaneji	computer
794	پخش	pæxʃ	broadcasting	3452	رادیویی	radijoji	radio
893	تلویزیون	televizijon	television	4003	لوح	lowh	tablet, disk
1082	تلفن	telefon	telephone	4223	موبایل	mobajl	mobile phone
1098	رادیو	radijo	radio				
1128	صفحه	sæfhe	page, screen, record	4698	دیسک	disk	disk
				5115	کامپیوتری	kampjuteri	computer
1272	پایگاه	pajgah	site	5577	کاست	kaset	cassette
1467	تلویزیونی	televizijoni	television	8092	نمایشگر	næmajeʃgær	monitor
1532	اینترنت	internet	internet	8111	ویدیو	video	video
1785	دوربین	durbin	camera	8148	وبلاگ	veblag	blog
1888	فناوری	fænaværi	technology	8697	کلیک	kelik	click
1908	تلفنی	telefoni	telephone	9065	پوشه	puʃe	folder
2149	کانال	kanal	channel	9252	فرکانس	ferekans	frequency
2505	الکترونیکی	elektroniki	electronic	10634	تلفن‌همراه	telefonehæmrah	mobile phone
2602	ماهواره	mahvare	satellite	10835	برنامه‌ساز	bærnamesaz	programmer
2784	الکترونیک	elektronik	electronics	11129	برنامه‌نویس	bærnamenevis	programmer
2900	حافظه	hafeze	memory	14501	فکس	fæks	fax
2951	اینترنتی	interneti	internet	16961	دیسکت	disket	diskette
3202	رایانه	rajane	computer	17194	گرامافون	geramafon	record player
3279	کامپیوتر	kampjuter	computer	18859	وب‌سایت	vebsajt	website

970 تصور tæsævvor *imagination* adj,n
- تصویر تهران با تصور قبلی ما قابل مقایسه نیست. — The image of Tehran does not compare to our previous imagination.
  91 | 823

971 شاعر ʃaʔer *poet* n
- او شاعر پارسی‌گوی هندی است — She is a Persian-speaking Indian poet.
  82 | 1678

972 اعتماد eʔtemad *trust* n
- او هم این را می داند و از اعتماد من سوء استفاده نمی کند. — He knows this too and he does not abuse my trust.
  87 | 1166

973 آرامش arameʃ *tranquility* n
- ثبات و آرامش جزیره‌را حتی توپهای امپراطوری نیز دیگر نمی‌توانند تامین کنند. — The island's stability and peace cannot even be provided by the empire's artillery.
  89 | 968

974 نفع næfʔ *profit, benefit* n
- این اختلافات چندان به نفع منافع ملی ما و همچنین کشورهای حوزه خلیج فارس نبود. — These differences are not in favor of our national interests or those of other countries in Persian Gulf region.
  90 | 891

975 فقر fæɣr *poverty* n

- حدود ۱٫۷ میلیارد نفر در جهان در فقر مطلق زندگی
میکنند. — About 1.7 billion people in the
world live in absolute poverty.

90 | 925

976 همکار hæmkɑr *colleague* n

- با او در تهران همکار بودم. — I worked with him in
Tehran.

91 | 819

977 اولویت owlævvijæt *priority* n

- توسعه ورزش همگانی از اولویتهای شهرداری در سال
جاری است. — The expansion of sport for
all is among City Hall's priorities for the
current year.

89 | 934

978 متخصص motexæsses *expert, specialist* adj,n

- شخصیت اصلی رمان مردی میانسال بود، متخصص در
تاریخ هنر بیزانس که برای ادامه تحقیقات خود با کشتی از
آمریکا به اروپا سفر می کرد. — The main character
of the novel was a middle-aged man, expert
in the history of Byzantine art, who traveled
to Europe and the USA by ship to continue
his research.

86 | 1284

979 صندوق sænduɣ *fund, box* n

- بانک جهانی و صندوق بینالمللی پول. — Word Bank
and International Monetary Fund.

83 | 1499

980 مشابه moʃɑbeh *similar* adj

- هر زن دیگری در سن او که حوادث مشابهی را از سر
گذرانده بود — Any woman at her age who had
been through the same incidents . . .

87 | 1198

981 فارسی fɑrsi *Persian* adj,n

- هر کاری بکنیم داریم فارسی حرف میزنیم. — Whatever
we do, we are speaking Farsi.

78 | 2062

982 نزدیکی næzdiki *proximity* adj,n

- گورستان خاوران در نزدیکیهای تهران است. — Khavaran
cemetery is in the proximity of Tehran.

90 | 895

983 رضایت rezɑjæt *satisfaction* n

- واقعاً از او کمال رضایت و امتنان را دارم. — Really I
am so thankful and satisfied with her.

93 | 591

984 نگرانی negærɑni *anxiety* n

- مادرم با نگرانی پرسید که مگر چه شده ؟ — My
mother anxiously asked, "What happened?"

82 | 1643

985 مؤثر mo?æsser *effective* adj

- شیوهای بسیار مفید و مؤثر است. — It's a very
effective and useful method.

82 | 1619

986 برجسته bærdʒeste *outstanding* adj

- عباس کیارستمی کارگردان برجسته ایرانی درگذشت.
— The prominent Iranian filmmaker Abbas
Kiarostami passed away.

89 | 961

987 قرن ɣærn *century* n

- از زمان انقلاب صنعتی یعنی از اواسط قرن نوزدهم تاکنون.
— Since the Industrial Revolution era, i.e the
middle of nineteenth century up to now.

76 | 2216

988 رسیدگی residegi *investigation* n

- بعد از رسیدگی به پرونده «کیارستمی» حرفهایی برای
گفتن دارم. — After investigating the Kiarostami
file, I have some words to share.

85 | 1353

989 ریال rijɑl *rial* n

- چون به خوبی می دانستم که دست کم هر سال سیصد هزار
ریال عایدات دارد. — Because I knew very well
that every year he earned at least three
hundred thousand rial.

72 | 2648

990 تصمیم گرفتن tæsmim gereftæn *decide* v

- تصمیم گرفتن سختترین کار دنیا است. — Making a
decision is the hardest thing in the world.

86 | 1247

991 اولیه ævvælijje *primary, original* adj

- ساکنان اولیه این منطقه اقوام تراکیه ای بودند.
— Thracian tribes were the original
inhabitants of this area.

85 | 1321

992 فنی fænni *technical* adj

- دچار اشکال فنی شد و خلاصه ماشین فعلا خراب دیگه.
— It had a technical problem and in short
the car is broken right now.

82 | 1597

993 خودرو xodrow *car* adj,n

- در حال حاضر خودروسازان جهانی در شرایطی به سرمی
برند که اگر نتوانند خود را با شرایط روز هماهنگ کنند،
محکوم به فنای صنعتی هستند. — At present, the
world automakers are in a position that if
they cannot adjust themselves to the existing
circumstances, they are doomed to industrial
failure.

66 | 3371

994 عرض ærz *width, saying* n

- سالن درازی بود به عرض حداکثر سه متر. — It was a
long hall with a width of at least three meters.

80 | 1829

995 مقدار meɣdɑr *amount* adv,n,q

- خانم به خانه رسید و از توی قوطی کوچکی یک پر و
مقداری روغن درآورد. — She got home and took
out a feather and some oil from a small box.

81 | 1750

996 عمده omde *main* adj
- نقش بسیار عمده ای دارد. — She has a very essential role.

82 | 1634

997 قول ɣowl *promise, saying* n
- اگر به قول شما این قرارگاه تا این حد موفق است ،چرا این همه انتقاد حول این نهاد است؟ — If as you are saying the camp is so successful, why is there so much criticism around it?

84 | 1389

998 سپرده seporde *entrusted, deposit* adj,n
- قرار است حفظ امنیت تا چندی دیگر به صورت کامل به عراقیها سپرده شود. — In the near future, security maintenance is supposed to be completely given to the Iraqis.

92 | 700

999 تجاری tedʒɑri *commercial* adj
- مراکز تجاری مدرنی در این شهر احداث شده اند. — Modern shopping centers have been built in this city.

82 | 1575

1000 ایتالیا italijɑ *Italy* pn
- در ایتالیا آشنا و فامیلی نداشتم. — I didn't have any friends or family in Italy.

73 | 2486

1001 درست dorost *right, correct* adj,adv
- این نام درست تر است. — This name is more correct.

75 | 2269

1002 قطع ɣætʔ *cut* n
- اگر این تولید به هر دلیل قطع شود شوک عظیمی در تامین برق کشور ایجاد خواهد شد. — If this production is interrupted for any reason, a huge shock in the supply of electricity will occur.

88 | 1022

1003 مأمور mæʔmur *agent, officer* n
- مأمور یقه ناصر را گرفت و از جا بلندش کرد و با غیظ چیزی گفت که ناصر معنی اش را نفهمید. — The officer took Naser's collar and lifted him from his seat and said something furiously that Naser did not understand.

84 | 1424

1004 ایالت ejɑlæt *state* n
- بی آنکه کسی متوجه شود روی معدن را پوشاند و عازم شهر ویلیامزبرگ در ایالت مریلند شد تا موضوع را برای بستگان و برخی از همسایگان بازگو کند. — Without anybody noticing, he covered the mine and went to Williamsburg in the state of Maryland to tell some of his family and friends about it.

80 | 1765

1005 امنیتی æmnijjæti *security* adj
- در یورش شبانه نیروهای امنیتی به دانشگاه بازداشت شد. — He was arrested during the security forces' nighttime raid on the university.

66 | 3286

1006 شکست ʃekæst *defeat, failure, break* n
- شکست سوریان و از دست دادن سهمیه المپیک. — Soryan's defeat and loss of Olympic quota spot.

75 | 2304

1007 تفاوت tæfɑvot *difference* n
- تفاوت میان یک صدف واقعی و نقاشی یک صدف چیست. — What's the difference between a real seashell and a drawing of a seashell?

83 | 1455

1008 همایش hæmɑjeʃ *conference* n
- برگزاری بیست و سومین همایش جشن گلریزان در خوزستان. — Holding the twenty third Golrizan celebration gathering in Khuzestan.

79 | 1917

1009 هفتم hæftom *seventh* adj,n
- حمید امجد در هفتم آذر ۱۳۴۷ در تهران زاده شد. — Hamid Amjad was born on the seventh of Azar, 1347.

86 | 1220

1010 کلاس kelɑs *class* n
- فردای اون روز، کلاس ما تماشایی بود. — The next day our class was spectacular.

84 | 1370

1011 روشنی rowʃæni *light* adj,n
- اشوزرتشت فروغ و روشنی ها و به پیروی آن آتش را برگزیده. — Zoroaster chose light and brightness, and following that, he chose fire.

96 | 348

1012 وجه vædʒh *manner* n
- نباید به هیچ وجه قشرهای جامعه را درگیر مناقشاتی کرد که تور آن را در سطح احزاب و گروه های سیاسی بسیار داغ و سوزان است. — Different social classes should never involve themselves in disputes where the temperature at the political party level is heated and incendiary.

87 | 1115

1013 ساختار sɑxtɑr *structure* n
- هر سوژه ای ساختار خاص خود می طلبد. — Every subject requires its own particular structure.

83 | 1450

1014 توافق tævɑfoɣ *agreement* adj,n
- همیشه با همسر خود توافق نظر داشته باشید و در اجرای قوانینی که تعیین می کنید، جدی باشید. — Always seek agreement with your spouse and be serious about implementing the rules you are setting.

80 | 1802

1015 كارگر kargær *worker* n
- از افزایش ۱۴ درصدی دستمزد کارگران راضی نیستیم. — We are not satisfied with the 14 percent increase in workers' wages.
- 86 | 1197

1016 قبلاً qæblæn *before* adv
- قبلاً ثابت شده‌است که توتون اثرات زیانباری بر ریه انسان وارد می‌سازد. — It has already been proven that tobacco causes damaging effects on human lungs.
- 90 | 844

1017 تمرین tæmrin *practice* n
- جمع کثیری از افسران ارشد آلمانی در حال انجام تمرینات جنگی بودند. — A large number of senior German officers were performing combat exercises.
- 88 | 1032

1018 عمر omr, omær *life, Omar* n,pn
- عمر من دارد تمام می شود. — My life is ending.
- 83 | 1505

1019 دارو daru *drug* n
- آیا استفاده از این دارو بی خطر است؟ — Is using this medication safe?
- 84 | 1371

1020 عقیده æɣide *belief* n
- ولی پدرم عقیده داشت که انسان ولو شاعر و ادیب هم باشد باید شغلی داشته باشد. — But my father also had the belief that a person, even if he is a poet or scholar, must also have a job.
- 88 | 1062

1021 آهن ahæn *iron* n
- هوای تهران مرطوب است و آهن ها زود پوسیده می شوند! — The weather in Tehran is humid and iron decays very quickly.
- 89 | 894

1022 کیلومتر kilometr *kilometer* n
- امکان ندارد بشود سالی ۱۵کیلومتر مترو ساخت! — It is not possible to build a 15 kilometer metro in one year!
- 87 | 1131

1023 محور mehvær *axis, dimension* n
- محور بعدی که سپاه به آن توجه ویژه‌ای دارد سرمایه انسانی است. — Another dimension that the IRGC pays special attention to is human capital.
- 87 | 1134

1024 ارتقا erteɣa *promotion, upgrade* n
- ارتقاء سطح علمی پزشکان متخصص و ارایه آخرین دستاوردهای علم پزشکی مربوط به این دو بیماری از جمله اهداف برپایی این همایش است. — Promoting the scientific level of specialized doctors and providing the latest achievements of medical science related to these two diseases are among the established goals of this conference.
- 87 | 1067

1025 استقبال esteɣbal *welcome* n
- برای سربازان نیز نشریات اختصاصی دیگری داریم که به شدت مورد استقبال این عزیزان قرار گرفته. — For the soldiers we have other specialized publications that have been extremely well received by these loved ones.
- 87 | 1078

1026 رضا reza *Reza* n,pn
- امام رضا(ع) در شهر مدینه به دنیا آمد. — Imam Reza was born in the city of Medina.
- 87 | 1070

1027 تأیید tæʔjid *confirmation* n
- با تکان سر حرف او را تأیید می‌کند. — He confirms her words with a nod of the head.
- 84 | 1418

1028 ایجاد کردن idʒad kærdæn *create* v
- زلزله بلوچستان پاکستان یک جزیره جدید ایجاد کرد. — The earthquake in Pakistani Balochistan created a new island.
- 87 | 1078

1029 نیازمند nijazmænd *needy, in need* adj,n
- بی‌شک نیازمند زمان خواهد بود. — Undoubtedly it will require time.
- 89 | 944

1030 انداختن ændaxtæn *throw* n,v
- جام می او را به زمین انداخت و شکست. — He threw his chalice to the ground and broke it.
- 77 | 2097

1031 واشنگتن vaʃængton *Washington* pn
- عملا کاخ سفید در واشنگتن را از مدار تاثیرگذاری خارج کنند. — To practically remove the White House in Washington from the orbit of effectiveness.
- 82 | 1527

1032 عربی æræbi *Arabic* adj,n
- معلم عبارتی عربی را بر تخته سیاه نوشت و بعد جدولی خط‌کشی کرد. — The teacher wrote an Arabic phrase on the blackboard and then drew a table.
- 76 | 2117

1033 همزمان hæmzæman *simultaneously* adj,adv
- نوروز همزمان با اعتدال بهاری است. — Nowruz coincides with spring equinox.
- 81 | 1661

1034 پنجم pændʒom *fifth* adj,n
- ایتالیا پنجمین کشور پرجمعیت اروپاست. — Italy is the fifth most populous country in Europe.
- 79 | 1853

1035 توانایی tævanaji *ability* n
- او اصلاً توانایی ذاتی و فطری در این باره را نداشت. — He didn't have innate or inherent ability in this regard at all.
- 84 | 1348

1036 صفر sefr *zero* n

- ا — گفتم صفر عدد نیست عدد از یک شروع می شود.
said zero is not a number, numbers begin from one.
86 | 1151

1037 شهری fæhri *urban* adj,n

- تهران به مدیریت یکپارچه شهری نیاز دارد. — Tehran needs an integrated urban management.
72 | 2581

1038 فقیر fæɣir *poor* adj,n

- کیسه های پول رو أورد و بین فقیر بیچاره ها قسمت کرد. — She brought out a sack of money and divided it among the poor, impoverished people.
93 | 570

1039 کشوری keʃværi *state, national* adj,n

- نتایج مسابقات کشوری کمان سنتی اعلام شد. — The results of the national traditional archery tournament were announced.
83 | 1414

1040 راستا rasta *direction* n

- سوال مهمی در این راستا مطرح است. — An important question is raised in this regard.
84 | 1345

1041 شرقی ʃærɣi *eastern* adj

- رشته کوه البرز به ۳ قسمت شرقی، مرکزی و غربی تقسیم می‌شود. — The Alborz mountain range is divided into 3 sections: western, central and eastern.
80 | 1703

1042 فکری fekri *mental, intellectual* adj,n,pn

- این بازی فکری با موس انجام میشود. — This brain game is played with a mouse.
88 | 972

1043 عمیق æmiɣ *deep* adj

- أنها درون چاله ای عمیق افتادند. — They fell into a deep pit.
89 | 884

1044 مطرح کردن mætræh kærdæn *propose, bring up* v

- مهمترین مشکلاتی که مردم با قالیباف مطرح کردند. — The most important issues that the people brought up to Ghalibaf.
90 | 773

1045 پوشش puʃeʃ *cover* adj,n

- او پوشش سیاه را بر سر بانو انداخت. — She dropped a black covering over the woman's head.
89 | 916

1046 سخنگو soxængu *spokesperson* n

- القاعده مرگ سخنگوی النصره در سوریه را تأیید کرد. — Al Qaeda confirmed the death of Al Nusra's spokesman in Syria.
84 | 1378

1047 مثلاً mæsælæn *for example* adv,conj

- مثلاً ذکر کنید که چرا شخص معروف است. — For example, mention why the person is famous.
68 | 2959

1048 محدود mæhdud *limited* adj

- تولید سبز: تولید با استفاده از فناوریهایی که آلودگی را محدود و یا حذف میکنند. — Green Production: production using technologies that limit or eliminate pollution.
85 | 1292

1049 وعده væʔde *promise* n

- تو چرا باید زندگی ات را با این وعده ها خراب کنی. — Why must you destroy your life with these promises?
90 | 772

1050 عزیز æziz *dear* adj,n,pn

- شهروندان عزیز موظف‌اند شناسنامه‌ی قبلی‌شان را از طریق پست به محل صدور ارسال دارند. — Our dear citizens are required to send their old IDs to the place of issue by post.
73 | 2420

1051 دوستی dusti *friendship* n

- نمایندگان ملل دستهایشان را به نشانه دوستی به طرف همدیگر دراز کرده‌اند. — The countries' representatives have stretched their arms towards each other as a sign of friendship.
92 | 679

1052 الله ællah *Allah, God* pn

- بسم الله الرحمن الرحیم. — In the name of God the compassionate the merciful.
70 | 2694

1053 امضا emzaʔ *signature* n

- قراردادهای صادرات نفت به ۳ کشور اروپایی امضا شد. — Contracts for oil exports to three European countries were signed.
82 | 1483

1054 ماست mast *yogurt* n,v

- نان و پنیر و ماست و سبزی. — Bread and cheese and yogurt and vegetables.
91 | 707

1055 برده bærde, borde *slave, carried* adj,v

- جهان امروز، ۴۶ میلیون برده دارد. — Today's world has 46 milion slaves.
86 | 1147

1056 سوخت suxt *fuel, burned* n,v

- سوخت‌های فسیلی به سه نوع اصلی تقسیم می‌شوند. — Fossil fuels are divided into three main types.
87 | 1064

1057 تحویل tæhvil *delivery, submission* n

- من برگه امتحانی را تحویل دادم و سوال آخر را بی‌جواب گذاشتم. — I turned in my answer sheet and left the last answer blank.
92 | 665

1058 رفع ræfʔ *removing* n
- سوءتفاهم‌های اجتماعی را رفع می‌کند. — It eliminates social misunderstandings.

83 | 1385

1059 باره bɑre *subject* n
- دیگر در این باره سخنی به میان نرفت مجلس متفرق شد و از هم جدا شدند و سیدجواد هم به کربلا آمد. — Nothing was said about it anymore, the assembly scattered and got separated from each other, and Sayyed Javad came to Karbala.

85 | 1235

1060 آنکه ɑnke *that which* conj
- به جای آنکه از او تشکر کند. — Instead of thanking him.

80 | 1730

1061 نگران negɑrɑn *anxious* adj
- مردم بیش از مسئولان نگرانند. — The people are more concerned than those responsible.

88 | 962

1062 لندن lændæn *London* pn
- وی از مدرسه پزشکی سنت ماری لندن فارغ‌التحصیل شد. — She graduated from St. Mary's Medical School in London.

77 | 2029

1063 تبلیغ tæbliɣ *propaganda, advertising* n
- سردار شما در صحبت‌هایتان از تبلیغات در زمان جنگ صحبت کردید. — Commander, in your talks, you spoke about advertising in wartime.

86 | 1110

1064 پسر pesær *son* adj,n
- پسرهای خواهر صاحب زمین برای دایی‌شان به رایگان کار می‌کنن. — The land owner's nephews work for their uncle at no charge.

70 | 2728

1065 انتشار enteʃɑr *publication* n
- شهرت نویسنده با انتشار داستان «پرواز شبانه» آغاز شد. — The author's fame commenced with the publication of the story "Night Flight."

79 | 1782

1066 پرسش porseʃ *question* n
- پاسخی که دریافت می کنید بستگی به پرسشی دارد که پرسیده اید. — The answer you will find depends on the question that you have asked.

87 | 1067

1067 مقاومت moɣɑvemæt *resistance* n
- جانم، گفتم که می رویم خودمان را آماده ی مقاومت بعدی بکنیم. — Dear, I said that we are going to prepare ourselves for the next resistance.

79 | 1754

1068 ظرف zærf *container, vessel* n
- زنان و دختران ده توی رودخانه ظرف و لباس می شستند. — Women and girls of the village were washing dishes and clothing in the river.

90 | 807

1069 قبول ɣæbul *accepting* adj,n
- باید قبول کنیم این صنعت را نمی توان با بسیاری از صنایع کشور مقایسه کرد. — We should accept that this industry cannot be compared with many industries in the country.

90 | 819

1070 تحلیل tæhlil *analysis* n
- شاهد عدم بررسی و تحلیل ابعاد این تصمیم هستیم. — We observe the lack of review and analysis of aspects of this decision.

85 | 1240

1071 قطعه ɣætʔe *piece* n
- سیاست: هنر تقسیم کیک تولد، به گونه ای که هر کس احساس کند بزرگ ترین قطعه را صاحب شده است. — Politics: the art of dividing a birthday cake in such a way that each person feels like they got the biggest piece.

85 | 1230

1072 معروف mæʔruf *famous* adj,n
- معروف‌ترین اثر وی شعر «کوچه» نام دارد. — His most famous work is the poem called "The Alley."

81 | 1571

1073 بهره bæhre *portion, interest* n
- چون نرخ تورم کاهش یافته پس به‌دنبال آن باید نرخ بهره نیز کم شود. — Since the inflation rate decreased, the interest rate must consequently also go down.

78 | 1882

1074 شاه ʃɑh *king, shah* n,pn
- شاهان و امیران همواره به او ارادت می‌ورزیدند. — Kings and emirs always expressed devotion to him.

75 | 2196

1075 ضد zedd *against, anti-* n
- به او قرص ضد افسردگی می‌دهند. — They give him anti-depressant pills.

77 | 2011

1076 اصفهان esfæhɑn *Esfahan* pn
- فارغ‌التحصیل کارشناسی ارشد در رشته فیزیک از دانشگاه اصفهان. — Master's in physics from the University of Isfahan.

78 | 1834

1077 هواپیما hævɑpejmɑ *airplane* n
- توی هواپیما چند تا گیلاس خوردی؟ — How many drinks did you have in the airplane?

80 | 1692

1078 شخصی ʃæxsi *personal* adj,n
- کسانی که منافع شخصی و فردی برای آنان از همه چیز مهم‌تر است. — People for whom personal and individual interests are the most important thing.

84 | 1292

1079 هشت hæʃt *eight* n
- هشت سالش بیشتر نیست. — He's not more than eight years old.

62 | 3579

1080 شکستن ʃekæstæn *break* adj,n,v
- صدای شکستن کاسه‌ای لعابی. — The sound of a glazed bowl breaking.
86 | 1106

1081 تشکیل دادن tæʃkil dadæn *form* v
- می خواست یک حزب سیاسی مستقل تشکیل بدهد. — He wanted to form an independent political party.
86 | 1153

1082 تلفن telefon *telephone* n
- یکی از دستگاه‌های تلفن گوشی نداشت. — One of the telephones didn't have a handset.
80 | 1696

1083 کلیه kolje, kollijje *kidney, all* n,q
- کلیه نواحی خلیج فارس در دوره‌های پیش از اسلام به ایران تعلق داشته است. — During the pre-Islamic period all areas of the Persian Gulf belonged to Iran.
86 | 1096

1084 فعلی feʔli *present* adj
- با مشکلات اقتصادی فعلی زندگی می کنند. — They live with their current economic difficulties.
86 | 1119

1085 امیدوار omidvar *hopeful* adj,v
- در پایان انتقادی کلی را عنوان می کنیم که امیدواریم تاثیر گذار باش. — At the end, we are bringing up a general criticism that we hope to be effective.
83 | 1349

1086 کارت kart *card* n
- محمد مختاری کارت زرد داشت. — Mohammad Mokhtari had a yellow card.
87 | 1012

1087 جذب dʒæzb *absorption* n
- لازم بود که واژه‌ها را جذب کند. — It was necessary for her to absorb the words.
84 | 1242

1088 خداوند xodavænd *god* pn
- خداوند متعال این توفیق را به ما عنایت فرموده است. — God almighty has granted us this opportunity.
84 | 1310

1089 تماس tæmas *contact* n
- با این ابزار امکان برقراری تماس مستقیم با مصاحبه شونده فراهم می‌گردد. — With this tool, there would be the possibility of obtaining direct contact with the interviewee.
86 | 1107

1090 مجمع mædʒmæʔ *assembly, convention* n
- مجمع عمومی این موضوع رو بررسی کرد. — The general assembly reviewed this issue.
80 | 1585

1091 خطرناک xætærnak *dangerous* adj
- ۴۰ ماده شیمیایی خطرناک در کشور وجود دارد. — There are 40 dangerous chemicals in the country.
91 | 694

1092 سالانه salane *annual* adj,adv
- میانگین بارش سالانه شهر بسیار پایین است. — The average annual precipitation of the town is very low.
85 | 1175

1093 روزی ruzi *someday, daily bread* n
- نگران روزی فردا نیستم. — I am not concerned about my daily bread for tomorrow.
80 | 1653

1094 بلند bolænd *long, high* adj
- خانم صادقی دستم را گرفت و مرا از جایم بلند کرد. — Ms. Sadeghi held my hand, and helped me stand up.
77 | 1920

1095 بیمارستان bimarestan *hospital* n
- تازه از بیمارستان مرخص شدم. — I have just been released from the hospital.
85 | 1210

1096 ذخیره zæxire *supply* n
- بدن انسان برای حفظ سلامتی خود همواره مقداری چربی به عنوان ذخیره انرژی در نقاط مختلف ذخیره می‌کند. — To maintain its own well being, the human body always stores a little bit of fat in various places as an energy reserve.
86 | 1063

1097 درجه dærædʒe *degree* n
- این وجود نازنین به این درجه از کمال رسیده است. — This dear existence has reached this degree of perfection.
79 | 1713

1098 رادیو radijo *radio* n
- داشتیم رادیو پیام را گوش می‌کردیم. — We were listening to *Radio Payam*.
85 | 1148

1099 سینما sinema *cinema* n
- او را قدیمی‌ترین عکاس سینمای ایران می‌دانند. — He is considered the oldest Iranian cinematographer.
71 | 2473

1100 پیش بینی piʃbini *prediction* n
- با توجه به پیش بینی هایی که صورت می‌گیرد. — With regard to all the predictions that are being made.
78 | 1816

1101 نفتی næfti *petroleum* adj
- سند همکاری نفتی ایران و هند امضا شد. — Iran and India signed an oil cooperation document.
81 | 1516

1102 دروازه dærvaze *gate, goal* n
- یونان می‌خواهد دروازه ورود گاز ایران به اروپا شود. — Greece wants to become the gateway for Iranian gas into Europe.
89 | 800

1103 شناسایی ʃenasaʔi *identification, reconnaissance* n

● روسیه آمریکا را به انجام پرواز شناسایی نزدیک مرزهایش متهم کرد. — Russia accused America of carrying out reconnaissance flights near its borders.

86 | 1114

1104 مبنا mæbna *base, basis* n

● برای من مبنای هر عملی ایمان است. — For me, faith is the basis of every action.

84 | 1224

1105 چینی ʧini *Chinese, china* adj,n

● یک عروسک چینی به قد آدم خریده بود. — She had purchased a human-sized china doll.

89 | 832

1106 تنظیم tænzim *regulation, adjustment* n

● این کتاب شامل هفده مقاله است که در سه بخش تنظیم شده است. — This book contains 17 articles which have been arranged in three parts.

83 | 1298

1107 حاکمیت hakemijjæt *rule* n

● آنها درپی غلبه یا حاکمیت برگیتی نبوده اند. — They were not after dominating or ruling the world.

83 | 1351

1108 نهایت næhajæt *extremity, end* n

● در نهایت زندگی خود را دگرگون می کنند. — Ultimately, they change their lives.

84 | 1230

1109 خویش xiʃ *self* pron

● خود را خالصانه در اختیار همکاران خویش قرار می‌دهند. — They sincerely put themselves at their colleagues' service.

75 | 1992

1110 شک ʃækk *doubt* n,pn

● بهروز شک داشت که مینا توسط یک ضارب به قتل رسیده بود. — Behrouz doubted that Mina had been killed by an assailant.

89 | 828

1111 اخیراً æxiræn *recently* adv

● این بیماری اخیراً گسترش زیادی یافته‌است. — This disease has increased greatly recently.

90 | 740

1112 بیانیه bæjanijje *statement* n

● بیانیه‌های رسمی ارتش ایالات متحده. — Official statements of the United States Army.

82 | 1387

1113 ذهن zehn *mind* n

● اولین راهی که به ذهن می‌رسد. — The very first thing that comes to mind.

83 | 1287

1114 مقابله moɣabele *confronting* n

● برای مقابله با این ترفند، هزینه درخواست‌ها، خدمات یا موارد اضافه را اعلام کنید. — To confront this trick, announce the expenses of the requests, services, or additional cases.

80 | 1552

1115 انجمن ændʒomæn *association* n

● در یکی از انجمن‌های ادبی از شاعری دعوت کردند که شعری بخواند. — In one of the literary societies they invited a poet to read a poem.

80 | 1564

1116 بچه bæʧʧe *child* n

● بچه‌ها با کیسه های پلاستیکی اومده بودند. — The children had come with plastic bags.

62 | 3354

1117 موقع mowɣeʔ *time* n

● در این موقع دختر جوان به سوی در اتاق شتافت و آن را بست. — At that moment the young girl rushed to the door of the room and closed it.

80 | 1587

1118 حمل hæml *shipping* n

● حمل و نقل عمومی رشد چشم گیری یافت. — Public transportation has grown significantly.

80 | 1508

1119 مصر mesr *Egypt* pn

● عمان را به مقصد اسکندریه مصر ترک کردم. — I left Oman for Alexandria, Egypt.

67 | 2755

1120 قضیه ɣæzijje *affair, theorem* n

● خودم قضیه را برایشان گفتم که مواظب باشند. — I told them about the matter myself so they would be careful.

87 | 974

1121 ضعیف zæʔif *weak* adj,n

● افراد چاق حافظه ضعیف‌تری دارند. — Fat people have a weaker memory.

90 | 757

1122 توجه کردن tævædʤʤoh kærdæn *pay attention* v

● به نشانه های خطر توجه کردن. — Paying attention to the signs of danger.

93 | 520

1123 زیبایی zibaji *beauty* adj,n

● زمانی که شهاب‌سنگ «فوکانگ» با سطح زمین برخورد کرد کوچکترین نشانه‌ای از زیبایی در آن مشاهده نمی‌شد. — When the Fukang meteorite hit the earth, not the smallest sign of its beauty was observed.

90 | 754

1124 واکنش vakoneʃ *reaction* n

● واکنش این زن، خارج از تصور بوده است. — This woman's reaction has been unimaginable.

85 | 1134

1125 لبنان lobnan *Lebanon* pn

● بچه‌ها را از دمشق دارند می‌فرستند به لبنان. — They are sending the children from Damascus to Lebanon.

76 | 1853

1126 آزمایش azmajeʃ *test* n

● انجام آزمایش تیروئید قبل از بارداری ضروریست. — Performing a thyroid exam before pregnancy is required.

85 | 1113

7 Emotion

Rank	Headword	Pronunciation	Gloss	Rank	Headword	Pronunciation	Gloss
533	رقابت	reɣabæt	competition	4020	خوشحالی	xoʃhali	happiness, joy
613	مهر	mehr	affection	4146	تنفر	tænæffor	aversion, hatred
955	خشونت	xoʃunæt	violence	4590	خصومت	xosumæt	enmity, animosity
984	نگرانی	negærani	anxiety	4934	دردسر	dardesær	trouble
1051	دوستی	dusti	friendship	4978	غرور	ɣorur	pride, vanity
1222	علاقه	ælaɣe	interest	5431	آسایش	asajeʃ	comfort
1253	عشق	eʃɣ	love	5480	بهت	boht	consternation
1526	تفاهم	tæfahom	understanding	5506	سردرگمی	særdærgomi	confusion
1691	ترس	tærs	fear	6093	خودخواهی	xodxahi	selfishness
1894	محبت	mohæbbæt	love	6741	شرم	ʃærm	shame
2030	شادی	ʃadi	joy	7044	دلسوزی	delsuzi	compassion
2073	راحتی	rahæti	comfort	7107	صمیمیت	sæmimijjæt	sincerity, intimacy
2099	وحشت	væhʃæt	panic	7290	انزجار	enzedʒar	disgust, aversion
2226	خودداری	xoddari	self-control	7822	احساساتی	ehsasati	sentimental
2586	داوری	daværi	judgment	8006	دلهره	delhore	fear
2859	شوق	ʃowɣ	eagerness	8257	بیزاری	bizari	dislike
2890	دشمنی	doʃmæni	hostility	8869	بیگانگی	biganegi	alienation
3109	صبر	sæbr	patience	9305	حسادت	hesadæt	jealousy
3192	شگفتی	ʃegefti	surprise	9510	خجالت	xedʒalæt	shame
3223	غم	ɣæm	sorrow, grief	10782	رنجش	rændʒeʃ	offense
3257	کشمکش	keʃmækeʃ	conflict	11107	رفاقت	refaɣæt	friendship
3334	نفرت	nefræt	hatred	13240	ترحم	tæræhhom	compassion
3336	انتقام	enteɣam	revenge	13767	عداوت	ædavæt	enmity, animosity
3651	خرسندی	xorsændi	satisfaction, contentment	13973	شعف	ʃæʔæf	glee
3678	کیف	kejf	intoxication	14509	گیجی	gidʒi	giddiness
3729	هراس	hæras	fear	16180	سوءتفاهم	suʔetæfahom	misunderstanding
3744	کینه	kine	grudge	16514	پررو	porru	cheeky
3793	افسردگی	æfsordegi	depression	17353	سرمستی	særmæsti	joy, ecstasy

1127 انفجار enfedʒar *explosion* n

- صدای انفجار لرزانش کرد. — The sound of the explosion made it shaky.
  84 | 1188

1128 صفحه sæfhe *page, screen, record* n

- صفحه را ورق زد. — She turned the page.
  80 | 1485

1129 پزشک pezeʃk *doctor* n

- برخی از بیماران مبتلا به دیابت نوع دوم تحت نظر پزشک معالج و یک متخصص تغذیه می‌توانند روزه بگیرند و از اثرات مفید روزه بهره‌مند شوند. — Some patients with type two diabetes can fast under the supervision of an attending physician and a nutrition specialist and benefit from the useful effects of the fast.
  83 | 1305

1130 انگلستان engelestan *England* pn

- از انگلستان به آمریکا اعزام شد. — He was dispatched from England to America.
  87 | 934

1131 گفته شدن gofte ʃodæn *be said* v

- رازهایی که گفته نشد. — Secrets that were not told.
  81 | 1411

1132 سنتی sonæti *traditional* adj
- ساختن سازهای سنتی هم هنر است و هم صنعت. — Making traditional musical instruments is both an art and industry.
- 85 | 1076

1133 مراجعه moradʒeʔe *reference* n
- یک روز یک نفر به وزارت ارشاد مراجعه می‌کند. — One day she will refer a person to the Ministry of Culture.
- 83 | 1278

1134 آگاهی agahi *awareness* n
- احتمالا از فعالیت های سیاسی و اجتماعی او آگاهی دارند. — They are probably aware of his political and social activities.
- 82 | 1315

1135 فلسطین felestin *Palestine* pn
- باید به فکر دیگر مسلمانان در لبنان و فلسطین باشیم. — Our thoughts should be on other Muslims in Lebanon and Palestine.
- 64 | 3071

1136 مخالفت moxalefæt *opposition* n
- ا — من مخالفت کردم چون می‌خواستم مخالفت کنم. disagreed because I wanted to disagree.
- 80 | 1539

1137 اندک ændæk *little* adj,adv,n,q
- اندک بی‌احترامی به حجاج ایرانی موجب عکس‌العمل ایران خواهد شد. — The slightest disrespect to the Iranian pilgrims will lead to a reaction from Iran.
- 86 | 998

1138 روستایی rustaji *villager, rural* adj,n
- دو مرد روستایی می خواستند برای یافتن شغل به شهر بروند. — Two villagers wanted to go to the city to find work.
- 86 | 978

1139 بیمار bimar *sick, patient* adj,n
- ساعت ۸ دم در بیمارستان بودم. — I was at the door of the hospital by 8.
- 80 | 1509

1140 فدراسیون fedrasijon *federation* n
- فدراسیون فوتبال بیش از ۱۳ میلیارد تومان بدهی دارد. — The Football Federation has more than 13 billion toman in debt.
- 80 | 1489

1141 نماز næmaz *prayer* n
- پیش از ظهر هم رفت نماز جمعه. — He went to Friday prayers before noon.
- 88 | 894

1142 تصریح tæsrih *stipulation, affirmation* n
- در تصریح این مدل ها چند چالش عمده وجود دارد. — There are some major challenges in specifying these models.
- 80 | 1530

1143 متن mætn *text* n
- این متن را امضا می کنی یا نه؟ — Are you going to sign this text or not?
- 81 | 1394

1144 مستقل mostæɣell *independent* adj
- ظهور سنت فکری مستقل علوم اجتماعی در آسیا. — The emergence of an independent intellectual tradition in the social sciences in Asia.
- 80 | 1507

1145 قاضی ɣazi *judge* n
- قطعاً کاربران خودشان قاضی بهتری هستند. — Their own users are definitely better judges.
- 86 | 1032

1146 پایتخت pajtæxt *capital* n
- این هشدار یک روز پیش از کریسمس به پایتخت‌های اروپایی ارسال شده است. — This warning was sent to the European capitals one day before Christmas.
- 81 | 1444

1147 کشیده keʃide *tall, slap* adj
- این گربه اندازه‌ای تقریباً مشابه با گربه اهلی اما کمی لاغرتر و بدنی کشیده‌تر دارد. — This cat is almost the same size as a domestic one but is slightly thinner and has an elongated body.
- 85 | 1091

1148 بازدید bazdid *visit* n
- بعد از بازدید، موفق نشد که مشکل پیش‌آمده را حل کند. — After the visit, she was not successful at resolving the problem at hand.
- 88 | 814

1149 چارچوب ʧarʧub *framework* n
- همیشه نمی توانیم با اصول و چارچوب فکری خود دیگران را مدیریت کنیم. — We cannot always manage others within our own intellectual framework and principles.
- 83 | 1248

1150 اتهام ettehâm *charge* n
- سه بار به اتهام دزدی بازداشت که دو بار تبرئه شد. — He was arrested three times on theft charges and was acquitted twice.
- 85 | 1120

1151 معمول mæʔmul *usual* adj
- نی از دسته سازهای محلی است و تقریبا در تمام نقاط ایران معمول و رایج است. — Ney is one of the folk instruments, and is common almost all around Iran.
- 93 | 460

1152 شهرستان ʃæhrestan *county* n
- امروز بعدازظهر به شهرستان می روم. — Today I will go to the country after lunch.
- 71 | 2283

1153 چندان tʃændan *so many, so* adv

- دلیلی هم که در پایان ذکر می‌شود چندان صریح آشکار و قابل فهم نیست. — And the reason that's being mentioned at the end isn't particularly clear, apparent or understandable.

86 | 1021

1154 هرگز hærgez *never* adv

- هرگز در هیچ مسابقه‌ای بازی نکرد. — She never played in a tournament.

84 | 1132

1155 محدودیت mæhdudijjæt *restriction* n

- برای پدیده هایی مثل اینترنت، اعمال محدودیت برای کودکان و نوجوانان لازم است یا نه؟ — For phenomena such as the internet, is it necessary to impose restrictions on children and adolescents or not?

88 | 850

1156 اجلاس edʒlas *session* n

- قصد دارد، در چارچوب اجلاس لیتوانی که ماه اکتبر برگزار می‌شود، توافقنامه تجارت آزاد با اتحادیه اروپا را امضا کند. — He plans, within the framework of the summit that will be held in Lithuania in October, to sign a free trade agreement with the European Union.

77 | 1687

1157 اکثر æksær *most* q

- اکثر افراد محل می‌دانند که سیسا رازی را درون خود پنهان دارد. — Most people in the area know that Sisa is keeping a secret.

87 | 945

1158 پیوند pejvænd *link* n

- پیوند بین ارز و سیاست‌های پولی و مالی. — The connection between currency and fiscal and monetary policy.

88 | 822

1159 بیرون birun *outside* adv,n

- او با عصبانیت از اتاق بیرون رفت و در را محکم بست. — He angrily went out of the room and slammed the door.

68 | 2492

1160 رود rud *river* n,v

- این شهر در جوار لشگرگاه مرکز ولایت هلمند و در محل تلاقی دو رود هیرمند و ارغنداب قرار گرفته است. — This city is located on the outskirts of Lashkargah, the capital of the Helmand province and at the confluence of two rivers, the Helmand and Arghandab.

78 | 1675

1161 تحمل tæhæmmol *tolerance* n

- تحملم بالاست. — I have a high tolerance.

92 | 528

1162 قهرمان ɣæhreman *champion* adj,n

- پدر کودک اصرار داشت استاد از فرزندش یک قهرمان جودو بسازد. — The boy's father insisted that the instructor make a judo champion out of his son.

77 | 1685

1163 حجم hædʒm *volume* n

- لبنیات که سرشار از کلسیم و ویتامین D هستند به حفظ و ساخت حجم عضلانی کمک می‌کنند. — Dairy products which are brimming with calcium and vitamin D help retain and build muscle volume.

85 | 1075

1164 اشتغال eʃteɣal *occupation* n

- ما با مشکلاتی چون اشتغال و ازدواج روبرو هستیم. — We are facing difficulties like employment and marriage.

86 | 957

1165 رعایت reʔajæt *observance* n

- با رعایت موارد لازم فرد دیابتی می‌تواند بیش از ۸۰ سال عمر کند. — By following the necessary regime, a diabetic person can live more than 80 years.

83 | 1200

1166 اراده erade *will* n

- هر چه اراده کند شدنی است. — Whatever she wills is achievable.

87 | 942

1167 قصد ɣæsd *intent* n

- فکر می کردم در این یکی دو روز تعطیل رییسم قصد دارد مرا به صرف شامی دعوت کند. — I was thinking my boss is planning to invite me for dinner over these couple of days off.

88 | 853

1168 اگرچه ægærtʃe *although* conj

- اگرچه گواهینامه دارم، از رانندگی می‌ترسم. — Although I have a license, I'm afraid of driving.

89 | 791

1169 وقوع voɣuʔ *occurrence* n

- این موضوع از زمان وقوع انقلاب اسلامی تا به امروز به خوبی مدیریت شده است. — From the time of the occurrence of the Islamic Revolution till today this subject has been well managed.

86 | 1003

1170 دیوان divan *court, book of poetry* adj,n

- دیوان حافظ را بردار و بیاور. — Get the Hafez collection of poems and bring it.

93 | 471

1171 سنی sonni, senni *Sunni, age* adj,n

- همه آنها سنی مذهب بودند. — All of them were Sunni.

89 | 728

1172 تدوین tædvin *compilation* n
- کتاب را تدوین می‌کردم. — I was editing a book.
- 84 | 1113

1173 پدیده pædide *phenomenon* n
- شکست نور یک پدیده اپتیکی است. — Refraction of light is an optical phenomenon.
- 83 | 1181

1174 لحظه læhze *moment* adj,n
- از هوش رفت پس لحظه‌ای به هوش آمد. — He fainted and then he woke up for a moment.
- 78 | 1572

1175 منتشر montæfer *published* adj
- هفته ای دو شماره منتشر می شد. — Each week two issues were published.
- 81 | 1348

1176 جهاد dʒæhad *jihad* n
- جهاد اقتصادی برنامه‌ی بلند مدت است یا استراتژی عملیاتی؟ — Is economic jihad a long term plan or an operational strategy?
- 89 | 759

1177 گرم gærm, geræm *hot, gram* adj,n
- بعد که دستهایش را گرم کرد، رفت سر صندوق زنش. — After warming up his hands, he went to his wife's safe.
- 81 | 1350

1178 الگو olgu *pattern* n
- پژمان برای من همیشه الگو بود. — Pezhman was always a role model for me.
- 85 | 1063

1179 خبرگزاری xæbærgozari *news agency* n
- دفتر خبرگزاری آناتولی در مصر بسته شد. — The Anadolu news agency office was closed in Egypt.
- 67 | 2525

1180 آسیب asib *injury, damage* n
- آسیب های ورزشی انواع مختلف دارند. — Athletic injuries have various types.
- 86 | 946

1181 سلامت sælamæt *health* adj,n
- خیلی متشکر قربانتان بروم به سلامت موفق باشید — Many thanks, I sacrifice myself for you, be healthy and successful.
- 85 | 1021

1182 خیر xejr, xæjjer *good/no, generous* adj,adv,n
- جان لاک معتقد بود که نوزاد موجود شریف و رام نشده است که که دارای موهبت درونی تشخیص خیر و شرّ می باشد. — John Locke believed that the newborn is a noble and undomesticated creature that has the inherent gift of distinguishing good and evil.
- 87 | 910

1183 قوی ɣævi *strong* adj
- تا سن 40 سالگی ارتباط برادران بسیار قوی است، اما به‌تدریج این ارتباط تضعیف می‌شود. — Up until 40 years of age, the brothers' relationship is very strong, but gradually, this relationship weakens.
- 85 | 1010

1184 بد bæd *bad* adj,adv,n
- شما بوی بد سیب زمینی‌ها را فقط برای یک هفته نتوانستید تحمل کنید. — You couldn't stand the bad odor of the potatoes for just one week.
- 75 | 1845

1185 ملاقات molaɣat *meeting* n
- آدرس محل کارش را یادداشت می کنم و برای فردا قرار ملاقات می گذاریم. — I'm taking a note of his workplace address and we are setting a meeting time for tomorrow.
- 90 | 663

1186 تجهیزات tædʒhizat *equipment* n
- فرمانده بخش ادوات و تجهیزات جنگی ایالات متحده نوشت: — The Commander of Equipment and Armaments of the United States wrote:
- 84 | 1125

1187 اسم esm *name* n
- آره اسم و فامیل هم بنویس. — Yes, write the first name and the last name too.
- 74 | 1877

1188 عربستان æræbestan *Arabia* pn
- سی شبه جزیره ی عربستان را دور زده. — Thirty days around the Arabian peninsula.
- 77 | 1654

1189 ضربه zærbe *impact, stroke* n
- هر کدام از این چوبهای گلف برای زدن ضربه‌های گوناگونی بکار می‌روند. — Each of these golf clubs is used for handling different strokes.
- 90 | 661

1190 مسکن mæskæn, mosækken *housing, sedative* n
- اما به هرحال کالاهای غیرقابل مبادله همچون هزینه مسکن، آموزش و ارتباطات نیز باید در فرمول محاسباتی وارد شوند. — However, in any case the untradable goods like housing, education, and communication expenses should also be included in the calculation formula.
- 76 | 1714

1191 مهدی mehdi, mæhdi *Mehdi, Mahdi* pn
- مهدی تاج رئیس فدراسیون فوتبال شد. — Mehdi Taj became the head of the Football Federation.
- 84 | 1108

1192 ترکیب tærkib *composition* n
- ترکیب خاصی از این دو شخصیت. — A specific composition of these two personalities.
- 85 | 1011

1193 عرضه ærze, orze *presenting/offering, capability* n
- عرضه جهانی نفت برای نخستین بار در سه سال گذشته کاهش یافت. — Global oil sales went down for the first time in three years.
- 79 | 1520

1194 شهرداری ʃæhrdari *municipality* n
● به شورای اسلامی و شهرداری سنندج هدیه نمود. — He gave a gift to the Islamic council and municipality of Sanandaj.
68 | 2465

1195 پیشرفته piʃræfte *advanced* adj
● پیشرفته‌ترین کفش ورزشی دنیا ساخته شد. — The world's most advanced sports shoes have been produced.
88 | 835

1196 بورس burs *stock exchange, scholarship* n
● آیا هیچ‌گونه بورس آموزشی در مدرسه کسب کردید؟ — Have you received any scholarship from school?
67 | 2542

1197 ششم ʃeʃom *sixth* adj
● ششمین مظنون بمب‌گذاری بروکسل دستگیر شد. — The sixth suspect in the Brussels bombing was arrested.
76 | 1712

1198 افزایش یافتن æfzajeʃ jaftæn *increase* v
● با اکتشاف منابع گاز طبیعی در دریای شمال ارز هلند افزایش یافت. — The value of the Dutch currency increased with the discovery of sources of natural gas in the North Sea.
85 | 1016

1199 جلو dʒelow *forward* adj,adv,n,prep
● ادبیات داستانی خیلی جلوتر از سینماست. — Literary fiction is well ahead of cinema.
68 | 2393

1200 چهارشنبه ʃæharʃæmbe *Wednesday* n
● چهارشنبه مثلاً، صبح زود می‌رود. — Wednesday, for example, he will leave early in the morning.
81 | 1284

1201 قلم ɣælæm *pen* n
● قلم را به دست گرفت. — She took the pen.
86 | 909

1202 سختی sæxti *difficulty* adj,n
● مدیریت بحران در تهران کار بسیار سختی است. — Crisis management is a very difficult task in Tehran.
89 | 706

1203 سیر، سجر sir, sejr *garlic/full, travel* adj,n,pn
● هرچی نگاش می کردی سیر نمی شدی. — However much you looked at her you wouldn't be satiated.
88 | 785

1204 شاخص ʃaxes *index* adj,n
● شاخص بورس‌های آسیایی کاهش یافت. — Asian stock indices went down.
78 | 1510

1205 مقدس moɣæddæs *holy* adj,n
● این پدر مقدس کسی را ندارد که برایش اعتراف کند. — This holy father does not have anyone to confess for him.
81 | 1275

1206 منتقل montæɣel *transferred* adj
● مجبور شدند به شیراز منتقلش کنند. — They were forced to transfer her to Shiraz.
90 | 639

1207 فوق fowɣ *above* adj
● نامه‌های الکترونیکی کلینتون حاوی اطلاعات فوق محرمانه بود. — Clinton's emails contained top secret information.
82 | 1229

1208 صدور sodur *issuance* n
● وزارت خارجه آمریکا با صدور بیانیه ای اعلام کرد. — US Department of State issuing a statement announced that . . .
83 | 1136

1209 نور nur *light* n
● زیر نور یک شمع مومی. — Under the light of a wax candle.
79 | 1468

1210 ارتباطی ertebati *communication* adj,n
● گوگل اپلیکیشن ارتباطی می‌سازد. — Google makes communication applications.
89 | 705

1211 آلمانی almani *German* adj,n
● آنه فرانک، یک یهودی آلمانی متولد شهر فرانکفورت بود. — Anne Frank was a German Jew born in the city of Frankfurt.
88 | 771

1212 صهیونیستی sehjunisti *Zionist* adj
● رژیم صهیونیستی عضو سازمان منع استفاده از سلاح های شیمیایی نیست. — The Zionist regime is not a member of the organization for the prohibition of the use of chemical weapons.
55 | 3643

1213 طرفدار tæræfdar *supporter, fan* adj,n
● هیچ طرفداری ندارند. — They don't have a supporter.
89 | 733

1214 محکوم mæhkum *sentenced* adj
● با استفاده از استدلال شما من دست متهم را به یک سال زندان محکوم میکنم! — Using your reasoning, I sentence the accused to one year in prison!
81 | 1316

1215 هنرمند honærmænd *artist* adj,n
● ما تعداد کمی هنرمند داریم. — We have a small number of artists.
81 | 1323

1216 فردا færda *tomorrow* adv,n
● فردا به شیراز می روم. — Tomorrow I will go to Shiraz.
71 | 2062

1217 سعید sæʔid *Said* adj,pn
● سعید ملایی به مدال برنز رسید. — Said Molai received the bronze medal.
88 | 766

1218 زندانی zendani *prisoner* adj,n
- من زندانی آزادشده‌ای هستم. — I am a freed prisoner.
- 80 | 1370

1219 تلاش کردن tælaʃ kærdæn *make effort* v
- تلاش می‌کنیم در انتخاب هیات رئیسه دایم این ترکیب را تغییر دهیم. — We strive to change the composition when selecting the permanent board of directors.
- 81 | 1283

1220 شکست خوردن ʃekæst xordæn *be defeated* v
- اردوان پنجم در این جنگ شکست خورد و کشته شد. — Artabanus V was defeated and killed in this war.
- 95 | 320

1221 مذاکره mozakere *negotiation* n
- این ترفندها، دامنه مذاکره طرف مقابل را حتی قبل از شروع مذاکره محدود می‌کند. — These tricks limit the extent of negotiation of the opposite side even before negotiation begins.
- 82 | 1223

1222 علاقه ælaɣe *interest* n
- موشی که علاقه زیادی به کندن تونل دارد. — A mouse that really likes to dig tunnels.
- 83 | 1159

1223 ایستادن istadæn *stand* n,pn,v
- صفر میان دایره‌ء چراغ خودش ایستاده بود. — Safar was standing inside a circle of his own light.
- 80 | 1324

1224 موج mowdʒ *wave* n
- پرتوهای لیزر دارای طول موج‌های متفاوتی هستند. — Laser beams contain various wavelengths.
- 84 | 1077

1225 اتخاذ ettexaz *adoption* n
- با تثبیت نرخ ارز و اتخاذ سیاست درهای باز، واردات افزایش یافت. — Imports increased by stabilizing the nominal exchange rate and adopting an open door policy.
- 87 | 823

1226 تقاضا tæɣaza *demand* n
- به دیدن فرزندانش رفتم و به آنها تسلیت گفتم و تقاضا کردم مرا سر قبر او بَرند. — Upon seeing his children, I went and gave my condolences, and requested that they take me to his grave.
- 82 | 1225

1227 لزوم lozum *need* n
- لزومی ندارد خودم عاشق شده باشم. — There's no need for me to be in love myself.
- 87 | 810

1228 معامله moʔamele *transaction* adj,n
- با پول معامله نمی کنم. — I do not make transactions with money.
- 85 | 996

1229 کمبود kæmbud *shortage* n
- ما با کمبود ارز روبرو هستیم. — We are faced with a shortage of currency.
- 85 | 982

1230 معمولاً mæʔmulæn *usually* adv
- چرا پیرترین افراد زنده معمولاً زن هستند؟ — Why are the oldest living people usually women?
- 82 | 1167

1231 بازسازی bazsazi *reconstruction* n
- بنا را برای بازسازی ویران خواهد ساخت. — He will destroy the building for reconstruction.
- 86 | 927

1232 مردمی mærdomi *popular* adj,n
- مردمی ترین دولت را داشتیم. — We had the most popular government.
- 76 | 1685

1233 شنیدن ʃenidæn *hear* n,v
- صدای همسایمان را شنیدیم. — We heard our neighbor's voice.
- 70 | 2131

1234 رنج rændʒ *pain* n
- زندگی رنج است ؛ یک رنج بی پایان! — Life is suffering, endless suffering!
- 89 | 726

1235 یوم jowm *day* n
- ۲۲ بهمن ۵۷ یوم الله بود. — 22nd Bahman of 1357 was the day of God.
- 91 | 549

1236 درس dærs *lesson* n
- درس‌هایی که می‌توان از قاتل‌ها فراگرفت. — Lessons that one can learn from murderers.
- 82 | 1196

1237 جدا dʒoda *separate* adj
- همان راه فرعی از اتوبان جدا می شد و به سمت اوین می رفت. — That same by-way separate from the motorway and went in the direction of Evin.
- 89 | 706

1238 ثروت særvæt *wealth* n
- حاضرم تمام ثروتم را بریزم به پای تو — I am ready to lay all of my wealth at your feet.
- 92 | 503

1239 بهداشت behdaʃt *hygiene* n
- تو بهداشت و سلامت مردم را می‌خواهي به خطر بیندازي. — You want to put people's health and hygiene in jeopardy.
- 78 | 1503

1240 سفیر sæfir *ambassador* n
- چرا سفیر اردن از تهران رفت؟ — Why did Jordan's ambassador leave Tehran?
- 84 | 1062

1241 مسلم moslem, mosællæm *Muslim, certain* adj,n,pn
- مسلم است او زنده است. — It is certain she is alive.
- 88 | 756

1242 پیوستن pejvæstæn *join* n,v

- پیوستن ایران به سازمان تجارت جهانی. — Iran joining the World Trade Organization.

88 | 739

1243 عظیم æzim *great* adj

- فرمانده قصد حمله به نیروی عظیمی از دشمن را داشت. — The commander intended to attack a great enemy force.

87 | 855

1244 آغاز کردن ɑɣɑz kærdæn *begin* v

- رسما فعالیت خود را آغاز کرده است. — She has formally begun her activity.

87 | 821

1245 مجدد modʒæddæd *renewed* adj

- برخی از تجار ایرانی، اقدام به واردات کالاهای ترکیه و صادرات مجدد آن به روسیه کرده‌اند. — Some Iranian merchants have imported Turkish goods and exported them again to Russia.

89 | 695

1246 نمایندگی næmɑjændegi *representation* n

- شعب و نمایندگی‌های خود را در ایران تعطیل کردند. — They closed their branches and agencies in Iran.

87 | 814

1247 درگیری dærgiri *involvement, engagement* n

- یکی از سربازان وظیفه را به محل درگیری قاچاقچیان و مأموران دولت فرستاده بودند. — They had sent one of the soldiers to the conflict location of drug dealers and government officials.

77 | 1517

1248 صحیح sæhih *correct* adj

- اگر این رنگها به نسبت صحیح مخلوط شوند. — If these colors are mixed in right proportions.

85 | 959

1249 همسر hæmsær *spouse* n

- همسر را به زندان می برند. — They will take my spouse to jail.

81 | 1224

1250 موسیقی musiɣi *music* n

- تا حالا در یک موسیقی ناب غرق شده ای! — Have you ever been drowned in pure music!

75 | 1685

1251 جدول dʒædvæl *table* n

- معلم عبارتی عربی را بر تخته سیاه نوشت و بعد جدولی خطکشی کرد. — The teacher wrote an Arabic word on the black board, then he drew a table.

80 | 1349

1252 شناخت ʃenɑxt *recognition, knowledge, knew* n,v

- بدون شناخت جوانان نمی توان برای آنان برنامه ریزی کرد. — One cannot plan for youth without understanding them.

83 | 1123

1253 عشق eʃɣ *love* n

- عشق و علاقه اش به او بیشتر شد. — His love and affection for her increased.

77 | 1517

1254 پنجاه pændʒah *fifty* n

- دویست و پنجاه سال پیش از میلاد. — 250 BCE.

56 | 3373

1255 بازی کردن bɑzi kærdæn *play* v

- بروس ویلیس در فیلم حماسی چینی بازی می‌کند. — Bruce Willis is playing a role in an epic Chinese film.

87 | 851

1256 لذا lezɑ *therefore* conj

- لذا از بیرون آمدن امتناع می کرد. — Therefore he refused to come out.

81 | 1220

1257 افزوده æfzude *added* adj

- تقاضای فرانسه برای کاهش مالیات بر ارزش افزوده رد شد. — France's demand for a reduction in value-added tax was rejected.

88 | 781

1258 بقیه bæɣijje *rest, remainder, balance* n,pron

- مرد جوان و بقیه جمعیت به قلب پیرمرد نگاه کردند. — The young man and the rest of the crowd looked at the old man's heart.

83 | 1122

1259 یار jɑr *sweetheart, friend, partner* n

- حتی مرگ هم‌یار و یاور احتیاج داشت و من همه یارانم را از دست داده بودم. — And even death needs a friend and helper and I had lost all of my friends.

91 | 554

1260 طبقه tæbæɣe *floor, stratum* n

- در طبقه سوم این خانه اتاق اجاره داده می‌شود. — On the third floor of this house, a room is being rented.

83 | 1096

1261 ثابت sɑbet *fixed* adj,n

- سکه‌های ایتالیایی به علت وزن و شکل ثابتشان محبوب بودند. — Italian coins were beloved for their weight and durable shape.

85 | 924

1262 دوشنبه doʃæmbe *Monday* n,pn

- روز دوشنبه، حدود ساعت 7 غروب، ستاره دنباله دار هالی دیده خواهد شد. — On Monday Halley's Comet will be seen at about 7 pm.

77 | 1500

1263 برادر bærɑdær *brother* n

- بعد هم نوبت به برادر رسید. — Next it was brother's turn.

76 | 1572

1264 فرودگاه forudgɑh *airport* n

- من در اداره کار دارم و نمی توانم برای دیدن خواهرم به فرودگاه بیایم. — I have work at the office, and I cannot go to the airport to see my sister.

86 | 849

1265 اشکال *eʃkal* difficulty n
- فقط یک اشکال کوچک، خیلی کوچک هست. — There is only one very small problem.
- 88 | 740

1266 سقوط *soɣut* fall n
- یعنی درست یکسال پیش از سقوط خلافت اسلامی و احتلال فلسطین از طرف انگلیس، به امضاء رسید. — In other words, it was signed just one year after the collapse of the Islamic caliphate and the British occupation of Palestine.
- 81 | 1247

1267 قدرتمند *ɣodrætmænd* powerful adj,n
- ایران به عنوان یک کشور اسلامی قدرتمند. — Iran as a strong Islamic country.
- 91 | 554

1268 سرباز *særbaz* soldier n
- در سال 1945 میلادی به وسیله سربازان روسی اسیر شد و به مسکو انتقال یافت. — In 1945 he was captured by Russian soldiers and transferred to Moscow.
- 78 | 1457

1269 معلم *moʔællem* teacher n
- معلم یکبار دیگر پرسید: آیا ظرف پر است؟ — The teacher asked again, "Is the container full?"
- 74 | 1782

1270 دستیابی *dæstjabi* access, achieving n
- نباید اجازه داد که حاشیه‌ها مانع از دستیابی به موفقیت شود. — One shouldn't allow the fringes to be an obstacle to achieving success.
- 85 | 972

1271 مفهوم *mæfhum* concept n
- شعر دارای مفهوم عاطفی می شود. — The poem has a romantic concept.
- 77 | 1502

1272 پایگاه *pajgah* base, site n
- پایگاه اطلاع رسانی دولت، از احضار محمود احمدی نژاد به دادگاه خبر داد و نوشت: — The government information center reported about summoning Mahmoud Ahmadinejad to the court and wrote . . .
- 80 | 1282

1273 پرورش *pærværeʃ* training, education, breeding n
- کرج یکی از مهمترین مناطق پرورش گل در ایران بوده است. — Karaj has been one of the most important areas of floriculture in Iran.
- 78 | 1406

1274 درک *dærk, dæræk* perception, hell n
- این واقعیت را درک کرد. — She understood this reality.
- 84 | 1035

1275 غذا *ɣæza* food n
- پیرمرد برای سفارش غذا به طرف صندوق رفت. — The old man went up to the cashier to order food.
- 80 | 1293

1276 شروع شدن *ʃoruʔ kærdæn* begin v
- مهاجرت خراسانیها به استان سیستان و بلوچستان از اوائل سده اخیر شروع شد. — The migration of people from Khorasan to the province of Sistan and Baluchistan began at the start of the last century.
- 86 | 845

1277 تخصصی *tæxæssosi* specialized adj
- فلسفه پژوهشی تخصصی است. — Philosophy is a specialized area of research.
- 86 | 891

1278 صدر *sædr* chest, top n,pn
- تکتازی این تیم در صدر جدول کماکان ادامه دارد. — This team's domination at the top of the charts still continues.
- 85 | 904

1279 اکبر *ækbær* greater, Akbar pn
- علی اکبر ولایتی. — Ali Akbar Velayati.
- 91 | 555

1280 خاطرنشان *xaterneʃan* reminder n
- ایشان خاطرنشان کردند: این حوادث مهم به برکت انقلاب اسلامی است. — He noted, "These are important events for the glory of the Islamic Revolution."
- 84 | 1031

1281 نوین *novin* new adj
- سفر رئیس‌جمهور به رم فصل نوینی را در روابط ایران-ایتالیا می‌گشاید. — The president's trip to Rome opens a new chapter in relations between Iran and Italy.
- 89 | 682

1282 مربی *moræbbi* coach n
- مربی وانمود کرد که حرف‌های او را نشنیده است. — The coach pretended not to have heard what he said.
- 80 | 1299

1283 محیط *mohit* environment n
- وزیر حفاظت محیط زیست و ذخایر طبیعی قزاقستان. — Kazakhstan's Minister of Environmental Protection and Natural Resources.
- 79 | 1334

1284 توضیح *towzih* explanation n
- برای توضیح عالم هستی نیازی به یک آفریدگار نیست. — There is no need for a creator in order to explain the world of existence.
- 87 | 813

1285 واقعاً *vaɣeʔæn* really adv
- آدم‌ها واقعاً به حرف‌هایی که می‌زنند اعتقاد دارند؟ — Do people really believe in what they say?
- 78 | 1421

1286 تبریز *tæbriz* Tabriz pn
- مسابقه ایران با قطر در تبریز برگزار شود. — The competition between Iran and Qatar took place in Tabriz.
- 83 | 1086

Frequency index 73

8 Family

Rank	Headword	Pronunciation	Gloss	Rank	Headword	Pronunciation	Gloss
214	زن	zæn	wife	4136	عمو	æmu	paternal uncle
282	خانواده	xanevade	family	4429	عروس	ærus	bride, daugher-in-law
859	دختر	doxtær	daughter	4480	داماد	damad	groom, son-in-law
883	پدر	pedær	father	4556	پیرمرد	pirmærd	old man
930	مادر	madær	mother	4727	پیرزن	pirzæn	old woman
943	جاری	dʒari	sister-in-law	6940	نوه	næve	grandchild
1064	پسر	pesær	son	7109	جد	dʒædd	ancestor
1249	همسر	hæmsær	spouse	7164	خاله	xale	maternal aunt
1263	برادر	bæradær	brother	7650	مهریه	mahrijje	bride's marriage portion
1316	نوجوان	nowdʒævan	teenager				
1780	ازدواج	ezdevadʒ	marriage	8751	یتیم	jætim	orphan
2296	شوهر	ʃowhær	husband	8769	بیوه	bive	widow
2300	بابا	baba	dad	8818	داداش	dadaʃ	older brother
2430	خواهر	xahær	sister	9066	مادربزرگ	madærbozorg	grandmother
3396	دایی	daji	maternal uncle	9359	پدربزرگ	pedærbozorg	grandfather
3693	طلاق	tælaɣ	divorce	9391	عمه	æmme	paternal aunt
3724	مامان	maman	mom	15828	جهیزیه	dʒæhizijje	dowry
3858	طفل	tefl	child	18644	مادرشوهر	madærʃowhær	mother-in-law
4033	عروسی	ærusi	marriage, wedding				

1287 تیر tir *arrow, Tir* n,pn

- هشتم تیرماه گذشته قرار بازداشت موقت رهامی و عبادی را صادر کرده بود. — Last month, on the eighth of Tir, the temporary detention order of Ebadi and Rahami was issued.

85 | 931

1288 قریب ɣærib *near, relative* adj,pn

- در کشور چین قریب به 300 میلیون خانوار زندگی می کنند. — Nearly 300 million households live in the country of China.

95 | 300

1289 مجله mædʒælle *magazine* n

- برای دریافت مجله لطفا مشترک شوید. — Please subscribe in order to receive a magazine.

88 | 720

1290 هماهنگی hæmahængi *harmony, coordination* n

- حمله به یمن با هماهنگی آمریکا صورت گرفت. — The attack on Yemen was conducted in coordination with America.

85 | 918

1291 پاسخ دادن pasox dadæn *reply* v

- دکتر ملک با لبخندی پاسخ داد. — Doctor Malek answered with a smile.

90 | 603

1292 پیشین piʃin *previous* adj

- دستاورد نسل پیشین را ناکافی خواهد انگاشت. — He will consider the achievements of the bygone generation as being insufficient.

87 | 805

1293 تغییر دادن tæɣjir dadæn *change* v

- اپل برای تغییر دادن اپلیکیشن‌هایش از ۴:۳ به ۱۶:۹ کار زیادی خواهد داشت. — In order to change its applications from 4:3 to 16:9, Apple will have a great deal of work.

92 | 491

1294 جامع dʒame? *comprehensive* adj,pn

- از پیام های کامل و جامع استفاده کنید. — Use complete and comprehensive messages.

85 | 945

1295 صحبت sohbæt *talk* n
- کمی با هم صحبت کردیم. — We talked together a little.
- 81 | 1199

1296 روزانه ruzane *daily* adj,adv
- روزانه میتونید این سوالات تان ارسال بفرمایید. — You can send your questions in daily.
- 86 | 819

1297 اصطلاح estelah *expression* n
- فرهنگ اصطلاحات راه و ترافیک انتشار یافت. — The Dictionary of Road and Traffic Terms was released.
- 86 | 870

1298 اعتراض eʔteraz *protest* n
- مرد به آرامی اعتراض کرد. — The man quietly protested.
- 64 | 2472

1299 توزیع towziʔ *distribution* n
- شبکه توزیع مواد مخدر ایجاد میکند. — He will create a drug distribution network.
- 83 | 1016

1300 وکیل vækil *attorney* n,pn
- در حال حاضر وکیل مهاجرت من است. — She is currently my immigration lawyer.
- 87 | 775

1301 امیر æmir *emir* n,pn
- این امیر وحشی، اخلاق و عادت پادشاهان را دارد، ساکت باشید. — This wild emir has the ethics and habits of the kings, be quiet.
- 80 | 1261

1302 اطمینان etminan *confidence* n
- بله قربان، اطمینان کامل دارم. — Yes sir, I have total assurance.
- 85 | 937

1303 کنگره kongere *congress* n
- عملیات حرارتی و سرامیکها و نسوزها از مباحث مورد بررسی در این کنگره بود. — Heat treating, ceramics, and Pyrex were the topics of discussion in this convention.
- 83 | 1074

1304 پیگیری pejgiri *follow-through* n
- شکایت مردم را چهکسی پیگیری میکند؟ — Who will follow up on people's complaints?
- 82 | 1097

1305 دقت deɣɣæt *accuracy* n
- دقت در نگهداری آن ضروری مینماید. — Its careful maintenance is essential.
- 86 | 846

1306 پرده pærde *curtain* n
- فردا از خانه بیرون نرفت و پشت پردهای پنهان شد. — The next day he didn't leave the house and hid behind a curtain.
- 88 | 740

1307 مثال mesal *example* n
- برای مثال درباره پاسخ به پرسش زیر، نظر شما چیست؟ — For example, what is your opinion concerning the answer to the below question?
- 80 | 1251

1308 رقیب ræɣib *competitor* adj,n
- رقیب آنها در این زمان، شرکتی به نام تایگر بود. — In those days their rival was a company named Tiger.
- 88 | 713

1309 ابراهیم ebrahim *Abraham, Ebrahim* pn
- داستان ابراهیم و اسماعیل. — The story of Abraham and Ishmael.
- 88 | 680

1310 فراهم کردن færahæm kærdæn *assemble* v
- تنها مشکل قیمت پیشنهادی و فراهم کردن ابزار لازم برای این انتقال است. — The only problem is the suggested price and to provide the necessary tools for this transfer.
- 89 | 628

1311 آرام aram *peaceful* adj,adv,pn
- کمی آرام می شوم. — I will calm down a little.
- 82 | 1085

1312 نیاز داشتن nijaz daʃtæn *need* v
- کار های غیرممکن به تلاش و تمرکز بیشتری نیاز دارد. — Impossible tasks require more effort and focus.
- 88 | 697

1313 نظیر næzir *equal* adv,n
- نظیر و همتا ندارد. — She has no peer or equal.
- 82 | 1111

1314 مرتبه mærtæbe *time, floor* n
- چند مرتبه باید بروم بیرون. — I should go outside a few times.
- 87 | 761

1315 برتر bærtær *superior* adj
- مسابقات فوتبال لیگ برتر. — Premier League football matches.
- 74 | 1697

1316 نوجوان nowdʒævan *teenager* adj,n
- سیگار های الکترونیکی میان نوجوانان بسیار پرطرفدار شدهاند. — Electronic cigarettes have become very popular among teenagers.
- 79 | 1308

1317 محله mæhælle *district* n,pn
- در همین محله ساکن هستم. — I am a resident of this very neighborhood.
- 88 | 730

1318 تحصیل tæhsil *study* n
- یک شخص جوان با تحصیلات عالی برای شغل مدیریتی در یک شرکت بزرگ درخواست داد. — A young person with higher education applied for a management position in a big company.
- 65 | 2399

1319 انگیزه æ ngize *motivation* n
- درباره هویت و انگیزه احتمالی این فرد توضیحی نداد. — This individual gave no explanation about personality or potential motivation.

85 | 920

1320 شکایت ʃekajæt *complaint* n
- هیچ کس هم شکایتی نکرد؟ — No one had a complaint?

87 | 755

1321 تحقیقاتی tæhɣiɣati *research* adj,n
- آژانس تحقیقاتی شریف راه‌اندازی می‌شود. — Sharif research agency will be launched.

88 | 688

1322 چهل ʧehel *forty* n
- چهل تا پرنده عاشق من هستند. — Forty birds are in love with me.

58 | 3038

1323 مدعی moddæʔi *plaintiff* adj,n
- این مرد مدعی است. — This man is the plaintiff.

87 | 741

1324 مقطع moɣættæʔ, mæɣtæʔ *broken, section* adj,n
- حساس‌ترین مقطع تاریخی. — The most critical point in history.

89 | 657

1325 فراوانی færavani *abundance* adj,n
- با مشکلات گوناگون و فراوانی روبه‌رو شده مبارزه میکند. — He struggles with copious and varying problems that he is faced with.

87 | 746

1326 سنگ sæng *rock* n
- هر کدام از این سنگ‌های کوچک حکاکی‌شده حدود 4 تا 5 میلیون تومان قیمت دارند. — Each of these small engraved stones cost 4–5 million toman.

78 | 1373

1327 سردار særdar *commander, general* n,pn
- سردار ، اگر من از گناهت بگذرم و آزادت کنم ، چه می کنی؟ — General, if I forgive your transgression and free you what will you do?

90 | 587

1328 مجازات modʒazat *punishment* n
- هر کشوری که مجازات اعدام را اجرا کند نمی‌تواند عضو اتحادیه اروپا باشد. — Any country that implements the death penalty cannot be a member of the European Union.

89 | 630

1329 حکایت hekajæt *story* n
- حکایت دیگری داشت. — She had another story.

88 | 720

1330 عضویت ozvijæt *membership* n
- به عضویت این سازمان در آمد. — She became a member of this organization.

86 | 797

1331 حساس hæssas *sensitive* adj
- در این شرایط حساس کجا هستی؟ — Where are you in these sensitive conditions?

87 | 790

1332 کارکنان karkonan *employees* n
- کارکنان بخش کشاورزی ایتالیا تظاهرات کردند. — Italy's agricultural sector workers protested.

85 | 874

1333 اغلب æɣlæb *often, frequently* adv,pron,q
- اغلب روزها را هم به قمار مشغول بود. — Most days he was also occupied with gambling.

82 | 1068

1334 معظم moʔæzæm *supreme* adj
- مقام معظم رهبری به مناطق محروم و دور افتاده توجه خاصی دارند. — The supreme leader pays special attention to deprived and remote regions.

81 | 1133

1335 الان ælan *now* adv
- من از الان در وسط یک نسل‌کشی هستم. — Now I am in the middle of a massacre.

64 | 2457

1336 قابلیت ɣabelijjæt *capability* n
- این شرکت قابلیت تعدیل بسیار خوبی را خواهد داشت. — This company will have a very good capacity to make adjustments.

88 | 720

1337 متحد mottæhed *united, ally* adj,n
- هر دو کشور قبل از انقلاب ایران متحد استراتژیک آمریکا بودند. — Before the Iranian revolution both countries were strategic allies of the USA.

71 | 1820

1338 عنصر onsor *element* n
- یک عنصر اصلی باران اسیدی است. — One fundamental element of rain is an acid.

81 | 1174

1339 حاشیه hæʃije *margin* n
- مدیرکل گردشگری مازندران در حاشیه این بازدید خاطرنشان کرد: — The general manager of Mazandaran Tourism on the sidelines of this visit noted that:

82 | 1064

1340 تعهد tæʔæhhod *commitment* n
- هشت صد تومان هم تعهد کرده بودند. — They had committed eight hundred toman.

84 | 923

1341 قلب ɣælb *heart* n
- لوریس چکناواریان تحت عمل جراحی قلب قرار گرفت. — Loris Tjeknavorian underwent heart surgery.

82 | 1069

1342 آدم ɑdæm *person* n,pn
- — آدم میتواند صحبت کند حالا خودم بهت تلفن میزنم. Humans can talk, so I'll call you myself.
59 | 2802

1343 فرا færa *beyond* adj,adv,prep
- — تنش این شهر را فرا گرفته است. Tension took over the city.
87 | 738

1344 قشر qeʃr *bark, stratum* n
- در نتیجه سن ازدواج برای هر دو قشر افزایش یافته است. — As a result, the marriage age for both classes has increased.
87 | 730

1345 اعدام eʔdam *execution* n
- بیستمین قاتل محکوم به مرگی بود که امسال در تگزاس اعدام شد. — He was the twentieth murderer sentenced to death that was executed in Texas this year.
93 | 385

1346 سایه saje *shadow* n
- — یه سایه پیدا نمیشه زیرش دراز بکشی. No shade to lay under will be found.
85 | 868

1347 کارمند karmænd *employee* n
- او تا نوزده سالگی درس حقوق خواند و پس از آن کارمند دولت شد. — He studied law till the age of nineteen and then became a government employee.
85 | 840

1348 شرکت کردن ʃerkæt kærdæn *participate* v
- در مدت چهار سال دبیرستان او در تمام تمرینها شرکت میکرد. — In his four years of high school he participated in all of the practices.
82 | 1039

1349 ادبیات ædæbijjɑt *literature* n
- — معلم ادبیات است. She's a literature teacher.
79 | 1282

1350 باد bɑd *wind, may (it) be* n,v
- در زمستان چون باد ندارد گرم است. — Because there is no wind in winter it is warm.
81 | 1138

1351 هجری hedʒri *A.H.* adj
- — بانو فخر عظمی ارغون ، متولد ۱۲۷۷ هجری. Mrs. Fakhr Ozma Arghavan, born in 1277 AH.
69 | 1962

1352 جستجو dʒostedʒu *search* n
- — توی گوگل جستجو کردم. I searched it on Google.
90 | 546

1353 جدایی dʒodɑji *separation* n
- — منتظر این جدایی ناگهانی نبوده است. She was not expecting this sudden separation.
94 | 355

1354 فلسطینی felestini *Palestinian* adj,n
- — به فلسطینی ها کمک کنید. You should help the Palestinians.
64 | 2390

1355 اصلاً æslæn *originally, by no means* adv
- — من اصلا حوصله اش را نداشتم. I didn't have any motivation for it.
62 | 2518

1356 تدبیر tædbir *measure, plan* n
- — وقتی که امید و تدبیر ، «بر باد رفته باشد» When hope and plans are "gone with the wind!"
87 | 718

1357 ایفا ifa *play* n
- — بیتردید اراده‌های انسانی هم نقش ایفا می‌کنند. Without a doubt human will also plays a role.
86 | 810

1358 ترک کردن tærk kærdæn *leave, abandon* v
- وقتی تماشاچیان ورزشگاه را ترک کردند مربی دید که پسر جوان تنها در گوشه‌ای نشسته است. — When the spectators left the stadium, the coach saw a young boy sitting alone in a corner.
92 | 420

1359 مهاجر mohɑdʒer *immigrant* adj,n,pn
- اولین گروه از این مهاجران روز چهارم آوریل به ترکیه بازگردانده می‌شوند. — The first group of these immigrants will be deported to Turkey on the 4th of April.
91 | 510

1360 حیات hæjɑt *life* n
- فلسفه های مادی قائل به آغاز و ختم حیات اجتماعی بشر در همین دنیا هستند. — Materialistic philosophies tell of the beginning and end of human social life in this world.
81 | 1086

1361 بستن bæstæn *close* n,pn,v
- — اکثر فروشگاه های فرانسه بسته بودند. Most of the stores in France were closed.
79 | 1229

1362 جزیره dʒæzire *island* n
- — ببخشید شما می‌دانید نام آن جزیره چیست؟ Excuse me, do you know the name of that island?
82 | 1049

1363 برقرار bærqærɑr *established* adj,n
- چه کسی می خواهد ارتباط برقرار کند و چه ویژگی‌هایی دارد؟ — What kind of person wants to establish communication and what characteristics does he have?
88 | 672

1364 قطر qotr, qætær *diagonal/diameter, Qatar* n,pn
- در وبسایت این شرکت آمده است که قطر دستگاه جدید ۷.۲ میلی متر خواهد بود. — On the company's website, it is mentioned that diameter of the new device would be 7.2 mm.
80 | 1210

1365 شور ʃur, ʃowr *salty/passion, deliberation* adj,n,pn
- از دریاچه های شور نیز نمک بدست می آورند. — They also obtain salt from saline ponds.

90 | 541

1366 دارایی daraji *property* n
- دارایی های استهلاک پذیر. — Depreciable assets.

87 | 738

1367 مهاجرت mohadʒeræt *emigration, immigration* n
- دلیل اصلی مهاجرت آنها مشخص نیست. — The main reason for their immigration is not clear.

89 | 591

1368 تقسیم tæɣsim *division* n
- سه شهر جدید به نقشه تقسیمات کشوری اضافه شد. — Three new cities were added to the country division map.

80 | 1155

1369 تکمیل tækmil *completion* n
- او برای تکمیل این دستگاه به پول نیاز داشت. — He needed money to complete this device.

87 | 724

1370 وسیع væsiʔ *large* adj
- او رفت و رفت تا به مزرعه ی وسیع رسید. — He went and went until he reached a vast farm.

82 | 1030

1371 اخلاق æxlaɣ *morality* n
- اخلاقم عوض شد. — My ethics changed.

89 | 634

1372 ضروری zæruri *necessary* adj
- در شرایط تورمی دوران جنگ، سیاست کنترل قیمت و دستمزد ضروری است. — In the inflationary conditions of wartime, a policy of controlling prices and wages is necessary.

83 | 979

1373 جشن dʒæʃn *celebration* n
- جشن نوروز در کاخ سفید به میزبانی میشل اوباما برگزار شد. — Michelle Obama hosted the Nowruz celebration in the White House.

85 | 856

1374 تخریب tæxrib *destruction* n
- شخصی مشغول تخریب دیوار قدیمی خانه اش بود. — Someone was busy demolishing their house's old wall.

85 | 830

1375 مسلح mosællæh *armed* adj
- نیروهای مسلح پشتوانه دستگاه دیپلماسی کشور هستند. — Armed forces are the backup for the country's diplomatic apparatus.

71 | 1771

1376 محفل mæhʔfel *social circle* n
- محفل کوچک خانواده هامون. — The small circle of our families.

91 | 477

1377 ذکر zekr, zækær *mention, penis* n
- نباید ذکر کرد. — It must not be mentioned.

78 | 1315

1378 حرکت کردن hærekæt kærdæn *move, set off* v
- بعضی از ما در خواب مرتب در یک دایره حرکت می کنند و برخی مرتب به زمین می افتند. — Some of us regularly move in a circle during sleep and some regularly fall onto the ground.

90 | 541

1379 حقوقی hoɣuɣi *legal* adj,n
- نظام حقوقی اردن بر پایه شرع اسلام و قوانین فرانسه می‌باشد. — Jordan's legal system is based on Islamic Sharia and French law.

84 | 926

1380 دریایی dærjaji *maritime* adj,n
- این خط لوله در مرز دریایی پاکستان شروع می‌کند. — This pipeline begins on the littoral border with Pakistan.

83 | 977

1381 فرایند færajænd *process* n
- فرایند اعطای بورس تحصیلی خارج از کشور به دانشجویان تغییر کرد. — The process for granting scholarships for study abroad changed.

83 | 964

1382 حریف hærif *opponent* n
- در همان دقیقه چهارم توسط اسکار گلزنی کرده و از حریف خود پیش افتادند. — In the fourth minute, they made a goal by Oscar, and they got ahead of their opponents.

78 | 1277

1383 بیمه bime *insurance* n
- من یه موقع واسه یه شرکت بیمه کارّ می‌کردم و اونا این آمار رُ منتشر کردن. — Once I was working for an insurance company, and they published the statistics.

77 | 1326

1384 جرم dʒorm, dʒerm *crime, substance* n
- تو مرتکب جرم شده‌ای. — You have committed a crime.

85 | 851

1385 جایزه dʒajeze *award* n
- یکی از کشاورزان منطقه ای، همیشه در مسابقه‌ها، جایزه بهترین غله را به دست می‌آورد. — One of the regional farmers always receives the prize for best grain in competitions.

79 | 1247

1386 دهم dæhom *tenth* adj,n,v
- نتایج رقابتهای دهمین جشنواره قرآنی منتشر شد. — The results of the tenth Koran Festival competition were released.

76 | 1452

1387 همسایه hæmsaje *neighbor* adj,n
- من از این همسایه را نمی توانم ببینم. — I cannot see this neighbor.

82 | 1030

1388 صف sæff *queue* n
- دست به سینه جلو تخت صف بستند. — Hands on their chests, they lined up in front of his throne.
- 93 | 402

1389 توصیه towsije *recommendation* n
- ا — من خواندن ادبیات معاصر را به شما توصیه می کنم. recommend that you read contemporary literature.
- 87 | 700

1390 اخلاقی æxlaɣi *moral, ethical* adj
- در هر طنزی دانش و نکتهٔ اخلاقی هست. — In every piece of satire there is knowledge and a moral point.
- 85 | 824

1391 بهمن bæhmæn *avalanche, Bahman* n,pn
- این نمایش نخستین بار در تاریخ سوم بهمن سال ۱۳۸۱ در سالن سایه اجرا شد. — For the first time this show was performed on the third of Bahman 1381 in Sayeh Theater.
- 81 | 1063

1392 توصیف towsif *description* adj,n
- هیچ نوشته‌ای‌قادر به توصیف این مکان زیبا و شگفت‌انگیز برای شما نیست. — No writing is capable of describing this beautiful and amazing location for you.
- 89 | 605

1393 کیلوگرم kilogræm *kilogram* n
- تنها ۴۵ کیلوگرم وزن دارد و توانست رقبای آمریکایی خود را پشت سر بگذارد. — He weighs only 45 kilograms, and was able to leave behind his American competitors.
- 78 | 1309

1394 نیویورک nijujork *New York* pn
- وقتی شما به شهر نیویورک سفر کنید، جالب ترین بخش سفر شما هنگامی است که پس از خروج از هواپیما و فرودگاه، قصد گرفتن یک تاکسی را داشته باشید. — When you travel to New York, the most interesting part of your trip is after leaving the airplane and the airport when you want to get a taxi.
- 80 | 1141

1395 موقت movæɣɣæt *temporary* adj
- ۶۵ رسانه خارجی مجوز فعالیت موقت در ایران گرفتند. — 65 foreign media received licenses for temporary operation in Iran.
- 87 | 693

1396 برنده bærænde *winner* adj,n
- اون برنده نیست. — He is not the winner.
- 88 | 642

1397 عملاً æmælæn *practically* adv,conj
- یادگیری زبان جدید عملاً غیر ممکن بود. — Learning a new language was practically impossible.
- 90 | 549

1398 دستاورد dæstaværd *achievement* n
- ضمن ارائه گزارشی از دستاوردهای علمی اش. — While presenting a report of his scientific achievements.
- 83 | 968

1399 گرد gærd, gerd, gord *powder/dust, round, champion* adj,n
- گرد و غبار به تهران می‌رسد. — The dust and haze reaches Tehran.
- 88 | 660

1400 سری seri, særi *series, a head* adj,n
- شامگاه جمعه یک سری حملات تروریستی به طور همزمان در چند منطقه پاریس روی داد. — Friday evening a series of simultaneous terrorist attacks took place in Paris.
- 83 | 959

1401 عقب æɣæb *back* adj,adv,n
- یک قدم به عقب برداشت و داد زد. — Took one step back and screamed.
- 81 | 1067

1402 رونق rownæɣ *boom* n
- روز به روز کسب و کارش بیشتر رونق گرفت. — Day by day her work flourished all the more.
- 90 | 514

1403 سبز sæbz *green* adj,n
- آن پرده زشت سبز رنگ را دیدم. — I saw that ugly green curtain.
- 80 | 1139

1404 بشر bæʃær *human* n
- آیا شامپانزه‌ها هم باید حقوق بشر داشته باشند؟ — Should chimpanzees also have human rights?
- 78 | 1274

1405 هنری honæri *artistic* adj
- برخی هم معتقدند، سانسور باعث رشد خلاقیت هنری می شود. — Some also believe censorship causes a growth of artistic creativity!
- 74 | 1548

1406 سرد særd *cold* adj
- حیف که این جا آب سرد نیست! — What a pity that there is no cold water here!
- 86 | 761

1407 دشوار doʃvar *difficult* adj
- حرف زدن برایم دشوار شده است. — Talking has become difficult for me.
- 87 | 711

1408 اتاق otaɣ *room* n
- مأمور ناصر را به اتاق پشتی برد و تمام لباسهایش را کند. — The officer took Naser to the backroom and took off all his clothes.
- 62 | 2406

1409 جبهه dʒebhe *front* n
- پروانه فروهر مدیر مسئول نشریه جبهه ملی ایران بود. — Parvaneh Forouhar was the managing editor of Iran's National Front magazine.
- 77 | 1353

1410 اعزام e?zam *dispatch* n

- بلاش سفیری نزد امپراتور روم اعزام داشت و به عمل کوربولو اعتراض کرد و سپس با سپاهی گران وارد بین النهرین شد. — Walagash sent an ambassador to the Roman Emperor and complained about Corbulo's act; then, with a big army, entered Mesopotamia.

86 | 787

1411 انتظار داشتن entezar daʃtæn *expect* v

- نباید انتظار داشت مشکلات در کوتاه مدت حل شود. — One should not expect problems to be solved in a short time.

92 | 395

1412 شیراز ʃiraz *Shiraz* pn

- تیمور با سپاهیان خود به سمت شیراز حرکت کرد. — Timur moved towards Shiraz with his troops.

84 | 902

1413 آره are *yes* adv

- آره پسرم، همیشه دوستت داشتم. — Yes, son, I have always loved you.

41 | 4452

1414 دسترسی dæstresi *accessibility* n

- بیش از ۷۰۰ میلیون نفر به آب سالم دسترسی ندارند. — More than 700 million people do not have access to safe drinking water.

86 | 782

1415 گزارشی gozareʃi *reporting* n

- عکسهای گزارشی و خبری باید خوب صادق، آگاهی دهنده و جالب بوده و دارای اثر شدید بوده یا قابل توجه باشند. — Good news and report photos should be honest, informative, interesting, and have strong influence or be significant.

83 | 924

1416 مصاحبه mosahebe *interview* n

- دخترک به من تلفن زد و خواست برای دیدار و مصاحبه بیاید خانه‌مان. — A little girl called me and asked to come to our house for a visit and an interview.

80 | 1102

1417 عبدالله æbdollah *Abdollah* pn

- فرزندانم عبدالله و سیاوش و زیباخانم خیلی از این بابت رنج می برند. — My children, Abdollah, Siavash, and Zibakhanom are suffering a great deal in this regard.

84 | 898

1418 احتمالی ehtemali *probable* adj

- بسیاری از مشکلات احتمالی برطرف خواهد شد. — Many of the potential problems will be resolved.

90 | 549

1419 بانو banu *lady* n

- او در برابر بانو زانو زد. — He knelt in front of the lady.

83 | 930

1420 روسی rusi *Russian* adj

- بیشتر مکاتبات اداری به زبان روسی انجام می‌شود. — Most official correspondence is conducted in Russian.

90 | 505

1421 فرمان færman *command* n

- هیچ کدام از سربازها موفق به انجام فرمان سرگروهبان نشد. — None of the soldiers were successful in carrying out the sergeant's order.

88 | 653

1422 کلمه kælæme *word* n

- مقالات بهتر است کمتر از ۵۰۰۰ کلمه باشند. — It is better for articles to be less than 5000 words.

73 | 1598

1423 منطقی mænteɣi *logical* adj,n

- این دلیل که به نظر شما منطقی می‌آید برای دیگران یک بهانه بی ارزش است تا دلیل. — This reason that seems logical to you is a worthless pretext to others rather than a reason.

86 | 773

1424 بالاخره bel?æxære *finally* adv,conj

- بالاخره پس از گذشت یک هفته بازی تمام شد. — After a week the game was finally finished.

83 | 944

1425 مالیات malijat *tax, taxes* n

- قانون مالیات های مستقیم. — Direct Tax Law.

82 | 999

1426 راهکار rahkar *strategy, solution* adj,n

- راهکار پیشنهادی شما برای حل این مشکل چیست؟ — What is your recommended solution to solve this problem?

86 | 746

1427 صحبت کردن sohbæt kærdæn *talk* v

- اوباما در عربستان در مورد ایران و داعش صحبت کرد. — In Saudi Arabia, Obama spoke about Iran and ISIL.

80 | 1119

1428 مادی maddi *material* adj

- آیا این عبادت هدف مادی دارد؟ — Does this worship have a material goal?

89 | 589

1429 تبادل tæbadol *exchange* n

- تبادل نظر و همکاری بیشتر کشور های مسلمان. — Further opinion exchange and cooperation between Muslim countries.

89 | 580

1430 اسپانیا espanja *Spain* pn

- انگلیس و اسپانیا از منطقه اروپا به طور مستقیم به جام‌جهانی صعود کردند. — From Europe, England and Spain climbed up directly to the World Cup.

72 | 1635

1431 آفریقا afriɣa *Africa* pn
- مسافرها را گروگان گرفت و هواپیما را به آفریقا برد. — He kidnapped the passengers and took the airplane to Africa.
- 74 | 1489

1432 نفوذ nofuz *influence* n
- عشق از قلب پیر مرد به قلب او نفوذ کرده بود. — The love from the old man's heart had influenced her heart.
- 81 | 1021

1433 یکشنبه jekʃæmbe *Sunday* n
- از روز یکشنبه در نگارخانه سعدآباد تهران در معرض دید عموم قرار گرفت. — Starting Sunday it will be displayed to the public at the Sa'dabad Gallery in Tehran.
- 77 | 1289

1434 ماهی mahi *fish, a month* n
- ماهی‌های قرمز را در رودخانه‌ها رها نکنید. — Don't release goldfish into the rivers.
- 78 | 1245

1435 ستاره setare *star* n,pn
- در چانه‌اش ستاره می درخشد. — The star twinkles on her chin.
- 87 | 710

1436 شعار ʃeʔar *slogan* n
- مردم با شعار «من انقلابی ام» به میدان آمدند. — People came to the square with the slogan "I am a revolutionary."
- 80 | 1096

1437 پایدار pajdar *stable* adj
- امنیت پایدار کشورمان مرهون خون شهیدان است. — Our country's stable security is indebted to the blood of martyrs.
- 88 | 601

1438 روانی rævani *fluency, psychotic* adj
- تاکنون نقش سه بیمار روانی را بازی کرده‌ام. — I have played the roles of three mental patients up to now.
- 84 | 876

1439 بندر bændær *port* n
- بسته شدن چند بندر صدور نفت در خلیج مکزیک. — The closing of several oil exporting ports in the Gulf of Mexico.
- 84 | 846

1440 بهانه bæhane *excuse* n
- به این بهانه که خودش زبان اسپانیایی بلد نیست. — With the excuse that he himself does not know Spanish.
- 82 | 997

1441 واسطه vasete *mediator* n
- آنها می‌گفتند ما بت‌ها را عبادت می‌کنیم تا میان ما و خدا واسطه باشند. — They said we worship the idols so that they act as intermediaries between us and God.
- 90 | 490

1442 منطق mænteɣ *logic* n
- تاریخ پر از منطق آن هاست. — History is full of their logic.
- 90 | 502

1443 شریف ʃærif *honorable* adj,pn
- مردم شریف کشور. — Honorable people of the country.
- 89 | 567

1444 چنان ʧenan *such* adv,n,pron
- چنان زار زدم که زن هایی که آنجا بودند همه متوجه من شدند. — I wept so much that all of the women who were there were aware of me.
- 79 | 1155

1445 آذربایجان azærbajdʒan *Azerbaijan* pn
- جمهوری آذربایجان و ارمنستان تداوم آتش‌بس در قره‌باغ را پذیرفتند. — The republics of Azerbaijan and Armenia accepted a continuation of the ceasefire in Karabakh.
- 79 | 1159

1446 دبیر dæbir *secretary* n
- دبیر کل فدراسیون بین‌المللی شیمی. — Secretary-General of the International Federation of Chemistry.
- 77 | 1276

1447 خروج xorudʒ *exit* n
- دقایقی بعد از خروج راننده از رستوران یکی از جوان ها به صاحب رستوران گفت: — A few minutes after the driver left the restaurant, one of the young people told the restaurant owner:
- 74 | 1475

1448 توجیه towdʒih *explanation, justification* n
- تاسیس بانک توجیه اقتصادی دارد؟ — Is establishing a bank economically justifiable?
- 90 | 532

1449 مشهور mæʃhur *famous* adj
- بعد از مدتی به نویسنده ای موفق و مشهور تبدیل گردد. — After some time she transformed into a successful and famous writer.
- 86 | 755

1450 تقدیر tæɣdir *destiny, appreciation* n
- ما از این اقدام تقدیر می کنیم. — We appreciate these actions.
- 88 | 633

1451 شبیه ʃæbih *similar* adj
- مترادف چینی‌اش باید چیز عجیبی بشود: چند هجای کوتاه و بلند که شبیه، درست شبیه جیغ است. — Its Chinese equivalent must be something strange: several short, loud syllables that are similar, that are just like a shriek.
- 87 | 699

1452 ماشین maʃin *machine, car* n
- آره برف پاک کن ماشین از کار افتاد. — Yeah, the windshield wiper of the car is broken.
- 74 | 1490

9 Female names

Rank	Headword	Pronunciation	Gloss	Rank	Headword	Pronunciation	Gloss
43	ایران	iran	Iran	4735	آفرین	ɑfærin	Afarin
1435	ستاره	setɑre	star	4980	پری	pæri	fairy, Pari
1521	شیرین	ʃirin	sweet	4984	ثمره	sæmære	fruit, offspring
2030	شادی	ʃɑdi	joy	5271	زهره	zohre	vesper
2159	شمسی	ʃæmsi	Shamsi	5329	فروغ	foruɣ	brightness
2650	زهرا	zæhrɑ	Zahra	5338	عالیه	ɑlije	supreme
3022	مریم	mærjæm	Maryam	5448	سارا	sɑrɑ	Sara
3031	رؤیا	roʔjɑ	dream	5534	گیتی	giti	world
3040	فاطمه	fɑteme	Fateme	5723	گوهر	gowhær	jewel
3050	پروانه	pærvɑne	butterfly	5761	سیمین	simin	silvery
3208	افسانه	æfsɑne	legend	5778	نازی	nɑzi	coquettish
3500	الهام	elhɑm	inspiration	5841	مروارید	morvɑrid	pearl
3622	نیکی	niki	goodness, good deed	5849	آذر	ɑzær	fire, Azar
3968	فرشته	fereʃte	angel	5916	لادن	lɑdæn	nasturtium
4025	ابریشم	æbriʃæm	silk	5938	مرجان	mærdʒɑn	coral
4137	معصومه	mæʔsume	Masume	5943	فروزان	foruzɑn	bright
4157	هاله	hɑle	halo, aura	6050	فرانک	færɑnæk	Faranak
4261	اکرم	ækræm	dearer	6075	ماری	mɑri	Marie
4325	لاله	lɑle	tulip	6158	لیلی	lejli	Leyli
4346	لیلا	lejlɑ	Layla	6206	خاتون	xɑtun	lady of rank
4350	نرگس	nærges	narcissus	6353	زینب	zejnæb	Zeynab
4491	یگانه	jegɑne	unique, sole	6385	نغمه	næɣme	melody
4557	آزاده	ɑzɑde	free, liberated	6426	عاطفه	ɑtefe	affection
4639	فرزانه	færzɑne	learned, wise	6729	مهری	mehri	Mehri
4640	پروین	pærvin	Parvin	6748	زینت	zinæt	ornament

1453 مایل mɑjel *willing* adj,n,v
- مایل نیست که در خانه ی خودش و یا خانه ی پسر ملاقات کند. — He is not inclined to meet in his own home or his son's home.
- 91 | 477

1454 روحیه ruhijje *mood, morale* n
- روحیه تان را از اول صبح تقویت کنید. — Lift up your spirit first thing in the morning.
- 91 | 471

1455 درست بودن dorost budæn *be right* v
- حدسم درست بود. — My guess was correct.
- 85 | 790

1456 تولیدی towlidi *manufactured, manufacturing* adj
- کرج دارای تعداد زیادی واحدهای تولیدی و صنعتی است. — Karaj has many industrial and manufacturing units.
- 83 | 899

1457 معتبر moʔtæbær *reliable, valid* adj
- افراد معتبر و قابل اعتمادی نیستند. — They are not reliable or credible individuals.
- 89 | 553

1458 تربیت tærbijæt *training, upbringing* n
- این اشخاص تربیت صحیحی ندارند. — These individuals do not have appropriate training.
- 74 | 1447

1459 ستاد setad *headquarters* n
- ● ستاد آسیب‌های اجتماعی در وزارت بهداشت راه اندازی شد. — The headquarters for social damages was launched within the Ministry of Health.
- 81 | 1041

1460 معاصر moɑʔser *contemporary* adj
- ● The — شاعر خوب معاصر که حالا مقیم آمریکاست. good contemporary poet who currently resides in America.
- 82 | 938

1461 قوت ɣovvæt, ɣut *strength, nourishment* n
- ● قوت حرف زدن هم نداشت. — She also did not have the power to speak.
- 91 | 473

1462 باب bab *gate, chapter* n
- ● باب چهارم. — Chapter 4.
- 86 | 704

1463 پرسیدن porsidæn *ask* v
- ● معلم از بچه‌ها پرسید: — The teacher asked the children:
- 64 | 2153

1464 جلوه dʒelve *revealing* n
- ● همایش جلوه‌های ویژه بصری سینما برگزار می‌شود. — A conference about special visual effects in film will be held.
- 90 | 485

1465 بخصوص bexosus *especially* adv,conj
- ● نور رنگ بخصوصی داشت. — The light had a particular color.
- 81 | 1012

1466 برقراری bæryærɑri *establishing* n
- ● برقراری امنیت به خودی خود انجام نمی شود. — Establishing security will not happen by itself.
- 86 | 723

1467 تلویزیونی televizijoni *television* adj
- ● این سازمان دارای یک شبکه تلویزیونی و یک شبکه رادیویی می‌باشد. — This organization has a radio network and a television network.
- 79 | 1147

1468 قصد داشتن ɣæsd dɑʃtæn *intend* v
- ● او اعلام کرد که قصد داره غذا بخوره. — He announced that he intended to eat food.
- 81 | 993

1469 طلب tælæb *demand, desire, -seeker* n
- ● ادبیات و هنر نیز مورد طلب است. — Literature and art are also in demand.
- 90 | 477

1470 محاکمه mohakeme *trial* n
- ● با تضمین محاکمه عادلانه به آمریکا باز می‌گردم. — I will return to America with the guarantee of a fair trial.
- 82 | 937

1471 استقرار esteɣrɑr *positioning, settlement* n
- ● دوره های استقرار و سکونت در هر محل طولانی‌تر و اغلب دائمی شد. — Periods of settlement and residence in each neighborhood become longer and often permanent.
- 85 | 752

1472 نظریه næzærijje *theory* n
- ● نظریه برابری قدرت خرید. — The theory of purchasing power parity.
- 77 | 1260

1473 هشدار hoʃdar *warning* n
- ● هشدار صندوق بین المللی پول به یونان. — International Monetary Fund warns Greece.
- 77 | 1250

1474 سالن salon *hall* n
- ● در این دوره از پیکارها که در سالن شماره دو خانه کشتی تهران برگزار شد، تیم ایران با کسب سه مدال طلا، دو نقره و دو برنز بر سکوی نخست ایستاد. — In this round of matches, which was held in Hall Number 2 of the Tehran House of Wrestling, the Iranian team won first place with three gold, two silver, and two bronze medals.
- 80 | 1037

1475 ثبات sobɑt, sæbbat *stability, clerk* n
- ● ثبات سیاسی و قدرت نظامی. — Political stability and military power.
- 79 | 1107

1476 مطبوعات mætbuat *press* n
- ● «بیگانه پرست» و «ماجراجو» را محمد ولی از فرمانده یاد گرفته بود و فرمانده هم از رادیو و مطبوعات ملی آموخته بود. — Mohammad Vali had learned "xenophile" and "adventurer" from the commander, and the commander had learned it from the radio and national media.
- 68 | 1799

1477 ورق væræɣ *sheet* n
- ● چرا مثل خرچنگ دفترم را ورق می زنید؟ — Why are you turning the pages in my notebook like a crab?
- 82 | 943

1478 نوبت nowbæt *turn* n
- ● اکنون نوبت آنان است. — Now it is their turn.
- 89 | 574

1479 خبر دادن xæbær dadæn *inform* v
- ● مخالفان اسد از اسارت یک ایرانی خبر دادند. — The Assad opposition reported the capture of an Iranian.
- 75 | 1343

1480 اداری edari *administrative* adj
- ● ساختار اداری ایران در تهران متمرکز شده‌است. — Iran's administrative structure is concentrated in Tehran.
- 77 | 1205

1481 استاندارد estandard *standard* adj,n
- باید فروش خود را با استانداردهای بالا مقایسه کنید. — You must compare your own sales with high standards.

82 | 950

1482 تولد tævællod *birth* n
- امروز روز تولد من است. — Today is my birthday.

88 | 626

1483 جایگزین dʒɑjgozin *replacement* adj,n
- قانون جدیدی جایگزین آن کرد. — The new law replaced that.

85 | 762

1484 بنده bænde *slave* n,pron,pn
- بنده بلد نیستم قلیان چاق کنم. — I, your humble servant, do not know how to light a hookah.

81 | 974

1485 ارض ærz *land* n
- ارض مقدس سامرا. — The sacred land of Samara.

88 | 589

1486 مدرک mædræk *document, evidence* n
- مهاجرین فاقد مدرک شناسایی. — Immigrants with no ID.

84 | 811

1487 مایه mɑje *source, cause, yeast* n
- اگر مایه زندگی بندگی است، دو صد بار مردن به از زندگی است. — If the stuff of life is servitude, dying two hundred times is better than living.

92 | 381

1488 برنامه‌ریزی bærnɑmerizi *planning* n
- برای موفقیت‌های آتی خود برنامه‌ریزی کنید و پیروزی‌های امروز خود را جشن بگیرید. — For your own future successes, engage in planning and celebrate today's victories.

80 | 1062

1489 نشریه næʃrijje *publication* n
- این پاسخی بود که آقای رودیارد کیپلینگ در سال 1889 از مسئولان نشریه سان فرانسیسکو اگزامینر دریافت کرد. — That was the response that Mr. Rudyard Kipling received from the editors of the *San Francisco Examiner* in 1889.

81 | 1000

1490 وارد کردن vɑred kærdæn *import, enter* v
- با وارد کردن ایمیل خود در فرم هفته‌نامه، مطالب جدید را به صورت هفتگی در ایمیل خود دریافت کنید! — By entering your e-mail address in the form for the weekly letter, you'll receive new articles in your e-mail on a weekly basis!

91 | 452

1491 تأکید کردن tæʔkid kærdæn *emphasize* v
- بوش بر افزایش فشار بر تهران تأکید کرد. — Bush emphasized increasing pressure on Tehran.

74 | 1441

1492 پل pol *bridge* n,pn
- از پل گذشت. — She crossed the bridge.

81 | 982

1493 ارزشمند ærzeʃmænd *valuable* adj
- ارزشمند ترین چیز های زندگی معمولاً دیده نمی شوند. — The most valuable things in life usually cannot be seen.

88 | 609

1494 یادگار jɑdegɑr *souvenir* n
- دخترم مواظبش باش یادگار اجدادیمونه. — Take good care of it, my daughter, it's our ancestral heirloom.

95 | 239

1495 معرفی شدن moʔærrefi ʃodæn *be introduced* v
- بهترین کشورها برای تحصیلات دانشگاهی معرفی شدند. — The best countries for higher education were introduced.

90 | 494

1496 درخت deræxt *tree* n
- اگر کوچه درخت داشت و نیمه‌تاریک نبود حتماً از آن طرف نمی‌رفتم. — If the street had trees and it wasn't half dark I would certainly go on that side.

77 | 1247

1497 استرالیا ostrɑlijɑ *Australia* pn
- استرالیا در حال حاضر حدود 1500 سرباز در افغانستان دارد. — Currently Australia has approximately 1,500 soldiers in Afghanistan.

85 | 769

1498 تمدن tæmæddon *civilization* n
- تمدن غربی بر آن مبتنی است. — Western civilization is based on that.

68 | 1773

1499 خاتمی xɑtæmi *Khatami* pn
- سید محمد خاتمی از سال ۱۳۷۶ تا ۱۳۸۴ در دو دوره پیاپی رئیس جمهور بود. — Seyed Mohammad Khatami was president for two consecutive terms from 1376 to 1384.

63 | 2165

1500 متوسط motævæsset *average* adj,n
- حالا با یکی از اهالی محل که مردی به سن و سال متوسطی هستند مصاحبه را شروع می کنم. — Now we will start the interview with one of the locals who is a middle aged man.

78 | 1147

1501 خواهان xɑhɑn *plaintiff, desirous* adj,n
- احمدی خواهان سرکوب بیشتر لرها بود. — Ahmadi was calling for further repression of the Lors.

84 | 802

1502 پنجشنبه pændʒʃæmbe *Thursday* n
- پنجشنبه به دکان نرفت. — He didn't go to the store on Thursday.

85 | 779

1503 عزم æzm *resolve* n

- کسی که دارای عزمی راسخ است جهان را مطابق میل خویش عوض می کند. ـ گوته. — A man with firm resolve can change the world to his liking. – Goethe.
93 | 336

1504 خلق xælɣ, xolɣ *creation/people, temper* n

- می‌خواستم بگم: ببینید، من هم می‌تونم انسان خلق کنم. — I wanted to say, "You see, I can also create humans."
84 | 805

1505 استفاده شدن estefade ʃodæn *be used* v

- همانطور که در بالا اشاره شد، چیپ A7 کاندیدای خوبی برای استفاده شدن در تبلت جدید است. — As was mentioned above, the A7 chip is a good candidate for use in the new tablet.
84 | 808

1506 کوشیدن kuʃidæn *attempt* v

- فرمانروایی که می‌کوشید تا مرزهای جنوبی کشورش را گسترش دهد، با مقاومت‌های سرداری محلی مواجه شد. — The ruler who strived to expand his country's southern borders came up against resistance by local commanders.
88 | 573

1507 همانند hæmanænd *similar* adv,n

- استانبول بعد از حمله اخیر همانند شهر ارواح شده است. — Istanbul has become like a ghost town after the recent attacks.
87 | 656

1508 لباس lebas *clothing* n

- در این مسابقه شرکت کنندگان باید با لباسهای سنتی حاضر شوند. — In this competition the participants need to be present in their traditional clothes.
74 | 1402

1509 سیما sima *face* n

- صدا و سیمای جمهوری اسلامی ایران. — Islamic Republic of Iran Broadcasting.
73 | 1434

1510 مبلغ mæblæɣ, mobælleɣ *amount, missionary* n

- وقتی به آن مرد گفته شد که آنها توانایی خرید زمینی به آن مبلغ را نداردند، او حاضر شد زمینش را به قیمت 57 سنت به کلیسا بفروشد. — When that man was told they didn't have the ability to buy land at that price, he was prepared to sell his land to the church for 57 cents.
80 | 1047

1511 تکلیف tæklif *task* adj,n

- بی تکلیف نیستم. — I am not without duties.
86 | 712

1512 گوناگون gunagun *various* adj

- کارشناسان ۶۶ مقاله از رشته‌های گوناگون را ارزیابی کردند. — Experts evaluated 66 articles on diverse subjects.
80 | 1019

1513 ریختن rixtæn *pour* adj,n,v

- داشت یواش یواش آب به سر و صورتش می زد که یکی از دهاتی ها به عنوان آب ریختن روی دستش آمد جلو و تکه کاغذی گذاشت توی جیب قبای میرزا. — He was slowly washing his head and face when one of the villagers came forward as though to pour water on his hands and put a piece of paper into the pocket of Mirza's cloak.
69 | 1742

1514 سلام sælam *hello, greeting* n

- سلام دوستای عزیزم. — Hello, my dear friends.
60 | 2368

1515 چشمگیر ʧeʃmgir *impressive* adj

- از آن زمان به بعد تعداد کانون های تفکر در جهان رشد چشمگیری پیدا کرد. — From that time on the number of think tanks in the world grew significantly.
88 | 603

1516 نابودی nabudi *destruction* n

- هوای آلوده سبب نابودی بافت‌های بدن می‌شود. — Polluted air causes the destruction of bodily tissues.
91 | 428

1517 فلسفه fælsæfe *philosophy* n

- من از فلسفه چی می دونم؟ — What do I know about philosophy?
78 | 1169

1518 جو ʤu, ʤow, ʤævv *stream, barley, atmosphere* n,pn

- کشت جو احتمالاً از اتیوپی و آسیای جنوب‌شرقی آغاز شده‌است. — Barley cultivation probably began in Ethiopia and Southeast Asia.
89 | 537

1519 مواجه شدن movaʤeh ʃodæn *be confronted* v

- با واقعیت مواجه شوید. — Face the reality.
82 | 900

1520 زود zud *soon* adj,adv

- بیا زودتر چیزها را ببینیم. — Come, let's see the things earlier.
73 | 1437

1521 شیرین ʃirin *sweet* adj,pn

- برخی از قندهای سنتزی شیرین‌ترند. — Some of the synthetic sugars are sweeter.
87 | 657

1522 حکومتی hokumæti *governmental* adj,n

- الگوی حکومتی ما مبتنی بر اسلام است. — Our governance model is based on Islam.
85 | 768

1523 حاکی haki *indicative* adj,v

- روزی تلگرامی به دستش رسید که خبر فوت پدر در آن بود و حاکی از این بود که پدر، تمام اموال خود را به او بخشیده است. — One day a telegram reached her which had news of her father's death indicating that he had left all of his property to her.
87 | 662

1524 رده ræde *category* n

- نام خود را در زمره بهترین‌های گلف در رده‌های سنی مختلف ثبت کرد. — He recorded his name amongst the best golfers in various traditional categories.

71 | 1565

1525 امیدوار بودن omidvar budæn *be hopeful* v

- امیدوارم که به هدف خود دست پیدا کند. — I hope he will reach his goal.

91 | 411

1526 تفاهم tæfahom *understanding* adj,n

- ایران و عراق در زمینه توسعه و حمایت از مدیریت دولتی و خدمات کشور یادداشت تفاهم همکاری امضا کرد. — Iran and Iraq signed a cooperative memorandum of understanding on development and support of the countries' administration and services.

90 | 492

1527 مطلوب mætlub *desirable, desired* adj

- بتوانیم تغییرات مطلوب را در افراد ایجاد کنیم. — We should be able to create the desired changes in individuals.

83 | 844

1528 قم ɣom *Qom* pn

- روز حادثه این مرد خودرو مرا از قم به مقصد کرج کرایه کرد. — On the day of the event, this guy rented my car from Qom bound for Karaj.

85 | 722

1529 جا گرفتن dʒa gereftæn *reserve, hold* v

- جا گرفتن در رده دوم. — Being in second place.

94 | 274

1530 شهادت ʃæhadæt *evidence, martyrdom* n

- امام حسن مجتبی علیه السلام توسط توطئه معاویه مسموم و به شهادت رسید. — Imam Hasan Mojtaba (AS) was poisoned and martyred by the plot of Muawiyah.

81 | 972

1531 اتمام etmam *completion* n

- اتمام دوران تحصیل. — The end of the period of education.

91 | 442

1532 اینترنت internet *internet* n,pn

- سایت اینترنتی در جمهوری اسلامی ایران مکلف است — A website in the Islamic Republic of Iran is obliged to . . .

84 | 770

1533 یاری jari *help* n

- تو را به یاری طلبیدم. — I requested your help.

91 | 409

1534 اظهار داشتن ezhar daʃtæn *express, declare* v

- شماری از منتقدان رادیو اظهار داشته‌اند رادیو زمانه زمانه هویت مشخصی پیدا نکرده. — A number of radio critics expressed that Radio Zamaneh has not found a clear identity.

72 | 1459

1535 جزو dʒozv *part, particle* n

- هر شب یک جزو می‌خواند. — Every night they read one part.

86 | 654

1536 فهرست fehrest *list* n

- در فهرست فاسد ترین کشورهای جهان قرار دارد. — It is on the list of the most corrupt countries in the world.

83 | 839

1537 خورشید xorʃid *sun* pn

- موهای بلندش که از زیر روسری کوچکش بیرون زده بود به نظرش طلایی تر از نور خورشید بود. — In his opinion, the long hair that had been poking out from under her small head scarf was more golden than sunlight.

86 | 671

1538 کمال kæmal *perfection* n,pn

- مرد در کمال نومیدی اونجا رو ترک کرد. — In complete despair, the man left that place.

86 | 693

1539 سبک sæbk, sæbok *style, light* adj,n

- هوا سبک بود و بهار زیر پوسته‌ء خاک خف کرده بود. — The air was light and spring lurked under the earth's crust.

83 | 843

1540 حقیقی hæɣiɣi *real* adj,pn

- وحدت حقیقی دارد. — It has a real unity.

90 | 490

1541 گمان goman *guess, belief* n

- فقط حدس و گمان است. — It's just guessing and speculation.

91 | 411

1542 مشاور moʃaver *consultant* adj,n

- برای حل این مشکل آنها شرکت مشاورین اندرسون را انتخاب کردند. — They picked the Andersen Consulting Company to solve their problem.

82 | 875

1543 دانشگاهی daneʃgahi *academic, university* adj,n

- فکر می کند با تحصیلات دانشگاهی می‌تواند آینده بهتری برای خودش بسازد. — He thinks he can build a better future for himself with a university education.

84 | 795

1544 قاچاق ɣaʧaɣ *contraband* n

- نوشیدنی های الکلی به طور قاچاق وارد ایران می‌شود. — Alcoholic beverages enter Iran as contraband.

82 | 905

1545 کجا kodʒa *where* adv,n,v
- میرزا باز من را کجا می‌بری؟ — Mirza, where else are you taking me?
63 | 2062

1546 تداوم tædavom *continuation* n
- به‌شدت نسبت به تداوم این خشونت‌ها اظهار نارضایتی کرده — He has strongly complained against the continuation of the violence.
87 | 622

1547 افتتاح eftetah *opening* n
- در سال 1368 این دبیرستان افتتاح شد. — This high school was inaugurated in 1368.
86 | 696

1548 طالبان taleban *Taliban* pn
- این رباعی را هم یکی از شاعران افغانی در زمان حکومت طالبان سروده است. — This quatrain was also composed by one of the Afghan poets from the time of the Taliban government.
55 | 2688

1549 ناحیه nahije *area* n
- داخل مدرسه بودیم که خبر شدیم پیرزنی تعادلش را از دست داده و از پله‌های خانه اشان به پایین سقوط کرده و دچار خونریزی بیرونی از ناحیه سر شده است. — We were inside the school when we were informed that the old woman had lost her balance, fallen down the stairs in her house, and is suffering internal bleeding in the head area.
72 | 1481

1550 سقف sæɣf *ceiling, roof* n
- سقف آن به اندازه دو طبقه ارتفاع داشت. — Its ceiling had a height of two stories.
86 | 650

1551 غنی ɣæni *rich* adj
- شهر بابک غنی ترین معادن مس ایران را دارا است — Shahr-e Babak has the richest copper mines in Iran.
88 | 546

1552 قطعاً qæt?æn *certainly* adv
- نان قطعاً گران می‌شود. — Bread is definitely getting expensive.
86 | 651

1553 سپاه sepah *army* n
- اولویت‌های سپاه در عرصه فرهنگی کدامند؟ — What are the army's priorities in the cultural arena?
86 | 648

1554 هشتم hæʃtom *eighth* adj,n
- هشتمین همایش سالانه انجمن سرطان ایران 30 آذر ماه برگزار می‌شود. — The Iran Cancer Society's eighth annual conference will be held on the 30th of Azar.
81 | 930

1555 درگیر dærgir *involved* adj
- از سال ۱۹۷۹ شوروی در جنگی طولانی و خونبار در افغانستان درگیر شد. — The Soviet Union got involved in a long and bloody war in Afghanistan from 1979 onwards.
90 | 447

1556 سکه sekke *coin* n
- سکه‌های ساسانی از طلا و نقره و مس بود. — Sasanian coins were made of gold, silver and copper.
81 | 929

1557 جنبش dʒombeʃ *movement* n
- اندکی از لرزش و جنبش باز دارم. — To keep it from moving and shaking a little.
72 | 1420

1558 سکوت sokut *silence* n
- او لحظه ای سکوت کرد. — He was quiet for a moment.
82 | 867

1559 دریافت کردن dærjaft kærdæn *receive* v
- مردم پیامک نوروزی روحانی را دریافت کردند. — People received Rowhani's Nowruz SMS.
84 | 741

1560 راه انداختن rah ændaxtæn *operate, launch* v
- دهقانان تظاهرات سنگینی علیه دولت به راه انداختند. — The farmers started heavy demonstrations against the government.
83 | 827

1561 احساس کردن ehsas kærdæn *feel* v
- آیا به طور مکرر احساس تشنگی می‌کنید؟ — Do you frequently feel thirsty?
87 | 626

1562 درمانی dærmani *therapeutic* adj
- فراهم کردن خدمات درمانی مناسب در مناطق محروم وظیفه ماست. — Providing appropriate health care services in underserved areas is our duty.
82 | 851

1563 حفظ کردن hefz kærdæn *protect, memorize* v
- بانک مرکزی مدیریت ذخایر ارزی را همواره انجام می‌دهد و سطح ذخایر را حفظ می‌کند. — The central bank always performs currency reserve management and maintains the level of the reserves.
92 | 382

1564 رویداد rujdad *event* n
- انقراض یک رویداد غیر معمول نیست. — Extinction is not an unusual occurrence.
84 | 749

1565 توقف tævæɣɣof *stop* n
- لحظه‌ای برای قدردانی از آن توقف می‌کنیم؟ — Will we stop for a moment to appreciate that?
86 | 646

1566 دیوار divar *wall* n
- کنار بخاری‌های دیواری، خوابشان می‌برد؟ — Will they fall asleep next to the wall heater?
76 | 1174

1567 پاریس paris *Paris* pn
- یک ساعت به پرواز پاریس گوتنبرگ مانده است. — One hour remained until the Paris-Gothenburg flight.
81 | 907

1568 تجدید tædʒdid *renewal* n
- The —— کاروانسرا ساخته یا تجدید بنا شده است. caravansary was built or renovated.

89 | 504

1569 ادب ædæb *politeness* n
- Up until —— تا بحال با تو با احترام و ادب حرف زده ام. now I've spoken to you with respect and courtesy.

85 | 729

1570 مبتنی mobtæni *based* adj
- آموزه‌های نوروز برستایش پروردگار مبتنی است. —— The lessons of Nowruz are based on praising God.

87 | 581

1571 علاقمند ælayemænd *interested* adj,n
- او هم به آقا فوق العاده علاقمند بود. She was also extraordinarily interested in the gentleman.

83 | 814

1572 درد dærd *pain* n
- با تریاک به عنوان یک داروی مسکن دردها آشنا شده بودند. —— They had got used to opium as a pain-relieving medicine.

71 | 1451

1573 مرور morur *review* adj,n
- به مرور زمان نیکی و بدی هم تغییر بیابد. With the passing of time both the good and the bad are changed.

88 | 549

1574 گفتنی goftæni *mentionable* adj
- گفتنی‌ها در این مورد زیاد است. There is a lot to be mentioned in this regard.

92 | 363

1575 روبرو شدن ruberu ʃodæn *meet* v
- همیشه برای روبرو شدن با رویدادهای غیرقابل پیش بینی آماده باشید. Always be prepared to encounter unforeseen events.

85 | 723

1576 چگونگی ʧegunegi *position, nature* n
- آثار مواد شبه‌افیونی بستگی به چگونگی مصرف دارو دارد. —— The effects of opioids depend on the circumstances of their consumption.

84 | 766

1577 واقعه vaye?e *event* n
- در تاریخ 12 اوت «22 مرداد» در بستر دریای بارنتس به گل نشست اما خبر این واقعه دو روز بعد اعلام شد. —— On the 12th of August (22nd of Mordad) it came to rest on the bed of the Barents Sea, but news of this incident was announced two days later.

84 | 765

1578 پیوسته pejvæste *connected, permanent* adj,adv
- زمان کمیتی پیوسته است. —— Time is a continuous quantity.

89 | 493

1579 کلام kælam *speech* n
- به یک شعر مناسب دیگر کلام را ختم کرد. With one more appropriate poem she finished her speech.

87 | 608

1580 روح ruh *spirit* n
- احساس کردم که روح خبیث پیرمرد، در من حلول کرده است —— I felt that the wicked spirit of the old man had been incarnated in me.

82 | 862

1581 اینک inæk *now* adv
- فقط اینک می‌فهمم که چقدر سخت و دشوار است برای اینکه یک چیزی انجام شود. It is only now that I understand how difficult it is for something to be done.

88 | 559

1582 الهی elahi *divine* adj,pn
- مرد دیگر حتما شایستگی نعمت های الهی را ندارد . . . —— The other man is certainly unworthy of divine blessings.

81 | 876

1583 منطقه‌ای mæntæye?i *regional* adj,n
- می‌توانند آزادانه در مورد حوادث منطقه‌ای و محلی گزارش تهیه کنند. —— They can freely report on local and regional events.

73 | 1335

1584 تفکر tæfækkor *thinking* n
- مبتنی بر تفکر شیعی است. It is based on Shia thought.

79 | 999

1585 ایمان iman *faith* n
- شکم گرسنه ایمان ندارد. A hungry stomach has no faith.

86 | 646

1586 تمایل tæmajol *tendency* n
- در صورت تمایل می توانید قسمتی از مصاحبه را گوش دهید یا دانلود نمائید. If you are so inclined, you can listen to or download part of the interview.

86 | 658

1587 آموختن amuxtæn *learn, teach* n,v
- قبل از ورود به مدرسه فارسی، انگلیسی و عربی را نزد پدر آموخت. Before he went to school, he learned Persian, English and Arabic at his father's side.

87 | 607

1588 سازنده sazænde *manufacturer, constructive* adj,n
- در تقویت جبهات نقش اساسی و سازنده داشت. He had a fundamental and productive role in strengthening the fronts.

86 | 627

1589 مشهد mæʃhæd *Mashhad* pn
- همان شب از مشهد حرکت کرد. They moved from Mashhad that very night.

82 | 861

1590 خاورمیانه xaværemijane *Middle East* pn
- کُویت کشوری در خاورمیانه است. — Kuwait is a middle eastern country.
72 | 1388

1591 مال mal *property* n
- چون تو مال من هستی! — Because you are mine!
76 | 1183

1592 احیا ehja *revival* n
- شاید بتوان با تغییراتی در این توافق آن را دوباره احیا کرد. — Maybe with these changes to the agreement it can be revived again.
87 | 588

1593 شیر ʃir *milk, lion* n
- هنوز دهانت بوی شیر می‌دهد. — Your breath still smells like milk.
78 | 1047

1594 مفید mofid *useful* adj
- می توانند اطلاعات مفیدی را در زمینه های مختلف در اختیار شما قرار دهند. — They can provide you with useful information in various fields.
84 | 728

1595 سیاه sijah *black* adj
- موهای سیاه بلندش روی پیشانی اش افتاده بود. — Her long black hair had fallen on her forehead.
72 | 1379

1596 پیمان pejman *pact* n,pn
- جنگ مجارها و عثمانی‌ها سرانجام با انعقاد پیمانی در سال ۱۶۹۹ پایان یافت. — The war between Hungarians and Ottomans finally ended with the conclusion of a treaty in the year 1699.
81 | 886

1597 سفید sefid *white* adj
- خیلی‌ها اسب سفید را دیده‌اند. — Many have seen the white horse.
77 | 1077

1598 کوتاهی kutahi *brevity, negligence* adj,n
- کوتاهی را در ایمنی پرواز از هیچکس نمی‌پذیرم. — I will not accept any misstep in flight safety from anyone.
90 | 422

1599 نبرد næbærd, næbord *battle, didn't carry* n,v
- نبردی دریایی که کمتر از آن یاد می‌شود. — A naval battle that's least remembered.
85 | 659

1600 خسارت xesaræt *damage* n
- خوزستان از جمله استان‌هایی است که در طول جنگ هشت ساله دچار خسارت فراوانی شد. — Khuzestan is among the provinces that suffered lots of damage during the 8 year war.
83 | 769

1601 معرض mæʔræz *exhibition hall, exposure* n
- چه کسانی بیشتر در معرض ابتلا به سندرم قلب شکسته هستند؟ — What people are more prone to suffering from the syndrome of a broken heart?
82 | 836

1602 باقی ماندن baγi mandæn *remain* v
- یکی از فواید پیاده روی این است که روحیه شما در طول روز بشاش باقی می ماند. — One of the benefits of walking is that your mood remains cheerful the rest of the day.
83 | 764

1603 چالش ʧaleʃ *challenge* n
- این شهر با چالش‌های مختلفی روبه‌روست. — This city is facing various challenges.
76 | 1137

1604 مطمئن motmæʔen *sure* adj
- مطمئنم که می تونی. — I am sure that you can.
85 | 689

1605 باغ baγ *garden* n
- امشب در فلان باغ مهمان تو هستیم. — Tonight we are your guest in such and such a garden.
78 | 1035

1606 حسینی hosejni *Hosseini* pn
- مراسم تاسوعا و عاشورای حسینی و دیگر مراسم های ملی ـ مذهبی نیز نیاز به مجوز دارد. — The Hossein-related ceremonies of Tasu'a and Ashura and other national-religious ceremonies also require a permit.
84 | 732

1607 نماد næmad *symbol* adj,n
- طی معاملات این هفته بورس، ۲۳۹ نماد بازدهی مثبت را نصیب سهامداران خود کردند . . . — During this week's stock transactions, 239 ticker symbols yielded positive returns for their shareholders . . .
88 | 537

1608 ماجرا madʒæra *adventure* n
- پسر پادشاه هم رفت ماجرا را رساند به گوش مادرش و مادرش هم به پادشاه گفت. — The king's son went and recounted the adventure to his mother, and his mother also told the king.
82 | 852

1609 نقد næγd *cash, critique* adj,n
- پول نقد داشتیم. — We had cash.
78 | 1030

1610 جناب dʒenab *excellency* n
- نه جناب اسم نوکرتان کاظم نیست رمضان است. — No sir. Your servant's name isn't Kazem, it's Ramezan.
81 | 886

1611 قرآن γorʔan *Koran* pn
- علوم دینی و قرآن را آموخت. — He studied the religious sciences and the Koran.
72 | 1389

10 Food

Rank	Headword	Pronunciation	Gloss	Rank	Headword	Pronunciation	Gloss
179	آب	ab	water	6590	گردو	gerdu	walnut
373	رشته	reʃte	noodle	6607	صبحانه	sobhane	breakfast
1054	ماست	mast	yogurt	6623	بادام	badam	almond
1203	سیر	sir	garlic	6643	سبزیجات	sæbzidʒat	vegetables
1275	غذا	ɣæza	food	6665	چنگال	ʧængal	fork
1365	شور	ʃur	salty	6712	آش	aʃ	thick soup
1434	ماهی	mahi	fish	6749	مزه	mæzze	taste
1521	شیرین	ʃirin	sweet	6752	کافه	kafe	cafe
1593	شیر	ʃir	milk	7087	توت	tut	mulberry
1635	گوشت	guʃt	meat	7460	ناهار	nahar	lunch
1640	نان	nan	bread	7496	کارد	kard	knife
1869	میوه	mive	fruit	7719	گلاب	golab	rose water
2250	تلخ	tælx	bitter	7840	موز	mowz	banana
2425	گندم	gændom	wheat	7955	حبوبات	hobubat	legumes
2426	برنج	berendʒ	rice	8077	گیلاس	gilas	cherry
2449	خام	xam	raw	8289	کباب	kæbab	kabob
2527	چای	ʧaj	tea	8752	فنجان	fendʒan	cup
2557	مرغ	morɣ	fowl	9119	سیبزمینی	sibzæmini	potato
2683	نمک	næmæk	salt	9177	دوغ	duɣ	yogurt drink
3037	قند	ɣænd	lump sugar	9368	بشقاب	boʃɣab	plate
3417	شیرینی	ʃirini	sweet, pastry	9556	ترشی	torʃi	pickles
3460	شام	ʃam	dinner	9782	هویج	hævidʒ	carrot
3630	رستوران	restoran	restaurant	10113	سرکه	serke	vinegar
4177	سبزی	sæbzi	greens	10123	لوبیا	lubija	bean
4383	فلفل	felfel	pepper	10496	گوساله	gusale	calf, veal
4538	سیب	sib	apple	10953	ادویه	ædvije	spices
4952	قهوه	ɣæhve	coffee	11058	آشپزی	aʃpæzi	cuisine
4957	کاسه	kase	bowl	11356	سوپ	sup	soup
5077	پخته	poxte	cooked	11742	پلو	polow	steamed rice
5081	نوشابه	nuʃabe	drink	12106	خامه	xame	cream
5298	پیاز	pijaz	onion	12555	کشک	kæʃk	whey
5314	آرد	ard	flour	12952	آلو	alu	plum
5335	انگور	ængur	grape	13043	خیار	xijar	cucumber
5854	پرتقال	porteɣal	orange	13173	آجیل	adʒil	roasted nuts, seeds
5902	بره	bærre	lamb	14070	آشپز	aʃpæz	cook
5988	آشپزخانه	aʃpæzxane	kitchen	16681	عدس	ædæs	lentil
6019	خاویار	xavijar	caviar	17067	آبمیوه	abmive	juice
6185	قاشق	ɣaʃoɣ	spoon	17262	فندق	fændoɣ	hazelnut
6213	شراب	ʃærab	wine	19771	شاهتوت	ʃahtut	black mulberry
6227	عسل	æsæl	honey				

1612 دخالت dexɑlæt *interference* n
- خیلی دارد دخالت میکند تو کار شماها. — He is interfering in your affairs a lot.
72 | 1359

1613 عزت ezzæt *esteem* n
- ایران کشوری بود که هر بخشی آهنگ جداگانه ای می نواخت؛ از عزت و عظمت ایران در آن دورانها خبری نبود. — Iran was a country every part of which played a separate song; there was no awareness of the glory and magnificence of Iran in those ages.
92 | 363

1614 یونان junɑn *Greece* pn
- آتن ثروتمندترین و بزرگترین ناحیه شهری یونان بود. — Athens was the wealthiest and largest urban area in Greece.
71 | 1415

1615 حافظ hafez *keeper, Hafez* n,pn
- می خواهید برایتان مثل حافظ غزل و مثل انوری قصیده بسازم. — You want me to write ghazals for you like Hafez and qasidas like Anvari.
83 | 774

1616 توپ tup *ball, cannon* n
- باید توپ زد! — The ball must be kicked!
86 | 624

1617 جبران dʒobrɑn *compensation* n
- می خواهم جبران کنم شما زندگی پسرم را نجات دادی. — I want to compensate you, you saved my son's life.
87 | 554

1618 پایانی pɑjɑni *final* adj,n
- او در سالهای پایانی با فقر دست به گریبان بود. — In the final years of life he was grappling with poverty.
74 | 1244

1619 جریمه dʒærime *fine* n
- بیست تومن جریمه دارد. — It has a fine of twenty toman.
84 | 714

1620 نفس næfæs, næfs *breath, spirit* n
- میرزا نفسی کشید. — Mirza took a breath.
79 | 970

1621 فن fæn *technique* n,pn
- دوره آموزشی اصول و فنون روزنامهنگاری برگزار میشود. — A training course in the principles and techniques of journalism will be held.
87 | 560

1622 روزه ruze *fast* adj,n
- من هم که روزه بودم و هوا هم گرم بود احساس خفگی می کردم. — I was fasting, it was hot, so I was feeling suffocated.
79 | 943

1623 نادیده گرفتن nɑdide gereftæn *overlook* v
- نقش تهران را نباید نادیده گرفت. — Tehran's role should not be ignored.
91 | 399

1624 اکثریت æksærijjæt *majority* n,q
- اکثریت مردم رومانی مسیحی هستند. — The majority of the people of Romania are Christian.
81 | 840

1625 بستر bestær *bed* n
- مقدار زیادی نفت خام در صخره‌های زیر بستر دریا وجود دارد. — There are large amounts of crude oil in the rock formations under the sea bed.
86 | 602

1626 شرح ʃærh *explaining* n
- شرح می دهم که تو چه جور جانم را نجات دادی. — I will describe how you saved my wife.
78 | 1028

1627 گرایش gerɑjeʃ *tendency* n
- یهودیان ایرانی در این کشور به سمت فعالیت در بخش خصوصی گرایش دارند. — Iranian Jews in this country are inclined towards activities in the private sector.
83 | 751

1628 ارشد ærʃæd *elder, senior* adj
- این تقریباً برای نخستین بار است که یک مقام ارشد دولتی به این صراحت از مخالفت عده‌ای در داخل کشور با لغو تحریم‌ها سخن گفته است. — This is pretty much the first time that a senior government official has talked with such candor about the opposition by a group within the country to the lifting of sanctions.
84 | 718

1629 سخن گفتن soxæn goftæn *speak, talk* v
- آیا ربطی بین سخن گفتن و موفقیت و محبوبیت می‌بینید. — Do you see a connection between speaking and success and popularity?
80 | 937

1630 فراز færɑz *top* n
- هواپیما بر فراز شهر شیراز چرخی زد و فرود آمد. — The plane circled once above the city of Shiraz and then landed.
91 | 374

1631 فاجعه fɑdʒeʔe *disaster* n
- پیکنیک بدون نمک یک فاجعه خواهد بود. — A picnic without salt will be a tragedy.
90 | 450

1632 متعلق mottæʔælleɣ *belonging* adj
- مهمانخانه کوچکی را که متعلق به مدیر مدرسه محلی بود. — It was a small guesthouse that belonged to the principal of the local school.
82 | 787

1633 مسیحی mæsihi *Christian* adj,n
- جمعیت مسلمانان اروپا تا سال ۲۰۵۰ با جمعیت مسیحیان در اروپا برابر می‌شود. — The Muslim population of Europe will match the Christian population by the year 2050.
90 | 449

1634 دوست داشتن dust dɑʃtæn *like* v

- من خیلی دوست دارم کنار ساحل قدم بزنم. — I really love to take walks along the beach.

72 | 1357

1635 گوشت ɡuʃt *meat* n

- کتاب آشپزی بدون گوشت را هم توی خانه دارم. — At home I also have the book about cooking without meat.

82 | 796

1636 بله bæle *yes* n

- گفتم بله ده سال پیش عمرش را داد به شما. — I said yes, he gave his life to you ten years ago.

72 | 1360

1637 برخوردار bærxordar *in possession of* adj,v

- در حال حاضر تولید از شرایط خوبی برخوردار نیست. — At the present, production is not enjoying very good conditions.

83 | 755

1638 فرش færʃ, forʃ *carpet, silt* n

- اولین تصمیم او هم خرید یک فرش و نیز یک صندلی ارگونومیک برای دفترش بود. — His first decision was to buy both a rug and an ergonomic chair for his office.

84 | 724

1639 آشنا aʃna *familiar* adj,n

- برای مدت طولانی از احوال اقوام و آشنایان خود بی خبر می‌ماندیم. — We have remained unaware of the state of our clan and out of touch with our relatives for a long time.

85 | 659

1640 نان nan *bread* n

- بوی نان تازه. — The smell of fresh bread.

77 | 1044

1641 ولایت velɑjæt *province* n

- این اثر تاریخی در یک کیلومتری شرق ولایت در بالای تپه موقعیت داشته و تقریبا 30 درصد آن تخریب شده است. — This historic site is located one kilometer east of the province at the top of a hill and nearly 30 percent of it has been destroyed.

56 | 2309

1642 باران bɑrɑn *rain* n

- صدای باران را نشنیدم. — I didn't hear the sound of the rain.

79 | 947

1643 مستقر mostæɣærr *established* adj

- مامور دیگری در آنجا مستقر بود. — Another agent was stationed there.

84 | 690

1644 قاتل ɣɑtel *killer* adj,n

- قاتلان وی تا کنون شناسایی و دستگیر نشده اند. — His killers have not been identified and arrested so far.

94 | 262

1645 انتها enteha *end* n

- به انتهای راهرو برسد. — He should arrive at the end of the corridor.

89 | 449

1646 راننده rɑnænde *driver* n

- راننده جان مسافرانش را نجات داد. — The driver saved the lives of his passengers.

82 | 784

1647 بیانگر bæjɑnɡær *expressive, indicative* adj,n

- بیانگر عدم توجه به ضوابط فوق الاشاره بود. — It was indicative of their lack of attention to the aforementioned criteria.

90 | 411

1648 خطاب xetab *address* n

- بارها او را گنج استراتژیک اسرائیل خطاب کرد. — He has repeatedly addressed him as Israel's strategic treasure.

89 | 487

1649 مصوبه mosævvæbe *legislation* n

- چون تکلیف آنها مشخص نبود و همه اینها با مصوبه دولت تعیین و تکلیف شد. — Because their duty was unclear, and they were all designated and tasked by government legislation.

81 | 865

1650 مغز mæɣz *brain* n

- دوزبانه‌ها مغزهای سریع‌تری دارند. — Bilinguals have faster brains.

82 | 806

1651 فرماندهی færmandehi *command* n

- فرماندهی کل قوا. — Commander in Chief.

90 | 422

1652 کانون kanun *focus, association* n

- با تشکیل این کانون‌ها در مساجد ما کارهای فرهنگی و هنری را بیش از پیش به درون روستاها نیز تسری خواهیم داد. — By forming these clubs in the mosques, we will spread cultural and artistic activities within villages more than ever.

80 | 905

1653 آشنایی aʃnaji *familiarity* n

- آشنایی من با ساز از اینجا شروع شد. — My familiarity with the instrument began here.

83 | 733

1654 درستی dorosti *correctness, truth* adj,n

- امروزه تلاشهایی برای از مودن درستی آنها در جریان است. — Today, efforts are underway to test their accuracy.

87 | 537

1655 خمینی xomejni *Khomeini* pn

- همیشه با سلام به محضر آقا امام زمان (عج) و امام خمینی (ره) شروع می‌کرد. — He would always start with a salute to the presence of Imam Mahdi and Imam Khomeini.

75 | 1153

1656 پولی puli *monetary* adj,n
- منطقه یورو، منطقه‌ای که در آن تنها واحد پولی رایج یورو است. — The Eurozone, a region where the only monetary unit is the Euro.
  85 | 661

1657 دنبال کردن donbal kærdæn *look for* v
- شما می‌توانید با دنبال کردن آنها به گذشته بازگردید. — You can return to the past by following them.
  88 | 486

1658 پشتیبانی poʃtibani *support* n
- ایران به پشتیبانی از سوریه ادامه می‌دهد. — Iran continues to support Syria.
  88 | 522

1659 ساحل sahel *shore* n
- به ساحل دریایی رسید. — She arrived at the shore of the beach.
  84 | 684

1660 سیصد sisæd *three hundred* n
- بیش از سیصد نفر در کنگو کینشازا کشته شده اند. — More than three hundred people were killed in Kinshasa in the Congo.
  51 | 2684

1661 مقررات moɣærrærat *regulations* n
- این کار مقرراتی دارد. — This work has regulations.
  82 | 806

1662 بانکی banki *banking* adj
- همه دارایی ها، از جمله حساب های بانکی اش مسدود شد. — All of his assets, including his bank accounts, were frozen.
  78 | 980

1663 مخفی mæxfi *hidden* adj
- اعضای یک سازمان مخفی هستند. — They are members of a secret society.
  94 | 232

1664 رو آوردن ru avordæn *turn* v
- برای تسکین آلام خود به مشروب رو آورده‌است. — He has turned to alcohol to relieve his ailments.
  89 | 451

1665 عدد ædæd *number* n
- یک عدد به آن اضافه شده! — A number has been added to it.
  82 | 792

1666 فرستادن ferestadæn *send* n,v
- با عجله فرستادند. — They sent it hurriedly.
  72 | 1270

1667 منتظر montæzer *waiting, expectant* adj
- منتظر نماندم که حرفی بزند. — I didn't expect her to say anything.
  79 | 943

1668 نحوه næhve *method* n
- کارهای زیادی را به نحوه شایسته انجام داد. — She accomplished a lot of work in an exemplary manner.
  78 | 959

1669 استعداد esteʔdad *talent* n
- مخصوصاً با استعداد فراوان شمسی حیف است که او نیمه کاره تحصیلش را رها کند. — Especially given Shamsi's great talent, it's a shame that she quit her education in the middle of things.
  85 | 640

1670 تشخیص tæʃxis *distinguishing, diagnosis* n
- تشخیص و درمان زودرس بیماری‌های اعصاب کودکان. — Early diagnosis and treatment of neurological disorders in children.
  77 | 997

1671 اینگونه ingune *this kind of* adv,pron
- اگر اینگونه عمل شود. — If it is practiced this way.
  81 | 845

1672 تابستان tabestan *summer* n
- گرمای شدید تابستان بر اکثر نقاط این کشور حکمفرما شده است. — The excessive heat of summer is rampant in most parts of the country.
  83 | 722

1673 خوش xoʃ *good* adj,adv
- چرا می‌گویند شاهنامه آخرش خوش است؟ — Why do they say that the end of the Shahname is good?
  73 | 1208

1674 بهره‌برداری bæhrebærdari *exploitation, operation* n
- خط متروی شهر آفتاب فردا به بهره‌برداری می‌رسد. — The Shahr-e Aftab metro line will be put into operation tomorrow.
  73 | 1198

1675 کره kære, kore, korre *butter, Korea/globe, foal* n,pn
- آب یکی از پاکترین و مقدس‌ترین منابع موجود روی کره خاکیست. — Water is one of the purest and most sacred resources in existence on the planet Earth.
  74 | 1157

1676 احتمالاً ehtemalæn *probably* adv
- پدر احتمالاً مي داند زنش نسبت به او چه نظري دارد. — The father probably knows what his wife's opinion is about him.
  82 | 768

1677 علامت ælamæt *mark* n
- من علامت زدم «نه» — I marked "No."
  83 | 732

1678 کوه kuh *mountain* n
- اگر می خواستی از بالای کوه ها ته دره را نگاه کنی، جویبار را مثل نخ سفیدی می دیدی. — If you wanted to look at the bottom of the valley from the top of the mountain, you would see the stream as a white thread.
  71 | 1317

1679 درآمدن dæramædæn *emerge* adj,v
- بعد از اینکه از زندان درآمدم منتقلم کردند شیراز. — After I came out of prison, they sent me to Shiraz.
  79 | 915

1680 ملک mælæk, mælek, melk *angel, king, estate* n,pn
- بازار املاک در رکود است. — The property market is in a slump.
81 | 805

1681 نامیدن namidæn *name* adj,v
- آنرا فلسفه عربی می‌نامیدند. — They used to call it Arabic philosophy.
81 | 811

1682 هشتاد hæʃtad *eighty* n
- هشتاد و سه سال دارد. — She is eighty-three years old.
54 | 2402

1683 انتخاباتی entexabati *electoral* adj,n
- هیچ پیشرفتی در عرصه اصلاحات انتخاباتی صورت نگرفته است. — No progress has been made in the area of electoral reform.
83 | 715

1684 امروزه emruze *nowadays* adv
- امروزه قصه ها نمایش تکراری اند و دعوت کردن تماشاچی برای دیدن یک فیلم دیگر چندان آسان نیست. — Nowadays, the stories are more or less repetitive and drawing in a viewer to watch another film is not so easy anymore.
80 | 868

1685 هفتاد hæftad *seventy* n
- دقیقا هفتاد و سه روز وقت دارم. — I have exactly seventy-three days.
55 | 2265

1686 بیگانه bigane *foreign, alien* adj,n
- صورتی که همیشه با من بیگانه بود — A face that was always foreign to me.
83 | 701

1687 مزیت mæzijjæt *advantage* n
- اکنون از این مزیت برخوردار است. — Now he enjoys this privilege.
86 | 570

1688 مهندسی mohændesi *engineering* adj,n
- از دانشگاه صنعتی امیر کبیر مهندسی کامپیوتر گرفت. — She received a computer engineering degree from Amirkabir University of Technology.
82 | 761

1689 وفاداری væfadari *loyalty* n
- وفاداری‌اش را به شاه اعلام کرد. — He announced his loyalty to the king.
97 | 119

1690 تک tæk, tok *single/attack, tip* adj,n
- چرا تک‌تک تماس‌ها برای آژانس امنیت ملی آمریکا مهم است؟ — Why is every single call important to America's National Security Agency?
83 | 690

1691 ترس tærs *fear* n
- ترس‌هایم را از من بگیر. — Take away my fears.
80 | 865

1692 آسان asan *easy* adj
- سؤال خیلی آسان بود و به راحتی به آن پاسخ دادند. — The question was very easy, and they answered it readily.
88 | 483

1693 رویکرد rujkærd *approach* n
- متأسفانه این رویکرد اکنون دنبال نمی شود. — Unfortunately this approach is not currently being pursued.
82 | 770

1694 فتح fæth *victory, conquest* n
- فتح نهایی آذربایجان و ارمنستان در سال 25 و فتح نهایی فارس در سال 92 هجری بود. — The final conquest of Azerbaijan and Armenia was in the year 25 and the final conquest of Persia was in the year 92 AH.
89 | 423

1695 جنگی dʒæŋi *military* adj,n
- حملات هوایی عربستان به بازار مستبا یمن جنایت جنگی بود. — The Saudi air strike at the Mastaba market in Yemen was a war crime.
84 | 677

1696 قاره ɣare *continent* n
- تمام قاره کشور من است. — The whole continent is my country.
82 | 744

1697 صادر sader *issued, exported* adj,n
- بزودی خبر به مدیر بردند و «نظر به مقتضیات اداری» حکم صادر گردید. — Very soon they notified the manager, and "considering administrative requirements" the verdict was issued.
87 | 508

1698 ترور teror *assassination* n
- فداییان اسلام ترور های متعددی را انجام دادند. — Fada'iyan-e Islam carried out numerous assassinations.
81 | 813

1699 ادبی ædæbi *literary* adj
- مفاخر بزرگ ادبی جهان اند. — They are great world literary figures.
83 | 723

1700 بازداشت bazdaʃt *arrest* n
- در حال حاضر این شش نفر را به اتهام آدم ربایی، قوادی و ارتباط نامشروع و اقامت غیرقانونی در کشور بازداشت می کنم. — Now, I arrest these six people on charges of kidnapping, pimping and illicit association, as well as illegal stay in the country.
81 | 783

1701 المپیک olæmpik *olympic, olympics* n,pn
- چرا اینجا رُ واسه المپیک زمستونی اجاره نمی‌دی تا خرج و مخارجتُ دربیاری؟ — Why not rent this place out for the Winter Olympics to make money for your expenses?
78 | 922

1702 مدل   model *model* n
- ● — از همین مدل برای من هم درست می کنی؟ Will you also make me one of this model for me?
  82 | 721

1703 مبارک   mobaræk *blessed* adj,pn
- ● مصرف نشاسته و پروتئین در ماه مبارک رمضان، انرژی بدن را تأمین می‌کند. — Consuming starch and protein during the holy month of Ramadan provides the body energy.
  73 | 1196

1704 ردیف   rædif *row* n
- ● کتاب فروش ردیف کتاب‌های شعر را نشان داد. — The bookseller pointed to the row of poetry books.
  87 | 539

1705 مقصد   mæɣsæd *destination* n
- ● بهتر بود مقصدتان را می فرمودید. — It would have been better if you had told me your destination.
  88 | 462

1706 گذراندن   gozærandæn *spend time, pass* adj,n,pn,v
- ● هر ایرانی روزانه ۵ تا ۹ ساعت را در شبکه‌های اجتماعی می‌گذراند. — Every Iranian spends daily 5 to 9 hours on social networks.
  84 | 668

1707 واردات   varedat *imports* n
- ● واردات، فروش و مصرف آدامس در سنگاپور ممنوع است. — Importation, sale and consumption of chewing gum is banned in Singapore.
  78 | 949

1708 تسهیلات   tæshilat *facilities, amenities* n
- ● تسهیلات ویژه برای سربازان متأهل ارائه شد. — Special facilities were provided to married soldiers.
  77 | 994

1709 احداث   ehdas *construction* n
- ● مطالعات احداث این سد از سال ۱۳۳۰ آغاز شد. — The construction studies of this dam began in the year 1330.
  74 | 1114

1710 کلان   kælan *big, macro-* adj
- ● بر برنامه ریزی کلان برای رفع آلودگی های ناشی از توسعه و صنعتی شدن کشور تاکید کرد. — He emphasized macro-planning for the elimination of pollution resulting from development and the industrialization of the nation.
  82 | 732

1711 عموم   omum *public, whole* n,q
- ● این تلفن برای عموم نیست. — This telephone is not for everybody.
  88 | 462

1712 اثبات   esbat *proof* n
- ● در حال حاضر نمی توان برتری یکی از این دو الگو را به اثبات رساند. — At present, the superiority of one of these two schemas cannot be proven.
  85 | 582

1713 استراتژی   estrateʒi *strategy* n
- ● در حقیقت استراتژی او به شکست منجر خواهد شد. — In reality, his strategy will lead to failure.
  84 | 665

1714 اردو   ordu *camp* adj,n
- ● از اردو و تمرین هم هیچ خبری نیست. — There are no signs of exercise or camping.
  73 | 1167

1715 گوش   guʃ *ear* n
- ● این سگ‌ها گوش‌های گرد بزرگی دارند. — These dogs have big round ears.
  71 | 1289

1716 استراحت   esterahæt *rest* n
- ● این هفته استراحت کن. — Rest this week.
  92 | 300

1717 سنگینی   sængini *weight* adj,n
- ● مثل این که چیزی روی زبانش سنگینی می کرد. — It was as if he had something heavy on his tongue.
  90 | 395

1718 مخصوص   mæxsus *special* adj
- ● هرکدام از این گوشتها بوی مخصوص دارد. — Each of these meats has its own specific smell.
  84 | 636

1719 نگاه کردن   negah kærdæn *look* v
- ● شازده کوچولو رفت و باز به گلهای سرخ نگاه کرد. — The little prince went and looked again at the red flowers.
  65 | 1585

1720 پژوهش   pæʒuheʃ *research* n
- ● پژوهش‌های زیادی نیز سیگار را از عوامل اصلی سرطان می‌دانند. — Much research also considers cigarettes to be one of the main causes of cancer.
  73 | 1173

1721 معین   moʔæjjæn, moʔin *determined, assistant* adj,pn
- ● روز حرکت را هم معین کرده اند. — They have determined the moving day.
  82 | 738

1722 ورزشکار   værzeʃkar *athlete* adj,n
- ● بهترین ورزشکاران سال ۲۰۱۵ فینا معرفی شدند. — The best FINA athletes of the year 2015 were introduced.
  87 | 514

1723 تحریم   tæhrim *sanction* n
- ● هزینه‌های واردات کالا به دلیل تحریم‌ها افزایش یافته است. — The costs of importing products have increased due to sanctions.
  62 | 1734

1724 وادار   vadar *persuaded* adj
- ● این کدام اجباری است که به نوشتن دارم و چه نیرویی است که پیوسته دستم را به سوی قلم برده و مرا وادار به نوشتن می‌کند؟ — What is this obligation that I have to write and what power is this that always carries my hand toward the pen and compels me to write?
  91 | 353

1725 جنایت dʒenajæt *crime* n
- آمریکا در میان کشورهای پیشرفته دارای آمار جرم و جنایت بالاتری بوده است. — America, among developed countries, has higher crime statistics.
- 74 | 1101

1726 تمام شدن tæmam ʃodæn *finish* v
- رادیو دمشق می‌گوید جنگ تمام نشده بلکه به تعویق افتاده. — Radio Damascus says the war has not ended, but rather been postponed.
- 79 | 848

1727 تبعه tæbæʔe *citizen* n
- چند تبعه افغان را دستگیر کردند. — They detained a few Afghan citizens.
- 85 | 585

1728 جواد dʒævad *Javad* pn
- آقای جواد بهزاد عزیز — Dear Mr. Javad Behzad.
- 89 | 430

1729 لایحه lajehe *bill* n
- لایحه نوسازی صنایع در مجلس بررسی شده است. — The bill for industry modernization has been investigated in parliament.
- 71 | 1230

1730 والیبال valibal *volleyball* n
- سالنها را به رشته هایی مانند والیبال وفوتبال اختصاص میدهند. — They are assigning halls to sports such as volleyball and soccer.
- 73 | 1138

1731 شعبه ʃoʔbe *branch* n,pn
- بانک ملی شعبه باکو. — The Baku branch of the National Bank.
- 81 | 777

1732 قطعی yætʔi *definite* adj
- نه، باید قول قطعی بدهی، می ترسم اگر پیشنهاد کنم، قبول نکنی. — No, you have to give your definite word. I'm afraid that if I suggest it, you won't accept.
- 86 | 550

1733 پیرامون piramun *perimeter* n,prep
- بگذاریم و پیرامون سایر مسائل صحبت کنیم. — Let's leave it and talk about the other issues.
- 81 | 770

1734 نیت nijjæt *intent* n
- نیت باید خیر باشه. — The intention must be good.
- 91 | 335

1735 پارک park *park* n
- میرزا داشت پارک می‌کرد. — Mirza was parking.
- 76 | 1003

1736 تابلو tablo *panel, sign* n
- روی تابلو خوانده می‌شد: من کور هستم لطفا کمک کنید. — The sign read, "I am blind please help."
- 86 | 560

1737 تخلف tæxællof *violation* n
- تخلف ناپذیری این سنتهای خاصّ الهی که همواره باید مورد توجه باشد . . . — The inexcusable violation of the special divine traditions, which always must be paid attention to . . .
- 84 | 652

1738 اندیشیدن ændiʃidæn *think* n,v
- من می‌اندیشم پس هستم. — I think, therefore I am.
- 83 | 665

1739 جنبه dʒæmbe *aspect* n
- استان تهران مانند برخی مناطق دیگر کشور ایران جنبه باستانی ندارد. — Tehran Province, like some other regions of the country, does not have any ancient attributes.
- 80 | 827

1740 خالی xali *empty* adj
- ظرف خالی را روی اجاق قرار دهید. — Put the empty container on the stove.
- 80 | 827

1741 برگزیده bærgozide *choice, elite* adj,n
- برگزیده المپیاد دانش آموزی، دانشجوی مهندسی هوا فضا. — The one chosen for the student olympiad: An aerospace engineer.
- 81 | 748

1742 پاک pak *pure* adj
- استکهلم پاک‌ترین پایتخت اروپایی شناخته شد. — Stockholm was recognized as the cleanest European capital.
- 83 | 673

1743 دی dej *Dey* n,pn
- اواسط دی ماه است. — It's the middle of Dey month.
- 74 | 1104

1744 ربودن robudæn *steal* adj,n,v
- ربودن چهار هواپیمای مسافربری عمل جنگی نیست، عمل تروریستی است. — Hijacking four commercial airliners is not an act of war, it is an act of terrorism.
- 92 | 311

1745 مخاطب moxatæb *viewer, reader* n
- مخاطب اینجاست. — Your audience is here.
- 80 | 816

1746 کاظم kazem *Kazem* pn
- ومحمد کاظم نجفی — dnA Mohammad Kazem Najafi.
- 94 | 219

1747 پذیرفته pæzirofte *accepted, admitted* adj,v
- اطلاعیه ثبت نام ویژه پذیرفته شدگان سال تحصیلی ۹۵-۹۴. — Announcement of the special register for those accepted for the schoolyear 94–95.
- 85 | 603

1748 دکترا doktora *doctorate* n
- محمد مصدق نخستین ایرانی دارنده ی مدرک دکترای رشته حقوق است. — Mohammad Mossadegh is the first Iranian holding a PhD in law.
- 92 | 312

1749 کیلو *kilo, kilogram* n
- دهها کیلو طلا و نقره در ساخت آن استفاده می‌شود. — Dozens of kilos of gold and silver were used in building it.
- 90 | 390

1750 نوار *nævar tape* n
- چمدانم را روی نوار نقاله می‌گذارد تا از زیر دستگاه بازرسی بگذرد. — He puts my suitcase on the conveyor belt to pass through the inspection machine.
- 81 | 760

1751 محمدی *mohæmmædi Mohammadi* adj,pn
- حبیب محمدی در سال ۱۳۳۶ به تهران مهاجرت کرد. — Habib Mohammadi immigrated to Tehran in 1336.
- 87 | 487

1752 مدنی *mædæni civic, civil* adj
- جامعه مدنی — Civil society.
- 81 | 750

1753 سفر کردن *sæfær kærdæn travel* v
- وزیر خارجه یونان در صدر هیاتی بلندپایه به ایران سفر کرد. — The Foreign Minister of Greece traveled to Iran as the head of a high-ranking delegation.
- 87 | 502

1754 انتظامی *entezami security* adj
- اولین بزرگراهی است که نیروی انتظامی در وسط جاده روی دریاچه باجه ایست بازرسی دارد. — It is the first highway where the police force has a checkpoint booth in the middle of the road on the lake.
- 75 | 1024

1755 تشریح *tæʃrih dissection, anatomy* n
- وضعیت را برای رأیس تشریح کرده ای؟ — Have you described the situation to the boss?
- 87 | 509

1756 ناظر *nazer observer* adj,n
- کسی ناظر این اتفاق نبود که به کمک بیاید؟ — Was there no one witnessing this event who could have helped?
- 81 | 765

1757 بیستم *bistom twentieth* adj,n
- این آبشار بیستمین آبشار بلند جهان است. — This waterfall is the world's twentieth tallest waterfall.
- 86 | 534

1758 راست *rast right* adj,adv,n
- خود زرتشت هم به گفته ی شاهنامه همان زمان در طرف راست گشتاسب نشسته بود. — Zoroaster himself, according to the Shahname, was seated at the same time at the right side of Goshtasp.
- 70 | 1250

1759 تعطیل *tæʔtil holiday* adj,n
- نگرانی‌ها از تعطیلی دولت آمریکا و تاثیر منفی آن بر رشد اقتصادی این کشور تاثیر زیادی بر قیمت طلا داشته است. — Concerns about the government shutdown in America and its negative impact on the country's economic growth had a significant impact on the price of gold.
- 84 | 611

1760 خرداد *xordad Khordad* n
- ماه خرداد رسید. — The month of Khordad has arrived.
- 70 | 1283

1761 فضایی *fæzaji space* adj,n
- هابل اولین تلسکوپ فضایی نبود. — Hubble was not the first space telescope.
- 83 | 653

1762 سلول *sellul cell* n
- گفته می شود این نوجوانان با بزرگسالان در یک سلول نگهداری می شوند. — It is said that adolescents are being kept in one cell with adults.
- 81 | 740

1763 آسمان *asman heaven* n
- به آسمان نگاه کرد. — She looked at the sky.
- 78 | 876

1764 نرم *nærm, norm soft, norm* adj
- پشم آلپاکا از پشم لاما نرمتر است. — Alpaca wool is softer than llama wool.
- 85 | 589

1765 ضرب *zærb multiplication, assault* n
- به ضرب گلوله به قتل رسید. — He was killed by the strike of a bullet.
- 89 | 395

1766 رأس *ræʔs head, top* n,pn
- در عربستان سعودی در رأس حکومت مرکزی، پادشاه قرار دارد. — In Saudi Arabia, the King is at the top of the central government.
- 87 | 482

1767 شغل *ʃoɣl job* n
- چه شغل‌هایی افسردگی می‌آورد؟ — What jobs cause depression?
- 84 | 601

1768 شهرک *ʃæhræk town* n
- کلانشهر تهران دارای محله‌ها و شهرک‌های گوناگونی است. — The Tehran metropolitan area contains a variety of neighborhoods and towns.
- 79 | 854

1769 دانشکده *daneʃkæde college, faculty* n
- مرد جوانی، از دانشکده فارغ التحصیل شد. — The young man graduated from the faculty.
- 85 | 587

1770 دوری *duri, dowri distance, plate* n
- دوری از او برای من و مادرش بزرگترین مصیبتها خواهد بود. — Being far away from him will be the greatest of tragedies for me and his mother.
- 92 | 301

11 Health

Rank	Headword	Pronunciation	Gloss	Rank	Headword	Pronunciation	Gloss
375	دكتر	doktor	doctor	4233	پرستار	pæræstar	nurse
566	خون	xun	blood	4599	جراح	dʒærrah	surgeon
603	بیماری	bimari	illness	5103	روانشناس	rævanʃenas	psychologist
840	درمان	dærman	treatment	5494	داروسازی	darusazi	pharmacology
847	پزشکی	pezeʃki	medical	5640	كلینیك	kelinik	clinic
934	سالم	salem	healthy	5797	اورژانس	urʒans	emergency
978	متخصص	motexæsses	specialist	5852	عفونت	ofunæt	infection
1019	دارو	daru	drug	6010	جنون	dʒonun	insanity
1095	بیمارستان	bimarestan	hospital	6269	مریض	mæriz	sick
1129	پزشک	pezeʃk	doctor	6750	سرماخوردگی	særmaxordegi	common cold
1139	بیمار	bimar	sick, patient	6790	داروخانه	daruxane	pharmacy
1181	سلامت	sælamæt	health	6887	فوت كردن	fowt kærdæn	die
1239	بهداشت	behdaʃt	hygiene	6895	شکستگی	ʃekæstegi	fracture
1438	روانی	rævani	psychotic	7331	سل	sel	tuberculosis
1670	تشخیص	tæʃxis	diagnosis	7873	تندرستی	tændorosti	health
1828	سلامتی	sælamæti	health	7983	سوختگی	suxtegi	burn
1901	زخمی	zæxmi	wounded	8715	سرخک	sorxæk	measles
1941	جراحی	dʒærrahi	surgery	8835	اسهال	eshal	diarrhea
1991	مجروح	mædʒruh	injured	8920	سرفه	sorfe	cough
2003	سرطان	særætan	cancer	9509	استفراغ	estefraɣ	vomiting
2080	بهداشتی	behdaʃti	hygienic	9637	بیهوشی	bihuʃi	unconsciousness, anesthesia
2144	مخدر	moxædder	narcotic	9735	داروساز	darusaz	pharmacist
2333	دارویی	daruji	pharmaceutical	10102	حامله	hamele	pregnant
2372	روحی	ruhi	spiritual, mental	10380	آمبولانس	ambulans	ambulance
3177	جسمانی	dʒesmani	corporeal, physical	10391	طاعون	taʔun	plague
3224	ویروس	virus	virus	11702	تندرست	tændorost	healthy
3246	فلج	fælædʒ	crippled	11808	فشارخون	feʃarexun	blood pressure
3277	معلول	mæʔlul	disabled, effect	12480	آسایشگاه	asajeʃgah	sanatorium
3366	زخم	zæxm	wound	12885	پارگی	paregi	cut
3441	قرص	ɣors	tablet	13057	آمپول	ampul	injection, ampoule
3504	طب	tebb	medicine	14328	آنفلوآنزا	anfluanza	flu
3512	تب	tæb	fever	14423	آبله	abele	smallpox, blister
3681	ایدز	ejdz	AIDS	15087	عمل‌جراحی	æmæledʒorahi	operation
3799	ویتامین	vitamin	vitamin	16919	عطسه	ætse	sneeze
4072	دیابت	dijabet	diabetes				

1771 معادل moʔadel *equivalent* adj
- ظاهرا این رقم معادل ضرری است که در این چند سال متحمل شده اند. — Apparently, this figure is equivalent to the loss they suffered in the last few years.
76 | 944

1772 اسماعیل esmaʔil *Ishmael, Esmail* pn
- استاد اسماعیل که حدود 100 سال قبل فوت نموده. — Professor Esmail who passed away around 100 years ago.
89 | 409

1773 طبیعت tæbiʔæt *nature* n
- توی راه از تماشای طبیعت لذت می‌بریم. — On the road we take pleasure in watching nature.
80 | 806

1774 قضائیه yæzaʔijje *judiciary* adj,n
- رئیسی دانشگاه علوم قضایی به کمک قوه قضائیه می‌آید. — The president of a university of judicial sciences comes to the help of the judiciary.
72 | 1144

1775 مگر mægær *by chance* adv,conj
- مگر تو بادام می‌خوری؟ — Do you eat almonds?
62 | 1674

1776 معماری meʔmari *architecture* n
- معماری برای افراد معلول جسمی. — Architecture for individuals with physical disabilities.
76 | 945

1777 شاخه ʃaxe *branch* n
- دختر پا گذاشت رو شاخه هاش و رفت بالا — The girl put her foot on its branches and climbed up.
85 | 586

1778 مواجه بودن movadʒe budæn *confront* v
- از زمانی که مرکز مبادلات ارزی ایجاد شده است ما با یک نرخ دیگر در بازار ارز کشور مواجه هستیم. — Since the center for currency exchange was established, we have had a different rate in the currency market.
84 | 613

1779 کاربرد karbord *application, use* adj,n
- به علت کاربرد سرب در بنزین، چرخه سرب غیر طبیعی شده است. — Due to the usage of lead in gasoline, the lead cycle has become unnatural.
85 | 570

1780 ازدواج ezdevadʒ *marriage* n
- قصد ازدواج داشتم. — I intended to get married.
78 | 852

1781 واقع شدن vaqeʔ ʃodæn *happen, be located* v
- باغ ارم در مرکز شهر شیراز و کنار خیابانی به همین نام واقع شده است. — Eram Garden is located in the center of the city of Shiraz and along a street by the same name.
79 | 834

1782 فهمیدن fæhmidæn *understand* v
- وقتی به اتاق برگشتم مرده مثل مرده ها روی زمین افتادم و دیگر هیچ چیز را نفهمیدم. — After returning to the room, I fell on the floor like the dead and did not understand anything.
58 | 1885

1783 مسکو mosko *Moscow* pn
- آره تو اینها رو به مسکو هم میفرستی الان. — Yeah, now you are sending them to Moscow too.
73 | 1096

1784 ارز ærz *foreign currency* n
- ارز دولتی بهش ندادند. — They did not give him government currency.
70 | 1236

1785 دوربین durbin *camera* adj,n
- چشمتان به دوربین باشد. — Your eyes should be on the camera.
87 | 475

1786 شصت ʃæst *sixty* n
- زنی بلند قد، با موهای جو گندمی و حدوداً شصت ساله بود. — She was a tall woman, with salt and pepper hair, and about sixty years old.
54 | 2124

1787 ورزشگاه værzeʃgah *stadium* n
- در های ورزشگاه ها به روی بانوان گشوده شد. — The doors of the stadium were opened for women.
80 | 774

1788 قبال yebal *opposite, facing* n
- آیا با بی‌توجهی و بی‌اعتنایی دیگران در قبال این استعدادها روبرو هستید. — Are you facing negligence and indifference of others towards these talents?
79 | 818

1789 وام vam *loan* n
- پیشنهاد افزایش وام مسکن را بررسی می کنیم. — We will review the suggestion to increase the housing loan.
77 | 916

1790 تظاهرات tæzahorat *protests* n
- نتیجه تظاهرات گسترده مردم این کشور بوده است. — It's been the result of the people's widespread demonstrations in this country.
55 | 2093

1791 تنش tæneʃ *tension* n
- ما خواهان هیچ نوع تنش در روابط با روسیه نیستیم. — We do not want any type of conflict in relation to Russia.
78 | 868

1792 نمایان nemajan *apparent, visible* adj
- هر چیزی نمایان است. — Everything is visible.
93 | 244

1793 پژوهشگر pæʒuheʃgær *researcher* adj,n
- پژوهشگران باید شکارچیان خوبی باشند. — Researchers should be good hunters.
74 | 1037

1794 مرتبط mortæbet *linked* adj
- پایگاه های مرتبط با برنامه سلاح های غیر کلاسیک سوریه. — Bases connected to Syria's unconventional weapons program.
83 | 626

1795 ایرنا irna *IRNA* pn
احمد رمضانپور نرگسی دیروز در گفتوگو با ایرنا اظهار. ... داشت — Yesterday in an interview with IRNA (Islamic Republic News Agency), Ahmad Ramazanpur Nargesi stated . . .
61 | 1744

1796 آباد abad *place* adj
— During the time of the Medes, the area of Ghazvin was inhabited. ناحیه قزوین در دوران ماد آباد بود.
78 | 851

1797 وابستگی vabæstegi *dependence* n
من هیچ وابستگی عاطفی به تو ندارم . — I am in no way emotionally dependent on you.
88 | 424

1798 تماشاگر tæmaʃagær *spectator* n
این فیلم با استقبال بسیار خوبی از سوی تماشاگران رو به رو شد. — The film was met with a very good reception from the audience.
80 | 778

1799 نماینده مجلس næmajændeje mædʒles *member of parliament* n
البته این نماینده مجلس توضیح بیشتری درباره نتایج این جلسه نداد. — Of course, this member of parliament did not give any further explanation about the results of the meeting.
80 | 755

1800 بومی bumi *native* adj,n
ما باید مدافع فرهنگ بومی و ملی خودمون باشیم. — We must defend our indigenous culture and our own nation.
85 | 575

1801 کانادا kanada *Canada* pn
پسر من کانادا درس می خواند. — My son is studying in Canada.
82 | 701

1802 ثروتمند servætmænd *wealthy* adj,n
برای چه میخواهید ثروتمند شوید؟ — Why do you want to be rich?
91 | 309

1803 ترسیم tærsim *drawing, tracing* n
اهداف سال آیندهی خود را ترسیم کنید. — Map out your goals for the coming year.
90 | 364

1804 خاطره xatere *memory* n
عشق تنها خاطره شیرین دوران زندگیم است. — Love is the only sweet memory from my lifetime.
79 | 802

1805 هسته hæste *nucleus, core* n
این امر ناشی از وجود میدان های مغناطیسی قابل توجه در داخل هسته های این ستارگان است. — This situation arises from the presence of remarkable magnetic fields inside the cores of these stars.
57 | 1931

1806 اتحاد ettehad *union, alliance* adj,n
وی از طریق این مذاکرات قصد داشت از اتحاد بین مخالفینش جلوگیری کند. — Through these talks, he intended to prevent an alliance between his opponents.
83 | 625

1807 مبادله mobadele *exchange* n
کلیه مبادلات باید رمزگذاری شود. — All exchanges must be encoded.
83 | 635

1808 حل شدن hæl ʃodæn *dissolve, be solved* v
همه مشکلات مملکت حل شده؟ — Have all of the country's problems been solved?
90 | 368

1809 سرویس servis *service* n
زمینه کاربرد این شبکه ها بسیار وسیع می باشد، پارامترهای کیفیت سرویس درآنها متفاوت است. — The application of these networks is very broad, the service quality parameters in them are different.
74 | 1016

1810 میانه mijane *middle* adj,n,pn
در حال حاضر با فروپاشی اتحاد شوروی رابطه فرهنگی میان ایرانیان و مردم آسیای میانه خصوصا فارسی زبانان از نو برقرار شده است. — Now with the collapse of the Soviet Union, the cultural relationship between Iranians and the people of Central Asia, specifically Persian speakers, has been re-established.
85 | 550

1811 برتری bærtæri *superiority, advantage* n
نماینده دانمارک در مجموع دو دیدار صاحب برتری یک بر صفر شد. — Denmark's representative was in the lead having scored 1–0 in both matches.
80 | 764

1812 دستی dæsti *manual, handmade, tame* adj,n
نیازی به ساخت آن به صورت دستی نیست. — There is no need to build it manually.
81 | 711

1813 حل کردن hæl kærdæn *solve* v
سرانجام یکی از آنها را حل کرد. — She finally solved one of them.
92 | 266

1814 گرچه gærtʃe *although* conj
این پیست گرچه کوچک است، ولی کمترین مسافت را تا مرکز شهر دارد. — Although this resort is small, it is closest to downtown.
82 | 655

1815 مهار mæhar *control* n
در شرایطی که قیمتها مهار شده بود. — While the prices were controlled.
89 | 389

1816 ظاهر *zaher appearance* n
- من هم قبول دارم که بعضی ها هستند که شاید ظاهر رفتارشون درست نباشه ولی دلشون پاکه. — I also accept that there are some whose behavior does not appear correct but their heart is pure.
84 | 573

1817 حلقه *hælγe ring* n
- راست می‌گفت، مرد حلقه به انگشت نداشت. — What he said was correct; the man didn't have a ring on his finger.
83 | 632

1818 فروختن *foruxtæn sell* adj,v
- دستگاه حفاری را به چندصد دلار فروختند. — They sold the drilling machine for a few hundred dollars.
78 | 858

1819 گلوله *golule bullet* n
- گلوله های گرد آهنی بود. — They were round, iron bullets.
88 | 443

1820 دامنه *damæne range, slope* n
- این شهر در دامنه کوه‌های زاگرس قرار دارد. — This city is located on the slope of the Zagros Mountains.
84 | 590

1821 بالغ *baleγ adult, mature* adj
- دو زن عاقل و بالغ دیگرشان کو؟ — Where are their other two mature and wise women?
83 | 643

1822 خواب *xab sleep, dream* n
- روزها در مزرعه کار می کردیم و شبها از خستگی زود خوابمان می برد. — During the days we would work on the farm and at night we would quickly fall asleep from exhaustion.
65 | 1453

1823 برگشتن *bærgæʃtæn return* adj,v
- از برگشتن بچه‌ها هم می‌توانم حرف بزنم. — I can talk about the return of the children.
68 | 1286

1824 نوری *nuri light, Nuri* adj,n,pn
- نوری پس از درگذشت آیت‌الله خمینی از این سمت استعفا داد. — After the death of Ayatollah Khomeini, Nuri resigned from this position.
84 | 567

1825 مهندس *mohændes engineer* n
- داریوش صابری دکتر است، نه مهندس. — Dariush Saberi is a doctor, not an engineer.
72 | 1089

1826 نخست‌وزیر *noxostvæzir prime minister* n
- نخست‌وزیر بریتانیا. — Prime Minister of Great Britain.
64 | 1501

1827 انقلابی *enγelabi revolutionary* adj,n
- وی افسر ارتش فرانسه و یکی از انقلابیان آن کشور بود. — He was a French Army officer and one of that country's revolutionaries.
72 | 1117

1828 سلامتی *sælamæti health* n,pn
- روباتی که به فکر سلامتی شماست. — The robot that thinks about your health.
89 | 394

1829 گوشه *guʃe corner* n
- پسر جوان تنها در گوشه ای نشسته است. — The lonely young boy is sitting alone in a corner.
77 | 887

1830 اساساً *æsasæn basically* adv
- رباب اساساً سازی محلی است. — The robab is basically a local musical instrument.
89 | 405

1831 مرزی *mærzi border* adj
- دادگاهی در مصر توافق مرزی قاهره و ریاض را باطل اعلام کرد. — An Egyptian court declared the Cairo and Riyadh border agreement void.
84 | 578

1832 لیگ *lig league* n
- هفته سیزدهم لیگ برتر. — The thirteenth week of the Premier League.
66 | 1370

1833 محیط زیست *mohitezist environment* n
- آژانس حفاظت از محیط زیست. — Enviromental Protection Agency.
77 | 891

1834 بغداد *bæγdad Baghdad* pn
- از معالجه اطبای کاظمین که مأیوس شدند یک روز به بغداد رفته و یک طبیب سنی مذهب را برای من به کاظمین آوردند. — One day, when they despaired of the Kadhimiya physicians' treatment, they went to Baghdad and brought a Sunni physician to Kadhimiya for me.
77 | 848

1835 صادر شدن *sader ʃodæn be exported, issued* v
- حکم بازداشت ۴۲ روزنامه نگار در ترکیه صادر شد. — Arrest warrants were issued for 42 journalists in Turkey.
83 | 639

1836 ناتو *nato NATO* pn
- از سال 2002 تا 2004 میلادی سفیر کشورش در ناتو و در اوایل دهه 80 سرکنسول ترکیه در حلب بوده است. — From 2002 to 2004, he was his country's ambassador to NATO and in the early 80's was Turkey's Consul General in Aleppo.
61 | 1647

1837 چپ *ʧæp left* adj,n
- چشم چپش را باز کرد. — She opened her left eye.
82 | 673

1838 غذایی *γæzaji food* adj
- صنایع غذایی در آمریکا به کاهش نمک فراورده‌ها ترغیب می‌شوند. — Food industries in America are being encouraged to reduce salt in products.
74 | 1007

1839 سد‌ sædd *dam, block* n

- 43% of — ۴۳ درصد مخزن سدهای کشور خالی است. the country's dam reservoirs are empty.

80 | 722

1840 لیست‌ *list* n

- لیست چیزهایی را که زنش خواسته بود دوباره با دقت خواند. — He carefully reread a list of things that his wife had requested.

88 | 426

1841 گران‌ geran *expensive* adj

- خاویار از گرانترین غذاهای جهان است. — Caviar is one of the world's most expensive foods.

81 | 680

1842 معنوی‌ mæʔnævi *spiritual* adj

- جامعه بختیاری نیز باید با همه توان هم از لحاظ مادی و هم معنوی به کمک خبرگزاری بیاید. — The Bakhtiari community should also come to the aid of journalism with all its power, both in a material and a spiritual sense.

84 | 579

1843 ترجمه‌ tærdʒome *translation* n

- آن را برای ناصر ترجمه کند. — To translate that for Nasser.

74 | 992

1844 کوشش‌ kuʃeʃ *effort* n

- خیلی کوشش کردم. — I made a big effort.

87 | 474

1845 جوانی‌ dʒævani *youth* adj,n

- ثروتی بهتر از جوانی نیست. — There is no better wealth than being young.

82 | 651

1846 یهودی‌ jæhudi *Jew, Jewish* adj,n,pn

- چون من یهودی نبودم، اعتراضی نکردم. — Because I am not Jewish I did not protest.

82 |656

1847 تحرک‌ tæhærrok *movement* n

- عمدتا تحرک اجتماعی دارند. — They largely have social mobility.

88 | 432

1848 رودخانه‌ rudxane *river* n

- شیر پرید تو رودخانه و خر را که در آب غوطه می خورد کشید بیرون. — The lion jumped into the river and pulled out the donkey, who had dived under the water.

78 | 831

1849 طلبیدن‌ tælæbidæn *call, ask, require* n,v

- مقابله با آلودگی هوای پایتخت، مدیریت می‌طلبد. — Dealing with air pollution in the capital requires management.

86 | 501

1850 فساد‌ fesad *corruption* n

- دشمن درصدد ازدیاد فساد در کشور است. — The enemy seeks to increase corruption in the country.

67 | 1346

1851 دقیقاً‌ dæɣiɣæn *exactly* adv

- منظور من هم دقیقاً همین بود. — That's exactly what I meant.

85 | 537

1852 معیار‌ meʔjar *standard* adj,n

- عملکرد گذشته بهترین معیار برای سنجش عملکرد آینده است. — The best gauge for evaluating future performance is past performance.

81 | 681

1853 روحانی‌ rowhani *cleric, Rowhani* adj,n,pn

- مایلم به موضوع روز عرصه سیاسی ایران و سفر روحانی به نیویورک اشاره کنم. — I am inclined to refer to the topic of the day: Iran's political arena and Rowhani's trip to New York.

77 | 845

1854 عمدتاً‌ omdætæn *chiefly* adv

- عمدتاً بر اثر مواجهه جهان اسلام با دنیای جدید، — Mainly due to the Islamic world's encounter with the new world.

85 | 518

1855 تالار‌ talar *hall* n

- پس از اتمام جلسه ، در حین پذیرایی از اساتید و متخصصان در تالار — At the end of the meeting, during the reception for professors and specialists in the hall . . .

78 | 815

1856 فرستاده‌ ferestade *sent, messenger* adj,n

- شاه عباس صفوی فرستادگانی را رهسپار لاهه کرد. — Shah Abbas sent emissaries headed to the Hague.

85 | 530

1857 وسط‌ væsæt *middle* n

- وسط سرش طاس بود. — The middle of his head was bald.

74 | 981

1858 حفاظت‌ hefazæt *protection* n

- او همواره مرا حفاظت می کند. — He always protects me.

77 | 868

1859 بشری‌ bæʃæri *human* adj,n

- امیدوارم خداوند بهترین سرنوشت را برای ایران و جامعه بشری رقم بزند. — May God bring the best destiny for Iran and human society.

82 | 633

1860 بها‌ bæha *price, cost, value* n

- بالاترین بها را دارد. — It has the highest value.

81 | 709

1861 مردی‌ mærdi *virility* n

- سخنان خسرو در ظاهر فریبنده و حاکی از مردی و بزرگواری بود. — Khosrow's words seemed deceptive and were indicative of dignity and manliness.

79 | 773

1862 کمکی komæki *auxiliary* adj,n
- عراق به مرز های مشترک خود با سوریه نیروهای کمکی
اعزام کرد. — Iraq has sent assistance forces to its shared border with Syria.
- 93 | 231

1863 امارت emaræt *emirate* n,pn
- شارجه یکی از هفت امارتی است که دولت امارات متحده
عربی را تشکیل می‌دهند. — Sharjah is one of the seven emirates that make up the United Arab Emirates.
- 84 | 557

1864 کرسی korsi *seat* n
- نتوانست بیش از یک سال بر این کرسی بماند. — He was not able to stay in this chair for more than a year.
- 85 | 539

1865 مواجه movadʒeh *confronting* adj,v
- بعضا در یک شعر بلند ما با چند تصویر مفهومی مواجه
می‌شویم. — Sometimes in a long poem we encounter several conceptual images.
- 84 | 560

1866 بازرگانی bazærgani *trade* adj,n
- در سال ۱۸۵۷ میلادی یک پیمان دوستی و بازرگانی میان
دو کشور در پاریس منعقد گردید. — In 1857, a treaty of friendship and trade between the two countries was signed in Paris.
- 75 | 949

1867 کریم kærim *generous, great* adj,pn
- فینالیست‌های مسابقات بین‌المللی قرآن کریم معرفی شدند
— The International Holy Koran Competition finalists were announced.
- 84 | 559

1868 چنانچه ʃenantʃe *if* conj
- چنانچه باور نمی کنی ، امشب مراقب باش. — If you don't believe it, keep an eye out this evening.
- 80 | 725

1869 میوه mive *fruit* n
- توی یخچال میوه نداشتیم. — We didn't have fruit in the refrigerator.
- 82 | 659

1870 تعقیب tæʔib *chase* n
- کریم خان زند در تعقیب خان قاجار تا تهران آمد.
— Karim Khan Zand in pursuit of Khan Qajar came all the way to Tehran.
- 89 | 394

1871 اخذ æxz *obtaining* n
- پس از اخذ مجوز از سازمان مدیریت و برنامه‌ریزی
کشور. — After obtaining permission from the State Management and Planning Organization.
- 85 | 543

1872 سینه sine *breast* n
- چنگیزخان با یک ضربه ی دقیق سینه ی شاهین را شکافت.
— Genghis Khan cleaved Shahin's chest with one precise strike.
- 79 | 759

1873 محسن mohsen *Mohsen* pn
- مهمان ها خیلی دلشان به حال محسن سوخت. — The guests greatly pitied Mohsen's condition.
- 83 | 601

1874 نگهداری negæhdari *preservation, safekeeping* n
- نگهداری نادرست مواد غذایی باعث بیماری می‌شود.
— Improper storage of food causes illness.
- 79 | 770

1875 قلبی ɣælbi *cordial, heart* adj
- نیمی از حمله‌های قلبی هیچ علامتی ندارند. — Half of all heart attacks have no symptoms.
- 83 | 612

1876 لغو læɣv *idle talk, nullification* n
- وزارت خزانه‌داری آمریکا تحریم‌ها علیه ایران در زمینه
خدمات و تجهیزات زیست محیطی را لغو کرد. — The United States Department of the Treasury repealed the sanctions against Iran on environmental services and equipment.
- 85 | 517

1877 نژاد neʒad *race* n
- بعلت وجود نژادهای مختلف در کشور دین واحدی وجود
ندارد. — There is no single religion in the country due to the existence of different races.
- 69 | 1186

1878 مرتکب mortækeb *perpetrator* adj
- مرتکب گناه شده است. — He has committed a sin.
- 94 | 202

1879 سایت sajt *site* n
- سایت‌هایی که مسائل اخلاقی را رعایت نکنند فیلتر می‌شوند.
— Sites that do not observe moral concerns will be filtered.
- 74 | 947

1880 خوزستان xuzestan *Khuzestan* pn
- قیمت مرغ در سایر استان‌های کشور به غیر از خوزستان
نیز سیر افزایشی داشته است. — The price of chicken in the rest of the nation's provinces, except Khuzestan, has also increased.
- 82 | 628

1881 خودی xodi *insider* adj,n
- نیروهای خودی در انجام مأموریت خود توفیق نیافتند.
— The Allied Forces did not succeed in their mission.
- 91 | 304

1882 یادداشت jaddæʃt *note* n
- هرچه می‌فهمید به مادر می‌گفت تا یادداشت کند.
— Everything he understood he told to his mother to make a note of it.
- 84 | 557

1883 آشنا شدن aʃna ʃodæn *be familiar, acquainted* v
- چندی بعد معلوم شد که او با زنی به نام سوزان آشنا شده و رابطه دارد. — After a while, it was revealed that he met a woman named Susan, and he had a relationship with her.
- 89 | 386

1884 اصرار esrar *insistence* n
- هر قدر دختر اصرار کرد که او را با خود ببرد، پسر قبول نکرد. — As much as the girl insisted that he take her with him, the boy did not accept.
- 84 | 572

1885 ایستگاه istgah *station* n
- در یک سحرگاه سرد ماه ژانویه، مردی وارد ایستگاه متروی واشینگتن دی سی شد و شروع به نواختن ویلون کرد. — On a cold morning in January, a man entered a metro station in Washington, D.C., and began playing the violin.
- 80 | 718

1886 روزگار ruzegar *times* n
- در روزگار قدیم پادشاهی بود. — In the old days there was a king.
- 81 | 687

1887 سراسری særasæri *nationwide* adj
- در دانشگاه سراسری مشغول به تحصیل شدند. — They started studying at the national universities.
- 84 | 567

1888 فناوری fænaværi *technology* n
- بنشین و از فناوری لذت ببر! — Sit down and enjoy the technology!
- 67 | 1267

1889 افق ofoɣ *horizon* n,pn
- افق باز هم سرخ رنگ و پوشیده از ابرهای سیاه بود. — The horizon was once again red and covered by black clouds.
- 90 | 333

1890 تکیه tekje *reliance, stress* n
- و به قول خودت همه شان با تکیه به قدرت ظلم. — As you said yourself, all of them relying on the power of tyranny.
- 64 | 1418

1891 اجرا کردن edʒra kærdæn *execute, perform* v
- فقط تعداد اندکی آهنگ‌های جدیدشان را اجرا کردند. — They only played a small number of their new songs.
- 89 | 370

1892 مشتری moʃtæri *customer, Jupiter* n,pn
- مشتریان دیگر با ناراحتی به آنها نگاه می کردند. — The other customers were looking at them uncomfortably.
- 80 | 716

1893 ظاهراً zaheræn *apparently* adv
- ظاهراً حق با شماست. — Apparently you have the right.
- 84 | 549

1894 محبت mohæbbæt *love* n
- سینما پیام صلح و محبت ایرانیان را به جهان می‌رساند. — Cinema delivers Iranians' message of love and peace to the world.
- 87 | 452

1895 بازیگر bazigær *actor* n
- بازیگر جوان پیشتازان فضا در حادثه ای عجیب درگذشت. — Young Star Trek actor dies in a strange accident.
- 79 | 766

1896 تشکیلات tæʃkilat *organization* n
- نیازمند تشکیلات حرفه ای است — It needs a professional organization.
- 79 | 756

1897 مذکور mæzkur *mentioned* adj
- نرخ ارز به سمت نرخ مذکور حرکت خواهد کرد. — The currency's price will move toward the aforementioned price.
- 72 | 1027

1898 شغلی ʃoɣli *job related* adj,n
- رئیس بانک جهانی از فرصت‌های شغلی می‌گوید. — The World Bank President talks about job opportunities.
- 84 | 533

1899 مسکونی mæskuni *residential* adj
- یک هواپیمای نظامی اندونزی در یک منطقه مسکونی سقوط کرد. — An Indonesian military plane crashed in a residential area.
- 81 | 668

1900 ورودی vorudi *entrance, input* adj,n
- ورودی تونل زیرزمینی. — Underground tunnel entrance.
- 87 | 446

1901 زخمی zæxmi *wounded* adj,n
- عباس زخمی شده و بی‌هوش است. — Abbas has been wounded and is unconscious.
- 72 | 1046

1902 زیان zijan *loss, harm* n
- زیان های جبران ناپذیری خواهیم دید. — We will incur irreparable losses.
- 86 | 488

1903 واگذار vagozar *transferred* adj,n
- هرگز نمی توان این امور را به وقت دیگری واگذار نمود . — These affairs can never be left to another time.
- 83 | 587

1904 قصه ɣesse *tale* n
- اما گه گاه که قصه‌ای می‌نوشتم می‌گفتی این قصه نیست، بیشتر یک گزارش است تا قصه. — But sometimes when I would be writing a story, you'd say that it wasn't a story, it was more a report than a story.
- 78 | 793

1905 مدال medal *medal* n
- تیم ایران با کسب سه مدال طلا، دو نقره و دو برنز بر سکوی نخست ایستاد. — The Iranian team topped the platform by obtaining three gold medals, two silvers, and two bronzes.

77 | 839

1906 ابهام ebham *ambiguity* n
- ابهامی وجود دارد. — An ambiguity exists.

87 | 427

1907 تولید شدن towlid ʃodæn *be produced* v
- اکثر این خودروها در کارخانه‌هایی تولید می‌شوند که ماحصل سرمایه‌گذاری مشترکی هستند. — The majority of these vehicles are produced in factories that are the result of joint ventures.

83 | 577

1908 تلفنی telefoni *telephone* adj
- روزی هفده بار با هم تلفنی حرف می زنند. — They used to talk to each other on the phone seventeen times a day.

88 | 401

1909 گرما gærma *heat* n
- می‌دانید گرما واقعاً ناراحت کننده است. — You know, the heat really is aggravating.

90 | 315

1910 مجدداً modʒæddædæn *once again* adv
- مرد اول درخواستش را دوبار دیگر تکرار می کند و مجدداً همان جواب را می شنود. — The first man repeats his request two more times and and hears the same answer again.

86 | 456

1911 کرمان kerman *Kerman* pn
- صدور فرش از گمرک استان کرمان آزاد است. — Carpet exportation through the customs of Kerman province is permitted.

79 | 724

1912 دانسته daneste *knowledge, known* adj,v
- حیف است دانسته‌هایم برود زیر خاک. — It is a pity to have my knowledge be buried.

86 | 482

1913 فولاد fulad *steel* n
- راه آهن دو ریل همراستا دارد که معمولاً از فولاد است. — Railroads have two parallel rails, which are usually made of steel.

79 | 726

1914 اقتدار eytedar *power* n
- اصلی‌ترین پایه اقتدار آن نظام محسوب می‌گردند. — They are the main basis of authority for the system.

85 | 491

1915 ماهه mahe *month* n
- بچه‌های ۶ تا ۱۰ ماهه هستند قادر در زیر آب به مدت ۵ دقیقه شنا کنند. — Children 6 to 10 months old are able to swim under water for 5 minutes.

82 | 605

1916 نگهبان negæhban *guard* adj,n
- نگهبان‌های مصری داشتند با هم گپ می‌زدند. — The Egyptian guards were chatting with each other.

73 | 1000

1917 نصب næsb *installing, installation* n
- تابلوی‌کوچک‌نصب‌شد. — A small sign was installed.

79 | 750

1918 بیننده binænde *viewer* n
- تحت تأثیر قرار دادن بیننده از اهداف اصلی و بسیار مهم محسوب می‌گردد. — Making an impression upon the viewer is considered one of the very important and main goals.

60 | 1605

1919 علنی ælæni *open, public* adj
- در ایران فعالیت علنی داشتند. — They were openly active in Iran.

83 | 569

1920 مشروع mæʃruʔ *permissible* adj,n
- با زنی دیگر روابط نامشروع داشت. — He had illegitimate relations with another woman.

84 | 549

1921 بیت bejt *distich, house* n
- پس از خواندن این بیت باز لحظه ای چند خاموش ایستاد. — After reading this verse, he again stood for a few moments in silence.

86 | 470

1922 رتبه rotbe *rank* n
- دانشگاه علم و صنعت رتبه اول دانشگاه‌های کشور شد. — The University of Science and Technology became the top ranked university in the country.

80 | 701

1923 ماهیت mahijjæt *nature, essence* n
- دانه های قهوه توانستند ماهیت آب را تغییر دهند. — Coffee beans were able to change the essence of water.

84 | 557

1924 دوستانه dustane *friendly* adj
- در محیطی دوستانه شما را به مقصد می‌رسانم. — I will take you to your destination in a friendly enviroment.

87 | 429

1925 جنگل dʒængæl *forest, jungle* n
- چرا باید جنگلها را حفظ کنیم؟ — Why should we protect the forests?

76 | 848

1926 حاج hadʒ *Haji* n
- حاج شیخ سعید قاضی یکی از نیکوکاران بزرگ است. — Hadj Sheikh Saeed Qazi is one of the main benefactors.

84 | 526

1927 حیوان hejvan *animal* n
- این حیوان همیشه در حال حرکت است و هیچ وقت در نقطه ای از آب ساکن نمی ماند. — This animal is always moving and never rests on one point of the water.

82 | 608

12 Last names

Rank	Headword	Pronunciation	Gloss	Rank	Headword	Pronunciation	Gloss
86	اسلامی	eslami	*Islamic*	2384	نیازی	nijazi	*Niazi*
170	بزرگی	bozorgi	*magnitude*	2454	واحدی	vahedi	*Vahedi*
233	ایرانی	irani	*Iranian*	2478	شیرازی	ʃirazi	*Shirazi*
396	زمانی	zæmani	*chronological*	2485	عظیمی	æzimi	*greatness, Azimi*
486	نظامی	nezami	*military*	2491	بیرونی	biruni	*external*
833	باقی	baɣi	*remaining*	2648	جعفری	dʒæʔfæri	*Jafari*
858	فردی	færdi	*individual*	2702	باستانی	bastani	*ancient*
871	قربانی	ɣorbani	*victim, sacrifice*	2710	افتخاری	eftexari	*honorary*
1039	کشوری	keʃværi	*state*	2718	درخشان	deræxʃan	*brilliant*
1042	فکری	fekri	*mental, intellectual*	2772	اقبال	eɣbal	*good luck, Eghbal*
1145	قاضی	ɣazi	*judge*	2773	توفیق	towfiɣ	*success*
1162	قهرمان	ɣæhreman	*champion*	2786	سعادت	sæʔadæt	*happiness*
1205	مقدس	moɣæddæs	*holy*	2834	رضایی	rezaji	*Rezai*
1359	مهاجر	mohadʒer	*immigrant*	2845	کریمی	kærimi	*Karimi*
1499	خاتمی	xatæmi	*Khatami*	2872	عزیزی	æzizi	*Azizi, dear*
1533	یاری	jari	*help*	2932	موسوی	musævi	*Mousavi*
1540	حقیقی	hæɣiɣi	*real*	2933	بازرگان	bazærgan	*merchant*
1582	الهی	elahi	*divine*	2949	فاتح	fateh	*victorious*
1606	حسینی	hosejni	*Hosseini*	3001	ظریف	zærif	*delicate*
1655	خمینی	xomejni	*Khomeini*	3003	آبادانی	abadani	*development*
1751	محمدی	mohæmmædi	*Mohammadi*	3036	فردوسی	ferdowsi	*Ferdowsi*
1824	نوری	nuri	*light*	3099	سعدی	sæʔdi	*Sa'di*
1828	سلامتی	sælamæti	*health*	3139	سروش	soruʃ	*angel*
1853	روحانی	rowhani	*cleric, Rowhani*	3142	مجاهد	modʒahed	*holy warrior*
1934	پهلوی	pæhlævi	*Pahlavi*	3155	حکیم	hækim	*wise person*
2011	طلایی	tælaji	*golden*	3219	رازی	razi	*Razi*
2057	جلالی	dʒælali	*Jalali*	3294	بهاری	bæhari	*spring*
2084	کشاورز	keʃaværz	*farmer*	3318	وزیری	væziri	*ministerial, Vaziri*
2234	طوفان	tufan	*storm*	3322	اصفهانی	esfæhani	*Esfahani*
2261	عراقی	eraɣi	*Iraqi*	3341	مرادی	moradi	*Moradi*
2295	هاشمی	haʃemi	*Hashemi*	3348	صمیمی	sæmimi	*intimate*
2298	گلستان	golestan	*rose garden, Golestan*	3365	تاجر	tadʒer	*merchant*
2324	برقی	bærɣi	*electric*	3385	انصاری	ansari	*Ansari*
2337	ریاضی	rijazi	*mathematical*	3408	بهبودی	behbudi	*improvement, gaining in health*
2372	روحی	ruhi	*spiritual, mental*	3435	رضوی	ræzævi	*Razavi*
				3453	سوری	suri	*Syrian*
2380	عباسی	æbbasi	*Abbasi, Abbasid*	3473	خیابانی	xijabani	*street*

(continued)

(continued)

Rank	Headword	Pronunciation	Gloss	Rank	Headword	Pronunciation	Gloss
3491	نوروزی	nowruzi	Nowruz	4283	خامنهای	xameneji	Khamenei
3526	صفوی	sæfævi	Safavid	4294	تختی	tæxti	Takhti
3540	تهرانی	tehrani	Tehrani	4297	جنگلی	dʒængæli	forest
3556	باقری	baγeri	Bagheri	4415	دوستدار	dustdar	devotee
3568	قاسمی	γasemi	Ghasemi	4456	یوسفی	jusefi	Yusefi
3581	نامدار	namdar	famous	4529	شکیبایی	ʃækibaji	patience, fortitude
3588	نصر	næsr	Nasr, help	4532	یزدی	jæzdi	Yazdi
3609	بهشتی	beheʃti	heavenly, Beheshti	4554	سالاری	salari	chiefship, -cracy, -archy
3625	شرف	ʃæræf	honor	4557	آزاده	azade	free, liberated
3637	غریب	γærib	strange	4569	مهاجرانی	mohadʒerani	Mohajerani
3854	بختیاری	bæxtijari	Bakhtiari	4574	اعتمادی	eʔtemadi	Etemadi
3859	کاشانی	kaʃani	Kashani	4598	صالحی	salehi	Salehi
3868	متولی	motævælli	custodian, administrator	4601	نجفی	nædʒæfi	Najafi
3925	کروبی	kærrubi	Karroubi	4690	ملکی	mæleki	Maleki
3957	ابراهیمی	ebrahimi	Ebrahimi, Abrahamic	4700	کاظمی	kazemi	Kazemi
3993	مجیدی	mædʒidi	Majidi	4712	لاریجانی	laridʒani	Larijani
3994	اکبری	ækbæri	Akbari	4718	مفیدی	mofidi	Mofidi, useful
4002	صادقی	sadeγi	Sadeghi	4722	قرآنی	γorʔani	Koranic
4024	شریعتی	ʃæriʔæti	Shariati	4732	حسابی	hesabi	proper
4062	تبریزی	tæbrizi	Tabrizi	4733	پهلوان	pæhlævan	champion, hero
4122	امیدی	omidi	Omidi	4735	آفرین	afærin	congratulations
4149	حیدری	hejdæri	Heidari	4781	امامی	emami	imam, Emami
4151	امینی	æmini	Amini	4810	علیزاده	ælizade	Alizadeh
4161	رفسنجانی	ræfsændʒani	Rafsanjani	4876	خرازی	xærrazi	haberdashery
4169	طباطبایی	tæbatæbaji	Tabatabai	4879	جنتی	dʒænnæti	Jannati
4186	حسنی	hosni, hæsæni	Hosni, Hasani	4919	استواری	ostovari	stability
4254	رحیمی	ræhimi	Rahimi	4946	محمودی	mæhmudi	Mahmudi
4272	فضل	fæzl	excellence, erudition	4956	ولایتی	velajæti	provincial
4275	سعیدی	sæʔidi	Saidi	4976	کلانتری	kælantæri	police station
				4998	سلطانی	soltani	Soltani

1928 قدیم γædim *old* adj,n
- بخش قدیم هرات شدیداً آسیب دید. — The old part of Herat was severely damaged.

80 | 695

1929 علیرضا ælireza *Alireza* pn
- چند هفته پیش علیرضا تلفنی به من گفته بود کلیدها به همان راحتی که در را باز می کنند قفل هم می کنند. — Several weeks ago, Alireza had said to me on the telephone that the keys that open the door, lock the door just as easily.

83 | 578

1930 یکصد jeksæd *one hundred* n
- یکصد تن مواد مخدر در کشور کشف شد. — One hundred tons of drugs were discovered in the country.

77 | 820

1931 کی kej, ki *when, who* adv
- شما کی هستید؟ — Who are you?
- 60 | 1586

1932 گزینه gozine *choice* n
- به نظر شما کدام گزینه پاسخ سوال وی است؟ — In your opinion which choice is the answer to her question?
- 84 | 548

1933 اعطا eʔta *giving* n
- بانک‌های دولتی چین هم معمولاً تسهیلات خود را به شرکت‌هایی اعطا می‌کنند که دولت چین در آنها سهام دارد. — Chinese government banks also generally grant their services to companies that the Chinese government has a share in.
- 84 | 528

1934 پهلوی pæhlævi, pæhluje *Pahlavi, next to* adj,n,pn
- در کلاس پهلوی من می‌نشست. — She used to sit next to me in class.
- 82 | 605

1935 فرض færz *assumption* n
- فرض محتمل دیگر در این مورد مربوط به روحیات خود نوجوانان است. — Another probable supposition in this matter is linked to the moods of the adolescents themselves.
- 82 | 600

1936 چقدر ʧeɣædr *how much* adv
- چقدر طول کشید. — How long did it take?
- 72 | 1024

1937 شایسته ʃajeste *worthy* adj
- چنانچه این خبر را شایسته تذکر می‌دانید، خواهشمند است کد . . . را همراه موضوع به آدرس . . . ارسال فرمایید. — If you consider this news worthy of mention, it is requested that you send code . . . along with the subject to address . . .
- 82 | 592

1938 افزون æfzun *exceeding* adj
- قدرت آن افزون شد. — Its power increased.
- 89 | 347

1939 حتماً hætmæn *certainly* adv
- حتماً برخی ردصلاحیت‌ها مرتبط با فساد بود. — Certainly some of the disqualifications were corruption-related.
- 67 | 1229

1940 حذف hæzf *elimination* n
- آیا می‌توان پرخاشگری را از رفتار افراد حذف نمود؟ — Can aggression be eliminated from individuals' behavior?
- 81 | 642

1941 جراحی dʒærrɑhi *surgery* adj,n
- پس از جراحی پدر نزد دکتر رفت و گفت . . . — After the surgery, father approached the doctor and said . . .
- 85 | 497

1942 منحصر monhæser *limited* adj
- من انسان منحصر به فردی هستم. — I am a unique person.
- 90 | 313

1943 استعفا esteʔfɑ *resignation* n
- متن استعفا نامه ام را بنویسم. — I should write the text of my resignation letter.
- 84 | 527

1944 منش mæneʃ *demeanor* n
- منش همیشه جوان دارد. — She always has a youthful disposition.
- 95 | 162

1945 معلوم mæʔlum *clear* adj
- معلوم بود بهترین لباس هایشان را پوشیده بودند. — It was clear they were wearing their best clothes.
- 77 | 807

1946 شوروی ʃowrævi *Soviet* pn
- بین تیم‌های برجسته‌ی امریکا و شوروی. — Between prominent U.S and Soviet teams.
- 76 | 815

1947 نود nævæd *ninety* n
- یازده هزار و نهصد و نود و نه ماهی کوچولو «شب به خیر» گفتند و رفتند خوابیدند. — Eleven thousand nine hundred ninety nine tiny fish said, "Good night" and went to sleep.
- 53 | 1951

1948 شکاف ʃekɑf *crack, gap* n
- شکاف هزینه و درآمد عمیق‌تر شد. — The gap between expenses and income became wider.
- 87 | 411

1949 بعید bæʔid *remote, unlikely* adj
- بعید نیست من چیز تازه‌ای بفهم. — It's not unlikely that I will understand something new.
- 92 | 265

1950 مشورت mæʃveræt *consultation* n
- اقدامات روحانی در سیاست خارجی با مشورت رهبری انجام می‌شود. — Rowhani's measures in foreign policy are conducted in consultation with the leader.
- 91 | 273

1951 نسخه nosxe *copy* adj,n
- قدیمی‌ترین نسخه آن در کتابخانه ملی پاریس نگهداری می‌شود. — Its oldest copy is kept in the National Library in Paris.
- 78 | 755

1952 پرنده pærænde *bird* n
- کمی بعد پرنده ها آمدند. — A little later the birds came.
- 77 | 790

1953 سعودی sæʔudi *Saudi* adj
- برخی از روحانیون تندروی سعودی با قانونی‌شدن «تعیین حداقل سن ازدواج» مخالفت می‌کنند. — Some hardline Saudi Clergymen oppose legalization of a "minimum marriage age."
- 86 | 447

1954 هیچگاه hiʧgah *never* adv
- ولی عجیب است که هیچگاه به گوش او توجه نمی‌کنی. — But it's strange that you never notice his ear.

89 | 368

1955 بلافاصله belafasele *immediately* adv
- بلافاصله مریض دیگری به مطب فرستاد. — He immediately sent another patient to the doctor's office.

86 | 457

1956 تبلیغاتی tæbliɣati *publicity, promotional* adj,n
- چطور از شر پیامک‌های تبلیغاتی خلاص شویم؟ — How do we get rid of SMS advertisements?

85 | 477

1957 برزیل berezil *Brazil* pn
- ولی به محض اعلام این توافق باراک اوباما، رسانه‌ها و کنگره به انتقاد از برزیل و ترکیه پرداختند. — However, as soon as Barack Obama's agreement was announced, media and congress criticized Brazil and Turkey.

76 | 810

1958 میراث miras *heritage* n
- میراث بشریت همین است. — This is humanity's inheritance.

72 | 986

1959 برپا bærpa *up, established* adj
- برپایی این جشنواره را عامل رقابت سالم در میان مراکز فرهنگی و هنری دانست. — He considered staging the festival as a factor in healthy competition among art and cultural centers.

85 | 476

1960 تعیین کردن tæʔin kærdæn *determine, appoint* v
- والدین می‌توانند صفات ژنتیکی از جمله رنگ چشم فرزند آینده خود را از پیش تعیین کنند. — Parents can predetermine the genetic traits of their future children, including eye color.

89 | 350

1961 موضوعی mowzuʔi *subject* adj,n
- تنوع موضوعی نقطه قوت جشنواره شعر نیاوران است. — Subject diversity is the strong point of the Niavaran Poetry Festival.

86 | 440

1962 جمهوری‌اسلامی dʒomhurije eslami *Islamic Republic* pn
- جمهوری‌اسلامی‌ایران تنها کشوری‌ست که هر دو المپیک (۱۹۸۰ و ۱۹۸۴) را تحریم کرده‌است. — The Islamic Republic of Iran is the only country that boycotted both the 1980 and 1984 Olympics.

48 | 2199

1963 کابینه kabine *cabinet* n
- با کابینه هاشمی رفسنجانی خداحافظی کرد. — He bid farewell to the cabinet of Hashemi Rafsanjani.

83 | 571

1964 بدهی bedehi *debt* n,v
- بدهی خود را به او می‌پردازد. — He will pay his own debt to her.

70 | 1088

1965 واژه vaʒe *word* n
- معمولاً واژه های پیام با حرف های دلش مطابقت نداشت. — Usually the words in the message did not match with the words in his heart.

77 | 802

1966 تلف tælæf *waste, casualty* n
- هر چه داشتی تلف شد. — Whatever you had perished.

81 | 632

1967 کویت kovejt *Kuwait* pn
- ناتو مرکز آموزش نظامی منطقه‌ای در کویت ایجاد می‌کند. — NATO is developing a regional military training center in Kuwait.

81 | 647

1968 قرمز ɣermez *red* adj,n
- پشت چراغ قرمز بودیم. — We were behind a red light.

79 | 723

1969 نظم næzm *order* n
- نظم و ترتیبی ندارید که عکس ها جابه جا نشوند؟ — Are you not organized enough to keep the pictures from moving around?

78 | 723

1970 رمضان ræmezan *Ramadan* n,pn
- اما ماه رمضان قبل از افطار که نمی شود کسی را دعوت کرد — However in the month of Ramadan one cannot invite someone over before Iftar.

80 | 661

1971 تفسیر tæfsir *commentary* n
- فقط تفسیر های خودش را قبول داشت. — He only accepted his own exegesis.

82 | 596

1972 تشکل tæʃækkol *formation, organization* n
- گسترش تشکل‌های علمی، ضروری است. — The expansion of scientific organizations is essential.

82 | 588

1973 پیشگیری piʃgiri *prevention* n
- برای پیشگیری از آسیب به مفاصل زانو و مچ پا کفشهای ورزشی متناسب با نوع هر ورزش بپوشید. — To prevent injury to the joints of the knee and ankle, wear the proper athletic shoes for the type of sport.

79 | 712

1974 شهریور ʃæhrivær *Shahrivar* n
- او — اواخر شهریور ماه امسال به ایران دیدن کرد. He visited Iran late in the month of Shahrivar this year.

79 | 692

1975 قبیل ɣæbil *kind, type* n
- از همین قبیل بکار می برم. — I use this very sort.

78 | 748

1976 تصویری tæsviri *video* adj,n
- اولین گزارش تصویری‌اش را در ۲۰ سالگی به چاپ رساند. — He published his first visual report when he was 20 years old.

85 | 473

1977 اندیشمند ændiʃmænd *thinker* adj,n
- اندیشمندان به روند تحولات اجتماعی کشور توجه دارند. — Thinkers are cognizant of the country's trend of social developments.

89 | 347

1978 برگشت bærgæʃt *return, returned* n,v
- راه برگشت را پیدا نمی‌کنند و درون قفس گیر می‌کنند. — They do not find their way back, and get stuck in a cage.

76 | 835

1979 مجاز modʒaz, mædʒaz *allowed, metaphor* adj
- شما مجاز نیستید. — You are not authorized.

84 | 510

1980 مأموریت mæʔmurijjæt *assignment, mission* n
- ماموریت مقابله با داعش ماموریت خطرناکی است. — The mission of confronting ISIS is a dangerous one.

78 | 721

1981 موزه muze *museum* n
- سیل در پاریس، موزه لوور را تعطیل کرد. — The flood in Paris shut down the Louvre museum.

72 | 964

1982 یورو juro *Euro* n,pn
- آیا تو حاضر بودی ۱۰۰ میلیون یورو برای بیل پرداخت کنی؟ — Would you pay 100 million Euros for Bill?

59 | 1559

1983 تحصیلی tæhsili *school* adj
- نحوه تاثیر سوابق تحصیلی در آزمون سراسری سال ۹۵ اعلام شد. — It was announced how educational background will influence the '95 university entrance exam.

74 | 897

1984 روان rævan *smooth* adj,n
- او پیکر خود را در آب روان می شوید. — He washes his body in the flowing water.

81 | 613

1985 بنیاد bonjad *foundation* n
- ساختمان این بنیاد در شمال غربی شهر ایروان قرار دارد. — The institution's building is located in northwestern Yerevan.

79 | 701

1986 بیکاری bikari *unemployment* n
- نرخ بیکاری در حال افزایش و سرمایه‌گذاری کشور با مشکلاتی همراه بوده. — Unemployment is rising and the country's investment is facing problems.

69 | 1081

1987 دستگیری dæstgiri *capturing, assist* n
- نیروهای امنیتی فرانسه و بلژیک به دنبال دستگیری او بوده‌اند. — French and Belgian security forces have been pursuing his arrest.

83 | 563

1988 زودی zudi *soon* n
- به زودی برایت پول می فرستم. — I will send money for you soon.

81 | 636

1989 پسندیدن pæsændidæn *approve* n
- اگر اینها همدیگرو دیدند و پسندیدند دیگه‌تمومه. — If they've seen each other and approved, then it's done.

91 | 265

1990 ناراضی narazi *dissatisfied* adj,n
- آیا از کار خود در ایران ناراضی هستی. — Are you dissatisfied with your job in Iran?

96 | 129

1991 مجروح mædʒruh *injured* adj,n
- توی جبهه‌ی جنگ مجروح شدم. — I was wounded on the battlefront.

85 | 495

1992 تولیدکننده towlidkonænde *producer* adj,n
- دولت حامی تولیدکنندگان است. — The government supports manufacturers.

75 | 828

1993 مصلحت mæslæhæt *expediency* n
- رئیس مجمع تشخیص مصلحت. — The head of the Expediency Discernment Council.

73 | 939

1994 تقدیم tæɣdim *present* n
- هر چی بفرماین تقدیم می کنم. — I will present you with whatever you request.

83 | 527

1995 جواب dʒævab *answer* n
- می خوای پرونده تو بیاره و جواب نامه تو بده؟ — Do you want him to bring your file and reply to your letter?

70 | 1025

1996 بشکه boʃke *barrel* n
- بیست دلار قیمت هر بشکه نفت افزایش پیدا کرد. — The price of oil has risen twenty dollars per barrel.

79 | 700

1997 نقاشی næɣɣɑʃi *painting* n
- همه نقاشی‌هایم را هدیه می‌کنم. — I am giving away all my paintings.
- 76 | 815

1998 خوشبختانه xoʃˈbæxtɑne *fortunately* adv
- خوشبختانه این مشکل قابل کنترل است. — Fortunately, this problem can be controlled.
- 83 | 531

1999 کودکی kudæki *childhood* n
- کودکی‌هایی که به تنهایی گذشت. — Childhoods which passed by in solitude.
- 85 | 470

2000 پاسخگو pasoxgu *answerable* adj,n
- چرا مسئولین پاسخگو نیستند؟ — Why are the authorities not accountable?
- 88 | 361

2001 ترکمنستان torkæmænestɑn *Turkmenistan* pn
- به کشور ترکمنستان عزیمت نموده است. — He has departed for the country of Turkmenistan.
- 86 | 451

2002 ضرر zærær *loss* n
- مذاکره با آمریکا چیزی جز ضرر ندارد. — Negotiations with America have done nothing but damage.
- 89 | 337

2003 سرطان sæɾætɑn *cancer* n
- میرزا دو ماه بعد سرطان کبدش عود کرد و مرد. — Two months later, Mirza's liver cancer recurred, and he died.
- 76 | 812

2004 شفاف ʃæffɑf *transparent* adj
- به طور شفاف می‌گویم. — I will say this transparently.
- 82 | 576

2005 سفارت sefɑræt *embassy* n
- پشت پرده حمله به سفارت عربستان چه کسی بود؟ — Who was behind the scenes of the attack on the Saudi Embassy?
- 79 | 683

2006 تحریک tæhrik *stimulation* n
- تحریک قوه خیال مخاطب. — Stimulating the creative imagination of the audience.
- 85 | 481

2007 قوم ɣowm *people* n
- دلم برای قوم و خویشم تنگ شده بود. — My heart had pined for my family and people.
- 73 | 913

2008 خراسان xorɑsɑn *Khorasan* pn
- خراسان از مراکز مهم موسیقی در میان تمدنهای بشری محسوب می شود. — Khorasan is considered one of the important centers for music among human civilizations.
- 70 | 1006

2009 قطار ɣætɑr *train* n
- شنوندگان گرامی هم اکنون من قطاری را از دور می بینم که از طرف جنوب به سمت ما می آید. — Dear listeners, at this moment I see a train in the distance that is coming our direction from the south.
- 86 | 430

2010 انکار enkɑr *denial* n
- ملموس نیست ولی واقعیتی غیر قابل انکار است. — It's not tangible, but an undeniable fact.
- 90 | 315

2011 طلایی tælɑji *golden* adj,pn
- دختركي با موهاي طلايي و چشمهاي سبز، بلند و باريك و سرد. — A little girl with blond hair and green eyes, tall, thin, and cold.
- 86 | 446

2012 همت hemmæt *ambition, magnanimity* n
- این کار بزرگ که با همت مردم قابل اجراست. — This great work that can be carried out by people's effort.
- 82 | 577

2013 اعتراف eʔterɑf *confession* n
- اعترافات زیر شکنجه معتبر نیست. — Confessions under torture are not reliable.
- 86 | 418

2014 تدریس tædris *teaching* n
- برنامه ریزان آموزشی طی سه دهه ی گذشته توجه خاصی به این پرسش داشته اند که چه چیز باید در مکاتب تدریس شود. — Over the last three decades, curriculum planners have paid special attention to what should be taught in schools.
- 69 | 1052

2015 همراهی hæmrɑhi *accompanying* n
- چند دقیقه صبر کنید من همراهیتون می کنم. — Wait for a few minutes, I will accompany you.
- 76 | 781

2016 آزاد شدن ɑzɑd ʃodæn *be freed* v
- وقتی آزاد شدی شاید بخواهی خاطرات دوران زندان را بنویسی. — When you are released you may want to write your memoirs about prison.
- 88 | 376

2017 متقابل motæɣɑbel *reciprocal* adj
- روسیه به تحریم‌های آمریکا پاسخ متقابل می‌دهد. — Russia gave a reciprocal answer to America's sanctions.
- 83 | 540

2018 پادشاه pɑdʃɑh *king* n
- محمد ظاهرشاه آخرین پادشاه افغانستان بود. — Mohammed Zahir Shah was the last king of Afghanistan.
- 66 | 1180

2019 تروریستی teroristi *terrorist* adj
- انفجار تروریستی در شمال بغداد ۶ کشته و ۱۴ زخمی برجای گذاشت. — The terrorist bombing in northern Baghdad killed 6 and left 14 injured.

66 | 1160

2020 نخبه noxbe *elite, genius* adj,n
- هر استعداد برتری نخبه نیست! — Not every great talent is a genius.

82 | 577

2021 ممنوع mæmnuʔ *forbidden* adj
- بندگی و سوداگری بنده در هر شکل که باشد ممنوع است. — Slavery and the slave trade shall be prohibited in all their forms.

82 | 551

2022 بیان کردن bæjan kærdæn *state, express* v
- رسانه ها چگونه حقایق غزه را بیان کردند؟ — How did the media state the facts of Gaza?

84 | 490

2023 تغییر کردن tæɣjir kærdæn *change* v
- اگر اجباری به تغییر نیست چرا تغییر کنیم. — If change is not required then why should we change?

90 | 299

2024 حداکثر hæddæksær *maximum* adv,n,q
- در تابستان حداکثر حرارت شهرستانهای ایرانشهر و زابل به ۵۰ درجه سانتیگراد می‌رسد. — In summer, the highest temperatures of Iranshahr and Zabol reach 50 degrees Celsius.

79 | 663

2025 نهم nohom *ninth* adj,n
- جواز حضور در نهمین دوره مسابقات جهانی جوانان تایلندرا گرفتند. — They got the permission to attend the ninth round of youth competitions in Thailand.

74 | 858

2026 دویست devist *two hundred* n
- دویست تا از خانه های شهر غارت شد. — Two hundred of the houses in the city were plundered.

54 | 1715

2027 شریک ʃærik *partner* adj,n
- شریک تجاری خوبی نیست. — He is not a good trade partner.

87 | 394

2028 فقیه fæɣih *Islamic jurist* adj,n
- اعضای شورای نگهبان از ۶ حقوقدان و ۶ فقیه تشکیل شده است. — Membership of the Guardian Council is composed of six lawyers and six Islamic jurists.

78 | 692

2029 ثابت کردن sabet kærdæn *prove* v
- چه طوری ثابت می کنی ، کار تو نبوده؟ — How are you going to prove it wasn't you?

92 | 229

2030 شادی ʃadi *joy* n,pn
- هر کجا هست عقل شادی نیست. — Everywhere there is reason, there is no happiness.

83 | 508

2031 داور davær *referee* n
- دقیقه 78 یوسف بخشی زاده بازیکن تیم بهمن به دلیل اعتراض به قضاوت داور از بازی اخراج شد. — At minute 78, Yousef Bakhshizadeh, a player on the Bahman team, was removed from the game for objecting to the referee's call.

80 | 641

2032 حیاتی hæjati *vital* adj,n
- وقتی حیاتی‌ترین مایع جهان مهلک می‌شود. — When the most vital fluid in the world turns fatal.

88 | 342

2033 تنوع tænævvoʔ *diversity* n
- تنوع مذهبی در شهر ارومیه بسیار زیاد است. — Religious diversity in the city of Urmia is very high.

84 | 471

2034 انجامیدن ændʒamidæn *end* adj,v
- درگیری دو کارگر نانوایی به قتل انجامید. — The fight between the two bakery employees ended in murder.

86 | 429

2035 تصرف tæsærrof *taking possession* n
- طلبکاران مغازه را تصرف کردند. — The creditors took possession of the shops.

85 | 458

2036 آسیایی ɑsijaji *Asian* adj
- دی کاپریو آخر هفته را با فیلها و اورانگوتان‌های آسیایی گذراند. — DiCaprio spent the weekend with elephants and Asian orangutans.

78 | 685

2037 ارشاد erʃad *guidance* n
- زمانی بود که وزارت ارشاد فقط به افراد متاهل مجوز نشر می‌داد. — There was a time when the Ministry of Culture and Islamic Guidance only gave publishing permits to married individuals.

71 | 963

2038 قدر ɣædr, ɣædær *magnitude, fate* n
- آن قدر که شما فکر میکنید سخت و بد نیست. — It is not as hard and as bad as you think.

70 | 989

2039 نسبی nesbi, næsæbi *relative, genealogical* adj
- عصمت یک امر نسبی است. — Chastity is a relative matter.

85 | 465

2040 مجوز modʒævvez *license* n
- وی عدم صدور مجوز برای اجرای متون خارجی را امری مثبت توصیف کرد. — He described the lack of issuance of licenses for performing foreign texts as a positive thing.

77 | 735

2041 پوشیدن puʃidæn *wear* n,v
- اکنون پوشیدن روسری در مدارس ترکیه مجاز اما در دانشگاه‌ها و سایر نهادهای عمومی ممنوع است. — At present wearing a scarf in Turkish schools is permitted but it is prohibited at universities and other public institutions.
78 | 687

2042 تشکر tæʃækkor *thanks* n
- از تمام زحمتاشون تشکر فراوان دارم. — I am very grateful for all of their trouble.
86 | 425

2043 صریح særih *explicit* adj,adv
- هشداری صریح بود. — It was a very explicit warning.
89 | 329

2044 جستن dʒæstæn, dʒostæn *jump, search* adj,n,v
- جستن این رابطه در دنیای واقع خطاست. — Seeking this relationship in the real world is a mistake.
74 | 820

2045 مقرر moɣærræɾ *arranged* adj
- تکالیف مقرر در آیین نامه مربوط. — Responsibilities stipulated in the relevant bylaws.
87 | 402

2046 اتفاقی ettefaɣi *accidental, occasional* adj,n
- زندگی معمولاً عجیب‌تر و اتفاقی‌تر از داستان است. — Life is usually stranger and more accidental than stories.
84 | 491

2047 رد کردن ræd kærdæn *reject* v
- مثل رد کردن آهنگی که که ... — Like rejecting a song that . . .
90 | 293

2048 صعود soʔud *rise* n
- در حال حاضر صعود فرانسه به عنوان تیم اول این گروه قطعی است. — At present, France's move to the top as the first team of the group is certain.
76 | 741

2049 سپردن sepordæn *deposit, entrust* n,v
- سپردن امور امنیتی به نیروهای ارتش و پلیس این کشور. — Giving security affairs responsibility to the army and police forces of this country.
80 | 608

2050 عجیب ædʒib *strange* adj
- خیلی چیزهای غریب و عجیب از او حکایت می کردند. — They relate a lot of interesting things about her.
77 | 731

2051 میلاد milad *birth* n
- کتیبه های معینی متعلق به قرن دوم پیش از میلاد کشف شده است. — Inscriptions definitely belonging to the second century before the birth (of Christ) have been discovered.
79 | 662

2052 فرق færɣ *difference* n
- فرق بین جوک و اصطلاح را هم که بهتر از من میدانید. — And you know the difference between a joke and an idiom better than I do.
77 | 733

2053 جانشین dʒaneʃin *successor, substitute* n
- جانشین امام خمینی نه مرجع است و نه امام. — The successor of Imam Khomeini is neither a marja nor an Imam.
86 | 412

2054 صادر کردن sader kærdæn *export, issue* v
- مقامهای انگلیسی بی‌درنگ دستور دستگیری او را صادر کردند. — English officials immediately issued the order for his arrest.
87 | 395

2055 متناسب motænaseb *elegant* adj
- استفاده از آیات و روایات متناسب با موضوع. — The use of verses and narrations appropriate to the subject.
83 | 524

2056 عقل æɣl *reason* n
- عقلش کجا رفته بود؟ — Where had their reason gone?
77 | 720

2057 جلالی dʒælali *Jalali* n,pn
- جلالی از سایپا برکنار شد. — Jalali was dismissed from Saipa.
86 | 417

2058 گشایش goʃajeʃ *opening, relief* n
- در مراسم گشایش همایش سراسری معلمان دوره آموزش ابتدایی. — In the opening ceremony of the nationwide gathering of elementary school teachers . . .
79 | 645

2059 پوست pust *skin* n
- از خوشحالی در پوست خود نمی گنجید. — He was so happy he couldn't fit in his own skin.
75 | 810

2060 خلیج xælidʒ *gulf* n
- خلیج بخشی از دریا است که در خشکی پیش رفته باشد. — A gulf is a part of the sea which has advanced onto the land.
73 | 876

2061 کوچکی kutʃæki *smallness* adj,n
- کوچکی و بزرگی تخم مرغها تأثیری در قیمت ندارد. — The smallness or bigness of the eggs has no effect on their price.
86 | 431

2062 آگاه agah *aware* adj,n
- خدا از غم‌های تو آگاه است. — God is aware of your sorrows.
82 | 548

2063 مشکوک mæʃkuk *doubtful, suspicious* adj

- این سه تن بخاطر مشکوک بودن شان از سوی نیرو های بین المللی مورد هدف قرار گرفتند. — These three people were targeted by international forces because they were suspicious.

92 | 215

2064 زاویه zavije *angle* n

- از هر زاویه میتوان عکس گرفت. — One can take a photo from any angle.

87 | 380

2065 بالا رفتن bala ræftæn *go up* v

- قیمت جهانی نفت بالا رفت. — The global price of oil increased.

82 | 531

2066 جلد dʒeld, dʒæld *volume, quick* n

- در کتابخانه این موزه بیش از ۵۰ هزار جلد کتاب وجود دارد. — There are more than 50 thousand volumes of books in this museum's library.

81 | 575

2067 مذهب mæzhæb *religion* n

- همه اقوام و مذاهب در آزادسازی خرمشهر شرکت داشتند. — All tribes and religions participated in the liberation of Khorramshahr.

82 | 550

2068 داوطلب davtælæb *volunteer, applicant* adj,n

- این آزمایش تاکنون روی ده داوطلب با موفقیت انجام شده است. — To date, this experiment has successfully been carried out on ten volunteers.

82 | 554

2069 ارتفاع ertefaʔ *altitude, height* n

- استوانه ای با 20 متر ارتفاع بود. — A cylinder with a height of 20 meters.

69 | 1004

2070 سیاستمدار sijasætmædar *politician* adj,n

- برای دولت و سیاستمداران آمریکا، ممکن است این جنگ عملا به پایان رسیده باشد. — For the American government and politicians it's possible that this war is effectively over.

83 | 512

2071 پیروز piruz *victorious* adj

- ملت کوبا در نهایت پیروز خواهد شد. — The nation of Cuba will ultimately be victorious.

81 | 568

2072 همبستگی hæmbæstegi *solidarity* n

- حج مظهر اتحاد و همبستگی مسلمانان با یکدیگر است. — Hajj is a manifestation of unity and solidarity of Muslims with each other.

86 | 407

2073 راحتی rahæti *comfort* adj,n

- به راحتی در کنار هم زندگی میکردند. — They were living together very comfortably.

80 | 625

2074 خصوصاً xosusæn *especially* adv,conj

- این شهر دارای میزان بارندگی بسیار، خصوصاً در بهار میباشد. — The city has a lot of precipitation, especially in the spring.

86 | 415

2075 پارس pars *bark, Pars* n,pn

- به صدای پارس سگی رفت طرف دریچهای که از طبقهی دوم به کوچه باز میشد. — She went towards the sound of the barking of a dog, towards a small door that opened from the second floor onto the alley.

81 | 574

2076 دوازده dævazdæh *twelve* n

- مینویسم که ساعت دوازده کنار رودخانه بودم، پهلوی یک نیمکت خالی. — I am writing that at twelve o'clock, I was by the river, beside an empty bench.

59 | 1424

2077 تبعیض tæbʔiz *discrimination* n

- باید شرایط مساوی و بدون تبعیض برای زنان و مردان در تصدی مشاغل حکومتی و سیاسی از جمله قضاوت دادگستری قائل شد. — Equal and non-discriminatory conditions must be granted for both men and woman in government and political jobs including the judiciary.

87 | 377

2078 مبارز mobarez *fighter* adj,n

- یک مبارز انعطاف پذیر است. — A warrior is flexible.

85 | 456

2079 پارلمان parleman *parliament* n

- رئیس جمهوری سودان با حضور در پارلمان این کشور دستور آزادی تمامی زندانیان سیاسی سودان را صادر کرد. — Attending the parliament, Sudan's president issued the order for the release of all Sudanese political prisoners.

73 | 861

2080 بهداشتی behdaʃti *hygienic* adj

- ۹ میلیارد دلار به بودجه بهداشتی بریتانیا افزوده میشود. — $9 billion will be added to Great Britain's health budget.

76 | 734

2081 تکنولوژی teknoloʒi *technology* n

- تکنولوژی محلی زیادی را در خودروهایمان به کار گرفتهایم. — We have made use of a lot of local technology in our cars.

76 | 739

2082 آزمون azmun *test* n

- نتایج اولیه آزمون دستیاری منتشر شد. — The initial results of the residency exam were released.

67 | 1092

13 Light verb constructions

Rank	Headword	Pronunciation	Gloss	Rank	Headword	Pronunciation	Gloss
115	نشان دادن	neʃan dadæn	show	990	تصمیم گرفتن	tæsmim gereftæn	decide
137	قرار گرفتن	γærar gereftæn	be located	1028	ایجاد کردن	idʒad kærdæn	create
162	وجود داشتن	vodʒud daʃtæn	exist	1044	مطرح کردن	mætræh kærdæn	propose
169	انجام دادن	ændʒam dadæn	accomplish	1081	تشکیل دادن	tæʃkil dadæn	form
217	دست دادن	dæst dadæn	shake hands, lose	1122	توجه کردن	tævædʒdʒoh kærdæn	pay attention
288	پیدا کردن	pejda kærdæn	find	1131	گفته شدن	gofte ʃodæn	be said
313	قرار دادن	γærar dadæn	put, place	1198	افزایش یافتن	æfzajeʃ jaftæn	increase
331	قرار داشتن	γærar daʃtæn	be located	1219	تلاش کردن	tælaʃ kærdæn	make effort
347	استفاده کردن	estefade kærdæn	use	1220	شکست خوردن	ʃekæst xordæn	be defeated
369	خارج شدن	xaredʒ ʃodæn	leave	1244	آغاز کردن	aγaz kærdæn	begin
395	ادامه دادن	edame dadæn	continue	1255	بازی کردن	bazi kærdæn	play
405	قرار بودن	γærar budæn	be supposed to	1276	شروع شدن	ʃoruʔ kærdæn	begin
462	انجام شدن	ændʒam ʃodæn	be done	1291	پاسخ دادن	pasox dadæn	reply
498	انتخاب کردن	entexab kærdæn	elect, choose	1293	تغییر دادن	tæγjir dadæn	change
614	عمل کردن	æmæl kærdæn	act, perform	1310	فراهم کردن	færahæm kærdæn	assemble
649	سال بودن	sal budæn	be years since	1312	نیاز داشتن	nijaz daʃtæn	need
670	آغاز شدن	aγaz ʃodæn	begin	1479	خبر دادن	xæbær dadæn	inform
713	اعلام کردن	eʔlam kærdæn	announce	1348	شرکت کردن	ʃerkæt kærdæn	participate
719	فکر کردن	fekr kærdæn	think	1358	ترک کردن	tærk kærdæn	leave, abandon
736	معرفی کردن	moʔærrefi kærdæn	introduce	1378	حرکت کردن	hærekæt kærdæn	move, set off
765	اتفاق افتادن	ettefaγ oftadæn	happen	1411	انتظار داشتن	entezar daʃtæn	expect
778	وارد شدن	vared ʃodæn	enter	1427	صحبت کردن	sohbæt kærdæn	talk
822	برخوردار بودن	bærxordar budæn	be in possession	1455	درست بودن	dorost budæn	be right
832	زندگی کردن	zendegi kærdæn	live	1468	قصد داشتن	γæsd daʃtæn	intend
838	اجازه دادن	edʒaze dadæn	permit	1490	وارد کردن	vared kærdæn	import, enter
841	کار کردن	kar kærdæn	work	1491	تأکید کردن	tæʔkid kærdæn	emphasize
861	کمک کردن	komæk kærdæn	help	1495	معرفی شدن	moʔærrefi ʃodæn	be introduced
881	باعث شدن	baes ʃodæn	cause	1505	استفاده شدن	estefade ʃodæn	be used
922	تبدیل شدن	tæbdil ʃodæn	convert	1519	مواجه شدن	movadʒeh ʃodæn	be confronted
941	سعی کردن	sæʔj kærdæn	try	1525	امیدوار بودن	omidvar budæn	be hopeful

Rank	Headword	Pronunciation	Gloss	Rank	Headword	Pronunciation	Gloss
1529	جا گرفتن	dʒa gereftæn	reserve, hold	2118	شروع کردن	ʃoruʔ kærdæn	begin
1534	اظهار داشتن	ezhar daʃtæn	express, declare	2120	حرف زدن	hærf zædæn	speak
1559	دریافت کردن	dærjaft kærdæn	receive	2127	بررسی کردن	bærræsi kærdæn	examine
1560	راه انداختن	rah ændaxtæn	operate, launch	2186	درک کردن	dærk kærdæn	comprehend
1561	احساس کردن	ehsas kærdæn	feel	2248	تأکید داشتن	tæʔkid daʃtæn	emphasize
1563	حفظ کردن	hefz kærdæn	protect, memorize	2188	تجربه کردن	tædʒrobe kærdæn	experience
1575	روبرو شدن	ruberu ʃodæn	meet	2196	جا گذاشتن	dʒagozaʃtæn	leave behind
1602	باقی ماندن	bayi mandæn	remain	2207	تأثیر گذاشتن	tæʔsir gozaʃtæn	leave impression
1623	نادیده گرفتن	nadide gereftæn	overlook	2277	متوجه شدن	motevædʒeh ʃodæn	notice
1629	سخن گفتن	soxæn goftæn	speak, talk	2288	تصور کردن	tæsavvor kærdæn	imagine
1634	دوست داشتن	dust daʃtæn	like	2306	شکست دادن	ʃekæst dadæn	defeat
1657	دنبال کردن	donbal kærdæn	look for	2309	تولید کردن	towlid kærdæn	produce
1664	رو آوردن	ru avordæn	turn	2335	خودداری کردن	xoddari kærdæn	refrain
1778	مواجه بودن	movadʒe budæn	confront	2411	تعریف کردن	tæʔrif kærdæn	define, describe
1781	واقع شدن	vaɣeʔ ʃodæn	happen, be located	2358	جلوگیری کردن	dʒelowgiri kærdæn	prevent
1719	نگاه کردن	negah kærdæn	look	2366	توضیح دادن	towzih dadæn	explain
1726	تمام شدن	tæmam ʃodæn	finish	2435	گزارش دادن	gozareʃ dadæn	report
1753	سفر کردن	sæfær kærdæn	travel	2447	استقبال کردن	esteybal kærdæn	welcome
1808	حل شدن	hæl ʃodæn	dissolve, be solved	2462	توصیف کردن	towsif kærdæn	describe
1813	حل کردن	hæl kærdæn	solve	2473	توصیه کردن	towsije kærdæn	recommend
1835	صادر شدن	sader ʃodæn	be exported, issued	2483	ترجیح دادن	tærdʒih dadæn	prefer
1883	آشنا شدن	aʃna ʃodæn	be familiar, acquainted	2488	نگه داشتن	negæh daʃtæn	keep
1891	اجرا کردن	edʒra kærdæn	execute, perform	2511	شناسایی کردن	ʃenasaji kærdæn	identify
1907	تولید شدن	towlid ʃodæn	be produced	2515	باز کردن	baz kærdæn	open
2022	بیان کردن	bæjan kærdæn	state, express	2746	رها کردن	ræha kærdæn	free, let go
2023	تغییر کردن	tæɣjir kærdæn	change	2518	جدا شدن	dʒoda ʃodæn	be separated
1960	تعیین کردن	tæʔjin kærdæan	determine, appoint	2520	شاهد بودن	ʃahed budæn	witness
2016	آزاد شدن	azad ʃodæn	be freed	2522	بالا بردن	bala bordæn	put up, raise
2029	ثابت کردن	sabet kærdæn	prove	2531	سال داشتن	sal daʃtæn	be years old
2047	رد کردن	ræd kærdæn	reject	2533	متوقف شدن	motevæɣɣef ʃodæn	stop
2054	صادر کردن	sader kærdæn	export, issue				
2065	بالا رفتن	bala ræftæn	go up				

(continued)

(continued)

Rank	Headword	Pronunciation	Gloss	Rank	Headword	Pronunciation	Gloss
2534	شرکت داشتن	ʃerkæt dɑʃtæn	participate, attend	3146	تحمیل کردن	tæhmil kærdæn	impose
2598	جمع شدن	dʒæmʔ ʃodæn	gather	3152	نابود کردن	nabud kærdæn	destroy
2612	حمله کردن	hæmle kærdæn	attack	3174	تشخیص دادن	tæʃxis dɑdæn	distinguish, diagnose
2626	ادعا کردن	eddeʔɑ kærdæn	claim	3193	به رسمیت شناختن	be ræsmijjæt ʃenɑxtæn	officially recognize
2633	قبول داشتن	qæbul dɑʃtæn	accept	3199	خوش آمدن	xoʃ ɑmædan	welcome
2638	تبدیل کردن	tæbdil kærdæn	convert	3211	تقسیم کردن	tæqsim kærdæn	divide, distribute
2668	مصرف کردن	mæsræf kærdæn	consume	3217	پی بردن	pej bordæn	discover, find out
2681	کنار گذاشتن	kenɑr gozaʃtæn	put away	3261	آسیب دیدن	asib didæn	be injured
2688	اعتراف کردن	eʔterɑf kærdæn	confess	3268	طول کشیدن	tul keʃidæn	last long
2695	تعطیل شدن	tæʔtil ʃodæn	shut down	3273	قبول کردن	qæbul kærdæn	accept
2703	فراموش کردن	færɑmuʃ kærdæn	forget	3275	یاد گرفتن	jad gereftæn	learn
2713	برخورد کردن	bærxord kærdæn	meet, collide	3299	تمایل داشتن	tæmajol dɑʃtæn	tend to, gravitate to
2719	متولد شدن	motævælled ʃodæn	be born	3301	دامن زدن	damæn zædæn	add fuel
2722	یاد کردن	jad kærdæn	remember	3325	پر کردن	por kærdæn	fill
2903	منتشر کردن	montæʃer kærdæn	publish	3399	تشکر کردن	tæʃækkor kærdæn	thank
2801	ساله بودن	sale budæn	be years old	3403	باور کردن	bavær kærdæn	believe
2803	حذف شدن	hazf ʃodæn	be eliminated	3492	بستگی داشتن	bæstegi dɑʃtæn	depend
2822	تلقی شدن	tælæqqi ʃodæn	be considered	3493	مقایسه کردن	moqajese kærdæn	compare
2850	گزارش شدن	gozareʃ ʃodæn	be reported	3363	جواب دادن	dʒævab dadæn	reply
2853	ظاهر شدن	zaher ʃodæn	appear	3412	بیرون آمدن	birun amædæn	emerge
3248	بزرگ شدن	bozorg ʃodæn	grow up	3443	اصلاح کردن	eslah kærdæn	reform, correct
2939	قطع شدن	qætʔ ʃodæn	be cut off, terminated	3476	شکایت کردن	ʃekajæt kærdæn	complain
2940	مشغول بودن	mæʃɣul budæn	be busy	3486	متوقف کردن	motævæqqef kærdæn	stop
2955	منتقل کردن	montæqel kærdæn	transfer, transmit	3487	مربوط بودن	mærbut budæn	be relevant
2995	باز شدن	baz ʃodæn	open	3514	تعلق داشتن	tæʔæloq dɑʃtæn	belong
3090	بازداشت شدن	bazdaʃt ʃodæn	be arrested	3536	به ثمر رساندن	be sæmær resandæn	bear fruit
3106	معلوم شدن	mæʔlum ʃodæn	become known	3557	عرضه کردن	arze kærdæn	present, offer, supply
3122	بنا بودن	bæna budæn	be supposed to	3563	کمک گرفتن	komæk gereftæn	get help
3132	تحمل کردن	tæhæmmol kærdæn	tolerate				
3134	طی کردن	tej kærdæn	journey				

Rank	Headword	Pronunciation	Gloss	Rank	Headword	Pronunciation	Gloss
3585	مصرف شدن	mæsræf ʃodæn	be consumed	4056	در زدن	dær zædæn	knock
				4063	حاکی بودن	haki budæn	indicate
3605	تحویل دادن	tæhvil dadæn	deliver, hand over	4077	توجیه کردن	towdʒih kærdæn	justify
3623	راضی بودن	razi budæn	be satisfied	4095	خریداری کردن	xæridari kærdæn	purchase
3645	آگاه بودن	agah budæn	be aware				
3650	قائل بودن	ɣael budæn	believe, profess	4114	درگیر شدن	dærgir ʃodæn	engage
3714	سؤال کردن	soʔal kærdæn	ask	4188	توسعه دادن	towseʔe dadæn	expand, develop
3722	گمان کردن	goman kærdæn	suppose	4191	گرفتار شدن	gereftar ʃodæn	get caught
3732	بلند شدن	bolænd ʃodæn	rise, grow	4116	پس گرفتن	pæs gereftæn	take back, withdraw
3747	گسترش دادن	gostæreʃ dadæn	expand	4166	صرف کردن	særf kærdæn	spend time, consume, conjugate
3750	فرا گرفتن	færa gereftæn	surround, learn				
3753	زنگ زدن	zæng zædæn	ring	4224	فرار کردن	færar kærdæn	escape
3764	تکرار کردن	tekrar kærdæn	repeat	4270	هدایت کردن	hedajæt kærdæn	guide
3767	تلقی کردن	tælæɣɣi kærdæn	consider	4281	دستور دادن	dæstur dadæn	order
3779	قطع کردن	ɣætʔ kærdæn	cut	4356	حذف کردن	hæzf kærdæn	eliminate, delete
3788	راه افتادن	rah oftadæn	set out				
3794	ارتباط داشتن	ertebat daʃtæn	be in contact	4291	رفتار کردن	ræftar kærdæn	behave
3800	جدا کردن	dʒoda kærdæn	separate	4293	واگذار کردن	vagozar kærdæn	hand over
3804	تشویق کردن	tæʃviɣ kærdæn	encourage	4296	آسیب رساندن	asib resandæn	cause injury
3847	توزیع شدن	towziʔ ʃodæn	be distributed	4311	اعتراض کردن	eʔteraz kærdæn	protest, object
3853	تماشا کردن	tæmaʃa kærdæn	watch, view	4336	سپری کردن	sepæri kærdæn	spend time
3864	طراحی کردن	tærrahi kærdæn	design	4347	پی گرفتن	pej gereftæn	follow up
3878	مرتکب شدن	mortækeb ʃodæn	commit	4443	دخالت کردن	dexalæt kærdæn	interfere
3941	رو شدن	ru ʃodæn	be exposed, bold	4537	گل زدن	gol zædæn	score a goal
4102	جمع کردن	dʒæmʔ kærdæn	collect	4379	پیاده کردن	pijade kærdæn	take apart, unload, execute
3959	خواستار شدن	xastar ʃodæn	demand	4381	رها شدن	ræha ʃodæn	be freed
3989	پرتاب کردن	pærtab ʃodæn	be thrown, launched	4391	رشد کردن	roʃd kærdæn	grow
3990	سوق دادن	sowɣ dadæn	guide, drive	4407	نابود شدن	nabud ʃodæn	be destroyed
3992	علاقه داشتن	ælaɣe daʃtæn	be interested	4420	تحلیل کردن	tæhlil kærdæn	analyze
3996	تعقیب کردن	tæʔɣib kærdæn	pursue	4426	ازدواج کردن	ezdevadʒ kærdæn	marry
4016	درست کردن	dorost kærdæn	correct, prepare	4459	چاپ کردن	tʃap kærdæn	print
				4464	گوش دادن	guʃ dadæn	listen
				4466	لازم داشتن	lazem daʃtæn	need

(continued)

(continued)

Rank	Headword	Pronunciation	Gloss	Rank	Headword	Pronunciation	Gloss
4474	تضمین کردن	tæzmin kærdæn	guarantee	4673	گرامی داشتن	gerami daʃtæn	honor
4507	اشتباه کردن	eʃtebah kærdæn	make a mistake	4687	درخواست کردن	dærxast kærdæn	request
4509	تحصیل کردن	tæhsil kærdæn	study	4771	صرف شدن	særf ʃodæn	be spent, consumed, conjugated
4519	ملی شدن	melli ʃodæn	be nationalized	4772	خسته شدن	xæste ʃodæn	become tired
4625	حساب کردن	hesab kærdæn	calculate, compute	4794	خواهش کردن	xaheʃ kærdæn	request
4560	راه رفتن	rah ræftæn	walk	4831	هزینه کردن	hæzine kærdæn	expend
4580	درگذشتن	dærgozæʃtæn	die	4880	انتقال دادن	enteɣal dadæn	transfer
4584	آگاه شدن	agah ʃodæn	be informed	4885	ذکر کردن	zekr kærdæn	mention, cite
4586	مطالعه کردن	motaleʔe kærdæn	read, study	4890	پنهان کردن	penhan kærdæn	hide
4607	رو کردن	ru kærdæn	turn to, look at	4862	کامل شدن	kamel ʃodæn	be completed, perfected
4637	بحث کردن	bæhs kærdæn	discuss	4958	تعلق گرفتن	tæʔælloɣ gereftæn	be given to, go to
4638	اثر گذاشتن	æsær gozaʃtæn	impress, affect	4961	خبر داشتن	xæbær daʃtæn	know, be aware
4648	ترجمه شدن	tærdʒome ʃodæn	be translated	4970	گریه کردن	gerje kærdæn	weep, cry
4649	تکمیل کردن	tækmil kærdæn	complete				
4651	اجازه خواستن	edʒaze xastæn	ask permission				

2083 آیت‌الله ajætollah *ayatollah* n

- با ریاست جمهوری آیت الله هاشمی و پایان جنگ، در دوران ایشان روابط تا حدودی بهبود پیدا کرد. — Under the presidency of Ayatollah Hashemi and with the end of the war, relations improved somewhat during his time.

64 | 1213

2084 کشاورز keʃaværz *farmer* n,pn

- انجمن حمایت از کشاورزان شهرستان اصفهان. — Society for the Support of Esfahan County Farmers.

82 | 552

2085 منصور mænsur *Mansour* pn

- ا — اسم منصور را چندین بار از علیرضا شنیده بودم. had heard Mansour's name from Alireza so many times.

92 | 227

2086 دیر dir, dejr *late, monastery* adj,adv,n,pn

- She — بخاطر دیر آمدنش معذرت خواهی کرد. apologized for coming late.

78 | 663

2087 ارزی ærzi *foreign* exchange adj

- معاملات ارزی با ایران را در سال ۲۰۰۸ قطع نمود. — They discontinued foreign exchange transactions with Iran in 2008.

75 | 775

2088 لطف lotf *kindness* n

- به لطف خدا مشکل رفع شد. — By the grace of God the problem was solved.

87 | 380

2089 ظهور zohur *appearance* n

- به زودی ظهور می کند. — He will appear shortly.

78 | 657

2090 گردش gærdeʃ *circulation* n

- اگر اصول واقعا اصول باشد ، نباید با گردش زمانه بگردد. — If a doctrine is really a doctrine, it shouldn't change over the course of time.

87 | 363

2091 معمولی mæʔmuli *ordinary* adj

- آیا نمک‌های دریایی بهتر از نمک‌های معمولی هستند؟ — Is sea salt better than ordinary salt?

87 | 386

2092 آبی abi *blue* adj,n
- آبی یک رنگ آرامش دهنده است. — Blue is a calming color.

74 | 807

2093 افغان æfɣɑn *Afghan* adj,n,pn
- مهاجران افغان به سال هاست که به دلیل نبود امنیت و کار به کشورهای همسایه مهاجرت شده اند. — For years, Afghan migrants have emigrated to neighboring countries due to a lack of security and work.

48 | 1939

2094 همدان hæmedɑn *Hamadan* pn
- اهل همدان بود. — She was from Hamedan.

81 | 560

2095 ثانیه sɑnije *second* n
- تمام روز یک ثانیه آرام نداشتم. — I didn't have one second of calm all day.

78 | 675

2096 تجاوز tædʒɑvoz *aggression* n
- اگر مرد بودن یعنی آدمکشی و قدرت طلبی و حق تجاوز به دیگران، من مرد نیستم. — If being a man means murdering, seeking power, and having the right to assault others, I am not a man.

78 | 669

2097 کارشناسی kɑrʃenɑsi *expertise, bachelor's degree* adj,n
- دوره کارشناسی مدیریت بازرگانی یکی از دوره های تحصیلی آموزش عالی است. — Bachelor of Business Administration is one of the higher education courses.

78 | 661

2098 سه‌شنبه seʃæmbe *Tuesday* n
- محمدحسین پورکاظمی روز سه‌شنبه به ایرنا گفت — On Tuesday Mohammad Hossein Pourkazemi told IRNA:

65 | 1129

2099 وحشت væhʃæt *panic* n
- دلت از وحشت پُر میشه. — Your heart fills with horror.

85 | 428

2100 جنجال dʒændʒɑl *tumult* n
- جنجال‌های سیاسی جهاد اقتصادی را به حاشیه رانده است. — Political controversies have pushed "economic jihad" to the side.

93 | 199

2101 کودتا kudetɑ *coup d'état* n
- کودتای نظامی آغاز شد. — The military coup d'état started.

86 | 389

2102 سنجش sændʒeʃ *measurement* n
- سازمان سنجش نمی‌خواهد کنکور حذف شود. — The assessment organization does not want the *konkur* exam to be removed.

88 | 331

2103 راندن rɑndæn *drive* adj,n,pn,v
- بیرون راندن پناهندگان فلسطینی بیانگر سیاستهای تبعیض نژادی سران اردن. — Expelling Palestinian refugees represents the racial discrimination policy of Jordan's leaders.

87 | 368

2104 مطابق motɑbeɣ *corresponding* adj
- تو از پنج نفر می‌خوای مطابق میل تو رفتار کنن. — You want five people to behave according to your desires.

72 | 859

2105 پاس pɑs *pass, guard, appreciation* n,pn
- در آخرین دقایق بازی پاس زیبایی به «رینکون» داد. — In the last minutes of the game he gave a nice pass to Rincón.

83 | 480

2106 ترویج tærvidʒ *promotion* n
- ترویج تولید ملی و حمایت از کار و سرمایه‌ی ایرانی، یک مسئله‌ی بلندمدت است. — The promotion of national production and support of Iranian work and investment is a long term issue.

88 | 347

2107 روایت revɑjæt *narrative* n
- داستان زوجی به نام مجید و پونه را روایت می‌کند. — It narrates the story of a couple named Majid and Puneh.

78 | 648

2108 اردن ordon *Jordan* pn
- تمام فرودگاه‌های مصر و سوریه و اردن و حتی عراق را بمباران کردند. — They bombed all of the airports in Egypt, Syria, Jordan, and even Iraq.

80 | 592

2109 مستند mostænæd *documentary* adj,n
- فیلم مستندی درباره ی تاریخچه ی ساخت تلسکوب نشان می دهد. — He will show a documentary film about the history of the making the telescope.

82 | 519

2110 پتروشیمی petroʃimi *petrochemistry* n
- صنعت پتروشیمی نیاز به سرمایه گذاری جدی دارد. — The petrochemical industry needs serious investment.

79 | 629

2111 واگذاری vɑgozɑri *settlement, transferring* n
- یکی از سازمان های پیشرو در بحث واگذاری امور به بخش خصوصی است. — One of the leading industries is in the debate about transferring its affairs to the private sector.

79 | 616

2112 میرزا mirza *scribe, Mirza* n,pn
- میرزا حسن شبها سیما را روی زانوهایش می نشاند و به
رسم دوران بچگی برایش کتاب می خواند. — At night,
Mirza Hasan would sit Sima down on his lap
like he would when she was a child and read
books to her.
53 | 1677

2113 ایده ide *idea* n
- رامبد جوان هنوز فکر و ایدههای تازه در سر دارد. —
Rambod Javan still has new thoughts and
ideas.
82 | 537

2114 حمید hæmid *Hamid* pn
- حمید هنوز راضی نشده بود. — Hamid still hadn't
been satisfied.
85 | 441

2115 آرزو arezu *wish* n
- آخرین آرزویم. — My last wish.
76 | 717

2116 شهرسازی ʃæhrsazi *urban development* n
- مدیرکل جدید راه و شهرسازی استان اصفهان منصوب شد.
— The new General Director of Roads and
Urban Development in Esfahan province was
appointed.
83 | 476

2117 جسد dʒæsæd *corpse* n
- تاکنون ده ها جسد از محل خارج شده است. — So far,
dozens of bodies have been removed from
the site.
84 | 470

2118 شروع کردن ʃoruʔ kærdæn *begin* v
- آنها شروع میکنند به شمارش. — They start counting.
76 | 721

2119 عوض ævæz *change* n
- اجازه بدهید عوضشان کنم. — Please let me change
them.
71 | 900

2120 حرف زدن hærf zædæn *speak* v
- میخوام باهات حرف بزنم. — I want to speak with
you.
54 | 1610

2121 اجتماع edʒtemaʔ *community* n
- انسان و اجتماع در شعر او حضور ندارد. — People
and society are not present in her poetry.
81 | 564

2122 خان xan *Khan* n
- دیدم حق با فتح الله خان است. — I realized Fathollah
Khan was right.
64 | 1183

2123 زمستان zemestan *winter* n
- بسیاری از افراد از سرمای پاییز و زمستان شکایت دارند.
— Many people complain of the fall and
winter cold weather.
81 | 557

2124 دبیرکل dæbirekol *secretary general* n
- حضرت بارون ادموند دو روچیلد دبیرکل اتحادیه طرفداران
اسرائیل. — His Excellency, Baron Edmond de
Rothschild, general secretary of the Union of
Supporters of Israel.
79 | 612

2125 هندی hendi *Indian, Hindi* adj,n
- پیرمرد هندی از کجا فهمیده من از چه تصمیمی گرفتم.
— Where did the old Indian man learn what
I decided?
85 | 413

2126 متقاضی motæɣazi *applicant* adj,n
- ایرانیها بیشترین متقاضی پناهندگی در بریتانیا بودهاند.
— Iranians formed the largest pool of
applicants for asylum in Britain.
80 | 587

2127 بررسی کردن bærræsi kærdæn *examine* v
- پوتین و اوباما اوضاع سوریه را بررسی کردند.
— Putin and Obama reviewed the
conditions of Syria.
84 | 441

2128 کیفی kejfi, kifi *qualitative, portable* adj
- نبود کنترل کیفی بازار مواد غذایی به طور حتم عواقب
جبران ناپذیری را به دنبال خواهد داشت. — The lack
of quality control in the food market will
certainly lead to irreparable consequences.
86 | 395

2129 موسی musa *Musa, Moses* pn
- من در خواب دیدم که حضرت موسی در راه به طرف من
آمد و مرا با خود به کوه طور برد. — I dreamed that
His Holiness, Moses came up to me on the
path and took me with him to Mount Sinai.
84 | 462

2130 اشغال eʃɣal *occupation* n
- مقام بسیار مهمی را اشغال می کند. — He occupies a
very important position.
74 | 774

2131 نشانی neʃani *address* n
- پیدا کردن نشانی. — Finding the address.
79 | 598

2132 دفاعی defaʔi *defensive* adj
- هر دستی سمت توانمندیدفاعی ایران دراز شود قطع
میکنیم. — We will cut off any hand extended
toward Iran's defense capabilities.
81 | 541

2133 صرفاً serfæn *merely, purely* adv
- در گذشته منطق صرفاً شاخهای از فلسفه شمرده میشد.
— In the past, logic was considered just a
branch of philosophy.
79 | 622

2134 هدیه hedje *gift* n
- آن را به من هدیه کردی. — You gave me that as a
gift.
86 | 382

2135 برف bærf *snow* n
- برف سرتاسر زمین ها را پوشانده است. — Snow has covered the whole ground.
- 81 | 529

2136 همگی hæmegi *all* pron,q
- مسلمانان همگی قرآن را بعنوان معجزه می‌دانند. — Muslims all consider the Koran a miracle.
- 83 | 486

2137 ابتکار ebtekar *initiative, innovation* n,pn
- ثبت اختراعات، ابتکارات و نوآوری‌ها در کشور به صورت واحد در می‌آید. — Registering inventions and innovations in the country will be unified.
- 86 | 397

2138 منتخب montæxæb *chosen, elected* adj,n
- به همه اعضای منتخب تبریک عرض نمود. — He congratulated all of the elected members.
- 81 | 533

2139 پیروی pejrævi *obedience, following* n
- او آزادی خواهان را به پیروی از غرب و دشمنی با اسلام متهم می‌کرد. — He would accuse the liberals of following the West and of being enemies of Islam.
- 88 | 333

2140 فریب færib *deception* n
- فریب خورده بودم. — I had been cheated.
- 88 | 318

2141 کتابخانه ketabxane *library* n
- بعد به سمت کتابخانه می روم و چند کتاب بر می دارم. — Then I will go to the library and pick up a few books.
- 78 | 644

2142 اختصاصی extesasi *special* adj
- روبات‌های صاحب شهر اختصاصی می‌شوند. — Robots will become the owners of an exclusive city.
- 91 | 252

2143 بابت babæt *matter, for* n,prep
- بابت تبریک های زیبای تولدم ازت ممنونم. — Thank you for the beautiful wishes for my birthday.
- 86 | 377

2144 مخدر moxædder *narcotic* adj
- کسی مواد مخدر مصرف می‌کند. — Someone is consuming narcotics.
- 70 | 916

2145 جداگانه dzodagane *separately* adj,adv
- دایکندی پیشتر یکی از ولسوالی‌های ولایت اروزگان بود ولی در تاریخ ۲۸ مارس ۲۰۰۴ به عنوان یک ولایت جداگانه تشکیل شد. — Daykundi was previously one of the districts of the Uruzgan Province, but on 28 March 2004, it was established as a separate province.
- 86 | 375

2146 بافت baft *context, texture, tissue* n
- کارنیتین در بافت عضلات و کبد ساخته می‌شود. — Carnitine is made in the liver and muscle tissue.
- 78 | 622

2147 دموکراسی demokrasi *democracy* n
- بعد کم کم به دوره دموکراسی رسیدند. — Then they slowly entered into the era of democracy.
- 72 | 850

2148 جنس dzens *gender, merchandise* n
- وقت خرید باید به جنس نگاه کرد. — While shopping one must check the merchandise.
- 83 | 488

2149 کانال kanal *channel, canal* n
- ماهواره را روشن می‌کنم و به لیست کانال‌ها نگاهی می‌اندازم. — I turn on the satellite (TV) and take a look at the list of channels.
- 86 | 389

2150 عازم azem *bound for* adj
- بلافاصله عازم سانفرانسیسکوی آمریکا شد. — He immediately departed for San Francisco in the United States.
- 90 | 279

2151 مدافع modafe? *defender* adj,n
- مدافعین حقوق بشر روسیه از اسنودن دفاع می‌کنند. — Russia's human rights defenders are defending Snowden.
- 83 | 483

2152 راجع radze? *referring* prep
- می‌خواهم راجع به آن روز با تو صحبت کنم. — I want to talk with you about that day.
- 84 | 433

2153 تنهایی tænhaji *loneliness* n
- حالا با شروع مدارس من بیشتر از هر زمانی احساس تنهایی می‌کنم. — Now that school has started I feel lonelier than ever.
- 80 | 562

2154 مراقبت moraɣebæt *supervision* n
- ازش مراقبت می‌کنی. — You will look after her.
- 85 | 415

2155 مرحوم mærhum *deceased* n
- میرزا عبدالحمید از دوستان قدیمی پدر مرحومم بود. — Mirza Abdol Hamid was one of my late father's old friends.
- 80 | 580

2156 متکی mottæki *dependent on* adj
- متکی به استعدادهای درونی. — Relying on internal talents.
- 88 | 337

2157 کابل kabol, kabl *Kabul, cable* n,pn
- به رغم بحران عراق حضور آمریکا در کابل افزایش می‌یابد. — Despite the crisis in Iraq, the American presence in Kabul is increasing.
- 51 | 1718

2158 موتور motor *engine, motorcycle* n

• پاسبان سوار بر موتور سیگارش را خاموش می کند. — The guard riding a motorcycle puts out his cigarette.

77 | 654

2159 شمسی ʃæmsi *solar* adj,pn

• در زمان جنگ تحمیلی و اوایل دهه 70 شمسی. — At the time of the imposed war and at the beginning of 70s in the solar calendar.

69 | 926

2160 فراموش færamuʃ *forgotten* adj,n

• هیچ وقت فراموش نمی کنم. — I will never forget.

88 | 336

2161 مصطفی mostæfa *Mostafa* pn

• مصطفی هاشمی‌طبا در گفت‌وگو با ایرنا گفت — In his talks with IRNA, Mostafa Hashemi Taba said . . .

85 | 398

2162 قمری ɣæmæri, ɣomri *lunar, turtle dove* adj

• شاعر عصر مشروطه متولد 1827 هجری قمری در قزوین بود. — The constitutional era poet was born in 1827 according to the lunar calendar in Qazvin.

70 | 886

2163 امیدواری omidvari *hopefulness* n

• جای امیدواری است. — There is room for hope.

79 | 583

2164 برابری bærabæri *equality* n

• وی در این کتاب به دفاع از برابری حقوق زن و مرد پرداخته‌است. — In this book, he has defended the equality of women's and men's rights.

84 | 448

2165 یازده jazdæh *eleven* n

• یازده سالم بود، بهگمانم. — I was eleven years old, I reckon.

60 | 1276

2166 میزبان mizban *host* adj,n

• کاپ اخلاق به بهترین تیم این مسابقات با نظر میزبان و کمیته اجرائی اهداء خواهد شد. — Based on the opinion of the host and the executive committee, the Ethics Cup will be given to the best team among the competitors.

69 | 926

2167 کیلومتری kilometri *kilometer* adj,n

• ارتش سوریه به ۲۵ کیلومتری فرودگاه الطبقه رسید. — The Syrian army arrived 25 km from the al-Tabaqa airport.

78 | 615

2168 عمرانی omrani *development* adj

• طرح های عمرانی. — Development projects.

79 | 594

2169 برطرف bærtæræf *eliminated* adj

• بی‌اعتمادی به آمریکا به این زودی برطرف نمی‌شود. — Distrust of America will not go away anytime soon.

83 | 481

2170 مطالبه motalebe *demanding payment* n

• ازش پنج هزار سکه ی طلا مطالبه می کنیم. — We demand five thousand gold coins from him.

83 | 481

2171 تضعیف tæzʔif *weakening* n

• بهتدریج این ارتباط تضعیف می‌شود. — This communication is gradually weakening.

86 | 382

2172 استراتژیک esteratezik *strategic* adj

• مرکز تحقیقات استراتژیک ریاست جمهوری. — Presidential Center for Strategic Research.

81 | 516

2173 مدرن modern *modern* adj

• رئیس جدید از نسل جامعه مدرن بود. — The new boss belonged to the modern generation of society.

77 | 655

2174 اعم æʔæm *more common, including* adj

• تمام مردم ایران اعم از شیعه و سنی در حقوق شهروندی در کشور مساوی و یکسان هستند. — All Iranian people have equal civil rights in the country, both Shia and Sunni.

85 | 413

2175 هماهنگ hæmahæng *harmonious* adj

• به نظر من باید با هم گفت‌وگو کنیم که با هم هماهنگ باشیم. — In my opinion, we should also discuss this so that that we are coordinated.

82 | 486

2176 جدیت dʒeddijæt *seriousness* n

• آدم وقتی با جدیت به کار مشغول باشد رنج و بیماری خود را نمی‌فهمد. — When a person is seriously occupied with work they don't understand their own suffering and infirmity.

93 | 189

2177 خلاصه xolase *summary* adj,n

• خلاصه چند تا چرک نویس نوشتم تا بالاخره یکی از آنها را پسندید گفت این خوب است. — In short, I wrote some drafts and finally he liked one and said this is good.

69 | 924

2178 تحمیل tæhmil *imposition* n

• سهامداران بدهی خود را به شرکت تحمیل کرده اند. — Shareholders have imposed their debt on the company.

87 | 334

2179 قدم ɣædæm *step* n

• امسال برای کمک به محیط زیست پنج قدم بردارید. — This year, take five steps to help the environment.

73 | 788

2180 متعهد motæ?æhhed *obliged, committed* adj
- حالا من خودم را متعهد می‌دانم. — I currently consider myself committed.
86 | 375

2181 اتوبوس otobus *bus* n
- با اتوبوس می‌رفت. — He was going by bus.
76 | 699

2182 دیپلماسی diplomasi *diplomacy* n
- لندن کانال های دیپلماسی خود با تهران را باز کرد. — London opened up diplomatic channels with Tehran.
89 | 302

2183 باند bɑnd *band, gang* n
- گزارش حاکی است پس از اعترافات اعضای این باند شیطانی، پرونده به شعبه ۷۷ دادگاه کیفری استان تهران ارسال شد. — The report states after the confessions of the members of this devilish band, the case was sent to the 77th branch of the criminal court of Tehran province.
85 | 419

2184 مهارت mæhɑræt *skill* n
- در هنر مهارت لازم را نداری. — Skill is not required in your art.
75 | 704

2185 نقض næɣz *violation* n
- فلسفه وجودی خود را نقض کرده است. — He has violated the philosophy of his own existence.
76 | 700

2186 درک کردن dærk kærdæn *comprehend* v
- ژنرال‌های پاکستانی خطر را درک کرده‌اند. — The Pakistani generals have sensed the danger.
87 | 353

2187 تعامل tæ?amol *interaction* n
- تعامل شما با شورای آینده شهر چگونه خواهد بود؟ — What will your interaction with the future city council be like?
81 | 517

2188 تجربه کردن tædʒrobe kærdæn *experience* v
- دنیای جدیدی را تجربه‌کردم. — I experienced a new world.
87 | 356

2189 فدرال federal *federal* adj
- این امر سبب تعطیلی بخشی از دولت فدرال آمریکا شد. — This became the reason for the partial shutdown of America's federal government.
90 | 268

2190 عمق omɣ *depth* n
- وسط حیاط ، یک حوض بزرگ بود و کم عمق. — In the middle of the courtyard was a large, shallow pool.
79 | 572

2191 تصمیم‌گیری tæsmimgiri *decision making* n
- باید ملت درباره آنها تصمیم‌گیری کند. — The nation should make a decision about them.
82 | 488

2192 حبس hæbs *prison* n
- برادر مرا به عنوان گروگان حبس کرده بودند. — They had imprisoned my brother as a hostage.
88 | 323

2193 دام dam *trap, livestock* n
- گربه هم رفت تو آشپزخانه کمین نشست و موشی را به دام انداخت. — The cat also went and sat in ambush in the kitchen and trapped a mouse.
81 | 514

2194 پیامبر pæjɑmbær *prophet* n,pn
- محمد پیامبر اسلام از طایفه قریش بود. — Mohammad, the Prophet of Islam, was of the tribe of Quraysh.
68 | 962

2195 شیمیایی ʃimijɑji *chemical* adj
- داعش بار دیگر در شمال عراق از سلاح شیمیایی استفاده کرد. — ISIS used chemical weapons in northern Iraq again.
83 | 473

2196 جا گذاشتن dʒɑgozɑʃtæn *leave behind* v
- فهرست خرید: لیستی که تهیه اش ساعت ها طول می کشد اما در فروشگاه به یاد می آورید که جا گذاشته اید. — Shopping list: a list whose preparation takes hours, but at the store you remember that you've left it somewhere.
86 | 384

2197 تعبیر tæ?bir *interpretation* n
- قرآن یک تعبیری دارد. — The Koran has one interpretation.
85 | 394

2198 دوش duʃ *shoulder, shower* adv,n
- زنان دوش به دوش مردان در اجتماع کار می کنند. — Women work side by side with men in the society.
86 | 371

2199 ایتالیایی itɑlijɑji *Italian* adj,n
- هیات عالی رتبه ایتالیایی وارد تهران شد. — The high-ranking Italian delegation arrived in Tehran.
83 | 471

2200 وزارتخانه vezɑrætxɑne *ministry* n
- می توان حضور خاتمی در این وزارتخانه را به دوره قبل و بعد از رحلت امام(ره) تقسیم کرد. — The presence of Khatami in this ministry can be divided into eras before and after the demise of the Imam.
77 | 656

2201 جغرافیایی dʒoɣrɑfjɑji *geographical* adj
- اطلاعات جغرافیایی من محدود است. — My geographic information is limited.
74 | 754

2202 محاسبه mohasebe *calculation* n
- روش‌های مختلفی برای محاسبه نرخ ارز به کار گرفته می‌شود. — Various methods are used to calculate the price of currency.
- 76 | 670

2203 متحده mottæhede *united* adj
- کشور امارات متحده عربی اولین میزبان این بازی‌ها در سال بود. — United Arab Emirates was the first host of the the games for the year.
- 69 | 906

2204 دانشجویی daneʃdʒuji *university student* adj
- پروژه های دانشجویی ممکن است با توجه به رشته تحصیلی و یا موضوع آنها متفاوت باشند. — Student projects may vary according to the course or subject.
- 80 | 555

2205 تبیین tæbjin *explanation* n
- توسعه متوازن بدون تبیین واقعیت‌ها ناممکن است. — Balanced development is impossible without explaining the facts.
- 82 | 481

2206 غیرقانونی ɣejrɣanuni *illegal* adj
- به اتهام اقامت غیرقانونی در شیراز دستگیر شده است. — He has been detained on the accusation of illegally residing in Shiraz.
- 83 | 453

2207 تأثیر گذاشتن tæʔsir gozaʃtæn *leave impression* v
- شخصیت همسران چه تأثیری بر زندگی مشترکشان می‌گذارد. — What kind of an impact can spouses' personality have on their married life?
- 89 | 276

2208 متوقف motevæɣɣef *stopped* adj
- دوباره ما را متوقف کرد. — He stopped us again.
- 88 | 314

2209 موسوم mowsum *called* adj
- یکی از شهرهای موسوم به اسکندریه را در این منطقه بنا کرد. — He built one of the cities named Alexandria in this region.
- 78 | 602

2210 تشویق tæʃviɣ *encouragement* n
- پدرش باز هم او را تشویق می‌کرد که به تمرین‌هایش ادامه دهد. — Her father encouraged her again to continue her exercises.
- 81 | 530

2211 خشم xæʃm *anger* n
- خشمش بیشتر می شد. — His rage was increasing.
- 80 | 532

2212 حس hess *sense, feeling* n
- مار ماهی حس بویایی بسیار قوی تری نسبت به سگ دارد. — The eel has a much stronger sense of smell than a dog.
- 73 | 753

2213 قضاوت ɣæzavæt *judgment* n
- شما خود قضاوت کنید. — Judge for yourself.
- 81 | 522

2214 یکسان jeksan *similar* adj,adv
- همه چیز یکسان است. — Everything is the same!
- 84 | 436

2215 ایمنی imæni *safety* adj,n
- در صورت ریزش باران، کلیه کارگران را با کلاه ایمنی به سالن نهار خوری ببرید . . . — In case of rain, bring all of the workers with safety helmets to the lunch room . . .
- 84 | 418

2216 گرفتار gereftar *caught, occupied* adj
- عربستان در گرداب خودساخته گرفتار شده است. — Saudi Arabia has been caught in a whirlpool of its own making.
- 87 | 351

2217 پیشنهادی piʃnehadi *proposed* adj,n
- مجلس افغانستان به وزیران پیشنهادی دولت رای اعتماد داد. — The Afghan parliament gave votes of confidence to the government's proposed ministers.
- 81 | 510

2218 روس rus *Russian* adj,n,pn
- او هم روس است. — She is also Russian.
- 84 | 421

2219 نشر næʃr *publishing* n
- در همان زمان نمایش تئاتر و نشر روزنامه به شیوه ساده انجام می‌گرفت. — During that time, theater showings and newspaper publishing were done in a simple way.
- 69 | 902

2220 زیارت zijaræt *pilgrimage* n
- روزی یکی از راجه‌های هندوستان برای زیارت به مشهد آمد. — One day, one of the Rajas of India came to Mashhad for a pilgrimage.
- 90 | 264

2221 مجید mædʒid *glorious, Majid* adj,pn
- آموزش روان خوانی قرآن مجید. — Teaching fluency in reading the Holy Koran.
- 78 | 596

2222 بمب bomb *bomb* n
- غربی‌ها که ایران را به استفاده از بمب هسته‌ای متهم می‌کنند باید برای اثبات خود دلیل داشته باشند. — Westerners that accuse Iran of using the atomic bomb need to have their own proof.
- 76 | 654

2223 سرخ sorx *red* adj,n
- به ندرت عصبانی می‌شد، وقتی هم می‌شد تمام صورتش سرخ می‌شد. — He would rarely get angry, but when he did his whole face would turn red.
- 73 | 751

2224 کلیدی kelidi *key* adj,n
- چگونه تعیین میشود؟ کلمات کلیدی متن — How are the key words of a text determined?

86 | 361

2225 سامان saman *orderliness* n,pn
- زندگی خود را به نحوی سر و سامان خواهید داد. — In a way you will bring order to your life.

87 | 334

2226 خودداری xoddari *self-control, restraint* n
- مرد دوم از رفتن به داخل مسجد خودداری می کند. — The second man refrained from going into the mosque.

87 | 325

2227 رئیسجمهور ræʔisdʒomhur *president* n
- رئیسجمهور درگذشت مرحوم علی دادمان را تسلیت گفت. — The president expressed his condolences for the death of the late Ali Dadman.

52 | 1591

2228 ورزیدن værzidæn *exercise* n,pn,v
- عشق ورزیدن برای او وجود ندارد. — Making love does not exist for him.

82 | 468

2229 تدارک tædarok *provision, preparation* n
- تدارک حمله نظامی آغاز شد. — Preparations for a military attack began.

84 | 418

2230 افراطی efrati *extremist* adj,n
- اولاند خواستار حمله به همه گروههای افراطی در سوریه شد. — Hollande called for attacks on all extremist groups in Syria.

85 | 385

2231 کتابی ketabi *bookish, flat* adj,n
- پس شما فرهیخته گرامی با نوشتن جملات تشویقی در بخش نظرات، جامعه را کتابیتر کنید. — So you, esteemed learned person, make society more literate by writing encouraging phrases in the comments section.

86 | 370

2232 یازدهم jazdæhom *eleventh* adj,n
- حمله های مرگبار یازدهم سپتامبر، چهره جهان را تغییر داد. — The deadly attacks of September eleventh changed the face of the world.

77 | 625

2233 پناه pænah *shelter* n
- آنانرا در پناه و چتر حمایت و محبت خویش قرارداد. — He has them under his shelter and loving and supportive umbrella.

87 | 331

2234 طوفان tufan *storm* n
- کشتی در طوفان شکست و غرق شد. — The ship broke in the storm and sank.

84 | 431

2235 درگذشت dærgozæʃt *death, died* n,v
- رییس جمهوری درگذشت آیت الله ملکوتی را تسلیت گفت. — The president expressed his condolences for death of Ayatollah Malakouti.

77 | 620

2236 حرم hæræm *sanctuary* n
- دو ایوان رو به شمال و جنوب راه ورود را به حرم یا مقصوره گنبددار مرکزی می گشودند. — Two porticos facing north and south opened the entryway to the sanctuary or central domed inner chamber.

87 | 329

2237 فوری fowri *immediate* adj,adv
- فوری خبردار می شویم. — We will be informed promptly.

85 | 406

2238 مقیم moɣim *resident* adj
- رئیس جمهور عراق از وی خواست از فلسطینیها مقیم عراق حمایت کند. — The Iraqi president asked him to support Palestinians residing in Iraq.

81 | 511

2239 خواننده xanænde *reader, singer* n
- اصولاً ویژگی ارکستری در این حجم و اندازه این است که با چند خواننده مختلف کار کند. — Basically, a trait of an orchestra of this size is that it works with several different singers.

75 | 680

2240 سپتامبر septambr *September* n
- نشست بعدی اوپک در ماه سپتامبر خواهد بود. — OPEC's next meeting will be in September.

78 | 613

2241 مسعود mæsʔud *Masoud* pn
- آقای مسعود شاکری. — Mr. Masoud Shakeri.

74 | 712

2242 ادا æda *coquettish, payment* n
- من میخوام حق مطلب ادا بشود. — I want the desired payment to be made.

87 | 339

2243 دریافتن dærjaftæn *perceive, receive* adj,v
- چون در این صورت کودک به دریافت هدیه عادت می کند. — Because in this case the child gets used to receiving gifts.

87 | 346

2244 چاره ʧare *remedy* n
- ایشان چارهای جز استعفا نداشت. — He had no choice but to resign.

83 | 438

2245 دشواری doʃvari *difficulty* adj,n
- ممکن است دشواری های بسیار زیادی را داشته باشد. — It is possible she will have a lot of difficulties.

86 | 351

14 Male names

Rank	Headword	Pronunciation	Gloss	Rank	Headword	Pronunciation	Gloss
109	علی	æli	Ali	2271	امین	æmin	honest, Amin
161	محمد	mohæmmæd	Mohammad	2383	صادق	sadeɣ	truthful
278	حسن	hæsæn	Hasan	2402	محمدرضا	mohæmmædreza	Mohammad Reza
730	عباس	æbbas	Abbas	2439	رسول	ræsul	messenger
795	محمود	mæhmud	Mahmoud	2441	یوسف	jusof, jusef	Joseph
834	حسین	hosejn	Hossein	2452	نعمت	neʔmæt	gift, blessing
862	احمد	æhmæd	Ahmad	2489	ناصر	naser	Nasser
1026	رضا	reza	Reza	2585	پرویز	pærviz	Parviz
1050	عزیز	æziz	Aziz	2645	صبا	sæba	zephyr
1191	مهدی	mehdi	Mehdi	2814	فرهاد	færhad	Farhad
1217	سعید	sæʔid	Said	2956	رحمت	ræhmæt	compassion
1241	مسلم	moslem	Muslim	2958	عارف	aref	Sufi, conoisseur
1279	اکبر	ækbær	Akbar	2963	مالک	malek	owner
1301	امیر	æmir	Amir	2987	نادر	nader	rare, Nader
1309	ابراهیم	ebrahim	Ebrahim	2988	سلیمان	solejman	Soleiman, Solomon
1311	آرام	aram	peaceful	3046	اصغر	æsɣær	Asghar
1342	آدم	adæm	Adam	3075	کسری	kæsra	Kasra
1391	بهمن	bæhmæn	avalanche, Bahman	3083	تقی	tæɣi	Taghi
1417	عبدالله	æbdollah	Abdollah	3085	خلیل	xælil	Khalil
1443	شریف	ʃærif	honorable	3195	مرتضی	morteza	Morteza
1538	کمال	kæmal	perfection	3227	داوود	davud	Davood
1721	معین	moʔin	Moin	3327	خسرو	xosrow	Khosrow
1728	جواد	dʒævad	Javad	3423	جعفر	dʒæʔfær	Jafar
1746	کاظم	kazem	Kazem	3439	شاهین	ʃahin	falcon, Shahin
1772	اسماعیل	esmaʔil	Ishmael, Esmail	3440	پویا	puja	dynamic
1867	کریم	kærim	generous, great	3475	جمال	dʒæmal	beauty, Jamal
1873	محسن	mohsen	Mohsen	3520	مراد	morad	desire, Morad
1929	علیرضا	ælireza	Alireza	3676	داریوش	darjuʃ	Darius
2085	منصور	mænsur	Mansour	3822	رحیم	ræhim	merciful, Rahim
2114	حمید	hæmid	Hamid	3880	حامد	hamed	Hamed
2129	موسی	musa	Musa, Moses	3883	شهریار	ʃæhrijar	monarch
2161	مصطفی	mostæfa	Mostafa	3934	بابک	babæk	Babak
2221	مجید	mædʒid	glorious, Majid	3982	قاسم	ɣasem	Ghasem
2225	سامان	saman	orderliness	4004	بهرام	bæhram	Bahram
2241	مسعود	mæsʔud	Masoud				
2265	هادی	hadi	conductor, Hadi				

Rank	Headword	Pronunciation	Gloss	Rank	Headword	Pronunciation	Gloss
4010	مهران	mehran	Mehran	4498	قربان	ɣorban	sacrifice
4042	محمدعلی	mohæmmædæli	Mohammad Ali	4579	نیکو	niku	good, fair
4103	عادل	adel	just	4592	همایون	homajun	Homayun
4105	عیسی	isa	Jesus	4677	رشید	ræʃid	well grown, Rashid
4176	نیما	nima	Nima	4702	مهرداد	mehrdad	Mehrdad
4242	وحید	væhid	Vahid	4703	بیژن	biʒæn	Bijan
4244	نوید	nævid	good news, Navid	4730	سلمان	sælman	Salman, Solomon
4414	مجتبی	modʒtæba	Mojtaba	4743	منوچهر	mænuʧehr	Manuchehr
4418	حبیب	hæbib	friend, lover, Habib	4817	رستم	rostæm	Rostam
4440	جمشید	dʒæmʃid	Jamshid	4902	بهزاد	behzad	Behzad
4469	بهروز	behruz	Behruz	4954	جهانگرد	dʒæhangærd	explorer
4484	فریدون	ferejdun, færidun	Fereydun	4974	کامران	kamran	Kamran
				4994	سیاوش	sijavæʃ	Siavash

2246 پیامد pejamæd *outcome* n
- پیامدهای هر یک از آنها بررسی می شوند. — The consequences of each and every one of them will be reviewed.
78 | 606

2247 حساسیت hæssasijjæt *sensitivity* adj,n
- اگزما از انواع حساسیت‌های پوستی است. — Eczema is one of the varieties of skin allergies.
83 | 459

2248 تأکید داشتن tæʔkid daʃtæn *emphasize* v
- دولت بر حمایت از تولید داخلی تاکید دارد. — The government emphasizes the support of domestic production.
86 | 371

2249 اخراج exradʒ *dismissal* n
- این کارگران نسبت به اخراج‌های خود معترضند و خواهان بازگشت به کار هستند. — These workers are protesting their layoffs, and demand their return to work.
76 | 646

2250 تلخ tælx *bitter* adj
- لبخند تلخی زد. — He smiled bitterly.
85 | 402

2251 متری metri *metric, meter* n
- دروازه ۱ متر عرض و یک و نیم متر طول دارد و در ارتفاع دو متری معلق است. — The gate is one meter wide and one and a half meters long, and is suspended at a height of two meters.
86 | 366

2252 صراحت serahæt *frankness* n
- با صراحت اعلام می‌کنیم که فلسطینیان را مسلح کردیم. — We are announcing plain and clear that we armed the Palestinians.
88 | 305

2253 بسیج bæsidʒ *mobilization, Basij* n
- نیرو و توانتان را برای رسیدن به این خواسته بسیج می‌کنید. — Mobilize all of your force and ability for achieving this request.
82 | 483

2254 بنگاه bongah *establishment* n
- در بیشتر بنگاه های مشمول قانون کار، سرنوشت افزایش حق مسکن همچنان نامعلوم است. — In most firms subject to labor laws, the fate of the increase in the right to housing remains unclear.
88 | 309

2255 پوشاندن puʃandæn *dress* adj,v
- زیبایی یعنی پوشاندن گیسوان. — Beauty means covering the tresses.
82 | 482

2256 نگرش negæreʃ *outlook* n
- نگرش سیاست گذاران. — The attitude of policy makers.
78 | 595

2257 برپایی bærpaji *erection, setting up* n
- پیش از برپایی حکومت منطقه‌ای کردستان عراق، آموزش عالی در این منطقه تنها به زبان عربی انجام می‌شد. — Before the establishment of the Kurdistan regional government of Iraq, higher education in this area was conducted only in Arabic.
79 | 562

2258 پرهیز pærhiz *avoidance* n
- ● — از خوردن غذاهای شور در این ماه پرهیز کنند. They should abstain from eating salty foods this month.
- 87 | 339

2259 درونی dæruni *inner* adj
- ● از گفتگوهای درونی خود، آگاه شوید. — Be aware of your own internal dialogues.
- 83 | 452

2260 فیلسوف filsuf *philosopher* adj,n
- ● اما این فیلسوف تو رو می شناسه! — But this philosopher knows you!
- 86 | 360

2261 عراقی erayi *Iraqi* adj,n,pn
- ● آینده‌ای تاریک کودکان عراقی را تهدید می‌کند. — A dark future threatens Iraqi children.
- 75 | 697

2262 اتمی ætomi *atomic* adj
- ● ایران سلاح های اتمی تولید نمی کند. — Iran will not produce atomic weapons.
- 73 | 752

2263 رانندگی ranændegi *driving* n
- ● کدام یک از دلایل زیر عامل بروز اکثر تصادفات رانندگی است. — Which one of the following reasons is the factor appearing in the most driving accidents?
- 79 | 565

2264 مصمم mosæmmæm *determined* adj
- ● الهام خیلی مصمم بود. — Elham was very determined.
- 91 | 226

2265 هادی hadi *conductor, Hadi* n,pn
- ● صدای هادی را شنیده بود. — He had heard Hadi's voice.
- 83 | 427

2266 خودکشی xodkoʃi *suicide* n
- ● مردم ایران همان زمان هم خودکشی تختی را باور نکردند. — Iranians, even at that time, did not believe Takhti's suicide.
- 85 | 375

2267 تروریسم terorism *terrorism* n
- ● این کار شما تروریسم است! — This work of yours is terrorism!
- 76 | 660

2268 رسماً ræsmæn *officially* adv
- ● رسماً شکست مذاکرات را اعلام کرد. — He formally announced the failure of the negotiations.
- 89 | 282

2269 عینی ejni *objective* adj
- ● شما بهتر است به حقایق عینی توجه داشته باشید. — You'd better pay attention to the objective facts.
- 85 | 386

2270 پیرو pejrow *follower* adj,n
- ● به پیروان اسلام «مسلمان» می‌گویند. — They call the followers of Islam "Muslims."
- 83 | 440

2271 امین æmin *honest, Amin* adj,pn
- ● دست کم، فعلاً قرار بود که درستکار و امین باشم. — At least for now, I was supposed to be honest and trustworthy.
- 86 | 343

2272 میل mejl, mil *desire, rod/mile* n
- ● میل شام داشتم. — I had a desire for dinner.
- 82 | 472

2273 خاتمه xateme *conclusion* n
- ● بحران در حال خاتمه یافتن است. — The crisis is ending.
- 85 | 373

2274 سازماندهی sazmandehi *organizing* n
- ● سازماندهی یکی از مهارتهای تفکر می باشد. — Organizing is one of of the thinking skills.
- 86 | 357

2275 وسعت vosʔæt *extent* n
- ● وسعت قلمرو آنها در زمان اوج قدرتشان از رود سند، در هند تا سلسله جبال هندوکش و از نورستان تا نزدیک بُست گسترش داشت. — The breadth of their territory at the height of their power spread from the river Sindh in India to the Hindu Kush mountain range and from Nuristan to near Bost.
- 80 | 515

2276 مقوله mæyule *category, topic* n
- ● امنیت اساسی ترین و اصلی ترین نیاز هر جامعه ای بوده و نقش پلیس در ایجاد این مقوله بر کسی پوشیده نیست. — Security is the most fundamental and most essential need in each community and the role of police in this issue is not lost on anybody.
- 79 | 566

2277 متوجه شدن motevædʒdʒeh ʃodæn *notice* v
- ● متوجه شد که آنچه انسان می گوید مهم نیست. — She realized that what people say is not important.
- 79 | 548

2278 پاره pare *torn, part* adj,n,q
- ● یک انار دیگر پاره شد. — Another pomegranate was cut open.
- 83 | 443

2279 شتاب ʃetab *haste* n
- ● شتاب داشت ، آن را زودتر ترک کند. — She was in a hurry to leave there more quickly.
- 88 | 290

2280 مجهز modʒæhhæz *well-equipped* adj
- کار بیمارستان زودتر از آنچه پیش بینی می‌شد به پایان رسید و به آخرین تجهیزات پیشرفته‌ی پزشکی مجهز شد. — The hospital job was finished sooner than had been anticipated, and was equipped with the latest advanced medical equipment.

85 | 368

2281 سرپرست sæɾpæɾæst *supervisor* n
- آیا فکر می کنید سرپرست شما یا رئیس شما اهمیتی به دلیل آن می دهد؟ — Do you think your boss or supervisor cares about the reason?

80 | 522

2282 عارضه ɑɾeze *incident* n
- این عارضه جدی‌تری است. — This is a more serious phenomenon.

71 | 809

2283 هکتار hektɑɾ *hectare* n
- مساحت این منطقه حدود ۶۲۰۰ هکتار است. — The area of this region is about 6,200 hectares.

75 | 663

2284 نسبتاً nesbætæn *relatively* adv
- کار نسبتاً پیچیده ای بود. — It was a relatively difficult task.

82 | 464

2285 خانوادگی xɑnevɑdegi *familial* adj,n
- سلمان با کودتای خانوادگی برکنار می‌شود. — Salman is being ousted through a family coup.

82 | 466

2286 توده tude *mass, Tudeh* n
- حزب توده غیرقانونی اعلام شد. — The Tudeh Party was declared illegal.

86 | 348

2287 شکوه ʃokuh, ʃekve *splendor, complaint* n
- در دوران او شاهنشاهی ساسانی یک دوره رونق و شکوه را تجربه کرد. — During his era, the Sasanian Empire experienced a period of prosperity and glory.

92 | 201

2288 تصور کردن tæsævvoɾ kæɾdæn *imagine* v
- هرگز تصور نکرده بودم که زمان بتواند به این آهستگی بگذرد. — I had never imagined that time could go by so slowly.

85 | 376

2289 نیروگاه niɾugɑh *power station* n
- تولید برق در نیروگاه‌های آبی را مختل کرده است. — It has disrupted hydroelectric power generation.

71 | 781

2290 ایراد iɾɑd *objection* n
- در باب نوشته های تو دو ایراد دارم . . . — I have two objections concerning your writings . . .

86 | 357

2291 مدیرعامل modiɾe ɑmel *managing director* n
- مدیر عامل بانک مسکن معتقد است باید شعبه‌های بانک گسترش یابد. — The CEO of Housing Bank believes that the bank branches should be increased.

77 | 620

2292 میهن mihæn *homeland* n
- برای میهن و مردم سرودن را آغاز نمودم. — I began to sing for my people and homeland.

90 | 236

2293 حرفه‌ای heɾfeji *professional* adj
- والدین او گرت و فرانسس هر دو از ورزشکاران حرفه‌ای به حساب می‌آمدند. — His parents, Garrett and Frances, were both considered professional athletes.

75 | 651

2294 صدد sædæd *intention* adj,n
- تلویزیون درصدد ارائه یک تصویر سیاه از اصلاح گران و روند اصلاح طلبی در کشور است. — Television seeks to provide a black image of the reformers and the country's reform process.

85 | 386

2295 هاشمی hɑʃemi *Hashemi* pn
- هاشمی برای روحانی نامه‌ای ارسال نکرده است. — Hashemi has not sent any letters to Rowhani.

71 | 789

2296 شوهر ʃowhæɾ *husband* n
- عکس شما را برداشت و پرسید شوهرتان است. — He picked up your photo and asked, "Is this your husband?"

65 | 984

2297 مکرر mokæɾɾæɾ *repeated* adj,adv
- نیروهای آمریکایی پس از پیروزی‌های مکرر، مکزیکو سیتی را اشغال کردند. — After repeated victories, the American forces took over Mexico City.

88 | 294

2298 گلستان golestɑn *rose garden, Golestan* n,pn
- مدیر کل میراث فرهنگی، صنایع دستی و گردشگری استان گلستان. — The managing director of Cultural Heritage, Handicrafts, and Tourism in the province of Golestan.

80 | 520

2299 فراری fæɾɑɾi *fugitive* adj,n
- هنوز چند ساعتی از ماجرا نگذشته بود که کارآگاهان موفق به ردیابی دو اعدامی فراری در روستایی در جاده بندر عباس شدند. — A few hours had not yet passed when the detectives successfully tracked down the two condemned fugitives in a village on the road to Bandar Abbas.

92 | 202

2300 بابا baba *dad* n

- ساعت ۵ صبح به بابا زنگ زدم. — I called Dad at five in the morning.

47 | 1729

2301 مخصوصاً mæxsusæn *especially* adv

- غذاهای فوری غربی نیز طرفداران زیادی مخصوصاً در میان جوانان و کودکان دارند. — Western fast food is popular especially among adolescents and children.

83 | 436

2302 مستمر mostæmærr *continuous* adj

- تنها راه به وجود آوردن تغییرات مستمر در زندگی داشتن یک هدف درازمدت است. — The only way to create constant changes in life is having a long-term goal.

84 | 401

2303 جانب dʒaneb *side, behalf* n

- من ملکی هستم که از جانب خدا مأمورم. — I am a king sent by God.

73 | 731

2304 راهنمایی rahnæmaji *guidance* adj,n

- با صمیمیتی که برایم نامنتظر بود، به من خوشامد گفت و مرا به اتاق پذیرایی راهنمایی کرد. — With a sincerity that was unexpected for me, she welcomed me and guided me to the living room.

76 | 635

2305 پراکنده pærakænde *dispersed* adj

- طی دو روز آینده بارش پراکنده باران در پاره‌ای از نقاط تهران پیش‌بینی می‌شود. — Over the next two days scattered showers are predicted in some parts of Tehran.

90 | 252

2306 شکست دادن ʃekæst dadæn *defeat* v

- نادرشاه مغول را شکست داد و دهلی را تصرف کرد. — Nader Shah defeated the Mongols and captured Delhi.

69 | 847

2307 منتهی montæhi, montæha *ending, but* adj,conj

- فلسفه هگل‌اش هم همین است، منتهی به شکل دیگری. — Hegel's philosophy is also like this yet in a different form.

86 | 340

2308 ابتدایی ebtedaji *elementary* adj,n

- مدارس ابتدایی شهر تهران و ری دوشنبه و سه‌شنبه تعطیل شد. — Rey and Tehran elementary schools were closed Monday and Tuesday.

80 | 504

2309 تولید کردن towlid kærdæn *produce* v

- تا اواخر سال‌های دهه 1970، چین سالانه کمتر از 3 هزار دستگاه خودروی سواری تولید می‌کرد. — Until the end of the 1970s, China produced fewer than three thousand passenger cars annually.

84 | 390

2310 محدوده mæhdude *perimeter* n

- یک دستگاه اتوبوس بین شهری با عبور از روی پای یک خانم جوان در محدوده ترمینال جنوب موجب قطع دو پای این شهروند تهرانی شد. — An intercity bus caused the legs of a citizen of Tehran to be cut off when it ran over the young woman's legs near the the the southern terminal.

78 | 567

2311 اسرائیلی esraʔili *Israeli* adj,n

- خبرنگار اسرائیلی جاسوس نبود. — The Israeli journalist was not a spy.

83 | 429

2312 متشکل motæʃækkel *consisting of* adj

- اکثریت آنها متشکل از شرکتهای چند ملیتی هستند. — The majority of them are formed as multinational corporations.

84 | 396

2313 افت oft *drop* n

- زمانی که عرضه یک کالا گسترش می‌یابد، افت قیمت را داریم. — When the supply of a product expands, we have a drop in the price.

83 | 432

2314 فرآورده færaværde *product* n

- تولید این فرآورده دارویی در ایران از خروج سالانه یک و نیم میلیون دلار ارز از کشور جلوگیری میکند. — The production of this pharmaceutical product in Iran prevents the country from pouring out one and half million dollars annually.

82 | 461

2315 عادلانه adelane *justly* adj,adv

- بازیگران بازار پولی باید در شرایط یکسان و عادلانه فعالیت کنند. — Players in the money market must operate in equal and just conditions.

87 | 320

2316 برج bordʒ *tower* n

- این شاعر در برج عاج خود نشسته است. — This poet is sitting in his own ivory tower.

83 | 430

2317 توکیو tokjo *Tokyo* pn

- جنوب غربی توکیو را تکان داد. — It shook the southwest of Tokyo.

84 | 394

2318 شی ʃeʔ *thing* n

- منکر وجود شی مورد ادعای شما است. — Denies the existence of the object of your claim.

89 | 270

2319 شاگرد ʃagerd *student* n

- جعفر جلو دکان نشسته بود، مثل شاگردی که منتظر استاد است. — Jafar sat in front of the store like a student waiting for the teacher.

64 | 1022

2320 چاه ʧah *well* n
- برو تو چاه. — Go into the well.

85 | 380

2321 تسلط tæsællot *dominance* n
- مدیر مدرسه تسلط کاملی به زبان انگلیسی نداشت. — The school's principal did not have a complete command of the English language.

82 | 456

2322 برگ bærg *leaf* n
- یک برگ دیگر را لگد کردم. — I kicked another leaf.

79 | 530

2323 خانوار xanevar *household* n
- در این کوچه تنگ و بن بست حدود پانزده خانوار زندگی می کردند. — In this narrow alley and dead end nearly fourteen or fifteen families used to live.

81 | 477

2324 برقی bærɣi *electric* adj,n,pn
- وسایل برقیتان را با راه رفتن شارژ کنید. — Charge your electronic appliances by walking.

93 | 156

2325 بازتاب baztab *reflection* adj,n
- بازتاب نور چراغ را دید. — She saw the reflection of the lamp's light.

87 | 322

2326 سینمایی sinemaji *cinematic* adj
- همکاری سینمایی ایران و چین آغاز شده است. — Cinematic cooperation between Iran and China has begun.

72 | 753

2327 خب xob *well* adv
- خب می‌دانم که حتماً ترجمه من اشکالاتی دارد، اما رمان به نظر شما چطور بود؟ — Okay, I know that my translation certainly had problems, but how was the novel in your opinion?

59 | 1196

2328 همگانی hæmeɡani *public, general* adj
- این جشن جمعی و همگانی است. — This is a general and collective celebration.

83 | 405

2329 خرج xærʤ *expense* n
- زن اول گفت «حالا که این جور شد، فقط می‌ماند خرج ملا، که آن را هم یک جوری جور می‌کنیم.» — The first woman said, "Now that that's taken care of, there's just the expense of the mullah, which we'll also sort out somehow."

80 | 504

2330 مملکت mæmlekæt *country* n
- استقلال این مملکت و عزت مستقلانه این مردم را پایکوب کرده بود. — The independence and independent dignity of this people had been trampled.

81 | 464

2331 تاجیکستان taʤikestan *Tajikistan* pn
- قیمت دارو در تاجیکستان گران است. — Medicine is expensive in Tajikistan.

80 | 496

2332 محتوا mohtæva *content* n
- بی بی سی مسئول محتوای سایت های دیگر نیست. — BBC is not responsible for the contents of other sites.

77 | 593

2333 دارویی daruji *pharmaceutical* adj,n
- همه گیاهان دارویی بی‌ضرر نیستند. — Not all medicinal herbs are harmless.

81 | 457

2334 صحن sæhn *courtyard, precinct* n
- آن جنازه را بطرف صحن مطهر میبردند. — They were carrying the body towards the Motahhar Courtyard.

89 | 260

2335 خودداری کردن xoddari kærdæn *refrain* v
- سفارت آمریکا از اظهار نظر در این باره خودداری کرد. — The US embassy refrained from any statement about that.

88 | 287

2336 آسمانی asemani *heavenly* adj,n
- سیاره یک جرم آسمانی است. — A planet is a celestial body.

91 | 221

2337 ریاضی rijazi *mathematical* adj,n,pn
- ایران، مقام چهارم المپیاد ریاضی جهان را کسب کرد. — Iran won fourth place in the world's Mathematical Olympiad.

85 | 373

2338 میر mir *emir, Mir* n,pn
- میرحسین موسوی به دلیل عارضه شدید قلبی به بیمارستان منتقل شد. — Mir Hossein Mousavi was taken to hospital due to a serious heart condition.

87 | 314

2339 قدردانی ɣædrdani *appreciation* n
- فریکسوس قوچ طلایی را به نشانه قدردانی برای زئوس قربانی کرد. — Phrixus sacrificed the golden ram as a token of appreciation to Zeus.

84 | 389

2340 ناب nab *pure* adj
- از طلای ناب ساخته شده بود؟ — Was it made out of pure gold?

93 | 173

2341 آبادی abadi *village, Abadi* n,pn
- کامو یکی از آبادی‌های کاشان است. — Kamu is one of the villages of Kashan.

87 | 309

2342 جور ʤur *sort* adj,n,pn
- چرا این جور نگاهم می کنند؟ — Why are they looking at me like this?

53 | 1397

2343 تخت tæxt *throne, bed, flat* n
- پس آرام روی تخت دراز کشید. — Then he slowly lay down on the bed.
- 76 | 600

2344 گیلان gilan *Gilan* pn
- جنگل‌های گیلان را همیشه به یاد داشته باشیم. — We will always remember the forests of Gilan.
- 77 | 567

2345 یکم jekom *first* adj,n
- فاصله خیابان یکم تا خیابان هفدهم برابر با ۱٫۸ کیلومتر می‌باشد. — The distance between First and Seventeenth Streets is 1.8 kilometers.
- 84 | 382

2346 ستون sotun *column* n
- یک ستون به ارتفاع شش متر. — One column with a height of six meters.
- 79 | 535

2347 کلید kelid *key, switch* n
- باک به او می‌گوید که کلید خانه را با خود نبرد. — Buck tells him not to take the house key with him.
- 76 | 598

2348 نحوی næhvi *syntactic, grammarian* adj,n
- ضمایر، کلماتی هستند که از نظر نحوی، یک واحد مستقل به حساب می‌آیند. — Pronouns are words that syntactically speaking are considered as an independent unit.
- 75 | 622

2349 ابتلا ebtela *affliction* n
- ابتلا به آلرژی. — Afflicted with allergies.
- 82 | 450

2350 رفاه refah *welfare, comfort* n
- به تدریج با افزایش سطح رفاه مردم در کشور های مختلف و به تبع آن ایجاد سلایق متنوع، خودروسازان به فکر ارائه مدل های جدیدتر، زیباتر و ایمن تر افتادند. — With the increase of the people's welfare in different countries and, following that, the emergence of diverse interests, automakers gradually began to consider providing newer, more attractive, and safer models.
- 80 | 496

2351 مغلوب mæɣlub *defeated* adj
- در آن بازی مغلوب اتلتیکومادرید شدند. — In that match they were beaten by Atlético Madrid.
- 86 | 341

2352 تشدید tæʃdid *intensification* n
- در پی تشدید آلودگی هوا کلیه مدارس و ادارات استان تهران شنبه تعطیل شد. — Following the intensification of air pollution, all schools and offices in Tehran Province were closed on Saturday.
- 72 | 709

2353 پژوهشی pæʒuheʃi *research* adj,n
- این مرکز پژوهشی-درمانی سالانه ۱۰۰۰۰۰۰ بیمار سرطانی را می‌پذیرد. — This therapy research center accepts 100,000 cancer patients annually.
- 78 | 561

2354 کاروان karevan *caravan* n
- بزرگترین خانه سیار کاروان جهان در عربستان سعودی ساخته شد. — The world's biggest caravan mobile home has been built in Saudi Arabia.
- 83 | 420

2355 بزودی bezudi *soon* adv
- چاپ دوم آن بزودی انتشار خواهد یافت. — Its second edition will be published soon.
- 87 | 307

2356 هوادار hævadar *supporter* adj,n
- سلمان خان از معدود هنرپیشه‌های بالیوود است که در میان طیف وسیعی از جامعه هند، هوادار دارد. — Salman Khan is one of the few Bollywood actors that has fans among a wide spectrum of of Indian society.
- 83 | 401

2357 نهضت nehzæt *movement* n
- نهضت اسلامی را را از پشت خنجر زدند. — They stabbed the Islamic movement in the back.
- 82 | 434

2358 جلوگیری کردن dʒelowgiri kærdæn *prevent* v
- با نیکوکاری از کارهای ناپسند جلوگیری کن. — Avoid indecencies through beneficence.
- 85 | 368

2359 حامل hamel *carrier* adj,n
- در هفته‌های اخیر محموله‌های کشتی حامل خوراک طیور در بنادر کشور لنگر انداخته بود. — In recent weeks, boat shipments carrying poultry feed had dropped anchor in the country's ports.
- 82 | 425

2360 نظرسنجی næzærsændʒi *opinion poll* n
- یک نظرسنجی در این سایت خبری انجام شد. — A survey was conducted on this news site.
- 84 | 375

2361 علیرغم ælaræɣm *despite* conj
- فرانسه، علی‌رغم اعتراض پزشکان، نظام‌بهداشتی‌اش را اصلاح می‌کند. — Despite objections from doctors, France is reforming its health system.
- 84 | 389

2362 اینکه inke *that* conj
- بچه ها از اینکه مجبور بودند، سیب زمینی های بدبو و سنگین را همه جا با خود حمل کنند، شکایت داشتند. — The children had complaints about the fact that they were required to carry smelly, heavy potatoes everywhere.
- 70 | 795

2363 شمارش ʃomareʃ *counting* n
- اولین سرشماری عمومی در سراسر امپراتوری عثمانی در سال ۱۸۴۴ تنها شهروندان مرد شمارش شدند. — In the first general census across the Ottoman Empire in the year 1844, only male citizens were counted.
- 90 | 223

2364 کوچه kutʃe *lane* n
- ماشینش را توی کوچه پارک می‌کرد. — He was parking his car in the alley.
- 66 | 911

2365 مرداد mordɑd *Mordad* n
- از مرداد پارسال تا امسال شرکت‌های خودروسازی بدترین سال حیات خود را سپری کرده‌اند. — From the month of Mordad of last year up until this year, automobile companies have been through the worst twelve months of their existence.
- 80 | 484

2366 توضیح دادن towzih dɑdæn *explain* v
- برنامه‌نویسی چیزی جز آنچه که توضیح دادم نیست. — Programming isn't anything but what I explained.
- 82 | 439

2367 ماندگار mandegar *lasting* adj
- عشق تنها حقیقت ماندگار است. — Love is the only lasting truth.
- 89 | 256

2368 خرد xeræd, xord *wisdom, small* adj,n
- مصاحبه‌کنندگان به اندازۀ کافی از خرد و هشیاری برخوردار بودند. — The interviewers had sufficient wisdom and consciousness.
- 81 | 472

2369 مردن mordæn *die* n,pn,v
- این جور مردن از هر جور مردنی راحت تر است. — This way of dying is more comfortable than other ways of dying.
- 66 | 902

2370 شانس ʃans *good luck* n
- شانس برنده شدن بیشتری دارد. — She has a higher chance of winning.
- 84 | 368

2371 خطا xætɑ *error* n
- این بار هم تیرش به خطا رفت. — This time her arrow also went astray.
- 80 | 496

2372 روحی ruhi *spiritual, mental* adj,n,pn
- دو سال پیش مادرش سرطان گرفت و وضع روحی ش باز هم بدتر شد. — Two years ago his mother developed cancer and her mental state also worsened.
- 79 | 506

2373 تجمع tædʒæmmoʔ *gathering* n
- گفتاری درباره تجمع جمعی از زنان مقابل سازمان ملل. — A talk about a group of women gathered in front of UN.
- 71 | 756

2374 مشغله mæʃɣæle *occupation* n
- پدرش باوجود مشغله بسیار ساعت‌هایی را در تنهایی به بازی کردن با او اختصاص می‌دادهاست. — Despite his job, his father devoted hours to play with him alone.
- 86 | 324

2375 کاخ kax *palace* n
- از جمله کاخ‌های معروف تهران می‌توان کاخ نیاوران را نام برد. — One can name Niavaran Palace among the famous palaces of Tehran.
- 72 | 702

2376 کردستان kordestan *Kurdistan* pn
- این رویداد متعلق به ملت کردستان است. — This event belongs to the nation of Kurdistan.
- 78 | 529

2377 شکوفایی ʃokufɑji *flowering* n
- پاییز در آلاسکا با شکوفایی گل‌های رنگارنگ آغاز شده است. — Autumn started in Alaska with colorful flowers blooming.
- 90 | 219

2378 گشودن ɡoʃudæn *open* n,v
- گشودن در کشور روی اقتصاد جهانی. — Opening the doors of the country to the global economy.
- 81 | 466

2379 غلط ɣælæt *mistake* adj,n
- غلط کردم. — I made a mistake.
- 83 | 405

2380 عباسی æbbɑsi *Abbasi, Abbasid* adj,pn
- تو هم سه عباسی دیگر را به من حلال کن. — You also remit to me 3 abbasis more.
- 89 | 259

2381 پانزده panzdæh *fifteen* n
- پانزده ساله بودم که او را نیز از دست دادم. — I was fifteen when I lost him too.
- 63 | 997

2382 کامیون kamjon *truck* n
- اکنون قطعات نمک به طور معمول توسط کامیون‌ها منتقل می‌شوند. — Now pieces of salt are normally transported by truck.
- 85 | 352

2383 صادق sadeɣ *truthful* adj,pn
- اگر تو درست و صادق باشی، مردم درست و صادق تو را پیدا می‌کنند. — If you are true and sincere, true and sincere people will find you.
- 83 | 409

2384 نیازی nijazi *needy, Niazi* n,pn
- آقای نیازی اشتباه بزرگی کرد. — Mr. Niazi made a big mistake.
- 83 | 406

2385 سیل sejl *flood* n
- ‏چهل سال قبل سیل آمده بود.‏ — Forty years ago a flood had come.
- 78 | 533

2386 گردشگری gærdefgæri *tourism* n
- ‏این دریاچه و کرانه‌های آن از جاذبه‌های گردشگری ارمنستان به شمار می‌آید.‏ — This lake and its coast are considered one of Armenia's touristic attractions.
- 77 | 564

2387 ناکامی nakami *frustration* n
- ‏با ناکامی‌های خود چه کنیم؟‏ — What shall we do with your failures?
- 87 | 299

2388 معضل moʔzæl *difficulty* n
- ‏موقعیت بحرانی می‌تواند معضلی باشد که شخص از حل آن ناتوان است.‏ — The crisis situation may be a predicament which the individual is incapable of solving.
- 74 | 641

2389 درآوردن dæraværdæn *extract, produce* adj,n,v
- ‏تکه کاغذی از کیف درآورد و روی آن چیزی نوشت.‏ — She took a piece of paper out of her bag and wrote something on it.
- 69 | 794

2390 بازرسی bazresi *inspection* n
- ‏بازرسی‌های مرزی در جبل‌الطارق ادامه دارد.‏ — Border inspections continue in Gibraltar.
- 81 | 463

2391 حامی hami *protector* adj,n
- ‏بزرگترین حامی شما بعد از خدا کیست؟‏ — After God, who is your biggest supporter?
- 78 | 527

2392 کلینتون kelinton *Clinton* pn
- ‏او ادعا می‌کرد که برای ۳۶ نفر از روسای آمریکا لباس دوخته است اما فقط اسم چند تن از آن‌ها را مانند کلینتون، اوباما و بوش بزرگ و کوچک بیان کرد.‏ — He claimed that he'd sewn clothes for 36 of America's presidents but only named a few of them, like Clinton, Obama, and big and little Bush.
- 81 | 458

2393 خوشحال xoʃhal *happy* adj,v
- ‏من از اینکه اینجا هستم خیلی خوشحالم.‏ — I am very happy to be here.
- 74 | 640

2394 مسافرت mosaferæt *travel* n
- ‏مسافرت بودم، رفته بودم یزد.‏ — I was on a trip; I'd gone to Yazd.
- 89 | 242

2395 محض mæhz, mæhze *pure, for/for the sake of* adj,n,prep
- ‏به محض ورود به شیراز کارش را در دانشکده آغاز کرد.‏ — As soon as she arrived in Shiraz, she began her job in the college.
- 81 | 447

2396 فوت fowt, fut *death, blow* n
- ‏پدرم امروز صبح فوت کرده است.‏ — This morning my father passed away.
- 88 | 280

2397 رهایی ræhaji *release* n
- ‏ژاپن پس از رهایی از جنگ، سیاست مسالمت آمیز در پیش گرفت.‏ — After being relieved of war, Japan adopted a peaceful policy.
- 83 | 390

2398 افسر æfsær *officer, crown* n
- ‏افسر پلیس بود و کلاهش زیر آفتاب برق می زد.‏ — It was a police officer and his hat was flashing in the sunlight.
- 85 | 355

2399 اقامت eɣamæt *stay* n
- ‏بهترین جای ممکن را برای استراحت و اقامت در اختیار این سلحشور یکه بگذارید.‏ — Put the best possible place for relaxing and settling down at the disposal of this unique warrior.
- 85 | 351

2400 نقره noɣre *silver* adj,n
- ‏همیشه سکه نقره را انتخاب می‌کرد.‏ — She would always select the silver coin.
- 79 | 494

2401 جانی dʒani *sincere, criminal* adj,n
- ‏با یک آدم جانی چقدر با احترام رفتار شد.‏ — How respectfully a criminal person was treated.
- 91 | 190

2402 محمدرضا mohæmmædreza *Mohammad Reza* pn
- ‏محمدرضا خاتمی برادر وی می گوید . . .‏ — His brother, Mohammad Reza Khatami, says . . .
- 74 | 627

2403 بنزین benzin *gasoline* n
- ‏در کانادا چقدر مالیات بنزین میدهید؟‏ — In Canada, how much do you pay in gas taxes?
- 75 | 605

2404 بستگی bæstegi *dependence* n
- ‏همه چیز در دنیا به شما بستگی دارد.‏ — Everything in the world depends on you.
- 90 | 233

2405 قاعده ɣaede *rule* n
- ‏از قاعده مستثنی نمی باشی.‏ — You are no exception to the rule.
- 77 | 554

2406 مجتمع modʒtæmæʔ *complex* n
- ‏این مجتمع ورزشی تفریحی برای ورزش دوستان و علاقمندان به ورزش شنا و فعالیت‌های ورزشی آبی و برای سرگرمی جوانان و مردم یزد احداث شده است.‏ — This sports complex was established for lovers of athletics, those interested in swimming and watersports, and for the youth and people of Yazd.
- 76 | 572

15 Materials

Rank	Headword	Pronunciation	Gloss	Rank	Headword	Pronunciation	Gloss
406	نفت	næft	oil	2960	کاشی	kaʃi	tile
551	خاک	xɑk	soil, dust	2968	سیمان	siman	cement
938	طلا	tæla	gold	3369	مایع	maje?	liquid
1021	آهن	ɑhæn	iron	4025	ابریشم	æbriʃæm	silk
1056	سوخت	suxt	fuel	4804	ماسه	mase	sand
1105	چینی	ʧini	porcelain	5219	نخ	næx	thread, string
1326	سنگ	sæng	rock	5300	پنبه	pænbe	cotton
1913	فولاد	fulad	steel	5456	پلاستیک	pelastik	plastic
2400	نقره	noɣre	silver	5793	خاکستر	xakestær	ash
2403	بنزین	benzin	gasoline	6274	آجر	adʒor	brick
2426	برنج	berendʒ	brass	6406	سرب	sorb	lead
2436	سیم	sim	wire	6427	طناب	tænab	rope, cord
2514	شیشه	ʃiʃe	glass	6551	زر	zær	gold
2611	روغن	rowɣæn	oil	6909	الماس	ælmas	diamond
2691	پارچه	parʧe	cloth, fabric	7133	آسفالت	asfalt	asphalt
2771	فلز	felez	metal	8015	پشم	pæʃm	wool
2871	چوب	ʧub	wood	8930	زغال	zoɣal	coal
2905	مس	mes	copper	9716	بلور	bolur	crystal
2910	کاغذ	kaɣæz	paper	18535	لاجورد	ladʒværd	lapis lazuli
2920	جواهر	dʒævaher	jewel				

2407 مراجع mæradʒe, moradʒe *references, visitor* n
- نام جدید ممکن است مراجعان قدیمی را سردرگم کند. — The new name might confuse old visitors.
83 | 390

2408 مقدم moɣæddæm, mæɣdæm *having priority, arrival* adj,n,pn
- تمدن اسلام بر سایر تمدن ها مقدم است. — Islamic civilization is at the forefront of other civilizations.
88 | 266

2409 شکنجه ʃekændʒe *torture* n
- زندانیان در زندانهای دولت شکنجه نمی شوند. — Inmates in government prisons are not tortured.
79 | 493

2410 کاستن kastæn *reduce* adj,n,v
- از دلایل رایج جویدن ناخن در کودکان می توان به کاستن از استرس، اضطراب و فشارهای عصبی و تنش های روزانه اشاره کرد. — Lessening stress, anxiety, nervous pressure, and day-to-day tensions can be mentioned among the reasons that children chew on their nails.
81 | 446

2411 تعریف کردن tæ?rif kærdæn *define, describe* v
- پرویز شاپور بیشتر لطیفه‌هایی را که تعریف می‌کرد، خودش می‌ساخت. — Most of the jokes that Parviz Shapur would tell he would make himself.
80 | 459

2412 ناپدید napædid *vanished* adj
- دو کوهنورد در تبت ناپدید شدند. — Two mountain climbers disappeared in Tibet.
90 | 223

2413 پارلمانی parlemani *parliamentary* adj
- اسد زمان برگزاری انتخابات پارلمانی را اعلام کرد. — Assad announced the date of parliamentary elections.
79 | 504

2414 سرشار særʃar *abundant* adj
- در آن روزهای سرشار از شادی و بی خیالی ، چه کسی می توانست او را متقاعد کند که زندگی پر از سختی هاست؟ — In those carefree days brimming with happiness who would convince her that life is full of difficulties?
87 | 296

2415 تبریک tæbrik *congratulations* n
- به مردم این کشور تبریک گفت. — He congratulated the people of this country.
84 | 375

2416 دایره dɑjere *circle* n
- با آن، می‌توان دایره‌هایی به شعاع بسیار کوچک ترسیم کرد. — With that, you can draw circles with very small radii.
  86 | 314

2417 مجری modʒri *executive* n
- از عادل فردوسی‌پور به‌عنوان یکی از بهترین مجریان و گزارشگران سیما تقدیر شد. — Adel Ferdosipour was appreciated as one of the best anchors and reporters of TV.
  83 | 385

2418 استخراج estexrɑdʒ *extraction* n
- نتایج این گزارش بر اساس اطلاعات فعلی استخراج شده است. — The results of this report have been extracted according to the current information.
  84 | 374

2419 کهن kohæn *old* adj
- این سرزمین کهن بود. — This land is ancient.
  79 | 504

2420 سراغ sorɑɣ *trace, beside, after* n
- هیچکس سراغ ما نیامد. — No one came to us.
  73 | 662

2421 موشک muʃæk *missile* n
- کره‌شمالی دو موشک میان‌برد آزمایش کرد. — North Korea tested two mid-range missiles.
  77 | 550

2422 مدار mædɑr *orbit, circuit* n
- مدار سیارات معمولاً بیضوی‌اند. — The orbits of planets are usually elliptical.
  85 | 346

2423 شهرت ʃohræt *renown* n
- روزنامه‌اش شهرت جهانی پیدا کرد. — Her newspaper gained worldwide fame.
  80 | 463

2424 ذهنی zehni *mental* adj
- با این کار یک تصویر ذهنی از مبلغی که درنظر دارید در ذهن خود می‌سازید و هدفتان را مشخص می‌کنید. — By doing this you create a mental image of the sum you are considering in your own mind and specify your goal.
  78 | 530

2425 گندم gændom *wheat* n
- گندم ها به زمین ریخت. — Wheat poured on the ground.
  79 | 493

2426 برنج berendʒ *rice, brass* n
- قیمت رسمی برنج ایرانی در بازار مشخص شد. — The official market price of Iranian rice was determined.
  84 | 367

2427 ترکیبی tærkibi *synthetic, compound, hybrid* adj,n
- اهورامزدا واژه‌های ترکیبی است و از اهورا و مزدا ساخته شده‌است. — Ahura Mazda is a compound word, made from Ahura and Mazda.
  89 | 248

2428 ژنرال ʒeneral *general* n
- یکی از دلایل اصلی موفقیت آقای ژنرال در استراتژی های نظامی اش ، توجه به مسئله ی مخابرات بود. — One of the main reasons for the general's success in his military strategy was his attention to the issue of intelligence.
  85 | 340

2429 فعلاً feʔlæn *at present* adv
- هوا فعلاً خنک می‌ماند. — For now, the air will remain cool.
  82 | 423

2430 خواهر xɑhær *sister* n
- غلط نکنم تو خواهر ما هستی. — If I'm not mistaken, you are our sister.
  75 | 595

2431 قدس ɣods *Jerusalem* pn
- ده‌ها فلسطینی از ساکنان شهر قدس نماز صبح را در مسجدالاقصی به جا آوردند. — Tens of Palestinian residents of Jerusalem did the morning prayer in Al-Aqsa Mosque.
  67 | 827

2432 کشتار koʃtar *killing* n
- ما از این کشتار شیعه و سنی به جان آمده ایم. — We are fed up with this Shia and Sunni killing.
  69 | 777

2433 درسی dærsi *instructional* adj,n
- به نظر می‌رسد که تمامی کتابهای درسی خود را از حفظ است. — It seems like he knows all of his school books by heart.
  52 | 1359

2434 مازندران mazændæran *Mazandaran* pn
- مرکز تحقیقات شیلاتی مازندران. — Mazandaran Fishery Research Center.
  78 | 502

2435 گزارش دادن gozareʃ dɑdæn *report* v
- افراد زیادی گزارش دارند که وی را دیده‌اند. — Many people reported that they have seen him.
  77 | 539

2436 سیم sim *wire* n
- هر جا پا می‌گذاری، سیم و کابل و لوله است. — Wherever you go there are a wires and cables and pipes.
  88 | 260

2437 اتومبیل otomobil *car* n
- پدرشان منزل و اتومبیلی دارد. — Their father has a house and an automobile.
  73 | 649

2438 فراگیر færagir *comprehensive* adj,n
- — «توارد» موضوعی فراگیر در ادبیات است. "Confluence" is a far-reaching subject in literature.

80 | 460

2439 رسول ræsul *messenger* n,pn
- حدیث رسول خدا. — the Hadith of God's Messenger.

77 | 542

2440 توانمندی tævanmændi *strength* n
- باید توانمندی‌هایمان را افزایش بدهیم. — We must increase our capabilities.

81 | 441

2441 یوسف jusof, jusef *Joseph* pn
- یوسف اعتصامی، در سال ۱۳۲۸ هجری قمری به عنوان نماینده مردم تبریز انتخاب شد. — Yousef Etesami was elected as the people's representative of Tabriz in 1328 AH.

81 | 430

2442 اختلال extelal *disruption* n
- این عدم تعادل باعث ایجاد اختلال در بازارهای مالی بین‌المللی می‌شود. — This lack of balance causes a disruption in international financial markets.

78 | 507

2443 شبانه ʃæbane *nightly* adj,adv
- شبانه بیانیه صادر می کردند. — They used to release a statement nightly.

86 | 307

2444 کلیسا kelisa *church* n
- به کلیسا هم می‌روند. — They also go to church.

81 | 421

2445 اولاً ævvælæn *first* adv,conj,n
- اولاً من همه داستان‌هایی را که نوشته شده، نخوانده‌ام. — First of all, I have not read all the stories that have been written.

85 | 343

2446 زلزله zelzele *earthquake* n
- در مورد زلزله و سیل حرف نمی‌زنیم. — We will not talk about the earthquake or the flood.

80 | 454

2447 استقبال کردن esteɣbal kærdæn *welcome* v
- ما با آغوش باز از این طرح استقبال می‌کنیم. — We welcome this plan with open arms.

86 | 315

2448 اعتباری eʔtebari *credit* adj,n
- خرید لوازم خانگی با کارت اعتباری آغاز شد. — The purchasing of household goods with credit cards began.

77 | 529

2449 خام xam *raw* adj
- گوشت خام باشه.حیووناکه گوشت پخته نمی خورن. — Let it be raw meat. Animals don't eat cooked meat.

78 | 518

2450 دیوید devid *David* pn
- فرد دیگر دیوید هورویتز بود. — The other person was David Horowitz.

87 | 275

2451 افکندن æfkændæn *throw* adj,n,v
- حادثه بر همه چیز سایه می‌افکند. — Incidents cast a shadow on everything.

88 | 259

2452 نعمت neʔmæt *gift, blessing* n,pn
- این نعمت هایی که به دست آورده ام همه مال خودم است، همه را خود درخواست کرده ام. — These blessings that I've brought upon myself are all my own, I sought them all myself.

88 | 249

2453 صلاحیت sælahijjæt *competence* n
- بطور کلی ناشران آزمونها آنها را فقط در اختیار روان شناسانی قرار می دهند که صلاحیت شغلی دارند. — Generally the publishers of these tests only give them to psychologists that have occupational qualifications.

74 | 606

2454 واحدی vahedi *modular, Vahedi* adj,n,pn
- آقای واحدی از شاعران شناخته شده ی این شهر است. — Mr. Vahedi is of the city's well-known poets.

89 | 228

2455 مالکیت malekijjæt *possession* n
- مالکیت این کمپانی، برخلاف اکثر شرکت‌های چینی، عمدتاً خصوصی است. — This company's ownership, unlike the majority of Chinese companies, is primarily private.

85 | 340

2456 پیدایش pejdajeʃ *genesis* n
- پیدایش مالکیت خصوصی. — The emergence of private property.

84 | 358

2457 منع mænʔ *forbidding* n
- سپاه را از ورود به سیاست منع کردند. — They banned the IRGC from entering politics.

85 | 324

2458 تساوی tæsavi *equality, tie* n
- بازی را به تساوی کشاند. — The game was tied up.

79 | 470

2459 محبوب mæhbub *popular, beloved* adj,n
- شاعران محبوب شما کدامند؟ — Which poets do you love?

90 | 224

2460 هلند holænd *Holland* pn
- همه شان غیر هلندی بودند. — All of them were non-Dutch.
79 | 465

2461 مسلط mosællæt *dominant* adj
- مسلط به روح مردم خاطره ی شهدا است. — The memory of the martyrs dominates the soul of the people.
89 | 232

2462 توصیف کردن towsif kærdæn *describe* v
- از آن ها خواست که بر اساس آنچه دیده بودند ، درخت را توصیف کنند. — He asked them to describe the tree according to how they had seen it.
90 | 212

2463 مساوی mosavi *equal, tie* adj
- آن را با دقت به دو تکه ی مساوی تقسیم کرد. — She carefully divided it into two equal pieces.
77 | 537

2464 نهصد nohsæd *nine hundred* n
- هزینه پرواز رفت و آمد به هند از نیویورک حدود نهصد دلار است. — The cost of round-trip flights from New York to India is around nine hundred dollars.
50 | 1408

2465 نما næma *front, shot* n
- چهار نما از یک تصویر. — Four views of one picture.
90 | 220

2466 ناشر naʃer *publisher* n
- ناشری کتابی را برای چاپ به وزارت ارشاد داد. — A publisher gave the book to the Ministry of Culture to print.
74 | 602

2467 مطلق motlæɣ *absolute* adj
- حاکم نیز در تنهایی مطلق به سر می برد. — The governor was also residing in absolute solitude.
83 | 382

2468 تجهیز tædʒhiz *equipping* n
- تجهیز شهروندان اسرائیلی به سلاح گرم. — Equipping Israeli citizens with firearms.
81 | 420

2469 تیره tire *dark, family, dash* adj,n
- نور تیره تر می شد. — The light was getting dimmer.
87 | 285

2470 تجلیل tædʒlil *honoring* n
- رئیس جمهور گرجستان سال نو را در افغانستان تجلیل می کند. — The president of Georgia will celebrate the new year in Afghanistan.
83 | 362

2471 توقع tævæɣɣoʔ *expectation* n
- توقعات خودتان را مدیریت کنید. — Manage your expectations.
85 | 330

2472 بارندگی barændegi *precipitation* n
- این حوضچه ها به هنگام بارندگی از آب باران پر می شود. — These small pools fill with rainwater when it rains.
82 | 396

2473 توصیه کردن towsije kærdæn *recommend* v
- پژوهشگران نوشیدن چای سبز را به افراد مسن توصیه می کنند. — Researchers recommend drinking green tea to the elderly.
87 | 275

2474 میسر mojæssær *possible* adj
- آنقدری که ممکن و میسر بوده — The extent to which it was possible and feasible . . .
86 | 300

2475 بوش buʃ *Bush* pn
- صدام محبوب دولت ریگان و بوش بود. — Saddam was the darling of the Reagan and Bush governments.
71 | 686

2476 تضمین tæzmin *assurance* n
- با تضمین محاکمه عادلانه به آمریکا باز می گردم. — I am returning to America with the guarantee of a fair trial.
79 | 476

2477 ظهر zohr, zæhr *noon, back* n
- نزدیک ظهر بود. — It was around noon.
76 | 543

2478 شیرازی ʃirazi *Shirazi* adj,pn
- شیرازی ها غذاهای متنوع و بسیار خوش طعم دارند. — Shirazi people have varied and very tasty dishes.
87 | 286

2479 خشک xoʃk *dry* adj
- صحرای نازکا یکی از خشک ترین مناطق زمین است. — The Nazca desert is one of the driest regions of the Earth.
75 | 563

2480 استوار ostovar *stable* adj
- ساختمان محکم و استوار سر جایش بود. — The building was firmly in place.
82 | 399

2481 تایلند tajlænd *Thailand* pn
- بین دو کشور ایران و تایلند هستیم. — We are between the two countries of Iran and Thailand.
80 | 432

2482 تخلیه tæxlije *evacuation, discharge* n
- دستورالعمل تخلیه اضطراری می بایست ساده باشد. — Emergency evacuation instructions must be simple.
85 | 320

2483 ترجیح دادن tærdʒih dadæn *prefer* v
- برای حفظ تعادل در تیم ترجیح دادم دی ماریا بماند. — In order to preserve equilibrium on the team I preferred that di María stay.
82 | 387

2484 الف ælef *alef* n,pn

• حرف الف که کلمه « الله » با آن شروع می‌شود. — The letter alef, with which the word "Allah" begins.

69 | 732

2485 عظیمی æzimi *greatness, Azimi* adj,pn

• بهرام عظیمی انیمیشن‌های خیابان‌های آرام را به پایان رساند. — Bahram Azimi finished the animations for "Easy Streets."

85 | 321

2486 پدید pædid *visible* adj,n

• دی ان ای در درون ژن ممکن است با اکسیژن آزاد که از سوخت مواد غذایی در سلول پدید می آید ترکیب شود. — DNA inside a gene can combine with free oxygen that comes into existence from burning food products in the cell.

78 | 480

2487 استخدام estexdam *employment* n

• دو سه شاگرد استخدام کرده بود. — Two or three apprentices were hired.

81 | 416

2488 نگه داشتن negæh dɑʃtæn *keep* v

• می بایست سر خود را به بالا نگه داشت و منتظر ماند. — He should have kept his head high and waited.

80 | 442

2489 ناصر nɑser *Nasser* pn

• پشت میز کارش نشست و به ناصر خیره ماند. — She sat down behind her work table and stared at Nasser.

81 | 429

2490 سرما særma *cold* n

• از سرما فهمیدم که دارد پائیز می‌شود. — From the cold I understood that it was becoming autumn.

82 | 382

2491 بیرونی biruni *external* adj,n,pn

• چرا لبه بیرونی خورشید بسیار گرمتر از سطح آن است؟ — Why is the outer edge of the sun much hotter than its surface?

85 | 319

2492 مسلماً mosællæmæn *certainly* adv

• مسلماً در این گزارش هویت فرد محفوظ باقی خواهد ماند. — Certainly the identity of the individual will remain protected in this report.

87 | 279

2493 نحو nɑhv *manner, syntax* n

• این تعبیر آخیر را به نحو دیگر هم می‌توان توجیه کرد. — This latter interpretation can also be explained in a different way.

84 | 339

2494 قاطع ɣɑteʔ *decisive* adj

• یکی از محور های اصلی کاری ما برخورد قاطع با متخلفین است. — One of the main points of our work is dealing firmly with offenders.

86 | 305

2495 لیبی libi *Libya* pn

• پایگاه‌های هوایی مهمی در لیبی است. — There are many important airbases in Libya.

54 | 1225

2496 دما dæma *temperature* n

• پس از آنکه دما به کمتر از 32 درجه سانتی‌گراد رسید، دستگاه را مجدداً روشن می‌کند. — After the temperature falls below 32 degrees centigrade, the device turns back on.

81 | 420

2497 والدین vɑledejn *parents* n

• 8.6% — ۸.۶ درصد والدین دانش‌آموزان بی‌سواد هستند. of students' parents are illiterate.

75 | 555

2498 جناح dʒenɑh *faction* n

• میان نظریات این دو جناح نشانه های زیادی از همسوئی دیده می شد. — Many signs of alignment could be seen between the theories of these two parties.

64 | 887

2499 برشمردن bærʃomordæn *enumerate* n,v

• برشمردن مزیتهای صنعت گردشگری ایران. — Enumerating the advantages of Iran's tourism industry.

83 | 377

2500 رکورد rekord *record* n

• این رکورد از سال ۱۹۹۳ تاکنون بی‌سابقه بوده است. — From 1993 to date, this record has been unprecedented.

79 | 458

2501 اردیبهشت ordibeheʃt *Ordibehesht* n

• در اردیبهشت ماه سال جاری برگزار شد. — It was held this year in the month of Ordibehesht.

81 | 411

2502 گرسنگی gorosnegi *hunger* n

• از شدت گرسنگی به حالت ضعف افتاده بود. — She had fallen into a weak state from severe hunger.

87 | 268

2503 زحمت zæhmæt *trouble* n

• من از همین تریبون از زحمات بی‌وقفت تشکر می‌کنم. — From this podium I thank your relentless efforts.

78 | 486

2504 تعلیم tæʔlim *teaching* n

• تعلیمات او، افراد تحصیل کرده شهری را بیشتر جذب می‌کرد. — His teachings educated urban people more.

67 | 799

2505 الکترونیکی elektroniki *electronic* adj

• اولین رایانه دیجیتال الکترونیکی ساخته شد. — The first digital electronic computer was built.

79 | 473

2506 بنیادی bonjadi *fundamental* adj
- امامت مفهومی بسیار بنیادی است. — "Imamate" is a very fundamental concept.
86 | 291

2507 ظلم zolm *oppression* n
- این چه ظلمی است. — What kind of tyranny is this?
86 | 302

2508 بیکار bikar *unemployed* adj,n
- ۵ میلیون نفر بیکار داریم. — We have five million unemployed people.
80 | 434

2509 کارگاه kargah *workshop* n
- عکاس از کارگاهش عکسها را آورد. — The photographer brought the photos from his studio.
79 | 461

2510 بو bu *smell* n,pn
- همچنین بوی ملایم آن طرفداران زیادی دارد. — Also its mild scent has many fans.
67 | 780

2511 شناسایی کردن ʃenasaji kærdæn *identify* v
- چاقی را به عنوان یک بیماری شناسایی کردند. — They identified obesity as a disease.
93 | 150

2512 دریاچه dærjatʃe *lake* n
- این دریاچه به عنوان یکی از مخوف ترین نقاط تانزانیا شناخته می شود. — This lake is recognized as one of the most dreadful spots in Tanzania.
76 | 537

2513 حریم hærim *confines* n
- دوست ندارم کسی به حریم احساسم نزدیک بشه. — I don't like to feel people in my personal space.
85 | 309

2514 شیشه ʃiʃe *glass, bottle* n
- برای فضاهای خصوصی نیز می‌توانید از شیشه‌های مات استفاده کنید. — Also, for private spaces, you can use opaque windows.
72 | 628

2515 باز کردن baz kærdæn *open* v
- درهای قلعه را باز کردند، خود را تسلیم ارتش اسلام کردند. — They opened the doors of the citadel, and submitted themselves to the army of Islam.
65 | 829

2516 غلبه ɣælæbe *triumph* n
- غلبه بر خجالت. — Overcoming shyness.
82 | 383

2517 باستان bastan *ancient* adj,n
- مدتی در موزه ایران باستان کار می کردم. — I used to work for a while in the Museum of Ancient Iran.
71 | 672

2518 جدا شدن dʒoda ʃodæn *be separated* v
- راه فرعی که از اتوبان جدا می شد. — The subsidiary road that was separated from the expressway.
84 | 334

2519 گمرک gomrok *customs* n
- یکی از مسائل واحدهای تولیدی مربوط به گمرک می‌شود. — One of the responsibilities of the production units is related to customs.
82 | 377

2520 شاهد بودن ʃahed budæn *witness* v
- بانک مرکزی در این زمینه آمار نگران‌کننده‌ای را ارائه داده و ما ۵ درصد رکود در سرمایه‌گذاری را شاهد هستیم. — The central bank has provided concerning statistics on this matter and we have witnessed a 5 percent slump in investment.
85 | 322

2521 تخصص tæxæssos *specialization, specialty* n
- چگونه از تخصص مشمولان سربازی در پادگان ها استفاده می شود؟ — How are the specialties of military conscripts used on bases?
87 | 265

2522 بالا بردن bala bordæn *put up, raise* v
- اگر خریدار هستید، همیشه می‌توانید قیمت را بالا ببرید. — If you are the buyer you can always increase the price.
84 | 346

2523 مد mædd, mod *high tide, fashion* n
- آخرین مد پاریس. — The latest fashion of Paris.
87 | 273

2524 متمرکز motæmærkez *concentrated* adj
- پرتوهای خورشید تا متمرکز نشوند نمی سوزانند. — Until they are concentrated, beams of sunlight will not burn.
81 | 397

2525 بینی bini *nose* n,v
- زنجیر توله سگ در دست خانم بود که بازوها و پاهای لخت و کفش پاشنه بلند داشت و از کنار ما گذشت عطر خوشایندی به بینی هایمان خورد. — The puppy's leash was in the woman's hand who had bare arms and legs and high-heeled shoes and as she passed by us, a pleasant fragrance met our noses.
78 | 474

2526 جزئیات dʒozʔijjat *details* n
- به جزئیات بیشتری اشاره شده است. — More details have been indicated.
81 | 415

2527 چای tʃaj *tea* n
- چرا چای را بدون قند می‌خوری؟ — Why do you drink tea without sugar?
76 | 543

2528 برخورداری **bærxordari** *having, enjoying* n

- دنیا فهمیده که برخورداری از انرژی هسته‌ای حق ما است.
  — The world has realized that having nuclear energy is our right.
  86 | 299

2529 مالزی **malezi** *Malaysia* pn

- برترینهای فوتبال آسیا فردا در مالزی معرفی میشوند و ایران با پنج نماینده در این مراسم حضور می یابد.
  — Top Asian soccer teams will be introduced tomorrow in Malaysia, and Iran will attend the ceremony with five representatives.
  79 | 455

2530 معاونت **moʔavenæt** *directorate, deputyship* n

- معاونت فرهنگی و ارتباطات سازمان میراث فرهنگی و گردشگری. — Communication and Cultural Directorate of Cultural Heritage and Tourism.
  72 | 638

2531 سال داشتن **sal daʃtæn** *be years old* v

- کریستین فقط هفده یا هیجده سال داشته و مرد سی و چند سال. — Christine was only seventeen or eighteen and the man was a bit over thirty.
  90 | 198

2532 مربوطه **mærbute** *relevant* adj

- — مسئول مربوطه آن ها را خیلی معطل کرد. The relevant official detained them for a long time.
  75 | 560

2533 متوقف شدن **motevæɣɣef ʃodæn** *stop* v

- — Stopping the متوقف شدن روند اصلاحات. process of reforms.
  83 | 362

2534 شرکت داشتن **ʃerkæt daʃtæn** *participate, attend* v

- — در تمامی جلسات محرمانه شرکت داشت. He participated in all confidential meetings.
  85 | 309

2535 گیاه **gijah** *plant* n

- — We used to eat این گیاه را با نمک می خوردیم. this plant with salt.
  73 | 617

2536 بارز **barez** *distinct, prominent* adj,pn

- — It was a clear نمونه ی بارزی از همین مسئله بود. example of this issue.
  86 | 288

2537 قلعه **ɣælʔe** *castle* n

- — This حالا این قلعه به یک تپه خاکی مبدل شده. fortress has transformed into an earthen hill.
  73 | 593

2538 نشاط **neʃat** *joy* n

- — They were از فرط شوق و نشاط بال و پر میزدند. flapping their wings from an excess of happiness and joy.
  87 | 271

2539 پنهان **penhan** *hidden* adj

- سیاره‌های غول‌پیکری که از دید پنهانند. — Giant planets that are not visible.
  67 | 784

2540 خط لوله **xætelule** *pipeline* n

- گروه دوم خط لوله با قطر 32 اینچ به پالایشگاه اصفهان و سپس با خط لوله ایی 24 اینچی به تهران و تبریز می آیند. — The second group of pipelines with a 32 inch diameter come to the Esfahan refinery and then to Tehran and Tabriz with the 24 inch diameter pipeline.
  81 | 405

2541 بنیان **bonjan** *structure* n

- از او آثاری در مورد بنیان‌های اخلاقی مارکسیسم به جا مانده است. — He left some works on the moral foundations of Marxism.
  87 | 258

2542 مشمول **mæʃmul** *included, subject to, draftee* adj,n

- مشمول مقررات قانون جدید نگردیدم. — I was not subject to the provisions of the new law.
  81 | 408

2543 نهادن **næhadæn** *put, place* n,v

- نظام جمهوری اسلامی ایران را بنیان نهادند. — He established the Islamic Republic of Iran.
  78 | 473

2544 گردن **gærdæn** *neck* n

- دو عمل جراحی مهم روی گردن او صورت گرفت. — Two major operations were performed on his neck.
  68 | 734

2545 پیشینه **piʃine** *background* n

- یا درباره پیشینه خانم مرحومه اطلاعاتی دارند. — Do they have any information about the deceased lady's background?
  88 | 243

2546 راز **raz** *secret, mystery* n,pn

- مثل گذشته راز دلت را با من در میان نمی گذاری. — As in the past you will not share the secret of your heart with me.
  82 | 389

2547 سلب **sælb** *divesting* n

- حق ندارد زبان مردمی را از او سلب کند. — One has no right to deprive a nation of its language.
  88 | 237

2548 کارنامه **karname** *report card* n

- در میان کارنامه ها چشمم به یک اسم آشنا افتاد. — My eye fell on a familiar name in the middle of the report cards.
  85 | 306

2549 بسکتبال **bæsketbal** *basketball* n

- تیم بسکتبال جوانان ایران. — Iran's youth basketball team.
  78 | 479

2550 نگریستن negæristæn *look* adj,n,v
- بعضی محققین به شکل متفاوتی به قضیه می‌نگرند. — Some scholars look at the case differently.
- 82 | 376

2551 شکر ʃekær, ʃokr *sugar, thanks* n
- خدا را شکر کنید که هنوز ایران نفت دارد. — Thank God that Iran still has oil.
- 78 | 473

2552 تعاونی tæʔavoni *cooperative* adj,n
- نخستین شرکت تعاونی خدمات گردشگری کشور در شهرستان رامسر آغاز بکار کرد. — The first cooperative tourism service started in the county of Ramsar.
- 77 | 496

2553 آشکار aʃkar *evident* adj
- بی اعتباری همه این معاهدات بسیار زود آشکار شد. — The unreliability of all of these treaties became clear very quickly.
- 71 | 665

2554 مشخصه moʃæxxæse *characteristic* adj,n
- سارا با خنده و کلماتی کشیده که مشخصه حالش سر جاش نیست و احتمالا مست کرده به من میگه. — Sara speaks to me with a laugh and slurred words that are characteristic of her not being well and probably being drunk.
- 77 | 509

2555 بحرین bæhrejn *Bahrain* pn
- بعدها به کشور بحرین مهاجرت کرد. — Later he emigrated to Bahrain.
- 54 | 1167

2556 خشن xæʃen *rough* adj
- نه اسلام خشن است و نه حکومت اسلامی. — Neither is Islam violent, nor is the Islamic government.
- 88 | 249

2557 مرغ morɣ *fowl* n
- تو بال مرغ را خوردی. — You ate a chicken wing.
- 70 | 690

2558 دهنده dæhænde *donor, -giving* n
- اسیدها دهندهٔ پروتون و قلیاها گیرندهٔ پروتون اند. — Acids are proton donors and alkalis are proton receptors.
- 75 | 549

2559 نهاده næhade *resource, input, placed* adj,v
- سایر نهاده‌های تولید ثابت هستند. — The rest of the production inputs are fixed.
- 85 | 300

2560 خاکی xaki *earthen, terrestrial* adj
- در دنیای خاکی شاید هیچ خوردنی لذیذتر و مفیدتر از میوه تازه موجود نباشد. — In this earthly world, there is perhaps no food more delicious and more beneficial than fresh fruit.
- 87 | 273

2561 سوار sævar *rider* adj,n
- سوار تاکسی بودم. — I was riding in a taxi.
- 79 | 451

2562 سالگرد salgærd *anniversary* n
- روز سالگرد ازدواج. — Wedding anniversary day.
- 80 | 413

2563 فاقد faɣed *lacking* adj,prep
- افغانستان راهی به دریاهای آزاد ندارد و بالطبع فاقد بندر و کشتیرانی است. — Afghanistan does not have a way to the open seas and naturally is lacking a port and shipping.
- 77 | 504

2564 سوختن suxtæn *burn* adj,n,v
- مربی در نهایت دلش به حال او سوخت و گفت: باشد می‌توانی بازی کنی. — The coach felt sorry for him and said, "Fine, you can play."
- 75 | 553

2565 میز miz *table* n
- روی میز باقی مانده بود. — It was left on the table.
- 64 | 830

2566 بلندی bolændi *height* adj,n
- به حزب الله لبنان نیز اجازه نمی دهد در این بلندی‌ها حضور پیدا کند. — They do not allow Hezbollah of Lebanon to be present in these heights.
- 84 | 335

2567 موظف movæzzæf *duty-bound* adj
- در نهایت براساس مصوبه این جلسه شرکت گاز استان مرکزی موظف شد حداقل نصف سوخت نیروگاه را تأمین کند. — Finally, based on this session's resolution, the Central Province's gas company was tasked with providing at least half of the powerplant's fuel.
- 81 | 389

2568 فرم form *form* n
- من از فرم سفارش کالا رو دادم به او. — I gave her the merchandise order form.
- 73 | 586

2569 میانگین mijangin *average* n
- میانگین طلاق در عربستان 35 درصد بیشتر از میانگین جهانی است. — The average divorce rate in Saudi Arabia is 35 percent higher than the world average.
- 81 | 395

2570 شاد ʃad *happy* adj,pn
- دلم شاد می شود وقتی که چشمک می زنی. — I get very happy when you wink at me.
- 85 | 308

2571 بنابر bænabær *according to* prep
- بنابر این، روایت مذکور معتبر است . . . — Thus, the aforementioned narrative is valid . . .
- 72 | 618

16 Nationalities

Rank	Headword	Pronunciation	Gloss	Rank	Headword	Pronunciation	Gloss
233	ایرانی	irɑni	Iranian	4143	ترکمن	torkæmæn	Turkmen
452	آمریکایی	ɑmrikɑji	American	4202	استرالیایی	ostrɑlijɑji	Australian
478	انگلیسی	engelisi	English	4449	برزیلی	berezili	Brazilian
698	ترک	tork	Turk	4475	کانادایی	kɑnɑdɑji	Canadian
942	عرب	æræb	Arab	4850	لبنانی	lobnɑni	Lebanese
952	فرانسوی	færɑnsævi	French	5870	بحرینی	bɑhrejni	Bahreini
1105	چینی	tʃini	Chinese	6150	لهستانی	læhestɑni	Polish
1211	آلمانی	ɑlmɑni	German	6540	بریتانیایی	beritɑnjɑji	British
1354	فلسطینی	felestini	Palestinian	6555	پرتغالی	porteɣɑli	Portuguese
1420	روسی	rusi	Russian	6701	کویتی	kovejti	Kuwaiti
2093	افغان	æfɣɑn	Afghan	7297	سوئدی	suʔedi	Swedish
2125	هندی	hendi	Indian	7420	الجزایری	ældʒæzɑjeri	Algerian
2199	ایتالیایی	itɑlijɑji	Italian	7610	ایرلندی	irlændi	Irish
2218	روس	rus	Russian	7677	بلژیکی	belʒiki	Belgian
2261	عراقی	erɑɣi	Iraqi	7832	آذری	ɑzæri	Azeri
2311	اسرائیلی	esrɑʔili	Israeli	7958	نروژی	norveʒi	Norwegian
2755	ژاپنی	ʒɑponi	Japanese	8055	اردنی	ordoni	Jordanian
2778	مصری	mesri	Egyptian	8285	کره‌ای	koreji	Korean
3285	پاکستانی	pɑkestɑni	Pakistani	8432	گرجی	gordʒi	Georgian
3388	افغانی	æfɣɑni	Afghan	8553	تایلندی	tɑjlændi	Thai
3442	اسپانیایی	espɑnjɑji	Spanish	8856	دانمارکی	dɑnmɑrki	Danish
3453	سوری	suri	Syrian	9189	اوکراینی	okrɑjni	Ukrainian
3708	ارمنی	ærmæni	Armenian	9525	آرژانتینی	arʒɑntini	Argentine
4087	تاجیک	tɑdʒik	Tajik	11714	مکزیکی	mekziki	Mexican
				12895	کلمبیایی	kolombijɑji	Colombian

2572 مطبوعاتی mætbuʔɑti *press* adj,n
- بیانیه مشترک مطبوعاتی صادر می‌کنیم. — We will issue a joint press statement.
73 | 604

2573 تأسف tæʔæssof *regret* n
- تأسف کافی نیست. — Regret is not enough.
85 | 302

2574 دسترس dæstres *access* n
- می‌توان رکوردهای در دسترس دیگر را جهت ویرایش انتخاب نمود. — Other accessible records may be selected for editing.
85 | 302

2575 تابع tɑbeʔ *citizen, follower* adj,n
- اگر ما قرار است تابع فرهنگستان باشیم، پس نمی شود از آن تخلف کرد. — If we are supposed to follow the Persian Academy, we cannot violate that.
81 | 390

2576 پیشتر piʃtær *before, further* adv
- قصه شیرینی بود و هر چه پیشتر می رفت شیرین تر می شد . . . — It was a sweet story and the further it went it became sweeter . . .
82 | 380

2577 همدیگر hæmdigær *each other* pron
- همه اینها مجموعه دستگاههایی است که در کنار همدیگر باید کار کنند. — All of these are a collection of devices that should work together.
80 | 430

2578 بزرگداشت bozorgdɑʃt *ceremony* n
- اول اردیبهشت روز بزرگداشت سعدی شیرازی شاعر بزرگ ایرانی. — The first of Ordibehesht is the celebration day of the great Iranian poet Sa'di Shirazi.
82 | 380

2579 صفت sefæt *adjective, quality* n
- كدام صفت را در دوستانتان بيشتر مى پسنديد؟ — Which attribute in your friends makes you happier?
79 | 440

2580 رم rom *Rome* pn
- شاه از رم بازگشت. — The shah returned from Rome.
82 | 368

2581 مو mu, mow *hair, vine* n
- با يک امريکايى مو بور بود . . . — He was with a blond-haired American . . .
64 | 826

2582 رمز ræmz *code* n
- اين اسم رمز را تكرار نكنيد. — Don't repeat this code name.
85 | 297

2583 تجزيه tædʒije *analysis, breakdown* n
- اگر منطقه يورو تجزيه شود، مديران كارخانه هاى فولكس واگن در آلمان ناگهان متوجه خواهند شد كه هزينه هايشان بر حسب مارك آلمان سر به فلك كشيده است. — If the Eurozone is dissolved, managers of Volkswagen factories in Germany will suddenly become aware that their costs in terms of the German mark are soaring.
80 | 414

2584 داير dajer *functioning* adj
- اين نمايشگاه تا تاريخ 30 خرداد 79 در محل كميسيون ملى يونسكو در ايران داير خواهد بود. — This exhibition will be functioning on the site of the national commission of UNESCO in Iran until the date of 30 Khordad 1379.
84 | 330

2585 پرويز pærviz *Parviz* pn
- پرويز ناتل خانلرى در شهريور ۱۳۶۹، در ۷۷ سالگى در تهران درگذشت. — Parviz Natel Khanlari passed away in Shahrivar of 1369 in Tehran, at the age of 77.
86 | 287

2586 داورى daværi *judgment, arbitration, refereeing* n
- داورى نهايى جايزه داستان تهران به پايان رسيد. — The final judgment of the Tehran Story Award ended.
81 | 393

2587 چطور ʃetowr *how* adv
- گرگ گفت «برايم تعريف كن ببينم چطور توانستى فلك را پيدا كنى و در راه به چه چيزهايى برخوردى؟» — The wolf said "Tell me how you could find heaven, and what did you encounter on the way?"
63 | 861

2588 قطعنامه yæt?name *resolution* n
- بعد از قبول قطعنامه از جبهه برگشت. — After accepting the resolution he returned from the front line.
70 | 679

2589 محكم mohkæm *solid* adj,adv
- گرانيت يكى از محكم ترين و سخت ترين سنگ ها مى باشد. — Granite is one of the most solid and hardest rocks.
76 | 504

2590 اسفند esfænd *Esfand* n
- در پانزدهم اسفند سال گذشته جلسه اى با حضور مسوولان ارشد كشور و نمايندگان استان در مجلس برگزار شد. — On the fifteenth of Esfand last year, a meeting was held with the nation's senior officials and representatives of the province in the parliament.
68 | 708

2591 راحت rɑhæt *comfort, comfortable* adj,adv
- سپس با خيال راحت به شيراز بازگشت. — He returned to Shiraz with peace of mind.
67 | 755

2592 تغذيه tæɣzije *feeding, nutrition* n
- قبل از آن كه مجبور به رژيم گرفتن بشويم، ورزش كنيم و مراقب تغذيه خود باشيم. — Before we are forced to diet, we should exercise and look after our own nutrition.
75 | 523

2593 پيكر pejkær *body* n
- اين سرزمين را از يک پيكر مى دانيم. — We consider this territory as one body.
85 | 304

2594 دوجانبه dodʒanebe *bilateral* adj
- ارتقاى روابط دوجانبه سياسى. — The promotion of bilateral political relations.
75 | 524

2595 شنا ʃena *swim* n
- يک استخر شنا هم ساخته بودند. — They had also built a swimming pool.
87 | 256

2596 آدمى ɑdæmi *human being* n
- نشانه آدميان بهشتى تبسم هميشگى است. — A permanent smile is a sign of heavenly human beings.
75 | 542

2597 گواهى govɑhi *certificate* n
- بايد نوشته شود ما امضاء كنندگان ذيل گواهى مى كنيم كه . . . — It should be written "We, the undersigned, certify that . . ."
90 | 186

2598 جمع شدن dʒæm? ʃodæn *gather* v
- تزريق انسولين در مبتلايان به ديابت موجب جمع شدن چربى در بدن و افزايش وزن است. — Injecting insulin in those who suffer from diabetes results in the aggregation of body fat and an increase in weight.
79 | 427

2599 بهشت beheʃt *heaven* n,pn
- آدم مهربانی مثل او حتما به بهشت می رفت. — A kind person such as him would certainly go to heaven.

82 | 375

2600 خریدن xæridæn *buy* n,v
- پول کافی هم برای خریدنش داشتیم. — We also had enough money to buy it.

61 | 913

2601 مضمون mæzmun *theme* n
- این مضمون یکی از مضامین اختصاصی و خیلی مهم و اساسی میباشد. — This theme is one of the dedicated themes and is very important and fundamental.

81 | 398

2602 ماهواره mahvare *satellite* n
- اخیراً روی آنتنهای ماهواره پارازیت میفرستند تا تصویرها دیده نشود. — Recently they have been jamming the satellite dishes so the pictures cannot be seen.

79 | 430

2603 حاوی havi *containing* adj
- امتحان حاوی دو سوال و بارم بندی از نمره بیست بود. — The test contained two questions and a maximum possible score of 20 points.

81 | 392

2604 سینا sina *Sina* pn
- فارابی و ابن سینا. — Farabi and Ibn Sina.

88 | 234

2605 عادت adæt *habit* n
- تو عادت داری هر کس رو که از نژاد خودت نیست، تحقیر کنی. — You are accustomed to mocking everyone who isn't of your own race.

79 | 439

2606 ابلاغ eblaɣ *notification* n
- خواستند تصمیم را به من ابلاغ کنند. — They wanted to notify me of their decision.

78 | 447

2607 چراغ tʃeraɣ *light* n
- پشت چراغ قرمز بودیم. — We were behind a red light.

69 | 675

2608 لایه laje *layer* n
- لباس همسر امپراتور بسیار زیباست و معمولاً با سیزده لایه از پارچه های ابریشمی دوخته می شود. — The emperor's wife's clothes are very beautiful and are usually sewn with thirteen layers of silk fabric.

79 | 445

2609 مناقشه monaɣeʃe *dispute* n
- این جزایر میان دو کشور مورد مناقشه هستند. — The islands between the two countries are in dispute.

87 | 259

2610 جسمی dʒesmi *physical* adj,n
- این هیجان تأثیر منفی بر سلامت جسمی و روانی خواهد گذاشت. — This excitement will have a negative effect on physical and mental health.

82 | 360

2611 روغن rowɣæn *oil* n
- نانتان توی روغن است. — Your bread is in the oil.

78 | 447

2612 حمله کردن hæmle kærdæn *attack* v
- به سوی نیروهای آمریکایی حمله کردند. — They attacked the US forces.

84 | 320

2613 هجوم hodʒum *attack* n
- هزاران نفر برای رفتن به سر کار هایشان به سمت مترو هجوم آورده بودند. — Thousands of people going to work had invaded the metro.

83 | 338

2614 متنوع motænævveʔ *varied* adj
- با این نرم افزار می توانید عکس های متنوع بگیرید. — You can take various types of pictures with this software.

81 | 376

2615 پشتوانه poʃtvane *backing* n
- باید پشتوانه امنیت ما باشد. — It should be a support for our security.

87 | 252

2616 یونانی junani *Greek* adj,n,pn
- سپس با یک کشتی یونانی راهی فرانسه شدم. — Then I set out for France on a Greek ship.

77 | 469

2617 رفتاری ræftari *behavioral* adj,n
- به عظمت روحی و ظرافتهای رفتاریاش پی بردم. — I realized the greatness of her spirit and her behavioral elegance.

80 | 414

2618 زنجان zændʒan *Zanjan* pn
- افق توسعه استان زنجان با واقعبینی شفاف و بدون غبار میگردد. — By having a realistic outlook, the development horizon for the province of Zanjan will become clear and unclouded.

80 | 418

2619 زور zur *force* n
- تمام زورش را جمع کرد. — He gathered all his strength.

75 | 531

2620 خانگی xanegi *homemade, domestic, interior* adj
- پخت شیرینی خانگی یک هنر اصیل است. — Baking homemade pastry is a noble art.

82 | 360

2621 قزاقستان yæzayestan *Kazakhstan* pn
- در گرجستان، ارمنستان، آذربایجان، قزاقستان، فلسطین، عراق، یمن، افغانستان، هندوستان، عمان، کویت، و عربستان یوزپلنگ وجود داشته است. — There have been cheetahs in Georgia, Armenia, Azerbaijan, Kazakhstan, Palestine, Iraq, Yemen, Afghanistan, India, Oman, Kuwait, and Saudi Arabia.
- 74 | 543

2622 مادرید mɑdrid *Madrid* pn
- مدیر موزه تاریخ طبیعی مادرید. — The director of the Natural History Museum in Madrid.
- 79 | 441

2623 یمن jæmæn, jomn *Yemen, auspiciousness* pn
- به دلایل امنیتی شبکه تلفن همراه در یمن را قطع کردند. — For security reasons, they shut down the cellular phone network in Yemen.
- 74 | 556

2624 تازگی tɑzegi *novelty, freshness, recently* n
- یک عامل سیا بهتازگی به ایران آمد. — A CIA agent recently came to Iran.
- 84 | 323

2625 بازگشتن bazgæʃtæn *return* n,v
- اولین گروه آزادگان به ایران بازگشتند. — The first group of those freed returned to Iran.
- 86 | 265

2626 ادعا کردن eddeaʔ kærdæn *claim* v
- همه ادعا کردند که دزدند. — Everyone alleged that they were thieves.
- 88 | 228

2627 توقیف towɣif *arrest, sequestration* n
- بسیاری از اموال توقیف شده در فرعون را در گنجینه ی تخت جمشید یافته اند. — They have found much of the pharaoh's seized property in the treasury at Persepolis.
- 77 | 466

2628 کرمانشاه kermanʃɑh *Kermanshah* pn
- شهرستان مرزی قصرشیرین از توابع استان کرمانشاه است. — The border county of Qasr-e Shirin is part of Kermanshah province.
- 80 | 401

2629 پیکان pejkɑn *arrow, Paykan* n,pn
- پیکانی که به پلیس انگلستان کمک کرد. — The Paykan which helped the UK police.
- 77 | 478

2630 نادرست nɑdorost *incorrect* adj
- اطلاعات نادرست را فعالانه و به سرعت تصحیح می کنیم. — We are actively and quickly correcting the incorrect information.
- 84 | 315

2631 بوشهر buʃehr *Bushehr* pn
- در تهران و بوشهر روز گذشته هیأتی عالیرتبه از ایران راهی مسکو شد. — Yesterday in Tehran and Bushehr a high-ranking commission departed Iran for Moscow.
- 75 | 511

2632 فیزیکی fiziki *physical* adj
- یک منبع واحد برای کل قوانین فیزیکی وجود دارد. — There is a single source for all physical laws.
- 82 | 365

2633 قبول داشتن yæbul dɑʃtæn *accept* v
- پاکدامنی او را همه قبول داشتند. — Everyone believed in his honesty.
- 83 | 342

2634 نایب najeb *deputy* n
- بهروز عباسیاقدم به عنوان نایب رئیس تعیین شد. — Behrouz Abbasi Aghdam was designated as the vice president.
- 84 | 314

2635 دهان dæhan *mouth* n
- هنگام تلفظ آنها دهان بیشتر باز میشود. — Their mouths become wider during pronunciation.
- 70 | 637

2636 لرستان lorestan *Lorestan* pn
- مثلا کسی که از استان لرستان آمده. — For example, someone who came from Lorestan province.
- 80 | 395

2637 امن æmn *safe* adj
- اتاق خواب کودک باید مکانی امن و راحت برای او باشد. — The child's bedroom must be a safe and comfortable place for him.
- 79 | 425

2638 تبدیل کردن tæbdil kærdæn *convert* v
- آن را به قدرت سیاسی و اقتصادی تبدیل کردند. — They changed it to a political and economic power.
- 85 | 292

2639 پیر pir *old* adj,n,pn
- پیرترین کلاغ آمریکایی در طبیعت تقریباً ۳۰ سال عمر کرده است. — The oldest American crow in nature lived approximately 30 years.
- 74 | 539

2640 عاشق aʃeɣ *lover* adj,n
- اما این چهل تا پرنده عاشق من هستند. — But these forty birds are in love with me.
- 72 | 587

2641 قیام ɣijam *rising* n
- وقتی کسی قیام می کند، حتما هدفی دارد. — When someone rises up, they surely have a goal.
- 75 | 517

2642 تقویم tæɣvim *calendar* n
- امروز ۲۲ مهر که بر اساس تقویم عربستان نهم ذیحجه همزمان با روز عرفه است. — Today, the 22nd of Mehr, which according to the Arabic calendar is the ninth of Dhu al-Hijjah as well the day of Arafah.
- 93 | 125

2643 امشب emʃæb *tonight* adv
- آخر بابا، امشب شب جمعه است. — Finally, man, tonight is Friday night.
70 | 651

2644 تبعید tæbʔid *exile* n
- به روسیه تبعید اش کردند. — They exiled him to Russia.
91 | 178

2645 صبا sæba *zephyr* n,pn
- اگر چراغ بمیرد صبا چه غم دارد. — If the lamp dies, what grief will Saba have.
92 | 153

2646 جانبه dʒanebe *-lateral* adj
- توافق دوجانبه نفتی ایران-چین. — Bilateral oil agreement between Iran and China.
70 | 629

2647 پرسپولیس perspolis *Persepolis* pn
- هفته سیزدهم لیگ برتر فوتبال پرسپولیس با ۲ گل به رده ۲ رسید. — In the thirteenth week of the Premier Soccer League, with two goals, Persepolis moved up to the second group.
66 | 742

2648 جعفری dʒæʔfæri *parsley, Jafari* adj,n,pn
- ظریف آزاد سازی فلوجه را به ابراهیم جعفری تبریک گفت. — Zarif congratulated Ibrahim al-Jaafari on the liberation of Fallujah.
86 | 265

2649 تثبیت tæsbit *stabilizing* n
- قیمت جهانی طلا پس از نوسانات شدید در ماه‌های اخیر اکنون بین ۱۲۵۰ تا ۱۴۰۰ دلار تثبیت شده است. — After severe fluctuations in the past months, the world price of gold has currently been stabilized between 1250 and 1400 dollars.
82 | 356

2650 زهرا zæhra *Zahra* pn
- سرکار خانم زهرا دریایی از لوس آنجلس. — Mrs. Zahra Daryai from Los Angeles.
80 | 390

2651 منظر mænzær *perspective* n
- از منظر قانونی بهتر است. — From a legal perspective, it is better.
86 | 278

2652 عملیاتی æmælijjati *operational* adj,n
- فرمانده کل ارتش در قرارگاه عملیاتی لشکر ۲۳ بازدید کرد. — The Commander-in-Chief visited the Division 23 Operating Base.
80 | 396

2653 پانصد pansæd *five hundred* n
- قریب به پانصد نفر در همان موقع کشته و سوخته شدند. — Around five hundred people were burnt and killed at the same time.
54 | 1086

2654 تدریجی tædridʒi *gradual* adj
- جنگ در افغانستان به صورت تدریجی در حال پایان یافتن است. — The war in Afghanistan is gradually coming to an end.
87 | 241

2655 فرود forud *landing* n
- در کویر فرود آمدند. — They landed in the desert.
84 | 310

2656 سرنشین særneʃin *passenger* n
- این هواپیما پنج تا هفت سرنشین داشت. — This airplane had five to seven passengers.
76 | 491

2657 چندانی ʃændani *quantitative, so much* adj
- بارندگی‌ها، تأثیر چندانی بر آب دریاچه ارومیه نداشتند. — The rainfall had no notable effect on Lake Urmia's water.
82 | 359

2658 پاسدار pɑsdar *guard* adj,n
- ولی ما پنج نفر پاسدار یزدی و برادران کمیته‌ی طبس باقی ماندیم. — However we five guardians from Yazd and brothers of the Tabas committee remained.
84 | 313

2659 فاز faz *phase* n
- فاز نهایی این مرکز در نیمه دوم امسال تکمیل خواهد شد. — The final phase of this center will be completed in the second half of this year.
80 | 391

2660 بارش bɑreʃ *precipitation* n
- چسبیده به هم توی تاریکی به تق تق بارش تگرگ روی شیروانی گوش دادیم. — Clinging to each other in the dark we listened to the rattle of the precipitation of hail on the gables.
78 | 447

2661 شمردن ʃemordæn *count* adj,n,v
- صد تومان شمرد و داد به پیرمرد. — He counted out 100 tomans and gave them to the old man.
77 | 471

2662 شهردار ʃæhrdar *mayor* n
- همه بجز شهردار از صحنه بیرون می‌روند. — Everyone except the mayor leaves the stage.
61 | 871

2663 خبرگان xebregan *experts* n
- مجلس خبرگان رهبری مجلسی متشکل از فقیه‌های «واجد شرایط» است. — The Assembly of Experts consists of "qualified" Islamic jurists.
78 | 430

2664 دروغ doruɣ *lie* adj,n
- دروغ‌ام کجا بود! — Where was my lie?
79 | 413

2665 مکتب mæktæb *school* adj,n
- خود من هم مثل تو می رفتم مکتب. — I myself, like you, used to go school.
72 | 579

2666 عواقب **ævaɣeb** *consequences* n
- می‌ماند تا عواقب باخت را تحمل کند. — She will remain until she can endure the consequences of losing.
- 91 | 175

2667 منعکس **monʔækes** *reflected* adj
- معیار باید منعکس کننده دیدگاه، فرهنگ و اهداف سازمان باشند. — The criteria must be reflective of the viewpoint, culture, and goals of the organization.
- 88 | 221

2668 مصرف کردن **mæsræf kærdæn** *consume* v
- صرفه جویی به معنای درست و مناسب مصرف کردن است. — Economization means proper and reasonable consumption.
- 85 | 280

2669 تحسین **tæhsin** *praise* n
- آثار او و تحسین‌های فراوانی را به خود جذب کرده‌اند. — His works have attracted much admiration.
- 90 | 189

2670 سلطه **solte** *domination* n
- چند قرن زیر سلطه‌ی ترک های عثمانی بود. — It was under the rule of the Ottoman Turks for several centuries.
- 77 | 457

2671 کارگردان **kargærdan** *director* n
- کوبریک جزء معدود کارگردان‌هایی بود که همواره در انتخاب فیلمنامه ریسک می‌کرد. — Kubrick was one of the few directors who always took a risk in choosing screenplays.
- 69 | 653

2672 رایج **rajedʒ** *current* adj
- شش اشتباه رایج در تربیت فرزند. — Six common mistakes in childrearing.
- 79 | 417

2673 نهایتاً **næhajætæn** *eventually* adv,conj
- نهایتاً این عملیات در ۸ فروردین آغاز شد. — Finally, this operation was launched on 8 Farvardin.
- 85 | 289

2674 مالیاتی **malijati** *tax* adj
- این یکی از بزرگ‌ترین کاهش‌های مالیاتی در تاریخ آمریکا بود. — This was one of the largest tax cuts in America's history.
- 78 | 430

2675 اقلیت **æɣællijæt** *minority* n
- در اقلیت بودند. — They were in the minority.
- 84 | 303

2676 تمرکز **tæmærkoz** *centralization, concentration* n
- تمرکزمان روی آینده است. — Our focus is on the future.
- 81 | 379

2677 رکن **rokn** *pillar, foot* n
- مردم در صحنه انتخابات نشان دادند که مهمترین رکن نظام هستند. — People on the scene of elections showed that they are the most important pillar of the system.
- 80 | 386

2678 اهدا **ehda** *offering* n
- رئیس جمهور نمی تواند بدون حکم قانون ملکیت های دولتی را بفروشد یا اهدا کند. — Without a legal ruling, the president cannot sell or donate state properties.
- 76 | 487

2679 دادگستری **dadgostæri** *justice* n
- نظرش این بود که کار به دادگستری خواهد کشید. — His opinion was that it would be taken to court.
- 73 | 550

2680 بدل **bædæl** *imitation* n
- می‌فهمم اصل چیست و بدل کدام است. — I understand which is the original and which is the substitute.
- 84 | 303

2681 کنار گذاشتن **kenar gozaʃtæn** *put away* v
- این کشورها به روشهای استفاده بهتر از انرژی و کنار گذاشتن صنایع و لوازم پرمصرف روی بیاورند. — These countries should turn towards more efficient ways of using energy and give up using non energy efficient industries and devices.
- 84 | 307

2682 میهمان **mihman** *guest* n
- خانه اش همیشه از میهمان و درویش پر بود. — His house was always full of guests and dervishes.
- 76 | 480

2683 نمک **næmæk** *salt* n
- قبل و بعد از غذا کمی نمک میل کنید. — Before and after eating, have a little bit of salt.
- 82 | 343

2684 همانطور **hæmantur** *as, just as* conj
- همانطور که رهبر انقلاب فرمودند ما باید سیاست را بشناسیم. — Just as the leader of the revolution said, we must understand politics.
- 79 | 419

2685 اعظم **æʔzæm** *greater, greatest* adj
- انگلا مرکل صدر اعظم آلمان. — Angela Merkel, Chancellor of Germany.
- 84 | 309

2686 خصوصیت **xosusijjæt** *characteristic* n
- تمدن ها و انسان این خصوصیت را دارند که هیچ دو نفری به هم شبیه نباشند و در عین حال همه به هم شبیهند. — Civilizations and humans have this characteristic that no two are identical to one another and at the same time all are similar to each other.
- 78 | 434

2687 بركت bærekæt *blessing* n
- — Give thanks برای بركت‌هایی که دارید شكرگزارید. for the blessings that you have.

89 | 194

2688 اعتراف كردن eʔteraf kærdæn *confess* v
- The Black نقابداران سیاه به 4 جنایت اعتراف كردند. Masks confessed to four crimes.

90 | 193

2689 منتقد montæyed *critic* adj,n
- دوما من اساسا یک منتقد نیستم بلكه فعال اجتماعی‌وفرهنگی — Secondly, I am not a critic, rather می‌باشم. I'm a social and cultural activist.

75 | 495

2690 نشاندن neʃandæn *seat* adj,n,v
- سازمان تاكسیرانی بارها و بارها اعلام كرده نشاندن دو — Taxi مسافر بر روی صندلی جلو ممنوع است. regulatory organizations have repeatedly announced that sitting two passengers on the front seat is prohibited.

86 | 268

2691 پارچه partʃe *cloth, fabric* n
- استفاده از پارچه‌های رنگی و روشن، ویژگی پوشاک زنان — Using bright colored fabrics is روستا است. the feature of women's clothing in villages.

82 | 354

2692 پوتین putin *Putin, boots* n,pn
- پوتین هایش گلی بود و خورشید پشت سرش پایین می آمد. — His boots were muddy, and the sun was setting behind him.

71 | 587

2693 قدمت yedmæt *age, antiquity* n
- نظام مردسالاری مثل نظام كشاورزی است كه ۶ هزار سال قدمت دارد و دیگر نقش بزرگی در جامعه بازی نمی كند. — The system of male domination is like the system of agriculture in that it's six thousand years old and no longer plays a large role in society.

84 | 293

2694 غیره yejre *other* adj,n
- نمایندگانی از كشور های آلمان ایتالیا كانادا انگلستان چین و غیره. — Representatives from Germany, Italy, Canada, England, China, etc.

77 | 447

2695 تعطیل شدن tæʔtil ʃodæn *shut down* v
- با تعطیل شدن كارخانه‌ها هزاران نفر بیكار می‌شوند. — With the factories being closed, thousands will be unemployed.

89 | 203

2696 رویارویی rujaruji *confrontation* n
- Lack عدم آمادگی برای رویارویی با رویدادهای زندگی. of preparation for facing the events of life.

84 | 309

2697 گرو gerow *pledge, pawn, mortgage* n
- اجناسی را كه به گرو می‌آوردند، به صورت مخفیانه، به زیر زمین انتقال می‌دادند. — They would secretly move the goods, which were brought as a pledge, to the basement.

89 | 201

2698 صلیب sælib *cross* n
- تا خانواده های اسرای فلسطین در مقابل مقر صلیب سرخ جهانی تجمع اعتراض آمیز برگزار كنند. — So the families of Palestinian prisoners hold their protest in front of the International Red Cross.

94 | 102

2699 چک ʧek *check, Czech* n,pn
- تعداد زیادی چک پول هم از دور و نزدیک به دست آنها می رسید. — A large number of bank checks, from both near and far, were reaching them.

78 | 433

2700 انحراف enheraf *deviation* n
- پاسخ انحرافی خوب پاسخی است. — A deviant answer is a good answer.

80 | 377

2701 تدریج tædriʒ *gradual* n
- پس از آن به تدریج مدرسه‌های بسیار دیگری در شهر ساخته شدند. — After that, many other schools were gradually built in the city.

78 | 429

2702 باستانی bastani *ancient* adj,pn
- این كشورهای دیگری كه تمدن های باستانی داشتند، كشورهای عراق، سوریه، مصر و شمال آفریقا، در طی مدت كوتاهی، اسلامی و عربی شدند. — These other countries that had ancient civilizations, the countries of Iraq, Syria, and North Africa, became Arab and Muslim over a short period of time.

71 | 602

2703 فراموش كردن færamuʃ kærdæn *forget* v
- هیچ وقت فراموش نمی كنم. — I will never forget.

75 | 490

2704 شنیده ʃenide *heard* adj
- كتابش را بر پایة شنیده‌هایش نوشته‌است. — He wrote his book based on all he heard.

75 | 490

2705 سرقت seryæt *theft* n
- شما رو متهم به سرقت كردم. — I accused you of theft.

73 | 535

2706 صادراتی saderati *export* adj
- عمده‌ترین محصول صادراتی این كشور مرفین یا تریاک است. — Morphine, or opium, is the main export product of the country.

82 | 338

2707 محرمانه mæhræmane *confidential* adj
- نتایج این آزمایش‌ها کاملا محرمانه است. — The results of these experiments are completely confidential.
88 | 229

2708 کیش kiʃ *faith, Kish* n,pn
- در کیش زرتشت مهر ایزد نور و روشنایی است. — In the Zoroastrian religion, Mithra is the god of light and luminosity.
81 | 366

2709 اصولی osul *principled, systematic* adj,n
- بنظر اصولی‌ترین راه حل همین است. — It seems like this is the most systematic solution.
81 | 372

2710 افتخاری eftexari *honorary* adj,n
- پروفسور لطفی‌زاده دارای ۲۵ دکترای افتخاری از دانشگاه‌های معتبر دنیاست. — Professor Lotfi Zadeh has 25 honorary doctorates from the world's prestigious universities.
94 | 111

2711 ساماندهی samandehi *systematization* n
- ساماندهی مدیریت. — Organizing the management.
79 | 402

2712 بریتانیا beritanja *Britain* pn
- سفارت بریتانیا در کابل و برخی از نهاد های دفاع از حقوق بشر به خاطر موجودیت شکنجه در زندان های افغانستان ابراز نگرانی کردند. — The British Embassy in Kabul and several institutions for the defense of human rights expressed concern over the existence of torture in prisons in Afghanistan.
78 | 426

2713 برخورد کردن bærxord kærdæn *meet, collide* v
- نیروهای امنیتی و نظامی در برخی نقاط با معترضان برخورد کردند. — Military and security forces clashed with protesters in some areas.
83 | 325

2714 فاش faʃ *frank, reveal* adj
- راز عروسم را فاش نکند. — She shoudn't reveal my bride's secret.
84 | 291

2715 جویا dʒuja *searching* adj,pn
- ما جویای حالت بودیم. — We were asking about you.
92 | 139

2716 سیا sija *CIA* pn
- سازمان سیا در زمان جنگ داخلی گواتمالا به دولت این کشور کمک می‌کرد. — During the civil war in Guatemala, the CIA assisted the country's government.
82 | 335

2717 ترافیک terafik *traffic* n
- حمله انتحاری به ریاست ترافیک کابل بیش از 20 کشته و زخمی برجای گذاشت. — A suicide attack on the Kabul Traffic Department left more than 20 dead and wounded.
70 | 606

2718 درخشان deræxʃan *brilliant* adj
- خطوط مورب درخشان را نمی‌دید. — He couldn't see the bright, diagonal lines.
84 | 307

2719 متولد شدن motævælled ʃodæn *be born* v
- وقتی متولد شدم شش کیلو وزن داشتم. — When I was born I weighed six kilos.
86 | 265

2720 رنگی rængi *colored* adj,n
- چهار پنجره آن دارای شیشه رنگی است. — Four of its windows have stained glass.
82 | 338

2721 تحکیم tæhkim *consolidation, strengthening* n
- گروه‌های رقیب افغان برای تحکیم موقعیت خویش و تصرف پایتخت وارد نبرد شدند. — Afghan rival groups started a battle to consolidate their position and capture the capital.
77 | 452

2722 یاد کردن jad kærdæn *remember* v
- یاد کردن از این روز بهانه‌ای است برای یادآوری جایگاه کشورمان در جهان. — Remembering this day is an excuse to remind us of our stance in the world.
81 | 358

2723 امت ommæt *Ummah* n
- شکاف سنگینی میان امت اسلام بر اساس این استراتژی پدید خواهد آمد. — Based on this strategy a huge gap will emerge within the Islamic nation.
82 | 333

2724 خلاقیت xælaɣijæt *creativity* n
- خلاقیت در آنها وجود ندارد. — No creativity exists in them.
82 | 343

2725 آفتاب aftab *sunshine* n
- زیر آفتاب ایستادم. — I stood under the sun.
74 | 523

2726 جذاب dʒæzzab *attractive* adj
- مردی که پشت میز پذیرش هتل ایستاده ، خوش قیافه و جذاب است. — The man standing behind the hotel reception desk is handsome and attractive.
82 | 328

2727 شوم ʃum *ominous* adj,v
- آیا جغد شوم است؟ — Is the owl a bad omen?
76 | 461

2728 طبیعتاً tæbiʔætæn *naturally* adv
- طبیعتاً آن‌ها که موفق‌تر هستند، سرشناستر هم خواهند بود. — Naturally, those who are more successful will be more renowned.
89 | 204

17 Nature

Rank	Headword	Pronunciation	Gloss	Rank	Headword	Pronunciation	Gloss
79	ماه	mah	moon	2149	کانال	kanal	channel, canal
179	آب	ab	water	2320	چاه	tʃah	well
243	زمین	zæmin	ground	2385	سیل	sejl	flood
372	گل	gol, gel	flower, mud	2512	دریاچه	dærjatʃe	lake
474	هوا	hæva	air	2535	گیاه	gijah	plant
551	خاک	xak	soil, dust	2838	دشت	dæʃt	plain
574	آتش	atæʃ	fire	2883	اقیانوس	oyjanus	ocean
625	دریا	dærja	sea	3295	دره	dærre	valley
1160	رود	rud	river	3580	بیابان	bijaban	desert
1224	موج	mowdʒ	wave	3643	چشمه	tʃeʃme	spring
1326	سنگ	sæng	rock	3647	بوستان	bustan	orchard
1362	جزیره	dʒæzire	island	4250	تالاب	talab	pond, wetlands
1435	ستاره	setare	star	4252	سیاره	sæjjare	planet
1439	بندر	bændær	port	4804	ماسه	mase	sand
1496	درخت	deræxt	tree	6005	غار	yar	cave
1537	خورشید	xorʃid	sun	6168	باتلاق	batlay	marsh
1605	باغ	bay	garden	7067	آبشار	abʃar	waterfall
1659	ساحل	sahel	shore	7184	علف	ælæf	grass
1678	کوه	kuh	mountain	7329	کاج	kadʒ	pine
1763	آسمان	asman	heaven	8112	بلوط	bælut	oak
1848	رودخانه	rudxane	river	8960	آتشفشان	atæʃfeʃan	volcano
1925	جنگل	dʒængæl	forest, jungle	9063	صدف	sædæf	seashell
2060	خلیج	xælidʒ	gulf	15427	آبراه	abrah	canal

2729 تماشا tæmaʃa *watching* n
- رفت؟ جاذبه‌هایی چه تماشای به باید «هنگام جزیره» در — On Hengam Island, what attractions should one go to see?
- 77 | 438

2730 تضاد tæzad *conflict* n
- انقلاب ما با آنچه در دنیا می گذرد در بنیاد فکری و اهداف در تضاد است. — In its intellectual foundation and goals, our revolution is in opposition to that which goes on in the world.
- 87 | 243

2731 فهم fæhm *understanding* n
- فهم شد؟ — Is it understood?
- 75 | 489

2732 صندلی sændæli *chair* n
- روی همین صندلی می نشستم. — I was sitting in this very chair.
- 71 | 589

2733 دیرینه dirine *old* adj,n
- روابط دیرینه خود با ایرانیان. — Its long-standing relations with Iranians.
- 90 | 183

2734 ساختمانی saxtemani *construction* adj,n
- می‌توان مصالح ساختمانی را دست‌کم در پنج رده تقسیم کرد. — Building materials can be divided into at least five categories.
- 76 | 459

2735 نوامبر novambr *November* n
- در نوامبر سال گذشته . . . — In November of last year . . .
- 86 | 256

2736 بشریت bæʃærijjæt *humanity* n
- خیانت علیه بشریت. — Treason against humanity.
- 87 | 243

2737 جاسوسی dʒɑsusi *espionage* adj,n
- جاسوسی کردن از کشورهای همسایه. — Espionage from neighboring countries.
74 | 513

2738 آنقدر ɑnɣædr *so much* adv
- یعنی آنقدر زود آمدم که هنوز هیچ کارمندی نیامده؟ — What you are saying is that I have come so early that no employees have arrived yet?
68 | 648

2739 مرجع mærdʒæʔ *authority* adj,n
- جمهوری اسلامی ایران در بالاترین مرجع تصمیم گیری جهانی تصویب می‌شود. — The Islamic Republic of Iran will be approved in the highest decision-making authority in the world.
82 | 328

2740 آزمایشی ɑzmɑjeʃi *experimental* adj,n
- نمونه آزمایشی این هواپیما در ۱۷ نوامبر ۱۹۵۶ پرواز کرد. — The prototype aircraft flew on November 17, 1956.
88 | 207

2741 تلقی tælæɣɣi *attitude, point of view* n
- ممکن است تلقی کسی این باشد که عالم از یک نقطه شروع شده است و به نقطه دیگری ختم می‌شود. — It's possible for someone's interpretation to be that the world started at one point and will end at another.
82 | 326

2742 حکمت hekmæt *philosophy, wisdom* n,pn
- البته حکمت خدا هم در این امداد حضور دارد. — Of course God's wisdom is also present in this relief.
79 | 387

2743 نجف nædʒæf *Najaf* pn
- در نهایت بعد از بیست سال اقامت در نجف و تحصیل در سطوح عالی به درجه اجتهاد رسیده است. — Finally, after twenty years of residing in Najaf and studying at the higher levels, he reached the level of ijtihad.
87 | 238

2744 صلاح sælɑh *salvation, advisable* n
- هر جوابی که خودت صلاح می‌دانی به او بده. — Give him whatever response that you yourself consider expedient.
87 | 231

2745 بدی bædi *evil* adj,n
- نماز ما را از بدیها دور می کند. — Prayers keep us away from evil.
73 | 519

2746 رها کردن ræhɑ kærdæn *free, let go* v
- سارقان فراری جسد همدستشان را رها کردند. — The fleeing thieves left the body of their accomplice behind.
84 | 286

2747 توهین towhin *insult* n
- من دوست ندارم اینجا به هیچ کس توهین بشه. — I don't want to insult anyone here.
87 | 229

2748 اردبیل ærdebil *Ardabil* pn
- در اردبیل سرباز وظیفه بود. — He was a soldier in Ardabil.
74 | 516

2749 همشهری hæmʃæhri *fellow citizen, Hamshahri* n,pn
- روزنامه همشهری. — Hamshahri newspaper.
53 | 1052

2750 سواری sævɑri *riding* adj,n
- دوچرخه سواری که بخواهد در کنار جاده حرکت کند مورد آزار رانندگان قرار می‌گیرد. — A biker who wants to bike along the road will be harassed by drivers.
80 | 377

2751 خرابی xærɑbi *destruction* n
- در اثر زلزله‌بم واقع در شهرستان بم در استان کرمان خرابی های زیادی به بار آمد. — The earthquake in Bam city in Kerman province caused a lot of destruction.
94 | 112

2752 اسیر æsir *captive* adj,n
- آمریکا در عملیاتی در صحرای طبس جهت‌آزادی جان گروگان‌های اسیر در ایران با شکست روبه‌رو شد و اسناد سری و مهمی در درون هلیکوپترها به جای مانده است. — America was confronted with failure in the Tabas Desert operation directed at the rescue of the hostages captive in Iran and classified and important documents were left inside the helicopters.
73 | 527

2753 تحقیقی tæɣiɣi *research* adj,n
- روزنامه‌نگاری تحقیقی چیست؟ — What is investigative journalism?
85 | 266

2754 ناتوانی nɑtævɑni *inability* n
- این زنان بیشتر به‌ظاهر خود می پردازند، مدام در باره ضعف و ناتوانی خود صحبت می کنند و ممکن است دچار حسادت شدید هم باشند. — These women pay more attention to their own appearance, continuously talk about their own weakness and inabilities, and are possibly experiencing extreme jealousy.
82 | 330

2755 ژاپنی ʒɑponi *Japanese* adj,n,pn
- منازل ژاپنی بنابر شرایط محیطی دارای فضایی خالی بین دیوار های چوبی هستند. — Japanese houses, in accordance with environmental conditions, have an empty space between wooden walls.
78 | 404

2756 فروپاشی forupɑʃi *collapse* n
- پس از فروپاشی اتحاد جماهیر شوروی، جنگ تشدید شد. — After the collapse of the Soviet Union, the war intensified.
80 | 370

2757 بحرانی bohrani *critical* adj,n
- ۷۵ درصد تالاب‌های کشور در وضع بحرانی قرار دارد. — 75% of the country's wetlands are in critical condition.
- 78 | 423

2758 دم dæm, dom *breath/near, tail* n,prep
- سرباز مأمور دم می‌خواست مرا راه ندهد، گفتم : «خود حاج آقا گفته‌اند، می‌توانم بیایم.» — The officer at the door wanted to not let me through, so I said, "Haj Agha himself said that I can come in."
- 60 | 838

2759 مکزیک mekzik *Mexico* pn
- مایا ها تمدن شگوفان و با عظمتی را در مکزیک پدید آوردند. — The Mayas created an amazing and majestic civilization in Mexico.
- 80 | 367

2760 جی dʒi, dʒej *g, j* pn
- محققان صنعت نفت ایران به فناوری تولید بنزین از گاز یا سوخت جی تی ال دست یافته اند. — Iran's oil industry researchers have achieved the technology of producing gasoline from gas or GTL fuel.
- 86 | 241

2761 اسب æsb *horse* n
- اسبش را به درختی بست و به قهوه خانه رفت. — He tied his horse to a tree and went to the coffeehouse.
- 70 | 579

2762 استاندار ostandar *governor-general* n
- نه تنها سردار و همسرش را بخشید ، بلکه او را به عنوان استاندار سرزمین جنوبی انتخاب کرد. — He not only forgave his commander and his wife, but chose him as the governor of the southern lands.
- 76 | 452

2763 معدود mæ?dud *few* adj,n,q
- داربی در شمار معدود کسانی قرار گرفت که سالانه بیش از یک میلیون دلار بیمه عمر می‌فروشند. — Darby was among the scant number of people who sell a million dollars' worth of life insurance each year.
- 88 | 212

2764 دراز deraz *long* adj
- علت عمر دراز سعدی نیز ایمان قوی او بود. — The reason for Sa'di's long life was also his powerful faith.
- 68 | 636

2765 چنانکه tʃenanke *as* conj
- چنانکه رهبر ارکستر می‌گوید. — As the conductor says.
- 78 | 401

2766 فزاینده fæzajænde *increasing* adj
- بانک مرکزی آمریکا اکنون با انتقادهای فزاینده مردم و رسانه ها مواجه است. — America's central bank is facing growing criticism from the people and media.
- 85 | 260

2767 راهنما rahnæma *guide* adj,n
- چشم از چراغ راهنما بر نمی داشت. — He would not take his eye off the guiding light.
- 86 | 257

2768 ارمنستان ærmænestan *Armenia* pn
- سر چشمه ی آن نزدیک رود ارس در سر زمین ارمنستان است. — Its source is near the Aras River in Armenia.
- 81 | 349

2769 ضبط zæbt *record* n
- صدایش را ضبط کردم. — I recorded her voice.
- 82 | 327

2770 تسهیل tæshil *facilitating* n
- تسهیل کمی یک سیاست نامتعارف پولیست. — Quantitative easing is an uncommon monetary policy.
- 84 | 284

2771 فلز felez *metal* n
- فلز متولدین فروردین آهن است. — The metal of those born in Farvardin is iron.
- 81 | 345

2772 اقبال eybal *good luck, Eghbal* n,pn
- خیلی خوش اقبال. — Very lucky.
- 84 | 281

2773 توفیق towfiɣ *success* n,pn
- خداوند چنین توفیقی به تو بدهد. — May God bless you with this good favor.
- 84 | 291

2774 مهاجم mohadʒem *invader, attacker, striker* adj,n
- هند برای مقاومت و دفاع از خود در برابر مهاجم هیچگونه سلاح و قدرتی ندارد. — India has no sort of power or weapons to resist and defend itself against an aggressor.
- 79 | 384

2775 آلودگی aludegi *pollution* n
- مهمترین علت آلودگی هوای تبریز، حمل و نقل درون‌شهری است. — The main cause of air pollution in Tabriz is urban transportation.
- 63 | 762

2776 آهان ahan *yes* adv
- آهان این نامه هم هست، . — Uh-huh, there is also this letter.
- 38 | 1593

2777 آواره avare *homeless* adj,n
- غریب و آواره ام. — I am a stranger and a vagrant.
- 80 | 364

2778 مصری mesri *Egyptian* adj,n,pn
- لاشه هواپیمای مصری پیدا شد. — The wreckage of the Egyptian plane was found.
- 69 | 609

2779 حماسه hæmase *epic* n
- وقتی مردم حرکت کردند حماسه خلق شد. — When people moved, they created epics.
- 84 | 291

2780 نوسان nævæsan *fluctuation* n
- نوسان نرخ. — Rate fluctuation.
- 76 | 452

2781 عصبی æsæbi *nervous* adj
- شما را عصبی کرد. — It made you nervous.
- 80 | 375

2782 کادر kadr *cadre* n
- همه چیز در کنترل دامپزشک و کادر متخصص است. — Everything is controlled by the veterinarian and specialist staff.
- 81 | 355

2783 صدام sæddam *Saddam* pn
- چنانچه صدام به سیاست فعلی خود ادامه دهد منطقه گرفتار یک فاجعه خواهد شد. — If Saddam continues his policy, the region is going to experience a disaster.
- 77 | 427

2784 الکترونیک elektronik *electronics* adj,n
- الکترونیک دانش مطالعهٔ عبور جریان الکتریکی در مواد مختلف. — Electronics is the field of study about the flow of electric current through various materials.
- 78 | 398

2785 پرچم pærtʃæm *flag* n
- باد گرم و خشکی می وزید و پرچم هایی که از تیرهای چراغ برق آویزان بودند آهسته تکان می داد. — A dry, warm wind was blowing and the flags hanging from the light poles fluttered slowly.
- 83 | 303

2786 سعادت sæʔadæt *happiness* n,pn
- در این دنیا اگر سعادتی است تنها نصیب دیوانگان است. — If there is happiness in this world it is fated only for the insane.
- 86 | 255

2787 یزد jæzd *Yazd* pn
- از یزد با اتوبوس رفتم تهران. — I went from Yazd to Tehran by bus.
- 70 | 577

2788 رابرت rabert *Robert* pn
- تنها ملاقات میان آلپاچینو و رابرت دنیرو. — The only meeting between Al Pacino and Robert De Niro.
- 90 | 166

2789 هسته‌ای hæsteji *nuclear* adj
- منع گسترش سلاح های هسته ای. — Banning the spread of nuclear weapons.
- 61 | 809

2790 عام am *common* adj,n
- حکم صادره صبح دیروز در ملاء عام و در محل وقوع قتل به اجرا درآمد. — Yesterday morning the sentence was carried out in public in the place where the murder occurred.
- 77 | 433

2791 فشرده feʃorde *pressed, concise* adj,n
- فشرده‌ترین آپارتمان جهان ساخته شد. — The world's most compact apartment was built.
- 87 | 227

2792 تایمز tajmz *Times* pn
- میدان تایمز در نیویورک، پر بازدید کننده‌ترین نقطه جهان با ۳۵ میلیون بازدیدکننده در سال است. — Times Square in New York is the most visited place in the world with 35 million visitors a year.
- 74 | 492

2793 برلین berlin *Berlin* pn
- آنکارا، سفیر خود را از برلین فراخواند. — Ankara recalled its ambassador from Berlin.
- 80 | 365

2794 مغرب mæɣreb *west, Maghreb, Morocco* n,pn
- بر اساس این گزارش، ابو دردار، یکی از فرماندهان گروه تروریستی القاعده در مغرب عربی . . . — Based on this report, Abu Derdar, one of the commanders of the terrorist group Al-Qaeda in the Islamic Maghreb . . .
- 85 | 257

2795 ابر æbr *cloud* n
- چرا این ابر جلو آفتاب را گرفته؟ — Why has this cloud gotten in front of the sun?
- 82 | 333

2796 بامداد bamdad *morning* n
- مرد هر بامداد از خانه بیرون میرود. — Each morning the man goes out of his house.
- 75 | 466

2797 مداخله modaxele *intervention* n
- حماس با مداخلات خارجی در امور داخلی یمن مخالف است. — Hamas opposes foreign interference in the internal affairs of Yemen.
- 67 | 658

2798 تعطیلی tæʔtili *vacation, closure* n
- این بحران باعث تعطیلی چند هفته‌ای بانک ها و ایجاد تظاهرات گسترده شد. — This crisis led to the closure of banks for several weeks and the creation of mass protests.
- 78 | 401

2799 احتیاج ehtijadʒ *need* n
- حالا یک واقعهٔ تاریخی دیگر پیش آمده بود که احتیاج به شناسنامه داشت و شناسنامه گم شده بود. — Now, another historical event had come up that he had a need for an ID and the ID had gone missing.
- 85 | 265

2800 همیشگی hæmiʃegi *perpetual* adj,adv
- این فرصت‌ها همیشگی نیست. — These opportunities are not forever.
- 86 | 244

2801 ساله بودن sɑle budæn *be years old* v
- من ۱۸ ساله بودم که حس مادری را تجربه کردم. — I was 18 years old when I experienced a sense of motherhood.

86 | 244

2802 اصیل æsil *noble* adj
- من دارای علاقه بسیار زیادی به موسیقی سنتی و اصیل ایرانی هستم. — I really like traditional and authentic Iranian music.

86 | 247

2803 حذف شدن hæzf ʃodæn *be eliminated* v
- ولی هرگز قابل حذف شدن نیست. — But it's never removable.

86 | 254

2804 غافل ɣɑfel *negligent, unaware* adj
- اما ارشمیدس که غافل از دور و برش بود همینطور داد و فریاد می‌کرد: یافتم، یافتم، یافتم . . . — But Archimedes, who was unaware of his surroundings, continued shouting, "Eureka, eureka, eureka . . ."

87 | 224

2805 تورم tæværrom *inflation* n
- تورم باید مهار شود. — Inflation must be contained.

76 | 435

2806 خزر xæzær *Caspian* pn
- حمایت آمریکا از انتقال گاز خزر به اروپا با تاکید بر حذف ایران از پروژه. — American support for transferring Caspian gas to Europe with an emphasis on eliminating Iran from the project.

69 | 592

2807 معرفت mæʔrefæt *knowledge* n
- شما با این همه زیبایی و کمال و معرفتی که داری چرا شوهر نمی کنی؟ — With all your beauty, perfection, and learning, why aren't you getting a husband?

71 | 554

2808 تعادل tæʔɑdol *balance* n
- هر تیم که زودتر تعادل تمامی افرادش بهم بخورد بازنده‌است. — Whichever team's members lose their balance sooner is the loser.

80 | 359

2809 سیزدهم sizdæhom *thirteenth* adj,n
- عینک اولین بار در قرن سیزدهم میلادی در اروپا استفاده شد. — Eyeglasses were used for the first time in Europe in the thirteenth century AD.

81 | 344

2810 سلسله selsele *chain* n
- نخستین جلسه از سلسله سخنرانی‌ها. — The first session in a series of talks.

69 | 589

2811 پادشاهی pɑdʃɑhi *kingdom, reign* n
- پس از سرنگونی پادشاهی ارمنستان در سال ۴۲۸ میلادی، این منطقه از نو بخشی از ایران شد. — After the overthrow of the Kingdom of Armenia in 428 AD, the region became a part of Iran again.

82 | 320

2812 جوی dʒui, dʒævvi *brook, atmospheric* adj,n
- با بهبود شرایط جوی در نیمه شمالی کشور موج جدیدی از سفرهای نوروزی آغاز شده است. — With the improvement of atmospheric conditions in the northern half of the country, a new wave of Nowruz trips have begun.

81 | 334

2813 نقص næɣs *defect* n
- تذکراتی به صاحبان این شرکت درباره رفع نقص فنی این خودرو داده‌ایم. — We have warned the owners of this company about solving the technical defect of this automobile.

86 | 242

2814 فرهاد færhɑd *Farhad* pn
- چند روز پیش فرهاد میرزا میگفت خسرو خان خیلی بی احتیاطی میکنه. — A few days ago, Farhad Mirza was saying that Khosrow Khan is being very imprudent.

82 | 321

2815 طرز tærz *manner* n
- این چه طرز راه رفتن است؟ — What manner of walking is that?

71 | 541

2816 کف kæf *bottom, palm, foam* n
- آنچه‌را در کف دارید آزادانه ببخشائید. — Give away all you have in hand.

71 | 549

2817 عید ejd *holiday* n
- اختصاص 30 میلیارد تومان برای ذخیره‌سازی میوه، به منظور جلوگیری از گرانی شب عید. — Allocation of 30 billion toman for fruit storage in order to prevent expensive prices on New Year's Eve.

74 | 490

2818 عشیره æʃire *nomadic tribe* n
- شیخ ما یک مرد قدرتمندی است . . . چقدر عشیره و قبیله دارد. — Our Sheikh is such a powerful man . . . oh how many clans and tribes he has.

88 | 202

2819 گراییدن gerɑjidæn *tend, incline* v
- زمانی که مکه فتح شد همه اقوام و قبایل به اسلام گراییدند. — When Mecca was conquered, all tribes and nations inclined toward Islam.

76 | 432

2820 یارانه jɑrɑne *subsidy* n
- یکسال پس از حذف یارانه نان. — One year after removing the subsidy on bread.

67 | 633

2821 مراقب moɣayeb *minder, attentive* adj,n
- از ش مراقبت کنه — Look after him.
- 90 | 169

2822 تلقی شدن tælæɣɣi ʃodæn *be considered* v
- انحصاری تلقی شدن صنعت خودرو ، به زیان خودروسازان — Monopoly in the automobile industry would incur losses for manufacturers and customers.
- 79 | 373

2823 شبه ʃebh, ʃæbe *quasi, night* adj,n,pn
- هنوز در صف بندی این طیف به راحتی می توان از دو دسته اصلاح طلبان واقعی و شبه اصلاح طلبان سخن گفت. — Still, along this spectrum one can easily speak of two branches of real reformists and quasi-reformists.
- 78 | 406

2824 گره gereh *knot, problem* n
- نخ یکی از کیسه‌ها را باز کرد و دوباره بست و سه گره روی هم زد. — He untied the thread of one of the bags and closed it again and tied three knots on top of one another.
- 80 | 365

2825 رکود rokud *stagnation, recession* n
- اقتصاد در وضعیت رکود و تورم بسیار بالا است. — The economy is in a state of stagnation and very high inflation.
- 77 | 417

2826 سریال serijal *series* n
- ماه مبارک رمضان فرا رسید و سریال های زیادی نیز به مناسبت این ماه در حال پخش هستند. — The blessed month of Ramadan arrived and in celebration of this month, there are many TV series airing.
- 72 | 531

2827 نوزدهم nuzdæhom *nineteenth* adj,n
- در قرن نوزدهم میلادی ارتباط این کشور با جهان غرب آغاز شد. — This country's relationship with the West began in the nineteenth century AD.
- 83 | 306

2828 ساحلی saheli *coastal* adj
- بیشتر جمعیت کشور در مناطق ساحلی زندگی می‌کنند. — Most of the country's population lives in coastal areas.
- 82 | 322

2829 مدرس modærres *teacher* n,pn
- این هفته با دکتر پرویز رزاقی، روان شناس و مدرس دانشگاه در این مورد گفت و گو می‌کنیم. — This week we will talk about this subject with Doctor Parviz Razaghi, a psychologist and university lecturer.
- 84 | 284

2830 امروزی emruzi *modern, contemporary* adj
- این رخدادی است که در بستر سیاسی امروزی ایران روی داده است. — This is an event that occurred within the context of present-day Iranian politics.
- 78 | 390

2831 متوسل motævæssel *seeking help* adj
- اگر هدف مهمی در پیش دارید ابتدا برای تحقق آن به دعا متوسل شوید و سپس آن را به خدا واگذار کنید. — If you have an important goal in mind, first, in order to realize it, resort to prayer and leave it to God.
- 93 | 117

2832 قطب ɣotb *pole* n
- به تازگی یک ماهواره کانادایی تصاویری از قطب جنوب زمین ارسال کرده است. — Recently, a Canadian satellite sent back images of Earth's South Pole.
- 83 | 301

2833 تأخیر tæʔxir *delay* n
- مراسم با یک هفته تأخیر برگزار شد. — The ceremony was held with a week-long delay.
- 78 | 392

2834 رضایی rezaji *Rezai* pn
- علیرضا رضایی سرپرست فدراسیون جهانی کشتی پهلوانی شد. — Alireza Rezaei became director of the World Wrestling Championship Federation.
- 83 | 306

2835 سیستان sistan *Sistan* pn
- موسیقی از دیرباز در زندگی مردم منطقه سیستان و بلوچستان حضوری فعال دارد. — From time immemorial music has had an active presence in the life of the people of the region of Sistan and Balochestan.
- 77 | 422

2836 پیاده pijade *pedestrian, on foot* adj,adv
- نمی دانم کی و کجا پیاده شدم. — I don't know when and where I got out.
- 77 | 418

2837 حین hin *time* n
- زنی مسن با موهای جوگندمی که تازه غذای خود را گرفته در گوشهء اتاق روی صندلی نشسته است، اما در حین خوردن غذا خوابش برده. — An elderly woman with graying hair has just gotten her food and sat down in a chair in the corner of the room, but she's fallen asleep while eating.
- 83 | 292

2838 دشت dæʃt *plain* n
- از دشت و کوه و بیابان گذشتند. — They crossed the plains, mountains, and desserts.
- 71 | 544

2839 صوتی sowti *acoustic* adj,n
- تهران آلوده‌ترین شهر جهان از نظر آلودگی صوتی است. — Tehran is the most polluted city in the world in terms of noise pollution.
- 89 | 176

2840 شکل‌گیری ʃeklgiri *formation* n
- توطئه‌ها علیه او نیز در حال شکل‌گیری است. — The conspiracy is also forming against him.
- 81 | 326

2841 دموکراتیک demokratik *democratic* adj
- باید مرکز توطئه ضد نهضت‌های دموکراتیک نباشد. — It must not be the center of the conspiracy against democratic movements.
- 75 | 446

2842 تأسیسات tæʔsisɑt *installations* n
- سران از تأسیسات هسته‌ای بازدید می‌کنند. — The leaders are visiting the nuclear installations.
- 81 | 338

2843 بدنی bædæni *physical* adj
- فقط دویدن برای سلامت بدنی شما کافی نیست. — Running alone is not enough for your physical health.
- 68 | 601

2844 ایستاده istɑde *standing* adj
- اسب‌ها می‌توانند به صورت ایستاده و نشسته بخوابند. — Horses can sleep standing and lying down.
- 68 | 613

2845 کریمی kærimi *Karimi* pn
- علی کریمی هم پنج میلیون تومان پاداش گرفت. — Ali Karimi also received a five million toman reward.
- 84 | 282

2846 معدنی mæʔdæni *mineral* adj
- هیلبرتز روشی یافته بود تا بتواند با استفاده از نور خورشید مواد معدنی در دریا را به سنگ آهک تبدیل کند. — Hilbertz had discovered a method for using sunlight to convert the mineral substances in the sea into limestone.
- 79 | 376

2847 خریداری xæridɑri *purchasing* n
- برو و شراب خریداری کن. — Go and buy wine.
- 81 | 324

2848 مقر mæɣærr, moɣerr *headquarters, confessing* n
- مقر اصلی فرماندهی عملیات نظامی ارتش آمریکا بر ضدعراق است. — The headquarters of America's military operations against Iraq.
- 82 | 306

2849 شایان ʃɑjɑn *worthy* adj,n
- شایان ذکر است. — It is worth mentioning.
- 87 | 211

2850 گزارش شدن gozɑreʃ ʃodæn *be reported* v
- پیش از این گزارش شده بود که هوا در این ناحیه خوب است. — Before it was reported that the weather in this region is good.
- 85 | 251

2851 فارغ fɑreɣ *free* adj
- اگر ما لحظه‌ای فارغ نیستیم. — If we are not free for a second.
- 78 | 398

2852 نقدی næɣdi *cash* adj,n
- بوکسرها هم از کمیته‌های ملی المپیک کشور خود جوایز نقدی دریافت می‌کنند. — Boxers also receive cash prizes from their National Olympic Committees.
- 80 | 345

2853 ظاهر شدن zɑher ʃodæn *appear* v
- آیا شما هنوز مجاز به ظاهر شدن در رادیو و تلویزیون‌های آمریکا نیستید. — Aren't you still allowed to appear on American television and radio?
- 78 | 395

2854 نوسازی nowsazi *renovating* n
- شخصی مشغول تخریب دیوار قدیمی خانه اش بود تا آن را نوسازی کند. — Someone was busy demolishing the old wall of their house so they could rebuild it.
- 78 | 397

2855 حج hædʒdʒ *Hajj* n
- هدیه ای را که در سفر حج برایش خریده بود. — The gift he had bought him on his Hajj pilgrimage.
- 84 | 274

2856 شباهت ʃæbɑhæt *similarity* n
- این حرف‌های شما خیلی شباهت دارد. — These words of yours have much similarity.
- 84 | 268

2857 آینه ɑjene *mirror* n
- به خودم در آینه نگاه کردم. — I looked at myself in the mirror.
- 73 | 497

2858 خونی xuni *blood* adj,n
- خونی که از شش‌ها می‌آید به سمت چپ قلب وارد می‌شود. — The blood that comes from the lungs, enters to the left side of the heart.
- 88 | 205

2859 شوق ʃowɣ *eagerness* n
- من با شوق فریاد می‌زدم. — I yelled enthusiastically.
- 89 | 191

2860 منظم monæzzæm *regular* adj
- لامپ‌ها را به طور منظم تمیز کنید. — Clean the light bulbs regularly.
- 77 | 402

2861 هموطن hæmvætæn *compatriot* n
- او از هموطنان محترم آذربایجانی است. — He is among our esteemed Azerbaijani countrymen.
77 | 417

2862 یکبار jekbar *once* adv
- فکر کردم بهتره یکبار دیگه بگم که من با اجبار حجاب موافق نیستم. — I thought it was better I say once more that I don't agree with compulsory hijab.
81 | 330

2863 رمان roman *novel* n
- شخصیت اصلی رمان مردی میانسال بود. — The main character of the novel was a middle-aged man.
72 | 510

2864 سفارش sefareʃ *order* adj,n
- گوشه ی دنج کافه ی کوچکی محل قرار مان بود؛ قهوه ای سفارش دادم. — The cozy corner of a small cafe was the location of our date; I ordered a coffee.
84 | 282

2865 اسد æsæd *Assad, Leo* pn
- در بحبوحه این فشارها اسد تصمیم گرفت — In the midst of this pressure, Assad decided . . .
77 | 408

2866 جزئی dʒozʔi *slight* adj,n
- این افراد به سرعت از جزئی‌ترین تغییرات در محیطشان آگاه می‌شوند. — These people quickly become aware of the slightest changes in their surroundings.
82 | 317

2867 مستقیماً mostæɣimæn *directly* adv
- شاخه اصلی آن مستقیماً به دریا می ریزد. — Its main branch flows directly into the sea.
85 | 262

2868 مبتلا mobtæla *suffering from* adj,n
- سال ها بعد، پسر همان اشراف زاده به ذات الریه مبتلا شد. — Years later, the same nobleman's son was stricken with pneumonia.
74 | 480

2869 بزرگسال bozorgsal *adult* adj,n
- روش تدریس بر یادگیری بی سوادان بزرگسال. — Teaching methodology for illiterate adults.
78 | 383

2870 بلژیک belʒik *Belgium* pn
- این رقابت‌ها مهر ماه امسال در بلژیک برگزار خواهد شد. — These competitions will be held in Belgium in the month of Mehr.
80 | 353

2871 چوب tʃub *wood* n
- باید این درخت را ببری و با چوبش برای بچه ام گهواره درست کنی. — You should cut down this tree and make a cradle out of it for my child.
77 | 413

2872 عزیزی æzizi *Azizi, dear* adj,pn
- من هم با جناب عزیزی موافقم. — I also agree with Mr. Azizi.
88 | 204

2873 اجباری edʒbari *mandatory* adj,n
- کویت آزمایش دی‌ان‌ای را برای همه اجباری کرد. — Kuwait made DNA tests mandatory for everyone.
87 | 222

2874 سرچشمه særtʃeʃme *source* n
- سرچشمه همه مشکلات و استرس‌های شما هم همین است. — This is the source of all of your problems and stress.
80 | 343

2875 بازنگری baznegæri *reappraisal* n
- بانک مرکزی اروپا بازنگری سیاست پولی خود را ضروری دانست. — European Central Bank considers its monetary policy review necessary.
82 | 303

2876 قزوین ɣæzvin *Qazvin* pn
- هر وقت می‌رفت قم یا قزوین در اطاقش را قفل می‌کرد. — Whenever he would go to Qom or Qazvin he would lock the door to his room.
77 | 415

2877 مشرف moʃærræf, moʃref *honored, near/ overlooking* adj,n,pn
- پنجره مشرف به پارکی است. — The window is overlooking a park.
87 | 217

2878 انعکاس enʔekas *reflection* n
- انعکاس تصویرش در آئینه. — The reflection of her picture in the mirror.
85 | 244

2879 محوری mehværi *pivotal* adj,n
- منافع محوری. — Core interests.
86 | 239

2880 قومی ɣowmi *ethnic* adj,n
- این مولفه ها باعث می شود که تنش ها قومی کاهش یافته و گروه ها و اقوام بتواند در کنار هم زندگی مسالمت آمیز نماید. — These components cause ethnic tensions to decrease and groups and nations to be able to live peacefully together.
73 | 496

2881 بازرس bazres *inspector* n
- مجمع عمومی عادی یک نفر را به عنوان بازرس اصلی و یک نفر را به عنوان بازرس علی البدل برای مدت یکسال انتخاب خواهد نمود. — The General Assembly will normally elect one person as chief inspector and one person as alternate inspector for a term of one year.
85 | 259

18 Politics

Rank	Headword	Pronunciation	Gloss	Rank	Headword	Pronunciation	Gloss
40	شهر	ʃæhr	city	2070	سیاستمدار	sijasætmædar	politician
90	دولت	dowlæt	government	2227	رئیس‌جمهور	ræʔisdʒomhur	president
103	سیاسی	sijasi	political	2286	توده	tude	mass, Tudeh
133	وزیر	væzir	minister	2762	استاندار	ostandar	governor-general
165	قانون	ɣanun	law	2841	دموکراتیک	demokratik	democratic
187	مجلس	mædʒles	parliament	3125	کمونیست	komonist	communist
219	جمهوری	dʒomhuri	republic	3188	مشروطه	mæʃrute	constitutional
223	سیاست	sijasæt	policy, politics	3190	صهیونیست	sæhjunist	Zionist
289	وزارت	vezaræt	ministry	3586	فرماندار	færmandar	governor
301	استان	ostan	province	3679	لیبرال	liberal	liberal
337	انتخابات	entexabat	elections	3698	فرمانداری	færmandari	governorship
412	حزب	hezb	party	3752	جمهوریخواه	dʒomhurixah	republican
470	دولتی	dowlæti	governmental	4125	شاهزاده	ʃahzade	prince
538	حکومت	hokumæt	government	4486	ولسوالی	volosvali	Afghan county
576	بین‌المللی	bejnolmelæli	international	4778	اساسنامه	æsasname	charter, constitution
711	کمیته	komite	committee	4780	سوسیالیست	sosijalist	socialist
785	جمهور	dʒomhur	republic	4824	کمونیستی	komonisti	communist
937	صلح	solh	peace	4921	جرگه	dʒærge	circle, jirga
1004	ایالت	ejalæt	state	5129	اصلاح‌طلب	eslahtælæb	reformist
1074	شاه	ʃah	king, shah	6217	والی	vali	governor
1152	شهرستان	ʃæhrestan	county	6557	محافظه‌کار	mohafezekar	conservative
1212	صهیونیستی	sehjunisti	Zionist	17145	اصول‌گرا	osulgera	fundamentalist
1826	نخست‌وزیر	noxostvæzir	prime minister				
1962	جمهوری‌اسلامی	dʒomhurije eslami	Islamic Republic				

2882 لیتر liter *liter* n
- بدن یک فرد بالغ بطور متوسط دارای ۴٫۷ تا ۵٫۷ لیتر خون می‌باشد. — The adult human body contains an average of 4.7 to 5.7 liters of blood.
82 | 314

2883 اقیانوس oɣjanus *ocean* n
- آیا در اعماق اقیانوس‌ها که بیش از ده کیلومتر عمق دارند و تاریکی مطلق حاکمه موجود زنده‌ای هست؟ — Are there any living creatures in the depths of the oceans, which are over ten kilometers deep and plunged in absolute darkness?
78 | 382

2884 یادگیری jadgiri *learning* n
- نخوردن صبحانه قدرت یادگیری را کاهش می‌دهد. — Skipping breakfast reduces learning ability.
63 | 716

2885 محرم mæhræm, mohærræm *close relative/confidant, Moharram* adj,n
- ماه محرم یک بار رفتم خونه. — Once I went home during the month of Moharram.
88 | 195

2886 قاهره ɣahere *Cairo* adj,pn
- برای تدریس در مدرسه دینی یهودیان به قاهره دعوت شد. — He was invited to Cairo to teach in the Jewish religious school.
72 | 506

2887 ممانعت momaneʔæt *prevention* n
- فرانسه مداخله نظامی خود را از روز جمعه گذشته و برای ممانعت از افتادن پایتخت به دست شبه نظامیان تندرو آغاز کرد. — France started its military intervention last Friday to prevent the capital from falling into the hands of extremist militants.
91 | 144.

2888 رقابتی reɣabæti *competitive* adj,n
- محیط رقابتی جهانی اطراف شما در چه شرایطی است؟ —
  What are the circumstances of the global
  competitive environment around you?
  82 | 298

2889 سوز suz *burning, pain* n
- در جمع آنها با سوز و درد این آهنگ را با خود زمزمه
  می‌کرد. — Among them, he was humming this
  song to himself, with burning and pain.
  83 | 285

2890 دشمنی doʃmæni *hostility* n
- دشمنی تو از کجاست؟ — Where does your enmity
  come from?
  84 | 271

2891 دندان dændan *tooth* n
- دندان قشنگی دارد. — She has beautiful teeth.
  73 | 479

2892 انسجام ensedʒam *cohesion* n
- فاقد تمرکز و انسجام هستند. — They lack focus and
  solidarity.
  86 | 240

2893 خلیفه xælife *caliph* n,pn
- هارون خلیفه مقتدری است که در دنیا کم پادشاهی آمده
  است که سعه ملکش به اندازه او باشد. —
  Haroun is a very powerful caliph, and
  there are few kings like him whose
  kingdom is so vast.
  65 | 651

2894 ترسیدن tærsidæn *fear* adj,n,v
- آن اوایل از خواب، سایه و تاریکی می ترسیدم، ولی حالا
  دیگر از هیچ چیز نمی ترسم. — At the beginning,
  I was scared of dreams, shadows, and
  darkness, but now I am not scared of
  anything.
  58 | 840

2895 جنسی dʒensi *sexual* adj,n
- روشن است که خشونت جنسی مشکلی جدی در سوریه
  است. — It is clear that sexual violence is a
  serious problem in Syria.
  79 | 369

2896 لوازم lævazem *equipment* n
- حقوق لباس و سلاح لوازم جنگی دریافت کردند. — They
  received salary, clothing, weapons, and
  military supplies.
  79 | 366

2897 وین vijen *Vienna* conj,pn
- نخستین روز گفتگوی مقامات ایران و آژانس بین المللی
  انرژی اتمی در وین در دو دور برگزار شد. — The first
  day of talks between Iranian officials and the
  International Atomic Energy Agency in
  Vienna was held in two rounds.
  86 | 236

2898 لوله lule *pipe, tube* n
- برای پیشگیری از یخزدگی لوله‌های آب چه باید کرد؟
  — What should one do in order to prevent
  water pipes from freezing?
  73 | 470

2899 دغدغه dæɣdæɣe *fear, anxiety* n
- دیگر دغدغه ای برایش ندارم. — I don't have any
  other concerns for him.
  79 | 362

2900 حافظه hafeze *memory* n
- نام فراموش شده را به حافظه ی من بازگرداند! — It
  returned the forgotten name to my memory.
  82 | 293

2901 تناقض tænaɣoz *contradiction* n
- علت این تناقض را در چه می‌بینید؟ — What do you
  see as being the cause of this contradiction?
  88 | 193

2902 مطلع mætlæʔ, mottæle *rising place, well-
  informed/witness* adj,n
- از این قضیه مطلع شد. — She was informed of this
  issue.
  83 | 292

2903 منتشر کردن montæʃer kærdæn *publish* v
- بر اساس اطلاعات جدیدی که سازمان سیا منتشر کرده
  آزمایش برخی هواپیماهای سری آمریکا در این مرکز انجام
  شده است. — According to new information that
  the CIA published, the testing of some secret
  American planes took place at this site.
  83 | 281

2904 مورخ moværræx, moværrex *dated, historian* n
- جلسه روز یکشنبه مورخ 1392/07/07. — A Sunday
  meeting, dated 7/7/1392.
  80 | 338

2905 مس mes, mæss *copper, touching* n
- شهربابک غنی ترین معادن مس ایران را دارا است.
  — Shahr-e Babak has the richest copper
  mines in Iran.
  75 | 433

2906 رسانه‌ای resaneʔi *media* adj,n
- چرا مردم به پیام‌های رسانه‌ای خاصی توجه می‌کنند و به
  بقیه بی توجه‌اند؟ — Why do people pay attention
  to certain media messages and disregard the
  rest?
  74 | 455

2907 تکراری tekrari *repetitious* adj
- این مباحث اکثراً تکراری بوده. — These discussions
  were mostly repeated.
  92 | 127

2908 اکتبر oktobr *October* n
- انقلاب اکتبر 1917 در روسیه. — The October 1917
  revolution in Russia.
  82 | 300

2909 مخابرات moxaberat *telecommunication* n
- شرکت مخابرات استان تهران — Telecommunication Company of Tehran.
83 | 285

2910 کاغذ kaɣæz *paper* n
- کاغذ هایش کمی زرد شده بود. — Its papers had turned a little yellow.
67 | 610

2911 عیار æjar *purity, Ayyar* n
- طلای ۱۸ عیار (۷۵۰) حاوی ۷۵ درصد طلاست. — 18 carat gold (750) contains 75 percent gold.
87 | 215

2912 کمرنگ kæmræng *pale* adj
- یک استکان چای کمرنگ برایش برد. — He took him a pale cup of tea.
92 | 122

2913 بیداری bidari *being awake* n
- البته با پیروزی انقلاب اسلامی و هوشیاری و بیداری ملت ایران که از این انقلاب ناشی شد، . . . — Certainly with the victory of the Islamic revolution and the alertness and awakeness of the Iranian nation that resulted from the revolution . . .
54 | 937

2914 انتقادی enteɣadi *critical* adj,n
- هر متفکر انتقادی‌ای نیز این گونه است. — Every critical thinker is like this.
88 | 191

2915 غرق ɣærɣ *drowning, sinking* adj,n
- آن روز کشتی دیگری غرق شد. — That day another boat sank.
82 | 307

2916 اضافی ezafi *additional* adj
- پول اضافی را به جیب می‌زد و دزد بود. — He would put the extra money into his pocket, and he was a thief.
86 | 221

2917 مساحت mæsahæt *surface area* n
- مساحت شهر در سال‌های پس از انقلاب به سرعت افزایش پیدا می‌کند. — The area of the city quickly increased in the years after the revolution.
76 | 409

2918 فروردین færværdin *Farvardin* n
- یعنی اول فروردین سال 1375 با 20 مارس مطابق بوده است. — This means the first of Farvardin 1375 corresponded with the 20th of March.
74 | 444

2919 ناشناس naʃenas *unidentified* adj,n
- از این سرباز ناشناس که حتی نامش را نمی دانست، یک قهرمان ساخت. — Of this unknown soldier, whose name he didn't even know, he made a hero.
90 | 156

2920 جواهر dʒævaher *jewel* n,pn
- موانع پیش روی تولید محصولات طلا و جواهر باید برداشته شود. — Obstacles to the production of gold and jewelry should be removed.
87 | 203

2921 صالح saleh *competent, righteous* adj,pn
- خدا گفت اگر در این شهر ۱۰ مرد صالح باشند آنها را عذاب نخواهد کرد. — God said if there are 10 righteous people in the city, He will not punish the city.
75 | 434

2922 رسالت resalæt *mission* n,pn
- یکی از مهمترین رسالت های اتاق های فکر تبیین رهنمودهای مقام معظم رهبری در عرصه های مختلف است. — One of the most important missions of think tanks is to explain the guidelines of the office of the Supreme Leader in various fields.
77 | 400

2923 ارومیه orumije *Urmia* pn
- در ارومیه این وضعیت چگونه است. — How is the situation in Urmia?
75 | 426

2924 خلع xælʔ *deposing* n
- همین الان بهترین فرصت است که او را خلع سلاح کنم. — Right now is the best opportunity for me to disarm him.
87 | 208

2925 نوآوری nowaværi *innovation* n
- در این فضایی که تشریح کردید، خودروسازان چینی چگونه دست به نوآوری می‌زنند؟ — In this atmosphere that you've described, how are Chinese automakers demonstrating innovation?
82 | 297

2926 انگار engar *as if* adv,conj
- انگار داشت با خودش حرف می زد: یا بودند . . . و ما می شناسیمشان . . . یا می شناختیمشان . . . بعضی ها را خیلی خوب . . . — He seemed to be talking to himself: "Or they were . . . and we know them . . . or we knew them . . . some of them quite well . . . "
54 | 906

2927 واضح vazeh *clear* adj
- من صدایتان را واضح شنیدم. — I heard your voice clearly.
81 | 319

2928 پکن pekæn *Beijing* pn
- اگر از پکن سه ساعت به سمت سواحل شرقی این کشور بروید، به شهر تیانجین می‌رسید. — If you go three hours from Beijing in the direction of the eastern coast of this country you will arrive at the city of Tianjin.
75 | 418

2929 گلی geli, goli *muddy, red* adj,n,pn
- خانه های گلی شمالی نمونه های بی مانند تاریخی هستند. — Mud houses in the north are unique historical examples.
87 | 206

2930 تعالی tæʔali, tæʔala *elevation, exalted* adj,n
- خداوند تبارک و تعالی. — God blessed and most high.
80 | 339

2931 پیکار pejkar *battle* n
- پیکار ما فقط برای دفاع از انسانیت است. — Our battle is only for the defense of humanity.
80 | 334

2932 موسوی musævi *Mousavi* pn
- تقریباً تمام دوران نخست وزیری میرحسین موسوی همزمان با جنگ ایران و عراق بود. — The premiership of Mir Hossein Mousavi was simultaneous with the Iran-Iraq war.
75 | 435

2933 بازرگان bazærgan *merchant* n,pn
- یک بازرگان آمریکایی ساکن کالیفرنیا گفته بود. — An American businessman living in California, said . . .
85 | 238

2934 صحت sehhæt *health, correctness* n
- چه اندازه صحت دارد؟ — How true is it?
81 | 310

2935 طبقاتی tæbæɣati *class* adj
- کمونیسم کارگری از این مبارزه طبقاتی سر بر میکند. — Worker-Communism emerges out of this class struggle.
87 | 199

2936 باقیمانده baɣimande *remainder* adj,n
- حل برخی مسائل باقیمانده در مذاکرات دشوار است. — It is difficult to solve some remaining issues in negotiations.
82 | 294

2937 ساختاری saxtari *structural* adj,n
- تغییرات ساختاری مهم در انتظار اقتصاد ایران است. — Important structural changes are expected in Iran's economy.
82 | 302

2938 سلیقه sæliɣe *taste* n
- البته این را می تواند فقط سلیقه شرقی باشد. — Of course this might only be an eastern taste.
85 | 244

2939 قطع شدن ɣætʔ ʃodæn *be cut off, terminated* v
- تیراندازی قطع شد. — Shooting stopped.
85 | 242

2940 مشغول بودن mæʃɣul budæn *be busy* v
- در باغهای اطراف شیراز به شکار مشغول بود. — He was busy hunting in the gardens around Shiraz.
87 | 213

2941 تخفیف tæxfif *discount* n
- در برخی از هتلها تا ۷۰ درصد تخفیف را شاهد هستیم. — We are seeing up to 70% discounts in some of the hotels.
88 | 191

2942 ائتلاف eʔtelaf *coalition* n
- اتحاد برای احیای دمکراسی که از ائتلاف احزاب سیاسی مخالف دولت پاکستان تشکیل شده است. — The alliance for the restoration of democracy was formed by a coalition of political parties opposed to Pakistan's government.
71 | 503

2943 مفاد mofad *substance* n
- مفاد ماده 2 قانون تجارت. — The contents of Article 2 of the trade law.
85 | 234

2944 اعزامی eʔzami *dispatched* adj
- نیروهای اعزامی حزب وحدت در آغاز موفق شدند. — In the beginning the deployed forces of the Unity Party were successful.
83 | 267

2945 شایعه ʃajeʔe *rumor* n
- شایعه افزایش نرخ بهره در آمریکا. — Rumor of rising interest rate in America.
77 | 392

2946 کاشان kaʃan *Kashan* pn
- کاسی ها در نیمه هزاره نخست پیش از میلاد در بخشهای گوناگون ایران امروزی پیشروی کردند و تا نزدیک کویر میانی و اصفهان و کاشان و مرز تهران امروزی پیش رفتند. — In the middle of the first millennium BC, the Kassites advanced into various parts of modern Iran, and nearly reached the central desert, and Esfahan, Kashan, and the borders of modern Tehran.
80 | 337

2947 انبوه æmbuh *crowded, thick* adj,n
- به آشپزخانه که رفتم، انبوه ظرفهای نشسته به من لبخند زدند. — When I went to the kitchen, a heap of sedentary dishes were smiling at me.
81 | 304

2948 گرفتاری gereftari *captivity, trouble, involvement* n
- ایران بیش از هر کشور دیگری با گرفتاریهای ناشی از مصرف تریاک غیرقانونی روبروست. — Iran, more than any other country, is faced with the problems caused by illegal drug use.
89 | 168

2949 فاتح fateh *victorious* adj,n,pn
- در دو هزار سال گذشته هیچ فاتح و کشور گشایی و یا نیروی مهاجم خارجی نتوانسته به زبان و فرهنگ ایرانی اثرات بنیادی بگذارد. — In the last two thousand years no victor, conqueror, or foreign invading force has been able to have a fundamental effect on Iranian culture or language.
89 | 171

2950 مارس mɑrs *March* n,pn

- ارتش مونته نگرو از ماه مارس سال 2010 میلادی در افغانستان حضور فعال دارد. — The army of Montenegro has had an active presence in the ISAF mission in Afghanistan since March 2010.

83 | 279

2951 اینترنتی interneti *internet* adj

- چین چند پایگاه اینترنتی دارد؟ — How many internet sites does China have?

70 | 525

2952 بیروت bejrut *Beirut* pn

- به همراه خانواده‌اش در محله‌ای مسیحی‌نشین در بیروت بسر می‌برد. — He lives with his family in a Christian neighborhood in Beirut.

77 | 381

2953 پله pelle *step* n

- بر پله‌ی جلو دکان نشسته بود. — She had sat down on the step in front of the store.

74 | 451

2954 گناه gonɑh *sin* n

- با علی که بودم احساس گناه می کردم. — I felt guilty for being with Ali.

73 | 454

2955 منتقل کردن montæɣel kærdæn *transfer, transmit* v

- چطور عطسه و سرفه بیماری را منتقل می‌کنند؟ — How do sneezing and coughing transmit disease?

88 | 196

2956 رحمت ræhmæt *compassion* n,pn

- خدا رحمتش کند. — May God have mercy on him.

71 | 513

2957 حجت hodʒdʒæt *reasoning, proof* n,pn

- امامان شیعه را حجت‌های خدا بر اهل دنیا و آخرت، معرفی کرده‌است. — He has introduced Shiite imams as proofs of God upon the people of the world and the hereafter.

76 | 412

2958 عارف ɑref *Sufi, conoisseur* adj,n,pn

- مرد تشنه، رمز عارف است که از بالای درخت آگاهی به جهان نگاه می‌کند. — The thirsty man symbolizes the mystic who looks at the world from the top of the tree of awareness.

84 | 259

2959 رغم ræɣm *spite* n

- دو تیم به رغم 90 دقیقه تلاش نتوانستند به دروازه راه یابند. — The two teams despite 90 minutes' effort could not make any goal.

75 | 427

2960 کاشی kɑʃi *Kashani, tile* n,pn

- با قالیچه های کردی و کاشی فرشش کرده بود. — He had covered it with tiles and Kurdish rugs.

86 | 225

2961 شورش ʃureʃ *rebellion* n,pn

- آروم نمی‌شینم. شورش می‌کنم. — I will not sit quietly. I will revolt.

82 | 297

2962 تقلید tæɣlid *imitation* adj,n

- تقلید او را می کند. — She imitates him.

82 | 285

2963 مالک mɑlek *owner* n,pn

- ژیلر مالک و مدیر یک شرکت بزرگ تولید لباس‌های کشباف در فرانسه بود. — Gillier was the owner and director of a large knitwear manufacturing company in France.

80 | 329

2964 چهارصد tʃæhɑrsæd *four hundred* n

- فردا صبح مجبور خواهد بود چهارصد پانصدتومانی به برف‌پاروکن‌ها بدهد. — Tomorrow morning she'll have to give four or five hundred toman to the snow shovelers.

52 | 970

2965 پرتاب pærtɑb *throw* n

- در هر پرتاب باید به زاویه توپ توجه داشت. — One must pay attention to the angle of the ball in every throw.

76 | 402

2966 سادگی sadegi *simplicity* n

- هرگز به عمر خود کسی را ندیده بودم که زبان فارسی را به این سادگی و روانی حرف بزند. — Never in my entire life had I seen someone who spoke Persian with such simplicity and facility.

83 | 271

2967 استمرار estemrɑr *continuity* n

- مردم برای استمرار موفقیت‌های نیروی انتظامی باید با آنان همکاری مناسبی داشته باشند. — For the continuance of the military's successes, the people must collaborate with it as appropriate.

84 | 263

2968 سیمان simɑn *cement* n

- بخش سیمان ما حدودا سه هزار و پانصد تن در روز تولید داریم. — In our cement department we have production of about three thousand five hundred tons per day.

70 | 523

2969 انحصار enhesɑr *monopoly* n

- صدور محصول ابریشم ایران و فروش آن در کشورهای اروپا در انحصار شاه قرار داشت. — Exporting Iran's silk products and selling them in European countries was part of the Shah's monopoly.

85 | 238

2970 همتا hæmtɑ *peer* n

- قیمت فروش خودرو فیات پنج برابر همتای هندی خود است. — The selling price of a Fiat automobile is five times that of its Indian counterpart.

78 | 361

2971 فلسفی fælsæfi *philosophical* adj
- این یک سؤال اقتصادی یا سیاسی نیست بلکه یک سؤال فلسفی است. — This is not an economic or political question, but rather a philosophical question.
- 76 | 403

2972 زبانی zæbani *verbal, lingual* adj,n
- نقش ادبیات موبایلی بر تحولات زبانی چقدر است؟ — How much of a role does cellphone literature play in language evolution?
- 79 | 345

2973 شکار ʃekar *hunting* n
- برای شکار بیرون رفتند. — They went outside to hunt.
- 79 | 339

2974 محوطه mohævvæte *enclosure, campus* n
- در محوطه دانشگاه دست به راهپیمایی زدهاند. — They marched on the university campus.
- 78 | 362

2975 گرامی gerami *esteemed* adj
- یادش گرامی باد و روحش شاد! — May his memory be honored and his spirit happy!
- 76 | 395

2976 مصاف mæsaf *battle* n
- کامران جمشیدوند و احمد سعیدی به مصاف حریف آمریکایی آمد. — Kamran Jamshidvand and Ahmad Saidi went against their American rival.
- 67 | 581

2977 سرانه særane *per capita* adj,n
- قطر دارای بیشترین درآمد سرانه در جهان شد. — Qatar has the highest per capita income in the world.
- 81 | 313

2978 داغ daɣ *hot* adj,n
- چای داغ و شیرین برایم بیاور. — Bring me hot sweet tea.
- 76 | 398

2979 کارکرد karkærd *performance, mileage* n
- در مکزیک و برزیل نیز همین شعار کارکرد داشته است. — Also, in Mexico and Brazil this slogan was effective.
- 78 | 367

2980 توازن tævazon *balance* n
- توازن معقولی بین سیاست های پولی و تولیدی این شرکت برقرار کند. — He should establish a reasonable balance between this company's monetary and production policies.
- 88 | 178

2981 کهنه kohne *old* adj
- در کتابخانههای عمومی نسخهای کهنه و پاره از آن دیوان را یافتم. — In a public library, I found an old tattered copy of that collection of poems.
- 79 | 336

2982 دانشآموز daneʃamuz *student* n
- دانشآموز فوقالعادهای است. — She is an extraordinary student.
- 62 | 699

2983 سیگار sigar *cigarette* n
- فقط سیگار خودم را روشن کردم. — I only lit my own cigarette.
- 69 | 539

2984 گریز goriz *escaping* n
- دیدم هیچ راه گریز و فراری نیست. — I saw that there was no escape route.
- 87 | 206

2985 ناگزیر nagozir *inevitable* adj,adv
- ناگزیر شد سه سال پیش از پایان دوره زمامداریش استعفا کند. — It became inevitable that he resign three years prior to the end of his term of rulership.
- 87 | 200

2986 نگارش negareʃ *authorship, writing* n
- لازم است در ارزش یابی نگارش و انشا به موارد زیر توجه شود. — It is necessary to pay attention to the subjects below in the evaluation of writing and composition.
- 82 | 289

2987 نادر nader *rare, Nader* adj,pn
- شعر «از این مرتع آهوانه بگریز . . . » از نادر ابراهیمی است. — The poem "Flee from this Deer Pasture" is by Nader Ebrahimi.
- 76 | 401

2988 سلیمان solejman *Soleiman, Solomon* pn
- سرانجام بلقیس به حقانیت حضرت سلیمان پی برد. — The Queen of Sheba finally realized the legitimacy of Solomon.
- 85 | 236

2989 بعداً bæʔdæn *later, then* adv,conj
- درباره تغییرات بعداً صحبت میکنم. — I will talk about changes later.
- 69 | 536

2990 آهنگ ahæng *tune* n
- هرگز نشنیده بودم آهنگ موتزارت را کودکی به این سن به این زیبایی بنوازد. — Never had I heard a child of this age play Mozart's music this beautifully.
- 72 | 474

2991 استخوان ostoxan *bone* n
- استخوان هایم از درد دارند می ترکند. — My bones are exploding from pain.
- 78 | 349

2992 صادرکننده saderkonænde *exporter* adj,n
- چین اولین صادرکننده بزرگ دنیا هست. — China is the largest exporter in the world.
- 77 | 376

2993 دستیار dæstjɑr *assistant* n
- Ahmad — قرار است احمد سنجری دستیار وی شود. Sanjari is supposed to be his assistant.
- 90 | 150

2994 لذت lezzæt *pleasure* n
- از شنیدن آواز در هم و بر هم پرندگان لذت فراوان می بردم. — I greatly enjoyed listening to the tangled song of the birds.
- 70 | 516

2995 باز شدن bɑz ʃodæn *open* v
- مدرسه ها دوباره باز شد. — The schools were reopened.
- 73 | 446

2996 واداشتن vadɑʃtæn *persuade, force* adj,n,v
- Forcing — واداشتن این ارتش به خروج از افغانستان. this army to leave Afghanistan.
- 91 | 135

2997 ممتاز momtɑz *super, top* adj
- در چنین شرایطی بود که شخصیتی ممتاز در نظام مدیریتی کشور توجه همگان را برانگیخت. — It was in such conditions that an outstanding personality in the country's administrative structure caught the attention of the public.
- 83 | 261

2998 پرتو pærtow *ray* n
- در پرتو مهتاب نگاهت بنشینم. — Let me sit in the ray of moonlight of your gaze.
- 80 | 319

2999 ارزان ærzɑn *cheap* adj,adv
- سیگار ارزان میکشید. — You smoke cheap cigarettes.
- 72 | 466

3000 سایپا sɑjpɑ *Saipa* n,pn
- وقتی کارگران ایران خودرو و سایپا پس از پایان کار از کارخانه خارج می شوند. — When the workers of Iran Khodro and Saipa leave the factory at the end of the work day.
- 73 | 442

3001 ظریف zærif *delicate* adj,pn
- لزوم اعمال کنترل ظریف تر بالا می رود. — The necessity of implementing more delicate control is increasing.
- 87 | 203

3002 غبار ɣobɑr *dust, haze* n
- زمین قبرستان پلید و غبار آلودی است. — The cemetery ground is unclean and dusty.
- 87 | 195

3003 آبادانی ɑbɑdɑni *development* n
- به عمران و آبادانی علاقه بسیار داشت. — He was very fond of construction and development.
- 91 | 133

3004 سرکوب særkub *suppression* n
- وقتی مرد میل به راضی کردن همسرش را از دست بدهد، احساسات محبت آمیز او خود به خود سرکوب می شود. — When a man loses his desire to satisfy his wife, his loving feelings will be suppressed by themselves.
- 60 | 730

3005 مدیترانه mediterane *Mediterranean* pn
- ناوگان ششم آمریکا هنوز هم در شرق مدیترانه مستقر میباشد. — The American sixth fleet is still based in the East Mediterranean.
- 89 | 173

3006 حدیث hædis *hadith* n
- غیر از این حدیث، احادیث دیگری میتواند دلیل این قاعده باشد. — Aside from this hadith, other hadiths may be the reason for this rule.
- 77 | 365

3007 بیم bim *fear* n
- مادر بیم زده او را نگاه کرد و در آشپزخانه را بست. — The mother, stricken with fear, looked at him, and shut the kitchen door.
- 86 | 219

3008 بهینه behine *optimum* adj
- در ایام خشکسالی مسئولین امور آب ، شعارهایی برای مصرف بهینه و صرفه جویی بکار می برند. — In times of drought the water authorities make use of slogans for optimal consumption and frugality.
- 80 | 314

3009 اردوگاه ordugɑh *camp* n
- این اردوگاه ها همگی در لهستان بودند. — These camps were all in Poland.
- 81 | 302

3010 شرکتکننده ʃerkætkonænde *participant* adj,n
- در جشنواره امسال به عنوان شرکتکننده حضور ندارم. — In this year's festival, I am not attending as a participant.
- 73 | 438

3011 سلطان soltɑn *sultan, king* n,pn
- بنیانگذار این دودمان سلطان محمود غزنوی بود. — The founder of this dynasty was Sultan Mahmoud Ghaznavi.
- 69 | 529

3012 هواپیمایی hævɑpejmɑji *aviation, airline* adj,n
- شرکت هواپیمایی امارات برترین شرکت هواپیمایی جهان در سال ۲۰۱۶ است. — Emirates airline is the best airline in the world in 2016.
- 82 | 281

3013 فوقالعاده fowɣolʔɑde *extraordinary* adj,adv
- فلامنکو یکی از غنیترین و فوقالعادهترین فرمهای موسیقی در جهان است. — Flamenco is one of the richest and most extraordinary forms of music in the world.
- 77 | 370

3014 خالص xɑles *pure* adj
- یخ را در لیوان پایه بلند کریستال، توی ویسکی خالص با سر انگشت می‌چرخاند. — With the tip of her finger, she swirled the ice in the long-stemmed glass around in the pure whisky.
- 86 | 210

3015 بینش bineʃ *insight* n
- جسورانه‌ترین ایده ممکن است بهترین بینش باشد. — It's possible the most daring idea is the best insight.
- 84 | 244

3016 ناتوان natævɑn *unable* adj
- هدف روزولت بهبودی وضع اقتصادی و اجتماعی ناتوان‌ترین و فقیرترین قشرها جامعه بود. — Roosevelt's goal was the economic and social improvements of the most incapable and the poorest parts of society.
- 90 | 156

3017 درواقع dærvɑɣeʔ *indeed* adv,conj
- ما درواقع در پی تحولاتی که . . . — In fact we are seeking changes that . . .
- 83 | 257

3018 بین الملل bejnolmelæl *international* adj
- یکی از اساتید روابط بین‌الملل می‌گوید — A professor of international relations says . . .
- 63 | 650

3019 اوپک opek *OPEC* pn
- برای شرکت در اجلاس سران اوپک اظهار امیدواری کرد. — He stated his hope to participate in the OPEC leaders' summit.
- 69 | 514

3020 ناچار nɑtʃɑr *compelled* adj,adv,n,v
- میرزا ناچار رفت. — Mirza was compelled to leave.
- 76 | 391

3021 روزافزون ruzæfzun *ever-increasing* adj
- او به مراجعه‌ روزافزون زنان به این مرکز اشاره کرده و فضای فعلی را ناکافی می‌داند. — He mentioned the ever increasing referral of women to this center and considers the current space insufficient.
- 84 | 242

3022 مریم mærjæm *Maryam* pn
- در کلیسای مریم مقدس در خیابان جمهوری. — In St. Mary's Church on Jomhuri Street.
- 69 | 518

3023 رواج rævɑdʒ *currency, circulation* n
- توجه به غزل سرایی در این دوره رواج یافت. — Regard for the composition of lyric poetry became prevalent in this period.
- 84 | 245

3024 ایلام ilɑm *Ilam* pn
- فرمانده سپاه پاسداران انقلاب اسلامی منطقه ایلام — The commander of the IRGC in the Ilam region.
- 79 | 323

3025 سرمربی særmoræbbi *head coach* n
- سرمربی تیم ملی شطرنج ایران معرفی شد. — The coach of Iran's national chess team was introduced.
- 72 | 458

3026 هرکس hærkæs *anyone, everyone* pron
- هرکس غرق در اندیشه بود. — Everybody was deep in thought.
- 84 | 243

3027 القاعده ælɣɑede *Al Qaeda* pn
- ما همانطور که با القاعده و طالبان مذاکره نکردیم با تروریستها نیز مذاکره نخواهیم کرد. — Just as we didn't negotiate with Al Qaeda and the Taliban, we also won't negotiate with terrorists.
- 69 | 514

3028 هزاره hezɑre *millennium, Hazara* n
- هزاره‌ها در زمان دوران صفوی و به اجبار به دستور شاه عباس به مذهب شیعه پیوستند. — Forced by the decree of Shah Abbas, Hazaras joined the Shia sect during the Safavid Period.
- 61 | 684

3029 ناو nɑv *naval vessel, drain* n
- ناوهای ایرانی خلیج عدن را ترک نمی‌کنند. — Iranian ships do not leave the Gulf of Aden.
- 80 | 317

3030 ناخالص nɑxɑles *impure, gross* adj
- توسعه را می توان برحسب افزایش تولید ناخالص ملی یا تولید ناخالص داخلی یا سطح استفاده از فن آوری وصنعتی شدن اندازه گرفت. — Development can be measured according to the increase of the gross national product or gross domestic product or the level of use of technology and industrialization.
- 80 | 318

3031 رؤیا roʔjɑ *dream* n,pn
- رؤیاهایتان را دنبال کنید! — Follow your dreams!
- 68 | 542

3032 خشکسالی xoʃksɑli *drought* n
- ۱۰ درصد ایران درگیر خشکسالی شدید است. — Severe drought is affecting 10 percent of Iran.
- 80 | 312

3033 خاصیت xɑsijjæt *property* n
- این کار چند خاصیت دارد. — This work has several properties.
- 81 | 302

3034 مسلحانه mosællæhɑne *armed* adj
- حرکات مسلحانه برای تأسیس دولتی در این منطقه بسیار واقع شده ولی هیچ یک پیروز نگشت. — A lot of armed movements to establish a government in this region have arisen, however none of them has been victorious.
- 85 | 227

3035 خیال xijɑl *imagination* n
- خیال دارد دیوانه ام. — She thinks I am crazy.
- 65 | 594

3036 فردوسی ferdowsi *Ferdowsi* pn
- بدخشان یکی از قدیمی‌ترین مناطقی است که در شاهنامه
  فردوسی از آن یاد شده است. — Badakhshan is one
  of the oldest regions that is mentioned in
  Ferdowsi's Shahname.
  79 | 327

3037 قند ɣænd *lump sugar* n
- سالمندان هنگام روزه گرفتن باید مراقب کاهش میزان آب
  بدن و کاهش قند خون باشند. — When fasting,
  older people should be wary of the
  decrease in the level of water and blood
  sugar in the body.
  75 | 404

3038 محافظت mohɑfezæt *protection* n
- از من محافظت کنید. — You should protect me.
  88 | 180

3039 کوبیدن kubidæn *pound, grind* n,v
- پا کوبیدند. — They stomped their feet.
  76 | 378

3040 فاطمه fɑteme *Fateme* pn
- بدین ترتیب فاطمه امروز از زندان آزاد خواهد شد. — Thus
  Fateme will be released from prison today.
  76 | 375

3041 تسلیت tæslijæt *condolences* n
- پیام تسلیت و همدردی شما عزیزان را خواندم. — I read
  the message of condolence and sympathy by
  you, loved ones.
  90 | 148

3042 بلوچستان bælutʃestɑn *Baluchestan* pn
- سرزمینی که اکنون بلوچستان نام دارد به اسم «مکا» مشهور
  بوده. — The land that is currently known as
  Balochistan has been known as Maka.
  81 | 302

3043 محرومیت mæhrumijjæt *deprivation, ban* n
- علت محرومیت روسیه از المپیک ریوچیست؟ — What is
  the reason for the exclusion of Russia from
  Rio Olympics?
  85 | 229

3044 نامگذاری nɑmgozɑri *giving a name* n
- ممنوعیت نامگذاری روسی در تاجیکستان اعلام شد.
  — The ban on giving Russian names was
  announced in Tajikistan.
  85 | 225

3045 پیشبرد piʃbord *progress* n
- در پیشبرد نهضت اسلامی نقشی به سزا ایفا کرد. — He
  had a significant role in promoting the
  Islamic movement.
  82 | 270

3046 اصغر æsɣær *Asghar* pn
- اصغر بیچاره، یادگار سینما و عکاسی ایران است.
  — Asghar Bichareh is a monument of Iran's
  cinema and photography.
  86 | 215

3047 کرزی kærzæj *Karzai* pn
- حامد کرزی. — Hamid Karzai.
  46 | 1066

3048 دولتمرد dowlætmærd *statesman, official* n
- بزرگ‌ترین وظیفه امروز دولتمردان تولید شغل است.
  — Today the greatest duty of authorities is
  job creation.
  81 | 296

3049 قلمداد ɣælæmdɑd *considered* adj,n
- در جلسات رسمی شهرستانی و استانی سرمایه گذاران را
  قلمداد می کنند. — At offical municipal
  and provincial assemblies, the investors are
  considered political entities.
  85 | 230

3050 پروانه pærvɑne *butterfly* n,pn
- به پروانه نگاه می کند. — She looks at the butterfly.
  74 | 413

3051 قدری ɣædri *a little, slight* adv,n,q
- وی قدری از اراضی آن را خریده بود. — He had
  bought some of those lands.
  80 | 313

3052 پیوست pejvæst *attachment, attached* n,v
- می‌توانید پیوست‌های شمارهٔ ۱ و ۲ کتاب را مطالعه کنید.
  — You can study Appendices 1 and 2 of
  the book.
  80 | 315

3053 نصیب næsib *share, lot, award* n
- مدال نقره کامپوند جهانی زنان نصیب ایران شد. — Iran
  was awarded the silver medal for
  International Women's Compound.
  85 | 229

3054 فی fi, fej *in/at/phi, Faye* pn
- مذاکره ایران و اروپا تنها راه‌حل رفع سوءتفاهمات فی مابین
  است. — Negotiation between Iran and Europe
  is the only solution to resolve mutual
  misunderstandings.
  79 | 328

3055 کرج kærædʒ *Karaj* pn
- کرج هم‌اکنون به‌عنوان یکی از کلان‌شهرهای کشور ایران
  به‌شمار می‌آید. — Karaj is now considered one of
  Iran's metropolises.
  74 | 417

3056 استدلال estedlɑl *reasoning* adj,n
- این استدلال از نظر علمی منطقی نیست. — From a
  scientific point of view this argument is not
  logical.
  79 | 334

3057 مکانی mækɑni *local* adj,n
- شهر همدان به علت موقعیت مکانی و جغرافیایی خود همیشه
  میزبان اقوام مختلف بوده‌است. — The city of
  Hamedan has always been the host of
  various ethnic groups due to its geographical
  location.
  83 | 255

19 Professions

Rank	Headword	Pronunciation	Gloss	Rank	Headword	Pronunciation	Gloss
133	وزیر	væzir	minister	2070	سیاستمدار	sijasætmædar	politician
368	فرهنگی	færhæŋgi	cultural, educational	2084	کشاورز	keʃaværz	farmer
420	حاکم	hakem	ruler	2124	دبیرکل	dæbirekol	secretary general
486	نظامی	nezami	military	2227	رئیس‌جمهور	ræʔisdʒomhur	president
503	معاون	moʔaven	assistant	2239	خواننده	xanænde	singer
521	دانشجو	daneʃdʒu	student	2281	سرپرست	særpæræst	supervisor
629	خبرنگار	xæbærnegar	reporter	2291	مدیر عامل	modire amel	managing director
798	محقق	mohæɣɣeɣ	scholar	2319	شاگرد	ʃagerd	student
830	بازیکن	bazikon	player	2398	افسر	æfsær	officer
852	نویسنده	nevisænde	writer	2428	ژنرال	ʒeneral	general
911	فرمانده	færmande	commander	2466	ناشر	naʃer	publisher
947	دانشمند	daneʃmænd	scientist	2487	استخدام	estexdam	employment
971	شاعر	ʃaʔer	poet	2508	بیکار	bikar	unemployed
976	همکار	hæmkar	colleague	2662	شهردار	ʃæhrdar	mayor
978	متخصص	motexæsses	expert, specialist	2671	کارگردان	kargærdan	director
1015	کارگر	kargær	worker	2762	استاندار	ostandar	governor-general
1046	سخنگو	soxæŋgu	spokesperson				
1129	پزشک	pezeʃk	doctor	2767	راهنما	rahnæma	guide
1145	قاضی	ɣazi	judge	2881	بازرس	bazres	inspector
1164	اشتغال	eʃteɣal	occupation	2904	مورخ	moværrex	historian
1215	هنرمند	honærmænd	artist	2933	بازرگان	bazærgan	merchant
1268	سرباز	særbaz	soldier	2982	دانش‌آموز	daneʃamuz	student
1269	معلم	moʔællem	teacher	2992	صادرکننده	saderkonænde	exporter
1300	وکیل	vækil	attorney	3025	سرمربی	særmoræbbi	head coach
1301	امیر	æmir	emir	3048	دولتمرد	dowlætmærd	statesman, official
1332	کارکنان	karkonan	employees	3078	تحلیلگر	tæhlilgær	analyst
1347	کارمند	karmænd	employee	3159	مدیرکل	modirekol	director general
1646	راننده	ranænde	driver				
1722	ورزشکار	værzeʃkar	athlete	3182	دستمزد	dæstmozd	wages
1793	پژوهشگر	pæʒuheʃgær	researcher	3290	بازنشسته	bazneʃæste	retired
1825	مهندس	mohændes	engineer	3365	تاجر	tadʒer	merchant
1826	نخست‌وزیر	noxostvæzir	prime minister	3390	سرهنگ	særhæŋg	colonel
1853	روحانی	rowhani	cleric	3494	حرفه	herfe	profession
1895	بازیگر	bazigær	actor	3497	نقاش	næɣɣaʃ	painter
1898	شغلی	ʃoɣli	job related	3586	فرماندار	færmandar	governor
1916	نگهبان	negæhban	guard	3595	طراح	tærrah	designer
1986	بیکاری	bikari	unemployment	3601	دیپلمات	diplomat	diplomat
1992	تولیدکننده	towlidkonænde	producer	3604	روزنامه‌نگار	ruznamenegar	journalist
2014	تدریس	tædris	teaching	3624	معمار	meʔmar	architect
2053	جانشین	dʒaneʃin	successor, substitute	3704	پروفسور	porofosor	professor

Rank	Headword	Pronunciation	Gloss	Rank	Headword	Pronunciation	Gloss
3850	سخنران	soxænran	speaker	4599	جراح	dʒærrah	surgeon
3886	قاچاقچی	qatʃaqtʃi	smuggler	5299	گزارشگر	gozareʃgær	reporter
3919	کارفرما	karfærma	employer	6042	شکارچی	ʃekartʃi	ʃekɪrʃi
3921	کارگزار	kargozar	agent	6082	آموزگار	amuzgar	teacher
3933	شاغل	ʃaɣel	employed	6442	سوداگر	sowdagær	trader, businessman
4132	فیلمساز	filmsaz	filmmaker	6709	امدادگر	emdadgær	relief worker
4195	سرتیپ	særtip	brigadier general	6769	کاوشگر	kavoʃgær	investigator
4417	خلبان	xælæban	pilot	7808	زرگر	zærgær	goldsmith
4458	صنعتگر	sænʔætgær	artisan	15011	تاریخنگار	tarixnegar	historian

3058 تعاون tæʔavon *cooperation* n
- تأسیس اتاق تعاون مشترک و برگزاری نمایشگاه های تخصصی مورد توجه قرار گرفت. — The establishment of a Chamber of Mutual Cooperation and holding specialized expositions was taken into consideration.
79 | 322

3059 گوی guj *ball* n
- گوی سبقت را از رقبای داخلی و خارجی خود برباید. — Outrun domestic and foreign competitors.
93 | 101

3060 کربلا kærbæla *Karbala* pn
- در کربلا هم زندگی می کرد. — He also used to live in Karbala.
87 | 189

3061 زرد zærd *yellow* adj,n
- سعید گفت: بقیه‌ی صورتم را رنگ زده بودم، سرخ و زرد و سبز. — Saeed said, "I had colored the rest of my face, red, and yellow, and green."
75 | 403

3062 ذره zærre *particle* n
- خودتان که دیدید ذره ای مسئولیت پذیر نیستند. — You saw it yourself, they are not responsible one bit.
73 | 435

3063 محاصره mohasere *blockade* n
- اماکن مسکونی در محاصره آب قرار گرفت. — The residential areas were surrounded by water.
77 | 358

3064 تناسب tænasob *proportion* n
- تناسب یکی از مفاهیم اصلی و پایه‌ای معماری است. — Proportion is one of the basic and core concepts in architecture.
85 | 221

3065 فجر fædʒr *dawn* n,pn
- برگزاری جشنواره فیلم فجر. — Holding of the Fajr Film Festival.
77 | 351

3066 میلان milan *Milan* pn
- دانشگاه میلان ایتالیا یکی از بهترین دانشگاههای ایتالیا می باشد. — University of Milan, Italy, is one of the best universities in Italy.
81 | 288

3067 وارداتی varedati *imported* adj
- قیمت چند خودروی وارداتی کاهش یافت. — The price of some imported cars dropped.
84 | 246

3068 نوروز nowruz *Nowruz* n,pn
- برای عید نوروز حتی یک روز هم تعطیل نداشتند. — They didn't even have one day off for the Nowruz holiday.
74 | 420

3069 اطلاعیه etelaʔijje *announcement* n
- در این اطلاعیه مبارزان فتح مقصر خوانده شدند. — In this statement Fatah fighters were announced guilty.
77 | 356

3070 بستری bestæri *admitted, confined to bed* adj,n
- مدت زمان بستری مهدی هاشمی منوط به نتیجه آزمایش‌هاست. — The duration of Mehdi Hashemi's hospitalization is subject to the test results.
86 | 208

3071 باختن baxtæn *lose* n,v
- فرانسویان جنگ را خودشان باختند. — The French lost the war.
84 | 238

3072 مسافت mæsafæt *distance* n
- مسافت مهاجرت آنها معادل هزار کیلومتر است. — Their migration distance is about a thousand kilometers.
88 | 177

3073 پیشرو piʃrow *progressive* adj,n
- حرکت تازه‌ای است که اینا نیوز پیشرو آن بوده. — It's a new movement that IBNA News has been pioneering.
- 91 | 136

3074 گیاهی gijahi *herbal, vegetable* adj,n
- آیا روغن‌های گیاهی واقعا سالم‌تر هستند؟ — Are vegetable oils really healthier?
- 80 | 311

3075 کسری kæsri, kæsra *deficit, Kasra* n,pn
- دولت متمایل به کاهش نرخ ارز اما با کسری شدید بودجه مواجه است. — The government desires a decrease in the foreign exchange rate, but is facing a severe budget deficit.
- 73 | 431

3076 جابجایی dʒabedʒaji *movement* n
- عجله‌ای برای جابجایی استانداران ندارم. — I am not in any hurry to switch the governors.
- 89 | 162

3077 تصادف tæsadof *accident* n
- معلوم شد اتومبیلی واژگون شده و جراثقالی آورده‌اند تا آن را از محل تصادف به جای دیگر حمل کنند. — It became apparent that a car had flipped over and they had brought a crane to move it from the site of the accident to another place.
- 77 | 355

3078 تحلیلگر tæhlilgær *analyst* n
- تحلیلگران نظامی معتقدند که این رکورد از سال ۱۹۹۳ تاکنون بی‌سابقه بوده است. — Military analysts believe that this record has been unprecedented from 1993 until now.
- 79 | 317

3079 تنگ tæng *narrow, tight* adj,n,pn
- اما خیابان تنگ تر از آن بود. — But the street was narrower than that.
- 72 | 440

3080 فیزیک fizik *physics* n
- رضا منصوری استاد فیزیک دانشگاه شریف. — Reza Mansouri, the professor of physics at Sharif University.
- 84 | 230

3081 دلاری dolari *dollar* adj,n
- خنجر ده میلیون دلاری قذافی در ترکیه کشف و ضبط شد. — Gaddafi's ten-million-dollar dagger was discovered and seized in Turkey.
- 73 | 418

3082 اشک æʃk *tear* n,pn
- پسر در حالی که اشک چشمانش را پر کرده پاسخ داد. — The boy answered as his eyes filled with tears.
- 71 | 458

3083 تقی tæɣi *Taghi* pn
- تقی بهرامی مدیرعامل انجمن تولیدکنندگان فولاد گفت — Taghi Bahrami, managing director of the steel manufacturers association, said . . .
- 92 | 107

3084 حفاری hæffari *excavation* n
- دستگاه حفاری را به چندصد دلار فروختند و با قطار به دیارشان برگشتند. — They sold the digging machine for several hundred dollars and took the train back to where they came from.
- 78 | 342

3085 خلیل xælil *Khalil* pn
- پیامبر اثر جبران خلیل جبران. — The Prophet by Kahlil Gibran.
- 93 | 105

3086 بقا bæɣa *survival* n
- برای بقا راه دیگری وجود دارد. — There is a another way for survival.
- 83 | 258

3087 ضربت zærbæt *blow, strike* n
- اما ماهی سیاه، همان وقت، خنجرش را کشید و به یک ضربت، دیواره ی کیسه را شکافت و در رفت. — But at the same time, the black fish drew his dagger and with one blow split the lining of the bag and ran off.
- 83 | 248

3088 اهواز æhvaz *Ahvaz* pn
- حتماً از اهواز آمده است. — He's certainly come from Ahwaz.
- 75 | 385

3089 بدیهی bædihi *evident, obvious* adj
- بدیهی است که من به دنبال درآمد بیشتری هستم. — It is evident that I am pursuing a higher salary.
- 80 | 300

3090 بازداشت شدن bazdaʃt ʃodæn *be arrested* v
- چهار تن دیگر از آنها در شهر کراچی مرکز ایالت سند پاکستان بازداشت شدند. — Four more of them were arrested in Karachi, the center of Sindh province in Pakistan.
- 76 | 371

3091 ریسک risk *risk* n
- ریسک سرمایه گذاری بین المللی در ایران کاهش یافته است. — The risk of international investment in Iran has lowered.
- 81 | 279

3092 ایسنا isna *ISNA* pn
- ایسنا در گزارشی از کاهش قیمت خودرو خبر داد. — ISNA announced the decrease of the price of automobiles in a report.
- 61 | 663

3093 ثمر sæmær *fruit, result* n

- ۹ — پنجاه سال طول می کشد تا درخت بلوطی ثمر دهد. It takes fifty years for an oak tree to bear fruit.

88 | 179

3094 مواجهه movadʒehe *confronting* n

- در مواجهه با بحران یورو؛ اروپا نه راه پس دارد، نه راه پیش. — In the face of the Euro crisis, Europe has neither a way back nor a way forward.

85 | 226

3095 راهبرد rahbord *strategy* n

- راهبرد ایران نابودی داعش و دیگر گروهک های تروریستی است. — Iran's strategy is to destroy ISIL and other terrorist groups.

81 | 286

3096 فریاد færjad *shout* n

- کسانی که حمام نرفته‌اند نمی‌دانند که فریاد در حمام چه انعکاس پرابهت و چندباره‌ای دارد. — People who haven't been to a bathhouse don't know that shouts in a bathhouse have impressive, reverberating echos.

74 | 399

3097 معترض moʔtærez *objector, protestor* adj,n

- کابل صحنه تجمع بی‌سابقه معترضان شد. — Kabul became the unprecedented rally scene of protesters.

54 | 821

3098 زباله zobale *garbage* n,pn

- لفاف کاغذی دور ساندویچ را توی سطل زباله می اندازم. — I will throw the paper wrapper around the sandwich into the waste basket.

71 | 466

3099 سعدی sæʔdi *Sa'di* pn

- من دوستدار برخی از شاعران ایرانی همچون سعدی هستم. — I'm a fan of some Iranian poets like Sa'di.

67 | 534

3100 جسم dʒesm *body* n

- از سلامت جسم و روح و روان خود برخوردار باشیم. — We have health of body, mind, and spirit.

80 | 295

3101 تحلیلی tæhlili *analytic, analytical* adj,n

- فلسفه تحلیلی چیست؟ — What is analytic philosophy?

67 | 536

3102 مکمل mokæmmel *complementary, supplementary* adj,n

- به کار بردن دارو را به عنوان روشی مکمل می‌دانند. — They consider the application of drugs as a complementary method.

85 | 220

3103 مزرعه mæzræʔe *farm* n

- سم غیرمجاز د.د.ت هنوز در برخی مزارع کشاورزی استفاده می‌شود. — The unauthorized pesticide DDT is still used in some farm fields.

84 | 228

3104 اندونزی ændonezi *Indonesia* pn

- آتشفشان «رینجانی» ده‌ها پرواز را در اندونزی لغو کرد. — The Rinjani volcano canceled dozens of flights in Indonesia.

74 | 396

3105 پایداری pajdari *endurance, resistance* adj,n

- این بنا از نظر سادگی، اندازه و پایداری، چشمگیر است. — This building is significant in terms of simplicity, size, and stability.

82 | 268

3106 معلوم شدن mæʔlum ʃodæn *become known* v

- تاریخ اکران فیلم جدید کلینت ایستوود معلوم شد. — The release date of Clint Eastwood's new film was revealed.

73 | 412

3107 امداد emdad *help* n

- کمیته امداد امام خمینی. — Imam Khomeini Relief Committee.

78 | 326

3108 بخاطر bexater *due to* prep

- این بخاطر کار و تمرین زیاد است. — This is because of practice and a lot of work.

70 | 476

3109 صبر sæbr *patience* n

- یک دقیقه صبر کن ببینم. — Wait just a minute and let me see.

72 | 445

3110 احضار ehzar *summons* n

- بعد وزیرش را احضار کرد و گفت «وزیر! ما نمی توانیم از پس این جانورهای عجیب و غریب و زبان نفهم بر بیاییم.» — Then he summoned his minister and said, "Minister! We can't overcome these outlandish and witless beasts."

85 | 220

3111 دعا doʔa *prayer* n

- همه به خاک بیفتید و دعا کنید، تا شاید او بماند. — Everyone fall to the ground and pray so that maybe he will stay.

66 | 546

3112 امتحان emtehan *test* n

- کسی در امتحان تقلب کرد. — Someone cheated on the test.

69 | 493

3113 حومه hume *outskirts* n,pn

- کالسکه در حومه ی شهر و در برابر پلکان کاخ توقف می کند. — The carriage stops in the outskirts of the city in front of the palace staircase.

85 | 216

3114 لب læb *lip* n

- با زبانت ، لب های خشکت را تر می کردی. — You were wetting your dry lips with your tongue.

57 | 749

3115 برنز boronz *bronze* adj,n
- به مدال برنز دست یافت. — He won the bronze medal.
- 75 | 387

3116 ناامنی naæmni *insecurity* n
- مرز ترکیه به دلیل ناامنی بسته شد. — The Turkish border was closed because of lack of security.
- 78 | 336

3117 طلبه tælæbe *seminary student* n
- من در این سنم تمام عمرم طلبه بودم. — At this age, I have been a student of theology all my life.
- 85 | 211

3118 متصل mottæsel *connected* adj
- اسکولرین یک آرامبخش است و در مغز به گیرنده های دوپامین متصل می شود. — Scoulerine is a 'sedative that is connected to dopamine receptors in the brain.
- 80 | 290

3119 رویه rævijje *method* n
- شاید بعضی با این رویه مخالف باشند. — Some may disagree with this approach.
- 75 | 376

3120 تهاجم tæhadʒom *aggression* n
- ۳۷ نفر در تهاجم طالبان به فرودگاه قندهار کشته شدند. — 37 people were killed in the Taliban attack on the Kandahar airport.
- 79 | 320

3121 نمره nomre *score* n
- فکر میکنید چه نمره ای خواهد داشت. — You think what would be your grade.
- 77 | 355

3122 بنا بودن bæna budæn *be supposed to* v
- بنا بود که سرمایه گذاری ما 6 / 2 درصد رشد داشته باشد. — Our investment was supposed to have 2.6 percent growth.
- 96 | 59

3123 تسریع tæsriʔ *expediting, speeding up* n
- مقادیر کم آن باعث تسریع تنفس می شود. — Small amounts of that cause accelerated breathing.
- 82 | 257

3124 اجتناب edʒtenab *avoidance* n
- از مذاکرات تهاجمی اجتناب کنید. — Avoid aggressive negotiations.
- 84 | 233

3125 کمونیست komonist *communist* adj,n
- سپس نوبت کمونیست‌ها شد. — Then it became the communists' turn.
- 83 | 241

3126 عظمت æzæmæt *majesty* n
- بعضیها اونو عظمت تمدن بشر مینامند. — Some call it the height of human civilization.
- 81 | 271

3127 قید ɣejd *restriction* n
- آخرین فتح بشر آزادی او از قید احتیاجات زندگانی خواهد بود. — The last triumph of mankind will be his release from the bond of life necessities.
- 81 | 271

3128 حزبی hezbi *party* adj,n
- مساجد نباید پایگاه دعواهای سیاسی و حزبی باشد. — Mosques should not be centers for partisan and political battles.
- 83 | 239

3129 بس bæs *enough* adj,adv
- یک بار بس است. — One time is enough.
- 68 | 511

3130 تایوان tajvan *Taiwan* pn
- ورود جهانگردان به تایوان به دنبال وقوع زلزله دو هفته گذشته در این جزیره به شدت کاهش یافته است. — The flow of tourists into Taiwan following the earthquake two weeks ago has severely declined.
- 77 | 353

3131 وفادار væfadar *faithful, loyal* adj
- این به آن معنا نیست که دریابندری به متن اصلی وفادار نیست. — This does not mean that Daryabandari is not faithful to the original text.
- 90 | 138

3132 تحمل کردن tæhæmmol kærdæn *tolerate* v
- درد و فشار زیادی را تحمل کرد. — She tolerated a lot of pain and pressure.
- 83 | 242

3133 محبوبیت mæhbubijjæt *popularity* n
- در بین افغانها محبوبیت دارد. — He is famous amongst Afghans.
- 87 | 186

3134 طی کردن tej kærdæn *journey* v
- طی کردن تمام این مراحل برایم لذت بخش است. — Going through all these processes is enjoyable for me.
- 82 | 267

3135 آرژانتین arʒantin *Argentina* pn
- آرژانتین خواستار پیوستن به ناتو شد. — Argentina requested to join NATO.
- 72 | 439

3136 شریعت ʃæriʔæt *sharia* n
- شریعت اسلامی، برای همه مسائل زندگی بشری پاسخی دارد. — Islamic Sharia has an answer for all issues of human life.
- 89 | 154

3137 دمشق dæmæʃɣ *Damascus* pn
- انفجار در مرکز دمشق هشت کشته بر جای گذاشت. — The explosion in the center of Damascus left eight people dead.
- 66 | 554

3138 خودگردان xodgærdan *autonomous* adj

- ما درخواست کشورهای عربی و خودگردان را برای اجرای آتش‌بس پذیرفتیم. — We accepted the autonomous and Arab countries' request for ceasefire.

71 | 458

3139 سروش soruʃ *angel, Soroush* n,pn

- بقیه اعضا به بحث پیرامون مطالب سروش می پرداختند. — The rest of the members would discuss the subjects mentioned by Soroush.

86 | 204

3140 محفوظ mæhfuz *protected* adj

- استفاده صلح آمیز از انرژی هسته‌ای برای جمهوری اسلامی ایران محفوظ است. — The peaceful use of nuclear energy is preserved for the Islamic Replic of Iran.

86 | 191

3141 منزله mænzele *just like* n

- به منزله یک موفقیت ملی است. — It is just like a national success.

89 | 156

3142 مجاهد modʒahed *holy warrior* adj,n,pn

- آن عالم مجاهد. — That learned warrior.

74 | 400

3143 استناد estenad *citing evidence* n

- رهبر انقلاب با استناد به این واقعیات نتیجه گرفتند. — Citing these facts the Supreme Leader came to a conclusion.

77 | 342

3144 مهمان mehman *guest* adj,n

- به مهمان ها بگویند مهمانی پادشاه افتاده به فردا. — Tell the guests that the king's party has been postponed till tomorrow.

73 | 419

3145 مخزن mæxzæn *reservoir, tank* n

- ایران دارای بزرگترین مخزن گازی جهان است. — Iran has the largest gas reserve in the world.

82 | 263

3146 تحمیل کردن tæhmil kærdæn *impose* v

- ابداع وتحمیل کردند. — They invented and imposed it.

87 | 177

3147 ترکی torki *Turkish* adj,n

- در مورد شمار سخنگویان به زبان ترکی آذربایجانی، اتفاق نظر وجود ندارد. — There is no consensus about the number of speakers of the Azeri Turkish language.

83 | 246

3148 تکامل tækamol *evolution* n

- در یک تقسیم بندی کلی می توان شهر ها را بر اساس دوران تکامل به سه دسته اصلی تقسیم کرد. — In a general classification, cities can be divided into three categories based on their periods of development.

70 | 474

3149 گرانبها gerɑnbæha *precious* adj

- در عوض چیز گرانبهای دیگری از تو می خواهم. — Instead, I want another valuable thing from you.

90 | 135

3150 شیوع ʃojuʔ *outbreak* n

- عامل شیوع بیماری‌های خطرناک. — The factor of an outbreak of dangerous diseases.

83 | 246

3151 تقابل tæɣabol *confronting* n

- بحث و جدل در مراحل اولیه مذاکره باعث ایجاد تقابل می‌شود که منجر به بن‌بست زودهنگام خواهد شد. — Disagreement and arguments in the initial stages of negotiations create opposition that will lead prematurely to a dead end.

84 | 234

3152 نابود کردن nabud kærdæn *destroy* v

- تو می خواهی نابودم کنی. — Do you want to destroy me?

92 | 108

3153 افشا efʃa *disclosure* adj,n,pn

- مبلغ این قرارداد افشا نشده است. — The amount in this contract has not been disclosed.

82 | 251

3154 آرمان ɑrman *ideal* n

- آرمان‌های انقلاب را گسترش دهد. — He should spread the ideals of the revolution.

74 | 385

3155 حکیم hækim *wise person* adj,n

- دوست کسی حکیم است که حکمت را دوست دارد. — A friend is someone who is wise and likes wisdom.

72 | 419

3156 کاربر karbær *labor intensive, user* n

- نیازی نیست که کاربر هر برنامه را به طور جداگانه آپدیت کند. — It is not necessary for the user to update every program separately.

76 | 353

3157 یکپارچه jekparʧe *whole, entirely* adj,adv

- ایران و افغانستان دارای یک ملت یکپارچه و واحد هستند. — Iran and Afghanistan form a united and integrated nation.

87 | 177

3158 فتنه fetne *sedition* n

- اجماع کلی مردم و نمایندگان بر محکومیت فتنه و فتنه‌گران است. — There is a general consensus among the people and representatives on the condemnation of sedition and the seditionists.

87 | 187

3159 مدیرکل modirekol *director general* n

- مدیرکل آژانس بین المللی انرژی اتمی. — Director General of the International Atomic Energy Agency.

67 | 527

3160 اینجابودن indʒabudæn *be here* v
- از اینجاست که مسیر نمایش عوض می‌شود. — It is here that the course of play changes.
- 81 | 267

3161 قیمتی qejmæti *costly, expensive* adj,n
- لاجورد نوعی سنگ قیمتی آبی‌رنگ است. — Lapis lazuli is a type of blue precious stone.
- 85 | 212

3162 انگشت æŋgoʃt *finger* n
- انگشت بر بینی گذاشته بود. — She had put her finger on her nose.
- 63 | 591

3163 منصوب mænsub *appointed* adj
- به مدیریت شرکت منصوب شد. — She was appointed to the company's management.
- 80 | 284

3164 بال bal *wing* n,pn
- بال‌های پرندهای باستانی در میانمار کشف شدند. — The wings of ancient birds were discovered in Myanmar.
- 74 | 388

3165 وحشتناک væhʃætnak *terrible* adj
- رستم پس از مدتی، به سرزمینی تاریک و وحشتناک رسید. — After some time, Rostam arrived in a dark and dreadful land.
- 88 | 169

3166 غزه ɣæze *Gaza* pn
- حضرت یوسف در جنگ غزه به ما کمک کرد. — The Prophet Joseph helped us in the Gaza war.
- 58 | 705

3167 شلیک ʃellik *firing* n
- هیتلر نیز برای خودکشی هم از سم و هم از شلیک گلوله استفاده کرد. — Hitler used both poison and a gunshot to commit suicide.
- 82 | 251

3168 ازبکستان ozbækestan *Uzbekistan* pn
- رئیس جمهوری پاکستان برای دیدار با اسلام کریم اف رئیس جمهوری ازبکستان دیروز وارد تاشکند شد. — Yesterday the president of Pakistan arrived in Tashkent for a visit with Islam Karimov, president of Uzbekistan.
- 79 | 308

3169 وحشی væhʃi *wild* adj,pn
- گل‌های وحشی که در مناطق بکر و دست نخورده بیشتر یافت می‌شوند. — Wild flowers which are found more in virgin, untouched areas.
- 86 | 193

3170 حماس hæmas *Hamas* pn
- رئیس دفتر سیاسی حماس در پایتخت اردن. — The head of Hamas's political office in the capital of Jordan.
- 67 | 513

3171 تابستانی tabestani *summer* adj
- این سنت از زمان المپیک تابستانی ۱۹۷۶ شروع شد. — This tradition began with the 1976 Summer Olympics.
- 85 | 212

3172 خنثی xonsa *neutral, neuter* adj
- موفق به خنثی کردن این بمبها شدند. — They were successful at neutralizing these bombs.
- 89 | 150

3173 آیت ajæt *miracle* n
- اگر این دو عدد را در هم ضرب کنیم عدد 3367 بدست می آمد که معجز آیت است. — If we multiply these two numbers together we get 3367, which is a miraculous omen . . .
- 71 | 440

3174 تشخیص دادن tæʃxis dadæn *distinguish, diagnose* v
- چگونه می‌توان اوتیسم را در کودک تشخیص داد؟ — How can one diagnose autism in a child?
- 80 | 285

3175 دسامبر desambr *December* n
- به دلیل اختلالات روانی در دسامبر سال 2012 در یک کلینیک روانی تحت درمان بوده است. — Due to psychological disorders, he received treatment in a mental health clinic in December 2012.
- 83 | 244

3176 روشنفکر rowʃænfekr *intellectual* adj,n
- حوزه دوم، روشنفکران دینی داخلی بود. — The second sphere was domestic religious intellectuals.
- 78 | 317

3177 جسمانی dʒesmani *corporeal, physical* adj
- امروز بعد از وخیم شدن اوضاع جسمانی‌اش، جان داد. — He died today, after his physical condition became critical.
- 82 | 250

3178 آرامی arami *tranquility, Aramaic* adj,n,pn
- زبان آرامی عضوی از زبان‌های سامی است. — The Aramaic language is a member of the Semitic languages.
- 82 | 246

3179 دایمی dajemi *permanent* adj
- توافق با ایران دایمی است. — The Iran deal is permanent.
- 77 | 332

3180 پناهنده pænahænde *refugee* adj,n
- منظورت اینه که پناهنده شیم؟ — You mean we should become refugees?
- 87 | 177

3181 سنگی sæŋgi *rocky* adj,n
- مجسمه‌های سنگی و برنزی بیشماری نیز از قهرمانان خود در میدان‌ها و معابر عمومی می‌گذاشتند. — They would also place countless bronze and stone statues of their heroes in the public paths and squares.
- 75 | 370

3182 دستمزد dæstmozd *wages* n
- افزایش شتابان نرخ اجاره مسکن که همواره بیشتر از افزایش دستمزد و حقوق است. — The rapid increase in the housing rental rate is always greater than the increase in wages and salaries.

81 | 265

3183 استانی ostani *provincial* adj,n
- می‌تواند سیاست‌های ملی را در مناطق استانی نیز، به اجرا بگذارد. — He can enforce national policies in provincial areas, too.

75 | 367

3184 نیک nik *good* adj,adv,n,pn
- ادبیات ایران همیشه تجلی نبرد دو سرشت نیک و بد بوده. — Iranian literature has always been the manifestation of the battle between good and evil.

82 | 257

3185 اتکا etteka *reliance* n
- اعتماد و قابلیت اتکا به دیگری. — Trust and the ability to rely on someone else.

82 | 248

3186 آزمایشگاه azmajeʃgah *laboratory* n
- تا کنون ماده تاریکی در آزمایشگاه‌ها مشاهده‌نشده است. — Until now, dark matter has not been observed in laboratories.

82 | 247

3187 ناگهان nagæhan *suddenly* adv,conj
- زن از این صدای ناگهانی، تکانی خورد. — The woman jolted from the sudden sound.

68 | 492

3188 مشروطه mæʃrute *constitutional* adj,n
- در دوره مشروطه اهمیت بیشتری یافت. — In the constitutional era it had more importance.

79 | 305

3189 غارت ɣaræt *looting* n
- انبار های حکومتی غارت شد. — The government warehouses were pillaged.

87 | 178

3190 صهیونیست sæhjunist *Zionist* adj,n
- شکایت من از بابت صهیونیست خواندن من نبود. — My complaint was not for me being called a Zionist.

55 | 764

3191 رایگان rajegan *free* adj
- پسر های خواهرِ صاحب زمین برای دایی‌شان به رایگان کار می‌کنند. — The sons of the landowner's sister work for their uncle for free.

82 | 249

3192 شگفتی ʃegefti *surprise* adj,n
- پل ایذه از شگفتی‌های قابل توجه تاریخی است. — The Izeh bridge is of the remarkable historical wonders.

86 | 191

3193 به رسمیت شناختن be ræsmijjæt ʃenaxtæn *officially recognize* v
- افغانستان را به رسمیت شناختند. — They officially recognized Afghanistan.

85 | 210

3194 زیست zist *life* n
- اینجا خانه‌ای خواهم ساخت و در آن خواهم زیست. — I will build a home here and live in it.

71 | 436

3195 مرتضی morteza *Morteza* pn
- در دور پنجم نیز مرتضی محجوب با پیروزی بر حریف خود هم چنان در صدر این رقابتها باقی ماند. — And in the fifth round, Morteza Mahjoub still remained at the top of the competition with a victory against his opponent.

76 | 350

3196 تعمیر tæʔmir *repair* n
- در حیاط داشتی بخاری را تعمیر می کردی. — You were repairing the heater in the courtyard.

85 | 204

3197 نهادینه næhadine *institutionalized* adj
- برای نهادینه شدن حضور زنان. — In order to institutionalize the presence of women.

83 | 232

3198 راستی rasti *indeed, truth* adj,adv,n
- راستی می خوای چیزی از خودم به تو قرض بدم. — Do you really want me to lend you something?

66 | 532

3199 خوش آمدن xoʃ amædan *welcome* v
- سلام به شما خانمها و آقایان به دنیای ورزش خوش آمدید. — Hello to you, ladies and gentlemen, welcome to the world of sports.

69 | 471

3200 آنگاه angah *then* adv,conj
- آنگاه به آهستگی چشمان را نیم باز نمود. — Then he slowly opened his eyes halfway.

74 | 376

3201 سده sæde *century* n
- منار جام سده های درازی به گونه ی یک زیبایی فراموش شده در خم دره در خاموشانه ایستاده بود. — The Minaret of Jam had quietly stood for long centuries as a kind of forgotten beauty in the bend of a valley.

76 | 342

3202 رایانه rajane *computer* n
- ویروسهای مخرب نیز می توانند از یک رایانه به رایانه دیگر منتقل شوند. — Destructive viruses can also be transferred from one computer to another.

70 | 440

3203 ست set *set* n
- ازبکستان در سه ست متوالی نتیجه را به چین تایپه واگذار کرد. — Uzbekistan lost to Chinese Taipei in three consecutive sets.

68 | 489

20 Religion

Rank	Headword	Pronunciation	Gloss	Rank	Headword	Pronunciation	Gloss
86	اسلامی	eslami	Islamic	1530	شهادت	ʃæhadæt	martyrdom
161	محمد	mohæmmæd	Mohammad	1580	روح	ruh	spirit
276	اسلام	eslam	Islam	1582	الهى	elahi	divine
278	حسن	hæsæn	Hasan	1585	ایمان	iman	faith
385	حوزه	howze	seminary	1589	مشهد	mæʃhæd	Mashhad
399	شهید	ʃæhid	martyr	1606	حسینی	hosejni	Hosseini, of Imam Hossein
460	امام	emam	imam	1611	قرآن	ɣorʔan	Koran
466	دینى	dini	religious	1633	مسیحی	mæsihi	Christian
524	رهبر	ræhbær	leader	1641	ولایت	velajæt	Governance, Guardianship
546	خدا	xoda	God	1655	خمینى	xomejni	Khomeini
552	جمعه	dʒomʔe	Friday	1728	جواد	dʒævad	Javad
564	مراسم	mærasem	ceremony	1746	کاظم	kazem	Kazem
626	حضرت	hæzræt	holiness	1751	محمدى	mohæmmædi	Mohammadi
666	رهبری	ræhbæri	leadership	1842	معنوى	mæʔnævi	spiritual
677	شیخ	ʃejx	sheikh	1846	یهودى	jæhudi	Jew, Jewish
679	حکم	hokm	order, sentence	1853	روحانى	rowhani	cleric, Rowhani
684	مسلمان	mosælman	Muslim	1920	مشروع	mæʃruʔ	permissible
691	سید	sejjed	descendant of prophet	1926	حاج	hadʒ	Haji
730	عباس	æbbas	Abbas	1962	جمهورىاسلامى	dʒomhurije eslami	Islamic Republic
788	مسجد	mæsdʒed	mosque	1970	رمضان	ræmezan	Ramadan
834	حسین	hosejn	Hossein	2028	فقیه	fæɣih	Islamic jurist
896	مذهبى	mæzhæbi	religious	2037	ارشاد	erʃad	guidance
897	میلادى	miladi	A.D.	2083	آیتالله	ajætollah	ayatollah
942	عرب	æræb	Arab	2089	ظهور	zohur	appearance (of Imam Mahdi)
1018	عمر	omær	Umar	2106	ترویج	tærvidʒ	promotion
1026	رضا	reza	Reza	2129	موسى	musa	Musa, Moses
1032	عربى	æræbi	Arabic	2159	شمسى	ʃæmsi	solar
1052	الله	ællah	Allah	2162	قمرى	ɣæmæri	lunar
1171	سنى	sonni	Sunni	2194	پیامبر	pæjambær	prophet
1176	جهاد	dʒæhad	jihad	2220	زیارت	zijaræt	pilgrimage
1182	خیر	xejr, xæjjer	good, generous	2221	مجید	mædʒid	glorious, Majid
1191	مهدى	mæhdi	Mahdi	2230	افراطى	efrati	extremist
1205	مقدس	moɣæddæs	holy	2236	حرم	hæræm	sanctuary
1235	یوم	jowm	day	2383	صادق	sadeɣ	Sadiq
1241	مسلم	moslem	Muslim	2407	مراجع	mæradʒe	references, Maraji (supreme legal authorities)
1294	جامع	dʒameʔ	Congregational, Friday				
1301	امیر	æmir	emir				
1417	عبدالله	æbdollah	Abdollah				

Rank	Headword	Pronunciation	Gloss	Rank	Headword	Pronunciation	Gloss
2439	رسول	ræsul	messenger	3771	آیین	ɑjin	religion, ceremony, ritual
2441	یوسف	jusof, jusef	Joseph	3822	رحیم	ræhim	merciful, Rahim
2444	کلیسا	kelisɑ	church	3923	آیه	ɑje	Koranic verse
2599	بهشت	beheʃt	heaven	3957	ابراهیمی	ebrahimi	Abrahamic
2641	قیام	ɣijam	rising	3968	فرشته	fereʃte	angel
2648	جعفری	dʒæʔfæri	Jafari	4036	نازل	nazel	delivered (heavenly book), sent down, appear (angel)
2650	زهرا	zæhrɑ	Zahra				
2698	صلیب	sælib	cross				
2708	کیش	kiʃ	faith, religion				
2723	امت	ommæt	Ummah	4105	عیسی	isɑ	Jesus
2739	مرجع	mærdʒæʔ	supreme legal authority	4164	قرائت	ɣærɑʔæt	recitation
				4187	شیعی	ʃiʔi	Shiite
2743	نجف	nædʒæf	Najaf	4211	حجاب	hedʒab	veil, hijab
2807	معرفت	mæʔrefæt	knowledge	4225	معاویه	moʔavije	Muawiyah
2855	حج	hædʒdʒ	Hajj	4261	اکرم	ækræm	dearer, his holiness
2885	محرم	mæhræm, mohærræm	close relative/ confidant, Moharram	4319	حرام	hæram	forbidden
2893	خلیفه	xælife	caliph	4324	خدایی	xodɑji	divine
2957	حجت	hodʒdʒæt	reasoning, proof	4359	علیه السلام	ælejhessælam	peace be upon him
3022	مریم	mærjæm	Maryam	4400	روحانیت	rowhɑnijæt	clergy
3046	اصغر	æsɣær	Asghar	4526	معنویت	mæʔnævijjæt	spirituality
3060	کربلا	kærbælɑ	Karbala	4562	امامت	emɑmæt	imamship
3142	مجاهد	modʒahed	holy warrior	4603	زائر	zɑʔer	pilgrim
3227	داوود	davud	Davood, David	4617	معصوم	mæʔsum	innocent
3287	عاشورا	ɑʃurɑ	Ashura	4711	بهایی	bæhaji	Bahai
3317	خاندان	xandɑn	clan	4722	قرآنی	ɣorʔɑni	Koranic
3359	حاجی	hadʒi	Hajji	4730	سلمان	sælmɑn	Salman
3423	جعفر	dʒæʔfær	Jafar	4849	عزاداری	æzadɑri	mourning
3634	مؤمن	moʔmen	devout, faithful, believer	4861	مکه	mække	Mecca
				4898	ابومسلم	æbumoslem	Abu Muslim
3658	اهل بیت	æhle bejt	Mohammad's family	4960	فتوا	fætvɑ	fatwa
3666	عبادت	ebɑdæt	worship	4975	رساله	resale	risala, scriptures
3673	سوره	sure	sura	5018	تشیع	tæʃæjjoʔ	Shi'ism

3204 شخصاً ʃæxsæn *personally* adv
• اسکندر شخصاً مردی را کشت که جانش را در نبرد گرانیک نجات داده بود. — Alexander personally killed a man who had saved his life in the Battle of the Granicus.
87 | 171

3205 کلاسیک kelɑsik *classic* adj
• بخشی از موسیقی معاصر افغانستان بر بنیاد موسیقی کلاسیک هندی استوار است. — A portion of contemporary music of Afghanistan is based on the foundation of classical Indian music.
78 | 307

3206 هتل hotel *hotel* n
• در هیچ هتلی راحت نیستم. — I am not comfortable in any hotel.
76 | 344

3207 عصب **æsæb** *nerve* n
- آلودگی صوتی تهدیدی است برای شنوایی و اعصاب. — Noise pollution is a threat to hearing and nerves.
- 84 | 219

3208 افسانه **æfsane** *legend* n,pn
- افسانه مهم نبود. — It was not an important myth.
- 70 | 454

3209 گریختن **gorixtæn** *flee* adj,v
- از خانه به جنگل گریختند. — They escaped from her house to the forest.
- 82 | 251

3210 مخرب **moxærreb** *destructive* adj
- مسئولیت رفتار های مخرب یا نادرست خود را بپذیرد. — He should accept responsibility for his own incorrect and destructive behaviors.
- 86 | 191

3211 تقسیم کردن **tæɣsim kærdæn** *divide, distribute* v
- جنگی در کار نبود تا پیروزی را تقسیم کنیم. — There was no war to share the victory.
- 85 | 202

3212 اقامه **eɣame** *setting up, holding* n
- نماز عید فطر به امامت مقام معظم رهبری اقامه شد. — Eid al-Fitr prayer was held with Supreme Leader as the prayer Imam.
- 89 | 147

3213 مهلت **mohlæt** *period of time, respite* n
- مهلت ثبت‌نام در کنکور دانشگاه آزاد تمدید شد. — The deadline to enroll in Azad University entrance exams was extended.
- 80 | 279

3214 سالروز **salruz** *anniversary* n
- رئیس مجلس شورای اسلامی در پیامی به مناسبت سالروز شهادت آیت‌الله مدرس بر حفظ حرمت و جایگاه مجلس تأکید کرد. — In a message on the occasion of the anniversary of the martyrdom of Ayatollah Modarres, the head of the Islamic Consultative Assembly underscored the preservation of the sanctity and standing of the Majles.
- 81 | 264

3215 آفریقایی **afriɣaji** *African* adj
- یک‌پنجم کودکان آفریقایی به واکسن دسترسی ندارند. — One in five African children do not have access to vaccines.
- 77 | 323

3216 پوشیده **puʃide** *covered, clothed* adj
- من فکر می‌کنم پوشیده‌ترین‌ها را انتخاب کرده‌اند. — I think they have selected the most covered ones.
- 76 | 338

3217 پی بردن **pej bordæn** *discover, find out* v
- باستان‌شناسان به راز های مقبره‌ای باستانی پی‌بردند. — Archaeologists have discovered the secrets of an ancient tomb.
- 82 | 251

3218 ارتکاب **ertekab** *committing* n
- به اتهام ارتکاب جنایت جنگی محاکمه شود. — He should be tried on the charge of committing war crimes.
- 85 | 195

3219 رازی **razi** *Razi* n,pn
- رازی از دانشمندان بزرگ ایرانی و کاشف الکل بود. — Razi was one of the great Iranian scientists and the discoverer of alcohol.
- 88 | 155

3220 راه‌حل **rahehæll** *solution* n
- راه‌حل‌های آمریکا، در افغانستان کارآمد نیست. — America's solutions in Afghanistan are not efficient.
- 73 | 393

3221 تمدید **tæmdid** *extension* n
- تمدیدهای مکرر نشان داد که هنوز مشکلاتی باقی مانده است. — Frequent renewals showed that there are still some remaining problems.
- 78 | 305

3222 ترانزیت **tranzit** *transit* adj,n
- ایران مسیر ترانزیت خارجی‌ها می‌شود. — Iran becomes a transit route for foreigners.
- 79 | 298

3223 غم **ɣæm** *sorrow, grief* n
- اگر تو عاشقی، غم را رها کن. — If you are in love, then let go of your sadness.
- 71 | 424

3224 ویروس **virus** *virus* n
- این ویروس سال گذشته در نیویورک موجب کشته شدن هفت نفر شد. — Last year in New York this virus led to the killing of seven people.
- 74 | 377

3225 تند **tond** *fast* adj,adv
- حالا خیلی تند حرف بزنید. — Now, speak very fast.
- 68 | 482

3226 حسب **hæsb** *quantity, agreement* n
- کلمه‌ی «استاد» را بر حسب پیشنهاد ایشان اختیار کردم. — I chose the word "Master" according to his suggestion.
- 75 | 356

3227 داوود **davud** *Davood, David* pn
- داوود دومین پادشاه اسرائیل به روایت عهد عتیق بود. — According to the Old Testament, David was the second king of Israel.
- 76 | 340

3228 مجرم **modʒrem** *guilty, criminal* adj,n
- زندانی، همیشه مجرم نیست. — A prisoner is not always a criminal.
- 85 | 207

3229 انحلال **enhelal** *liquidation* n
- مدارک لازم جهت انحلال شرکت چیست؟ — What are the required documents for liquidating a company?
- 87 | 169

3230 هفدهم hevdæhom *seventeenth* adj,n
- در سده هفدهم هلندی‌ها در این جا قلعه‌ای ساختند. — In the seventeenth century the Dutch built a fortress here.
81 | 260

3231 گردان gærdan, gordan *turning, battalion* n
- یک گردان جدید برای انجام عملیات تشکیل شد. — A new battalion was formed for the operation.
90 | 131

3232 هفتگی hæftegi *weekly* adj,adv,n
- این گروه به صورت هفتگی با شاه دیدار می‌کنند. — This group visits with the Shah weekly.
89 | 149

3233 کاندیدا kandida *candidate* n
- از وی به عنوان کاندیدای ریاست‌جمهوری نام برده می‌شود. — They refer to him as a presidential candidate.
75 | 351

3234 خندیدن xændidæn *laugh* v
- او خندیدن خود را حس نکرده است. — She has not felt her own laughter.
52 | 817

3235 قایم γajem *firm, hidden* adv,n
- توی جیب شلوارش قایم می کرد. — He was hiding it in the pocket of his pants.
76 | 332

3236 امپراتوری emperaturi *empire* n
- جنگ نخست جهانی را جنگ مرگ امپراتوری‌ها می‌دانند. — They consider World War I to be the war of the death of empires.
85 | 203

3237 اوکراین okrajn *Ukraine* pn
- پخش برنامه‌های اروپای آزاد در اوکراین قطع شد. — Free Europe broadcasts were stopped in Ukraine.
79 | 290

3238 مبادرت mobaderæt *undertaking* n
- خیلی ها مبادرت به ادامه مصرف این داروی پر عارضه می کنند. — Many attempt to continue taking this highly hazardous medication.
88 | 152

3239 مشاوره moʃavere *consultation* n
- هدف ما فقط مشاوره است. — Our goal is just consultation.
77 | 317

3240 بسنده bæsænde *sufficient, content* adj
- چقدر زیباست که به همین مقدار فقط بسنده کنیم. — How beautiful it is to be content with only this amount.
90 | 131

3241 درج dærdʒ *insertion, incorporation* n
- در ایران هدف های کلی آموزشی از طریق شوراهای برنامه ریزی در کتاب های روش تدریس یا راهنمای معلم درج می گردد. — In Iran, general academic goals are incorporated by planning councils into teaching methodology books and teacher's guides.
77 | 316

3242 الجزایر ældʒæzajer *Algeria* pn
- در کشور الجزایر این تحول به یک شکل دیگر انجام گرفت. — In Algeria, this development took place in another way.
77 | 315

3243 انفرادی enferadi *individual, solitary* adj,n
- به سه سال حبس انفرادی محکوم شد. — He was sentenced to three years in solitary confinement.
81 | 253

3244 عقد æγd *(marriage) contract* n
- دختر را عقد کردند. — They married the girl.
80 | 281

3245 توطئه towteʔe *conspiracy* n
- ساتی برزن نیز در این توطئه شرکت داشت. — Sati Barzan was also involved in this conspiracy.
62 | 596

3246 فلج fælædʒ *crippled* adj,n
- یک بار کنار کسی که پاهایش فلج بود نشسته بودم. — Once, I was sitting next to someone whose legs were paralyzed.
90 | 133

3247 مهربان mehræban *kind, gentle* adj,pn
- آیا گولن یک صوفی مهربان است؟ — Is Gulen a gentle Sufi?
74 | 364

3248 بزرگ شدن bozorg ʃodæn *grow up* v
- بچه ها بزرگ می شوند دیگر به ما احتیاج ندارند. — Children will get bigger and no longer need us.
78 | 298

3249 چشم‌انداز tʃeʃmændaz *perspective* n
- چشم‌انداز او تا نوک دماغ اوست. — His outlook only goes as far as the tip of his nose.
72 | 396

3250 ویتنام vijetnam *Vietnam* pn
- شش ماه پیش از ویتنام برگشت. — He returned from Vietnam six months ago.
83 | 224

3251 لازمه lazeme *requisite, precondition* adj,n
- لازمه خروج از بحران بیکاری، سرمایه‌گذاری بخش خصوصی است. — Private sector investment is the requirement to get out of the unemployment crisis.
85 | 203

3252 استانبول estambol *Istanbul* pn
- در استانبول چند روزی توقف داشت. — She stopped for a few days in Istanbul.
84 | 213

3253 سهمیه sæhmijje *quota, share* n
- The — سهمیه سوخت خودروهای عمومی تغییر نمی‌کند.
  fuel quota for public vehicles will not change.
  75 | 353

3254 ارگان organ *organ* n
- آنان همچنین در مذاکرات بروکسل بر سر تشکیل یک ارگان
  نظارتی مشترک توافق کردند. — They also agreed
  upon the formation of a joint supervisory
  organ at the negotiations in Brussels.
  74 | 357

3255 عنایت enajæt *favor* n
- با عنایت به این که در شش ماهه دوم سال طبق روال گذشته
  صادرات استان افزایش چشمگیری خواهد داشت. — Thanks
  to the fact that the second six months of the
  year passed routinely, the province will have a
  significant increase in exports.
  81 | 249

3256 محیطی mohiti *environmental* adj,n
- تغییرات شدید شتاب جاذبه و شرایط محیطی تأثیری بر آن
  ندارد. — It is not affected by sharp changes in
  the acceleration of gravity and environmental
  conditions.
  68 | 461

3257 کشمکش keʃmækeʃ *conflict* n
- کشمکش گسترده طرفداران دربار و دولت در مجلس هفدهم
  موجب شد تا دکتر مصدق انحلال مجلس را به رفراندوم
  گذارد. — The widespread conflict between the
  court and the government in the 17th
  Parliament led to Dr. Mosaddegh putting the
  dissolution of the parliament to a referendum.
  87 | 163

3258 تعجب tæʔædʒdʒob *surprise* n
- خیلی تعجب کردم. — I was very suprised.
  69 | 456

3259 مرتب moræۦtæb *orderly, arranged* adj,adv
- پس همه چیز مرتب است. — Then everything is
  arranged.
  76 | 337

3260 اصولاً osulæn *in principle* adv
- اصولاً طراحی ابعاد مختلفی دارد. — In principle the
  design has different dimensions.
  75 | 340

3261 آسیب دیدن asib didæn *be injured* v
- کشتی آسیب دید و نزدیک بود غرق گردد. — A boat
  was damaged and close to sinking.
  87 | 165

3262 ت te *letter te* n,pn
- ت. تا سر حد امکان — D. As far as possible.
  61 | 599

3263 سکو sækku *platform* n
- بچه که دیگر جلو سکو رسیده بود با تعجب به میرزا نگاه کرد.
  — The boy, who had once again come to the
  platform, looked at Mirza with astonishment.
  79 | 278

3264 روزمره ruzmærre *routine* adj
- امروز دیگر ابزاری مانند رایانه و پدیده هایی مثل اینترنت
  یکی از اجزای زندگی روزمره ما شده اند. — Today
  tools like the computer and phenomena
  such as the internet have become fixtures of
  everyday life.
  84 | 217

3265 اشراف æʃraf, eʃraf *noblemen, being in high position* n
- او یک اشراف زاده است. — He is born of the
  nobility.
  89 | 136

3266 دموکرات demokrat *democrat* adj,n
- دیکتاتورها نیز گاهی دموکرات می شوند. — Dictators
  also occasionally become democrats.
  76 | 328

3267 آبادان abadan *Abadan* pn
- گرد و خاک آبادان به ۶۶ برابر حد استاندارد رسید. — Air
  dust in Abadan reached 66 times the
  standard limit.
  78 | 299

3268 طول کشیدن tul keʃidæn *last long* v
- فقط دو دقیقه طول کشیده است. — It has only lasted
  two minutes.
  74 | 359

3269 تانک tank *tank* n
- چرا نفت ایران در تانک و هواپیمایی می‌سوزد... — Why is
  the oil of Iran burning in tanks and airplanes . . .
  87 | 171

3270 پویایی pujaji *dynamism* n
- دانشگاه‌های کشور فاقد پویایی است. — The country's
  universities lack dynamism.
  90 | 127

3271 علامه ællame *erudite, Allameh* n,pn
- علامه جعفری پس از یازده سال اقامت در نجف، به ایران
  بازگشت. — Allameh Jafari returned to Iran
  after eleven years living in Najaf.
  85 | 192

3272 ستایش setajeʃ *praise* n
- مرا ستایش کنید. — You should praise us.
  86 | 177

3273 قبول کردن ɣæbul kærdæn *accept* v
- پیر مرد قبول نکرد. — The old man did not agree.
  76 | 331

3274 فاکتور faktor *invoice, factor* n
- در این آزمایش چندین فاکتور در نظر قرار گرفته شده است.
  — In this experiment, several factors have
  been taken into consideration.
  87 | 162

3275 یاد گرفتن jad gereftæn *learn* v
- بنابر اظهارات خود صدام، او چیز های زیادی از عمویش یاد
  گرفت. — Based on Saddam's own statements,
  he learned many things from his uncle.
  70 | 427

3276 برون borun *outside* adj,adv,n,prep
- تا از رواج شایعه و انحراف افکار عمومی توسط رسانه‌های برون مرزی جلوگیری شود. — To prevent spreading rumors and the deviation of public opinion by cross-border media.
83 | 218

3277 معلول mæʔlul *disabled, effect* adj,n
- سعی بر آن دارد که از معلول به علت احتمالی پی برد. — Through its effects he tries to figure out the probable cause.
80 | 264

3278 پرتغال porteɣal *Portugal* pn
- تیم ملی پرتغال فرصت دارد. — Portugal's national team has an opportunity.
73 | 373

3279 کامپیوتر kampjuter *computer* n
- تبلت‌ها سریع‌تر از انتظار جای کامپیوترهای شخصی را گرفتند. — Tablets replaced personal computers much faster than expected.
70 | 434

3280 دایم dajem *permanent* adj,adv
- برای اقامت دایم اقدام کرده ام و منتظر نتیجه ام. — I have applied for permanent residence and I am waiting for the result.
78 | 292

3281 سنا sena *senate* n,pn
- هیلاری کلینتون اولین همسر رئیس جمهور در آمریکاست که وارد سنا شده. — Hillary Clinton is the first First Lady in America to enter the Senate.
76 | 322

3282 هیاهو hæjahu *tumult* n
- گوشم را محکم به در می چسباندم که صدای هیاهو و شادی بچه ها را بشنوم . . . — I put my ear to the door to listen to the sound of the children's fanfare and happiness . . .
90 | 126

3283 دویدن dævidæn *run* adj,n,v
- از دویدن بر روی سطوح یخ زده و پیاده روی در پیاده روهای تاریک و دوچرخه‌سواری در خیابان‌های شلوغ بپرهیزید. — Avoid running on frozen surfaces, walking on dark sidewalks, and bicycling on busy streets.
65 | 508

3284 سطحی sæthi *superficial* adj,n
- ولی عیب بزرگش این است که سطحی است. — But his major problem is that he is superficial.
77 | 317

3285 پاکستانی pakestani *Pakistani* adj
- ۲۰ هزار پاکستانی در وزارت کشور بحرین شاغلند. — 20 thousand Pakistanis are employed in Bahrain's Interior Ministry.
67 | 483

3286 هموار hæmvar *flat, smooth, paved* adj
- مسیر هموار است. — The path is paved.
84 | 212

3287 عاشورا aʃura *Ashura* n
- عاشورا فقط یک بار در عالم اتفاق افتاده است. — Ashura has only happened one time in the world.
83 | 223

3288 استبداد estebdad *tyranny* n
- هاشم خان با استبداد و بیرحمی ، حکومت راند. — Hashem Khan ruled despotically and without mercy.
82 | 235

3289 سپاهان sepahan *Sepahan* n,pn
- قدرت سپاهان بر هیچکس پوشیده نیست. — The strength of Sepahan is no secret.
73 | 371

3290 بازنشسته baznefæste *retired* adj,n
- چند سال باید کار کنید تا بازنشسته شوید؟ — How many years do you have to work until you retire?
71 | 405

3291 وطن vætæn *homeland* adj,n,pn
- دفاع از وطن وجیبه تمام اتباع افغانستان است. — Defending the homeland is an obligation of all citizens of Afghanistan.
70 | 430

3292 ناراحتی narahæti *discomfort* n
- سارا با ناراحتی به اتاق خوابش رفت. — Upset, Sara went to her room.
79 | 286

3293 داستانی dastani *fictional* adj,n
- او ۳۰ کتاب داستانی نوشت. — He wrote 30 fiction books.
75 | 338

3294 بهاری bæhari *spring* adj,pn
- بهار طبیعت و شکوفایی غنچه های بهاری را گرامی می دارند. — They cherish nature's spring and the blossoming of spring buds.
93 | 87

3295 دره dærre *valley* n
- مثل باد از دره ها گذشت و مثل سیل از تپه ها سرازیر شد. — It passed through the valleys like the wind and flowed from the hills like a flood.
70 | 426

3296 احسان ehsan *charity, Ehsan* n,pn
- محمد رمضان پور و احسان خدادادی اعضای تیم ملی برای حضور در جام جهانی ژیمناستیک تهران هستند. — Mohammad Ramezanpour and Ehsan Khodadadi are members of the national team to appear in Tehran's Gymnastics World Cup.
82 | 230

3297 ناچیز natʃiz *worthless* adj
- آیا صدهزار تومان رقم ناچیزی است. — Is one hundred thousand toman a small amount?
81 | 253

3298 ديپلماتيک *diplomatik diplomatic* adj
- افريقاى جنوبى سرگرم بررسى برقرارى مناسبات ديپلماتيک با بغداد است. — South Africa is currently investigating establishing diplomatic ties with Baghdad.

79 | 279

3299 تمايل داشتن *tæmajol daʃtæn tend to, gravitate to* v
- فقط 40 درصد شهروندان به خريد كالاهاى ايرانى تمايل دارند. — Only 40 percent of citizens are willing to buy Iranian goods.

89 | 134

3300 ممنوعيت *mæmnuʔijjæt prohibition* n
- امروز پنتاگون اين ممنوعيت را برداشت. — Today the Pentagon lifted this ban.

82 | 232

3301 دامن زدن *damæn zædæn add fuel* v
- بايد از دامن زدن به اضطراب و ترس فرزندانشان بپرهيزند. — They should avoid provoking anxiety and fear in their children.

86 | 184

3302 كارگردانى *kargærdani direction* n
- اين فيلم را محمد حسن ناظرى كارگردانى كرده است. — Mohammad Hassan Nazeri has directed this film.

66 | 485

3303 اندام *ændam organ, figure* n
- زيبايى سيما و اندام و گيسوان او را ستوده اند. — They have praised the beauty of her visage, figure, and locks.

84 | 204

3304 راهبردى *rahbordi strategic* adj,n
- به دليل قرار گرفتن در موقعيت راهبردى و ترانزيتى از اهميت فراوانى برخوردار است. — It is of great importance due to its strategic and transport position.

70 | 417

3305 مديون *mædjun indebted* adj
- پاسخ آمد: اشتباه مى كنى. تو مديون او هستى! — The answer came: "You're mistaken. You are indebted to him!"

90 | 121

3306 مليت *mellijjæt nationality* n
- دانشگاه‌هاى ايران از ۱۰۳ مليت دانشجو دارند. — Iranian universities have students of 103 nationalities.

85 | 193

3307 يونسكو *junesko UNESCO* pn
- دغدغه اصلى يونسكو در سال آينده. — The main concern of UNESCO in the coming year.

77 | 302

3308 هوش *huʃ intelligence* n
- عوامل بسيار زيادى در روند كاهش هوش و حافظه مؤثر هستند. — Many factors have the effect of reducing intelligence and memory.

68 | 452

3309 تونس *tunes Tunisia, Tunis* pn
- گفته مى‌شود شيخ راشد الغنوشى و جنبش النهضه تونس نيز با ارسال پيام تبريک براى اين هنرمند ارزشمند، از او خواستند در اين راه ثابت قدم بماند. — It is said that Sheikh Rached Ghannouchi and the Ennahda Movement of Tunisia, having sent a congratulatory message to this valuable artist, have asked that he stay firmly on this path.

67 | 475

3310 برخاستن *bærxastæn get/rise up* adj,n,v
- آنها مى‌توانستند نظر مشخصى ارائه نمايند تا بر نابرابرى‌هاى جامعه به مبارزه برخيزند. — They managed to present a specific opinion in order to rise up to fight against the inequalities of society.

75 | 335

3311 زند *zænd radius, ulna, Zand* pn,v
- طايفة زند گروهى بودند با معيشت شبانى. — The Zand tribe was a group with a herding livelihood.

73 | 362

3312 مه *mæh, meh, me moon, fog, May* n
- صداى زير زنگ ساعت شمس العماره را از درون مه پاييزى شنيد. — He heard the high-pitched sound of the chime of the clock of Shams-ol-Emareh from within the autumn fog.

78 | 299

3313 دبيرستان *dæbirestan high school* n
- اين پسر در هنگام ورود به دبيرستان هم لاغرترين دانش آموز كلاس بود. — When this boy started high school, he was also the skinniest student in class.

81 | 241

3314 جماعت *dʒæmaʔæt assembly* n
- به خود گفتم به به به ، جماعت مسلمين از خواب بيدار شده اند. — I said to myself, "My my, the congregation of Muslims has awoken from slumber."

79 | 278

3315 صنفى *senfi guild, trade* adj
- امروز نزديک به ۸۰۰ واحد صنفى در تهران وجود دارد. — Today there are nearly 800 trade units in Tehran.

72 | 382

3316 تحرير *tæhrir writing* n
- ميزبان گل را در گلدانى كه از آشپزخانه آورده جا داد و آنها را روى ميز تحرير كوچكى نزديک پنجره گذاشت. — The host put the flower in a vase that he had brought from the kitchen and placed it on a small writing desk near the window.

84 | 201

3317 خاندان *xandan clan* n
- بايكوت انتخابات كويت به نفع خاندان سلطنتى تمام مى‌شود. — The boycott of Kuwait elections ended in favor of the royal family.

76 | 317

3318 وزیری væziri *ministerial, Vaziri* n,pn
- وزیری سمفونی نفت را به مناسبت ملی شدن صنعت نفت ایران ساخت. — Vaziri composed the Oil Symphony on the occasion of the nationalization of Iran's oil industry.
- 75 | 338

3319 بلوک boluk, belok *district, block* n
- نخستین بلوک سهام بانک پارسیان به فروش رسید. — The first block of Parsian Bank shares was sold.
- 88 | 145

3320 آنکارا ankara *Ankara* n,pn
- برای رفتن به استانبول باید نخست با اتومبیل به آنکارا برود. — In order to go to Istanbul he must first drive to Ankara.
- 72 | 384

3321 پرش pæreʃ *jump* n
- چرا پرش کردی که بریزد روی میز؟ — Why did you jump and make it spill on the table?
- 89 | 133

3322 اصفهانی esfæhani *Esfahani* adj,pn
- مردم اصفهان به زبان پارسی و لهجه اصفهانی سخن می‌گویند. — The people of Esfahan speak Persian with an Esfahani accent.
- 85 | 188

3323 کلیات kollijjɑt *generalities, general works* n
- این موتورها از نظر کلیات شباهت زیادی با موتور اتومبیل‌ها دارند. — These engines in general are very similar to car engines.
- 84 | 210

3324 هماکنون hæmæknun *just now* adv
- هماکنون بسیاری از کشورها و هیئت‌های تجاری آماده سفر به ایران و گسترش روابط اقتصادی هستند. — Many countries and trade councils have already traveled to Iran and are spreading economic relations.
- 63 | 534

3325 پر کردن por kærdæn *fill* v
- می‌گویند فرم‌ها را پر کنید. — They say: "Fill out the forms."
- 77 | 313

3326 تعدیل tæʔdil *modification* n
- تعدیل نرخ ارز براساس تورم. — Adjusting the price of currency based on inflation.
- 77 | 312

3327 خسرو xosrow *Khosrow* pn
- خسرو را من می‌شناسم. — I know Khosrow.
- 79 | 277

3328 پاسخگویی pɑsoxguʔi *responding* n
- پاسخگویی به تهدیدها در هر سطحی حیاتی است. — Responding to threats on every level is vital.
- 77 | 311

3329 خوراک xorɑk *food* n
- پس خوراک شماها، شب و روز، بادام است؟ — So your food, day and night, is almonds?
- 84 | 204

3330 پنجره pændʒere *window* n
- پنجره را باز کرد. — She opened the window.
- 64 | 528

3331 البرز ælborz *Alborz* pn
- در دامنه جنوبی رشته کوه‌های البرز جای دارد. — It is located along the southern slopes of the Alborz mountain range.
- 79 | 276

3332 بست bæst *clip, sanctuary, closed* pn,v
- برای محکم کردن شیلنگ‌های گاز حتما باید از بست‌های فلزی استفاده شود. — For tightening gas hoses, certainly metal clamps must be used.
- 66 | 491

3333 حرمت hormæt *sanctity* n
- حرمتش را نگه می‌دارند. — They will maintain their honor.
- 79 | 273

3334 نفرت nefræt *hatred* n
- بهروز از این اسم نفرت داشت. — Behruz hated this name.
- 85 | 187

3335 روشنگری rowʃængæri *enlightenment* n
- عصر روشنگری دوران آزاداندیشی است. — The Age of Enlightenment is the period of free thought.
- 94 | 75

3336 انتقام enteɣɑm *revenge* n
- انتقام می‌گیرین یا می بخشین؟ — Are you going to take revenge or forgive?
- 88 | 144

3337 نفی næfj *negation* n
- نفی تحجر، روح سیاسی اسلام را غالب می‌کند. — Rejection of fanaticism makes the political spirit of Islam dominant.
- 82 | 228

3338 رایزنی rɑjzæni *consultation* n
- رایزنی برای انتخاب رئیس شورای شهر. — Consultation for the election of the chairman of the city council.
- 71 | 396

3339 ظاهری zaheri *apparent, superficial* adj,n
- همه حرف‌هایش ظاهری است. — All of his words are superficial.
- 81 | 240

3340 نامناسب nɑmonɑseb *inappropriate* adj
- از انتشار عکس‌های نامناسب بپرهیزید. — Refrain from publishing inappropriate pictures.
- 81 | 247

3341 مرادی moradi *Moradi* pn
- سهراب مرادی با طلا بازگشت. — Sohrab Moradi returned with gold.

86 | 175

3342 کور kur *blind* adj,n
- میرزا گفت: «کور که نیستم.» — Mirza said, "I am not blind."

74 | 346

3343 انبار ænbar *storehouse* n
- انباری می‌یابد که به او به ارث رسیده است. — He will find a warehouse that he has inherited.

78 | 288

3344 شناسنامه ʃenasname *identity card* n
- هزینه دریافت و تعویض شناسنامه اعلام شد. — Fees for receiving and replacing identity cards were announced.

78 | 281

3345 تعویق tæʔviɣ *delay, postponement* n
- تکمیل ساخت زیربنای این شهر با مقداری تعویق در دهه ۱۹۸۰ به پایان رسید. — Construction of the city's infrastructure was completed with some delay in the 1980s.

83 | 213

3346 خروجی xorudʒi *exit, output* adj,n
- ترافیک در خروجی‌های تهران نیمه سنگین است. — Traffic is semi-heavy at Tehran exits.

81 | 238

3347 بیهوده bihude *futile* adj,adv
- چه بیهوده است! — How pointless!

85 | 185

3348 صمیمی sæmimi *intimate* adj,pn
- آنها چشمانی درشت و صورتهایی مردانه و صمیمی دارند. — They have harsh eyes and intimate, manly facial features.

87 | 158

3349 متولد motævælled *born* adj,n
- انیشتین متولد چه ماهی است؟ — In what month was Einstein born?

81 | 244

3350 ذیل zejl *appendix, following, below* adj,n
- رشته‌های این دانشکده به شرح ذیل می‌باشند: — The college programs include the following:

67 | 471

3351 برانگیخته bæræŋgixte *stimulated, excited* adj,n,v
- این موضوعی است که باعث برانگیخته‌تر شدن خشم حاکمیت شد. — This is the matter which provoked the anger of the government.

90 | 124

3352 کوفی kufi *Kufic, Kofi* adj,pn
- مالک اشتر رهبر کوفیان بود. — Malik Ashtar was the leader of people of Kufa.

72 | 377

3353 گردشگر gærdeʃgær *tourist* n
- ارزانی نرخ اسکان، گردشگران زیادی را جذب کرد. — Inexpensive accommodation rates attracted many tourists.

80 | 252

3354 یادآور jadavær *reminder, memento, reminiscent* adj
- روز آزادی خرمشهر یادآور فتح فاتحان بر بلندترین فراز هاست. — Khorramshahr Liberation Day commemorates the conquest of conquerors on the highest of peaks.

66 | 483

3355 ارزنده ærzænde *valuable* adj
- برای ما پیشنهادهای ارزنده خود را بفرستید. — Send us your valuable suggestions.

84 | 207

3356 عموماً omumæn *generally* adv
- داستانهای مثنوی عموماً با فرهنگ ایران آن روزگار منطبق بوده‌است. — Masnavi stories were generally consistent with the Iranian culture of those days.

82 | 228

3357 دستورالعمل dæsturolʔæmæl *instructions* n
- دستورالعمل جدید مصرف آنتی بیوتیک‌ها ابلاغ شد. — New instructions were issued for taking antibiotics.

80 | 257

3358 بهره‌گیری bæhregiri *utilization* n
- خصوصاً با بهره‌گیری از استعداد شخصی مربیان. — Especially by taking advantage of the coaches' personal talent.

78 | 281

3359 حاجی hadʒi *Hajji* n,pn
- مادر «حاجی‌بابای اصفهانی» را خوانده بود. — His mother had read "Hajji Baba of Ispahan."

62 | 548

3360 گوشی guʃi *receiver, headphones, phone* n
- چطور گوشی‌های اندروید هک می‌شوند؟ — How are Android phones being hacked?

62 | 557

3361 بنیانگذار bonjangozar *founder* n,pn
- وی معتقد است آموزش جامعه‌شناسی باید ابن‌خلدون را به‌عنوان پدر بنیانگذار خود محسوب کند. — He believes that the instruction of sociology should count Ibn Khaldun as its founding father.

82 | 221

3362 گفتمان gofteman *discourse, dialogue* n
- این بحث در گفتمان‌های فیلسوفان همچنان ادامه دارد. — This discussion still continues in the discourse of philosophers.

79 | 268

21 Simple verbs

Rank	Headword	Pronunciation	Gloss	Rank	Headword	Pronunciation	Gloss
2	بودن	budæn	be	714	بخشیدن	bæxʃidæn	forgive, give
9	شدن	ʃodæn	become	752	کشاندن	keʃandæn	drag, pull
14	خواستن	xastæn	want	774	نشستن	neʃæstæn	sit
16	داشتن	daʃtæn	have	786	کشیدن	keʃidæn	pull, draw
17	کردن	kærdæn	do	850	افتادن	oftadæn	fall
19	بایستن	bajestæn	must	903	کشتن	koʃtæn	kill
23	توانستن	tævanestæn	be able	967	فرمودن	færmudæn	order, say
24	رسیدن	residæn	arrive	1030	انداختن	ændaxtæn	throw
34	گرفتن	gereftæn	take	1080	شکستن	ʃekæstæn	break
37	گفتن	goftæn	say	1223	ایستادن	istadæn	stand
42	دادن	dadæn	give	1233	شنیدن	ʃenidæn	hear
87	دانستن	danestæn	know	1242	پیوستن	pejvæstæn	join
93	آمدن	amædæn	come	1361	بستن	bæstæn	close
99	یافتن	jaftæn	find	1463	پرسیدن	porsidæn	ask
112	آوردن	aværdæn	bring	1513	ریختن	rixtæn	pour
128	رفتن	ræftæn	go	1587	آموختن	amuxtæn	learn, teach
147	بردن	bordæn	take	1666	فرستادن	ferestadæn	send
192	رساندن	resandæn	deliver	1681	نامیدن	namidæn	name
194	گذاشتن	gozaʃtæn	put, leave	1706	گذراندن	gozærandæn	spend time, pass
202	دیدن	didæn	see				
211	پرداختن	pærdaxtæn	pay, engage in	1738	اندیشیدن	ændiʃidæn	think
				1744	ربودن	robudæn	steal, kidnap
257	گذشتن	gozæʃtæn	pass	1782	فهمیدن	fæhmidæn	understand
277	افزودن	æfzudæn	add	1818	فروختن	foruxtæn	sell
280	خواندن	xandæn	read	1849	طلبیدن	tælæbidæn	call, ask, require
305	نمودن	nemudæn	show, do				
310	زدن	zædæn	beat, strike	2034	انجامیدن	ændʒamidæn	end
315	نوشتن	neveʃtæn	write	2041	پوشیدن	puʃidæn	wear
316	ساختن	saxtæn	build	2044	جستن	dʒæstæn, dʒostæn	jump, search
494	شایستن	ʃajestæn	be possible, deserve	2049	سپردن	sepordæn	deposit, entrust
505	ماندن	mandæn	stay	2103	راندن	randæn	drive, repulse
604	گردیدن	gærdidæn	turn				
658	گشتن	gæʃtæn	turn	2228	ورزیدن	værzidæn	exercise
686	خوردن	xordæn	eat	2255	پوشاندن	puʃandæn	dress
689	پذیرفتن	pæziroftæn	accept	2369	مردن	mordæn	die
705	شناختن	ʃenaxtæn	know, recognize	2378	گشودن	goʃudæn	open
				2410	کاستن	kastæn	reduce

(continued)

(continued)

Rank	Headword	Pronunciation	Gloss	Rank	Headword	Pronunciation	Gloss
2451	افکندن	æfkændæn	*throw*	4327	بافتن	bɑftæn	*weave*
2543	نهادن	næhadæn	*put, place*	4361	نوشیدن	nuʃidæn	*drink*
2550	نگریستن	negæristæn	*look*	4438	گرویدن	gerævidæn	*adopt a belief*
2564	سوختن	suxtæn	*burn*	4513	گنجاندن	gondʒandæn	*pack, include*
2600	خریدن	xæridæn	*buy*	4623	گرداندن	gærdandæn	*rotate, manage*
2661	شمردن	ʃemordæn	*count*	4633	پریدن	pæridæn	*jump, fly*
2690	نشاندن	neʃandæn	*seat*	4647	سنجیدن	sændʒidæn	*measure*
2894	ترسیدن	tærsidæn	*fear*	4665	زیستن	zistæn	*live*
3039	کوبیدن	kubidæn	*pound, grind*	4697	آمیختن	ɑmixtæn	*mix*
3071	باختن	bɑxtæn	*lose*	4755	جنگیدن	dʒængidæn	*fight*
3209	گریختن	gorixtæn	*flee*	4758	کاهیدن	kahidæn	*detract*
3234	خندیدن	xændidæn	*laugh*	4766	چرخیدن	tʃærxidæn	*turn*
3283	دویدن	dævidæn	*run*	4769	تابیدن	tabidæn	*shine, twist*
3782	خوابیدن	xɑbidæn	*sleep*	4802	پیچیدن	piʃidæn	*twist*
3814	پیمودن	pejmudæn	*measure, traverse*	4818	درخشیدن	deræxʃidæn	*shine*
3873	دوختن	duxtæn	*sew*	4833	پاشیدن	pɑʃidæn	*scatter, sprinkle*
4104	نواختن	nævaxtæn	*play*	4852	هراسیدن	hærasiden	*fear*
4203	چیدن	tʃidæn	*pick, pluck, set*	4936	پختن	poxtæn	*cook*

3363 جواب دادن dʒævab dadæn *reply* v
• زنم به جای جواب دادن گفت: «چرا اذیت می کنی؟»
— Instead of answering, my wife said: "Why are you being a bother?"
59 | 612

3364 نارضایتی narezajæti *dissatisfaction* n
• در دوران پس از کودتا نارضایتی‌هایی در بسیاری از نقاط ایران بوجود آمد. — In the aftermath of the coup, grievances arose in many parts of Iran.
79 | 273

3365 تاجر tadʒer *merchant* n,pn
• رهبر جدید طالبان تاجری تحت حمایت پاکستان است. — The new leader of the Taliban is a Pakistan-backed businessman.
78 | 283

3366 زخم zæxm *wound* n
• چرا نمک به زخم می پاشید؟! — Why are you rubbing salt in the wound?!
77 | 306

3367 مداوم modavem *continuous* adj
• شرکت اصلی به صورت مداوم در این منطقه فعالیت نمی‌کرد. — The main company was not continuously active in this region.
81 | 247

3368 بازاری bazari *businessman* adj,n
• در این مراسم اصناف و بازاریها شرکت نکردند. — Traders and Bazaar merchants did not participate in the ceremony.
88 | 140

3369 مایع maje? *liquid* adj,n
• آب به صورت مایع وجود داشت. — Water existed as a liquid.
78 | 288

3370 کارایی karaji *efficiency* n
• برد این سری موشکها بلند بوده و از کارایی بالایی برخوردار بودند. — This series of missiles was long-range and high performance.
84 | 203

3371 سکونت sokunæt *residence* n
• فعلاً در تهران سکونت دارد. — She currently resides in Tehran.
82 | 223

3372 رایانه‌ای rajaneji *computer* adj
• نوید برهانی قهرمان اولین جشنواره ملی بازی‌های رایانه‌ای شد. — Navid Borhani was champion of the first National Computer Games Festival.
78 | 289

3373 بزرگوار bozorgvar *generous, honorable* adj,n
- چه کسی بزرگوار نیست؟ — Who is not honorable?

74 | 340

3374 چهارچوب tʃæhartʃub *frame, framework* n
- عشق چهارچوبی ندارد. — Love has no boundaries.

84 | 196

3375 ناقص naɣes *defective* adj
- سرمایه گذاری در خودرو و پتروشیمی به صورتی ناقص صورت گرفته است. — Investment in automobiles and petrochemicals has taken place incompletely.

86 | 167

3376 گازی gazi *gas* adj
- بخاری گازی از مدارس پایتخت حذف می‌شود. — Gas heaters are being removed from the capital's schools.

72 | 368

3377 صدمه sædme *injury* n
- من دست دختر را طوری از کوزه در می‌آورم که نه کوزه بشکند و نه دستش صدمه ببیند. — I'll get the girl's hand out of the urn in such a way so the urn won't break and her hand won't be hurt.

80 | 259

3378 پنهانی penhani *secret* adj,adv,n
- معامله پنهانی بین ایران و آمریکا وجود ندارد. — There is no secret deal between Iran and America.

88 | 143

3379 شورشی ʃureʃi *rebel* adj,n,pn
- شورشیان طرفدار مسکو در اوکراین را کنترل کنید. — Control the pro-Moscow rebels in Ukraine.

71 | 387

3380 انزوا enzeva *isolation* n
- آیا ممکن است سال‌ها در گوشه انزوا بماند و خودش را نشان ندهد — Is it possible that he would remain in his corner of isolation for years and never show himself . . .

85 | 179

3381 کد kædd, kod *toil, code* n
- سورس کد برنامه های اجرایی . . . — The source code of the executable programs . . .

79 | 269

3382 جزء dʒozʔ *part, detail, ingredient* adj,n
- بنده هم جزء این عده بودم. — I was also part of this group.

65 | 495

3383 مظلوم mæzlum *oppressed* adj,n
- ایران همواره درکنار ملت‌های مظلوم است. — Iran has always been alongside the oppressed nations.

80 | 253

3384 مترو metro *metro* n
- خط ۶ مترو امسال راه‌اندازی می‌شود. — Metro Line 6 will be launched this year.

77 | 291

3385 انصاری ænsari *Ansari* pn
- ساسان انصاری به پرسپولیس پیوست. — Sasan Ansari joined Persepolis.

76 | 309

3386 تدارکاتی tædarokati *logistical, supply* adj
- حمله به خودروی تدارکاتی ناتو در پاکستان یک کشته برجای گذاشت. — Attacks on NATO supply vehicles in Pakistan left one killed.

83 | 208

3387 اعتیاد eʔtijad *addiction* n
- آیا ورزش در درمان اعتیاد مؤثر است؟ — Is exercise effective in treating addiction?

71 | 397

3388 افغانی æfɣani *Afghan* adj,n
- پناهندگان افغانی در ایران بیمه می‌شوند. — Afghan refugees in Iran will have insurance.

60 | 579

3389 پاییز pajiz *autumn* n
- باد خنک شب پاییز از پنجره باز ماشین توی صورتم می‌خورد. — The cool night air of autumn came through the car's open window and grazed my face.

80 | 247

3390 سرهنگ særhæng *colonel* n
- یکدفعه چشمش به سرهنگ افتاد. — Suddenly his eye fell on the colonel.

79 | 269

3391 هوشمند huʃmænd *clever* adj
- استفاده از انواع مختلف سیستم‌های هوشمند در پزشکی رو به افزایش است. — The use of various types of intelligent systems in medicine is increasing.

83 | 206

3392 گیرنده giærænde *recipient, receiver* adj,n
- گیرنده‌هایتان را خاموش کنید. — Turn off your receivers.

79 | 266

3393 معقول mæʔɣul *reasonable* adj,n
- بین ساعت هفت تا دوازده، ساعت‌های معقول و منطقی‌تری یه. — The hours between seven and twelve are more reasonable and logical hours.

83 | 217

3394 دوازدهم dævazdæhom *twelfth* adj,n
- با 3 امتیاز به رده دوازدهم سقوط کردند. — With three points, they fell to twelfth place.

70 | 406

3395 مرده morde *dead, lifeless* adj,n
- ساکنان تپه ارسطو مردگانشان را در کنار خود دفن می‌کردند. — Aristotle Hill residents buried their dead beside them.

62 | 544

3396 دایی daji *maternal uncle* n,pn
- هنوز از پله‌ها بالا نرفته بودیم که در باز شد و دایی سرش را بیرون آورد. — We still hadn't gone up the stairs when the door opened and Uncle stuck his head out.

70 | 402

3397 طیف tejf *spectrum* n
- این طیف افراد مورد توجه بیشتر مدیریت شهرداری قرار گرفته. — This spectrum of individuals has garnered more attention from the municipal management.
79 | 272

3398 پیچیدگی piʃidegi *twist, complexity* n
- حتی اگر پیچیدگی‌ها را تشخیص دهند. — Even if they can recognize the complexities.
86 | 173

3399 تشکر کردن tæʃækkor kærdæn *thank* v
- مرد اول از او بطور فراوان تشکر می کند و هر دو راهشان را به طرف مسجد ادامه می دهند. — The first man thanked him a lot, and they both continued their way to the mosque.
75 | 324

3400 هیجان hæjædʒan *excitement, emotion* n
- مدیریت بر هیجانات یکی از مهارت‌های زندگی محسوب می‌شود. — Managing excitement is considered one of life's skills.
77 | 299

3401 فرنگی færængi *European, Western* adj
- لباس فرنگی بر تن داشت. — He had European clothes on.
76 | 312

3402 ناامیدی naomidi *hopelessness* n
- ازدواج آنان سرشار از یاس و ناامیدی بود. — Their marriage was full of despair and hopelessness.
89 | 136

3403 باور کردن bavær kærdæn *believe* v
- توقع داری دروغت را باور کنم؟ — Do you expect me to believe your lie?
69 | 426

3404 لهستان læhestan *Poland* pn
- دو کشور ایران و لهستان دو موافقت نامه اقتصادی امضا کردند. — The two nations of Iran and Poland have signed a pair of economic agreements.
72 | 364

3405 سگ sæg *dog* n
- گربه‌ها و سگ‌ها اشعه فرابنفش را می‌بینند. — Cats and dogs can see ultraviolet radiation.
60 | 578

3406 سازش sazeʃ *reconciliation, compromise* n
- این آدما اهل مدارا و سازش نیستند. — These people are not ones for tolerance and compromise.
84 | 195

3407 کلمبیا kolombija *Colombia* pn
- کلمبیا راهی جام جهانی شد. — Colombia is headed to the World Cup.
81 | 238

3408 بهبودی behbudi *improvement, gaining in health* n,pn
- چاوز از بهبودی‌اش خبر داد. — Chavez announced his recovery.
90 | 122

3409 بیل bil *shovel* pn
- این کار توسط بیل مکانیکی انجام خواهد گردید. — This work will be done by the mechanical shovel.
80 | 254

3410 سالیانه salijane *annually* adj,adv,n
- شرکت تنها 25 بیلیون دلار فروش سالیانه داشت. — The company alone had 25 billion dollars' worth of sales annually.
81 | 239

3411 آشکارا aʃkara *explicitly* adv
- آشکارا نظرات خود را ابراز کرده‌اند. — They have openly expressed their opinions.
90 | 116

3412 بیرون آمدن birun amædæn *emerge* v
- از دهانش بیرون می آمد. — It was coming out of his mouth.
68 | 429

3413 کنون konun *now* adv,n
- تا کنون نتوانسته ام قسم بخورم. — Till now I have not been able to make promises.
69 | 420

3414 خستگی xæstegi *fatigue* n
- خستگی مفرط روانی جسمانی. — Excessive psychological and physical exhaustion.
75 | 318

3415 فقدان feydan *loss, lack* n
- لذت فقدان رنج است. — Pleasure is the absence of pain.
74 | 336

3416 بازمانده bazmande *survivor* adj,n
- حالا فروهر اصلی که در تمامی کتیبه ها و مجسمه های باستان هست — بازمانده از باستان Now, the Faravahar which is in all of the inscriptions and statues surviving from ancient times . . .
82 | 220

3417 شیرینی ʃirini *sweet, pastry* adj,n
- بزودی شیرینی عروسی را خواهیم خورد. — Soon we will eat wedding candy.
75 | 323

3418 ناامید naomid *hopeless* adj,adv,n
- ما در مورد اینان ناامید نیستیم. — We are not despairing of them.
88 | 142

3419 والا vala, vaʔella *eminent, otherwise* adj,conj
- زود آب برسان به من والا می میرم. — Get me water soon; otherwise, I die.
68 | 436

3420 ابد æbæd *eternity* adj,n

• از داشتن گنجینه‌های طبیعی تا ابد محروم خواهیم ماند. — We will be left deprived of the natural treasures forever.

90 | 118

3421 مختصر moxtæsær *brief* adj,n

• مختصر از هر چیز می ترسم. — In short, I am afraid of everything.

79 | 267

3422 کاربردی kɑrbordi *applied, functional* adj,n

• معماری و عکاسی، به عنوان هنرهای کاربردی در نظر گرفته می‌شوند. — Architecture and photography are considered applied arts.

80 | 251

3423 جعفر dʒæʔfær *Jafar* pn

• جعفر داشت می‌خندید. — Jafar was laughing.

59 | 592

3424 تاریک tɑrik *dark* adj

• شب ها توی اتاق تاریک روی همین صندلی می نشستم. — Nights I would sit in a dark room on this very chair.

72 | 368

3425 رسمیت ræsmijjæt *state of being official/formal* n

• شناختن این گروه‌ک های مسلح و بدون رسمیت کلید حل و فصل اکثر درگیری های موجوده است. — Identifying these armed and unofficial groups is the key to resolving most of the existing conflicts.

83 | 210

3426 خالق xɑleɣ *creator* n

• خردی و کوچکی بشر در برابر خالق عظیم. — Puniness of humans in the face of the great creator.

89 | 127

3427 کوی kuj *quarter, alley, street* n

• این ناحیه دارای 3 محله کوی نصر، شهر آرا و تهران ویلا می باشد. — This region has three districts: Nasr Alley, Shahr-e Ara and Tehran Villa.

68 | 435

3428 همدلی hæmdeli *empathy, sympathy* n

• همه با هم همدلی، همفکری و همکاری می‌کنند. — Everyone is being sympathetic, likeminded, and cooperative.

79 | 269

3429 عمان ommɑn *Oman* pn

• دریای عمان و خلیج فارس محل حمل و نقل جهانی نفت محسوب می‌شود. — The Gulf of Oman and the Persian Gulf are considered the spot for global transportation of oil.

79 | 259

3430 مستحکم mostæhkæm *fortified* adj

• آیا جبهه طالبان مستحکم تر خواهد شد؟ — Will the Taliban lines become more fortified?

83 | 212

3431 قله ɣolle *peak* n

• خورشید داشت بی صدا و سنگین به سوی مغرب پایین می‌رفت تا پشت بلندترین قله پنهان شود. — The sun was quietly and heavily descending to the west to hide behind the tallest peak.

77 | 291

3432 سواد sævɑd *literacy* n,pn

• نه ، سواد ندارم. — No, I am not literate.

73 | 355

3433 سیزده sizdæh *thirteen* n

• سیزده فروردین متعلق به تیر ایزد باران است. — The thirteenth of Farvardin belonges to Tir, the god of rain.

57 | 624

3434 متعال motæʔɑl *exalted, almighty* adj

• این اراده خداوند متعال است. — This is the will of God Almighty.

77 | 287

3435 رضوی ræzævi *Razavi* adj,pn

• استان خراسان رضوی. — Razavi Khorasan Province.

85 | 181

3436 فروشگاه foruʃgɑh *shop* n

• فروشگاه‌های لوازم آرایشی در تهران ۸ برابر کتابفروشی‌ها هستند. — There are 7 times more makeup supply stores than bookstores in Tehran.

77 | 294

3437 گرجستان gordʒestɑn *Georgia* pn

• کشور گرجستان یکی از کشور های قاره اروپا است. — The nation of Georgia is one of the countries of the European continent.

79 | 264

3438 بخت bæxt *luck* n

• بخت بد ما را ببین. — Look at our bad luck!

78 | 279

3439 شاهین ʃɑhin *falcon, Shahin* pn

• این موضوع کنجکاوی پادشاه را برانگیخت و دستور داد تا پزشکان و مشاوران دربار، کاری کنند که شاهین پرواز کند. — This matter ignited the king's curiosity and he ordered the doctors and court advisers to do something so the falcon could fly.

83 | 201

3440 پویا pujɑ *dynamic* adj,pn

• ایران بزرگترین و پویاترین وزارت اطلاعات را دارد. — Iran has the largest and most dynamic Ministry of Intelligence.

83 | 204

3441 قرص ɣors *tablet* adv,n

• قرص‌های لاغری «شیشه» دارند. — Weight loss pills contain "crystal."

74 | 340

3442 اسپانیایی espanjaji *Spanish* adj,n
- گونهٔ اسپانیایی گیتار آکوستیک با عنوان «گیتار فلامنکو» شناخته می‌شود. — The Spanish version of acoustic guitar is known as "flamenco guitar."
75 | 321

3443 اصلاح کردن eslah kærdæn *reform, correct* v
- باید خودش را اصلاح کند. — He should rehabilitate himself.
90 | 114

3444 فیلیپین filipin *Philippines* pn
- حدود هفتصد هزار نفر در فیلیپین آسیب رسانده و بیش از شصت و نه هزار نفر نیز با از دست دادن خانه و کاشانه های خود در اردوگاه‌های موقت زندگی میکنند. — Approximately 700,000 people were injured in the Philippines and more than 69,000 are also living in temporary camps after losing their homes.
78 | 278

3445 لاتین latin *Latin* adj,n,pn
- در حال حاضر این کتابخانه مشتمل بر کتاب فارسی، لاتین و عربی است. — Currently, the library contains books in Arabic, Latin and Persian.
64 | 489

3446 نوزاد nowzad *newborn* n
- نوزاد شش ماهه — Six month old newborn.
74 | 340

3447 توافقنامه tævafoɣname *written agreement* n
- بر ضد توافقنامه دوم اوسلو رای داد. — He voted against the second Oslo Accord.
72 | 370

3448 باراک barak *Barack, Barak* pn
- ایهود باراک نخست وزیر اسرائیل در مورد صلح جدی نیست. — Ehud Barak, Israel's prime minister, is not serious about peace.
76 | 307

3449 ترانه tærane *song* n
- محتوای ترانه‌ها هم اغلب مردانه است. — The content of the ballads is also usually masculine.
84 | 196

3450 تپه tæppe *hill* n
- تپه ها به هم نزدیکتر شد. — The hills became closer together.
68 | 428

3451 مقصر moɣæsser *guilty* adj,n
- خودش را مقصر می دانست. — He blamed himself.
87 | 159

3452 رادیویی radijoji *radio* adj
- برنامه‌های رادیویی داعش از پایگاه نظامیان خارجی پخش می‌شود. — ISIS radio programs are broadcast from foreign military bases.
83 | 211

3453 سوری suri *Syrian* adj,n,pn
- سوری‌ها نباید به ترکیه بازگردانده شوند. — Syrians should not be returned to Turkey.
63 | 513

3454 بمباران bombaran *bombardment* n
- بمباران بیمارستان جنایت جنگی است. — Bombing hospitals is a war crime.
80 | 245

3455 نابود nabud *destroyed* adj
- تو می خواهی نابودم کنی. — Do you want to destroy me?
89 | 129

3456 برچیدن bærʃidæn *pack up, remove* adj,n
- به سرعت سفره را برمی‌چیدند و به کار ادامه می‌دادند. — They would pack up the table quickly and continue to work.
92 | 89

3457 چرخ ʧærx *wheel, turn* n
- چرخ ابزاری است گرد که کاربردهای گوناگون دارد. — The wheel is a round tool that has various uses.
76 | 297

3458 تحقیر tæhɣir *contempt* n
- او همه ما را تحقیر می کند. — He disdains all of us.
85 | 184

3459 نشان دهنده neʃandehænde *indicator* n
- لباس آن‌ها نشان دهنده شخصیتشان است. — Clothing is an indicator of their personality.
73 | 346

3460 شام ʃam *dinner* n,pn
- در این فاصله مادر سفره ی شام را مهیا می کرد. — In this season mom would prepare the dinner spread.
67 | 445

3461 اوباما obama *Obama* pn
- وی در پایان گفتگو به موضوع مذاکرات میان اوباما و روحانی نیز اشاره کرد. — At the end of the interview she also alluded to the subject of negotiations between Obama and Rowhani.
56 | 645

3462 سربازی særbazi *military service* n,pn
- به نظر من سربازی تمرین زندگی است. — In my opinion, military service is a practice for life.
85 | 180

3463 جامه dʒame *clothes* n
- به من بگو این زیباترین جامهٔ من است. — Tell me this is my loveliest garb.
87 | 149

3464 میزبانی mizbani *hospitality* n
- فدراسیون کشتی درخواست خود را برای میزبانی جام‌های جهانی ارائه داد. — The Wrestling Federation presented its request for hosting the World Cup.
75 | 308

3465 برعکس bær?æks *vice versa* adj,adv,conj

- باید اشاره کرد مصرف زیاد ویتامین در حاملگی اثرات بسیار مضر برای جنین دارد و برعکس مصرف فولیک اسید که کپسول‌های هماتینیک موجود است مفید است. — It should be mentioned that taking an excessive amount of vitamins will have very negative results on the fetus, but on the other hand taking folic acid which can be found in hematinic capsules is beneficial.
- 81 | 232

3466 موجودی mowdʒudi *stock, inventory* n

- موجودی‌ها را اعلام کنید. — Announce the inventory.
- 85 | 180

3467 شایع ʃaje? *widespread* adj

- کم اشتهایی در شرایط افسردگی کاملاً شایع است. — Lack of appetite during depression is entirely common.
- 83 | 201

3468 فروند færvænd *counter for ships and planes* n

- دو فروند هلیکوپتر در یک طرف جاده و چهار فروند در طرف دیگر جاده قرار داشت. — Two helicopters were on one side of the road and four were on the other.
- 76 | 305

3469 تردد tæræddod *coming and going* n

- ممنوعیت تردد خودرو‌های فاقد استانداردهای آلاینده مصوب. — The prohibition of car traffic lacking the approved emissions standards.
- 77 | 292

3470 شستن ʃostæn *wash* adj,n,v

- کیشا شستن زمین را تمام کرد. — Kisha finished scrubbing the ground.
- 64 | 485

3471 توأم tow?æm *linked* adj

- عدالت باید توأم با کرامت باشد. — Justice should be accompanied with dignity.
- 83 | 205

3472 رسم ræsm *custom* n

- دنیا رسم رفاقت را از یاد برده است. — The world has forgotten the tradition of companionship.
- 87 | 146

3473 خیابانی xijabani *street* adj,n,pn

- تعداد معتادان خیابانی ۱۰ برابر شده است. — The number of street addicts increased ten-fold.
- 78 | 268

3474 مملو mæmlovv *full* adj

- زندگی، مملو از تغییر و تحول است. — Life is full of change and transformation.
- 87 | 151

3475 جمال dʒæmal *beauty, Jamal* n,pn

- حکایت پادشاهی که بسیار صاحب جمال بود. — The story of a king who was very handsome.
- 84 | 194

3476 شکایت کردن ʃekajæt kærdæn *complain* v

- اردوغان از طنزپرداز آلمانی شخصاً شکایت کرد. — Erdogan personally criticized a German satirist.
- 87 | 152

3477 تبعیت tæbæ?ijjæt *following* n

- آن مکاتب و موسسه ها نیز از مقرره ها و برنامه های دولتی تبعیت می کند. — These schools and institutions also adhere to government regulations and programs.
- 84 | 186

3478 تیراندازی tirændazi *shooting* n

- به مردم تیراندازی می کنیم. — We will shoot at the people.
- 75 | 319

3479 سرپرستی særpæræsti *supervision* n

- سرپرستی دانشجویان را دکتر حمیدرضا فرهادی یکی از اساتید دانشگاه صنعتی شریف به عهده داشت. — Dr Hamidreza Farhadi, one of the professors of Sharif University of Technology, was responsible for supervising the students.
- 82 | 215

3480 ارجاع erdʒa? *reference* n

- ارجاعات از موارد مهم ساختار یک مقاله علمی است. — References are one of the important items in the structure of a scientific article.
- 79 | 259

3481 مترجم motærdʒem *translator* n

- او رسماً مترجم خانواده اش شد. — He officially became his family's translator.
- 75 | 309

3482 رشت ræʃt pn

- شهرهای بزرگ کشور مثل اصفهان تبریز مشهد کرمان رشت تهران. — Big cities of the country like Esfahan, Tabriz, Mashhad, Kerman, Rasht, and Tehran.
- 75 | 318

3483 گردهمایی gerdehæmaji *conference* n

- محل گردهمایی های سالانه مردم بوده است. — This has been the annual gathering place for people.
- 77 | 288

3484 مضاعف moza?æf *double* adj

- اهمیتی مضاعف پیدا می کند. — It will achieve double importance.
- 84 | 186

3485 اختراع extera? *invention* n

- معتقد بود به زودی دستگاهی اختراع می‌شود که می‌تواند افکار انسان را به تصویر تبدیل کند. — He believed that a device would soon be invented that could transform humans' thoughts into images.
- 82 | 220

3486 متوقف کردن motævæɣɣef kærdæn *stop* v
- بانک‌ها اعطای وام به مردم را متوقف کردند. — Banks stopped granting loans to people.
- 86 | 165

3487 مربوط بودن mærbut budæn *be relevant* v
- آنچه به ادبیات مربوط است. — That which is relevant to literature . . .
- 86 | 165

3488 سالمند salmænd *old* adj,n
- مرد سالمند و بالا بلندی که کلاه مشکی به سر دارد آهسته قدم می زند. — The tall elderly man who is wearing a black hat is walking slowly.
- 76 | 301

3489 تخصیص tæxsis *allocation* n
- در صورت تخصیص کامل این اعتبار شرکت مترو می‌تواند به فعالیت‌های خود ادامه دهد. — In case of the full allocation of the credit, Metro Company will be able to continue its activities.
- 77 | 288

3490 مونیخ munix *Munich* pn
- برنده مدال طلای المپیک مونیخ. — The Munich Olympic gold medal winner.
- 81 | 228

3491 نوروزی nowruzi *Nowruz* adj,pn
- سفره هفت‌سین از سفره‌های نوروزی است. — The haft-sin spread is one of the Nowruz tables.
- 73 | 342

3492 بستگی داشتن bæstegi daʃtæn *depend* v
- بنابراین همه چیز در دنیا به شما بستگی دارد. — Therefore, everything in the world depends on you.
- 82 | 215

3493 مقایسه کردن moɣajese kærdæn *compare* v
- این اعداد مقایسه کن. — Compare these numbers.
- 86 | 163

3494 حرفه herfe *profession* n
- حرفه روزنامه نگاری. — The journalistic profession.
- 71 | 373

3495 کارگری kargæri *labor, workers* adj,n
- حقوق کارگری تنها ۱۰ روز ماه کفاف می‌دهد. — A laborer's income covers only 10 days of living a month.
- 80 | 235

3496 جانباز dʒanbaz *disabled war veteran* adj,n
- در استان خراسان 6 هزار جانباز دارای ضایعه اعصاب و روان وجود دارند. — In Khorasan province, there are 6,000 veterans who have neurological and physiological injuries.
- 77 | 284

3497 نقاش næɣɣaʃ *painter* adj,n
- باید از نقاشهای ساختمان بپرسم. — I must ask the building's painters.
- 79 | 256

3498 لقب læɣæb *title* n
- نام و یا لقب وی ذکر نشده است. — Her name and/or nickname has not been mentioned.
- 82 | 207

3499 غالب ɣaleb *prevailing, most* adj,n,q
- بالاخره گرسنگی بر او غالب شد. — Finally hunger overcame him.
- 81 | 224

3500 الهام elham *inspiration* n,pn
- الهام گرفته ایم. — We have been inspired.
- 67 | 423

3501 اسکناس eskenas *banknote* n
- توی جیب شلوارش فقط اسکناس داشت. — In his pants pocket he only had banknotes.
- 79 | 249

3502 مغازه mæɣaze *shop* n
- کم کم از تعداد مغازه ها کم می شد. — Slowly the number of stores was decreasing.
- 70 | 382

3503 مزبور mæzbur *aforesaid* adj
- در سخنرانی مزبورش بر نکات مهمی انگشت گذاشته است. — In his aformentioned speech he pointed out important points.
- 71 | 362

3504 طب tebb *medicine* adj,n
- تحصیلات طب من شروع شد. — My medical education began.
- 81 | 227

3505 هوشیاری huʃjari *vigilance, alertness* n
- او اکنون برای بازیابی هوشیاری‌اش دارو مصرف می‌کند. — He is now on medication to recover alertness.
- 84 | 186

3506 مصادف mosadef *coinciding, meeting* adj
- اول ژانویه مصادف با دی ماه سال جاری. — The first of January coinciding with Dey month of the current year.
- 89 | 120

3507 نمادین næmadin *symbolic* adj
- در برخی جمهوری‌های آسیای میانه همچون ترکمنستان و ازبکستان حتی نشانه‌های نمادین دموکراسی هم وجود ندارد. — In some Central Asian republics, such as Turkmenistan and Uzbekistan, there are no signs of even symbolic democracy.
- 86 | 157

3508 شادمانی ʃadmani *rejoicing* n
- جشن و شادمانی خیابان های رُم را فراگرفت. — The celebrations and rejoicing spread to the streets of Rome.
- 91 | 99

3509 مفصل mæfsal, mofæssæl *joint, lengthy* adj,n
- به طور مفصل به استدلال پرداخت. — She put forth a detailed argument.
- 86 | 156

3510 ته tæh *bottom, end* n
- از ته دل دعا کرد. — He prayed from the bottom of his heart.

52 | 706

3511 شانزدهم ʃɑnzdæhom *sixteenth* adj,n
- امروز شانزدهم فروردین، برابر با پنج آوریل، ساعت نه شب است. — Today is the 16th of Farvardin, which is equivalent to April 5th, at nine o'clock at night.

75 | 304

3512 تب tæb *fever* n
- بله، تب داری. — Yes, you have a fever.

84 | 190

3513 اعتصاب eʔtesab *strike* n
- تصمیم گرفته است به اعتصاب غذا پایان دهد. — He decided to end the hunger strike.

62 | 508

3514 تعلق داشتن tæʔæloɣ dɑʃtæn *belong* v
- فراموش میکنند به کجای افغانستان تعلق دارند شمالش یا جنوب. — They forget what part of Afghanistan they belong to, the north or the south.

84 | 182

3515 پنداشتن pendɑʃtæn *suppose* adj,n,v
- سربازانش مردمش جوانانش حتی کودکانش آمریکا را برترین و بزرگترین کشور دنیا میپندارند. — Its soldiers, its people, its youth, even its children, consider America the best and greatest country in the world.

77 | 280

3516 هجدهم hedʒdæhom *eighteenth* adj,n
- جام هجدهم والیبال آسیا با ۱۶ تیم برگزار میشود. — The eighteenth Asian Volleyball Cup will be held with 16 teams.

80 | 234

3517 تئاتر teʔɑtr *theater* n
- از تئاتر خوشم نمیآد. — I do not like theater.

59 | 553

3518 عهد æhd *promise, treaty* n
- با خدای خود عهد بسته ام. — I have made a covenant with God himself.

72 | 355

3519 گرگان gorgɑn *Gorgan* pn
- دوباره به گرگان بازگشتم و مدتی در آن شهر ماندم. — I returned to Gorgan, and stayed for a while in that city.

78 | 267

3520 مراد morɑd *desire, Morad* n,pn
- جناب آقای مراد عزیز. — Dear Mr. Morad.

82 | 210

3521 تاکسی tɑksi *taxi* n
- راننده تاکسی بود. — He was a taxi driver.

74 | 324

3522 متحمل motæhæmmel *suffering* adj
- متحمل زیانهای فراوانی میشوند. — They will sustain immense losses.

84 | 183

3523 خونین xunin *bloody* adj
- ابرهای سرگردان غروب، خونین به نظر میرسند. — The clouds wandering about the sunset look bloody.

79 | 253

3524 کوبا kuba *Cuba* pn
- مجمع ملی کوبا لایحه اصلاحات در اقتصاد کمونیستی را تصویب کرد. — The National Assembly of Cuba ratified the bill for reforms in its communist economy.

71 | 370

3525 فقه feɣh *Islamic law* n
- بر همین اساس در فقه اسلامی زرتشتیان در کنار یهودیان و مسیحیان قرار گرفته اند. — On the same grounds, in Islamic jurisprudence, Zoroastrians are positioned next to Jews and Christians.

76 | 286

3526 صفوی sæfævi *Safavid* adj,pn
- اکنون این مسجد صفوی توسط کارشناسان میراث فرهنگی ایران مرمت و ساماندهی میشود. — Now the Safavid mosque is being reconstructed and renovated by experts in Iran's Cultural Heritage.

74 | 316

3527 شرعی ʃærʔi *religiously correct* adj
- ایشان رعایت قانون را یک تکلیف شرعی میدانستند. — He considered obeying the law a religious duty.

73 | 330

3528 منحرف monhæref *deviant* adj
- آقای بی گناهی که منحرف شد. — A sinless man who was perverted.

85 | 170

3529 تصدی tæsæddi *taking charge* n
- صادقلو از فعالان ستاد روحانی در انتخابات ریاست جمهوری بوده و برای تصدی کرسی استانداری گلستان به عنوان یکی از سه گزینه مورد نظر اصلاح طلبان استان معرفی شده بود. — Sadeghloo was one of the people active on Rowhani's staff during the presidential elections, and was presented as one of the three choices being considered by the reformists in the province for the governorship of Golestan.

79 | 252

3530 ضوابط zævabet *criteria* n
- حفظ ضوابط و مقررات از هر چیزی مهم تر است. — Maintaining criteria and regulations is more important than anything.

72 | 342

3531 دارنده dɑrænde *possessor* adj,n
- دارندگان کارت حرفهای روزنامهنگاری «بیمه» میشوند. — Professional journalist card holders will receive "insurance."

78 | 260

22 Sports

Rank	Headword	Pronunciation	Gloss	Rank	Headword	Pronunciation	Gloss
39	دو	dow	running	1895	بازیگر	bazigær	player
121	تیم	tim	team	1905	مدال	medal	medal
285	بازی	bazi	game, play	2031	داور	davær	referee
372	گل	gol	goal	2105	پاس	pas	pass
384	مسابقه	mosabeγe	competition	2371	خطا	xæta	foul
490	فوتبال	futbal	soccer	2400	نقره	noγre	silver
569	استقلال	esteγlal	Esteghlal F.C.	2549	بسکتبال	bæsketbal	basketball
688	جام	dʒam	cup	2586	داوری	daværi	refereeing
823	کشتی	koʃti	wrestling	2595	شنا	ʃena	swimming
830	بازیکن	bazikon	player	2647	پرسپولیس	perspolis	Persepolis F.C.
880	ورزشی	værzeʃi	athletic, sporty	2774	مهاجم	mohadʒem	striker, forward
923	قهرمانی	γæhremani	championship	3025	سرمربی	særmoræbbi	head coach
938	طلا	tæla	gold	3115	برنز	boronz	bronze
961	ورزش	værzeʃ	sport	3478	تیر اندازی	tirændazi	shooting
1096	ذخیره	zæxire	reserve	3740	تنیس	tenis	tennis
1102	دروازه	dærvaze	goal	3885	فیفا	fifa	FIFA
1162	قهرمان	γæhreman	champion	4141	فوتسال	futsal	indoor soccer
1282	مربی	moræbbi	coach	4447	استخر	estæxr	pool
1385	جایزه	dʒajeze	award	4929	هندبال	hændbal	handball
1396	برنده	bærænde	winner	5190	بازنده	bazænde	loser
1616	توپ	tup	ball	5569	دروازه‌بان	dærvazeban	goalkeeper
1722	ورزشکار	værzeʃkar	athlete	10257	زورخانه	zurxane	Iranian traditional gym
1730	والیبال	valibal	volleyball	17958	والیبالیست	valibalist	volleyball player
1787	ورزشگاه	værzeʃgah	stadium				
1832	لیگ	lig	league				

3532 اشتیاق eʃtijaγ *eagerness* n
- او فهمید که اشتیاق می‌تواند به طلا تبدیل شود. — He realized that avidity can be turned into gold.
- 86 | 162

3533 جاذبه dʒazebe *attraction* n
- سه هزار جاذبه گردشگری در کشور شناسایی شد. — Three thousand tourist attractions in the country were identified.
- 75 | 305

3534 زادگاه zadgah *birthplace* n
- در کنار جاده ، چراغ های زادگاهش سوسو می زنند. — On the side of the road the lights of his birthplace were flickering.
- 84 | 189

3535 ختم xætm *completing* n
- ترقی شما در زندگی از ذهن‌تان شروع و به همانجا ختم می‌شود. — Your advancement in life begins and ends with your mentality.
- 76 | 293

3536 به ثمر رساندن be sæmær resandæn *bear fruit, achieve* v
- به ثمر رساندن اهداف سیاست خارجه آمریکا در این کشور . . . — To achieve America's foreign policy objectives in this country . . .
- 81 | 219

3537 حوالی hævali *vicinity* n
- در حوالی میدان ، بساطش را پهن کرده بود ؛ فریب می فروخت. — He had laid out his stall on the outskirts of the square and was selling deception.
- 82 | 211

3538 انصاف ensaf *equity* n
- انصاف داشته باشید، حاجی. — Be fair, Hajji.
87 | 148

3539 پیراهن pirahæn *shirt* n
- پیراهن مرا بگیر. — Take my shirt.
75 | 302

3540 تهرانی tehrani *Tehrani* adj,pn
- ۶۷٪ تهرانی‌ها فارس و فارسی زبان هستند. — 67% of Tehranis are Persian and speak Persian.
73 | 331

3541 عمران omran *construction* n,pn
- ارقام سنگینی برای عمران و آبادانی هزینه می‌شود. — Heavy figures are being spent on construction and development.
77 | 278

3542 قاجار γadʒar *Qajar* adj,pn
- باغ وزیر حجت آباد رضوانشهر در زمان قاجار و توسط میرزا محمد مستوفی بنا شده. — The Hojjat Abad-e Vazir gardens of Rezvanshahr were built during the Qajar period by Mirza Mohammad Mostowfi.
73 | 336

3543 تاکتیک taktik *tactic* n
- این تاکتیک وی چه مطلبی را می رساند؟ — What question does this tactic of his convey?
83 | 190

3544 تشییع tæʃjiʔ *accompanying* n
- در مراسم تشییع جنازه پایش بر روی یخها سرخورد. — During the funeral ceremony he slid on the ice.
88 | 134

3545 بکارگیری bekargiri *utilization, application, employment* n
- مجلس بکارگیری بازنشستگان در دستگاه‌ها را ممنوع کرد. — Parliament banned the employment of retirees in institutions.
86 | 163

3546 برگرفته bærgerefte *taken up, adapted* adj,n
- لایحه حمایت از خانواده برگرفته از قرآن است. — The Family Protection Bill is adapted from the Quran.
86 | 159

3547 خریدار xæridar *buyer* n
- هند دومین خریدار بزرگ نفت ایران شد. — India became the second-largest purchaser of Iran's oil.
75 | 299

3548 زیربنایی zirbænaji *infrastructural* adj,n
- مسایل زیربنایی وجود دارند. — Issues exist with infrastructure.
83 | 193

3549 برآورد bæravord *estimate* n
- برآوردی از میزان خسارت طوفان و سیل به محیط زیست تهران نداریم. — We do not have any estimate of the storm and flood damage to Tehran's environment.
67 | 420

3550 سرگرم særgærm *amused, busy* adj
- دکتر ملک چنان سرگرم بیمارستان و بیماران مختلف شده بود که به هیچ وجه گذر روزهای هفته را متوجه نمی شد. — Doctor Malek had become so occupied with the hospital and the various patients that he was oblivious to the passing of days.
78 | 263

3551 معطوف mæʔtuf *inclined, focused* adj
- عملکرد آن‌ها خیلی معطوف به نتیجه نیست. — Their performance is not focused on the result.
79 | 247

3552 سودان sudan *Sudan* pn
- کودتا در سودان ناکام ماند — Coup in Sudan failed.
61 | 516

3553 ازا eza *stead, exchange* n
- یعنی به ازا هر 27 دستگاه خودرو یک تصادف داشته ایم. — This means that for each 27 vehicles we have had an accident.
75 | 302

3554 هرات hærat, herat *Herat* pn
- فرماندار استان هرات. — Governor of Herat Province.
45 | 834

3555 فینال final *final* n
- با شکست حریفی لهستانی خود راهی دیدار فینال شد. — With the defeat of his Polish adversary, he headed to the final match.
62 | 494

3556 باقری baγeri *Bagheri* pn
- گل ایران را کریم باقری به ثمر رساند. — Karim Bagheri scored Iran's goal.
84 | 186

3557 عرضه کردن ærze kærdæn *present, offer, supply* v
- عرضه کردن مواد غذایی مشخص. — Supplying specific food products.
81 | 225

3558 متأثر motæʔæsser *saddened, affected by* adj
- زبان پالمیری نیز متأثر از عربی بود. — The language of Palmyra was also affected by Arabic.
81 | 215

3559 عکاس ækkas *photographer* adj,n
- عکاس به تندی عکس ها را گرفت. — The photographer was rapidly taking pictures.
80 | 229

3560 یخ *jæx ice* n
- چوب خشک و مثل یخ سرد شده است. — The wood has become dry and cold as ice.
78 | 257

3561 ناگهانی *nagæhani sudden* adj
- از زمان مرگ ناگهانی پدر و مادرشان با هم زندگی می‌کنند. — Since the sudden death of their parents they are living together.
80 | 237

3562 حمام *hæmmam bath, bathroom* n
- او رفت در حمام را باز کرد. — He went and opened the door of the bathroom.
68 | 408

3563 کمک گرفتن *komæk gereftæn get help* v
- از طریق کمک گرفتن از برخی کشورهای خارجی. — Through getting help from some foreign countries.
90 | 105

3564 باطل *batel null, void* adj,n
- زندگی که در آن خدا مرکز نباشد بی هدف و باطل است. — Life that does not have God at its center is meaningless and vain.
76 | 282

3565 گفتار *goftar speech* n
- گفتار بی‌فایده بود. — Talking was useless.
69 | 383

3566 انشا *enʃa composition* n
- معلم گفته بود بنویسیم انشا. — The teacher had said that we should write a composition.
92 | 87

3567 آستانه *astane threshold* n
- در آستانه مرگ هستم. — I am on the threshold of death.
68 | 396

3568 قاسمی *γasemi Ghasemi* pn
- ثریا قاسمی سال ۱۳۱۹ در تهران متولد شد. — Soraya Ghasemi was born in 1319 in Tehran.
81 | 221

3569 رزمنده *ræzmænde warrior* adj,n
- بعد از نماز حضرت آیت الله صدوقی برای رزمنده ها صحبت می کردند. — After prayers, His Holiness Ayatollah Sadoughi spoke to combatants.
83 | 196

3570 انس *ons friendship, intimacy* n
- از کودکی با هنر انس داشت. — From childhood, he was interested in art.
91 | 97

3571 استثنایی *estesnaji exceptional* adj,n
- سردار سلیمانی یک پدیده استثنایی است. — General Soleimani is an exceptional phenomenon.
82 | 201

3572 صمیمانه *sæmimane sincerely* adj,adv
- به‌حضور حضرتعالی‌صمیمانه‌تبریک‌میگویم. — I sincerely extend my congratulations to your honor.
86 | 153

3573 صداقت *sedaγæt honesty* n
- او عمرش را با صداقت و فعالیت می گذراند. — He spends his life with integrity and activity.
82 | 207

3574 خورشیدی *xorʃidi solar* adj,n,pn
- بزرگترین نیروگاه خورشیدی جهان در دبی ساخته می‌شود. — The world's largest solar power plant will be built in Dubai.
81 | 223

3575 بازنشستگی *bazneʃæstegi retirement* n
- خدمات صندوق بازنشستگی بهبود نمی‌یابد. — Pension Fund services are not improving.
79 | 250

3576 فراموشی *færamuʃi oblivion, amnesia* n
- برای درمان فراموشی چه باید کرد؟ — What can be done to treat amnesia?
83 | 188

3577 کنسرت *konsert concert* n
- کنسرت در تالار حافظ شهر شیراز برگزار خواهد شد. — The concert will be held in Hafez Hall in the city of Shiraz.
78 | 252

3578 سفارتخانه *sefaræetxane embassy* n
- گاردین امروز خبری با عنوان بازگشایی سفارتخانه های ایران و لندن هموار شد را به عنوان تیتر خود بر گزید. — Today, the Guardian selected an article with the title "Way Paved for the Reopening of the Embassies in Iran and London" as its headline.
84 | 178

3579 کام *kam palate, goal, com* n
- شیرینی این پیروزی، کام مردان را نیز شیرین خواهد کرد. — Sweetness of this victory will also sweeten men's palates.
80 | 232

3580 بیابان *bijaban desert* n,pn
- اطراف مدرسه بیابان بود. — Around the school was a desert.
76 | 289

3581 نامدار *namdar famous* adj,n
- برخی از کاندیداهایی که نامدار نیز هستند. — Some of the candidates who are famous too.
88 | 129

3582 دیدنی *didæni worth watching, spectacular* adj
- روستای اروشکی یکی از دیدنی‌ترین و زیباترین روستاهای دیلمان است. — Arushki is one of the most spectacular and the most beautiful villages in Daylaman.
67 | 414

3583 زیستی *zisti life, vital, biological* adj
- تأثیر زیستی آن‌ها چندان مشخص نیست. — Their biological effects are not that clear.
81 | 216

3584 راهپیمایی rɑhpejmɑji *march, rally* n
- راهپیمایی روز قدس آغاز شد. — The Jerusalem Day rally began.

69 | 380

3585 مصرف شدن mæsræf ʃodæn *be consumed* v
- تعداد سیگارهایی که در حال مصرف شدن است قاچاق می‌باشد. — A number of cigarettes that are consumed are smuggled.

85 | 162

3586 فرماندار færmɑndɑr *governor* n
- تغییر فرمانداران یا استانداران ربطی به انتخابات ندارد. — The change in governors has no connection with the elections.

80 | 231

3587 مصرفی mæsræfi *consumer* adj
- واردات کالاهای مصرفی از آمریکا ممنوع است. — The importation of consumer goods from America is banned.

78 | 259

3588 نصر næsr *Nasr, help* n,pn
- نصر نخستین کسی بود که ملاصدرا را به جهان انگلیسی زبان معرّفی کرد. — Nasr was the first person who introduced Mulla Sadra to the English-speaking world.

89 | 120

3589 صرفه‌جویی serfedʒuji *economizing, conservation* n
- صرفه‌جویی لازم است. — Conservation is necessary.

79 | 240

3590 اتفاقاً ettefɑqæn *by chance, in fact* adv
- اتفاقاً در آن روز، پیامبر خانه نبود. — In fact, on that day, the prophet was not home.

69 | 383

3591 ملاک melɑk, mællɑk *criterion, landowner* n
- داشتن خودرو و خانه ملاک قطع یارانه‌ها نیست. — Auto and home ownership is not a criterion for cutting subsidies.

80 | 234

3592 کفایت kefɑjæt *adequacy* n
- البته این اهرم به تنهایی کفایت نمی‌کند. — Of course by itself this leverage will not suffice.

86 | 160

3593 فاسد fɑsed *rotten, corrupt* adj
- بحران غذایی به خاطر مدیریت فاسد جهانی است. — The food crisis is due to corrupt global management.

82 | 206

3594 مارک mɑrk *mark, brand* n,pn
- اکثر این فرآورده‌های غیربهداشتی حتی در داخل کشور تولید و با مارک‌های خارجی روانه فروشگاه‌ها می‌شود. — Most of these non-hygienic products are even produced inside the country, and sent to stores as foreign brands.

77 | 263

3595 طراح tærrɑh *designer* n
- طراح لباس های شیک و گران قیمت. — The designer of chic and expensive clothing.

78 | 259

3596 ذوب zowb *fusion, melting* adj,n
- با ذوب کردن برف آب تهیه کردیم. — We procured water by melting snow.

77 | 261

3597 باختری bɑxtæri *western, Bactrian* adj
- زبان بلخی یا باختری زبانی منقرض شده است. — The language of Balkh, or Bactrian, is an extinct language.

74 | 303

3598 زمانه zæmɑne *era, age* n
- دوره زمانه عوض شده است. — The times have changed.

82 | 208

3599 سازندگی sɑzændegi *development, construction* n
- اولویت اصلی بسیج سازندگی چیست؟ — What is the main priority of Basij Construction?

69 | 384

3600 نصف nesf *half* n
- نامزد بیش از نصف آراء را بدست آورد. — The candidate received more than half the votes.

70 | 370

3601 دیپلمات diplomɑt *diplomat* n
- دیپلمات‌های سعودی خاک ایران را ترک کردند. — Saudi diplomats left Iranian soil.

79 | 245

3602 متمادی motæmɑdi *protracted, long* adj
- منابع نامشروعی که طی سالیان متمادی در داخل کسب کرده بودند. — The illegal sources that they had gained locally over many years.

90 | 112

3603 چهارده tʃæhɑrdæh *fourteen* n
- بازگشت آیت‌الله خمینی به ایران پس از چهارده سال تبعید — Ayatollah Khomeini's return to Iran after fourteen years of exile.

60 | 520

3604 روزنامه‌نگار ruznɑmenegɑr *journalist* n
- عصر آن روز، روزنامه‌نگار به آن محل برگشت و متوجه شد که کلاه مرد کور پر از سکه و اسکناس شده است. — That evening, the journalist returned to that place and realized the blind man's hat had been filled with coins and bills.

76 | 284

3605 تحویل دادن tæhvil dɑdæn *deliver, hand* over v
- من برگه امتحانی را تحویل دادم و سوال آخر را بی‌جواب گذاشتم. — I turned in my answer sheet and left the last answer blank.

85 | 171

3606 گمنام gomnam *unknown* adj
- در این انتخابات نیز حضور چهره‌های گمنام می‌تواند موجب تحول و شگفتی شود. — In these elections, the presence of unknown faces can cause change and surprise.
91 | 95

3607 تصاحب tæsahob *taking possession* n
- پس از آن نیروهای شوروی شهر‌بند تصاحب کردند. — After that, the Soviet forces took over the city.
89 | 114

3608 تألیف tæʔlif *compilation* n
- لسان العرب، تألیف ابن منظور، جامع‌ترین فرهنگ زبان عربی که در قرن هفتم هجری تدوین یافته است. — *The Arabic Language*, compiled by Ibn Manzur, was the most comprehensive Arabic dictionary compiled in the 7th century AH.
76 | 276

3609 بهشتی beheʃti *heavenly, Beheshti* adj,pn
- بهشتی — این استاد جدید هم امیدی نداشت. — Beheshti also didn't have any hope in this new professor.
77 | 258

3610 مبهم mobhæm *ambiguous* adj
- بچه های کلاس هم مانند معلم از این نقاشی مبهم تعجب کردند. — Like the teacher, the students in the class were surprised by the ambiguous painting.
82 | 200

3611 پذیرا pæzira *welcoming* adj
- سالانه صدها هزار مسافر را پذیرا میشود. — Hundreds of thousands of travelers are received annually.
85 | 164

3612 ارمغان ærmæɣan *souvenir* n
- بهترین ارمغان حج معرفت و خودشناسی است. — The best souvenir of Hajj is wisdom and self-discovery.
84 | 177

3613 اشغالی eʃɣali *occupied* adj
- عثمانیها به ناچار پیرانشهر و دیگر مناطق اشغالی ایران را تخلیه کردند. — The Ottomans had to evacuate Piranshahr and other occupied regions of Iran.
62 | 483

3614 پنالتی penalti *penalty* n
- علی کریمی پنالتی را از دست داد. — Ali Karimi missed the penalty.
81 | 207

3615 زنگ zæng *bell, ring* n
- صبح پنج شنبه خودم زنگ زدم. — I myself called on Thursday morning.
68 | 390

3616 ششصد ʃeʃsæd *six hundred* n
- شش هزار و ششصد و شصت و شش شیشه شراب شکست. — Six thousand six hundred and sixty six bottles of wine broke.
52 | 654

3617 هوشیار huʃjar *alert* adj
- رییس جمهور اسبق آمریکا هوشیار است. — The former president of the United States is astute.
88 | 131

3618 حسینیه hosejnijje *assembly hall* n
- در کنار مسجد حسینیه نیز احداث شده است. — Next to the mosque, a Hoseinie was built.
90 | 108

3619 تعلیق tæʔliɣ *suspension* n
- این مراسم به حالت تعلیق درآمده. — This ceremony has been suspended.
76 | 272

3620 قلمرو ɣælæmrow *realm* n
- یورشی ناگهانی را به قلمرو اروپا و بازارهای نوظهور آغاز کرده است. — A sudden push to European territory and emerging markets has begun.
73 | 315

3621 محسوس mæhsus *perceptible* adj
- تغییرات حالا کاملاً محسوس و مشهود بودند. — The changes were now entirely tangible and obvious.
83 | 184

3622 نیکی niki *goodness, good deed* n,pn
- با این حال، از آنان به نیکی یاد میشود. — But they have left behind a good reputation.
89 | 116

3623 راضی بودن razi budæn *be satisfied* v
- پدرش از او راضی نبود. — His father was not happy with him.
77 | 262

3624 معمار meʔmar *architect* n
- معماران برگزیده معرفی می‌شوند. — Hand-picked architects will be introduced.
82 | 194

3625 شرف ʃæræf *honor* n,pn
- رقاصی باز شرف دارد. — Dancing is honorable again.
87 | 139

3626 توسل tævæssol *resorting* n
- توسل به زور در ایران را باید کنار گذاشت. — They should stop resorting to force in Iran.
86 | 146

3627 کرامت kæramæt *generosity, dignity* n
- غیرمسلمانان هم صاحب کرامت و حقوق هستند. — Non-Muslims have dignity and rights too.
84 | 176

3628 حذفی hæzfi *elimination, playoff* adj
- جام حذفی فوتبال ایران نام مسابقات فوتبال در ایران است. — The Iranian Football Elimination Cup is the name of a football playoff competition in Iran.

78 | 253

3629 گنبد gombæd *dome* n,pn
- این بنای مستطیل شکل با گنبد کبود دارای یک شبستان و پلکانی تا قاعده گنبد در حیاط می باشد. — This rectangular building with a blue dome has a bedchamber with a stairway to the base of the dome in the courtyard.

68 | 385

3630 رستوران restoran *restaurant* n
- سه جوان موتور سیکلت سوار هم به رستوران آمدند. — Three young people riding motorcycles also came to the restaurant.

79 | 241

3631 اجاره edʒare *rent* n
- در طبقه سوم این خانه اتاق اجاره داده می شود. — A room is rented out on the third floor of this house.

82 | 204

3632 اکتشاف ektefaf *exploration* n
- در طول تاریخ روشهای مختلفی برای اکتشاف نفت بکار برده شده است. — Throughout history, various methods have been used to discover oil.

80 | 223

3633 چربی tʃærbi *fat* n
- لبنیات پرچربی ممکن است از دیابت پیشگیری کند. — Fatty dairy products may prevent diabetes.

74 | 308

3634 مؤمن moʔmen *devout* adj,n
- نقطهٔ آغاز خرابی یک آدم مؤمن کجاست؟ — Where is the starting point of failure for a person of faith?

76 | 277

3635 گمرکی gomroki *customs* adj
- برای گرفتن پروانه سبز گمرکی از سایت چه اقداماتی باید انجام داد؟ — What steps must be taken in order to get the green customs file from the website?

81 | 213

3636 اسبق æsbæɣ *preceding* adj
- نخست وزیر اسبق فرانسه. — Former French prime minister.

84 | 169

3637 غریب ɣærib *strange* adj,n,pn
- حرفهای غریب و عجیب زد. — He spoke strange words.

76 | 272

3638 منشی monʃi *secretary* n,pn
- او همچنین برای نوشتن و تایپ گزارشاتش به کمک یک منشی نیاز داشت. — He also needed a secretary to help him write and type his reports.

80 | 228

3639 شانه ʃane *comb, shoulder* n
- شانه اش را تا کنار گوش بالا کشید. — She stretched her shoulder up to the edge of her ear.

68 | 388

3640 معاف moʔaf *exempt* adj
- آپارتمان من معاف از هر افزایش سکونتی شده. — My apartment has been exempted from any residential increase.

88 | 130

3641 بهره وری bæhreværi *productivity* n
- این سیستم موجب افزایش بهره وری می شود. — The system leads to an increase in productivity.

80 | 226

3642 صنف senf *guild, trade* n
- اگر افراد زیادی در یک صنف مشکلی را مطرح میکنند باید به نظر آنها احترام بگذاریم. — If many people in a trade raise a problem then we must respect their opinion.

79 | 241

3643 چشمه tʃeʃme *spring* n
- چشمه آبگرم مکانی است که به صورت مداوم آب گرم یا داغ از زمین خارج میشود. — A hot spring is a place where warm or hot water continuously comes out of the ground.

70 | 358

3644 خراب xærab *broken, demolished* adj
- ساختمان دارد خراب می شود. — The building is being destroyed.

64 | 446

3645 آگاه بودن agah budæn *be aware* v
- از میان مراجعه کنندگان اکثریت آنها از خطر ازدواج فامیلی آگاه بودند. — The majority of visitors were aware of the risk of consanguineous marriage.

88 | 129

3646 محال mohʃl *impossible* adj,n
- گفتم شیطان چنان در پوست تو رفته است که بتوان با تو دو کلمه حرف حساب زد. — I said that the Devil is so deep inside your skin that it's impossible to be able to speak two whole words to you.

87 | 138

3647 بوستان bustan *orchard* n,pn
- میدانی فرق گلستان و بوستان چیست؟ — Do you know what the difference between between the Golestan and Bustan is?

74 | 302

3648 استعمار esteʔmar *colonialism* n
- استعمار غرب در خاورمیانه. — Western colonialism in the Middle East.

80 | 228

3649 احتیاط ehtijat *caution* n
- در گوشه ای ایستادم و به احتیاط دستمال را باز کردم. — I stood in a corner and carefully opened the handkerchief.
82 | 196

3650 قائل بودن qael budæn *believe, profess* v
- او برای تکامل تکنولوژی اهمیت زیادی قائل است. — He places great importance on technology development.
84 | 179

3651 خرسندی xorsændi *satisfaction, contentment* n
- نتایج انتخابات ونزوئلا موجب خرسندی ملت و دولت ایران شد. — The Venezuela election results brought joy to the Iranian nation and government.
87 | 139

3652 تظاهرکننده tæzahor konænde *protester* n
- پلیس هنگ کنگ به سوی تظاهرکنندگان گاز اشک آور شلیک کرد. — The Hong Kong police fired tear gas at demonstrators.
54 | 613

3653 مطهر motæhhær *pure, holy* adj,pn
- در حرم مطهر بنیانگذار جمهوری اسلامی ایران. — In the holy shrine of the founder of the Islamic Republic of Iran.
79 | 231

3654 تمدنی tæmæddoni *civilization* adj,n
- به این گرایش تمدنی شان افتخار می‌کنند. — They are proud of this trend of their civilization.
83 | 186

3655 پیشروی piʃrævi *progress* adj,n
- ترکیه از پیشروی های کردها در برابر داعش در سوریه نگران است. — Turkey is concerned about the Kurds' advancement against ISIS in Syria.
87 | 138

3656 تکنیک teknik *technique* n
- او همواره تکنیک ها و تاکتیک های خود را می سنجد. — He is always testing his techniques and tactics.
73 | 307

3657 ری rej *Rey* pn
- در اطراف شهر ری مسجدی بود. — Around Rey city there was a mosque.
78 | 248

3658 اهل بیت æhle bejt *Mohammad's family* n
- این مردی که مخلص اهل بیت پیغمبر است. — This man who is devoted to the household of the Prophet.
85 | 161

3659 پالایشگاه palajeʃgah *refinery* n
- همچنین بخش دیگری از نفت خام مورد نیاز این پالایشگاه از منابع کشورهای آسیای میانه فراهم می شود. — And another part of this refinery's required crude oil is provided by resources in Central Asian countries.
72 | 324

3660 گور gur *tomb* n,pn
- این سه گور دسته جمعی متعلق به دوره صدام است. — These three mass graves belong to Saddam's period.
73 | 309

3661 دیار dijar *land* n
- در این دیار به کسی امیدی نداریم. — In this land we have no hope for anyone.
82 | 193

3662 معافیت moʔafijjæt *exemption* n
- معافیت گمرکی برای حجاج. — Customs exemptions for pilgrims.
79 | 238

3663 مخابراتی moxaberati *telecommunication* adj
- تمامی دکل‌های مخابراتی تهران بررسی خواهد شد. — All of Tehran's cell towers will be examined.
82 | 192

3664 تفکیک tæfkik *separation* n
- تفکیک دین از حکومت و حکومت از دین. — The separation of religion from government and government from religion.
74 | 294

3665 خواجه xadʒe *eunuch, master* n,pn
- روزی شاه خواجه را دستگیر کرد و دست و پایش را بست. — One day the king had the eunuch arrested and his hands and feet bound.
73 | 310

3666 عبادت ebadæt *worship* n
- به عبادت مشغول باشد. — He should occupy himself with worship.
73 | 307

3667 پافشاری pafeʃari *insistence, persistence* n
- دمشق بر حفظ حقوق کامل خود پافشاری می‌کند. — Damascus is insisting on maintaining its full rights.
88 | 129

3668 همسو hæmsu *in line with* adj
- با ما در افکار همسو نیستند. — They are not aligned with our thinking.
88 | 123

3669 مغایر moɣajer *contrary* adj
- دولت‌هایی که عموماً مغایر با دمکراسی و عدالت اجتماعی هستند. — They are governments that are generally opposed to democracy and social justice.
85 | 157

3670 موش muʃ *mouse, rat* n,pn
- چند روز پیش موش آمد تو آشپزخانه ما. — A few days ago the mouse came into our kitchen.
69 | 367

3671 صحرا sæhra *fields, desert* n
- تو هم دختر را بفرست با آنها برود به صحرا. — You too send your daughter to the desert with them.
76 | 274

3672 قبیله yæbile *tribe* n
- در نتیجه مردم مسلمان از هر قوم و قبیله و مذهب و نژاد و زبانی هم در کشورهای خود باید وحدت و همبستگی ملی خود را حفظ و تقویت کنند. — In conclusion, Muslims of every ethnicity, tribe, religion, race, and language must preserve and strengthen national unity and solidarity in their own countries.
- 77 | 261

3673 سوره sure *sura* n
- در قرآن از نور یاد شده و سوره ای به همین نام در آن وجود دارد. — In the Koran light was mentioned and there is a chapter by the same name.
- 66 | 408

3674 ماهانه mahane *monthly* adj,adv,n
- شما ماهانه چقدر حقوق دریافت می کنی؟ — How much is your monthly salary?
- 87 | 142

3675 آزار azar *torture, torment* n
- بچههایتان واقعاً دارند همه را آزار میدهند. — Your children are really vexing everybody.
- 75 | 280

3676 داریوش darjuʃ *Darius* pn
- با مرگ داریوش و پیروزی اسکندر. — With Darius's death and Alexander's conquest.
- 75 | 277

3677 تور tur *net, tour* n
- پنجرهها تور سیمی دارند. — The windows have screens.
- 91 | 93

3678 کیف kif, kejf *bag, intoxication* n,pn
- سیما هنوز نمیداند یک پسربچه در کیف مادر او یک زنجیر طلا گذاشته تا خودش را از اتهام دزدی خلاص کند. — Sima still doesn't know that a boy has placed a gold chain in his mother's purse to save himself from accusations of theft.
- 67 | 391

3679 لیبرال liberal *liberal* adj,n
- سوسیالیستها نگران لیبرالتر شدن قوانین هستند. — Socialists are concerned about laws becoming more liberal.
- 85 | 156

3680 ژنو ʒenev *Geneva* pn
- شنیدهام نردهای که دور دریاچه شهر ژنو است بیش از صد سال پیش کار گذاشته شده و هنوز هم صحیح و سالم به جای خودش باقی است. — I've heard that the fence around Lake Geneva was put into place more than a hundred years ago, and is still in good working order.
- 86 | 148

3681 ایدز ejdz *AIDS* n
- در مورد بیماری ایدز و هپاتیت . . . — Regarding AIDS and hepatitis . . .
- 69 | 365

3682 خیانت xijanæt *treachery* n
- این گونه اقدامات امنیت کشور را به خطر انداخته و خیانت محسوب میگردد. — This type of action has put the security of the nation in danger and is considered treason.
- 78 | 239

3683 فقره fæɣære *vertebra, case, incidence* n
- وقوع یک فقره قتل به کلانتری انقلاب اطلاع داده شد. — One count of murder was reported to the Enghelab police station.
- 80 | 213

3684 دزد dozd *thief* n
- من دزد نیستم. — I am not a thief.
- 65 | 422

3685 تزیین tæzjin *decoration* n
- در قاب پنجره ها با شیشه های رنگی تزیین گردیده اند. — The window frames are decorated with colored glass.
- 86 | 145

3686 ضریب zærib *factor, ratio, index* n
- ضریب گلیسمیک چیست؟ — What is glycemic index?
- 74 | 292

3687 انزلی ænzæli *Anzali* pn
- پسماندها، تالاب انزلی را تخریب میکند. — Waste is destroying the Anzali Wetlands.
- 84 | 176

3688 کالیفرنیا kalifornija *California* pn
- اهل کالیفرنیایین؟ — Are you from California?
- 80 | 224

3689 مبدأ mæbdæʔ *origin* n
- برج میلاد مبدأ سفرهای تهرانگردی میشود. — Milad Tower is becoming the starting point for touring Tehran.
- 81 | 208

3690 مبدل mobæddæl *transformed* adj,n
- آنوقت جایی در تهران پنهان می شدم و با لباس مبدل خودم را به جنوب می رساندم. — At that point I was hiding somewhere in Tehran and with a change of clothes, I got myself to the South.
- 80 | 223

3691 مادری mɑdæri *maternal* adj,n
- من از سرزمینهای پدری و مادری رانده شده ام. — I have been driven from the land of my father and mother.
- 82 | 191

3692 تذکر tæzækkor *reminder, notice* n
- احتیاجی به تذکر نبود. — It didn't need to be mentioned.
- 83 | 180

3693 طلاق tælɑɣ *divorce* n
- چی، طلاق بگیرم؟ — What, should I get a divorce?
- 71 | 329

23 Time

Rank	Headword	Pronunciation	Gloss	Rank	Headword	Pronunciation	Gloss
22	سال	sal	year	1296	روزانه	ruzane	daily
30	روز	ruz	day	1314	مرتبه	mærtæbe	time, floor
35	پیش	piʃ	before	1395	موقت	movæɣɣæt	temporary
52	قبل	ɣæbl	before	1434	ماهی	mahi	a month, per month
53	مدت	moddæt	term, period				
79	ماه	mah	month	1520	زود	zud	soon
83	زمان	zæman	time	1618	پایانی	pajani	final
96	بار	bar	turn, time	1684	امروزه	emruze	nowadays
118	بعد	bæ?d	then, after	1954	هیچگاه	hiʃgah	never
132	دوره	dowre	period	2095	ثانیه	sanije	second
163	پایان	pajan	end	2355	بزودی	bezudi	soon
180	آینده	ajænde	future	2443	شبانه	ʃæbane	nightly
201	امروز	emruz	today	2477	ظهر	zohr	noon
242	ساعت	sa?æt	hour, time	2562	سالگرد	salgærd	anniversary
269	هفته	hæfte	week	2642	تقویم	tæɣvim	calendar
332	تاریخ	tarix	history	2643	امشب	emʃæb	tonight
388	دقیقه	dæɣiɣe	minute	2830	امروزی	emruzi	modern, contemporary
396	زمانی	zæmani	chronological				
407	دوران	dowran	period, era	2989	بعداً	bæ?dæn	later, then
410	وقت	væɣt	time	3028	هزاره	hezare	millennium
411	وقتی	væɣti	when	3200	آنگاه	angah	then
414	فصل	fæsl	season	3201	سده	sæde	century
417	شب	ʃæb	night	3214	سالروز	salruz	anniversary
499	دهه	dæhe	decade	3264	روزمره	ruzmærre	routine
511	عصر	æsr	afternoon, age, era	3410	سالیانه	salijane	annually
				3598	زمانه	zæmane	era, age
609	قبلی	ɣæbli	previous	3674	ماهانه	mahane	monthly
656	امسال	emsal	this year	3711	پارسال	parsal	last year
672	هنگام	hengam	time	3783	یکسال	jeksal	one year
707	گاه	gah	time	3967	بعدازظهر	bæ?dæzzohr	afternoon
732	بعدی	bæ?di	next	3976	دیشب	diʃæb	last night
918	صبح	sobh	morning	4534	هرگاه	hærgah	whenever
940	دیروز	diruz	yesterday	4604	موقتی	movæɣɣæti	temporary
987	قرن	ɣærn	century	4731	فصلی	fæsli	seasonal
1016	قبلاً	ɣæblæn	before	4911	سحر	sæhær	dawn
1033	همزمان	hæmzæman	simultaneously	5059	موعد	mow?ed	deadline
1092	سالانه	salane	annual	5227	درازمدت	derazmoddat	long-term
1117	موقع	mowɣe?	time	5266	درسال	dærsal	per year, annually
1174	لحظه	læhze	moment				
1216	فردا	færda	tomorrow	5366	سالجاری	saledʒari	This year, current year

Rank	Headword	Pronunciation	Gloss	Rank	Headword	Pronunciation	Gloss
5475	بلندمدت	bolændmoddæt	long-term	12156	وقتیکه	væɣtike	when
6031	زودهنگام	zudhengam	premature, early	12297	پریشب	pæriʃæb	the night before last
6283	شبانه‌روز	ʃæbaneruz	24 hours	12408	همه‌ساله	hæmesale	perennial, annually
6739	زمانیکه	zæmanike	when	12847	همه‌روزه	hæmeruze	everyday
6842	ماهیانه	mahijane	monthly	12878	صدساله	sædsale	centenary, centennial
7379	موقتاً	movæɣɣætæn	temporarily				
7472	کوتاهمدت	kutahmoddæt	short term	12987	نیمه‌شب	nimeʃæb	midnight
8672	ناگاه	nagah	suddenly	14056	بیگاه	bigah	untimely
9048	روز قبل	ruzeɣæbl	the day before	14340	هرازگاهی	hæræzgahi	occasionally, once in a while
9303	هرساله	hærsale	each year, every year	14601	زمان‌بندی	zæmanbændi	timing, scheduling
9718	دوسالانه	dosalane	biennial	14896	پس‌فردا	pæsfærda	the day after tomorrow
10016	گه‌گاه	gægah	occasionally, from time to time	15682	یک‌شبه	jekʃæbe	over night
				15840	سالنامه	salname	calendar
10096	عقربه	æɣræbe	hand (clock)	16380	فرداشب	færdaʃæb	tomorrow night
10365	هنگامیکه	hengamike	when	17060	دیرهنگام	dirhengam	late
10700	زودگذر	zudgozær	temporary	18315	طولانی‌مدت	tulanimoddat	long-term
11016	سحرگاه	sæhærgah	dawn, early morning, daybreak	19153	قبل از	ɣæblæz	before
				19520	یکمرتبه	jekmærtæbe	once, suddenly
11524	بموقع	bemowɣeʔ	on time	19662	موقعیکه	mowɣeʔike	when

3694 اشرف æʃræf *nobler, noblest, Ashraf* adj,pn
- انسان اشرف مخلوقات است. — Humans are the noblest of creatures.
- 81 | 210

3695 افراط efrat *excess* n
- افراط در مصرف برخی غذاها سبب مسمومیت غذایی می‌شود. — Excess consumption of certain foods causes food poisoning.
- 83 | 181

3696 اعلا æʔla *superior* adj,pn
- فرشهای اعلا. — Exquisite rugs.
- 91 | 93

3697 مختل moxtæll *confused* adj
- پیرمرد کاملاً مختل شده بود. — The old man was entirely confused.
- 86 | 152

3698 فرمانداری færmandari *governorship* n
- بودجه ۹۳ شهرداری تهران به فرمانداری ارسال شد. — The 1393 Tehran Municipal budget was sent to the governor's office.
- 85 | 153

3699 دوچرخه doʧærxe *bicycle* n
- هر روز دوچرخه سواری کنی — To ride your bike every day.
- 75 | 274

3700 معکوس mæʔkus *reversed* adj
- در جوامع امروز ممکن است نقش‌های سنتی زن و مرد معکوس شود. — In today's societies, it's possible for the traditional roles of women and men to be reversed.
- 87 | 134

3701 تریاک tærjak *opium* n
- البته خودش می‌گوید غیر از تریاک، حشیش و الکل هم مصرف می‌کرد. — Of course he himself says that besides opium he also used to consume hashish and alcohol.
- 82 | 192

3702 سرتاسر særtasær *throughout* n,q
- برف سرتاسر زمین ها را پوشانده است. — Snow has totally covered the ground.
- 88 | 123

3703 قانع ɣaneʔ *convinced* adj,pn

• هیچ وقت نتوانستم خودم را قانع کنم که او را شناختم.
— I could never convince myself that I knew her.

83 | 184

3704 پروفسور porofosor *professor* n

• جان گابریلی پروفسور روانشناسی دانشگاه استانفورد گفت.
— John Gabrieli, professor of psychology at Stanford University said . . .

78 | 237

3705 یاس jɑs, jæʔs *jasmine, despair* n

• بوی عطر یاس از چادر نماز سایه توی ریه هام می‌پیچد.
— The scent of jasmine from the prayer chador wrapped my lungs in a shadow.

86 | 148

3706 تکذیب tækzib *denial, contradiction* n

• کتاب را تصدیق نکنید و تکذیب نکنید. — Neither confirm nor deny the book.

78 | 239

3707 ساری sɑri *sɑri, Sɑri, contagious* pn

• سیل به صدها هکتار زمین کشاورزی شهرستان ساری آسیب رساند. — Flooding damaged hundreds of hectares of agricultural land in Sari.

82 | 196

3708 ارمنی ærmæni *Armenian* adj,n

• ارمنستان اعلام کرد شهروندان ارمنی منطقه قره باغ باید استقلال داشته باشند. — Armenia announced that Armenian citizens of the Karabakh region should have independence.

83 | 175

3709 ناکام nɑkɑm *frustrated* adj

• تلاش سه مرد برای ربودن یک فروند هواپیمای مسافربری شرکت هواپیمایی پادشاهی اردن ناکام ماند. — The attempt by three men to hijack a Royal Jordanian Airlines commercial airliner failed.

83 | 179

3710 کرانه kerane *shore* n

• ادامه درگیری‌ها در کرانه باختری و غزه به شدت بر میزان سرمایه گذاری در منطقه تاثیر گذاشته است. — Continuation of clashes in the West Bank and Gaza has strongly affected the amount of investment in the region.

72 | 312

3711 پارسال pɑrsɑl *last year* adv

• تو اینُ پارسال هم گفتی. — You also said that last year.

73 | 304

3712 نشانگر neʃɑngær *marker* adj,n

• می دانی هر زخمی نشانگر انسانیت است. — You know, each wound is an indication of humanity.

79 | 229

3713 معاینه moʔɑjene *examination* n

• ما در حال آماده کردن یک مریض برای معاینه هستیم. — We are in the process of preparing a patient for examination.

74 | 289

3714 سؤال کردن soʔɑl kærdæn *ask* v

• از مردم سؤال کردم که آن مرد کیست؟ — I asked people, "Who is that man?"

83 | 177

3715 تبصره tæbsere *note, clause* n

• پس از آنکه تبصره‌هایی به شرایط اولیه رقابت افزوده شد. — After some waivers were added to the existing conditions of competition.

71 | 328

3716 شناور ʃenɑvær *floating* adj,n

• پرنده‌ها در پرتو نور شناورند. — The birds are floating in a beam of light.

79 | 226

3717 بالقوه belɣovve *potential, potentially* adj,adv

• هشت خطر بالقوه‌ای که زمین را ناامن می‌کند. — Eight potential dangers that make the Earth unsafe.

78 | 240

3718 تسلیحات tæslihɑt *armaments* n

• دشمن رسانه را جایگزین تسلیحات نظامی کرده است. — The enemy has replaced military weapons with media.

78 | 237

3719 شجاعت ʃodʒɑʔæt *courage* n,pn

• خیلی خوشحال شد و به شجاعت پسر کوچکش آفرین گفت. — He became very happy and congratulated his small son for his bravery.

85 | 159

3720 انتصاب entesɑb *appointment* n

• اعضای شورای ملی می توانند به عنوان وزیر انتصاب گردند. — Members of the National Council can be appointed as minister.

86 | 141

3721 شاکی ʃɑki *plaintiff* adj,n

• اغلب شاکی‌ها زن‌هایی بودند که شوهرها ولشان کرده بودند و رفته بودند. — Many times the complainants were women whose husbands had left them and gone away.

84 | 166

3722 گمان کردن gomɑn kærdæn *suppose* v

• مردم گمان کردند که او می خواهد آن زن را ارشاد و راهنمائی کند. — People assumed he wanted to guide that woman.

78 | 244

3723 خلال xelɑl *interval, pick* n

• در خلال سه سال اخیر. — During the last three years.

81 | 200

3724 مامان maman *mom* n
- راستی مامان این را میخواستم بهت بگویم. — Mom, actually I wanted to tell you this.

45 | 764

3725 جرج dʒordʒ *George* pn
- لئو اشنایدر در حال حمل چمدان دیگر جرج وارد میشود. — Leo Schneider enters carrying another of George's suitcases.

74 | 295

3726 حقوق‌بشر hoɣuɣebæʃær *human rights* n
- کمیسر جدید حقوق‌بشر سازمان ملل معرفی شد. — The new United Nations High Commissioner for Human Rights was introduced.

48 | 702

3727 آژانس aʒans *agency* n
- لیست تورهای خارجی آژانس را در زیر مشاهده می فرمایید. — You may view the agency's list of foreign tours below.

65 | 410

3728 اهانت ehanæt *insult* n
- کارکنان ارتش اهانت به مقدسات مسلمانان را محکوم کردند. — Army staff condemned insulting the religious sanctities of Muslims.

80 | 213

3729 هراس hæras *fear* n
- داشتن تردید، هراس و احساس عدم امنیت خاطر طبیعی است. — Having doubt, fear, and feelings of insecurity is natural.

84 | 168

3730 تاریکی tariki *darkness* adj,n
- چرا تو تاریکی نشستی؟ — Why did you sit in the dark?

66 | 399

3731 محضر mæhzær *notary public, presence* n
- همه عالم محضر و حریم خداست. — All the world is God's territory and a place for his presence.

87 | 128

3732 بلند شدن bolænd ʃodæn *rise, grow* v
- 4 دقیقه قبل صدای منصوریان برای چه بلند شد؟ — Why did Mansourian raise his voice four minutes ago?

52 | 627

3733 رخداد roxdad *happening* n
- شخصیت‌های فرهنگی سیاسی و اجتماعی نیز به تحلیل این رخداد پرداختند. — Cultural-political and social characters also began to analyze this event.

83 | 174

3734 هیچگونه hiʧgune *no way* adv
- کسی که قابل نمودن هیچگونه ایمان و ایقان نباشد از درک فیض و رحمت هم محروم می ماند. — Anyone

who is incapable of any sort of faith or conviction shall remain deprived of the understanding of grace and mercy.

77 | 248

3735 چهاردهم ʧæhardæhom *fourteenth* adj,n
- چهاردهمین همایش باستان‌شناسی ایران برگزار می‌شود. — The fourteenth Conference of Iranian Archaeology will be held.

75 | 274

3736 خنده xænde *laughter* n
- با خنده فرزندش دردهایش تسکین می‌یافت. — With her child's laughter, her pain subsided.

58 | 520

3737 مجسمه modʒæssæme *statue* n
- او مثل مجسمه مانده بود. — He remained like a statue.

73 | 296

3738 پتانسیل potansijel *potential* n
- ایران در حوزه گردشگری مذهبی، پتانسیل بالایی دارد. — Iran has high potential in the area of religious tourism.

83 | 172

3739 غفلت ɣeflæt *neglect* n
- سال ها به غفلت گذشت. — It was neglected for years.

78 | 231

3740 تنیس tenis *tennis* n
- قراردادهای بسیاری نیز با ورزشکارهای معروف تنیس بسته شد. — Many contracts were also concluded with famous tennis players.

65 | 414

3741 مهیا mohæjja *ready* adj
- تمام امکانات اولیه حتماً برای آنها مهیا باشد. — All the basic necessities must be ready for them.

85 | 152

3742 الکساندر æleksandr *Alexander* pn
- شاعر بزرگ الکساندر پوشکین. — The great poet Alexander Pushkin.

90 | 101

3743 سرود sorud *song, sang* n,pn,v
- آوازی نیست که نخواند و تصنیف و سرودی نیست که نداند. — There is no song that he didn't sing and no ballad or anthem which he did not know.

82 | 186

3744 کینه kine *grudge* n
- بوی بد کینه و نفرت، قلب شما را فاسد می کند. — The bad smell of grudges and hatred corrupts your heart.

87 | 135

3745 کوره kure *furnace* n
- حتی کوره‌های آجرپزی تجدید بنا شد. — Even the brickyard furnaces were rebuilt.

82 | 189

3746 گرمی *gærmi warmth* adj,n,pn
- گرمی هوا باعث توسعه جنگل‌های انبوه گردید. — The heat of the air caused the development of thick forests.
- 84 | 162

3747 گسترش دادن *gostæreʃ dadæn expand* v
- رژیم بحرین سرکوب تظاهرات مردمی را گسترش داد. — The Bahraini regime expanded repression of public protests.
- 82 | 190

3748 متخلف *motæxællef offender* adj,n
- بی سوادی و فرهنگ عدم برخورد جدی با متخلفان قانون را از عوامل عمده افزایش خشونت در برابر زنان می دانند. — They consider illiteracy and a culture of not seriously confronting violators of the law as one of the primary factors for the increase in violence against women.
- 84 | 168

3749 دانه *dane seed, grain* n
- پس از مدتی این دانه کوچک شن که ماده سختی آن را پوشانده — After a while, this small grain of sand which is covered with a hard material . . .
- 63 | 430

3750 فرا گرفتن *færa gereftæn surround, learn* v
- زنان افغانستانی به فرا گرفتن تعلیمات نظامی و کار کردن در ارگان های دولتی علاقمند اند. — Afghan women are interested in military training and working in government agencies.
- 81 | 205

3751 گاردین *gardijen Guardian* pn
- روزنامه میل اند گاردین چاپ آفریقای جنوبی. — *Mail & Guardian* newspaper published in South Africa.
- 85 | 149

3752 جمهوریخواه *dʒomhurixah republican* adj,n
- هشت نفر از اعضای حزب جمهوریخواه آمریکا که نامزد انتخابات ریاست جمهوری این کشور هستند . . . — Eight members of the American Republican party who are candidates for this country's presidential elections . . .
- 70 | 339

3753 زنگ زدن *zæng zædæn ring* v
- البته من به آزاده زنگ میزنم. — Of course I will call Azadeh.
- 46 | 736

3754 تزریق *tæzriɣ injection* n
- مبتلایان به دیابت نوع ۱ (وابسته به انسولین) که در روز چند نوبت لازم است انسولین تزریق کنند. — Those suffering from type I diabetes (dependent on insulin) need to inject insulin several times a day.
- 82 | 190

3755 مانور *manovr maneuver* n
- اطمینان حاصل کنید که جایی برای مانور باشد. — Make sure that there is room for the maneuver.
- 82 | 190

3756 همجوار *hæmdʒævar neighboring* adj
- اولویت اصلی در روابط دیپلماتیک باید معطوف به کشورهای همجوار باشد. — The main priority in diplomatic relations should be focused on neighboring countries.
- 90 | 100

3757 فرو *foru down* adj,prep
- با آرامش در صندلی‌اش فرو رفت. — He slowly sank in his chair.
- 71 | 321

3758 کاشتن *kaʃtæn plant* n,v
- جو را بیش از غلات دیگر می‌کاشتند. — They would plant barley more than other grains.
- 85 | 157

3759 برکنار *bærkenar removed* adj
- سفیر ترکیه در امارات برکنار شد. — The Turkish Ambassador to the UAE was dismissed.
- 85 | 158

3760 تار *tar dim, string, lute* adj,n
- در دوران کودکی و ابتدا از پدرش تار نوازی را آموخت. — In childhood, he learned first from his father to play tar.
- 71 | 323

3761 ریاضیات *rijazijjat mathematics* n
- او از همان ابتدای تحصیل استعداد و علاقه ای عمیق به ریاضیات داشت. — From the beginning of his studies, he had deep talent and interest in mathematics.
- 80 | 212

3762 مستلزم *mostælzem requiring* adj,n
- نقد مستلزم همدلی و همزبانی است. — Criticism requires empathy and compassion.
- 76 | 261

3763 موضعی *mowzeʔi local* adj,n
- کوکائین اولین بی‌حس کننده موضعی طبیعی است. — Cocaine is the first natural local anesthetic.
- 88 | 115

3764 تکرار کردن *tekrar kærdæn repeat* v
- تکرار کردن جملات و عباراتی که مثبت هستند، می توانند به افراد انرژی بدهند. — Repeating sentences and phrases that are positive can energize a person.
- 80 | 211

3765 سمینار *seminar seminar* n
- این روزها هرجا که نگاه می‌کنید، سمینار است و کنفرانس و کنگره و سمپوزیوم و از این قبیل مجامع. — Everywhere you look these days, there's a seminar, or a conference, or an assembly, or a symposium, and other such gatherings.
- 74 | 277

3766 دوگانه dogane *double* adj
- بازی های دوگانه. — Two-sided games.

82 | 181

3767 تلقی کردن tælæɣɣi kærdæn *consider* v
- او را به عنوان یکی از بزرگترین رهبران جهان غرب تلقی می‌کند. — They regard him as one of the greatest leaders of the western world.

81 | 192

3768 زیرساخت zirsaxt *infrastructure* n
- زیرساخت‌هایی که به مدیریت بحران کمک می‌کند. — Infrastructure that will help with crisis management.

74 | 284

3769 اعلامیه eʔlamijje *announcement* n
- اعلامیه‌ء مشترک میان جمهوری اسلامی افغانستان و جمهوری مردم چین در مورد تاسیس مشارکت و همکاری استراتژیک. — Joint declaration between the Islamic Republic of Afghanistan and the People's Republic of China on the establishment of a strategic partnership.

73 | 294

3770 سرشناس særʃenas *well-known* adj
- هنرمند سرشناس ایرانی. — A prominent Iranian artist.

82 | 184

3771 آیین αjin *religion, ceremony, ritual* n
- آیین بدرقه عباس کیارستمی روز یکشنبه ۲۰ تیر برگزار شد. — Abbas Kiarostami's farewell ceremony was held on Sunday, the 20th of Tir.

62 | 441

3772 ادغام edɣam *integration, merger* n
- به‌تازگی پیشنهاد ادغام چندین خودروساز اروپایی را به منظور ایجاد «یک فولکس‌واگن دیگر» مطرح کرده است. — It has recently brought up the proposal for the merger of several European automakers so as to create "another Volkswagen."

74 | 284

3773 ستم setæm *cruelty* n
- بیشتر دوران فرمانروایی او سراسر بی رحمی و ستم بر مردم گذشت. — Most of his reign passed in brutality and oppression of the people.

85 | 150

3774 دفعه dæfʔe *time* n
- ده سال پیش دفعه اولی که پسرمان را گرفته بودند. — Ten years ago when for the first time they had arrested our son.

53 | 598

3775 خشکی xoʃki *dryness, dry land* adj,n
- رفت و رفت تا به خشکی رسید. — He went and went until he reached dry land.

83 | 178

3776 وارده varede *received* adj
- عمرالبشیر اتهامات وارده به نظامیان سودان را رد کرد. — Omar al-Bashir rejected the charges lodged against Sudan's military.

80 | 211

3777 زوج zowdʒ *pair, couple* adj,n
- ای زوج خوشبخت، امیدوارم به پای هم پیر شوید. — O fortunate couple, I hope you grow old at each other's feet.

78 | 233

3778 معادله moʔadele *equation* n
- معادله اقتصادی آمریکا هنوز به تعادل نرسیده است. — America's economic equation still has not been solved.

80 | 203

3779 قطع کردن ɣætʔ kærdæn *cut* v
- رییس بخش حرف او را قطع کرد. — The section chief cut off his speech.

78 | 230

3780 اقلیم eɣlim *climate* n
- تغییر اقلیم با جنگل‌های مازندران چه کرده است؟ — What has climate change done to Mazandaran's forests?

83 | 169

3781 گریبان geriban *collar* n
- گریبان پیراهنشان شکافی داشت. — The collar of their shirts had a cut.

87 | 130

3782 خوابیدن xabidæn *sleep* n,v
- مردی در قبر وسطی خوابیده بود. — A man was lying in the middle grave.

55 | 559

3783 یکسال jeksal *one year* adv,n
- دو فضانورد آمریکایی و روسی پس از یکسال به زمین بازگشتند. — Two Russian and American astronauts returned to Earth after one year.

76 | 260

3784 نژادی neʒadi *racial* adj
- تبعیض نژادی در آمریکا یک واقعیت است. — Racial discrimination is a reality in America.

81 | 201

3785 گوناگونی gunaguni *diversity, variety* adj,n
- در این سرزمین گوناگونی ادیان و اقوام بسیار فراوان بود. — There was an abundance of diversity of religions and ethnic groups in this land.

80 | 212

3786 پاپ pap *Pope* adj,n,pn
- اسقف‌ها یا پاپ هر چی می‌خوان بگن. — The bishops and the Pope say whatever they want.

75 | 268

3787 همینطور hæmintowr *also, likewise* conj
- برای من هم همینطور بود. — It was the same for me too.
65 | 399

3788 راه افتادن rah oftadæn *set out* v
- امام کفش را به دست گرفت و پای برهنه به راه افتاد. — The imam took his shoes in hand and set out on his way barefoot.
52 | 614

3789 حرارت hæraræt *heat* n
- باید حرارت را بیشتر کرد. — The heat must be increased.
65 | 399

3790 منتها montæha *extremity, but* adv,conj,n
- فردا هم همین کار را تکرار کن، منتها به جای لباس سفید، لباس سبز بپوش. — Tomorrow do the same thing, but instead of white clothes, wear green.
82 | 184

3791 قسم yæsæm, yesm *oath, sort* n
- چرا به جان هفت برادرت قسم نمی خوری؟ — Why don't you swear on the life of your seven brothers?
69 | 351

3792 فرعی fær?i *secondary* adj
- آنوقت‌ها خانه ما واقع در یک کوچه فرعی منشعب از یک خیابان اصلی بود. — At that time our house was situated on a subsidiary road branching off of the main street.
76 | 255

3793 افسردگی æfsordegi *depression* n
- رژیم غذایی سالم خطر افسردگی را کاهش می‌دهد. — A healthy diet reduces the risk of depression.
77 | 246

3794 ارتباط داشتن ertebat daftæn *be in contact* v
- این افراد همچنین با شبه‌نظامیان عراقی در سوریه ارتباط داشتند. — These individuals also had a connection with Iraqi militants in Syria.
84 | 166

3795 نمایشگاهی næmajefgahi *exhibition* adj,n
- مجموعه نمایشگاهی شهر آفتاب ۱۴ اردیبهشت افتتاح می‌شود. — The Shahr-e Aftab exhibition collection will open on 14 Ordibehesht.
78 | 228

3796 یقین jæyin *certain* n
- شاه یقین کرد که راضی در این کار هست. — The king made certain that there was secrecy in this work.
84 | 163

3797 ژانویه ʒanvije *January* n
- تحریم‌های ایران احتمالا تا ژانویه برداشته می‌شوند. — The Iran sanctions will likely be lifted in January.
79 | 216

3798 غیبت yejbæt *absence* n
- امام مهدی در پس پرده غیبت زندگی خود را شروع کرده‌است. — Imam Mahdi began his life behind a veil of absence.
84 | 162

3799 ویتامین vitamin *vitamin* n
- آلبالو میوه‌ای کم کالری و سرشار از ویتامین C است. — The sour cherry is a low-calorie fruit that is brimming with vitamin C.
66 | 380

3800 جدا کردن dʒoda kærdæn *separate* v
- اگر هر دو به یک راه قدم بگذارید کشته خواهید شد و اگر راهتان را از هم جدا کنید به مقصود خواهید رسید. — If you both walk down the same path, you will be killed, but if you take different paths, you will reach your objective.
83 | 174

3801 مکالمه mokaleme *dialogue* n
- میتونی یه مکالمه کوتاه داشته باشی. — You can have a short conversation.
84 | 164

3802 اضطراب ezterab *anxiety* n
- زنش دم پنجره با اضطراب به این ور و آن ور نگاه می کند. — His wife was sitting at the edge of the window anxiously looking this way and that.
72 | 298

3803 واجد شرایط vadʒede færajæt *eligible, qualified* adj
- بیش از 50 میلیون نفر واجد شرایط رای دادن هستند. — More than 50 million people are eligible to vote.
84 | 156

3804 تشویق کردن tæfviy kærdæn *encourage* v
- او را تشویق می‌کرد که به تمرین‌هایش ادامه دهد. — She used to encourage him to continue his exercises.
85 | 151

3805 تربیتی tærtibi *disciplinary, systematic, ordinal* adj
- چطور نکات تربیتی را در مورد بچه‌ها اعمال کنیم؟ — How should we apply disciplinary points on children?
70 | 335

3806 سرمایه‌گذار særmajegozar *investor* adj,n
- بیش از ۷۰ سرمایه‌گذار خارجی در سال ۹۳ وارد این بازار شده‌اند. — More than 70 foreign investors have entered this market in the year 93.
72 | 307

3807 مکتوب mæktub *written, letter* adj
- ایران و بوئینگ برای خرید هواپیما به توافق مکتوب رسیده‌اند. — Iran and Boeing have come to a written agreement for purchasing aircraft.
82 | 179

3808 هفتصد hæftsæd *seven hundred* n

- جمشید پادشاهی عادل و زیبارو بود که نوروز را بر پا
داشت و هفتصد سال بر ایران پادشاهی کرد. —
Jamshid was a just and handsome king, who
established Nowruz and reigned over Iran for
seven hundred years.

52 | 596

3809 دگرگونی degærguni *transformation* n

- در قرن بیستم پیدایش کامپیوتر موجب دگرگونی و رشد
سریع حسابداری شد. — In the twentieth century,
the emergence of the computer resulted in
the rapid growth and transformation of
accounting.

75 | 270

3810 غیرنظامی γejrnezami *civilian* adj,n

- به کشته شدن هزاران غیرنظامی منجر خواهد شد. — It
will lead to the death of thousands of
civilians.

70 | 324

3811 هندوستان hendustan *India* pn

- از هندوستان برای ما چه سوغاتی آورده ای؟ — What
souvenir have you brought for us from India?

74 | 282

3812 طنز tænz *satire* adj,n

- مثل همیشه در حال پرسه زدن در وب بودم که به وبلاگ
سیاسی برخورد کردم. طنز — As always, I was
roaming the web when I encountered a blog
of political satire.

73 | 292

3813 تمجید tæmdʒid *praise* n

- در تعریف و تمجید از فرزندتان افراط نکنید. — Do not
go to extremes in praising and admiring your
child.

91 | 88

3814 پیمودن pejmudæn *measure, traverse* adj,n,v

- مسافتی طولانی را پیمودند تا به مقصد رسیدند. — They
traveled a long distance to reach the
destination.

80 | 204

3815 اقصی æγsa *farther* adj,n

- افراد ثروتمند معمولا به اقصی نقاط جهان سفر می‌کنند.
— Rich people usually travel around the
world.

92 | 73

3816 پوستر poster *poster* n

- پوستر اول عکسی فوق العاده زیبا از حکیم ارد بزرگ
است. — The first poster is an excellent picture
of Hakim Orod Bozorg.

84 | 160

3817 نی nej *straw, flute* n

- می‌گفت برو نی مرا بیاور. — He used to say,
"Go and bring that flute of mine."

80 | 199

3818 ذوق zowγ *good taste, enthusiasm* n

- آن وقتها که جوان بودم ذوق زندگی داشتم. — In those
days when I was young I had enthusiasm
for life.

80 | 199

3819 تروریست terorist *terrorist* adj,n

- وی از آنها به عنوان تروریست اسم می برده. — He had
named them as terrorists.

65 | 389

3820 ذات zat *essence* n

- منطق اصلاحات در ذات و هویت انقلاب نهفته است.
— The logic of reforms is hidden in the very
essence and identity of the revolution.

82 | 178

3821 کبیر kæbir *great, adult* adj,pn

- زیرا بنا به فرموده بنیان گذار کبیر انقلاب امام (ره) همه باید
سیاسی باشیم ولی سیاست زده نباشیم. — For as the
Imam, the great founder of the revolution
stated, everyone must be political but must
not be politicized.

79 | 215

3822 رحیم ræhim *merciful, Rahim* pn

- خداوند رحمان و رحیم است. — God is
compassionate and merciful.

70 | 331

3823 بازگرداندن bazgærdandæn *repatriate* adj,n

- مداخله دولت اندونزی در بازگرداندن پناه جویان تیمور
شرقی به این منطقه را محکوم کرد. — He
condemned the Indonesian government's
interference in returning the East Timorese
asylum seekers to the region.

83 | 167

3824 متوالی motævali *successive* adj

- به تدریج دولت هخامنشی بر اثر اختلافات درونی بین شاه
و شاهزادگان و جنگهای متوالی در غرب ایران از یک
سو و خوشگذرانی شاهان از سوی دیگر، ضعیف گشت.
— The Achaemenid goverment gradually
grew weak due to internal conflicts
between the king and princes and
consecutive wars in western Iran on one
hand and because of the hedonism of the
kings on the other.

82 | 186

3825 موافقتنامه movafeγætname *agreement* n

- ایران و لهستان دو موافقتنامه همکاری اقتصادی امضاء
کردند. — Iran and Poland signed two
economic cooperation agreements.

82 | 182

3826 تسخیر tæsxir *conquest* n

- آنها آسمان را هم تسخیر می‌کنند! — They will even
conquer the sky!

83 | 174

3827 بزرگراه bozorgrah *expressway, highway* n
- عدد، به نام خیابان‌های اصلی و بزرگراه‌های تهران اضافه می‌شود. — Numbers will be added to the names of the main streets and highways of Tehran.
65 | 397

3828 مصنوعی mæsnuʔi *artificial* adj
- محسن خان پای مصنوعی اش را از زانو جدا کرده و روی میز گذاشته است. — Mohsen Khan separated his artificial leg at the knee and placed it on the table.
77 | 237

3829 موشکی muʃæki *missile* adj
- جنگ‌روانی دشمنان تأثیری بر ارتقاء توان موشکی ایران ندارد. — The enemies' psychological war has no effect on Iran's missile capability upgrade.
60 | 460

3830 بهادار bæhadar *valuable* adj
- سازمان بورس و اوراق بهادار. — Securities and Exchange Organization.
68 | 354

3831 الجزیره ældʒæzire *Al Jazeera* n,pn
- اما نکته جالب توجه بازتاب آغاز این روابط در برخی از رسانه‌های خارجی همچون ، گاردین ،بی بی سی ، الجزیره ، وجروزالم پست بود. — An interesting point, however, is the attention to the start of these relations as reflected in some of the foreign media, like *The Guardian*, BBC, *Al Jazeera*, and *The Jerusalem Post*.
67 | 357

3832 وصل væsl *union, joining* n
- سوند بهش وصل کرده بودند. — They had attached a catheter to him.
79 | 212

3833 نیل nil, nejl *indigo/Nile, attainment* n,pn
- تلاش یا کار انسان اهمیت بسیار زیادی در نیل به اهداف دارد. — Human effort or work is very important in achieving goals.
76 | 247

3834 پانزدهم panzdæhom *fifteenth* adj,n
- در پانزدهم اسفند سال گذشته جلسه‌ای با حضور مسوولان ارشد کشور و نمایندگان استان در مجلس برگزار شد. — On the fifteenth of Esfand of last year, a meeting was held in Parliament with the country's senior officials and provincial representatives in attendance.
73 | 283

3835 استحکام estehkam *solidness, strength* n
- استحکام نیروهای مسلح را مهم‌ترین عامل برای حفظ امنیت نظام اسلامی می داند. — He considers the strength of the armed forces to be the most important factor for maintaining the security of the Islamic system.
85 | 151

3836 مهره mohre *marble, bead, vertebra* n,pn
- از تصورش مهره های پشتم تیر می کشد. — The vertebrae in my back are prickling from imagining it.
83 | 171

3837 مربع moræbbæʔ *square* adj,n
- اما مستطیل نیست، مربع است. — But it's not rectangular, it's square.
73 | 285

3838 توانمند tævanmænd *capable* adj
- به دست متخصصان توانمند داخلی طراحی و ساخته شده اند. — Designed and built by the capable hands of local experts.
83 | 164

3839 نقدینگی næɣdinegi *liquidity* n
- مدیریت نقدینگی یکی از بزرگ‌ترین چالش‌هایی است که سیستم بانک‌داری با آن روبرو است. — Liquidity management is one of the biggest challenges the banking system is facing.
75 | 261

3840 مغزی mæɣzi *cerebral* adj
- ۹۰ درصد از سکته‌های مغزی قابل‌پیشگیری هستند. — 90 percent of strokes are preventable.
73 | 285

3841 چراکه ʧerake *because* conj
- از فردا نمی‌ترسم چراکه دیروز را دیده‌ام و امروز را دوست دارم. — I'm not afraid of tomorrow because I've seen yesterday and I like today.
80 | 198

3842 آتی ati *upcoming* adj
- دختران درباره سرنوشت آتی خود تصمیم می‌گیرند. — Girls make decisions about their own future fate.
70 | 327

3843 جواز dʒævaz *license* n
- ایران جواز حضور در مرحله نهایی را کسب کرد. — Iran received permission to attend the final.
86 | 140

3844 کفش kæfʃ *shoe* n
- کفش‌هایم کو؟ — Where are my shoes?
61 | 447

3845 متفکر motæfækker *thinker, thoughtful* adj,n
- این متفکر آمریکایی در ادامه گفت: آمریکا می‌گوید ایران تهدیدی برای جهان است. — This American intellectual continued by saying, "America says Iran is a threat to the world."
77 | 233

3846 عاری ari *bereft, free* adj
- عاری از هرگونه عوارض جانبی خواهد بود. — It will be free from any side effects.
87 | 121

3847 توزیع شدن towziʔ ʃodæn *be distributed* v
- اگر تولید مواد غذایی به صورت عادلانه در جهان توزیع شود. — If food is distributed fairly in the world.
85 | 148

24 Days (in day order)

Rank	Headword	Pronunciation	Gloss	Rank	Headword	Pronunciation	Gloss
476	شنبه	ʃæmbe	*Saturday*	1200	چهارشنبه	tʃæharʃæmbe	*Wednesday*
1433	یکشنبه	jekʃæmbe	*Sunday*	1502	پنجشنبه	pændʒæmbe	*Thursday*
1262	دوشنبه	doʃæmbe	*Monday*	552	جمعه	dʒomʔe	*Friday*
2098	سه‌شنبه	seʃæmbe	*Tuesday*				

3848 خوشنویسی xoʃnevisi *calligraphy* n
- جایزه بزرگ خوشنویسی برگزار می‌شود. — The Calligraphy Grand Prix will be held.

79 | 208

3849 تکه tekke *piece* n
- تکه‌ها را جمع کرد و توی یک دستمال ریخت. — He gathered up the pieces and dumped them into a napkin.

61 | 439

3850 سخنران soxænran *speaker* n
- من تنها سخنران این جلسات نیستم. — I am not the only speaker at these meetings.

82 | 174

3851 مشروط mæʃrut *conditional* adj
- قبولی مشروط چیست؟ — What is conditional acceptance?

82 | 176

3852 کندی kondi, kenedi *slowness, Kennedy* n,pn
- بارش شدید باران موجب توقف و کندی تردد قطارها در سمنان شد. — Heavy rainfall caused stopping and slowing in Semnan's train traffic.

82 | 176

3853 تماشا کردن tæmaʃa kærdæn *watch, view* v
- او را تماشا می‌کردند. — They were watching him.

79 | 215

3854 بختیاری bæxtijari *Bakhtiari* adj,pn
- این موضوع چه ربطی به ما بختیاری ها دارد. — What does this subject have to do with us Bakhtiaris?

73 | 288

3855 کنوانسیون konvansijon *convention* n
- عضویت در این کنوانسیون ها را بپذیریم و مقررات بین المللی را رعایت کنیم — For us to accept membership in these conventions and observe international regulations.

75 | 255

3856 ثبت‌نام sæbtenam *enrollment* n
- اونها میگن هیچکس توی مسکو بدون ثبت‌نام زندگی نمیکنه. — They say no one in Moscow lives without signing up.

78 | 222

3857 نهفته næhofte *hidden* adj
- نوزادان به احساس نهفته در صدا پی می‌برند. — Infants sense the emotions hidden within the voice.

80 | 197

3858 طفل tefl *child* n
- هر طفل مکتبی می‌داند که عدد با یک شروع می‌شود. — Every schoolboy knows that the numbers begin with 1.

71 | 308

3859 کاشانی kaʃani *Kashani* adj,pn
- در طی این دوران، کاشانی مرجع تقلید فدائیان اسلام شد. — During this period, Kashani became the grand ayatollah of Fadaiyan-e Islam.

83 | 161

3860 مشهود mæʃhud *evident* adj
- اما خصومت دولت بوش با ایران همچنان باقی و مشهود است. — But the Bush administration's animosity toward Iran is still remaining and obvious.

80 | 195

3861 کود kud *fertilizer, manure* n
- ایران به فناوری تولید سموم و کودهای بیولوژیک دست یافت. — Iran gained the technology to manufacture biological fertilizers and pesticides.

89 | 101

3862 رفاهی refahi *welfare, leisure* adj
- این پارک در جنوب شهر قرار دارد و دارای تأسیسات تفریحی و رفاهی است. — The park is located south of the city and has leisure and recreational facilities.

80 | 198

3863 شیکاگو ʃikago *Chicago* pn
- در ماه می، پاکستان در نشست سران ناتو در شیکاگو دعوت نشد. — In May, Pakistan was not invited to the conference of the heads of NATO in Chicago.

82 | 172

3864 طراحی کردن tærrahi kærdæn *design* v
- آقای دنیزلی تمرینات خیلی خوبی رو طراحی کردن. — Mr. Denizli has designed very good exercises.

87 | 126

3865 جذابیت dʒæzzabijjæt *attractiveness, charm* n
- جذابیت خود را از دست می دهند. — They lose their charm.
- 84 | 153

3866 نوجوانی nowdʒævani *adolescence* adj,n
- او بیشتر دوران نوجوانی خود را در پرورشگاه بسر برد. — He lived most of his youth in the orphanage.
- 84 | 153

3867 فلزی felezzi *metal* adj
- رفتم تا روی نیمکت فلزی کنار سالن بنشینم. — I went to sit on the metal bench next to the auditorium.
- 75 | 257

3868 متولی motevælli *custodian, administrator* n,pn
- متولی وقف کیست؟ — Who is the time keeper?
- 73 | 276

3869 مساعد mosaʔed *favorable* adj
- ایجاد شرایط مساعد برای به کارگیری سرمایه انسانی. — Creating favorable conditions for the deployment of human capital.
- 76 | 239

3870 گرامیداشت geramidaʃt *honoring* n
- اسرائیل از تمبر گرامیداشت «کوروش کبیر» رونمایی کرد. — Israel unveiled the stamp honoring Cyrus the Great.
- 82 | 172

3871 گنجینه gændʒine *treasury* n
- آیات قرآن همچون گنجینههایی است. — The verses of the Koran are like a treasure.
- 84 | 160

3872 سلطنت sæltænæt *monarchy* n
- تیگران سوم بر تخت سلطنت ارمنستان نشست. — Tigranes III sat on the throne of the Kingdom of Armenia.
- 67 | 357

3873 دوختن duxtæn *sew* adj,n,v
- مادر سراسیمه به اتاق دوید، سوزن را بالا برد و به سرعت به دوختن مشغول شد. — Mother ran headlong into the room, picked up the needle and quickly got busy sewing.
- 74 | 270

3874 فرضیه færzijje *hypothesis* n
- فرضیههای زیاد در زمینه علت مرگ او مطرح شد. — A lot of hypotheses were raised regarding the cause of her death.
- 75 | 255

3875 قد γædd *height* n
- با یک امریکانی مو بور بود، مو بور و بلند قد و چهارشانه. — He was with a blond haired American, tall, and broad shouldered.
- 65 | 379

3876 خزانه xæzane *treasury* n
- دیشب دزدها خزانه پادشاه را خالی کردهاند. — Last night thieves emptied the king's treasury.
- 82 | 175

3877 پیشی piʃi *cat, precedence* n
- کرزای با هزار رای از سایر رقبای انتخاباتی خود پیشی گرفته است. — Karzai with one thousand votes has surpassed his other electoral rivals.
- 89 | 107

3878 مرتکب شدن mortækeb ʃodæn *commit* v
- انگلیس خطای بزرگی در روابط دو جانبه مرتکب شد. — Britain made a big mistake in bilateral relations.
- 85 | 140

3879 راهاندازی rahændazi *making operational* n
- دانشگاه مجازی قرار بود تا پایان سال جاری در کشور راهاندازی شود. — The virtual university was supposed to be put into operation in the country by the end of this year.
- 63 | 411

3880 حامد hamed *Hamed* pn
- حامد کرزای رئیس جمهور فعلی افغانستان. — The current President of Afghanistan, Hamid Karzai.
- 58 | 482

3881 انتقالی enteγali *transferred* adj
- حکومت انتقالی عراق. — Iraqi Transitional government.
- 69 | 331

3882 دود dud *smoke* n
- دود را توی صورت ناصر فوت کرد. — She blew smoke into Nasser's face.
- 71 | 307

3883 شهریار ʃæhrijar *monarch* n,pn
- شهریار عارف نیست، بیشتر عاشق است. — Shahriyar is not a mystic, he is more a lover.
- 71 | 302

3884 جدال dʒedal *conflict* n
- این جدال نه تنها روزهای متوالی که حتی ممکن است هفتهها نیز ادامه پیدا کند. — This dispute might go on for several days and even weeks.
- 87 | 120

3885 فیفا fifa *FIFA* pn
- فیفا محرومیت تیم پیروزی را لغو کرد. — FIFA canceled the exclusion of the winning team.
- 79 | 212

3886 قاچاقچی γaʧaγʧi *smuggler* adj,n
- افریقا هدف جدید قاچاقچیان است. — Africa is the new smugglers' target.
- 74 | 264

3887 ساختگی saxtegi *forged* adj
- دولت اردوغان مخالفان را با اتهامات ساختگی دستگیر می
  کند. — Erdogan's government arrests
  opposition activists with false accusations.
  90 | 89

3888 باخت baxt *losing, loss, lost* n,v
- فقط یک باخت (مقابل انگلستان) داشتند. — They had
  only one loss (against England).
  71 | 305

3889 ریز riz *tiny* ad
- با خط خیلی ریز دور آن تصویر قلبی کشیدم. — With a
  very thin line, I drew a picture of a heart
  around it.
  72 | 293

3890 مهرماه mehrmah *Mehr* n
- این نمایشگاه چهار روزه از مهرماه افتتاح می‌شود.
  — This four–day exhibition will be open from
  the month of Mehr.
  71 | 302

3891 عثمانی osmani *Ottoman* adj,n,pn
- ترکان عثمانی — — Ottoman Turks.
  85 | 143

3892 اتصال ettesal *connection, joint* n
- او با اتصال سیم ها ماشین را روشن کند. — She
  should start the car by connecting the wires.
  72 | 295

3893 قضا ɣæza *judgment, past due* n
- کسی که نماز قضا دارد باید در خواندن آن کوتاهی نکند.
  — A person who has an unsaid prayer past
  due should not fail to say it.
  76 | 242

3894 منافق monafeɣ *hypocritical, hypocrite* adj,n
- مردان منافق و زنان منافق. — Hypocrite men and
  hypocrite women.
  77 | 226

3895 تبع tæbæʔ *follower, following* n
- به تبع اتفاقی که افتاده بود از لحاظ روحی هم افت کرده
  بودم. — Following the event that had taken
  place, I had felt down spiritually as well.
  85 | 141

3896 موضع‌گیری mowzeʔgiri *adopting a position* n
- موضع‌گیری ناآگاهانه درباره توافق ژنو نکنید. — Do not
  take positions regarding the Geneva
  Agreement unknowingly.
  77 | 231

3897 خوشی xoʃi *joy* adj,n
- انسان توانست برای نخستین بار خوشی‌ها و رنج‌های
  خود را با صدا نمایش دهد. — For the first time
  man could express his pains and
  pleasures with sound.
  72 | 291

3898 عاطفی ɑtefi *emotional* adj
- چطور روابط عاطفی را سالم نگهداریم؟ — How can
  we maintain healthy emotional relationships?
  75 | 256

3899 فراخواندن færaxandæn *invite, summon* adj,v
- این سفردرپی تصمیم مصر به فراخواندن سفیر خود از
  اسرائیل صورت گرفته است. — This trip took place
  following Egypt's decision to recall its
  ambassador from Israel.
  84 | 152

3900 گستره gostære *expanse* n
- این طرح ها گستره وسیعی از نفت و گاز و پتروشیمی تا
  راهسازی ذوب آهن کشتیرانی کشاورزی و گردشگری را
  شامل میشود. — These plans include a broad
  range of oil, gas, petrochemical, road
  construction, iron smelting, shipping,
  agriculture, and tourism.
  86 | 134

3901 مداوا modava *medical treatment* n
- باید مورد مداوا قرار بگیرند. — They should be
  treated.
  90 | 89

3902 نهادی næhadi *institutional* adj,n
- واقعیت اجتماعی زن ایرانی در مقایسه با ۳۰ سال گذشته
  دچار تغییرات اساسی و نهادی شده است. — The social
  reality of Iranian women has undergone
  substantial and institutional changes over the
  last 30 years.
  84 | 155

3903 کماکان kæmakan *as before, still* adv
- برف کماکان می‌بارد. — It is still snowing.
  83 | 164

3904 لبخند læbxænd *smile* n
- لطفاً با لبخند وارد شهر ما شوید. — Please enter our
  city with a smile.
  59 | 464

3905 اتریش otriʃ *Austria* pn
- کشور های پیشرفته غربی مثل سویس، اتریش و فرانسه
  بخش عظیمی از رفاه اجتماعی و اقتصادی خود بر رو سود
  ناشی از توریسم متکی کرده‌اند. — A large part of the
  social and economic welfare of advanced
  western countries like Switzerland, Austria,
  and France has relied on profits resulting
  from tourism.
  69 | 328

3906 ملحق molhæɣ *joined* adj
- خوشحالم که جناب آقای فردوسی پور هم به جمع ما ملحق
  شدند. — I am glad Mr. Ferdowsipur also
  joined us.
  89 | 103

3907 منكر monker, monkær *denying, detestable/vice* adj,n
- امر به معروف و نهی از منكر نشانه احساس مسئولیت اجتماعی است. — To promote virtue and prevent vice is an indication of feeling socially responsible.
78 | 222

3908 جغرافیا dʒoɣrafija *geography* n
- علوم نقشه‌برداری شاخه‌ای از جغرافیا است. — Surveying is a branch of geography.
65 | 383

3909 تاج tadʒ *crown* n
- هنوز فرزندی ندارم كه پس از من صاحب تاج و تخت بشود. — I still don't have a child to inherit my crown and throne after me.
76 | 236

3910 تراز tæraz *level* n
- تراز آب دریاچه ارومیه یک متر افزایش یافت. — Lake Urmia's water levels rose by one meter.
86 | 133

3911 شكننده ʃekænænde *fragile* adj,n
- هر چند این روند بر اقتصاد شكننده اروپا بویژه فرانسه و آلمان تأثیر مخربی خواهد گذاشت. — Although this trend will have a particularly destructive effect on the fragile economy of France and Germany.
90 | 88

3912 اجماع edʒmaʔ *consensus* n
- با یک اجماع ملی می‌توان به معنی واقعی هدفمندی یارانه‌ها رسید. — The true meaning of targeted subsidies can be arrived at by a national consensus.
83 | 166

3913 قرارگاه ɣærargah *army camp* n
- وقتی داشتند از یه قرارگاه به قرارگاه دیگه‌ای منتقلش می‌كردند نجاتش دادیم. — We rescued him while they were transferring him from one camp to another.
88 | 109

3914 حیاط hæjat *yard* n
- كبوتر های وحشی در حیاط قدم می زنند. — The wild pigeons are walking in the yard.
60 | 439

3915 ترقی tæræɣɣi *progress, rise* n,pn
- من امیدوارم كه وی همچنان راه ترقی خود را ادامه دهد. — I am hopeful that she will continue on her path of progress.
74 | 260

3916 متشكر motæʃækker *thankful, grateful* v
- بچه ها متشكریم. — Thank you, guys.
55 | 523

3917 مجال mædʒal *opportunity* n
- مجالی برای انجام این منظور به دست نمی آمد. — A good opportunity would not present itself for this purpose.
83 | 163

3918 پایبند pajbænd *fettered, loyal* adj
- پرزیدنت پوتین به این هدف پایبند خواهد بود. — President Putin will be committed to this goal.
80 | 191

3919 كارفرما karfærma *employer* n
- صبح روز بعد كارفرما من را به اتاقش احضار كرد. — The following morning, the employer summoned me to his office.
79 | 210

3920 عرق æræɣ, erɣ *sweat, blood vessel* n
- پشتش خیس عرق شده. — His back was soaked with sweat.
67 | 347

3921 كارگزار kargozar *agent* adj,n
- محمد هاشمی از حزب كارگزاران استعفا كرد. — Mohammad Hashemi resigned from the Executives (of Construction) Party.
72 | 288

3922 ماشینی maʃini *mechanical* adj,n
- هم اكنون بیش از چهارصد واحد از كارخانه‌ها به تولید فرش ماشینی اشتغال دارند — There are currently more than four hundred factories engaged in machine-made carpet production.
86 | 133

3923 آیه aje *Koranic verse* n
- معنی آیه این است — This verse means . . .
64 | 390

3924 مجارستان mædʒarestan *Hungary* pn
- هلند ۸ بر یک مجارستان را شكست داد. — The Netherlands beat Hungary 8-1.
80 | 189

3925 كروبی kærrubi *Karroubi* pn
- در دیدار آقای كروبی با مقامات عالی رتبه ایتالیا. — Mr. Karroubi's meeting with Italian high-ranking officials.
64 | 385

3926 قطبی ɣotbi *polar* adj
- تغییرات جوی به طرز عجیبی بر زندگی خرس‌های قطبی تأثیر گذاشته است. — Climate change has affected the lives of polar bears in a strange way.
90 | 93

3927 دیجیتال didʒital *digital* adj
- سینمای دیجیتال تیغ دولبه است. — Digital cinema is a double-edged sword.
76 | 241

3928 تابعیت tabeʔijjæt *citizenship* n
- حدس میزنم پایه تابعیت است. — I guess it is the basis for citizenship.
86 | 128

3929 استثنا estesnɑ *exception* n
- این حکمی کلی است استثناهایی هم دارد. — This is a general edict, it also has exceptions.
81 | 184

3930 ویران virɑn *ruined* adj
- کشورمان ویران شده است. — Our country has been destroyed.
79 | 204

3931 اصابت esɑbæt *hitting* n
- تیرش به سنگ اصابت می‌کرد. — His arrows were striking the stone.
87 | 116

3932 مصرف‌کننده mæsræfkonænde *consumer* adj,n
- صرفاً در بازار داخلی مصرف‌کننده دارد. — It only has consumers in the domestic market.
73 | 271

3933 شاغل ʃɑɣel *employed* adj,n
- افرادی که در بخش‌ها شاغل هستند. — The people who are employed in different divisions.
79 | 208

3934 بابک bɑbæk *Babak* pn
- گزارش نیویورک تایمز از بابک زنجانی برای این سرمایه دار ایرانی، تحریم ها طلا بودند. — The New York Times report about Babak Zanjani: for this Iranian capitalist, sanctions were gold.
84 | 147

3935 عنان enan, ænan *rein, Annan* pn
- کوفی عنان وارد تهران شد. — Kofi Annan arrived in Tehran.
65 | 372

3936 مقصود mæɣsud *purpose* n
- مقصود دشمن چگونه حاصل میشود؟ — How are the enemy's goals accomplished?
73 | 277

3937 اشغالگر eʃɣalgær *occupier, occupying* adj,n
- نیروهای امنیتی بحرین با همدستی نیروهای اشغالگر سعودی به سرکوب مردم پرداخته اند. — In collaboration with the occupation forces of Saudi Arabia, Bahraini security forces have suppressed people.
61 | 431

3938 غالباً ɣalebæn *frequently* adv
- پادشاهان غالباً در آن سکنا می‌گزیدند. — Kings would often settle there.
72 | 285

3939 انضباط enzebɑt *discipline* n
- ایجاد ثبات اقتصادی و برقراری نظم و انضباط مالی. — Stabilizing the economy and establishing financial discipline.
88 | 106

3940 وضوح vozuh *clarity* adj,n
- انگشتان دست هام به وضوح می لرزند. — My fingers were clearly trembling.
86 | 129

3941 رو شدن ru ʃodæn *be exposed, bold* v
- دستمزد بازیگران مشهور ایرانی رو شد. — The earnings of famous Iranian actors were exposed.
76 | 232

3942 دادستان dɑdestɑn *public prosecutor* n
- وظایف و اختیارات دادستان کدامند؟ — What are the duties and authorities of a prosecutor?
78 | 215

3943 دربند dærbænd *Darband, captive* adj,pn
- سپاه بزرگ او تار و مار و پسرش نیز پس از آن دربند و اسیر شد. — His great army was routed and his son was captured and then imprisoned.
91 | 81

3944 اشتراک eʃterɑk *participation, subscription, commonality* n
- ایران و لبنان اشتراکات زیادی دارند. — Iran and Lebanon have a lot in common.
67 | 337

3945 عرفان erfɑn *Sufism, mysticism* n
- سعدی یکی شخصیت‌های بزرگ عرفان ایران. — Sa'di is one of the great figures of mysticism in Iran.
75 | 249

3946 زانو zɑnu *knee, bend* n
- میرزا بر دو زانو نشست. — Mirza sat on both knees.
69 | 311

3947 سامانه sɑmɑne *system* n
- دانشمندان مشغول آزمایش روی سامانه نوینی هستند که قادر به شناسایی اثر انگشت است. — Scientists are engaged in testing a new system that is able to identify fingerprints.
55 | 512

3948 دلخواه delxɑh *desired, ideal* adj,n
- خواستم درسی به تو داده باشم تا بدانی همیشه اوضاع طبق دلخواه شما پیش نمی‌رود. — I wanted to teach you a lesson that things will not always happen according to your desires.
84 | 146

3949 خونریزی xunrizi *bleeding, bloodshed* n
- وقتی هر روز در صدر اخبار کشور جنگ و خونریزی باشد چگونه می‌توان شاد بود و شاد زندگی کرد؟ — When war and bloodshed are at the top of the country's news every day, how can one be happy and live a happy life?
- 83 | 154

3950 هشتصد hæʃt sæd *eight hundred* n
- نزدیک هشتصد نفر دیگر در این حملات کشته و هزار نفر نیز مجروح شدند. — Nearly eight hundred more people were killed and a thousand injured in the attacks.
- 52 | 561

3951 بلندپایه bolændpaje *high-ranking* adj
- یک مقام بلندپایه — A high-ranking official.
- 78 | 212

3952 منصفانه monsefane *just, fair* adj,adv
- به نظر آنها قیمت بسیار منصفانه بود — In their opinion, the price was very fair.
- 87 | 121

3953 موکول mowkul *depending, postpone* adj
- موکول کردن تنبیه به آینده — Postponing the punishment to the future.
- 81 | 179

3954 مقیاس meɣjas *scale* n
- زمین لرزه نخست صبح چهارشنبه با شدت 5 درجه در مقیاس ریشتر روی داد. — The first earthquake occurred on Wednesday morning with a magnitude of 5 on the Richter scale.
- 70 | 300

3955 دامن damæn *skirt* n
- باز دامن کتش را کشید. — She tugged at the skirt of her coat again.
- 71 | 288

3956 کناره kenare *edge, bank* n
- کناره‌های رود سن در پاریس در سال ۱۹۹۱ وارد فهرست میراث جهانی یونسکو شد. — The banks of the Seine in Paris entered the UNESCO World Heritage List in 1991.
- 81 | 182

3957 ابراهیمی ebrahimi *Ebrahimi, Abrahamic* pn
- از گسترده‌ترین دین‌های جهان می‌توان از دین‌های ابراهیمی نام برد. — One can name the Abrahamic religions as the most widespread religions in the world.
- 77 | 224

3958 فوریه fevrije *February* n
- از ماه فوریه بزرگترین خریدار کنجاله سویای این کشور محسوب می‌شود. — Since February, it has counted as the largest purchaser of this country's soybean oil cakes.
- 81 | 179

3959 خواستار شدن xastar ʃodæn *demand* v
- وی در سال ۲۰۱۴ خواستار پایان دادن به جنگ داخلی سوریه شد. — In 2014 he called for an end to Syria's civil war.
- 52 | 556

3960 نامشروع namæʃruʔ *unlawful* adj
- بعد از حضور غیرقانونی و نامشروع نظامی عربستان در بحرین. — After the illegal, illegitimate military presence of Saudi Arabia in Bahrain.
- 91 | 78

3961 آلوده alude *polluted* adj
- موتور هوا را هم آلوده می‌کند. — The motor also pollutes the air.
- 69 | 318

3962 آسانی asani *ease* adj,n
- از قابلیت‌های این برنامه آسانی کار با آن می‌باشد. — One of the capabilities of this program is the ease with which one can work with it.
- 83 | 163

3963 دعوا dæʔva *quarrel* n
- روزی نبود که بی دعوا و مرافعه بگذرد. — Not a day went by that there wasn't an argument or quarrel.
- 74 | 257

3964 پرسنل personel *personnel* n
- در این همایش یکصدنفر از مسئولین و پرسنل امدادگران و داوطلبان جمعیت هلال احمر حضور داشتند. — A hundred officials and staff workers of the Red Crescent volunteers and rescuers attended this conference.
- 80 | 185

3965 خشمگین xæʃmgin *angry* adj
- رستم از این بی اعتنائی خشمگین شد. — Rostam was furious at this indifference.
- 84 | 150

3966 مسی mesi *copper* adj
- در ظروف مسی غذاهای اسیدی و ترش نپزید. — Do not cook acidic and sour foods in copper vessels.
- 89 | 100

3967 بعدازظهر bæʔdæzzohr *afternoon* adv,n
- امروز بعدازظهر به شهرستان می‌روم تا با آنها دیداری تازه کنم. — This afternoon I'm going to the countryside to have another visit with them.
- 69 | 315

3968 فرشته fereʃte *angel* n,pn
- فرشته رحمتی است که از آسمان به زمین افتاده است. — The merciful angel that has fallen from heaven to earth.
- 79 | 202

3969 منسجم monsædʒem *coherent* adj
- طرحی منسجم را ارائه نماییم. — We should present a coherent design.
- 82 | 166

3970 دوهزار dohezar *two thousand* n
- مرد دو هزار چهره نام یک مجموعه تلویزیونی ایرانی است. — *The Man of Two-Thousand Faces* is the name of an Iranian television series.
- 52 | 558

3971 ثانیاً sanijæn *secondly* adv,conj,n
- ثانیاً من گفتم راجع به اهمیت کتاب حرف بزند. — Secondly, I told him to talk about the importance of books.
- 80 | 190

3972 پاکی paki *cleanliness, purity* adj,n
- برای آزمون پاکی، او میبایست از آتش میگذشت. He — had to pass through fire as a test of purity.
- 88 | 107

3973 سوژه suʒe *subject* n
- سوژه این گزارش را خودش به من داده بود. — She had given me the topic of this report herself.
- 84 | 146

3974 چهلم ʧehelom *fortieth* adj,n
- چهلمین دوره آموزش عکاسی دیجیتال برگزار میشود. — The fortieth course of digital photography training will be held.
- 94 | 56

3975 لغت loɣæt *word* n
- اگر لغت انگلیسیاش یادم نمیآمد ولش میکردم. — If I couldn't recall the English word I would let it go.
- 72 | 276

3976 دیشب diʃæb *last night* adv
- هاشمی دیشب گفت نمیآید. — Last night Hashemi said he would not come.
- 65 | 359

3977 کوهستان kuhestan *highland, mountain country* n
- به کوهستان خوش آمدید. — Welcome to the mountains.
- 81 | 175

3978 توانا tævana *able, mighty* adj,pn
- وی علاوه بر رشته ی تحصیلی اش روانشناسی، در نویسندگی، موسیقی شناسی و نقاشی نیز بسیار توانا بود. — In addition to her field of study, psychology, she was also very capable in writing, musicology, and painting.
- 79 | 196

3979 فراکسیون fraksijon *parliamentary group* n
- او نخستین رئیس فراکسیون زنان بود و در انتقال گزارشهای مربوط به این فراکسیون نقش فعالی داشت. — She was the first chairperson of Women's group, and she had an active role in transmitting the reports of this group.
- 59 | 442

3980 تیرماه tirmah *Tir* n
- شنبه سوم تیرماه 46 — Saturday, the third of month of Tir, 1346.
- 69 | 313

3981 مصوب mosævvæb *ratified, approved* adj
- نرخ مصوب گوشت مرغ امسال افزایش یافته بود. — The approved price for chicken had increased this year.
- 72 | 281

3982 قاسم ɣasem *Ghasem* pn
- اسمم ابوالقاسمه، اما همه قاسم صدام میزنن. — My name is Abolghasem, but everyone calls me Ghasem.
- 77 | 220

3983 روشنایی rowʃænaji *brightness* n
- پر از روشنایی است. — It is full of light.
- 80 | 188

3984 فرمول formul *formula* n
- میخوای فرمول اتم کشف کنی. — Do you want to discover the atom's formula?
- 79 | 196

3985 ریالی rijali *Rial-based* adj
- پاداش ۱۰۰ میلیون ریالی مسافران المپیک ریو پرداخت شد. — The 100 million-rial bonuses were paid to the Rio Olympics travelers.
- 78 | 205

3986 دوام dævam *durability* n
- این حکومت تقریباً از سال 1300 تا 630 قبل از میلاد دوام یافته است. — This government lasted from approximately 1300 to 630 BCE.
- 74 | 251

3987 پاداش padaʃ *reward, bonus* n
- فرهنگیان باید پاداش پایان خدمت دریافت کنند. — Educators must receive end of service bonuses.
- 81 | 173

3988 وزنه væzne *weight* n
- وزنه برداری رو دنبال میکنند. — They follow weightlifting.
- 76 | 228

3989 پرتاب کردن pærtab ʃodæn *be thrown, launched* v
- تظاهرکنندگان به سوی ساختمان شهرداری سنگ و بطری پرتاب کردند. — Protesters threw rocks and bottles at the city office.
- 90 | 84

3990 سوق دادن sowɣ dadæn *guide, drive* v
- پسر خوانده ام مرا به سمت اسلام سوق داد. — My adopted son led me towards Islam.
- 84 | 144

3991 دفع dæfʔ *repelling, fend off* n
- روسیه برای دفع حملات اتمی آمادگی دارد. — Russia is prepared to fend off nuclear attacks.
- 76 | 235

3992 علاقه داشتن ælaɣe dɑʃtæn *be interested* v
- آنها علاقه داشتند بر اساس سیاست‌ها و تصمیم‌های خودشان بخشی از این انقلاب را سانسور کنند. — They were interested in censoring parts of this revolution based on their own policies and decisions.
87 | 117

3993 مجیدی mædʒidi *Majidi* pn
- مجیدی در هندوستان فیلم می‌سازد. — Majidi is making a film in India.
82 | 170

3994 اکبری ækbæri *Akbari* pn
- عزت‌الله اکبری به مدال نقره دست یافت. — Ezatollah Akbari won the silver medal.
86 | 125

3995 مؤسس moʔæsses *founder* adj,n
- صادق نوروزی یکی از اعضای مؤسس آن بود. — Sadegh Nowruzi was one of its founding members.
80 | 184

3996 تعقیب کردن tæʔɣib kærdæn *pursue* v
- آنان را تعقیب کرد و در کنار نهروان با آنان رودررو قرار گرفت. — He followed them and confronted them at Nahrevan.
92 | 65

3997 یکسانی jeksɑni *equality, uniformity* adj,n
- بر اساس شاخص های آماری میزان شباهت و یکسانی آنها نشان داده می شود. — By statistical indices the level of their similarities and identicality is demonstrated.
90 | 90

3998 جیب dʒejb, dʒib *collar/sine, pocket* n
- بلیط توی جیبم بود. — The ticket was in my pocket.
61 | 418

3999 فایده fɑjede *benefit* n
- این همه کتاب و فیلم بی فایده بود. — All of these films and books were useless.
69 | 313

4000 برهان borhɑn *proof, logic* n
- این خیلی مهم است که خدا را با دلیل و برهان قبول داشته باشیم. — It is very important that we accept God by reason and logic.
87 | 120

4001 اذعان ezʔɑn *admission* n
- فرماندهان ارشد ارتش آمریکا همیشه به این نکته اذعان کرده‌اند. — Top military commanders of the USA have always confessed that . . .
80 | 184

4002 صادقی sɑdeɣi *Sadeghi* pn
- در برزیل، ایمان صادقی صاحب مدال طلا شد. — Iman Sadeghi won a gold medal in Brazil.
81 | 180

4003 لوح lowh *tablet, disk* n
- کتابشناسی ملی ایران از سال 1376 به بعد به‌صورت لوح فشرده منتشر می شود. — The National Bibliography of Iran from 1376 onwards will be released as a CD.
73 | 256

4004 بهرام bæhrɑm *Bahram* pn
- بهرام بیضایی در سال ۱۳۱۷ به دنیا آمد. — Bahram Beyzai was born in 1317.
56 | 485

4005 بجای bedʒɑje *instead of* prep
- این میوه‌ها را بجای قند و شکر مصرف کنید! — Instead of sugar and sugar cubes, eat these fruits!
74 | 253

4006 متقاعد motæɣɑed *convinced* adj
- اما در آن روزهای سرشار از شادی و بی خیالی، چه کسی می‌توانست او را متقاعد کند که زندگی پر از سختی‌هاست؟ — But in those days brimming with happiness and abandon, who could have convinced him that life is full of hardships?
86 | 126

4007 فرهنگسرا færhæŋgsærɑ *cultural center* n
- این فرهنگسرا دارای ساختمان اختصاصی برای سینما است. — This cultural center has a building dedicated to cinema.
62 | 397

4008 شانزده ʃɑnzdæh *sixteen* n
- یک نوجوان شانزده ساله در ارتباط با تیراندازی مونیخ بازجویی شد. — A sixteen-year-old teenager was interrogated in connection with the shooting in Munich.
55 | 496

4009 پوند pond *pound* n
- یک پوند بریتانیا اکنون برابر با ۱٫۳۳ دلار آمریکاست. — One British pound is currently equal to 1.33 U.S. dollars.
76 | 229

4010 مهران mehrɑn *Mehran* pn
- مهران مدیری همراه با پیمان قاسمخانی خالقان این مجموعه هستند. — Mehran Modiri along with Peyman Ghasemkhani are the creators of this series.
85 | 135

4011 ترمیم tærmim *repair, restore* n
- ارتباط بین شورای شهر و شهرداری ترمیم شد. — The relationship between the city council and the mayor's office was repaired.
76 | 231

4012 تحریف tæhrif *distortion, falsification* n
- نمی‌توان با سانسور و تحریف، حقایق را از مردم پنهان کرد. — One cannot hide the truth from the people with censorship and falsification.
87 | 119

25 Persian months (by month order)

Rank	Headword	Pronunciation	Gloss	Rank	Headword	Pronunciation	Gloss
2918	فروردین	færværdin	Farvardin, Aries	613	مهر	mehr	Mehr, Libra
2501	اردیبهشت	ordibeheʃt	Ordibehesht, Taurus	4714	آبان	aban	Aban, Scorpio
1760	خرداد	xordad	Khordad, Gemini	5849	آذر	azær	Azar, Sagittarius
1287	تیر	tir	Tir, Cancer	1743	دی	dej	Dey, Capricorn
2365	مرداد	mordad	Mordad, Leo	1391	بهمن	bæhmæn	Bahman, Aquarius
1974	شهریور	ʃæhrivær	Shahrivar, Virgo	2590	اسفند	esfænd	Esfand, Pisces

4013 اسکان eskan *resettlement, accommodation* n
- اسکان زائران، مهمترین مسئله سفر اربعین امسال است. — Accommodations for pilgrims is the most important issue of the Arbaeen trip this year.

86 | 121

4014 لیسانس lisans *bachelor's degree* n
- لیسانس خود را در سال 1131 در این مکان گرفتند. — He received his bachelor's in this location in the year 1131.

74 | 248

4015 شجاع ʃodʒaʔ *brave, courageous* adj,pn
- دیپلماتهای شجاعمان قابل اعتماد هستند. — Our brave diplomats are reliable.

84 | 145

4016 درست کردن dorost kærdæn *correct, prepare* v
- به خانه رفت و کمی آش در دیگ درست کرد. — She went home and made a bit of stew in the pot.

61 | 405

4017 وخیم væxim *serious* adj
- میگوید حال یکی از دوستانش خیلی وخیم است و باید او را ببرد بیمارستان. — He says that one of his friends is in a very grave state, and he must take him to the hospital.

69 | 309

4018 تسلیحاتی tæslihati *armament* adj
- پارلمان اروپا خواستار تحریم تسلیحاتی عربستان شد. — The European Parliament called for an arms embargo on Saudi Arabia.

81 | 172

4019 القا elɣa *suggestion, induction* n
- القای پیام به مخاطب، یکی از سخت ترین کارها در دنیاست. — Impressing a message on an audience is one the most difficult tasks in the world.

83 | 156

4020 خوشحالی xoʃhali *happiness, joy* n
- بنظر نمیرسد که این خوشحالی طولانی مدت باشد. — It does not seem that this happiness will last long.

76 | 225

4021 تعرض tæʔærroz *offensive, aggression* n
- این ادعاها یک ادعای تعرض نیست. — These claims are not a claim of aggression.

84 | 145

4022 چوبی ʧubi *wooden* adj,n
- این تالار یک مربع کامل است و یک گنبد بسیار زیبای چوبی دارد. — This hall is a perfect square and has a beautiful wooden dome.

78 | 202

4023 شیطان ʃejtan *Satan, naughty* n,pn
- شیطان بزرگ قابل اعتماد نیست. — The Great Satan is not credible.

72 | 271

4024 شریعتی ʃæriʔæti *Shariati* n,pn
- شریعتی از دانشگاه علامه رفت. — Shariati left Allameh University.

81 | 168

4025 ابریشم æbriʃæm *silk* n,pn
- جنس آن از ابریشم و آلومینیوم و چوبهای فوقالعاده سبک و محکم بود. — Its material was of extraordinarily light and strong wood, aluminum and silk.

83 | 156

4026 تندرو tondrow *fast, extremist* adj,n
- بعید است تندروها کمکی به دولت آقای روحانی بکنند. — It is unlikely that the extremists will help Mr. Rowhani's government.

86 | 128

4027 حول howl *power, area, around* n
- ساعت حول و حوش 5 بعدازظهر بود. — It was around five in the afternoon.

81 | 175

4028 اصالت esalæt *authenticity, originality, gentility* n
- مدارک دانشگاهی اصالت ندارند. — Academic degrees lack authenticity.
- 81 | 171

4029 مابقی mabæɣi *remainder* n
- بخش محدودی از این ارتفاعات در استان تهران و مابقی در استان مازندران واقع شده‌است. — A limited portion of these heights is located in Tehran and the rest in Mazandaran province.
- 88 | 100

4030 دبیرخانه dæbirxane *secretariat* n
- به دبیرخانه جشنواره رسید. — It reached the secretariat of the festival.
- 75 | 238

4031 فدا feda *sacrifice* adj,n
- معلم جوان جانش را فدای نجات دانش‌آموزان کرد. — The young teacher sacrificed his life to save his students.
- 79 | 195

4032 دانمارک danmark *Denmark* pn
- فیلمساز مطرح دانمارک سینمای اولین فیلم انگلیسی خودرا می‌سازد. — Famous Danish film director makes her first English film.
- 79 | 191

4033 عروسی ærusi *marriage, wedding* n
- می خواهم عروسی کنم. — I want to get married.
- 66 | 339

4034 همسایگی hæmsajeɣi *neighborhood, proximity* n
- همسایگی با یک رقیب فرصت است یا تهدید؟ — Is proximity with a competitor an opportunity or a threat?
- 92 | 67

4035 خداحافظی xodahafezi *saying goodbye* n
- دردناک‌ترین خداحافظی‌ها آنهایی هستند که هرگز نه گفته شدند و نه توضیح داده شدند. — The most painful goodbyes are the ones that were never said nor explained.
- 65 | 350

4036 نازل nazel *low, humble, sent down* adj
- هنر قاجاری در سطح نازل‌تری نسبت به هنر دوره‌های قبلی ارزیابی می‌شود. — Qajar art is valued lower compared to the art of previous periods.
- 84 | 145

4037 روانشناسی rævanʃenasi *psychology* n
- آینده روانشناسی در کشور ما روشن و امیدبخش است. — Psychology has a hopeful and bright future in our country.
- 67 | 326

4038 کیست kist *who is, cyst* v
- اکثریت کیست‌ها خوش‌خیم هستند. — The majority of cysts are benign.
- 77 | 212

4039 نبی næbi *prophet* adj,n,pn
- آیا محمد را به‌عنوان خاتم انبیاء قبول دارید؟ — Do you accept Mohammad as the Seal of the Prophets?
- 76 | 223

4040 جانشینی dʒaneʃini *succession, substitution* n
- از سال 1701 جنگهای جانشینی اسپانیا شروع شد. — The War of the Spanish Succession began in 1701.
- 89 | 95

4041 ولادیمیر veladimir *Vladimir* pn
- ولادیمیر پوتین رئیس جمهور روسیه. — Russian President Vladimir Putin.
- 74 | 247

4042 محمدعلی mohæmmædæli *Mohammad Ali* pn
- محمدعلی اینانلو کارشناس مطرح محیط زیست درگذشت. — Mohammad Ali Inanloo the famous environmental expert passed away.
- 73 | 257

4043 افزار æfzar *tool* n
- البته سخت افزار هم مهم است. — Of course hardware is also important.
- 74 | 247

4044 نامزدی namzædi *engagement, nomination* n
- هنوز نامه های دوران نامزدی را نگه داشته و مطالعه می کنند. — They have still kept the letters from the time of their engagement, and read them.
- 78 | 199

4045 سروده sorude *sung, poem* adj,n,v
- اشعار این آلبوم از سروده‌های حافظ و باباطاهر هستند. — Hafez and Baba Taher's poems are lyrics of this album.
- 80 | 182

4046 معبر mæʔbær, moʔæbber *thoroughfare, dream interpreter* n
- بین میدان قدس تا سر پل تجریش یک معبر پیاده ایجاد می‌شود. — Between Ghods Square to the Tajrish Bridge a pedestrian passageway will be constructed.
- 76 | 224

4047 ناشناخته naʃenaxte *unknown* adj
- حوزه فناوریهای نوین ناشناخته است. — The domain of new technologies is unknown.
- 81 | 175

4048 تراکم tærakom *compression, density* n
- اندازه جمعیتها و همچنین تراکم آنها افزایش یافت. — The size of the populations, and also their density, increased.
- 68 | 314

4049 بدنه bædæne *body, frame* n
- ۵ مبتکر بریتانیایی، خودرویی با بدنه تمام مقوایی طراحی کردند. — 5 British inventors designed a car with an all-cardboard body.
- 73 | 252

4050 بدهکار bedehkar *debtor, indebted* adj,n
- یعنی آن قدر به حکومت بدهکار بوده که اموالش را ضبط کرده اند؟ — In other words he is in so much debt to the government that they have confiscated his property?
- 85 | 134

4051 یادآوری jadaværi *reminder* n
- — در اینجا یادآوری چند نکته ضروری است. Here it is necessary to recall a few points.
- 71 | 275

4052 حیث hejs *respect* n
- — از این حیث مشابه سوئد و بلژیک است. In this respect it is similar to Sweden and Belgium.
- 60 | 418

4053 صفا sæfa *purity* n,pn
- زن قباد با اینکه کمی چل و خل بود، اما اهل هو و جنجال نبود و با بقیه اهل خانه در صلح و صفا زندگی می کرد. — Even though Ghobad's wife was a little dim-witted and nuts, she wasn't one to cause trouble and lived with the rest of the household in peace and serenity.
- 82 | 160

4054 دیکتاتوری diktatori *dictatorship, dictatorial* adj,n
- مقصود از دیکتاتوری نوع قدرتی است که چند تا از این مشخصات را دارا باشد. — By dictatorship we mean a kind of power which has some of these features.
- 71 | 273

4055 زیربنا zirbæna *infrastructure* n
- زیربنای تشکیل این حکومت را دین‌سالاری شکل داده‌است — Theocracy has formed the infrastructure of this government.
- 77 | 212

4056 در زدن dær zædæn *knock* v
- صدای قدم ها و بعد در زدن او را شنیدیم. — I heard the sound of his steps, and then, the sound of his knocking.
- 74 | 240

4057 فوریت fow?rijjæt *urgency* n
- خواستم به فوریت عینک را بردارم. — I wanted to pick up my glasses with urgency.
- 80 | 183

4058 همگام hæmgam *marching together* adj
- شاه که آمادگی آن را نداشت تا بتواند خود را با درخواست ملی گرایان همگام نماید. — The Shah lacked the preparation to be able to align himself with nationalists' demands.
- 86 | 121

4059 سناریو senarijo *scenario, screenplay* n
- چرا آمریکا این سناریو را مطرح ساخته و باراک اوباما هم به دفاع از آن پرداخته‌است؟ — Why did America raise this scenario and why has Barack Obama supported it?
- 76 | 218

4060 واجب vadʒeb *necessary* adj
- این سوره از ۷ آیه تشکیل شده و در هر نماز واجب و مستحب دو بار خوانده می‌شود . . . — This sura is made up of seven verses and is read twice in each required and recommended prayer . . .
- 85 | 133

4061 دریغ deriɣ *regret, pity* adv,n
- با دریغ و افسوس، خبر درگذشت شاعر بزرگ را دریافت کردم. — With sorrow and regret, I received the news of the great poet's death.
- 82 | 155

4062 تبریزی tæbrizi *Tabrizi* adj,pn
- تبریزی‌ها با بلیط الکترونیکی وارد ورزشگاه شدند. — Tabrizis entered the stadium with electronic tickets.
- 79 | 188

4063 حاکی بودن haki budæn *indicate* v
- مذاکرات انگلیس و روسیه حاکی از اختلاف نظرها در مورد سوریه است. — Britain and Russia's negotiations indicate a difference of opinion on the topic of Syria.
- 71 | 277

4064 بازگشایی bazgoʃaji *reopening* n
- این تونل در شهریور ماه امسال بازگشایی می شود. — The tunnel will be reopened in Shahrivar this year.
- 77 | 210

4065 تلگراف telegraf *telegraph* n
- ایستگاه فرستنده تلگراف بی سیم. — Wireless telegraph transmitter station.
- 88 | 100

4066 جعلی dʒæ?li *forged* adj
- یک نامه جعلی برای آن بکار برد. — He used one fake letter for that.
- 85 | 126

4067 نرم‌افزار nærmæfzar *software* n
- این سوالی است که از یک مهندس نرم‌افزار پرسیده می‌شود — This is a question that is posed to a software engineer, and as a result it has a technical answer. در نتیجه پاسخی فنی نیز دارد.
- 73 | 255

4068 پادگان padegan *garrison, barracks, base* n
- استان‌های مصر تبدیل به پادگان‌های نظامی شدند. — Egyptian provinces were turned into military bases.
- 88 | 104

4069 سرور sorur, særvær *server joy, leader, server* n,pn
- سرور ویکی‌لیکس حراج می‌شود. — WikiLeaks server goes on auction.
- 85 | 129

4070 گرانی gerani *expensive, high prices* adj,n
- گرانی‌های فزاینده رنج‌آور است اما صبوری کنید. — Rising inflation is painful, but be patient.
- 82 | 157

4071 بیمارستانی bimarestani *hospital* adj,n
- عفونت بیمارستانی چیست؟ — What is hospital-acquired infection?

84 | 142

4072 دیابت dijabet *diabetes* n
- مادر من از سال هاست که واریس و دیابت داره. — My mother has had varicose veins and diabetes for years.

70 | 280

4073 مقاوم moɣavem *resistant* adj
- مقاوم‌ترین شیشه نشکن تلفن‌همراه تولید میشود. — The most resistant shatterproof glass for cellphones will be produced.

84 | 143

4074 کوهستانی kuhestani *mountainous* adj
- سرعت مجاز اتوبوس‌ها در جاده‌های کوهستانی باید کاهش یابد. — The speed limit on mountainous roads should be reduced for buses.

68 | 306

4075 فیلمنامه filmname *screenplay* n
- آقای فراهانی مشغول خواندن این فیلمنامه بود. — Mr. Farahani was in the process of reading this film script.

67 | 320

4076 سمنان semnan *Semnan* pn
- استانهای تهران سمنان البرز قزوین — Tehran, Semnan, Alborz, and Ghazvin provinces.

71 | 275

4077 توجیه کردن towdʒih kærdæn *justify* v
- رفتار حسنی قابل توجیه کردن بود. — Hassani's behavior was justifiable.

91 | 74

4078 برگرداندن bærgærdandæn *return* adj,n,v
- لیبی مسافران مصری را به کشورشان برگرداند. — Libya returned the Egyptian passengers to their country.

75 | 230

4079 رها ræha *loose, free* adj
- مرد دوم را همانجا رها کند. — To set the second man free right there.

76 | 220

4080 پستی posti *postal* adj,n
- افزایش تعرفه‌های پستی غیرقانونی است. — Increase in postal rates is illegal.

75 | 226

4081 کتبی kætbi *written* adj
- نامه ی کتبی خواسته اند. — They wanted a written letter.

86 | 119

4082 مولوی mowlævi *Rumi* pn
- رقیب مولوی فریاد زد: «این سرکه نیست بلکه شراب است» — One of Mowlavi's friends shouted, "This is not vinegar, but wine!"

73 | 247

4083 کمپانی kompani *company* n
- فعالیت این کمپانی در زمینه‌های عطر و ادکلن و پوشاک آقایان و خانم‌ها و کفش و محصولات چرمی بود. — This company was active in the areas of perfume, cologne, men and women's clothing, shoes, and leather goods.

72 | 266

4084 پیک pejk, pik *courier, spades* n
- یک پیک موتوری. — A motorcycle messenger.

90 | 88

4085 امکان‌پذیر emkanpæzir *possible* adj
- این به دو شکل امکانپذیر است. — This is possible in two forms.

74 | 237

4086 برجا bærdʒa *stable, fixed* adj
- بار دیگر رکورد قهرمان جهان رضازاده برجا ماند. — Once again the world champion Rezazadeh's record remained in place.

73 | 245

4087 تاجیک tadʒik *Tajik* adj,pn
- از پدری پشتون و مادری تاجیک در شهر مزار شریف افغانستان به دنیا آمد. — He was born to a Pashtun mother and a Tajik father in Mazar-e Sharif, Afghanistan.

83 | 147

4088 دریافتی dærjafti *received, receipt* adj
- چطور اطلاعات دریافتی را مدیریت کنیم؟ — How to manage the received information?

78 | 198

4089 ضمناً zemnæn *incidentally* adv,conj
- ضمناً عکس ها با نام شخص ارسال کننده در وب سایت نمایش داده می شود. — By the way, the photos will be displayed on the website with the name of the person sending them.

82 | 158

4090 رزمی ræzmi *combat* adj
- هوانوردی نظامی دربرگیرنده فعالیتهای رزمی و نیز مأموریت‌های پروازی که برای پشتیبانی نظامی انجام می‌شوند می‌باشد. — Military aviation includes combat activities and also flying missions which are performed for military support.

81 | 169

4091 تعویض tæʔviz *replacing* n
- تعویض تکنولوژی نیروگاه می‌تواند در کاهش آلایندگی مؤثر باشد. — Replacing the power plant's technology would be effective in the reduction of emissions.

78 | 196

4092 چاقی ʃaɣi *obesity* n
- چاقی در مردان خطرناک‌تر از زنان است. — Obesity in men is more dangerous than in women.

83 | 148

4093 صعودی soʔudi *ascending, upward* adj

● Fuel — مصرف بنزین همچنان رشد صعودی دارد. consumption continues to have rising growth.

84 | 141

4094 فلان folan *so and so, such and such* adj, n,pron

● فلان کار را باید بکنی. — You have to do such and such work.

62 | 380

4095 خریداری کردن xæridɑri kærdæn *purchase* v

● برو و شراب خریداری کن. — Go and buy wine.

81 | 166

4096 بوسنی bosni *Bosnia, Bosnian* pn

● سربازان بوسنی در عملیات رزمی 'آیساف' در افغانستان شرکت می کنند. — Bosnian soldiers participate in ISAF combat operations in Afghanistan.

83 | 151

4097 روانه rævane *bound for* adj

● جوانان امروز مانند رزمندگان گذشته روانه جبهه‌ها می‌شوند. — Today's youth, like the warriors of the past, will be sent to the frontlines.

77 | 208

4098 المپیاد olæmpijɑd *Olympics* n

● چهارمین المپیاد دانش آموزی واحدهای آموزشی در تهران. — The fourth students' Olympiad of educational centers in Tehran.

83 | 151

4099 موازات movɑzɑt *parallel* n

● طرح ساخت کانال جدیدی به موازات کانال سوئز آغاز شد. — Plans to build a new canal parallel to the Suez Canal began.

84 | 138

4100 خاور xɑvær *east* n,pn

● قومی به نام کاسی از خاور به فلات ایران راه یافتند. — A tribe called the Kassites found their way to the Iranian Plateau from the east.

83 | 143

4101 انسانیت ensɑnijjæt *humanity* n

● انسانی است که به دست خودش از مسیر انسانیت منحرف شده. — He is a person who has been diverted from the path of humanity by his own hand.

85 | 131

4102 جمع کردن dʒæmʔ kærdæn *collect* v

● شب، شام که خورده شد و سفره را جمع کردند. — At night, after the dinner was eaten, they put away the eating mat.

65 | 340

4103 عادل ɑdel *just* adj,pn

● انسان‌های عادل و منصف، به تقوا نزدیکترند. — Just and fair people are nearer to piety.

76 | 211

4104 نواختن nævɑxtæn *play* adj,n,pn,v

● رافائل میناسکانیان در یادبود استاد درگذشته‌اش پیانو می‌نوازد. — Raphael Minaskanian plays piano in memory of his late master.

82 | 160

4105 عیسی isɑ *Jesus* pn

● من خواب دیدم که عیسی آمد. — I had a dream that Jesus came.

77 | 202

4106 خیریه xejrijje *charitable* adj

● هدف انسان از شرکت در کارهای خیریه چیست؟ — What are people's objectives in participating in charitable activities?

84 | 134

4107 کمین kæmin *ambush* n

● هرگز از کمین دشمنان غافل نشوید. — Don't ever be caught unawares by the enemy's ambush.

91 | 71

4108 مسدود mæsdud *obstructed* adj

● این جهانگرد همچنین نوشته که در آن زمان آب رودخانه هریرود تغییر مسیر داده و از داخل پسته‌زار کنار پل می گذشته و راه را مسدود کرده بود. — This traveler also wrote that at that time the water of the Harirud River changed its course and passed through the pistachio grove next to the bridge and had blocked the road.

82 | 154

4109 کنفدراسیون konfederɑsijon *confederation* n

● عضویت یک پزشک زن ایرانی در کنفدراسیون طب ورزشی آسیا. — Membership of an Iranian female doctor in the Asian Sports Medicine Federation.

77 | 200

4110 یورش joreʃ *attack* n

● در سال 2197 پیش از میلاد به میان رودان (عراق امروزی) یورش بردند و بر اکد چیره شدند. — In the year 2197 BCE, they attacked Mesopotamia (modern-day Iraq), and triumphed over the Akkadians.

82 | 158

4111 تراکتورسازی trɑktorsɑzi *tractor manufacturing* n

● باشگاه تراکتورسازی در سال ۱۳۴۹ با حمایت کارخانه تراکتورسازی تبریز تاسیس شد. — Tractor Club was founded in 1349 with the support of Tabriz Tractor Factory.

76 | 214

4112 شایستگی ʃɑjestegi *merit* n

● It — هیچ مهارت یا شایستگی خاصی را تست نمی کند. doesn't test any specific skill or competency.

81 | 168

4113 نزاع nezɑʔ *quarrel* n

● سخن شما موجب نزاع و دعوا است. — Your talk causes argument and controversy.

87 | 109

4114 درگیر شدن dærgir ʃodæn *engage* v
- آمریکا مایل به درگیر شدن در منطقه با قدرتی چون چین نیست. — America is not willing to come to blows with powers such as China in the region.
83 | 146

4115 سرمایه‌داری særmajedari *capitalism, capitalist* n
- استثمار سرمایه‌داری به مرحله‌ای رسید که فهم سرمایه‌دارانه از نیروی کار غلبه یافت. — The capitalist exploitation reached a stage in which the capitalists' conception of the work force prevailed.
56 | 457

4116 پس گرفتن pæs gereftæn *take back, withdraw* v
- رییس جمهور یمن استعفایش را پس گرفت. — The Yemeni president withdrew his resignation.
85 | 129

4117 پاکسازی paksazi *purging, purification* n
- باکتری‌ها در پاکسازی آب‌ها و خاک‌های آلوده به آلاینده‌های نفتی و شیمیایی کاربرد وسیعی دارند. — Bacteria have extensive application in cleaning waters and soils contaminated with petroleum and chemical pollutants.
74 | 231

4118 ملزم molzæm *obliged, bound* adj
- دیلی تلگراف ملزم به پرداخت غرامت شد. — The Daily Telegraph was obliged to pay compensation.
85 | 129

4119 عوام ʔævam *common people* n
- سازندهٔ تراژدی باید زبانی را به کار گیرد که در مرز باریک بین زبان عوام و زبان خواص واقع باشد. — The producer of tragedy must use language that falls in the narrow range between the language of nobles and commoners.
86 | 120

4120 ایجاب idʒab *obligation* n
- اهمیت این بحران ایجاب کرد که با جناب آقای دکتر بشاراسد رییس جمهور سوریه مصاحبه کنی. — The importance of this crisis required you to interview Bashar Al Assad, Syrian president.
80 | 179

4121 رومانی romani *Romania* pn
- هم اکنون هزاران خرس در جنگل‌های رومانی زندگی می‌کنند. — Still today thousands of bears live in the forests of Romania.
75 | 221

4122 امیدی omidi *Omidi* n,pn
- فراگیری سه‌تار را نزد علی امیدی در یزد آغاز کرده است. — He began learning setar with Ali Omidi in Yazd.
82 | 159

4123 سلطنتی sæltænæti *royal* adj,n
- مردم اسپانیا خواستار برچیده شدن نظام سلطنتی شدند. — Spanish people were calling for the abolition of the monarchy.
76 | 212

4124 اخلال exlal *disruption* n
- اخلال در زندان جرم است. — Disruption in prison is a crime.
90 | 85

4125 شاهزاده ʃahzade *prince* n,pn
- شاهزاده ابراهیم رفت به شکار. — Prince Ebrahim went hunting.
71 | 270

4126 تطبیق tætbiq *comparison* adj,n
- این برنامه چطور با برنامه جهانی جنرال‌موتورز تطبیق پیدا خواهد کرد؟ — How will this plan match up with global plan of General Motors?
59 | 414

4127 فروشی foruʃi *for sale* adj,v
- این خودرو فروشی نیست. — This car is not for sale.
76 | 213

4128 تعمیق tæʔmiq *fathoming, deepening* n
- بر تعمیق همکاریهای اقتصادی تاکید کرده اند. — They emphasized deepening economic cooperation.
81 | 160

4129 اضطراری ezterari *forced, emergency* adj
- پارلمان ترکیه رسماً وضعیت اضطراری ۳ ماهه را تصویب کرد. — The Turkish Parliament formally approved the 3-month state of emergency.
77 | 202

4130 بی‌سابقه bisabeye *unprecedented* adj
- موج بی‌سابقه گرما چین را فرا گرفت. — An unprecedented heat wave took hold of China.
63 | 364

4131 مظهر mæzhær *manifestation, symbol* n
- از سوی دیگر این نیرو باید مظهر اعتماد و مهربانی نسبت به مردم باشد. — On the other hand, this force should be a symbol of trust and kindness towards people.
75 | 224

4132 فیلمساز filmsaz *filmmaker* n
- عده ای از نویسندگان وفیلمسازان روسی. — A number of Russian writers and filmmakers.
72 | 257

4133 ملا molla, mælæ? *mullah, assembly* n
- مختصر مقصود من ذکر یک شاهکار مرحوم ملا بود. — In short, my intention was to mention a masterpiece of the late Mullah.
59 | 409

4134 بارسلونا barselona *Barcelona* pn
- بارسلونا قهرمان جام باشگاه‌های جهان شد. — Barcelona won the Club World Cup.
72 | 259

4135 درخشش deræxʃeʃ *brilliance* n
- درخشش ستارگان زیباست. — The brilliance of the stars is beautiful.

83 | 147

4136 عمو æmu *paternal uncle* n
- عمو زنجیرباف بلند شو. — Get up uncle Zanjirbaf!

61 | 387

4137 معصومه mæʔsume *Masume* pn
- معصومه عباسی روز شنبه در گفت وگو با ایرنا افزود. — On Saturday Masume Abbasi in an interview with IRNA added . . .

79 | 183

4138 دهکده dehkæde *village* n
- همان شب آن دهکده را ترک کرد. — The same night he left the village.

80 | 174

4139 جانبی dʒanebi *lateral, side* adj,n
- آیا داروهای ضد افسردگی عوارض جانبی دارند؟ — Do antidepressants have side effects?

79 | 182

4140 کمر kæmær *waist* n
- اندازه دور کمر نشان دهنده ریسک ابتلا به بیماری کبد است. — Waist size indicates risk of developing liver disease.

69 | 284

4141 فوتسال futsal *indoor soccer* n
- تیم ملی فوتسال ایران در اولین بازی خود در رقابتهای جامجهانی کوچک مقابل آرژانتین به تساوی رسید. — Iran's national futsal team tied Argentina in their first game in the mini world cup tournament.

71 | 268

4142 مفهومی mæfhumi *conceptual* adj,n
- آثار مفهومی جشنواره فجر تکراری است. — The conceptual works in Fajr Visual Arts Festival are repetitive.

80 | 169

4143 ترکمن torkæmæn *Turkmen* adj,n,pn
- علاوه بر زبان فارسی، به ترکی قزلباش و ترکمنی نیز تسلط دارد. — In addition to Persian, she also has a command of the Qizilbash Turkish and Turkmen languages.

85 | 129

4144 ویرانی virani *destruction* n
- غرب ویرانی سوریه را میخواهد. — The West desires the destruction of Syria.

85 | 121

4145 محموله mæhmule *shipment* n
- این محموله با مجوز رسمی از آمریکا بارگیری شده بود. — This cargo had been loaded with an official permit from America.

72 | 252

4146 تنفر tænæffor *aversion, hatred* n
- شباهت خشم و تنفر در چیست. — What is the similarity between anger and hatred?

92 | 63

4147 ابری æbri *cloudy* adj,n
- هوای کرکوک ابری است. — Kirkuk weather is cloudy.

87 | 109

4148 حائز hɑez *possessing, holding, eligible* adj
- ایران حائز رتبه اول قطعی اینترنت منطقه شد. — Iran holds first place in internet outages in the region.

76 | 207

4149 حیدری hejdæri *Heidari* pn
- علیرضا حیدری نایب رئیس فدراسیون کشتی شد. — Alireza Heidari became the vice president of Wrestling Federation.

81 | 162

4150 زمره zomre *group* n
- او که در زمره سرداران ممتاز سپاه داریوش بود، — As he was an elite level commander in Darius's army . . .

79 | 183

4151 امینی æmini *Amini* pn
- مهناز امینی در یک روز دومین طلا را هم شکار کرد. — Mahnaz Amini hunted for her second gold in one day.

83 | 141

4152 همزیستی hæmzisti *coexistence* n
- ایران خواهان همزیستی مسالمت آمیز در منطقه است. — Iran calls for peaceful coexistence in the region.

88 | 98

4153 حدوداً hodudæn *approximately* adv,q
- در ۱۹۰۰، عبور از اقیانوس اطلس حدوداً پنج روز به طول میانجامید. — In 1900, crossing the Atlantic Ocean would take about five days.

84 | 138

4154 شنونده ʃenævænde *listener* n
- در واقع شنونده را برای شنیدن خبر نهایی آماده میکند. — In fact, it prepares the listener to hear the final news.

80 | 170

4155 هیچکس hitʃkæs *nobody* pron
- در این پروسه هیچکس صاحب پول نشده است. — In this process, no one has had control over the money.

68 | 297

4156 کیسه kise *bag* n
- این کیسه پلاستیکی متعلق به دو مسافر بوده است. — This plastic bag belonged to two passengers.

64 | 338

4157 هاله hɑle *halo, aura* n,pn
- هاله سفید رنگ درخشانی در اطراف ماه میدرخشد. — A bright white halo shines around the moon.

90 | 83

4158 دری *Dari adj,n,pn*

- آن چیزی که به عنوان زبان دری شناخته می‌شود با زبان
  فارسی رایج در ایران تفاوتی ندارد. — What is known
  as Dari language isn't any different from the
  Persian language spoken in Iran.

  57 | 436

4159 ضمانت *zemɑnæt guarantee n*

- فرمودند من برای تو ضمانت درخت خرما در بهشت می‌
  کنم. — He stated, "For you, I guarantee a
  palm tree in paradise."

  83 | 144

4160 مشت *moʃt fist n,q*

- مشت محکمی به دهان دشمن است. — It is a strong
  fist into the mouth of enemy.

  67 | 310

4161 رفسنجانی *ræfsændʒɑni Rafsanjani pn*

- اکبر هاشمی رفسنجانی از ۱۳۶۸ تا ۱۳۷۶ در دو دوره
  پیاپی رئیس جمهور بود. — Akbar Hashemi
  Rafsanjani was president from 1368 to 1376
  in two consecutive terms.

  64 | 341

4162 جنین *dʒænin fetus n*

- زنان باردار در سه ماه اول بارداری به ویژه هشت هفته
  اول به دلیل تشکیل سلول‌های مغزی جنین نباید روزه
  بگیرند. — Pregnant women should not fast
  during the first trimester of their pregnancy
  and specifically in the first eight weeks
  because of the formation of the fetus's
  brain cells.

  72 | 248

4163 اراک *ærak Arak pn*

- بزرگترین شهر و مرکز استان مرکزی شهر اراک می‌باشد.
  — Arak is the largest city and the capital of
  Markazi province.

  72 | 248

4164 قرائت *yærɑʔæt recitation n*

- در پایان نشست نامه‌ای به امضای نماینده مجلس خطاب به
  رئیس جمهوری قرائت شد. — At the end of the
  session, a letter signed by the Majles
  representative and addressed to the
  president was read.

  63 | 349

4165 همفکری *hæmfekri exchanging ideas n*

- تجربه نشان داده که با همفکری کارها بهتر پیش می‌رود.
  — Experience has shown that with
  exchanging ideas things get done better.

  90 | 80

4166 صرف کردن *særf kærdæn spend time, consume,
  conjugate v*

- در برخی از افعال هنگام صرف کردن فعل، حروف صدا
  دار تغییر می‌کند. — When some verbs are
  conjugated, the vowels change.

  86 | 111

4167 سفره *sofre tablecloth n*

- مادر سفره‌ی شام را مهیا می کرد. — Mother was
  preparing the dinner spread.

  69 | 283

4168 اینطور *intur this way adv*

- اینطور کار کردن را بسیار دوست دارم. — I like
  working this way a lot.

  60 | 385

4169 طباطبایی *tæbɑtæbɑji Tabatabai pn*

- طباطبایی سرپرست فدراسیون وزنه برداری شد.
  — Tabatabai became the head of the
  Weightlifting Federation.

  81 | 162

4170 اهرم *æhrom lever n,pn*

- به عنوان اهرم فشار بر ایران به شمار می‌آورد.
  It is being considered as leverage against Iran.

  86 | 113

4171 گریه *gerje cry n*

- گریه خوب است یا بد؟ — Is crying good or bad?

  57 | 421

4172 شهروندی *ʃæhrvændi citizenship adj,n*

- دسترسی آزاد به اطلاعات حق شهروندی است. — Free
  access to information is a right of citizenship.

  83 | 144

4173 جنجالی *dʒændʒɑli tumultuous adj*

- دادگاه محاکمه او یکی از جنجالی‌ترین دادگاه‌های اواخر قرن
  بیستم بود. — His court trial was one of the most
  controversial trials in the late twentieth century.

  86 | 110

4174 معاهده *moʔɑhede treaty n*

- مطابق به معاهده استراتیژیک میان هر دو کشور به
  همکاری‌های خود حتی پس از سال 2014 نیز ادامه میدهیم.
  — In accordance with the strategic treaty
  between both countries we are continuing
  our cooperation even after 2014.

  72 | 249

4175 حیرت *hejræt amazement n*

- مرد با حیرت پرسید. — The man asked with
  surprise.

  79 | 178

4176 نیما *nima Nima pn*

- تو فقط تا فردا با مایی، نیما؟ — Are you only with us
  until tomorrow, Nima?

  52 | 491

4177 سبزی *sæbzi greens n*

- مادر لیلا سبزی خرد می‌کرد. — Leila's mother was
  chopping greens.

  75 | 217

4178 گستردگی *gostærdegi span n*

- این ایالت با وجود گستردگی، کم‌جمعیت ترین ایالت پاکستان
  است. — This state, despite its size, is
  Pakistan's most sparsely populated province.

  77 | 202

26 Dari months (by month order)

Rank	Headword	Pronunciation	Gloss	Rank	Headword	Pronunciation	Gloss
1118	حمل	hæmæl	*Aries*	245	میزان	mizan	*Libra*
12791	ثور	sowr, sæwr	*Taurus*	10535	عقرب	æɣræb	*Scorpio*
	جوزا	dʒowza, dʒæwza	*Gemini*	6861	قوس	ɣows, ɣæws	*Sagittarius*
2003	سرطان	særætan	*Cancer*	307	جدی	dʒædi	*Capricorn*
2865	اسد	æsæd	*Leo*	11311	دلو	dælv, dælw	*Aquarius*
17507	سنبله	sombole, sombolæ	*Virgo*	18000	حوت	hut	*Pisces*

4179 مرکب mærkæb, morækkæb *horse, compound/ ink* adj,n
- مرکب و قلمی. — Pen and ink.

79 | 181

4180 بنی bæni *sons, Bani* n,pn
- بنی‌آدم اعضای یکدیگرند. — Human beings are members of a whole.

81 | 159

4181 پیاپی pejɑpej *consecutive* adj
- کافی است چند عکس پیاپی بگیرید تا نرم افزار عکس ها را به هم وصل کند و شما بتوانید ۳۶۰ درجه کامل را ببینید. — All you have to do is take a number of pictures one after the other so that the software joins them together and you can see 360 degrees around.

71 | 260

4182 بادی bɑdi *wind, air* adj,n
- در نیروگاه بادی، توربین بادی اصلی ترین جزء به حساب می آید. — In wind power plants the wind turbine is the major component.

87 | 105

4183 دربار dærbɑr *royal court, palace* n
- این پیمان روسیه و آلمان موجب خشم مردم و دربار ایران شد. — This treaty between Russia and Germany angered the people and the royal court of Iran.

72 | 243

4184 واکنشی vɑkoneʃi *reactive, reflexive* adj,n
- شرطی‌شدن واکنشی چیست؟ — What is respondent conditioning?

84 | 135

4185 استرس estres *stress* n
- به این دلیل که خیلی چیزها را در مورد آن مطلب نمی دانید، به خود استرس ندهید. — Due to the fact that you do not know much about this topic, don't stress yourself out.

68 | 287

4186 حسنی hosni, hæsæni *Hosni, Hasani* n,pn
- حسنی مبارک، رئیس جمهور این کشور برکنار شد. — Hosni Mubarak, the country's president, was ousted.

70 | 273

4187 شیعی ʃiʔi *Shiite* adj
- بحث فلسفه تاریخ اجتماعی بشر مبتنی بر تفکر شیعی است. — The debate on the philosophy of mankind's social history is based on Shiite thought.

82 | 148

4188 توسعه دادن towseʔe dɑdæn *expand, develop* v
- برنامه صلح آمیز هسته‌ای را توسعه می‌دهیم. — We are developing a peaceful nuclear program.

89 | 89

4189 پلاستیکی pelɑstiki *plastic* adj
- خرید و فروش اسلحه پلاستیکی در افغانستان ممنوع شد. — Plastic arms trade was banned in Afghanistan.

84 | 134

4190 رحم ræhm, ræhem *compassion, womb* n
- خدایا به تو پناه می برم. به بچه های من رحم کن. — Oh God, I seek refuge in you. Have mercy on my children.

75 | 220

4191 گرفتار شدن gereftɑr ʃodæn *get caught* v
- من در چنگال احساسی گرفتار شده بودم. — I had been seized by a clutch of emotions.

84 | 128

4192 مشتاق moʃtɑɣ *eager* adj,n,pn
- مردم روستا بسیار مشتاق شده بودند. — The people of the village had become excited.

84 | 128

4193 ایثار isɑr *altruism, sacrifice* n
- اگر روح ایثار و خطاپوشی در میان زن و مرد حاکم باشد. — If the spirit of sacrifice and forgiveness prevails between women and men . . .

87 | 108

4194 بخیر bexejr *good* adv
- صبح بخیر آقای کاسترو. — Good morning, Mr. Castro.

53 | 472

4195 سرتیپ særtip *brigadier general* n
- سرتیپ همش مسخره میکنه. — The brigadier general does everything in a ridiculous way.

84 | 127

4196 غرفه ɣorfe *booth* n
- در کنار آن ایوان ها و غرفه های قدیمی وجود دارد. — There are pavilions and porches next to it.

76 | 206

4197 ذاتی zati *inherent, intrinsic* adj
- مبارزه با جرم ماموریت ذاتی نیروی انتظامی است. — Crime-fighting is the intrinsic mission of law enforcement.

79 | 180

4198 کتیبه kætibe *inscription* n
- این خط برای نوشتن کتیبههای هخامنشی به کار رفتهاست. — This script was used for writing Achaemenid inscriptions.

66 | 308

4199 کنارهگیری kenaregiri *resignation* n
- آماده کنارگیری هستم. — I am ready to step down.

70 | 263

4200 وقف væɣf *religious endowment, devotion* n
- همه ی زندگی اش را وقف شوهر بیمارش کرد. — All of his life was devoted to her sick husband.

85 | 124

4201 بازجویی bazdʒuji *interrogation* n
- اف بی ای هیلاری کلینتون را برای بازجویی احضار میکند. — The FBI summoned Hillary Clinton for questioning.

73 | 235

4202 استرالیایی ostralijaji *Australian* adj,n
- زن ۶۳ ساله استرالیایی مادر شد. — 63-year-old Australian woman becomes a mother.

82 | 144

4203 چیدن tʃidæn *pick, pluck, set* adj,n,v
- در حال تاب خوردن، سیب را از درخت میچیند. — While swinging, she picks an apple from the tree.

67 | 299

4204 عامه amme *public* n,q
- فرهنگ عامه روی رفتار و کردار اجتماعی تاثیر میگذارد. — Public culture affects social behavior and conduct.

69 | 278

4205 تأثیرگذار tæʔsirgozar *impressive, effective* adj
- دیپلماسی تأثیرگذار ریشه در حرکتهای فرهنگی دارد. — Effective diplomacy is rooted in cultural movements.

73 | 238

4206 قانونگذاری ɣanungozari *legislation* n
- توهین به مجلس در طول تاریخ قانونگذاری بیسابقه بود. — Insulting the parliament was unprecedented in legislative history.

77 | 192

4207 کلاً kollæn *totally* adv
- کلاً جمعیت زرتشتیان جهان را بیش از دویست و ده هزار نفر ندانستهاند. — They have not estimated the total world population of Zoroastrians to be more than two hundred and ten thousand.

81 | 160

4208 مظنون mæznun *suspect* adj,n
- پلیس با فرد مظنون رفتار خشنی دارد و سپس اتاق را ترک میکند. — The police officer acts in a violent manner with the suspect and leaves the room . . .

84 | 129

4209 باشکوه baʃokuh *magnificent* adj
- انتخاباتی باشکوه برگزار شد. — A magnificent election was held.

82 | 145

4210 رویتر rujter *Reuters* pn
- رویتر گزارش می دهد. — Reuters reports.

60 | 380

4211 حجاب hedʒab *veil* n
- زنان محجبه ادارات دولتی ترکیه از این پس میتوانند با حجاب اسلامی در سر کار خود حاضر شوند. — From now on, hijab wearing women in Turkish government offices will be able to go to their place of work with the Islamic hijab.

67 | 298

4212 شن ʃen *gravel* n
- استاد دوباره دست به جعبه برد و چند مشت شن را برداشت و داخل لیوان ریخت. — The professor put his hand in the box again, picked up a few handfuls of sand, and poured them into the cup.

79 | 179

4213 راضی razi *satisfied* adj
- از کدام یک از آنها مشخصاً راضی هستید؟ — Which of them are you satisfied with, specifically?

85 | 117

4214 تست test *test* n
- تست کلینیکی در حال انجام است. — Clinical testing is in progress.

76 | 206

4215 بیتوجهی bitævædʒohi *inattentiveness* n
- این میدان نیز مانند سایر بناهای تاریخی اصفهان مورد بیتوجهی قرار گرفت. — Like the rest of the historical monuments in Isfahan, this square was neglected.

80 | 166

4216 سازوکار sazokar *mechanism* n

- تلاشی برای ایجاد یک سازوکار شفاف به منظور گسترش عضویت در شورای امنیت صورت نمی‌گیرد. — An effort was not made to create a transparent mechanism for expanding membership in the Security Council.

83 | 136

4217 خرم xorræm *green, lush* adj,pn

- این بهشت به شکل باغی سبز، خرم و زیبا مجسم می‌شده است. — This paradise was imagined in the form of a beautiful, lush and green garden.

76 | 202

4218 ریزش rizeʃ *spilling, precipitation* n

- در صورت ریزش باران، کلیه کارگران را با کلاه ایمنی به سالن نهار خوری ببرید. — In case of rain, bring all of the workers with safety helmets to the lunch room.

81 | 156

4219 نابسامانی nabesamani *chaos* n

- چه کسانی مسئول نابسامانی ها هستند؟ — Who is responsible for the chaos?

85 | 123

4220 عرفات æræfat *Arafat* pn

- اولین میهمان خارجی که بلافاصله پس از انقلاب به تهران آمد، یاسر عرفات بود. — The first foreign guest who came to Tehran immediately after the revolution was Yasser Arafat.

67 | 302

4221 تصفیه tæsfije *purging, purifying* n

- آب حاوی موادالی و بیولوژیک به فرآیندهای خاص تصفیه نیاز دارد. — The water containing biological and organic materials requires special treatment processes.

84 | 133

4222 ناخواسته naxaste *unwanted* adj,adv

- خواسته یا ناخواسته من هم سوار بر موج سیاسی کشور شدم. — Whether I liked it or not, I too was riding the country's political wave.

79 | 176

4223 موبایل mobajl *mobile phone* n

- صدای زنگ موبایل قطع می شود ... — The ringing of the cell phone stops . . .

86 | 115

4224 فرار کردن færar kærdæn *escape* v

- حیوانات دیگر از ترس فرار می‌کردند. — The other animals were running away out of fear.

73 | 238

4225 معاویه moʔavije *Muawiyah* pn

- آیا ای معاویه میدانی علی کیست؟ — Hey Moavieh, do you know who Ali is?

53 | 476

4226 شمس ʃæms *sun, Shams* pn

- شمس پهلوی در ۱۰ اسفند ۱۳۷۴ در سن ۷۸ سالگی درگذشت. — Shams Pahlavi died on 10 Esfand 1374 at the age of 78.

78 | 186

4227 هی hej *hey, continuously, keep* adv,pn

- هی اصرار می کرد بیا بریم یه جا بشینیم حرف بزنیم. — He kept insisting we go sit somewhere and talk.

48 | 549

4228 صادقانه sadeɣane *truthful, truthfully* adj,adv

- صادقانه مذاکره کنید. — Negotiate honestly!

82 | 145

4229 مسافربری mosaferbæri *passenger (service)* adj,n

- هواپیمای مسافربری کانادا مجبور به فرود اضطراری شد. — Canada passenger jet was forced to make an emergency landing.

83 | 136

4230 کرمجنوبی korejeʤonubi *South Korea* pn

- کرمجنوبی در دو بازی آینده خود میزبان سوریه است. — South Korea would host Syria for its two future games.

53 | 473

4231 ادیب ædib *literary scholar* adj,n,pn

- او انسانی فرهیخته و ادیب بود. — He was a literary scholar and a sophisticated person.

79 | 172

4232 بانی bani *sponsor, builder* n

- چون این بنا بسیار کهنه‌است نمی‌توان بانی آن را معلوم کرد. — Since the building is very old, its builder cannot be determined.

82 | 147

4233 پرستار pæræstar *nurse* n,pn

- پرستاران ایرانی کجا می‌روند؟ — Where do Iranian nurses go?

65 | 317

4234 متغیر motæɣæjjer *variable* adj,n

- میزان نیاز کشور به واردات برنج متغیر است. — The country's need for rice imports is variable.

66 | 306

4235 مستعد mostæʔedd *talented* adj

- بسیار قابل و مستعد است. — She is very able and talented.

81 | 154

4236 محو mæhv *obliterated* adj

- این مشکلات محو و فراموش خواهند شد. — These problems will be erased and forgotten.

78 | 187

4237 اهتمام ehtemam *endeavor* n

- به اهتمام و نظارت الله وردی خان. — With Allahverdi Khan's dedication and supervision.

78 | 181

4238 گاو gav *cow, bull, ox* n
- گاوها دو نفر را در پامپلونا شاخ زدند. — Bulls gored two people in Pamplona.
66 | 307

4239 انتخابیه entexabije *electoral* adj,n
- حوزه انتخابیه تهران. — Tehran electoral constituency.
67 | 289

4240 قبولی γæbuli *acceptance* adj,n
- میزان قبولی‌ها پایین بود. — The passing rate was low.
80 | 167

4241 شانگهای ʃanghaj *Shanghai* pn
- سازمان همکاری شانگهای. — Shanghai Cooperation Organization.
77 | 190

4242 وحید væhid *Vahid* pn
- در این بازی وحید شمسایی به عنوان بهترین بازیکن انتخاب شد. — Vahid Shamsaei was elected as the best player in the game.
80 | 165

4243 تعرفه tæʔrefe *tariff* n
- باید تعرفه پارچه پایین بیاید. — The tariff for fabric should be reduced.
69 | 268

4244 نوید nævid *good news, Navid* n,pn
- رمان حسادت نوید ظهور یک نویسنده صاحب سبک را می‌داد. — The novel *La Jalousie* promised the advent of a stylist.
81 | 153

4245 محکومیت mæhkumijjæt *conviction, condemnation* n
- قوه قضائیه هیچ گونه اقدامی برای محکومیت آنان به عمل نیاورده. — The judicial branch has not done anything for their convictions.
78 | 181

4246 دردناک dærdnak *painful* adj
- مورچه آتشین، دردناک‌ترین نیش را در میان حشرات دارد. — Fire ants have the most painful sting among all insects.
84 | 127

4247 ریاض rijaz *Riyadh* pn
- در سال 2011 نیز ریاض خواستار خرید 200 عراده تانک لئوپارد 2 از آلمان شده بود که این امر با مخالفت‌هایی در داخل آلمان مواجه شد. — In 2011, Riyadh had also requested to buy 200 Leopard 2 tanks from Germany which was met with objections within Germany.
78 | 184

4248 موادمخدر mævademoxæder *narcotics* n
- مهم‌ترین محل اثر موادمخدر بر مغز است. — The most significant effect of narcotics is on the brain.
48 | 534

4249 تعلق tæʔælloγ *attachment, belonging* n
- فراموش میکنن به کجای افغانستان تعلق دارند شمالش یا جنوب. — They forget what part of Afghanistan they belong to, the north or the south.
80 | 159

4250 تالاب talab *pond, wetlands* n
- یک دسته از پرندگان فلامینگو روز شنبه در تالاب بوجاق زیبا کنار فرود آمدند. — On Saturday, a group of flamingos landed next to the Bujagh wetlands in Zibakenar.
74 | 221

4251 اسکار oskar *Oscar* pn
- در همان دقیقه چهارم توسط اسکار گلزنی کرده و از حریف خود پیش افتادند. — In the fourth minute, Oscar scored them a goal and they outstripped their opponent.
76 | 203

4252 سیاره sæjjare *planet* n
- تهران به صورت آلوده ترین شهر سیاره زمین درآمده. — Tehran has become the most polluted city on planet Earth.
75 | 206

4253 خسته xæste *tired* adj
- من از این بحث خسته شده‌ام. — I have grown tired of this discussion.
69 | 265

4254 رحیمی ræhimi *Rahimi* pn
- محمدرضا رحیمی به اوین بازگشت. — Mohammad Reza Rahimi returned to Evin prison.
78 | 181

4255 اذیت æzijjæt *harassment* n
- صحنه‌های شکنجه و بازجویی اذیتم کرد. — The interrogation and torture scenes bothered me.
82 | 144

4256 کلاه kolah *hat* n
- کلاه از سر برداشته بود. — He had removed his hat.
60 | 369

4257 معتاد moʔtad *addicted* adj,n
- شوهرم معتاد بود. — My husband was an addict.
69 | 265

4258 رهگذر ræhgozær *passerby* n
- شاید برای یک رهگذر ساده تماشای این صحنه ها ساده به نظر برسد ولی برای ما درد آور است. — Perhaps for a simple passerby, it seemed simple to witness that scene, but for us, it was painful.
81 | 153

4259 عکاسی ækasi *photography* n
- کتاب عکاسی ماکرو و کلوزآپ منتشر شد. — A close-up and macro photography book was released.
79 | 169

4260 پنجه **pændʒe** *hand, claw, paw* n,pn
- از هر پنجنشان چند هنر می‌ریخت. — Artistry poured forth from all of their hands.

74 | 216

4261 اکرم **ækræm** *dearer* adj,pn
- پیامبر اکرم تصمیم گرفت که کار آنان را یکسره کند. — Dearest Prophet decided to adjudicate their work.

68 | 279

4262 تلخی **tælxi** *bitterness* adj,n
- تمام تلخی دنیا را من غارت کرده ام. — I have plundered all of the world's bitterness.

83 | 137

4263 طبعاً **tæbʔæn** *naturally* adv
- طبعاً آدم‌های مجنونی مثل من را نیز بیشتر به خود جذب می‌کرد. — He naturally attracted insane people like me more.

76 | 200

4264 فراغت **farayæt** *leisure* n
- در اوقات فراغت تابستان گذشته. — During last summer's leisure time.

69 | 272

4265 دال **dal, dall** *letter dal, indicative* adj,n
- مدارک دال بر گناهکار بودن متهم است. — The documents are the indication of the guilt of the accused.

88 | 91

4266 میثاق **misay** *promise, convention* n
- با خدا میثاق بسته‌اند. — They have made a promise to God.

84 | 128

4267 کشتیرانی **keʃtirani** *shipping* n
- رودخانه در قسمت سفلی خود از ساحل تا نزدیکی اهواز قابل کشتیرانی است. — The river in its lower part from the coast to near Ahvaz is good for shipping.

85 | 117

4268 خدشه **xædʃe** *scratch, blemish* n
- واردکردن خدشه به استقلال این کشور. — To compromise the independence of the country.

86 | 111

4269 قیاس **yijas** *analogy, comparison* n
- آیا ایرانیان در قیاس با دیگر ملل افراد باهوشی هستند؟ — Are Iranians smart people in comparison to other nations?

84 | 122

4270 هدایت کردن **hedajæt kærdæn** *guide* v
- مسافر بی‌تجربه هواپیما را هدایت کرد. — An inexperienced passenger steered the plane.

84 | 122

4271 موازی **movazi** *parallel* adj
- به شکل موازی روی آنها کار می‌کنند. — They work on them in a parallel manner.

78 | 175

4272 فضل **fæzl** *excellence, erudition* n,pn
- کسانی که خود دارای فضل و دانش بودند، فرزندانشان را خودشان آموزش می‌دادند. — Those who had erudition and knowledge taught their children themselves.

77 | 187

4273 مدام **modam** *continuous* adj,adv
- مدام اشک می‌ریختم. — I wept continuously.

69 | 267

4274 رانده **rande** *driven, expelled* adj,v
- شیطان در این روز خوار و حقیرتر و رانده‌تر و در خشمناک‌ترین اوقات خواهد بود. — On this day, Satan will be more despised and cast off, and will be at his most furious moments.

83 | 133

4275 سعیدی **sæʔidi** *Saidi* pn
- طنز در سروده‌های محمدشریف سعیدی، اغلب تلخ است. — Satire in Mohammad Sharif Saeedi's poems is often bitter.

84 | 129

4276 مقطعی **mæɣtæʔi** *sectional, improvised* adj,n
- ناشران این مجلات هم بیشتر به دنبال اهداف کوتاه مدت و مقطعی بوده اند. — The publishers of these magazines have been more interested in short-term and improvised goals.

83 | 137

4277 لحن **læhn** *tone* n
- این جمله را با لحنی دیگر ادا کرد. — She said this sentence with a different tone.

72 | 238

4278 بنیادین **bonjadin** *fundamental, basic* adj
- از ذرات بنیادین تا بزرگ ترین سیاره ها را دربر می‌گیرد. — It includes all the fundamental particles to the largest planets.

80 | 164

4279 سپاس **sepas** *gratitude* n
- من ترا شکر و سپاس می‌گویم. — I thank you.

76 | 193

4280 نوبه **nowbe** *shivering, turn* n
- این ناحیه‌ها نیز به نوبه خود به ۵۴ شهرستان تقسیم شده‌اند. — These districts are in turn divided into 54 cities.

83 | 135

4281 دستور دادن **dæstur dadæn** *order* v
- بارندگی که شروع شد دستور دادم بخاری ها را از هفت صبح بسوزانند. — When the rain started I ordered them to light the heaters at seven in the morning.

75 | 205

4282 ایرلند irlænd *Ireland* pn
- وزیر دارایی ایرلند تاکید کرده است کسری بودجه در سال جاری همچنان طبق برنامه است. — Ireland's Finance Minister emphasized that the budget deficit in the current year is still in accordance with the plan.
- 81 | 149

4283 خامنه‌ای xameneji *Khamenei* pn
- هم اکنون آیت الله خامنه‌ای فرمانده کل قوا جمهوری اسلامی ایران می‌باشد. — Ayatollah Khamenei is currently the Commander in Chief of the Islamic Republic of Iran.
- 51 | 483

4284 بدو bædv *beginning* n
- او در بدو تولد به زردی مبتلا شد. — He had jaundice from birth.
- 78 | 176

4285 کاستی kasti *decrease, shortcoming* n
- بازیکنان ما به شدت تلاش می‌کنند تا کاستی‌ها و کمبودی‌های خود را برطرف کنند. — Our players are working hard to fix their flaws and shortcomings.
- 76 | 195

4286 واکسن vaksæn *vaccine* n
- بعد از تزریق واکسن او را به بیمارستان شریعتی انتقال دادهاند. — After the vaccination they transferred him to Shariati Hospital.
- 76 | 193

4287 دامی dami *livestock* adj,n
- علوم دامی، شاخه‌ای از مهندسی کشاورزی بشمار می‌آیند. — Animal science is considered a branch of agricultural engineering.
- 85 | 118

4288 حماسی hæmasi *epic* adj
- آلبوم منظومه‌های حماسی منتشر شد. — The album *Epic Poems* was released.
- 84 | 122

4289 رنگین rængin *colored* adj
- یک فنچ نر بالغ رنگین‌تر و معمولاً به راحتی از فنچ ماده قابل تشخیص است. — An adult male finch is more colorful and usually more easily recognizable than female finches.
- 89 | 84

4290 کمربند kæmærbænd *belt* n,pn
- انگار داشت کمربندش را باز می‌کرد. — As if he was unbuckling his belt.
- 80 | 156

4291 رفتار کردن ræftar kærdæn *behave* v
- کوروش کبیر با همه به نیکی و داد رفتار کرد. — Cyrus the Great acted with kindness and justice towards everybody.
- 74 | 212

4292 سوگند sowgænd *oath* n
- به سوگندی که در مجلس خوردید وفادار باشید. — Be faithful to the oath you took in parliament.
- 76 | 196

4293 واگذار کردن vagozar kærdæn *hand over* v
- واگذار کردن کارها یک مهارت است. — Delegating tasks is a skill.
- 79 | 165

4294 تختی tæxti *Takhti* pn
- جهان پهلوان «تختی» یکی از اسطوره های ورزش ایران است. — World champion Takhti is one of the legends of Iranian sports.
- 81 | 152

4295 مازاد mazad *surplus* adj,n
- به علت حاصلخیزی زمین های کشاورزی در اکثر تولیدات آن مازاد بر نیاز استان است و صادر می گردد. — Due to the fertility of its farmlands, most of its products are surplus to the needs of the province and are exported.
- 72 | 237

4296 آسیب رساندن asib resandæn *cause injury* v
- عینک‌های آفتابی ارزان به چشم آسیب می‌رساند. — Cheap sunglasses harm the eyes.
- 86 | 105

4297 جنگلی dʒængæli *forest* adj
- درهای پارک جنگلی یاس در تهران به روی شهروندان باز شد. — Jasmine Natural Park in Tehran opened its doors to the public.
- 75 | 207

4298 تجلی tædʒælli *manifestation* n
- خداوند به موسی فرمود بر کوهی تجلی می کنم ، اگر کوه بر جای خود ماند آنگاه می توانید مرا ببینید. — God said to Moses,"I will become manifest on a mountain, if the mountain remains in its place, you will be able to see me."
- 78 | 176

4299 ایوان ejvan *portico* n,pn
- پدر و مادر پشت به ما بودند، توی ایوان. — Our mom and dad were behind us on the porch.
- 66 | 298

4300 تخم toxm *egg, seed* n
- یک دانه تخم سیب داد. — She gave one apple seed.
- 74 | 217

4301 خم xæm, xom *bend, jar* adj,n
- با پایین آمدن پرده خم می شدند. — They bowed with the lowering of the curtain.
- 58 | 384

4302 جنازه dʒenaze *corpse* n
- در این موقع پسرکی که نزدیک جنازه دختر ایستاده بود، گفت «بروید کنار!» — At that moment a little boy who was standing near the corpse of the girl said, "Move aside!"
- 76 | 198

4303 وزش væzeʃ *blowing* n

- وزش بادها در شهر مشهد بیشتر در جهت جنوب شرقی به شمال غربی است. — The direction of the wind blowing in Mashhad is mainly from the southeast to northwest.

73 | 220

4304 هواشناسی hævaʃenasi *meteorology* n

- هواشناسی البرز نسبت به وقوع سیل هشدار داد. — Alborz Meteorology warned of the incidence of flood.

80 | 159

4305 سرنگونی særneguni *overthrow* n

- رهبری الترابی را به همدستی با شورشیان دارفور و تلاش برای سرنگونی دولت از طریق اقدام مسلحانه متهم کرده است. — Al-Turabi leadership has been accused of collaboration with the Darfur insurgents and trying to overthrow the government through armed action.

65 | 310

4306 راسخ rasex *firm* adj,pn

- عزم راسخ ایران برای مبارزه با قاچاق و عرضه مواد مخدر. — Iran's strong determination to fight drug trafficking and supply.

91 | 64

4307 پدیدار pædidar *visible* adj,n

- این نشانه درست در شب چهاردهم ماه پدیدار خواهد شد. — This sign will appear right on the fourteenth night of the month.

84 | 126

4308 آواز avaz *call, song* adj,n

- اول چند تا آواز انگلیسی خواندم. — At first I sang a few English songs.

68 | 273

4309 فرسوده færsude *worn out* adj

- کمتر از یک درصد تاکسی‌های فرسوده نوسازی شدند. — Less than one percent of old taxis were renovated.

65 | 310

4310 سرطانی særætani *cancerous, cancer* adj

- داروهای بیماران سرطانی رایگان نیست. — Medicines for cancer patients are not free.

79 | 169

4311 اعتراض کردن eʔteraz kærdæn *protest, object* v

- مقامات انگلیس به این اقدام وی اعتراض کردند. — English officials objected this action of his.

77 | 184

4312 اطرافیان ætrafijan *entourage* n

- سوالاتی که اطرافیان امام ازش می‌پرسن. — The questions Imam's entourage ask him.

81 | 145

4313 آزمایشگاهی azmajeʃgahi *laboratory* adj

- شبکه آزمایشگاهی تشخیص اچ‌آی‌وی در کشور افتتاح شد. — An HIV diagnostic laboratory network was opened in the country.

82 | 140

4314 مرمت mæræmmæt *restoration* n

- محققان آلمانی تخت سلیمان را مرمت می‌کنند. — German researchers are restoring Takht-e Solyeman.

71 | 246

4315 سرشماری særʃomari *census* n

- در مرحله سوم طرح سرشماری اتباع افغانی. — In the third round of the census plan of Afghan nationals.

70 | 256

4316 فداکاری fædakari *selfless devotion* n

- سربازان نمادهای برجسته صداقت و فداکاری هستند. — Soldiers are symbols of outstanding honesty and dedication.

81 | 147

4317 فقید fæɣid *deceased* adj

- رفیق حریری نخست وزیر فقید لبنان. — Rafik Hariri, late prime minister of Lebanon.

84 | 121

4318 سبد sæbæd *basket* n

- نامه را انداخت توی سبد. — She dropped the letter in the basket.

77 | 183

4319 حرام hæram *forbidden* adj

- دشمنی و جنگ بین دو گروه مسلمان ممنوع و حرام است. — Enmity and war between two Muslim groups is forbidden and haram.

76 | 192

4320 شعله ʃoʔle *flame* n,pn

- لحظه ای شعله، ریش و سبیلش را روشن کرد. — For a moment the flame lit his beard and mustache.

76 | 193

4321 برآمدن bæramædæn *rise* n,v

- در این روز آتش بزرگی بر افروخته می‌شود، که تا صبح زود و برآمدن خورشید روشن نگه داشته می‌شود. — On this day a huge fire is kindled, which is kept lit till early morning and the sunrise.

76 | 197

4322 پیری piri *old age* n

- من قبل از اینها باید به این شغل‌ها فکر می‌کردم نه حالا سر پیری . . . . — I should have thought about these careers beforehand and not now, at the cusp of old age.

78 | 177

4323 تأمل tæʔæmmol *contemplation* n

- بدون تأمل جواب می دهد. — He answers without hesitation.

75 | 205

27 Islamic months (by month order)

Rank	Headword	Pronunciation	Gloss	Rank	Headword	Pronunciation	Gloss
2885	محرم	mohærræm	Muharram	4839	رجب	rædʒæb	Rajab
1036	صفر	sæfær	Safar	5002	شعبان	ʃæʔban	Sha'ban
19346	ربیع‌الاول	ræbiʔolævvæl	Rabi' al-awwal	1970	رمضان	ræmezan	Ramadan
19776	ربیع‌الثانی	ræbiʔossani	Rabi' al-thani	11964	شوال	ʃævval	Shawwal
N/A	جمادی‌الاول	dʒomadijolævvæl	Jumada al-awwal	N/A	ذیقعده	ziyæʔde	Dhu al-Qa'dah
N/A	جمادی‌الثانی	dʒomadijossani	Jumada al-thani	N/A	ذیحجه	zihædʒdʒe	Dhu al-Hijjah

4324 خدایی xodaji *divine* adj,pn,v
- نبرد و مبارزه در نیروهای مسلح رنگ خدایی دارد. — The battle and fight in the armed forces has a divine hue.
81 | 151

4325 لاله lale *tulip* n,pn
- از دور مثل باغ پر از گل و لاله رنگارنگ بنظر می‌آمد. — From far away, it looked like a garden full of colorful flowers and tulips.
82 | 136

4326 متجاوز motædʒavez *aggressor, exceeding* adj,n
- شما متجاوز از هفت هزار تومان زباله را بدون اجازه دولت فروخته‌اید؟ — You've sold over seven thousand tomans' worth of garbage without the government's authorization?
83 | 128

4327 بافتن baftæn *weave* adj,n,v
- بافتن یک جفت قالیچه. — Weaving a pair of rugs.
77 | 187

4328 سانحه sanehe *accident* n
- ترکیدن یکی از لاستیکهای هواپیمای مسافربری کنکورد عامل اصلی وقوع سانحه سقوط آن بوده است. — The bursting of one of the Concorde airliner's tires had been the main cause of the crash.
74 | 208

4329 نامعلوم namæʔlum *unknown* adj
- تشکیل دولت جدید باعث ناامیدی شهروندان این کشور نسبت به آینده سیاسی نامعلوم کشورشان شده است. — Formation of the new government has caused disappointment among its citizens regarding the uncertain political future of their country.
91 | 64

4330 محرک mohærrek *stimulus, motor, trigger* adj,n
- در صورتی که اجتناب از محرک‌ها کافی نباشد، استفاده از دارو توصیه می‌شود. — If trigger avoidance is insufficient, use of medication is recommended.
76 | 196

4331 سنگاپور sængapur *Singapore* pn
- تیم بسکتبال جوانان قطر در یک بازی دور از انتظار با نتیجه 65 به 55 بر سنگاپور غلبه کرد. — Qatar's youth basketball team prevailed over Singapore in a game exceeding expectations with a score of 65 to 55.
80 | 160

4332 سرو særv, serv *cypress, serve* n
- درخت های کاج و سرو کاشته شده است. — Pine and cypress trees have been planted.
75 | 204

4333 متعادل motæʔadel *moderate* adj
- مجموعه بسیار متعادل و هماهنگ است. — It is a very balanced and harmonious collection.
81 | 147

4334 بهزیستی behzisti *social welfare* adj,n
- اولین همایش بررسی راههای پیشگیری از اعتیاد با حضور مدیرکل سازمان بهزیستی کردستان در بیجار برگزار شد. — The first seminar investigating ways to prevent addiction, attended by the Director General of the social welfare organization of Kurdistan, took place in Bijar.
64 | 308

4335 پیگرد pejgærd *legal action, prosecution* n
- متخلفین تحت پیگرد قانونی قرار می‌گیرند. — The offenders are placed under judicial prosecution.
86 | 104

4336 سپری کردن sepæri kærdæn *spend time* v

- اکثر ایرانیان نوروز را با کورش کبیر در تخت جمشید سپری کردند. — The majority of Iranians spent the New Year by Cyrus the Great in Persepolis.

80 | 153

4337 فراگیری færagiri *comprehensiveness, learning* n

- مصرف صبحانه فراگیری مغز را افزایش میدهد. — Eating breakfast increases your brain's ability to learn.

75 | 202

4338 منشور mænʃur *charter, prism* n,pn

- منشورسازمان ملل. — United Nations Charter.

82 | 137

4339 بسیجی bæsidʒi *member of Basij* adj,n

- متأسفانه این فاجعه منجر به شهادت ۱۳ تن از بسیجیهای حاضر در مسجد شد. — Unfortunately, this disaster led to the martyrdom of 13 Basijis who were present in the mosque.

71 | 234

4340 بایرن bajern *Bayern* n,pn

- فصل آینده کاپیتان بایرن مونیخ خواهد بود. — He would be next season's captain for Bayern Munich.

70 | 243

4341 واریز variz *depositing* n

- لیست هزینه ها رو بده تا به حسابش واریز کنیم. — Provide the list of gifts so we can make a deposit into his account.

79 | 164

4342 برکناری bærkenari *dismissal* n

- فدراسیون فوتبال برکناری کیروش را تکذیب کرد. — Football Federation denied dismissal of Queiroz.

74 | 210

4343 غروب ɣorub *sunset* n

- نزدیک غروب رو به مادر بر زمین نشست. — Around sunset he sat on the floor facing his mother.

67 | 277

4344 نویسندگی nevisændegi *writing* n

- نویسندگی را به عنوان حرفه برگزید. — He chose writing as a career.

90 | 70

4345 صید sejd *hunting, fishing, game* n

- همچنین تعیین گونههای مختلف جهت صید از اهداف این بخش میباشد. — Also, determination of the different species for hunting is the goal of this division.

74 | 211

4346 لیلا lejla *Layla* pn

- لیلا گفت «راستش نمیدونم.» — Leyla said, "Honestly, I don't know."

52 | 455

4347 پی گرفتن pej gereftæn *follow up* v

- راه خودمان را پی گرفته ایم. — We have followed our own path.

85 | 111

4348 ویلیام viljam *William* pn

- ویلیام کیسی رئیس سازمان اطلاعاتی آمریکا سیا بود. — William Casey was the director of the Central Intelligence Agency (CIA).

78 | 168

4349 عذرخواهی ozrxahi *apology* n

- ثانیا از این بابت عذرخواهی میکنم. — Secondly, I apologize for this.

82 | 139

4350 نرگس nærges *narcissus* n,pn

- دخترها روبهروی هم نشسته بودند و گلبرگهای یک گل نرگس را به نوبت میکندند. — The girls were sitting across from each other, taking turns plucking the petals of a narcissus flower.

61 | 341

4351 لرزه lærze *earthquake, tremor* n

- لب لرزه داشت. — His lips trembled.

86 | 105

4352 سرازیر særazir *downhill, descend* adj

- تروریستها به سوریه سرازیر شدهاند. — Terrorists have rushed into Syria.

81 | 144

4353 راد rad *rad, Rad, generous* pn

- مهدی مرتضوی راد از تهران. — Mehdi Mortazavi Rad from Tehran.

88 | 87

4354 تنگه tænge *straits, channel* n,pn

- تنگه هرمز در امنیت کامل است. — The Straits of Hormoz enjoy complete security.

80 | 154

4355 ایالتی ejalæti *provincial, state* adj,n

- یک وزیر ایالتی پاکستان در انفجار تروریستی کشته شد. — A Pakistani provincial minister was killed in the terrorist bombing.

86 | 105

4356 حذف کردن hæzf kærdæn *eliminate, delete* v

- باید رقبا را از مسیر حذف کنید. — You must remove the competitors from the path.

89 | 78

4357 آدرس adres *address* n

- نام و آدرس مدرسه را از او می گیرد. — He will get the name and address of the school from her.

71 | 238

4358 ناتمام natæmam *incomplete* adj

- این بحث ناتمام ماند. — The discussion remained unfinished.

91 | 64

4359 عليه السلام **ælejhessælam** *peace be upon him* expression

- يكى از نكات آموزنده زندگى على عليه السلام همين مبارزه با خوارج است. — One of the educational points of the life of Ali, peace be upon him, is that very battle with the Kharijites.

63 | 321

4360 تبار **tæbar** *lineage* n

- همه ما عاشق ميهن و تبار پاك خويش هستيم. — We all love our pure ancestry and homeland.

80 | 153

4361 نوشيدن **nuʃidæn** *drink* n,v

- بدون توجه به تشنگى آب بنوشيد. — Regardless of thirst, drink water.

75 | 196

4362 سهامدار **sæhamdar** *shareholder* n

- شما دوست داشتيد سهامدار صنعت خودرو مى شديد؟ — Do you wish you had become a shareholder in the automotive industry?

69 | 255

4363 زنجيره **zændʒire** *chain* n

- طولانى‌ترين زنجيره آتشفشانى در جهان كشف شد. — The longest volcanic chain in the world was discovered.

80 | 155

4364 مدينه **mædine** *Medina* pn

- مصادف خوشحال و خوشوقت به مدينه برگشت. — Mossadef, happy and pleased, returned to Medina.

68 | 263

4365 شكم **ʃekæm** *stomach* n

- مى روند توى شكمش. — They will go into his stomach.

58 | 372

4366 قاطعانه **ɣateʔane** *decisive, decisively* adj,adv

- با متخلفان قاطعانه برخورد خواهد شد. — Violators will be dealt with firmly.

89 | 79

4367 ارباب **ærbab** *master* n

- جعفر گفت: «خوب، حالا برويد بيرون تا من با ارباب حرف بزنم.» — Jafar said, "Okay, now go outside so I can talk with the master."

59 | 365

4368 خلاق **xællaɣ** *creative* adj

- جمع بندى تجارب و نظرات خبرگان و افراد خلاق ميسر نيست. — Summarizing the opinions and experiences of experts and creative people is not possible.

80 | 152

4369 تفريحى **tæfrihi** *recreational* adj

- جاذبه‌هاى تاريخى تفريحى و طبيعى فراوانى دارد. — It has plenty of historical, recreational, and natural attractions.

76 | 189

4370 برگه **bærge** *index card, clue, dried fruit* n

- هنوز 200 هزار برگه رأى متعلق به اتريشى هاى مقيم خارج شمارش نشده است. — Two hundred thousand voting ballots belonging to Austrians residing abroad have not yet been tallied.

75 | 201

4371 دفن **dæfn** *burial* n

- البته در دين مقدس ما سوزاندن جسد جايز نيست و ما اجساد رفتگان خود را دفن مى‌كنيم. — Of course, in our sacred religion, the burning of bodies is not allowed, and we bury the bodies of our deceased.

76 | 184

4372 بخار **boxar** *steam* n

- حداكثر بخار آب موجود در جو ۴–۳ درصد است. — The maximum water vapor in the atmosphere is 3–4 percent.

79 | 160

4373 غزل **ɣæzæl** *ghazal* n

- سيمين بهبهانى بانوى غزل ايران درگذشت. — Simin Behbahani, Iran's Lady of Ghazals, has died.

71 | 229

4374 ايستادگى **istadegi** *resistance* n

- اين تظاهرات و ايستادگى مردم مشت محكمى بر دهان ياوه گويان خواهد زد. — These demonstrations and the perseverance of the people will hit the nonsense talkers in the mouth with a firm fist.

67 | 269

4375 تاريخچه **tarixtʃe** *short history* n

- تاريخچه ايده‌هاى اقتصادى. — A history of economic concepts.

79 | 162

4376 روال **ræval** *procedure* n

- امور بيمارستان نيز روال خود را داشت. — The hospital's affairs also had their own routine.

82 | 135

4377 شناس **ʃenas** *acquaintance, -ologist* n

- يك روز زن و شوهر جوانى كه هر دو زيست شناس بودند طبق معمول براى تحقيق به جنگل رفتند. — Once a young couple who were both biologists went to the forest, as usual, for research.

79 | 164

4378 متداول **motædavel** *in common use* adj

- نشانه‌هاى متداول آن شامل قدم زدن، — Its common symptoms include pacing . . .

80 | 149

4379 پياده كردن **pijade kærdæn** *take apart, unload, execute* v

- هر چه تعداد مدير بيشتر باشد، پياده كردن قوانين راحت تر خواهد بود. — The more managers there are, the easier applying the rules will be.

89 | 79

4380 اسمی esmi *nominal* adj,n
- فقط از نظر اسمی باهم شباهت دارند. — They are only similar to each other in name.

  68 | 258

4381 رها شدن ræha ʃodæn *be freed* v
- پس از لحظه‌ای کیف از دستش رها شد. — After a moment, the bag was released from her hand.

  75 | 195

4382 گشوده goʃude *opened, open* adj
- سر در دانشگاه تهران نمادی از کتابی باز و گشوده در برابر دیدگان است. — Tehran University's main entrance is a symbol of an open book in the sight of beholder.

  78 | 166

4383 فلفل felfel *pepper* n
- نمک و فلفل به میزان لازم. — The requisite amount of salt and pepper.

  89 | 80

4384 مجاور modʒaver *adjacent, neighboring* adj,n
- جنگل مجاور روستایشان پر از میمون بود. — The forest neighboring their village was full of monkeys.

  80 | 148

4385 جهش dʒæheʃ *jumping, mutation* n
- پایان یافتن هزاره دوم با جهش های علمی، اقتصادی و فرهنگی بسیاری همراه بود. — The end of the second millennium was accompanied by many scientific, economic, and cultural leaps.

  80 | 148

4386 غنا ɣæna *wealth, Ghana* n,pn
- مخالفان دولت در اطراف پایتخت غنا در اعتراض به افزایش قیمت سوخت و هزینه های زندگی تظاهرات کردند. — Ghana's government opposition groups protested around the capital against the increase in fuel prices and the high cost of living.

  83 | 125

4387 توماس tomas *Thomas* pn
- این روزها بسیار علاقه مند به خواندن آثار توماس برن شده‌ام. — These days I have become very interested in reading Thomas Byrne's works.

  82 | 137

4388 بازده bazdeh *yield* n
- در حالی که بازده دارایی داخلی و خارجی به نرخ بهره و انتظارات تغییر نرخ ارز وابسته است . . . — Since the return on domestic and foreign assets is dependent on the interest rate and expectations of change in currency value . . .

  77 | 181

4389 شطرنج ʃætrændʒ *chess* n
- شطرنج بازی کنیم. — We should play chess.

  74 | 205

4390 معجزه moʔdʒeze *miracle* n
- داروساز گفت «متاسفم دخترجان، ولی ما اینجا معجزه نمی فروشیم.» — The pharmacist said, "I'm sorry, dear girl, but we don't sell miracles here."

  76 | 184

4391 رشد کردن roʃd kærdæn *grow* v
- آنها پس از 2 هفته مشاهده کردند که پوست سر ترمیم شده و موها نیز در حال رشد کردن است. — After 2 weeks they noticed that the scalp was restored and the hair was growing.

  78 | 170

4392 وصف væsf *description* n
- به این سپیدی نگاه کن، ببین چقدر وصف ناپذیره! — Look at this whiteness, see how indescribable it is!

  77 | 173

4393 صاف sɑf *flat* adj
- تا دست‌هایش نلرزد یا نبیند که می‌لرزد نامهٔ مچاله شده را صاف کرد. — So her hands wouldn't shake, or so she wouldn't see that they're shaking, she smoothed out the crumpled letter.

  71 | 232

4394 شاخ ʃax *horn, branch* n
- شاخهای بسیار تیزی دارد. — It has very sharp horns.

  71 | 231

4395 پالایش pɑlɑjeʃ *refining* n
- پالایش نفت بندرعباس. — Bandar Abbas oil refining.

  82 | 137

4396 تمایز tæmajoz *distinction* n
- وجه تمایز ترک اعتیاد با درمان اعتیاد در چیست؟ — What distinguishes quitting an addiction from treating an addiction?

  76 | 188

4397 خرده xorde *bit, fragment* adj,n
- می‌بینند که پرندگان تمام خرده‌های نان را خورده‌اند. — They see that the birds have eaten all the breadcrumbs.

  75 | 189

4398 بالندگی bɑlændegi *growth, exuberance* n
- تئاتر، عامل بقا و بالندگی ملت‌هاست. — Theater is the survival and growth factor of nations.

  90 | 74

4399 هدفمند hædæfmænd *targeted, purposeful* adj
- انسان هدفمند همیشه موفق است. — A goal-oriented person is always successful.

  71 | 228

4400 روحانیت rowhɑnijæt *clergy* n
- روحانیت همیشه پناهگاه مردم بوده است. — The clergy have always been a refuge for people.

  68 | 256

4401 وصول vosul *collection* n
- عاقبت پول ها وصول شد. — Finally the money was collected.
- 81 | 142

4402 استانداری ostandari *governor generalship* n
- سیدحسین هاشمی استانداری تهران را تحویل گرفت. — Seyyed Hossein Hashemi accepted the governorship of Tehran.
- 74 | 206

4403 ذیربط ziræbt *relevant* adj
- از طریق مراجع ذیربط پیگیر حق و حقوق قانونی خود هستیم. — We are pursuing our legal rights through the relevant authorities.
- 72 | 221

4404 مرتفع mortæfæʔ, mortæfeʔ *removed, elevated* adj
- ساختمان های مرتفع. — Tall buildings.
- 76 | 187

4405 شیمی ʃimi *chemistry* n
- دکتر کسلر استاد شیمی این دانشکده. — Doctor Kessler, professor of chemistry in this college.
- 77 | 173

4406 سطر sætr *line* n
- همه ی اطلاعاتی که به دست آورده ام از چند سطر بیش تر نیست. — All the information that I have gathered is no more than a few lines.
- 86 | 99

4407 نابود شدن nabud ʃodæn *be destroyed* v
- سقوط یکی از آنها باعث نابود شدن دیگری میشود. — The collapse of one of them can lead to the loss of the other one.
- 87 | 95

4408 قانون‌اساسی ɣanune æsasi *constitution* n
- درصدی از شرکت کنندگان در نظرسنجی معتقد بودند که رای مثبت به قانون‌اساسی عراق اوضاع امنیتی کشور را بهبود می‌بخشد. — A percentage of participants in a survey believed that an affirmative vote for the Iraq constitution will improve the country's security situation.
- 49 | 482

4409 بلیت belit *ticket* n
- بلیت سینما — A cinema ticket.
- 67 | 263

4410 فرقه ferɣe *sect* n
- جامعه لبنان عمدتا از دو فرقه مسلمان سنی و شیعه و مسیحیان مارونی تشکیل می‌شود. — The society in Lebanon generally consists of two Muslim sects, Sunni and Shia, and Maronite Christians.
- 82 | 132

4411 محصور mæhsur *fenced, besieged* adj
- اما واقعیت آن است که محصور بودن در خشکی و نداشتن راه ارتباطی با آبهای آزاد همچنان مهمترین چالش پیش روی ترکمن هستند. — But the fact is that being landlocked and not having access to the open sea is still the most important challenge facing the Turkmen.
- 87 | 90

4412 اعتلا eʔtela *raising, exaltation* n
- مقدم دانستن منافع جمع بر منافع شخصی را زمینه ساز اعتلا و پیشرفت کشور خواندند. — They called the prioritization of the interests of the whole over those of the individual the grounds for the exaltation and progress of the country.
- 85 | 108

4413 لیکن likæn *but* conj
- جغرافی یک بخش از علوم اجتماعی است، لیکن نمی توان گفت، که با علوم طبیعی بدون ارتباط است. — Geography is part of the social sciences, but it cannot be said that it has no connection to the natural sciences.
- 71 | 227

4414 مجتبی modʒtæba *Mojtaba* pn
- پسر سید مرتضی و آقا مجتبی رفتند پشت درختا و دیگه پیداشون نشد، دو نفر اومدند و منو بردند تو یه راهروی تاریک. — The son of Seyyed Morteza and Mr. Mojtaba ducked behind the trees and disappeared, and two people came and took me into a dark corridor.
- 79 | 155

4415 دوستدار dustdar *devotee, fan* adj,n,pn
- آیا تو اینقدر زن پرستی یا بیزار از مرد ، که دوستدار زنان دیگری؟ — Are you that much of a worshipper of women or are you loathsome of men and thus a lover of other women?
- 79 | 155

4416 کاوش kavoʃ *excavation* n
- تا پیش از حفاریها و کاوشهای باستان شناسان افسانه‌ها و تصورات گوناگونی در مورد برج بابل وجود داشت. — Prior to archaeological explorations and excavations, there were various conceptions and legends about the Tower of Babel.
- 73 | 207

4417 خلبان xælæban *pilot* n
- به گفته پلیس خلبان این هلیکوپتر یکی از کشته‌شدگان است. — According to the police, the helicopter's pilot is one of those who were killed.
- 75 | 189

4418 حبیب hæbib *friend, lover, Habib* n,pn
- یادبودی از شاعر آذربایجانی میرحبیب ساهر. — A memorial to the Azerbaijani poet, Mir Habib Saher.
- 68 | 260

4419 بم bæm *bass, deep, Bam* adj,pn
- صدایش گرفته و بم بود. — His voice was gruff and bass.
- 73 | 214

4420 تحلیل کردن tæhlil kærdæn *analyze* v
- بتوان واقعیتها را تحلیل کرد و اختلاف نظرها را از بین برد. — To be able to analyze the facts and eliminate differences of opinion.

90 | 68

4421 جنگنده dʒæŋgænde *warrior* adj,n
- علت سقوط این جنگنده نیروی هوایی هند در دست بررسی است. — The reason for the crash of the Indian air force fighter is under investigation.

72 | 216

4422 تشریفات tæʃrifɑt *formalities* n
- به دستور وی جشن نوروز را با تشریفات زیاد برگزار نمودند. — Under his command, the Nowruz celebration was held with much formality.

84 | 116

4423 سازه sɑze *factor, structure* n
- سازه‌های کامپوزیتی در ایران کلید می‌خورند. — Composite structures in Iran will be launched.

78 | 166

4424 سرا særɑ *house* n
- (ایران ای سرای امید) از شعرهای سایه است. — "Iran, Oh House of Hope" is one of Sayeh's poems.

81 | 143

4425 هفده hevdæh *seventeen* n
- مریم بیش از هفده سال است که در زندان به سر می برد. — Maryam has been in prison for more than seventeen years.

59 | 353

4426 ازدواج کردن ezdevɑdʒ kærdæn *marry* v
- هنوز فرصت ازدواج کردن پیدا نکرده ایم! — We have not had the opportunity to get married yet!

57 | 374

4427 بکارگیری bekɑrgiri *utilization, hiring, employment* n
- طرح ممنوعیت بکارگیری بازنشستگان به انجام می رسد؟ — Will the ban on employment of retirees be accomplished?

81 | 136

4428 تلفیق tælfiɣ *combination* n
- نورپردازی در تئاتر، تلفیقی از خلاقیت و تکنیک است. — Theatrical lighting is a combination of creativity and technique.

69 | 249

4429 عروس ærus *bride, daugher-in-law* n
- هر دو عروس شده بودند. — Both had become brides.

60 | 344

4430 مدد mædæd *help* n
- می‌تواند به روشن شدن بیشتر موضوع مدد رساند. — It can contribute to further clarify the issue.

82 | 132

4431 سومالی somɑli *Somalia* adj,pn
- چهاردهمین محموله کمکهای بشردوستانه کشورمان وارد فرودگاه موگادیشو پایتخت سومالی شد. — Our country's fourteenth humanitarian aid cargo landed at Mogadishu airport, the capital of Somalia.

52 | 435

4432 خاموش xɑmuʃ *silent, extinguished* adj
- موبایلش خاموش بود. — His cell phone was turned off.

68 | 257

4433 غرض ɣæræz *motive, grudge* n
- نمی دانست مقصودم فقط شوخی و خنده است یا غرض دیگری دارم. — He didn't know if my aim was just to joke and laugh or if I had another intent.

69 | 242

4434 خودروسازی xodrowsɑzi *automobile manufacturing* n
- شرکت‌های خودروسازی موظفند از ابتدای سال خودرو — At the start of the year, automakers will be responsible for producing cars according to this standard. بر اساس این استاندارد تولید کنند.

61 | 322

4435 شمشیر ʃæmʃir *sword* n
- یک بار هم با شمشیر تهدید اش کردم. — One time I also threatened him with a sword.

73 | 206

4436 معالجه moʔɑledʒe *medical treatment* n
- هیچ کدام نتوانستند معالجه اش کنند. — No one could cure him.

80 | 148

4437 منعقد monʔæɣed *signed, coagulated* adj
- حتی نمایندگانی از تیم ما به پرتغال سفر کردند اما قراردادی منعقد نشد. — Some representatives of our team even traveled to Portugal, but no contract was concluded.

80 | 146

4438 گرویدن gerævidæn *adopt a belief* v
- حدود 80 مسلمان ایرانی و افغان در آلمان به مسیحیت گرویدند. — About 80 Iranian and Afghan Muslims converted to Christianity in Germany.

73 | 205

4439 مساعدت mosɑʔedæt *assistance* n
- مساعدت در تامین خطوط اعتباری مناسب برای بازارهای هدف صادراتی. — Assistance in providing appropriate credit lines for export target markets.

77 | 173

4440 جمشید dʒæmʃid *Jamshid* pn
- این مصاحبه در هفتهنامه محلی تخت جمشید در شهر مرودشت منتشر شده است. — This interview has been published in the local weekly *Takhte Jamshid* in the city of Marvdasht.

78 | 161

4441 دگرگون deɡærɡun *changed, transformed* adj
- موفقیت افراد را دگرگون می کند. — Success changes people.
77 | 169

4442 پنتاگون pentagon *Pentagon* pn
- سخنگوی پنتاگون گفت هیچ یک از جت‌های عراقی هدف قرار نگرفتند. — The Pentagon's spokesperson said that none of the Iraqi jets were targeted.
74 | 198

4443 دخالت کردن dexalæt kærdæn *interfere* v
- در زندگی خصوصی مردم نباید دخالت کرد. — One must not interfere in people's private lives.
79 | 159

4444 مارتین martin *Martin* pn
- کشف فلز آلومینیوم توسط مارتین حال شیمیدان آمریکایی. — The discovery of aluminum by Martin Hall, an American chemist.
86 | 103

4445 محکمی mohkæmi *solidity* adj
- تنگستن باعث محکمی، و وجود کروم و نیکل سبب ضدزنگ شدن فولاد می‌شود. — Tungsten provides strength, and the presence of chromium and nickel makes the steel stainless.
86 | 96

4446 علمیه elmijje *scientific* adj
- مجمع مدرسین و محققین حوزه علمیه قم نیز از شرکت در انتخابات خودداری کردند. — The Assembly of Qom Seminary Teachers and Researchers also refrained from participation in the elections.
79 | 159

4447 استخر estæxr *pool* n,pn
- استخرش خیلی بزرگ است. — Its pool is very large.
76 | 178

4448 بام bam *roof* n
- فلات پامیر به نام بام دنیا معروف است. — The Pamir plateau is known as the roof of the world.
69 | 245

4449 برزیلی brezili *Brazilian* adj
- درام برزیلی برنده بزرگ جشنواره توکیو شد. — The Brazilian drama became the big winner of Tokyo Festival.
80 | 143

4450 فلوریدا florida *Florida* pn
- فلوریدا را یک مهره مهم برای پیروزی در انتخابات به حساب می‌آورد. — He considers Florida key to winning the election.
87 | 92

4451 سکته sekte *stoppage, stroke* n
- وی دچار خونریزی مغزی شده و یا اینکه سکته مغزی کرده است. — He is suffering from a cerebral hemorrhage, or has had a stroke.
72 | 215

4452 عفو æfv *pardon* n
- مرا باید عفو کنی. — You must forgive me.
79 | 151

4453 تحمیلی tæhmili *imposed, forced* adj,n
- نوسانات نرخ ارز در زمان جنگ تحمیلی. — Currency price fluctuations during the the the imposed war.
75 | 188

4454 تهاجمی tæhadʒomi *aggressive* adj,n
- نگاه تهاجمی در راهبردها و تجهیزات ما وجود ندارد. — There is no aggressive vision in our strategies or equipment.
84 | 111

4455 نقلیه næɣlijje *transport* adj
- اولین بزرگراهی است که وسایل نقلیه شاخ به شاخ با هم تصادف می کنند. — It's the first highway where vehicles crash head on.
69 | 241

4456 یوسفی jusefi *Yusefi* pn
- علی یوسفی به مدال برنز دست یافت. — Ali Yousefi received a bronze medal.
86 | 96

4457 عیب ejb *fault* n
- نقش اصلی آنها در پی بروز خطا و عیب در شبکه مشخص می‌شود. — Their main role is determined after the emergence of mistakes and faults in the network.
64 | 288

4458 صنعتگر sænʔætɡær *artisan* n
- صنعتگر باید ثروتمند باشد. — Artisans should be rich.
84 | 116

4459 چاپ کردن tʃap kærdæn *print* v
- بعضی از روزنامه‌ها عکس اش را در صفحه اول چاپ کردند. — Some of the newspapers printed his picture on the front page.
79 | 155

4460 خطبه xotbe *sermon, homily* n
- خطبه می خواند. — He will read the sermon.
75 | 186

4461 تجربی tædʒrobi *experimental* adj
- ویرجینیا وولف نویسنده رمان‌های تجربی است. — Virginia Woolf is the author of experimental novels.
75 | 189

4462 سازگار sazeɡar *compatible* adj
- از دیدگاه بوم‌شناسی، توریسم از هر صنعت تولیدی دیگری ارجح‌تر است زیرا با محیط‌زیست سازگارتر و دوست‌تر است. — From an ecological perspective, tourism is preferable to any manufacturing industry because it is more compatible with and friendly to the environment.
78 | 165

4463 استقامت esteɣɑmæt *resistance* n
- ایمان و اسلام و استقامت در راه حمایت و گسترش اسلام. — Faith, Islam and perseverance along the path to support the spread of Islam.
80 | 150

4464 گوش دادن guʃ dɑdæn *listen* v
- هر چه خاتمی می‌گوید را نباید گوش داد. — One must not listen to everything that Khatami says.
57 | 362

4465 هنگفت hengoft *exorbitant* adj
- زیان‌های هنگفت یا سودهای هنگفت. — Enormous losses or enormous profits.
86 | 101

4466 لازم داشتن lazem dɑʃtæn *need* v
- هر چه لازم داشتند خرید و برگشت خانه. — He bought all they needed and returned home.
79 | 155

4467 قزاق ɣæzzɑɣ *Cossack, Kazakh* adj,n
- قرار بود او توسط پزشکان قزاق و خارجی مورد بررسی قرار گیرد. — He was supposed to be examined by Kazakh and foreign doctors.
91 | 63

4468 کاش kɑʃ *I wish* adv
- کاش حقیقت را می‌گفتم . . . — I wish I had said the truth . . .
61 | 325

4469 بهروز behruz *Behruz* pn
- از روزی که به بهروز خبر آوردند که سیما خودکشی کرده حالش دگرگون شد ولی هنوز مرگ سیما را کاملا باور نکرده بود. — From the day that they brought Behruz the news that Sima had committed suicide, his demeanor changed, but he still hadn't completely accepted Sima's death.
74 | 199

4470 وای vɑj *oh, alas* adv
- وای کجا بروم کجا مخفی شوم؟ — Oh, where should I go, where should I hide?
53 | 407

4471 اختلاس extelas *embezzlement* n
- مرا به جرم اختلاس و سرقت اموال دولتی به محاکمه هم بکشند . . . — They'll also try me for embezzlement and theft of state property . . .
81 | 134

4472 مرگبار mærgbɑr *deadly* adj
- مننژیت بخصوص در کودکان هنوز شایع خطرناک و مرگبار است. — Meningitis, especially in children, is still common, dangerous and fatal.
85 | 105

4473 زننده zænænde *repulsive, striker* adj,n
- به شکل غیراخلاقی و زننده آنان را بازداشت کردند. — They were arrested in an immoral and repulsive manner.
89 | 76

4474 تضمین کردن tæzmin kærdæn *guarantee* v
- کار خود را تضمین نمی کند. — He does not guarantee his own work.
88 | 85

4475 کانادایی kanadaji *Canadian* adj
- اعتراض بومیان کانادایی گسترش می‌یابد. — Canadian indigenous protest spreads.
81 | 135

4476 درحالی‌که dærhalike *while, as* conj
- 86 درصد از ثروتمندان عاشقانه مطالعه می‌کنند، در حالی‌که 26 درصد از مردمان فقیر عاشق مطالعه هستند. — 86% of wealthy people read with passion, while 26% percent of the poor are passionate about reading.
47 | 484

4477 تاب tab *endurance* n
- تو باید احتضار را تاب بیاوری. — You must bear the agony.
76 | 180

4478 مجموعاً mædʒmuʔæn *altogether* adv,n
- به واسطه سه اتهام در پرونده‌اش مجموعاً به 15 سال حبس محکوم شد. — Due to the three charges in the case, he was sentenced to a total of 15 years in prison.
87 | 89

4479 پیچ piʃ *bend, vine, screw* n
- برای رسیدن به این روستای کوهستانی زیبا و بکر باید از مسیر سخت و دشوار با پیچ‌های خطرناک عبور کرد. — To reach to this beautiful and pristine mountain village, one must take a difficult route with dangerous curves.
73 | 207

4480 داماد damad *groom, son-in-law* n,pn
- عروس و داماد هنوز از حجله نیامده اند. — The bride and groom haven't come out of the bridal chamber yet.
72 | 212

4481 مین min *mine* n
- پاکسازی مناطق آلوده به مین و مواد منفجره. — Cleaning the areas contaminated with mines and explosives.
76 | 176

4482 سانسور sansur *censorship* n
- خودتو سانسور نکن پژمان. — Don't censor yourself, Pezhman.
84 | 110

4483 برملا bærmæla *exposed* adj
- اما این مساله نیز با انتشار کتاب یاد شده برملا شد. — However, this issue also was revealed with the publication of the mentioned book.
94 | 41

28 French months (by month order)

Rank	Headword	Pronunciation	Gloss	Rank	Headword	Pronunciation	Gloss
3797	ژانویه	ʒɑnvije	January	11204	ژوئیه	ʒuʔije	July
3958	فوریه	fevrije	February	5072	اوت	ut	August
2950	مارس	mɑrs	March	2240	سپتامبر	septɑmbr	September
5582	آوریل	ɑvril	April	2908	اکتبر	oktobr	October
3312	مه	me	May	2735	نوامبر	novɑmbr	November
8340	ژوئن	ʒuʔæn	June	3175	دسامبر	desɑmbr	December

4484 فریدون ferejdun, færidun *Fereydun* pn
- از آن روز که دوستی من و فریدون مشیری آغاز شد. — From that day my friendship with Fereydun Moshiri began.
- 78 | 163

4485 بسزا beseza *appropriate, well-deserved, considerable* adj
- در مدرسه‌سازی سهم بسزایی داشتند. — They had a significant role in building schools.
- 81 | 136

4486 ولسوالی volosvali *Afghan county* n
- ولسوالی جوند دارای ۳۸۰ قریه می‌باشد. — Jawand district has 380 villages.
- 41 | 577

4487 گم ɡom *lost, missing* adj
- بروید گم بشوید! — Go, get lost!
- 64 | 285

4488 پارسی pɑrsi *Parsi, Persian* adj,n,pn
- رودکی پدر شعر پارسی محسوب می‌گردد. — Rudaki is considered the father of Persian poetry.
- 72 | 212

4489 پایبندی pɑjbændi *adherence, compliance* n
- آژانس پایبندی ایران به تعهداتش را تأیید کرد. — The agency confirmed Iran's compliance with its obligations.
- 78 | 158

4490 مار mɑr *snake* n
- همه مارها سمی نیستند. — Not all snakes are venemous.
- 69 | 237

4491 یگانه jeɡɑne *unique, sole* adj,pn
- اهورامزدا همان خدای یگانه است. — Ahura Mazda is the one and only God.
- 75 | 188

4492 فوراً fowræn *immediately* adv
- علی سلمان باید فوراً آزاد شود. — Ali Salman must be released immediately.
- 74 | 189

4493 گله ɡælle, ɡele *flock/herd, complaint* n
- دید گله آهویی به چرا مشغول است و یکی از آن ها طوق طلا به گردن دارد. — He saw that the herd of deer was busy grazing, and one of them had a gold collar around its neck.
- 72 | 210

4494 شبهه ʃobhe *doubt* n
- هیچ شک و شبهه ای در کار نیست. — No doubt or uncertainty is necessary.
- 74 | 193

4495 زیست‌محیطی zistmohiti *environmental* adj
- آن بخش از فعالیت‌هارا که مغایر با هنجارهای زیست‌محیطی تشخیص می‌دهد تعطیل کند. — To stop the part of activities he considers to be against environmental norms.
- 77 | 164

4496 ورا værɑ *beyond* n,prep,pron
- چند دهه دیگر از ورای وقایع سیاسی حال حاضر، از آیت الله خمینی چطور یاد خواهد شد؟ — A few decades from now, beyond the present political events, how will Ayatollah Khomeini be remembered?
- 74 | 190

4497 هجده hedʒdæh *eighteen* n
- خواندن این کتاب برای افراد زیر هجده سال، ممنوع است و هر کس ناراحتی قلبی یا بیماری عصبی دارد، آن را نخواند. — Reading this book is prohibited for the people under eighteen years of age, and anyone who has a heart or neurological disease should not read this book.
- 56 | 370

4498 قربان ɣorban *sacrifice* n,pn
- آن زمان «عید قربان» است که گوشت قربانی فراوان می‌شود. — That is during "Sacrifice Feast" when there is an abundance of sacrificial meat.
- 52 | 414

4499 دفترچه dæftærtʃe *notebook* n

- زمان و محلّ سردردرا در یک دفترچه یادداشت نموده و
  بکوشید در اولین مراحل بروز سردرد جلوی آن را بگیرید.
  — Note the time and location of the
  headache in a notebook and try to prevent it
  at the first signs of onset.

77 | 170

4500 مثنوی mæsnævi *Masnavi* n,pn

- مثنوی مولوی حاصل نبرد انسان با نفس درونی خویش
  است. — Rumi's Masnavi is the result of the
  human battle with its inner spirit.

73 | 200

4501 اسارت esaræt *captivity* n

- شمار زیادی از فرماندهان طالبان به اسارت نیروهای جبهه
  متّحد درآمدند. — A large number of Taliban
  commanders were captured by forces of the
  United Front.

78 | 160

4502 شدیداً ʃædidæn *severely* adv

- با هر اقدامی علیه امنیت مرزی شدیداً برخورد میکنیم.
  — We will deal severely with any action
  against border security.

78 | 155

4503 سیطره sejtære *control, predominance* n

- در برابر سیطره‌ی عمیق و وسیع شرکت‌های چند ملیتی
  قدرتی ندارند. — They don't have any power
  against the deep and wide dominance of
  multinational corporations.

75 | 180

4504 تاکتیکی taktiki *tactical* adj,n

- دشمنان هیچگاه قادر به برآورد توان عملیاتی و تاکتیکی
  ایران نخواهند بود. — The enemies will never be
  able to estimate Iran's tactical and
  operational capabilities.

80 | 141

4505 یکپارچگی jekpartʃegi *integrity* n

- آذربایجان به پناهگاه اصلی و مرکزی برای یکپارچگی
  صفویان تبدیل گشت. — Azerbaijan turned into a
  core and central haven for the integrity of the
  Safavids.

86 | 96

4506 موجودیت mowdʒudijjæt *existence, presence,
integrity* n

- گروه تروریستی داعش در بدخشان افغانستان اعلام
  موجودیت کرد. — The terrorist group ISIS
  announced its presence in Badakhshan,
  Afghanistan.

69 | 235

4507 اشتباه کردن eʃtebah kærdæn *make a mistake* v

- اولین هدف در این دیدگاه اجتناب از اشتباه کردن است.
  — The first goal of this approach is to avoid
  making mistakes.

69 | 240

4508 بازدهی bazdehi *result, productivity, efficiency* n

- چطور بازدهی کارمندان را افزایش دهیم؟ — How can
  we increase employee productivity?

76 | 173

4509 تحصیل کردن tæhsil kærdæn *study* v

- در آن جا تحصیل کردند. — They studied there.

81 | 137

4510 آرامگاه aramgah *grave* n

- اونجا تنها یک آرامگاه بود. — There was only one
  tomb there.

61 | 316

4511 خیره xire *dazzled, staring* adj,adv

- با مهربانی خیره می‌شوم در چشمهایش و به سادگی سایه ی
  خودم می خندم. — With kindness I stare in his eyes,
  and I laugh at the simplicity of my own shadow.

58 | 349

4512 تعبیری tæʔbiri *interpretive* n

- آنها با نگرش تعبیری به معنی مخالف بودند. — They were
  against the interpretive approach to meaning.

86 | 95

4513 گنجاندن gondʒandæn *pack, include* adj,n,v

- گنجاندن درس‌هایی در کتب درسی دانش‌آموزان.
  — Inclusion of some lessons in the
  students' textbooks.

82 | 126

4514 حراست hærasæt *protection* n

- مرا به اتاق حراست راهنمایی کرد. — He led me to
  the security post.

84 | 111

4515 جولای dʒulaj *July* n

- در جولای برگزار شد. — It was held in July.

81 | 137

4516 مردود mærdud *rejected, failed* adj

- آخر سال مردود شدیم — We failed the final test.

86 | 94

4517 فیلیپ filip *Philip* pn

- واقعاً تحت تأثیر بازی فیلیپ لام قرار گرفتم. — I have
  been really impressed by Philipp Lahm's play.

89 | 75

4518 خلوت xælvæt *seclusion, privacy* adj,n

- موقعی که دور و بر دختر خلوت شد، گربه با او حرف زد.
  — When it got quiet around the girl, the cat
  talked with her.

74 | 189

4519 ملی شدن melli ʃodæn *be nationalized* v

- همه مخالف ملی شدن بودند. — Everybody was
  against nationalizing.

82 | 126

4520 تکان tækan *shake, shock* n

- تکان‌های زمین بین ۴ تا ۱۰ دقیقه ادامه داشته‌است.
  — The aftershocks have continued for
  4–10 minutes.

82 | 129

4521 دنباله dombale *continuation* n
- درباره متفقین در دنباله همین داستان بعداً صحبت می کنیم. — We will talk later about the allies in the sequel to this story.
- 74 | 190

4522 متضاد motæzadd *opposite* adj
- دو عنصر متضاد که با یکدیگر در حال کشاکش هستند. — Two contrasting elements that are in conflict with each other.
- 84 | 111

4523 ربع rob? *quarter* n
- یک ربع بعد، جلوی ساختمان دادگاه بودم. — A quarter of an hour later, I was in front of the courthouse.
- 77 | 165

4524 جمع‌آوری dʒæm?aværi *collection* n
- خیابان‌ها پر از آشغال‌هایی بود که آنهارا جمع‌آوری نشده بود. — The streets were full of uncollected trash.
- 61 | 311

4525 فاضلاب fazelab *sewage* n
- اداره آب و فاضلاب — Water and Wastewater organization.
- 65 | 274

4526 معنویت mæ?nævijjæt *spirituality* n
- در دنیای امروز از معنویت سخن گفته می‌شود. — In today's world one talks about spirituality.
- 79 | 151

4527 مصداق mesdaɣ *proof, typical specimen* adj,n
- بارزترین مصداق عدالت قضایی است. — The most striking example of justice is judicial justice.
- 78 | 155

4528 هخامنشی hæxamæneʃi *Achaemenian* adj,pn
- الواح هخامنشی متعلق به ایران است. — The Achaemenid tablets belong to Iran.
- 66 | 260

4529 شکیبایی ʃækibaji *patience, fortitude* n
- سپاسگزارم ؛ به خاطر شکیبایی. — Thank you for your patience.
- 89 | 73

4530 اثرگذار æsærgozar *impressive* adj,n
- مار در آیین مهر و اژدها در فرهنگ ایرانی، نقشی بنیادین و اثرگذار دارند. — Snakes in Mithraism and dragons in Iranian culture have a fundamental and awe-inspiring role.
- 82 | 127

4531 دلسوز delsuz *compassionate* adj,n
- خانم قشقایی از پرستاران دلسوز بیمارستان هستند. — Ms. Qashqai is one of the caring nurses in the hospital.
- 80 | 139

4532 یزدی jæzdi *Yazdi* adj,pn
- پیرمرد یزدی با لهجه شیرینش تعریف میکنه. — The old Yazdi man tells the story with his sweet accent.
- 79 | 148

4533 بخشش bæxʃeʃ *donating, pardon* n
- بخشش بهتر است. — Forgiveness is better.
- 85 | 100

4534 هرگاه hærgah *whenever* adv
- هرگاه نیاز به کمک دارید، قدم پیش بگذارید و درخواست کمک کنید. — Whenever you require help step forward and ask for assistance.
- 68 | 240

4535 معیشتی mæ?iʃæti *subsistence* adj
- اولویت، رسیدگی به مشکلات معیشتی مردم است. — Addressing people's subsistence problems is the priority.
- 78 | 154

4536 نظاره nezare *observation* n
- متاسفانه این گل زیبا را خیلی به ندرت می توان نظاره کرد. — Unfortunately, one can so rarely behold this beautiful flower.
- 90 | 69

4537 گل زدن gol zædæn *score a goal* v
- در دقایق پایانی قدرت بهادری نیز برای ایران گل زد. — In the final minutes, Ghodrat Bahadori also scored a goal for Iran.
- 81 | 132

4538 سیب sib *apple* n
- از درخت سیب بوی تازگی فواره می زد. — The smell of freshness effervesced from the apple tree.
- 64 | 284

4539 شفافیت ʃæffafijjæt *transparency* n
- موسسه شفافیت بین المللی. — Transparency International Institute.
- 74 | 188

4540 جنابعالی dʒænabeali *your excellency* pron
- جهت ملاقات جنابعالی با شهردار محترم تهران. — For your excellency's meeting with the honorable mayor of Tehran.
- 75 | 177

4541 امانت æmanæt *honesty, consignment* n
- راستی، کی اونقدر احمق بود که اون کتاب رو بهت امانت داد؟ — By the way, who was that stupid to give that book to you?
- 80 | 143

4542 گارد gard *guard* n
- او یک گارد محافظ ایجاد کرد که به آنها دستمزد خوبی می‌داد. — He created a protective guard which he paid a good wage.
- 87 | 90

4543 عبرت ebræt *lesson, example* n
- مادر که عبرت گرفته بود. — The mother who had learned her lesson.
- 81 | 131

4544 یخچال jæxtʃal *refrigerator* n
- چطور غذا را در یخچال سالم نگهداریم؟ — How to keep food healthy in the fridge?
- 75 | 181

4545 سیاستگذاری sijasætgozari *policy making* n
- ساختار سیاستگذاری بانک مرکزی باید اصلاح شود. — The Central Bank policymaking structure must be reformed.

75 | 184

4546 بیدار bidar *awake* adj
- شاید هم بیدار باشد و دارد نگاهمان می‌کند. — Maybe she's awake and is looking at us now.

68 | 243

4547 جنایتکار dʒenajætkar *criminal* adj,n
- احتمال می‌رفت مرد جنایتکار در آنجا مخفی باشد. — The criminal was possibly hiding there.

85 | 104

4548 گوسفند gusfænd *sheep* n
- گوسفندان به خانه‌ها و خودرو مردم در بریتانیا حمله کردند. — Sheep attacked people's homes and cars in Britain.

70 | 226

4549 صرفه særfe *profit, advantage* n
- به‌صرفه نیست. — It is not economical.

68 | 245

4550 فروشنده foruʃænde *salesperson, vendor* n
- فروشندگان بزرگ چگونه عمل می‌کنند؟ — How do great salespeople act?

68 | 241

4551 مصیبت mosibæt *tragedy* n
- یک کوه هم طاقت ندارد اینقدر مصیبت را تحمل کند. — A mountain doesn't have the staying power to endure this much disaster.

82 | 121

4552 وکالت vekalæt *lawyering, power of attorney* n
- تعدادی از اعضای آن علاوه بر وکالت فعالیت سیاسی هم می‌کنند. — A number of its members besides being lawyers are also political activists.

82 | 122

4553 مرتع mærtæʔ *pasture* n
- مرتع در روستا متعلق به کل روستا است. — The pasture in the village belongs to the entire village.

72 | 202

4554 سالاری salari *chiefship, -cracy, -archy* pn
- سروری و سالاری مفاهیمی ضددموکراتیک اند. — Lordship and chiefship are anti-democratic concepts.

74 | 186

4555 تفرقه tæfreɣe *discord, division* n
- تفرقه در عراق به نفع منطقه نیست. — Division in Iraq will not benefit the region.

78 | 158

4556 پیرمرد pirmærd *old man* n
- پسر این پیرمرد دستگیر شد. — The old man's son was arrested.

56 | 359

4557 آزاده azade *free, liberated* adj,n,pn
- انسانهای آزاده متعهد و خلاق. — Free, committed, and creative humans.

64 | 276

4558 قایق ɣajeɣ *boat, canoe* n
- من هرگز به فروش این قایق فکر نکرده بودم. — I had never thought about selling this boat.

78 | 153

4559 ممیز momæjjez *auditor, decimal point, censor* adj,n,pn
- روند رشد سخت گیری‌های ممیزان بسیار بالا رفته‌است. — The growth process of censors' rigidity has greatly increased.

78 | 152

4560 راه رفتن rah ræftæn *walk* v
- آنها نخستین کسانی شدند که بر روی سطح ماه راه رفتند. — They became the first people to walk on the surface of the moon.

61 | 303

4561 مخدوش mæxduʃ *altered, blemished* adj
- حوادثی از این قبیل نمی تواند روابط عمیق کشور را مخدوش نماید. — Incidents of this kind cannot tarnish the country's deep ties.

80 | 135

4562 امامت emamæt *imamship, Imamah* n
- انحراف از مسیر حق و امامت به این نقطه اوج رسیده بود. — Deviation from the path of righteousness and the Imamah had reached this tipping point.

80 | 140

4563 دوبار dobar *twice* adv
- پستچی همیشه دوبار زنگ می‌زند — *The Postman Always Rings Twice.*

79 | 143

4564 عزیمت æzimæt *departure* n
- احمدی نژاد پیش از عزیمت، درباره اهداف سفرش گفت. — Ahmadinejad spoke about the objectives of his trip before departure.

82 | 124

4565 سهیم sæhim *involved, shareholder* adj
- یکی از اثرات توسعه سیاسی در جامعه این است که مردم احساس می کنند که در تصمیم گیری ها سهیم هستند. — One of the effects of political development in society is that people feel like they have a role in decision-making.

81 | 127

4566 بازبینی bazbini *inspection, review* n
- سناتورهای آمریکایی لایحه بازبینی توافق هسته‌ای را به کنگره ارائه کردند. — US senators presented the nuclear deal review bill to Congress.

83 | 113

4567 وبا væba *cholera* n

● علل گوناگونی برای ویرانی شهر اهواز بیان شده است از جمله بروز بیماری وبا و طاعون و شکسته شدن سد. — Different causes have been expressed for the ruin of the city of Ahvaz, among them the outbreak of cholera, the plague and the breaking of the dam.

72 | 201

4568 ناگوار nagovar *unpleasant* adj

● می توانم درک کنم که حرفهام چقدر برایش تلخ و ناگوار است. — I can understand how bitter and unpleasant my words are for him.

86 | 94

4569 مهاجرانی mohadʒerani *Mohajerani* pn

● حشمت مهاجرانی مدیر تیمهای ملی فوتبال ایران شد. — Heshmat Mohajerani became the manager of Iran's national football teams.

60 | 313

4570 مکلف mokællæf *obliged* adj

● دولت خود را متعهد و مکلف به احیای دریاچه ارومیه می‌داند. — The government sees itself committed and obliged to restore Lake Urmia.

72 | 203

4571 افتتاحیه eftetahijje *inaugural* n

● گفته می شود که در مراسم افتتاحیه این نمایشگاه صدها هنرمند و هنر دوست حضور داشتند. — It's said that hundreds of artists and art lovers were present at the gallery's opening ceremony.

80 | 135

4572 نابرابری nabærabæri *inequality* n

● نابرابری در آمدی افزایش یافت. — Income inequality increased.

80 | 138

4573 متوسطه motævæssete *middle, secondary (school)* adj,n

● مسابقه‌های دانش آموزان دختر دوره متوسطه شهر تهران — The competition of Tehran female high school students.

73 | 191

4574 اعتمادی eʔtemadi *Etemadi* n,pn

● نخستین ترانه‌های وی با خوانندگی خشایار اعتمادی اجرا می‌شد. — His first songs were performed by Khashayar Etemadi as the vocal.

74 | 186

4575 قصر ɣæsr *palace* n,pn

● من قصر می‌خواهم با استخر، و اتاق‌هاش هم همه‌شان باید چلچراغ داشته باشند. — I want a palace with a pool, and its rooms must all have chandeliers.

68 | 242

4576 شهریورماه ʃæhriværmah *Shahrivar* n

● انتظار این است که نرخ تورم شهریورماه نسبت به مردادماه روند کاهشی بیشتری را نشان دهد. — The

expectation is that the inflation rate in the month of Shahrivar will demonstrate a greater downward trend relative to the month of Mordad.

78 | 150

4577 جرئت dʒorʔæt *daring, courage* n

● هیچکس جرأت تعدی ندارد. — Nobody dares infringe.

73 | 198

4578 قذافی ɣæzafi *Gaddafi* pn

● ولادیمیر پوتین رئیس جمهوری روسیه روز دوشنبه دعوت معمر قذافی رهبر لیبی را برای سفر به این کشور پذیرفت. — On Monday Russian President Vladimir Putin accepted Libyan leader Muammar Gaddafi's invitation to travel to that country.

51 | 416

4579 نیکو niku *good, fair, well* adj,adv,pn

● برای کسانی که در تاریکی راه خود را گم کرده اند بسیار نیکو باشد — For people who have lost their way in the darkness it would be very good.

84 | 111

4580 درگذشتن dærgozæʃtæn *die* v

● پرویز شاهینخو درگذشت. — Parviz Shahinkhou passed away.

86 | 92

4581 هرمزگان hormozgan *Hormozgan* pn

● استان هرمزگان در جنوب ایران واقع شده‌است. — Hormozgan province is located in southern Iran.

78 | 151

4582 پیگیر pejgir *persistent* adj

● پیگیر مشکلات دختران شین آبادی هستم. — I am following up on the problems of the Shinabadi girls.

86 | 96

4583 کلامی kælami *verbal* adj,n

● مجموع روابطی را که از طریق گفتن و گفتگو حاصل می شود ارتباط کلامی می گویند. — The relations that result from speaking and conversation are called verbal communication.

70 | 217

4584 آگاه شدن agah ʃodæn *be informed* v

● دانش آموزان باید نسبت به پژوهش و نوآوری آگاه شوند. — Students should be informed about research and innovation.

86 | 91

4585 بازو bazu *arm* n

● به خاطر داشته باشید احساس درد در ناحیه قفسه سینه ، انه های زود بازو و شانه چپ ممکن است یکی از نش رس حمله قلبی باشد. — Remember that pain in the left shoulder, arm and the area of your ribcage is one of the signs preceding a heart attack.

75 | 180

4586 مطالعه کردن motɑleʔe kærdæn *read, study* v

- پژوهشگر نمی تواند تاثیر تمام متغییر ها را بر یکدیگر
مطالعه کند. — A researcher cannot study the effect of all of the variables on each other.

77 | 158

4587 نامطلوب nɑmætlub *undesirable* adj

- عواملی نامطلوب ومشکلاتی پیچیده — Undesirable factors and complex problems.

78 | 153

4588 تمیز tæmiz *clean, discernment* adj,adv

- خدمتکار خانه را تمیز کرده بود. — The servant had cleaned the house.

75 | 175

4589 وفاق vefɑɣ *harmony* n

- او نه تنها نزدیکان خود را نکشت، بلکه یگانگی و وفاق را در خانواده ی اشکانی بر پایه ی استوار قرار داد. — Not only did he not kill his relatives, rather he put unity and consensus in the Parthian family on a firm pedestal.

78 | 155

4590 خصومت xosumæt *enmity, animosity* n

- افزایش تحریم‌ها به خصومت بیشتر می‌انجامد. — Increasing the sanctions would lead to more animosity.

85 | 97

4591 مختص moxtæss *special* adj

- این امر مختص صنایع خودروسازی نیست. — This is not specific to the automotive industry.

85 | 98

4592 همایون homɑjun *Homayun* pn

- ا — ده روز آزگار از منزل همایون قدم بیرون نگذاشتم. didn't set foot out of Homayun's home for ten whole days.

79 | 147

4593 رفیق ræfiɣ *pal* adj,n,pn

- به نظر من رفیق خود را یافته ام. — In my opinion I have found my own friend.

64 | 273

4594 ملموس mælmus *tangible* adj

- با استفاده از اقدام پژوهشی می توان موقعیت های نامعین ملموس مربوط به اقدام ها و عملیات آموزشی را مشخص کرد. — By using the scientific method, the tangible but indefinite positions related to educational steps and methods can be determined.

79 | 145

4595 نیرومند nirumænd *powerful* adj,pn

- به خوبی می‌دانید که یک لبخند گرم، چه سلاح نیرومندی است. — You know well what a powerful weapon a warm smile is.

80 | 141

4596 پررنگ porræng *conspicuous, prominent* adj,adv

- آنهارا واضح و پررنگ نوشت. — He wrote them clear and bold.

86 | 91

4597 زمستانی zemestɑni *winter* adj

- پکن میزبان المپیک زمستانی ۲۰۲۲ شد. — Beijing will host the 2022 Winter Olympics.

83 | 112

4598 صالحی sɑlehi *Salehi* pn

- آمانو با صالحی دیدار کرد. — Amano met with Salehi.

68 | 239

4599 جراح dʒærrɑh *surgeon* adj,n

- مشهورترین جراح روسیه و حتی اروپا می‌خواد با شما صحبت کنه، فرصت رو از دست ندین. — The most famous surgeon in Russia, or even Europe, wants to speak to you; do not miss the opportunity.

80 | 138

4600 نیجریه nidʒerije *Nigeria* pn

- وزیر امور خارجه کشورمان همچنین در دیدار همتایان خود از تایلند، نامیبیا، سودان، و نیجریه تلاش کرد زمینه‌های توسعه مناسبات سیاسی اقتصادی را گسترش دهد. — In meetings with his counterparts from Thailand, Namibia, Sudan, and Nigeria, our nation's minister of foreign affairs endeavored to expand the fields of development of political and economic relations.

75 | 174

4601 نجفی nædʒɑfi *Najafi* pn

- ابوالحسن نجفی درگذشت. — Abolhassan Najafi passed away.

71 | 212

4602 زرین zærrin *golden* adj

- لوح سیمین کشف شد و تلاش وسیع و مستمر برای کشف لوح زرین نیز ادامه دارد. — The silver tablet was discovered and continued and wide ranging efforts to uncover the golden tablet are also ongoing.

77 | 162

4603 زائر zɑʔer *pilgrim* pn

- عکس های زیر توسط زائران خانه خدا عکاسی شده و در رسانه های خارجی و داخلی منتشر شده اند. — The pictures below were taken by pilgrims to the house of God and published in domestic and foreign media.

69 | 225

4604 موقتی movæɣɣæti *temporary* adj

- می‌دانید این مطب موقتی است و من فقط چند ماهی در شیراز می مانم. — You know that this clinic is temporary and I will only stay in Shiraz for a few months.

86 | 90

4605 باکو bɑku *Baku* pn

- روزنامه ملت چاپ باکو چندی پیش نوشت . . . — Mellat newspaper, published in Baku, recently wrote . . .

76 | 168

4606 ارادت eradæt *devotion* n
- مردم را شایسته عشق و ارادت و خدمت می دانستند.
— They believed people deserve love, devotion, and service.
86 | 93

4607 رو کردن ru kærdæn *turn to, look at* v
- سپس امام به اصحابش رو کرده گفت. — Then the Imam turned to his companions and said . . .
58 | 333

4608 چمن tʃæmæn *grass, lawn* n
- اما هنگامی که دارید چمن ها را می زنید . . . — In the time that you have you will mow the lawn . . .
76 | 164

4609 خرمشهر xorræmʃæhr *Khorramshahr* pn
- آزادسازی خرمشهر که نزدیک هم هست. — The liberation of Khorramshahr which is close too.
69 | 230

4610 وان vɑn *bathtub, Van* n,pn
- پس از ۵ ساعت مسافرت با کشتی بر روی دریاچه وان به ایستگاه تات وان می رسند. — After 5 hours travel by ferry on Lake Van they arrive at Tatvan Terminal.
86 | 90

4611 بانکداری bɑnkdɑri *banking* n
- مهارت های ارتباطی باید در صنعت بانکداری تقویت شود. — Communication skills must be improved in the banking industry.
71 | 205

4612 بلغارستان bolɣɑrestɑn *Bulgaria* pn
- در این نمایشگاه آثاری از کشورهای روسیه، انگلیس، سوئد، بلغارستان، یونان، ایتالیا، اتریش، آلمان و فرانسه نیز به نمایش گذاشته می شوند. — In this exhibition, works from the countries of Russia, England, Sweden, Bulgaria, Greece, Italy, Austria, Germany and France will also be shown.
79 | 147

4613 منزوی monzævi *reclusive* adj,pn
- جمهوری اسلامی نه فقط منزوی نیست، بلکه در دنیا با چشم تکریم و احترام به جمهوری اسلامی و به ایران اسلامی و به ملت عزیز ما نگریسته میشود. — Not only is the Islamic Republic not secluded, but in the world the Islamic Republic, Islamic Iran, and our beloved country is viewed with reverent and respectful eyes.
86 | 95

4614 کارآمد kɑrɑmæd *skillful, efficient* adj
- این نظام مالی جهانی دیگر کارآمد نیست. — This global financial system is not efficient anymore.
69 | 225

4615 یکباره jekbɑre *all at once* adj,adv
- پیر مرد در حالی که این دعا را با خود زمزمه می کرد و می رفت، یکباره یک گره از گره های دامنش گشوده شد و گندم ها به زمین ریخت. — As the old man was

murmuring prayers to himself and going along, all of a sudden one of the knots from his skirt came undone, and wheat poured to the ground.
81 | 125

4616 حیطه hite *domain* n
- در حیطه وظایف وزارت کشاورزی بود. — It was among Ministry of Agriculture duties.
73 | 195

4617 معصوم mæʔsum *innocent* adj,n
- طفل معصوم محکوم شد. — The innocent child was condemned.
76 | 166

4618 الزام elzɑm *necessity, requirement* n
- در فنلاند الزام ورود به خدمت از سن ۱۹ سالگی آغاز می‌شود. — The entry into service requirement starts at age 19 in Finland.
73 | 191

4619 قرقیزستان ɣerɣizestɑn *Kyrgyzstan* pn
- قسمت اعظم این سرزمین متعلق به تاجیکستان و قرقیزستان و قسمت هایی هم جز قلمرو افغانستان و پاکستان است. — A large part of this land belongs to Tajikistan and Kyrgyzstan and sections are also part of the territory of Afghanistan and Pakistan.
69 | 221

4620 مفاسد mæfɑsed *evils, corruption* n
- دادگاه مفاسد اقتصادی باید علنی باشد. — Economic corruption courts must be open to the public.
85 | 100

4621 زیرزمینی zirzæmini *underground* adj
- ساخت اولین پارک زیرزمینی جهان آغاز شد. — Construction of the world's first underground park has begun.
75 | 172

4622 تنگنا tæŋnɑ *bottleneck, difficulty* n
- از طریق وسایل ارتباط جمعی به تنگنا و مسائلی بر می‌خورد. — Through the mass media it faces problems and bottlenecks.
81 | 130

4623 گرداندن gærdɑndæn *rotate, manage* v
- سریع رویم را می‌گردانم به طرف دیگر. — I quickly turn my face to the other side.
77 | 160

4624 حسی hessi *sensory* adj
- پوست به عنوان سیستم حسی با محیط خارج عمل می‌کند. — The skin acts as a sensory interface with the outside world.
78 | 152

4625 حساب کردن hesɑb kærdæn *calculate, compute* v
- همیشه می‌توان به عنوان دوستی باوفا روی او حساب کرد. — One can always count on him as a faithful friend.
80 | 134

4626 حوصله howsele *patience* n
- خیلی حوصله داری. — You have a lot of patience.
- 61 | 298

4627 کاپیتان kapitan *captain* n
- تیم سوئد از دقیقه 79 با اخراج پاتریک اندرسون کاپیتان خود ده نفره شد. — The Swedish team was down to 10 people from minute 79 with the expulsion of Patrik Andersson, its captain.
- 80 | 132

4628 اکتفا ektefa *contenting oneself, finding sufficient* n
- از این جهت تنها به گرفتن نشانی از آن زن اکتفا کرده و به مادرید رفتم. — Hence, merely getting the address from that woman sufficed and I left for Madrid.
- 83 | 111

4629 شادابی ʃadabi *freshness* adj,n
- گردو باعث شادابی پوست می‌شود. — Walnuts promote freshness of the skin.
- 85 | 99

4630 سیار sæjjar *mobile* adj,pn
- تعداد ۹۵ مدرسه سیار عشایری در استان فارس فعالیت می‌کنند. — 95 nomadic mobile schools are active in Fars province.
- 85 | 99

4631 بروکسل bruksel *Brussels* pn
- دوازده کشور تولیدکننده لباس‌های آماده در بروکسل گردهم آمدند. — Twelve countries that produce ready-to-wear clothing met in Brussels.
- 75 | 171

4632 هلندی holændi *Dutch* adj,n,pn
- هلندی‌ها پل فولادی چاپ می‌کنند. — The Dutch are printing steel bridges.
- 82 | 119

4633 پریدن pæridæn *jump, fly, evaporate* n,v
- مانند زنبور در فصل پاییز می مانم که توان پریدن ندارند. — I am like bees in the fall that can not fly.
- 54 | 368

4634 یقیناً jæɣinæn *certainly* adv,conj
- در صورت خطا در محاسبه یقیناً شکست خواهید خورد. — In the event of a miscalculation you will certainly lose.
- 85 | 96

4635 قطره ɣætre *drop* n
- هر قطره خون که توی آب می‌چکید یک گل سرخ می‌شد. — Each drop of blood that dripped into the water would become a rose.
- 67 | 240

4636 دست‌اندرکار dæstændærkar *involved* n
- اصلاً خوب نیس من دس اندرکار باشم. — It's absolutely not a good idea for me to be involved.
- 72 | 193

4637 بحث کردن bæhs kærdæn *discuss* v
- در مورد مباحث روز بحث کردند. — They discussed the topics of the day.
- 77 | 159

4638 اثر گذاشتن æsær gozaʃtæn *impress, affect* v
- بدون اثر گذاشتن در دستاورد زندگی. — Without affecting the life achievements.
- 84 | 105

4639 فرزانه færzane *learned, wise* adj,n,pn
- ما خواهان همکاری با این مرد فرزانه هستیم. — We would like to cooperate with this wise man.
- 80 | 135

4640 پروین pærvin *Parvin* pn
- دیوان اشعار پروین اعتصامی ترکیبی از دو سبک و شیوه لفظی و معنوی آمیخته با سبکی مستقل است. — The poetry of Parvin Etesami is a combination of two verbal and spiritual techniques mixed with an independent style.
- 81 | 129

4641 ربطی ræbti *linking, connecting* adj,n
- افعال بودن، شدن، و مشتقات این افعال ، افعال ربطی هستند. — The verbs 'be', 'become' and the derivatives of these verbs are called linking verbs.
- 73 | 189

4642 تمامیت tæmamijjæt *integrity* n
- دفاع از تمامیت ارضی. — The defense of territorial integrity.
- 77 | 155

4643 بی‌نظیر binæzir *unique, unparalleled* adj,pn
- خدمات دولت در حوزه بهداشت، بی‌نظیر است. — The government's services in the area of healthcare are unmatched.
- 76 | 163

4644 ساکت saket *silent, extinguished* adj,pn
- حیاط ساکت بود. — The yard was quiet.
- 58 | 320

4645 شر ʃærr *evil* adj,n
- خدا جهان را آفریده است که یاور او در نبرد با شر باشد. — God created the world so it will be His aid in the battle with evil.
- 74 | 176

4646 وقفه væɣfe *pause* n
- مبارزات انتخاباتی خود را پس از یک هفته وقفه با حمله به رقیب خود جورج بوش از سر گرفت. — After a week-long interval, he resumed his election campaign with an attack against his opponent George Bush.
- 80 | 130

4647 سنجیدن sændʒidæn *measure* n,v
- معیاری برای سنجیدن هنر. — A criterion for evaluating art.
- 80 | 130

29 Transport

Rank	Headword	Pronunciation	Gloss	Rank	Headword	Pronunciation	Gloss
47	راه	rah	way, road	2354	كاروان	karevan	caravan
344	سفر	sæfær	travel	2364	كوچه	kuʧe	lane, alley
634	پرواز	pærvaz	flight	2382	كاميون	kamjon	truck
796	خيابان	xijaban	street	2561	سوار	sævar	rider
823	كشتى	keʃti	ship	2655	فرود	forud	landing
873	مسافر	mosafer	traveler, passenger	2656	سرنشين	særneʃin	passenger
1077	هواپيما	hævapejma	airplane	2717	ترافيك	terafik	traffic, traffic jam
1264	فرودگاه	forudgah	airport	3384	مترو	metro	metro
1452	ماشين	maʃin	car	3427	كوى	kuj	quarter, alley, street
1492	پل	pol	bridge	3689	مبدأ	mæbdæʔ	origin
1646	راننده	ranænde	driver	3699	دوچرخه	doʧærxe	bicycle
1705	مقصد	mæɣsæd	destination	3827	بزرگراه	bozorgrah	expressway, highway
1885	ايستگاه	istgah	station	4417	خلبان	xælæban	pilot
2009	قطار	ɣætar	train	4558	قايق	ɣajeɣ	boat, canoe
2150	عازم	azem	leaving, departing, setting off	7011	موتورسيكلت	motorsiklet	motorcycle
2158	موتور	motor	engine, motorcycle	10478	كالسكه	kaleske	carriage
2181	اتوبوس	otobus	bus	13329	مهماندار	mehmandar	steward
				13807	درشكه	doroʃke	carriage

4648 ترجمه شدن tærdʒome ʃodæn *be translated* v
- از فارسى به عربى ترجمه شده و در قاهره به چاپ رسيده است. — It was translated from Persian to Arabic and published in Cairo.
  79 | 137

4649 تكميل كردن tækmil kærdæn *complete* v
- فضانوردان ديسكاورى ساختمان ايستگاه فضايى را تكميل مى‌كنند. — Discovery astronauts are completing construction of the space station.
  88 | 79

4650 شاهنامه ʃahname *Shahname* pn
- ا — من رستم رو خيلى دوست دارم شاهنامه بى‌نظيره. really like Rostam; the *Shahname* is unparalleled.
  71 | 201

4651 اجازه خواستن edʒaze xastæn *ask permission* v
- در مدينه از معاويه اجازه خواستند. — In the city of Medina, they asked for Muawiyah's permission.
  85 | 99

4652 لااقل laʔæɣæl *at least* adv,conj
- لااقل چند دقيقه وقت لازم دارد. — It requires at least a few minutes time.
  73 | 187

4653 پذيرايى pæziraji *reception, entertainment* n
- ايلام و خوزستان آماده پذيرايى از بازديدكنندگان اين مناطق شدند. — Ilam and Khuzestan were ready for the reception of visitors to these areas.
  69 | 216

4654 توهم tævæhhom *hallucination, fantasy* n
- رهبران انگليس در اين توهم به سر مى برند. — British leaders are living in this illusion.
  86 | 86

4655 مفاخر mæfaxer *sources of pride* n
- فردوسى از مفاخر ادبيات جهان است. — Ferdowsi is one of the stars of world literature.
  92 | 51

4656 ماهر maher *skillful* adj
- به مدد دستان ماهر دكتر به زندگى دوباره دست مى‌يافتند. — With the help of the doctor's skilled hands, they would once again gain life.
  83 | 109

4657 وجدان vodʒdan *conscience* n
- وجدان من ناراحت باشه؟ — Should my conscience be troubled?
71 | 200

4658 گذرنامه gozærname *passport* n
- گذرنامه اش را از جیب بیرون آورد و به او داد. — He pulled his passport from his pocket and gave it to him.
81 | 128

4659 پناهگاه pænahgah *shelter* n
- حالا ما باید این تله را بدل کنیم به پناهگاه. — Now we must change this trap into a refuge.
86 | 91

4660 شاهی ʃahi *kingship, royal* adj,n,pn
- اردشیر بر تخت شاهی نشست و برای چهار سال شاهنشاه ایران بود. — Ardeshir sat on the royal throne, and for four years was the Shah of Iran.
72 | 194

4661 برگزیدن bærgozidæn *pick* n,v
- نمایندگان خود را برگزیدند. — They elected their representatives.
79 | 143

4662 نمودار nemudar *diagram, visible* n
- یک جفت چشمی نمودار گردید. — A pair of eyepieces appeared.
65 | 256

4663 آقایی aɣaji *gentlemanly behavior, mastery, Aghaei* n,pn
- ثریا آقایی حریف قدرتمندی از مالزی را شکست داد. — Soraya Aghaei defeated a strong opponent from Malaysia.
85 | 97

4664 نمایشنامه næmajeʃname *play* n
- چندین نمایشنامه و فیلم بر اساس آن ساخته شده‌است. — A few plays and movies have been made based on it.
71 | 205

4665 زیستن zistæn *live* adj,n,v
- در ارتفاعات مرکزی افغانستان می زیستند. — They used to live in the highlands of central Afghanistan.
81 | 126

4666 هاشم haʃem *Hashem* pn
- هاشم اطمینان داشت که عباس کور است. — Hashem was positive that Abbas was blind.
80 | 134

4667 مؤلفه moællefe *component* n
- مفهوم فضا مؤلفه‌های سنتی خود را از دست داده است. — The concept of space has lost its traditional components.
74 | 174

4668 عمارت emaræt *building* n
- قناری کوچک با آن بال‌های زرد و قشنگش می‌آمد و می‌نشست روی سر شیر سنگی روبروی عمارت شهرداری و شروع می‌کرد به خواندن. — The tiny canary with its pretty yellow wings would come and sit upon the stone lion facing town hall and begin singing.
68 | 231

4669 همانا hæmana *indeed* adv
- بعد از ۲۰ سال انتظار مردم فنوج به مهم‌ترین خواسته خود که همانا شهرستان شدن فنوج بود رسیدند. — After twenty years of waiting, the people of Fanuj got their most foremost desire, which had unequivocally been for Fanuj to become a county.
75 | 167

4670 شیفته ʃifte *infatuated, fascinated* adj,n
- انسان شیفته مادیت، کوته‌نظر و کم‌عمل می‌شود. — A human obsessed with materialism is shortsighted and low functioning.
84 | 101

4671 پوهنتون pohæntun *university* n
- برای تحصیلاتِ پوهنتونی به لبنان رفته و در پوهنتون امریکایی بیروت ادامه تحصیل داد. — For higher education he went to Lebanon, and continued his studies at the American University of Beirut.
41 | 530

4672 تکثیر tæksir *multiplication, reproduction* n
- این مراکز برای نیل به هدف خود، انواع متعدد آزمون‌ها را جمع آوری و تکثیر می کند. — These centers gather and reproduce numerous types of tests to achieve their goal.
78 | 145

4673 گرامی داشتن gerami daʃtæn *honor* v
- نشان دهنده علاقه و اعتقاد اجتماعی و مذهبی مردم به گرامی داشتن اماکن مذهبی است. — It represents the people's religious and social belief and interest in honoring religious sites.
83 | 111

4674 تخمین tæxmin *estimate* n
- خسارات وارده را بیش از یک میلیون دلار تخمین زدند. — They estimated the incurred damages to be more than one million dollars.
72 | 190

4675 پهنه pæhne *stretch of land, area* n,pn
- پهنه دفاعی ایران مستحکم‌تر می‌شود. — Iran's defensive zone is becoming stronger.
85 | 93

4676 همچنانکه hæmtʃenanke *as* conj
- همچنانکه به دوران اخیر نزدیک می‌شویم، نوشته‌ها در مورد کلیبر کمتر میشود. — As we get closer to recent times, there are fewer writings about Kaleybar.
86 | 89

4677 رشید ræʃid *well* grown, *Rashid* adj,pn
- شما از جهت قانونی بالغ و رشید هستید. — Legally you are mature and grown-up.
- 81 | 121

4678 سرگردان særgærdan *wandering, vagrant* adj
- سرگردان به زن آبی پوش نگاه کرد. — He looked at the woman in blue confusedly.
- 79 | 138

4679 دزدی dozdi *theft, burglary* adj,n
- هدیه سارق به خواهرش، راز دزدی‌های سریالی را فاش کرد. — The thief's gift to his sister revealed the secret of the serial burglaries.
- 73 | 188

4680 زشت zeʃt *ugly* adj
- لوازم آرایشی: ابزاری که زن زیبا را زشت و زن زشت را زشت تر نشان می دهد. — Cosmetics: a tool to make a beautiful woman look ugly and an ugly woman uglier.
- 76 | 162

4681 بازیافتن bazjaften *recycle, recover* adj,n,v
- نیل به رستگاری از طریق بازیافتن یگانگی با خود، دیگران و طبیعت است. — Attaining righteousness is through regaining unity with oneself, others, and nature.
- 71 | 199

4682 چادر tʃador *tent, chador* n
- من به تو چادر می دهم. — I will give you a chador.
- 62 | 283

4683 استکبار estekbar *arrogance* n
- انسان در رفتارش استکبار را نشان می‌دهد. — Humans exhibit arrogance in their behavior.
- 64 | 260

4684 خطیر xætir *important, dangerous* adj
- وظیفه خطیر ما. — Our solemn duty.
- 86 | 86

4685 اطلاق etlaɣ *calling a name* n
- به عصر اعراب پیش از اسلام اطلاق می شود. — Refers to the pre-Islamic era of Arabs.
- 70 | 205

4686 چاقو tʃaɣu *knife* n
- این کارگران توسط چاقو به شکل فجیع به قتل رسیده اند. — These workers were gruesomely murdered by knife.
- 74 | 175

4687 درخواست کردن dærxast kærdæn *request* v
- رئیس از جوان درخواست کرد تا دستهایش را نشان دهد. — The chief asked that the young man show his hands.
- 84 | 99

4688 کوچ kutʃ *migration* n
- ز این رو برادران باهم کوچ نمی‌کنند. — That's why the brothers don't migrate together.
- 84 | 104

4689 پیشگام piʃgam *pioneer* adj,n
- فیلم‌های اروپایی همیشه پیشگام هنر فیلم بوده‌اند. — European films have always pioneered the art of cinema.
- 83 | 112

4690 ملکی melki, mæleki *real estate, Maleki* adj,n,pn
- آیت الله میرزا جواد ملکی تبریزی. — Ayatollah Mirza Javad Maleki Tabrizi.
- 62 | 282

4691 تل tæll, tel *hill/pile, headband* n,pn
- او دستور داد تا تل بزرگی از هیزم در بابل فراهم آورند. — He ordered a large pile of firewood to be gathered in Babylon.
- 84 | 104

4692 متمایز motæmajez *distinct* adj
- در نتیجه آنها را از کارگران متمایز می سازد. — As a result it distinguishes them from the workers.
- 77 | 150

4693 ابداع ebda? *innovation* n
- این کلمه ابداع بزرگ اوست. — This word is her great innovation.
- 75 | 170

4694 پروردگار pærværdegar *Creator* n,pn
- فاطمه شاگرد مستقیم پروردگار بود. — Fatemeh was a direct student of God.
- 73 | 182

4695 ساقط saɣet *fallen, miscarried, lapsed* adj
- وقتی رژیم شاه ساقط شد. — When the Shah's regime was overthrown.
- 88 | 72

4696 رشوه reʃve *bribery, bribe* n
- می‌دانم، اما خودتان که می‌دانید ما رشوه قبول نمی‌کنیم. — I know, but you yourself know that we do not accept bribes.
- 77 | 155

4697 آمیختن amixtæn *mix* adj,n,v
- بعد از ورود اسپانیایی‌ها در قرن شانزدهم به مکزیک، این سنت با باورهای مسیحی آمیخته شد. — After the arrival of the Spanish to Mexico in the sixteenth century, the tradition was mixed with Christian beliefs.
- 75 | 166

4698 دیسک disk *disk* n
- باید ابتدا آن را روی دیسک سخت ذخیره کرد. — First, it needs to be saved on a hard disk.
- 84 | 102

4699 ماریا marija *Maria* pn
- این مایه مباهات من است که ماریا و خانواده اش مرا پذیرفت. — It is an honor that Maria and her family accepted me.
- 86 | 85

4700 کاظمی kazemi *Kazemi* pn
- کاظمی برکنار شد. — Kazemi was dismissed.
- 71 | 199

4701 پلیسی polisi *police* adj,n
- یک فیلم پلیسی است. — It's a detective film.

78 | 142

4702 مهرداد *Mehrdad* pn
- آقای مهرداد پولادی. — Mr. Mehrdad Puladi.

67 | 232

4703 بیژن biʒæn *Bijan* pn
- بیژن زنگنه وزیر نفت ایران در پایان این مذاکرات گفت. — Iranian Oil Minister, Bijan Zangeneh, at the end of the talks said . . .

81 | 123

4704 تنزل tænæzzol *decline, decrease* n
- یک تأثیر منفی بچه دار شدن می تواند این باشد که شوهر، از شخص شماره یک همسر خود، به شخص شماره دو تنزل می کند. — A negative effect of having children can be that a husband is downgraded by his spouse from a primary position to a secondary position.

81 | 121

4705 صدم sædom *hundredth* adj,n
- مراسم صدمین سالگرد قتل عام ارامنه در سراسر جهان برگزار شد. — The commemoration of the 100th anniversary of the Armenian genocide was held around the world.

70 | 208

4706 آشتی aʃti *reconciliation* n
- سپهری میکوشد نوعی آشتی بین سنت و مدرنیته ایجاد کند. — Sepehri strives to create a kind of reconciliation between tradition and modernity.

76 | 162

4707 مبادا mæbada *lest* adv
- از سوی دیگر مسئولان بیمارستان نیز حتی کمترین نیاز های او را اجابت می کردند تا مبادا حرف رفتن از او بشنوند. — On the other hand, the hospital officials responded to even his slightest need lest they hear talk of leaving from him.

71 | 198

4708 پیشتاز piʃtaz *pioneer, front-running* adj,n
- این خودرو با فاصله زیادی از رقبا در بازار انگلستان پیشتاز است. — This car leads its competitors in the English market by a wide margin.

81 | 126

4709 جعل dʒæʔl *forgery* n
- زیر نور ماوراء بنفش تلالو خاصی دارد و مانع از جعل اسکناس میشود. — Under ultraviolet light, it has a certain glint that prevents forging banknotes.

81 | 121

4710 ترجیح tærdʒih *preference* n
- ا — هزار بار مرگ را بر آن زندگی ترجیح میدهم. prefer death a thousand times over to such a life.

85 | 92

4711 بهایی bæhaji *Bahai* n,pn
- در سال ۱۹۱۹ اولین معبد بهاییان در عشقآباد تاسیس شد. — The first Baha'i temple in Ashgabat was founded in 1919.

84 | 102

4712 لاریجانی laridʒani *Larijani* pn
- لاریجانی آزادسازی شهر فلوجه را تبریک گفت. — Larijani congratulated the liberation of Fallujah.

67 | 234

4713 مهربانی mehræbani *kindness* adj,n
- دستش را با مهربانی روی شانههای پسر گذاشت. — She put her hands kindly on the boy's shoulders.

76 | 158

4714 آبان aban *Aban* n
- ۲۸ آبان ۱۳۲۵ خورشیدی. — The 28th of Aban 1325 in the solar calendar.

64 | 263

4715 پروسه prose *process* n
- این پروسه درحال حاضر دارای کاستی های جدی است. — Currently this process has serious deficiencies.

49 | 418

4716 رسوایی rosvaji *disgrace, scandal* n
- یک شکست و رسوایی بزرگ برای این رژیم محسوب می شود. — It is considered a failure and a huge scandal for the regime.

74 | 175

4717 مشتمل moʃtæmel *containing* adj
- فصل اول و دوم کتاب مشتمل بر بحث های مقدماتی است. — The first and second chapters of the book contain introductory discussions.

77 | 150

4718 مفیدی mofidi *Mofidi, useful* adj,pn
- بدرالسادات مفیدی روزنامهنگار ایرانی و دبیرانجمن صنفی روزنامهنگاران ایران است. — Badrolsadat Mofidi is an Iranian journalist and secretary of the Association of Iranian Journalists.

86 | 84

4719 بازاریابی bazarjabi *marketing* n
- بازاریابی سینمایی چیست؟ — What is cinematic marketing?

64 | 258

4720 مفصلی mæfsæli *joint, articular* adj
- استحمام در آن موجب بهبود بیماریهای عصبی، مفصلی و رماتیسم میشود. — Bathing in it improves rheumatism, and joint and neurological diseases.

79 | 137

4721 اظهارنظر ezharnæzær *comment* n
- این اظهارنظر درباره قیمت خودرو درست نبود. — That comment about the price of cars was not correct.

71 | 198

4722 قرآنی yorʔani *Koranic* adj
- ربنای شجریان معروف‌ترین تلاوت‌های قرآنی اوست. — Shajarian's Rabana is one of his most famous Koranic recitations.
66 | 236

4723 ملایم molajem *gentle* adj
- آفتاب ملایم می‌تابید. — The sun was shining softly.
81 | 121

4724 مقبره mæɣbære *tomb* n
- می‌گن مقبره ی کوروش اصلا مال کوروش نیست. — They say that Cyrus's tomb doesn't actually belong to Cyrus.
64 | 262

4725 نثر næsr *prose* n
- این رمان به نثری سلیس و روان نوشته شده است. — This novel has been written in a very fluent prose.
59 | 308

4726 مجزا modʒæzza *separate* adj
- آزمون تحقیق در دو مرحله مجزا صورت گرفت. — The research test took place in two separate phases.
78 | 142

4727 پیرزن pirzæn *old woman* n
- پیرزن از کاریز بر می گشت. — The old woman was returning from the aqueduct.
50 | 399

4728 آگهی agæhi *advertisement* n
- آگهی و اعلانی درباره ی تک نوازی آینده به منزل همه ی شاگردان فرستادم. — I sent advertisements and notifications of the upcoming musical solo to all of the students' homes.
67 | 229

4729 باردار bardar *pregnant, loaded* adj
- زن باردار شد. — The woman got pregnant.
80 | 129

4730 سلمان sælman *Salman* pn
- همچو سلمان در مسلمانی بکوش. — Just like Salman put effort in being a Muslim.
80 | 125

4731 فصلی fæsli *seasonal* adj,n
- آلرژی‌های فصلی را با این مواد غذایی کنترل کنید. — Control seasonal allergies with these foods.
78 | 142

4732 حسابی hesabi *proper, quite* adj,adv,n,pn
- دسته دلقک‌ها داستان زن‌های نان آور خانواده و مردهای حسابی خوشگذران است. — Guignol's Band is the story of breadwinner women and quite jovial men.
53 | 369

4733 پهلوان pæhlævan *champion, hero* adj,n,pn
- تا حالا خیلی از پهلوان ها هوس این کار را کرده اند و خودشان را به کشتن داده اند. — Until now many heroes have desired this work and have given themselves to killing.
82 | 114

4734 وگرنه vægærnæ *otherwise* conj
- شاید هم گفته، وگرنه از کجا می‌دانست؟ — She might have said it, how else would he know?
71 | 199

4735 آفرین afærin *well done, bravo* n,pn
- آفرین دخترم. — Well done my daughter.
67 | 232

4736 شوک ʃok *shock* n
- یک شوک فیزیکی به او وارد شده. — He was afflicted with a physical shock.
80 | 131

4737 بازهم bazhæm *again* adv
- جیب‌برهای حرفه‌ای باز هم به دام افتادند. — Professional pickpockets were caught again.
77 | 153

4738 مکعب mokæʔæb *cube* n
- چهار مناره کوتاه آجری به صورت مکعب در بالای این نما با طاق تزیینی همراه می باشد. — Four short brick minarets in the form of a cube at the top of the facade are accompanied by a decorative arch.
72 | 191

4739 تیتر titr *headline* n
- از تیتر یک روزنامه خیلی خوشم اومد، — I liked the headline of a newspaper a lot.
77 | 150

4740 اینچنین inʧenin *such* adv,pron
- بدیهی است که باید اینچنین بشود. — It is evident that it must be this way.
88 | 72

4741 راستین rastin *true* adj
- عشق باید توان پرتاب انسان به سوی هدفهای راستین را داشته باشد. — Love should be capable of launching a man towards his true goals.
87 | 82

4742 منزلت mænzelæt *status* n
- حقوق اساسی بشر و منزلت و ارزش انسان را در منشور سازمان ملل متحد مورد تایید مجدد قرار داده‌اند. — The fundamental right of mankind and the status and value of the person has been reconfirmed in the United Nations' charter.
78 | 142

4743 منوچهر mænuʧehr *Manuchehr* pn
- به گفته منوچهر منطقی برآوردها حاکی است. — According to Manouchehr Manteghi estimates suggest that.
61 | 284

4744 چرخش ʧærxeʃ *turn, rotation* n
- سرعت چرخش یک کهکشان چقدر است. — What is the speed of rotation of a galaxy?
82 | 112

4745 بازیگری bɑzigæri *acting* n
- She — وی علاقه ی بسیار زیادی به بازیگری دارد. really likes acting.
73 | 184

4746 همگرایی hamgerɑji *convergence* n
- همگرایی نور به معنی رسیدن پرتوهای موازی نور در یک نقطه مشترک به هم است. — Convergence of light means reaching of parallel rays of light together at a common point.
75 | 165

4747 چرخه ʧærxe *reel, cycle* n
- تکمیل چرخه سوخت هسته ای. — Completing the nuclear fuel cycle.
69 | 209

4748 پیشاپیش piʃɑpiʃ *in advance* adv,n
- پیشاپیش از زحمات شما متشکرم. — Thank you in advance for your efforts.
88 | 76

4749 جنایی dʒenɑji *criminal* adj
- نویسنده داستان‌های جنایی به اتهام قتل دستگیر شد. — A crime fiction writer was arrested on charges of murder.
73 | 177

4750 مجریه modʒrijje *executive* adj
- این مشکل در قوه مجریه نیز هست و سیاستهای اقتصادی کشور در چند سال اخیر متغیر و متحول بوده است. — This problem also exists in the Executive Branch and the country's economic policies have been variable and evolving in the last few years.
72 | 190

4751 درود dorud *greeting* n,pn,v
- درود بر همه شما خانواده های عزیز. — Greetings to all of you, dear families.
76 | 157

4752 عصبانیت æsæbɑnijjæt *anger* n
- عصبانیت من به خاطر مشکلات مالی بود. — My anger was due to financial problems.
76 | 159

4753 مگاواتی megɑvɑt *megawatt* adj,n,pn
- قرارداد احداث یک نیروگاه هزار مگاواتی در جنوب تهران نیز تقریباً نهایی شده است. — The contract for construction of a thousand-megawatt power plant south of Tehran is almost finalized.
75 | 162

4754 زیروبمی zirobæmi *pitch, tone* adj,n
- دراین زبان‌ها زیروبمی در کلمات تک‌هجایی باعث تغییر معنی می‌شود. — In these languages, tone in monosyllabic words changes the meaning.
46 | 447

4755 جنگیدن dʒæŋgidæn *fight* adj,n,v
- برای بیش از یک دهه با آنها جنگیدند. — They fought for more than a decade with them.
75 | 161

4756 محبوس mæhbus *imprisoned* adj,n
- یک سال در زندان خانگی محبوس می کند. — He put him under house arrest for one year.
91 | 56

4757 جم dʒæm, dʒom *Jamshid/Jam, motion/wag* n,pn
- در سن ۹۲ سالگی در بیمارستان جم تهران درگذشت. — He died at age 92 at Tehran's Jam Hospital.
83 | 105

4758 کاهیدن kɑhidæn *decline, alleviate* v
- تا حدودی از مشکلات مربوط به حفاظت از محیط زیست در ایران می‌کاهد. — To some extent it alleviates problems related to environmental protection in Iran.
84 | 102

4759 عرفانی erfɑni *Sufist, mystic* adj
- جنبه عرفانی و اعتقادی آن بسیار عمیق است. — Its believing and mystical side is very deep.
71 | 194

4760 پسته peste *pistachio* n
- قبلاً قیمت پسته تقریبا دو برابر انار بود. — The price of pistachios used to be twice that of pomegranates.
75 | 160

4761 ترغیب tærɣib *persuasion* n
- روابط دو جانبه را ترغیب کرده است. — He encouraged bilateral relationships.
74 | 175

4762 کوهی kuhi *mountain* adj,n,pn
- نابودی جمعی بزهای کوهی سایگا ادامه دارد. — The mass destruction of Saiga antelope continues.
81 | 118

4763 تشریفاتی tæʃrifɑti *ceremonial* adj,n
- هیچ بندی از قانون اساسی، تشریفاتی نیست. — None of the constitution clauses is ceremonial.
88 | 73

4764 پیتر piter *Peter* pn
- «پیتر پن» از کجا آمد؟ — Where did Peter Pan come from?
83 | 108

4765 ترانزیتی trɑnziti *transit* adj
- راه ترانزیتی اصفهان - بندر امام کوتاه می‌شود. — The Isfahan – Bandar-e Emam transit route is getting shorter.
81 | 121

4766 چرخیدن ʧærxidæn *turn* v
- چرخیدن کلید در قفل. — The key turning in the lock.
65 | 242

4767 نزول nozul *fall, descent* n
- از منزلت انسانی خود نزول کرده است. — His human dignity has declined.
80 | 127

4768 افشار _æʃʃɑr Afshar_ pn
- نادرشاه افشار رو سر چ می کنم ، نجات دهنده ایران از چنگال یه مشت غارتگر ... — I'm searching for "Nader Shah Afshar," the savior of Iran from a pack of pillagers.
79 | 136

4769 تابیدن _tɑbidæn shine, twist_ adj,v
- در زمستان نور خورشید به داخل اتاقهای نشیمن می‌تابید. — In winter, sunlight would shine into the living rooms.
78 | 140

4770 مصونیت _mæsunijjæt immunity_ n
- رییس جمهور کرزی می‌گوید مسئله مصونیت قضایی سربازان را به مردم واگذار خواهد کرد. — The president, Hamid Karzai, says that the issue of judicial immunity for soldiers will be left to the people.
70 | 202

4771 صرف شدن _særf ʃodæn be spent, consumed, conjugated_ v
- یک سال و پنج ماه برای چاپ این کتاب وقت صرف شد. — A year and five months were spent to print this book.
86 | 83

4772 خسته شدن _xæste ʃodæn become tired_ v
- هی نالیدند، تا اینکه خسته شدند. — They kept whining till they got exhausted.
70 | 199

4773 رابط _rɑbet intermediary, connector_ adj,n
- شیلنگ های رابط. — Connector hoses.
87 | 76

4774 یهود _jæhud Jewry_ pn
- عید حنوکا یادآور یکی از معجزات در تاریخ یهود است. — Hanukkah commemorates one of the miracles of Jewish history.
70 | 203

4775 صدراعظم _sædreʔæzæm chancellor_ n
- آنگلا مرکل صدراعظم آلمان. — German Chancellor Angela Merkel.
76 | 155

4776 شیری _ʃiri milk, dairy_ adj,n,pn
- یک سوم جمعیت جهان راه شیری را نمی‌بینند. — One-third of the world's population does not see the Milky Way.
82 | 115

4777 شگفت _ʃegeft amazing_ adj,n
- پدر که از این جواب پسرش شگفت زده شده بود پرسید چرا نمی توانی؟ — The father who had been amazed by his son's answer asked, "Why can't you?"
77 | 151

4778 اساسنامه _æsɑsnɑme charter, constitution_ n
- فعالیت‌های اقتصادی هلال احمر مطابق اساسنامه است. — Red Crescent economic activities are in accordance with its charter.
78 | 143

4779 بندری _bændæri port_ adj,n
- دریادار سیاری وارد شهر بندری چینگ دائو شد. — Admiral Sayyari entered the port city of Qingdao.
86 | 82

4780 سوسیالیست _sosijɑlist socialist_ adj,n
- نامزد سوسیالیست‌ها شهردار پاریس شد. — The socialist candidate was elected mayor of Paris.
72 | 186

4781 امامی _emɑmi imam, Emami_ adj,pn
- یونس امامی صاحب مدال برنز شد. — Yunes Emami won the bronze medal.
80 | 127

4782 نتانیاهو _netɑnjɑhu Netanyahu_ pn
- تنها زمانی که ما نتانیاهو را تحت فشار بگذاریم می توانیم به یک واسطه واقعی در منطقه تبدیل شویم. — Only when we put Netanyahu under pressure can we turn into a real intermediary in the region.
74 | 169

4783 طبع _tæbʔ nature_ n
- طبع مزاحی داشت. — He had a joking nature.
74 | 169

4784 سست _sost weak_ adj
- عرق سردی بر تن و بدنم نشست و پایم سست شده. — A cold sweat fell on my body and my foot got weak.
81 | 117

4785 ژنتیکی _ʒenetiki genetic_ adj
- رایانه‌ها طب ژنتیکی را متحول می‌کنند. — Computers have revolutionized genetic medicine.
75 | 162

4786 احقاق _ehɣɑɣ rectifying_ n
- هدف از این اعتصاب احقاق حقوق کارکنان بخش خدمات مترو بوده است. — The goal of this strike was restoring the rights of the Metro service workers.
86 | 87

4787 عینک _ejnæk glasses_ n,pn
- بذار ببینم، عینکم کو! — Let me see, where are my glasses?
60 | 286

4788 دوحه _dowhe Doha_ pn
- حضور کشور های عرب در کنفرانس اقتصادی دوحه. — The presence of Arab nations in the Doha Economic Conference.
79 | 131

4789 جوار _dʒævɑr proximity_ n
- در جوار ما زوجی به همراه دو کودک خود نشسته اند. — A couple along with their two children are sitting in our vicinity.
80 | 123

4790 دیوانه _divɑne crazy_ adj,n
- دیوانه شده‌ای مگر؟ — Have you gone crazy or what?
54 | 344

4791 بلا bæla, bela *disaster, without* n,prep,pn
- چه بلایی سر خودش آورده بود! — What a calamity he had brought upon himself!
- 69 | 208

4792 ناجا nadʒa *Iranian police* pn
- فرمانده ناجا — Iranian police force commander.
- 79 | 133

4793 نوزده nuzdæh *nineteen* n
- در تقویم بهائی هر ماه، نوزده روز و هر سال نوزده ماه دارد. — In the Bahá'í calendar each month has nineteen days, and each year is nineteen months.
- 58 | 310

4794 خواهش کردن xahe∫ kærdæn *request, beg* v
- دعا کردند و خواهش کردند. — They prayed and begged.
- 58 | 310

4795 مؤلف moʔallef *author, compiler* adj,n
- بزرگداشت مؤلفان، بزرگداشت علم و دانش است. — A tribute to the authors is a tribute to science and knowledge.
- 72 | 186

4796 کویر kævir *salt desert* n
- هلیکوپترها بین راه طبس و یزد، در کویر فرود آمدند. — The helicopters landed in the desert on the way from Tabas to Yazd.
- 71 | 192

4797 اکثراً æksæræn *mostly* adv
- هم اکنون اهالی استان مرکزی اکثراً مسلمان و شیعه هستند. — Now the people of Central Province are mostly Shia Muslims.
- 74 | 172

4798 ارضی ærzi *territorial, land* adj
- مالکیت ارضی یک پیشرفت تعیین کننده بود که آثار شرا آشکار میکند. — Property ownership was a decisive improvement which reveals its effects.
- 78 | 142

4799 بیچاره bit∫are *helpless* adj,n
- بیچاره موهایش به کلی سفید شده. — Poor thing, her hair has gone totally gray.
- 56 | 327

4800 بشار bæ∫ar *Bashar* pn
- سعودیها به مخالفین بشار اسد کمک میکنند. — The Saudis are helping Bashar Assad's opponents.
- 62 | 268

4801 تعارض tæʔaroz *antagonism, opposition* n
- این تعارض در رفتار و گفتار شماست. — This conflict is in your behavior and speech.
- 76 | 156

4802 پیچیدن pit∫idæn *twist, turn* v
- آن دو از پیاده رو پیچیدند توی کوچهای که به خیابان اصلی میرسید. — Those two turned from the sidewalk into an alley that led to the main road.
- 59 | 292

4803 انحصاری enhesari *exclusive, monopoly* adj,n
- قدرتی انحصاری که میتواند قاعده عرضه و تقاضای بازار را برهم بزند . . . — A monopolistic power that can disturb the law of market supply and demand . . .
- 80 | 122

4804 ماسه mase *sand* n
- معادن شن و ماسه از فردا اجازه فعالیت دارند. — Sand and gravel mines will be allowed to operate by tomorrow.
- 79 | 132

4805 مخاطره moxatere *peril, risk* n
- به دنبال زندگی خود بروند اما در این راه هر یک با مخاطره ای خاص روبه رو می شوند. — To follow their own lives, but each one will face a specific danger on this path.
- 81 | 121

4806 ولیعهد væliʔæhd *crown prince* n
- شاهزاده عبدالله ولیعهد عربستان. — Crown Prince Abdullah of Saudi Arabia.
- 84 | 98

4807 کیفری kejfæri *penal, criminal* adj,n
- دیوان کیفری لاهه یک جنایتکار جنگی صربستان را آزاد کرد. — The International Criminal Court released a Serbian war criminal.
- 75 | 162

4808 فرضی færzi *hypothetical* adj
- آمریکا همواره به یک دشمن فرضی نیاز دارد. — America always needs a hypothetical enemy.
- 86 | 82

4809 متعارف motæʔaref *common* adj
- روش متعارف برای درمان این بیماری استفاده از انواع داروهاست. — The standard method of treatment for this illness is using different types of medications.
- 82 | 112

4810 علیزاده ælizade *Alizadeh* pn
- عباسعلی علیزاده در گفت وگو با ایرنا افزود — Abbas Ali Alizadeh said in an interview with IRNA . . .
- 77 | 148

4811 نوپا nowpa *newly established, toddler* adj
- ما به انرژی به خصوص در کشورهای دارای اقتصاد نوپا نیاز داریم. — We need energy, especially in countries with emerging economies.
- 88 | 69

4812 پسندیده pæsændide *admirable, approved* adj,v
- بسیار پسندیده و مطلوب است. — It is very admirable and desirable.
- 86 | 84

4813 دریچه dæri∫e *window, valve, vent* n
- ساختار و عملکرد دریچههای قلبی با یکدیگر متفاوت است. — Structure and function of heart valves differ from each other.
- 76 | 154

30 War

Rank	Headword	Pronunciation	Gloss	Rank	Headword	Pronunciation	Gloss
152	نیرو	niru	*force*	2421	موشک	muʃæk	*missile*
263	جنگ	dʒæng	*war*	2428	ژنرال	ʒeneral	*general*
302	دفاع	defaʔ	*defense*	2752	اسیر	æsir	*captive*
393	مرگ	mærg	*death*	2942	ائتلاف	eʔtelaf	*coalition*
399	شهید	ʃæhid	*martyr*	3029	ناو	nav	*naval vessel, battleship*
404	امنیت	æmnijæt	*security*	3063	محاصره	mohasere	*blockade*
486	نظامی	nezami	*military*	3071	باختن	baxtæn	*lose*
534	حمله	hæmle	*attack*	3167	شلیک	ʃellik	*firing, shooting*
553	عملیات	æmælijat	*operation*	3231	گردان	gordan	*battalion*
598	پلیس	polis	*police*	3269	تانک	tank	*tank*
622	پیروزی	piruzi	*victory*	3390	سرهنگ	særhæng	*colonel*
733	زندان	zendan	*prison*	3454	بمباران	bombaran	*bombardment*
776	تسلیم	tæslim	*surrender*	3462	سربازی	særbazi	*military service*
789	دشمن	doʃmæn	*enemy*	3496	جانباز	dʒanbaz	*disabled war veteran*
823	کشتی	keʃti	*ship*	3819	تروریست	terorist	*terrorist*
946	سلاح	selah	*weapon*	3826	تسخیر	tæsxir	*conquest, conquer, capture*
955	خشونت	xoʃunæt	*violence*	4068	پادگان	padegan	*garrison, barracks, base*
1006	شکست	ʃekæst	*defeat, failure*	4201	بازجویی	bazdʒuji	*interrogation*
1127	انفجار	enfedʒar	*explosion*	4417	خلبان	xælæban	*pilot*
1176	جهاد	dʒæhad	*jihad*	4421	جنگنده	dʒængænde	*fighter aircarft*
1268	سرباز	særbaz	*soldier*	4481	مین	min	*mine*
1337	متحد	mottæhed	*ally*	4501	اسارت	esaræt	*captivity*
1409	جبهه	dʒebhe	*front*	4557	آزاده	azade	*Iranian released (Iran-Iraq) war captives*
1530	شهادت	ʃæhadæt	*martyrdom*	4976	کلانتری	kælantæri	*police station*
1548	طالبان	taleban	*Taliban*	5257	سنگر	sængær	*trench*
1553	سپاه	sepah	*army, IRGC*	5265	انهدام	enhedam	*destruction, demolition*
1599	نبرد	næbærd	*battle*	5592	ملوان	mælævan	*sailor, seaman*
1616	توپ	tup	*cannon*	5614	جاسوس	dʒasus	*spy*
1694	فتح	fæth	*victory*	5922	تفنگ	tofæng	*gun, rifle*
1698	ترور	teror	*assassination*	7881	آزادسازی	azadsazi	*liberalization, liberation*
1700	بازداشت	bazdaʃt	*arrest*	7891	رژه	reʒe	*parade, march*
1819	گلوله	golule	*bullet*	7919	خمپاره	xompare	*mortar shell*
1881	خودی	xodi	*friendly*	9889	مسلسل	mosælsæl	*machine gun*
1991	مجروح	mædʒruh	*injured*	12435	تیمسار	timsar	*general*
2101	کودتا	kudeta	*coup d'état*				
2130	اشغال	eʃɣal	*occupation*				
2195	شیمیایی	ʃimijaji	*chemical*				
2222	بمب	bomb	*bomb*				
2262	اتمی	ætomi	*atomic*				
2267	تروریسم	terorism	*terrorism*				

4814 عصبانی æsæbani *angry* adj
- He — نقش یک آدم عصبانی را در سریال‌ها ایفا می‌کرد. used to play the role of an angry person in the series.

61 | 276

4815 خلیج‌فارس xalidʒefars *Persian Gulf* pn
- الان به راحتی می‌توان به کشورهای حاشیه خلیج‌فارس رفت و یک خودرو خرید. — Now one can easily go to one of the countries around the Persian Gulf and purchase a car.

51 | 373

4816 ارجمند ærdʒomænd *valuable, esteemed* adj,pn
- شما در چشم ما دارای مقامی ارجمند و برجسته بودید. — In our eyes you had an elevated and significant position.

63 | 257

4817 رستم rostæm *Rostam* pn
- می‌بخشید، شما از کجا فهمیدید اسم بچه رستم است؟ — Pardon me, how did you know that the child's name is Rostam?

75 | 157

4818 درخشیدن deræxʃidæn *shine* adj,n,v
- مثل درخشیدن برق. — Like the shine of lightning.

83 | 104

4819 کنکور konkur *entrance exam* n
- نتیجه‌ی کنکور که آمد، همان سال اول در یکی از رشته‌های ممتاز دانشگاه تهران قبول شد. — When the results of the college entrance exams came out, she was accepted into one of the distinguished fields of study at Tehran University that same year.

76 | 154

4820 نرخ تورم nerxetæværom *inflation rate* n
- آخرین نرخ تورم 12 ماهه در مردادماه و به میزان 39 درصد بود. — The last 12-month inflation rate was in Mordad at 39%.

75 | 163

4821 فعل feʔl *verb* n
- آخرین فعل جمله‌های استاد امجدی را تکرار کرد. — She repeated the final verb of professor Amjadi's sentences.

62 | 268

4822 نشیب næʃib *descent, downhill* n
- سرعت اینترنت این روزها فراز و نشیب دارد. — Internet speed these days has its ups and downs.

85 | 89

4823 مسالمت mosalemæt *conciliation, non-violence* n
- علی‌رغم داشتن تاریخی آشفته و گاه خون‌آلود با هم به آرامش و مسالمت زندگی می‌کنند. — Despite a turbulent and sometimes gory history, they live together in peace and harmony.

62 | 268

4824 کمونیستی komonisti *communist* adj
- در واقع مارکس درباره خصوصیات جامعه کمونیستی صحبت زیادی نکرده است. — In fact Marx did not talk much about the particulars of communist society.

80 | 120

4825 اسکی eski *ski* n
- پیست اسکی توچال پنجمین پیست اسکی مرتفع جهان است. — Tochal ski resort is the world's fifth highest resort in the world.

71 | 191

4826 گزیده gozide *chosen, selected, excerpt* adj,n
- گزیده‌هایی از برنامه «سه ستاره» از شبکه سه سیما پخش می‌شود. — Excerpts of the program "Three Stars" will be broadcast on TV3.

85 | 91

4827 موجی mowdʒi *wavy, shell-shocked* adj,n
- موهاش، موجی بود موجی تر از دریا. — Her hair was wavy; wavier than the sea.

77 | 142

4828 خیز xiz *rise, leap, swelling* n,pn,v
- فتنه گران برای مقابله با ارزشهای انقلاب اسلامی خیز برداشته‌اند. — Mutineers have risen up to confront the values of the Islamic Revolution.

79 | 130

4829 دستخوش dæstxoʃ *gratuity, prone, subject to* adj,n
- هوای تهران و بسیاری از شهرها دستخوش تغییرات چشمگیر شده است. — Tehran and many other cities' weather have undergone significant changes.

81 | 115

4830 بازگشته bazgæʃte *returned* adj
- خطر تروریست‌های غربی بازگشته از سوریه، اروپا را تهدید می‌کند. — The danger of western terrorists returned from Syria threatens Europe.

83 | 102

4831 هزینه کردن hæzine kærdæn *expend* v
- ایرانی‌ها چقدر از درآمد خود را هزینه بنزین می‌کنند. — How much of their income do Iranians expend on gasoline?

77 | 143

4832 خیام xæjjam *Khayyam* pn
- ما در این کشور فردوسی و مولانا و خیام و حافظ داریم. — We have Ferdowsi and Rumi and Khayyam and Hafez in this country.

58 | 297

4833 پاشیدن paʃidæn *scatter, sprinkle* adj,n,v
- روی هم آب می‌پاشیدند. — They were sprinkling water on each other.

74 | 166

4834 پوستی pusti *(made of)* skin, fur adj
- مراقب بیماری‌های پوستی ناشی از استخر باشید. — Watch out for skin diseases coming from pools.

84 | 93

4835 پایانه pajane *terminal* n
- بازسازی پایانه خارگ. — Reconstruction of Kharg terminal.
76 | 149

4836 سره sære *pure* adj,n
- زبان پارسی شیوه دیگر نوشتن یا گفتن زبان فارسی است که بیشتر در نوشته‌های ادبی یا سره به کار می‌رود. — "Parsi" is another way of writing or pronouncing the "Farsi" language, which is used more in pure or literary writings.
44 | 447

4837 نگه negæh *hold, look* n
- می بایست سر خود را به بالا نگه داشت و منتظر ماند. — One should keep his head high and wait.
74 | 162

4838 پوشاک puʃak *clothing* n
- ۱۰ هزار تولیدکننده پوشاک از مرکز شهر منتقل می‌شوند. — Ten thousand clothing manufacturers will relocate from the city center.
71 | 190

4839 رجب ræd͡ʒæb *Rajab* n,pn
- روز سوم رجب سال دویست و پنجاه و چهار. — Third of Rajab of the year two hundred and fifty-four.
88 | 73

4840 اقتضا eɣteza *exigency, necessity* n
- به اقتضای شرایط اقدامات لازم را در مورد تنگه هرمز انجام میدهیم. — Due to circumstances, we will take the necessary measures in the Strait of Hormuz.
84 | 94

4841 درهم derhæm, dærhæm *dirham, mixed* adj,n,pn
- متوجه تصویری پیچیده و درهم می‌شوید. — You will notice a complex and mixed image.
69 | 204

4842 احتساب ehtesab *calculation* n
- این مجموعه نزدیک به ده هزارمتر بدون احتساب زمین های اطراف آن وسعت دارد. — The complex is close to ten thousand meters, excluding the surrounding land area.
85 | 90

4843 پیشه piʃe *craft, profession* n
- بافت تور های ماهیگیری نیز از دیگر پیشه‌های مردمان شهر سوخته بوده‌است. — Weaving fishing nets was also one of the other vocations of people in Burnt City.
67 | 218

4844 آری ari *yes* n,v
- البته او گفت، آری. — Of course he said yes.
75 | 158

4845 تام tam *full, Tom* adj,pn
- چون شباهتی تام بفرزندانم داشت . . . — Because he bore a total resemblance to my children . . .
80 | 124

4846 خودروساز xodrowsaz *auto worker/maker* n
- این وضعیت شرایط را برای خودروسازان داخلی مشکل نموده است. — This situation has made conditions difficult for domestic automakers.
48 | 397

4847 منحل monhæll *dissolved* adj
- رییس جمهور اختیار داره که مجلس را منحل کند. — The president has the authority to dissolve the parliament.
85 | 91

4848 تیپ tip *brigade, type* n
- تمام تیپ های شخصیتی به یک اندازه ارزشمند هستند. — All personality types are equally valuable.
80 | 119

4849 عزاداری æzadari *mourning* n
- اولین شب مراسم عزاداری حضرت فاطمه زهرا (س) برگزار شد. — The first night of the mourning ceremonies of Hazrat Fatemeh Zahra was held.
81 | 112

4850 لبنانی lobnani *Lebanese* adj,n
- بیش از نیمی از لبنانی‌ها در بیروت زندگی می‌کنند. — More than half of the Lebanese live in Beirut.
78 | 135

4851 تعصب tæʔæssob *prejudice* n
- تبعیضات نژادی و تعصبات قومی به اوج رسیده بود. — Racism and ethnic prejudice came to the highest peak.
76 | 150

4852 هراسیدن hærasidæn *fear* n,v
- از انتقام این گروه مسلح می‌هراسند. — They fear retaliation by this armed group.
79 | 131

4853 جراحت d͡ʒerahæt *wound* n
- یکی از همراهانش بر اثر اصابت خرده شیشه جراحت مختصری برداشت. — One of his companions suffered from minor injuries because of being hit by glass particles.
81 | 117

4854 شوخی ʃuxi *joke* n
- تو با من شوخی میکنی؟ — Are you joking with me?
68 | 210

4855 پلاک pelak *license plate, plaque* n
- پلاک میکروبی میتواند موجب تحریک و تورم لثه شود. — Microbial plaque can result in irritation and swelling of the gums.
73 | 174

4856 رجوع rod͡ʒuʔ *reference* n
- به چه کسی می‌توان رجوع کرد؟ — To whom can one refer?
70 | 194

4857 گزینش gozineʃ *selection* n

- این فرایند گزینش را از هم اکنون در سیاست های بهداشتی برخی کشورها می بینیم. — As of now, we are seeing this selection process in the health policies of some countries.

72 | 178

4858 جانور dʒɑnevær *animal* n

- این چه جور جانوری است. — What kind of an animal is this?

67 | 216

4859 ذهنیت zehnijæt *mentality* n

- این ذهنیت چندان هم دور از واقعیت نبود. — This mentality was really not that far from reality.

67 | 218

4860 اجبار edʒbɑr *compulsion, obligation* n

- بهبود کیفیت محصولات کشاورزی یک اجبار جهانی است. — Improving the quality of agricultural products is a global obligation.

81 | 118

4861 مکه mække *Mecca* pn

- اجتماع بزرگ مسلمانان در شهرهای مقدس مکه و مدینه است. — A big assembly of Muslims is in the holy cities of Mecca and Medina.

67 | 221

4862 کامل شدن kɑmel ʃodæn *be completed, perfected* v

- با کامل شدن تحقیقات موضع اش را اعلام کند. — To announce its stance after the completion of investigations.

85 | 86

4863 عروقی oruɣi *vascular* adj

- سینوزیت، بیماری‌های عروقی و فشار خون را شدت می‌دهد. — Sinusitis intensifies vascular disease and high blood pressure.

78 | 134

4864 خوشایند xoʃɑjænd *pleasant, pleasure* adj,n

- این برایم خوشایند است. — It is pleasant to me.

84 | 95

4865 سرایت serɑjæt *contagion, transmission* n

- می ترسم دیوانگی آنها به من هم سرایت کرده باشد. — I'm afraid their insanity has spread to me, too.

76 | 147

4866 بازگو bɑzgu *retelling* n

- جک نتیجه را برای دوستش ماکس بازگو می کند. — Jack retells the result for his friend Max.

82 | 106

4867 مستبد mostæbed *despotic, tyrant* adj,n

- ثانی آباچا حاکم مستبد سابق نیجریه اختلاس کرده است. — Sani Abacha, former authoritarian ruler of Nigeria, had committed embezzlement.

86 | 82

4868 ورشکستگی værʃekæstegi *bankruptcy* n

- منجر به زیان و ورشکستگی واحدهای تولیدی گردد. — It led to losses and the bankruptcy of the production units.

61 | 269

4869 حراج hærɑdʒ *sale* n

- . . . و چهارمین اثر گران این حراج بود. — . . . was the fourth most expensive work in this auction.

87 | 77

4870 مجازی mædʒɑzi *virtual, metaphorical* adj

- در دنیای مجازی دارای طیف گسترده ای از مخاطبین خواهد بود. — In the virtual world it will have a wide spectrum of audiences.

65 | 234

4871 مثابه mæsɑbe *similar* n

- این اصلاحات را به مثابه کودتای در برابر خواسته مردم میدانند. — They consider these reforms as a coup against what the people want.

71 | 186

4872 قالی ɣɑli *carpet, rug* n

- سیگارم را چاق کردم و با صاحب خانه از قالی هایش حرف زدیم. — I lit my cigarette and talked with the owner of the house about his carpets.

71 | 187

4873 نارسایی nɑræsɑji *inadequacy, insufficiency, failure* n

- نوشابه‌های گازدار خطر نارسایی قلب را بالا می‌برند. — Carbonated drinks raise the risk of heart failure.

76 | 148

4874 تیز tiz *sharp, fast* adj

- نگاه تند و تیزی به صورتم انداخت. — She took a quick look at my face.

75 | 155

4875 مشی mæʃj *gait, manner* n

- آمریکا خط مشی ما در قبال فلسطین را تعیین نمی‌کند. — America does not determine our policy toward Palestine.

86 | 80

4876 خرازی xærrɑzi *haberdashery, Kharazi* pn

- خرازی بر حمایت ایران از مبارزات مردم فلسطین تاکید کرد. — Kharazi emphasized Iran's support for the struggles of the people of Palestine.

66 | 229

4877 هامبورگ hɑmburg *Hamburg* pn

- هامبورگ بزرگترین شهر بی‌خودروی جهان است. — Hamburg is the world's largest car-free city.

78 | 138

4878 مندرج mondæredʒ *inserted, printed* adj

- طبق اطلاعات مندرج در طرح جامع ناحیه ارومیه، — According to the information written in the Urmia regional master plan . . .

68 | 207

4879 جنتی dʒænnæti *Jannati* pn
- آیت الله جنتی رییس مجلس خبرگان شد. — Ayatollah Jannati became the head of the Assembly of Experts.
81 | 111

4880 انتقال دادن enteɣal dadæn *transfer* v
- ویرا به بیمارستان سینا انتقال دادند. — He was transferred to Sina hospital.
76 | 150

4881 پیمانی pejmani *contractual* adj,n
- شرایط تبدیل وضعیت کارکنان پیمانی به رسمی اعلام شد. — The conditions for changing the status of contract employees into official employees were announced.
88 | 69

4882 یگان jegan *detachment, unit* n,pn
- این یگان مهندسی بود. — It was an engineering unit.
75 | 154

4883 خوار xar *contemptible* adj,pn
- خودش رو خوار و خفیف کند. — He puts down and humiliates himself.
86 | 80

4884 بسط bæst *extension* n
- بسط همکاریهای تجاری و اقتصادی بین دو کشور. — The expansion of trade and economic cooperation between the two countries.
77 | 138

4885 ذکر کردن zekr kærdæn *mention, cite* v
- مسائلرا از اولویت‌های منطقه ذکر کردند. — They mentioned the issue as one of the priorities in the region.
75 | 153

4886 خوی xuj, xoj *habit/temperament, sweat/Khoy* n,pn
- محیطرا در خلق و خوی مردم مؤثر میداند. — He considers environment to have an effect on people's mood.
81 | 117

4887 شعاع ʃoʔaʔ *ray, beam* n,pn
- ادامه اوضاع نابسامان اقتصادی در این منطقه این کشور را نیز تحت شعاع قرار می دهد. — Continuation of the poor economic conditions in this region will cast a shadow on this country too.
82 | 106

4888 گربه gorbe *cat* n
- گربه فرمانده شورشیان چچن گم شد. — The Chechen insurgent commander's cat was lost.
61 | 270

4889 توکل tævækkol *trust* n,pn
- با دست خالی فقط با امید به خدا و توکل به خدا. — With bare hands, only with hope in God and trust in God.
85 | 89

4890 پنهان کردن penhan kærdæn *hide* v
- حالا من را پنهان کن. — Now hide me.
78 | 131

4891 هفته‌نامه hæftename *weekly publication* n
- این مصاحبه در هفته‌نامه‌ی محلی تخت جمشید در شهر مرودشت منتشر شده است. — This interview was published in the local weekly paper of Marvdasht, *Takhte Jamshid*.
65 | 236

4892 مسن mosenn *elderly* adj
- افراد مسن که از سلامت جسمانی برخوردارند و داروی خاصی مصرف نمی کنند — The elderly who are healthy and do not take any specific medications . . .
84 | 91

4893 کاربری karbæri *function, use* n
- بسیاری از زمین‌ها میتوانند کاربری‌های بهتری از کاربری حمل و نقلی داشته باشند. — Many lands can have better uses than transportation.
78 | 136

4894 لطمه lætme *injury, damage* n
- به اقتصاد لطمه می‌زند. — It hurts the economy.
79 | 125

4895 اندوه ænduh *grief* n
- شادی و اندوه از یکـدیگر جدا نیستند. — Happiness and sadness are not separate from each other.
78 | 132

4896 گذرگاه gozærgah *crossing point, passageway* n
- این گذرگاه اول اکتبر افتتاح میشود. — This pathway will open the first of October.
83 | 97

4897 سهل sæhl *easy* adj,n,pn
- قوانین عرضه عمومی کتاب باید سهلتر شود. — The rules for public offering of books should be easier.
85 | 85

4898 ابومسلم æbumoslem *Abu Muslim* pn
- ابومسلم یک تیم واقعی از خراسان است. — Abu Muslim is a real team from Khorasan.
82 | 107

4899 راحل rahel *deceased* adj
- باید رئیس جمهوری مومن متعهد و کارآمد انتخاب کنیم تا آرمان‌های امام راحل و رهبر معظم انقلاب اسلامی محقق و کشور ما از گذشته بهتر شود. — We must elect a faithful, committed, and efficient president so the ideals of the late Imam and great leader of the Islamic Revolution are realized and our country becomes better than in the past.
78 | 134

4900 اطلاع‌رسانی etela?ræsani *information science* n
- پیشرفت‌های خوبی که در عرصه اطلاع‌رسانی بوجود آمده است. — Good progress has been made in the area of information science.

61 | 265

4901 مزار mæzar *shrine, tomb* n
- میریم به مزار شهدا به نیابت از همه شما. — We are going to the graves of the martyrs on behalf of all of you.

70 | 187

4902 بهزاد behzad *Behzad* pn
- بهزاد فراهانی می‌خواهد چه نمایشی اجرا کند؟ — Which play does Behzad Farahani want to perform?

71 | 180

4903 استعمال este?mal *utilization* n
- استعمال آن از طرف تو واقعاً جایز نمی باشد. — You are actually not authorized to use it.

74 | 161

4904 استعماری este?mari *colonial* adj
- از سیاست استعماری فرانسه در آن ناحیه آزرده بود. — He was unhappy with French colonial policy in that region.

70 | 187

4905 شل ʃæl, ʃol, ʃel *lame, loose, Shell* adj,pn
- اما با شنیدن صدای خش‌خش دستش شل شد. — But upon hearing a rustling sound, his hand became lame.

78 | 132

4906 کیهان kejhan *universe* n,pn
- کوچکترین ستارگان کیهان چیستند؟ — What are the smallest stars in the universe?

71 | 184

4907 بسا bæsa *many, often* adv
- چه بسا افرادی با قلم و زبان خود حرف‌هایی را در بین مردم مطرح می کنند — How often do people bring up discussions in public with their own tongue and pen!

76 | 143

4908 تخریبی tæxribi *destructive* adj
- تنها پنج درصد از ویروس‌ها دارای اثرات تخریبی هستند. — Only five percent of viruses have destructive effects.

84 | 94

4909 اورانیوم uranijom *uranium* n
- فعالیت مشترک برای غنی‌سازی اورانیوم. — Joint activities to enrich uranium.

77 | 138

4910 جیمز dʒejmz *James* pn
- جیمز وات اولین سازنده ماشین بخار نیست. — James Watt isn't the first inventor of the steam engine.

75 | 154

4911 سحر sæhær, sehr *dawn, magic* n,pn
- پسر پادشاه کله سحر بیدار شد. — The king's son woke at the crack of dawn.

70 | 188

4912 کاریکاتور karikatur *caricature, cartoon* n
- نخستین مسابقه کشوری کاریکاتور با موضوع صبحانه برگزار می‌شود. — The first national caricature contest on breakfast will be held.

75 | 152

4913 صداوسیما sedavæsima *radio and television* n,pn
- رییس سازمان صداوسیما. — Head of Islamic Republic of Iran Broadcasting.

73 | 165

4914 سیلاب sejlab *flood waters* n
- اطراف ساختمانهای مهم بانکوک کیسه های شنی قرار داد شده است تا از آنها در برابر سیلاب محافظت کند. — Sandbags had been put around the important buildings in Bangkok to protect them from flooding.

82 | 104

4915 تعیین‌کننده tæ?jinkonænde *decisive* adj
- بازار عرضه و تقاضا تعیین‌کننده سرنوشت نرخ ارز خواهد بود. — Market supply and demand will determine the future exchange rate.

70 | 188

4916 فراخوان færaxan *invitation, summons* n
- فراخوان مقاله. — Call for papers.

79 | 125

4917 منوط mænut *dependent* adj
- عضویت افتخاری انجمن منوط به پیشنهاد یکی از اعضای هیئت مدیره و پذیرش اکثریت آراء این هیئت است. — Honorary membership in this society depends on a recommendation from one of the members of the board of directors and a majority vote of acceptance by this board.

80 | 117

4918 پرشور porʃur *passionate* adj
- از مال دنیا یک قلم داشت یک سر پرشور و دلی که عاشق بود. — From the wealth of the world he had a pen, a passionate head and a heart which was in love.

76 | 147

4919 استواری ostovari *stability* adj,n,pn
- قله دماوند در فرهنگ کشور ایران مظهر پایداری و استواری است. — Mount Damavand is a symbol of stability and solidity in Iranian culture.

90 | 56

4920 اطاعت eta?æt *obedience* n
- حالا هرچه به او بگویم اطاعت می کند. — Now he will obey whatever I say to him.

68 | 201

4921 جرگه dʒærge *circle, jirga* n
- بعداً به جرگه بزرگان پیوستند. — Later they joined the circle of important people.
45 | 421

4922 بلوغ boluɣ *puberty, maturity* n
- به علت بلوغ صدایش به حد کافی کلفت و زشت شده بود. — Due to maturity, his voice had become thick and ugly enough . . .
79 | 127

4923 درگذشته dærgozæʃte *deceased* adj,n
- از بزرگترین بناهای یادبود درگذشتگان جنگ در جهان است. — It is one of the greatest war memorials in the world.
82 | 102

4924 تندیس tændis *statue* n
- تندیس ۳۵ متری مائو خبرساز شد. — The 35-meter statue of Mao made headlines.
79 | 124

4925 دمکراسی demokrasi *democracy* n
- برای پیشرفت دمکراسی در این کشور به او رای دهند. — They should vote for him in order to advance democracy in this country.
72 | 172

4926 سانتیمتر santimetr *centimeter* n
- به عرض ۹۵ سانتیمتر و طول ۴۵۰۰ سانتی متر است. — It's 95 centimeters wide and 4500 centimeters long.
73 | 166

4927 بهسازی behsazi *improving living conditions* n
- ولی این پایان عملیات بهسازی هست. — But this is the end of improvement operations.
78 | 130

4928 خلل xelæl *crack, defect* n
- ایجاد خلل در عالم طبیعت است. — Causing disturbance in the world of nature.
85 | 83

4929 هندبال hændbɑl *handball* n
- تیم ملی هندبال جوانان جمهوری اسلامی ایران در برابر ژاپن قرار گرفت. — The national youth handball team of the Islamic Republic of Iran was placed against Japan.
72 | 171

4930 ارگ ærg, org *citadel, organ* n,pn
- الان توی ارگ فقط یک قسمت از حرمسرا باقی مانده که فقط باعث دردسر است. — Right now there's only a portion of the harem left in the citadel, which is just a headache.
66 | 216

4931 الکتریکی elektriki *electric* adj
- به آنها شوک الکتریکی داده شده است. — They have been given electric shocks.
65 | 226

4932 اقیانوسیه oχjɑnusije *Oceania* pn
- جزایر سلیمان در نیمکره جنوبی در قاره اقیانوسیه و شمال شرقی استرالیا و جنوب خط استوا واقع شده است. — The Solomon Islands are located in the southern hemisphere in the continent of Oceania, northeast of Australia and south of the equator.
78 | 131

4933 جورج dʒordʒ *George* pn
- حتی کتاب مزرعه حیوانات جورج اورول هم زمانی به خاطر این دلیل رد شد که «فروش داستان‌های حیوانات در آمریکا غیرممکن است.» — Even the book *Animal Farm* by George Orwell was rejected at the same time because "It's impossible to sell stories about animals in America."
78 | 131

4934 دردسر dærdesær *trouble* n
- این مسئله همیشه باعث دردسر میشه. — This issue always causes headaches.
68 | 202

4935 گمراه gomrɑh *misled* adj
- افکار عمومی نیز گمراه میشود. — Public opinion also will be misled.
90 | 55

4936 پختن poxtæn *cook* n,v
- وسایل پختن آن را آماده کن. — Prepare the cooking utensils for it.
73 | 164

4937 تکمیلی tækmili *supplementary, graduate* adj
- طرح سنجش و پذیرش دانشجو در دوره‌های تحصیلات تکمیلی تایید شد. — The plan for assessing and accepting students in graduate programs was determined.
79 | 122

4938 خطه xette *territory, country* n
- مردمان این خطه از کشور پهناور ایران. — The people of this region of the vast country of Iran.
83 | 101

4939 سناتور senator *senator* n
- ارسال نامه ۴۷ سناتور به ایران باعث شرمندگی من است. — The sending of the letter of 47 senators to Iran caused me to be ashamed.
72 | 174

4940 آموخته ɑmuxte *learned, accustomed* adj,n,v
- آمدهایم یاد بگیریم و آموخته‌هایمان را نشان دهیم. — We have come to learn and show what we have learned.
72 | 170

4941 آهسته ɑheste *slow, slowly* adj,adv
- رفیق عزیز، تو یه کمی آهسته صحبت می کنی. — Dear friend, you speak a little slowly.
55 | 313

4942 فرمایش færmajeʃ *command, remark* n
● We — ما نباید فرمایش امام (ره) را فراموش کنیم. should not forget the remarks of Imam (RIP).
78 | 128

4943 مسافرتی mosaferæti *travel* adj,n
● آمریکا هشدارهای مسافرتی درباره ویروس زیکا را تغییر می‌دهد. — America is changing the travel warnings regarding the Zika virus.
84 | 92

4944 حیثیت hejsijjæt *prestige* n
● ما آبرو و حیثیت داریم. — We have esteem and prestige.
77 | 140

4945 غیردولتی ɣejrdowlæti *non-governmental* adj
● فعالیت‌های زیست محیطی غیردولتی نیز لغو شده است. — The non-governmental environmental activities have also been canceled.
66 | 216

4946 محمودی mæhmudi *Mahmudi* pn
● محمدرضا محمودی قهرمان مسابقات اسنوکر تک فریم شد. — Mohammad Reza Mahmoudi won the single frame snooker championship.
81 | 112

4947 آفرینش afærineʃ *creation* n
● همه آفرینش وابسته به الوهیت اوست. — All of creation is dependent on his divinity.
72 | 175

4948 ین jen *yen* n
● این محموله قاچاق که 37 میلیارد ین ارزش دارد. — The smuggled goods worth 37 billion yen.
80 | 120

4949 آفت afæt *calamity, blight* adj,n
● آفت، ۴۰ میلیون درخت شمشاد را نابود کرد. — The pest destroyed 40 million boxwood trees.
71 | 178

4950 دیرین dirin *old, ancient* adj
● از روزگاران دیرین انسان‌ها به دنبال مکان خوش آب و هوا و سرسبز برای سکنی بودند. — Since ancient times human beings have been looking for places with good climate and flourishing lands for settlement.
90 | 58

4951 کاردانی kardani *professional skill, 2-year degree* adj,n
● به کسی که این دوره را با موفقیت به پایان برساند، مدرک کاردانی اعطا می‌شود. — An Associate's Degree is granted to those who successfully complete this course.
88 | 64

4952 قهوه ɣæhve *coffee* n
● قهوه ی مجانی هم بهمون می دن. — They give us free coffee too.
65 | 227

4953 بابل babel, babol *Babylon/Babel, Babol* pn
● نشست دوستداران میراث فرهنگی کشور در بابل برگزار شد. — The country's Cultural Heritage admirers' meeting was held in Babol.
76 | 142

4954 جهانگرد dʒæhangærd *tourist, explorer* adj,n,pn
● بهترین راه برای جذب هر چه بیشتر جهانگرد. — The best way to attract more tourists.
72 | 174

4955 لفظ læfz *word* n
● حکومت سلطنتی یا جمهوری صرفاً اختلاف در لفظ نیست. — Monarchy or republic is not merely a difference in expression.
73 | 164

4956 ولایتی velajæti *provincial, Velayati* adj,n,pn
● ولایتی به سوریه رفت. — Velayati visited Syria.
63 | 241

4957 کاسه kase *bowl* n
● هزینه ی یک بشقاب و یک کاسه را پرداخت کردم. — I paid for the cost of one plate and one bowl.
64 | 237

4958 تعلق گرفتن tæʔelloɣ gereftæn *be given to, go to* v
● جایزه نوبل اقتصادی ۲۰۱۵ به آنگوس دیتون تعلق گرفت. — Angus Deaton was awarded the 2015 Nobel prize for economics.
74 | 154

4959 جهانگردی dʒæhangærdi *tourism* n
● در نهایت با توجه به مقاصد افراد، اشکال مختلفی از جهانگردی مذهبی شکل می‌گیرد. — Overall, taking into account the individuals' destinations, various problems develop from religious tourism.
67 | 212

4960 فتوا fætva *fatwa* n
● مرحوم پدرم خیلی امروزی بود، فتوا داد که برای خودش موسیقی حلال است. — My late father was very modern and gave a religious edict to himself that music was permissible.
79 | 124

4961 خبر داشتن xæbær daʃtæn *know, be aware* v
● ۷۰ درصد دیابتی‌ها از بیماری خود خبر ندارند. — 70% of diabetics are unaware of their illness.
64 | 232

4962 تمهید tæmhid *scheme, maneuver* n,pn
● این نشانه‌ها در تمهیدات زبان‌شناسی بکار می‌روند. — These signs are used in linguistic maneuvers.
79 | 121

31 Weather

Rank	Headword	Pronunciation	Gloss	Rank	Headword	Pronunciation	Gloss
414	فصل	fæsl	season	3312	مه	meh	fog
474	هوا	hæva	air	3389	پاییز	pajiz	autumn
506	برق	bærɣ	lightning	3560	یخ	jæx	ice
584	بهار	bæhar	spring	3780	اقلیم	eɣlim	climate
1097	درجه	dærædʒe	degree	3789	حرارت	hærɑræt	heat, temperature
1177	گرم	gærm	hot, warm	4147	ابری	æbri	cloudy
1350	باد	bad	wind	5071	خنک	xonæk	cool
1406	سرد	særd	cold	5106	بارانی	barani	rainy
1642	باران	baran	rain	5217	رعد	ræʔd	thunder
1672	تابستان	tabestan	summer	5516	طوفانی	tufani	stormy
1909	گرما	gærma	heat	5599	نسیم	næsim	breeze
2123	زمستان	zemestan	winter	5727	رطوبت	rotubæt	humidity
2135	برف	bærf	snow	6720	آفتابی	aftabi	sunny
2234	طوفان	tufan	storm	7510	شبنم	ʃæbnæm	dew
2385	سیل	sejl	flood	11443	تگرگ	tægærg	hail
2490	سرما	særma	cold	11809	ژاله	ʒale	dew
2496	دما	dæma	temperature	12418	تندباد	tondbad	gale, hurricane
2645	صبا	sæba	zephyr	13128	تندر	tondær	thunder
2795	ابر	æbr	cloud				
3032	خشکسالی	xoʃksali	drought				

4963 لفظی læfzi *verbal* adj,n
- این دو با هم درگیری لفظی پیدا می‌کنند. — These two are having a verbal clash with each other.
83 | 97

4964 شیشه‌ای ʃiʃeʔi *glass* adj,n
- بطری‌های شیشه‌ای برای نخستین بار در مصر باستان مورد استفاده قرار گرفت. — Glass bottles were used for the first time in ancient Egypt.
81 | 110

4965 منتفی montæfi *no longer probable, canceled* adj
- سفرش به کشور آلمان منتفی شده است. — His trip to Germany has been canceled.
82 | 102

4966 انعقاد enʔeɣad *coagulation, conclusion* n
- انعقاد معاهده ترکمانچای بین ایران و روسیه. — Conclusion of the Turkmenchay Treaty between Iran and Russia.
79 | 120

4967 چلسی ʧelsi *Chelsea* pn
- چلسی قهرمان جام اتحادیه انگلیس شد. — Chelsea won the EFL Cup.
71 | 176

4968 پایینی paʔini *downstairs, lower* adj
- ۲۰ تا ۲۵ دندان در فک پایینی دارند. — They have 20 to 25 teeth in the lower jaw.
87 | 75

4969 ننه næne *mom* n
- واژه ننه به عنوان برابر برای مادر بهکار می‌رود. — The word nane, is used as a synonym for mother.
43 | 439

4970 گریه کردن gerje kærdæn *weep, cry* v
- کاش گریه نمی‌کرد. — If only she hadn't cried.
54 | 315

4971 رغبت reɣbæt *desire, inclination* n,pn
- توریست با رغبت وارد کشور شود. — A tourist should enter the country willingly.
79 | 123

4972 رسوب rosub *sedimentation, sediment* n

• رسوبات و فاضلاب مهم‌ترین معضل تالاب انزلی است. — Sediment and waste are the most important problems of Anzali Lagoon.
70 | 186

4973 چتر tʃætr *umbrella, parachute* n

• این چیدمان هنری در سنت‌پترزبورگ از ۵۰۰ چتر رنگی ساخته شده است. — The art installation was created in St. Petersburg with more than 500 colorful umbrellas.
83 | 97

4974 کامران kɑmrɑn *Kamran* pn

• کامران جمشیدی رئیس گروه مترجمین مؤسسه است. — Kamran Jamshidi is the head of the translators' group at the institute.
76 | 142

4975 رساله resɑle *letter, treatise* n

• با مداد ابرو در حاشیه آن رساله نوشته اند. — They had written with eyebrow pencil in the margin of the dissertation.
70 | 182

4976 کلانتری kælɑntæri *police station* n,pn

• ۷۰درصد کلانتری‌ها دوربین دارند. — Seventy percent of police stations have cameras.
73 | 165

4977 سارق sɑreɣ *thief* n

• سارق کو؟ — Where's the thief?
70 | 187

4978 غرور ɣorur *pride, vanity* n

• کشاورز با غرور جواب داد : «بله». — The farmer answered with pride, "Yes."
73 | 163

4979 ملکه mæleke *queen* n

• دیوید بکام که با خانواده‌اش در کاخ ملکه انگلستان حاضر شده بود. — David Beckham, who was present with his family in the palace of the Queen of England.
73 | 164

4980 پری pæri, pori *fairy/Pari, fullness* n,pn

• پَری از موجودات خیالی و افسانه‌ای فرهنگ عامه و خرافات مردم است. — Fairies are imaginary and mythical creatures from folklore and people's superstition.
75 | 151

4981 راکتور reɑktor *reactor* n

• در مجموع دارای چهار راکتور هسته ای است. — It has a total of 4 nuclear reactors.
75 | 148

4982 طبل tæbl *drum* n

• اسرائیل بر طبل جنگ با ایران میکوبد. — Israel beats the drums of war with Iran.
89 | 59

4983 ترابری tærɑbæri *transportation* n

• وزیر راه و ترابری برکنار شد. — The Minister of Roads and Transportation was dismissed.
76 | 145

4984 ثمره sæmære *fruit, offspring* n,pn

• معاویه که به مجموع از ثمره کار و بحث خشنود بود. — Muawiyah, who was pleased with the overall results of work and discussion.
82 | 101

4985 سوزان suzan *burning* adj,pn

• آفتاب سوزان. — Burning sun.
84 | 87

4986 بویراحمد bojeræhmæd *Boyer Ahmad* pn

• مردم بویراحمد از قوم لر هستند. — The people of Boyer Ahmad are Lor.
73 | 159

4987 زین zin *saddle, from this* conj,n

• زین پس آسمان ایران برای پهبادهای دشمن ناامن است. — From now on, the Iranian sky is unsafe for enemy drones.
77 | 137

4988 مقتدر moɣtæder *powerful, strong* adj

• فردی مقتدر و بی‌پروا و جسور بود. — He was a strong, fearless, and bold individual.
77 | 133

4989 وفا væfɑ *loyalty* n

• میرزا که وفا ندارد. — Mirza has no loyalty.
78 | 125

4990 خودکفایی xodkæfɑji *self-sufficiency* n

• ایران در پیچیده ترین علوم دفاعی به خودکفایی رسیده است. — Iran has attained self-sufficiency in the most complex defense sciences.
71 | 173

4991 بیات bæjɑt *stale* adj,n,pn

• فقط نان بیات می‌خرید. — He would only buy stale bread.
88 | 67

4992 بریده boride *cut, clipping* adj,v

• سر بریده بود. — He was beheaded.
73 | 160

4993 پلید pælid *dirty, evil* adj,n

• برخی از کشورهای همسایه، مجری نیات پلید غربی‌ها هستند. — Some neighboring countries are the henchmen for Western evil intentions.
93 | 39

4994 سیاوش sijɑvæʃ *Siavash* pn

• سیاوش اکبرپور مهاجم تیم فوتبال تراکتورسازی تبریز. — Siavash Akbarpour, the striker of Tractor Sazi soccer team of Tabriz.
84 | 88

4995 هیچکدام hiʧkodɑm *none, neither* pron
- ایران از هیچکدام از قطعنامه‌های شورای حکام راضی نبوده است. — Iran has not been satisfied with any of the Board of Governors' resolutions.
  85 | 86

4996 کثیر kæsir *numerous, abundant* adj,n,pn
- الآن عده کثیر آنها در فلسطین به سر می برند. — Now a large number of them reside in Palestine.
  78 | 127

4997 خواهش xɑheʃ *request* n
- خواهشت را قبول می کنم. — I will accept your request.
  77 | 132

4998 سلطانی soltɑni *royal* adj,n,pn
- کاخ مسعودیه کاخ سلطانی بود. — Masoudieh was a royal palace.
  81 | 105

4999 بجز bedʒoz *except* conj
- این مرکز همه روزه بجز ایام تعطیل آماده ارائه خدمات هستند. — This center is ready to provide service every day except holidays.
  84 | 92

5000 برادری berɑdæri *brotherhood, fraternity* n
- جشن نوروز تقویت پیوندهای برادری است. — The Nowruz celebration is the strengthening of brotherhood bonds.
  84 | 92

Alphabetical index

> **Word family head,** pronunciation, *gloss,* pos, rank

آب	ab *water* n,pn 179		آشنا	aʃna *familiar* adj,n 1639
آباد	abad *place* adj 1796		آشنا شدن	aʃna ʃodæn *be familiar, acquainted* v 1883
آبادان	abadan *Abadan* pn 3267		آشنایی	aʃnaji *familiarity* n 1653
آبادانی	abadani *development* n 3003		آشکار	aʃkar *evident* adj 2553
آبادی	abadi *village, Abadi* n,pn 2341		آشکارا	aʃkara *explicitly* adv 3411
آبان	aban *Aban* n 4714		آغاز	aɣaz *beginning* n 270
آبی	abi *blue* adj,n 2092		آغاز شدن	aɣaz ʃodæn *begin* v 670
آتش	atæʃ *fire* n 574		آغاز کردن	aɣaz kærdæn *begin* v 1244
آتی	ati *upcoming* adj 3842		آفت	afæt *calamity, blight* adj,n 4949
آخر	axær *final* adj,adv,conj,n 188		آفتاب	aftab *sunshine* n 2725
آدرس	adres *address* n 4357		آفریقا	afriɣa *Africa* pn 1431
آدم	adæm *person* n,pn 1342		آفریقایی	afriɣaji *African* adj 3215
آدمی	adæmi *human being* n 2596		آفرین	afærin *congratulations* n,pn 4735
آذربایجان	azærbajdʒan *Azerbaijan* pn 1445		آفرینش	afærineʃ *creation* n 4947
آرام	aram *peaceful* adj,adv,pn 1311		آقا	aɣa *mister* n,pn 135
آرامش	arameʃ *tranquility* n 973		آقایی	aɣaji *gentlemanly behavior, mastery* n, pn 4663
آرامگاه	aramgah *grave* n 4510			
آرامی	arami *tranquility, Aramaic* adj,n,pn 3178		آگاه	agah *aware* adj,n 2062
آرزو	arezu *wish* n 2115		آگاه بودن	agah budæn *be aware* v 3645
آرژانتین	arʒantin *Argentina* pn 3135		آگاه شدن	agah ʃodæn *be informed* v 4584
آرمان	arman *ideal* n 3154		آگاهی	agahi *awareness* n 1134
آره	are *yes* adv 1413		آگهی	agæhi *advertisement* n 4728
آری	ari *yes* n,v 4844		آلمان	alman *Germany* pn 594
آزاد	azad *free* adj 235		آلمانی	almani *German* adj,n 1211
آزاد شدن	azad ʃodæn *be freed* v 2016		آلودگی	aludegi *pollution* n 2775
آزاده	azade *free, liberated* adj,n,pn 4557		آلوده	alude *polluted* adj 3961
آزادی	azadi *freedom* n 321		آمادگی	amadegi *readiness, preschool* n 890
آزار	azar *torture, torment* n 3675		آماده	amade *ready* adj 421
آزمایش	azmajeʃ *test* n 1126		آمار	amar *statistics* adj,n 520
آزمایشگاه	azmajeʃgah *laboratory* n 3186		آمدن	amædæn *come* adj,v 93
آزمایشگاهی	azmajeʃgahi *laboratory* adj 4313		آمریکا	amrika *America* pn 107
آزمایشی	azmajeʃi *experimental* adj,n 2740		آمریکایی	amrikaji *American* adj 452
آزمون	azmun *test* n 2082		آموختن	amuxtæn *learn, teach* n,v 1587
آژانس	aʒans *agency* n 3727		آموخته	amuxte *learned, accustomed* adj,n,v 4940
آسان	asan *easy* adj 1692		آموزش	amuzeʃ *teaching* n 493
آسانی	asani *ease* adj,n 3962		آموزشی	amuzeʃi *educational* adj 849
آستانه	astane *threshold* n 3567		آمیختن	amixtæn *mix* adj,n,v 4697
آسمان	asman *heaven* n 1763		آن	an *that* n,pron,pn 13
آسمانی	asemani *heavenly* adj,n 2336		آنجا	andʒa *there* adv,n 775
آسیا	asija *Asia* n,pn 529		آنچه	antʃe *that which* pron 516
آسیایی	asijaji *Asian* adj 2036		آنقدر	anɣædr *so much* adv 2738
آسیب	asib *injury, damage* n 1180		آنگاه	angah *then* adv,conj 3200
آسیب دیدن	asib didæn *be injured* v 3261		آنکارا	ankara *Ankara* n,pn 3320
آسیب رساندن	asib resandæn *cause injury* v 4296		آنکه	anke *that which* conj 1060
آشتی	aʃti *reconciliation* n 4706		آهان	ahan *yes* adv 2776

آهسته	aheste *slow, slowly* adj,adv 4941	
آهن	ahæn *iron* n 1021	
آهنگ	ahæng *tune* n 2990	
آواره	avare *homeless* adj,n 2777	
آواز	avaz *call, song* adj,n 4308	
آوردن	aværdæn *bring* adj,n,v 112	
آیا	aja *whether* adv,conj 323	
آیت	ajæt *miracle* n 3173	
آیت‌الله	ajætollah *ayatollah* n 2083	
آینده	ajænde *future* adj,n 180	
آینه	ajene *mirror* n 2857	
آیه	aje *Koranic verse* n 3923	
آیین	ajin *religion, ceremony, ritual* n 3771	
ائتلاف	e?telaf *coalition* n 2942	
ابتدا	ebteda *beginning* adv,n 468	
ابتدایی	ebtedaji *elementary* adj,n 2308	
ابتلا	ebtela *affliction* n 2349	
ابتکار	ebtekar *initiative, innovation* n,pn 2137	
ابد	æbæd *eternity* adj,n 3420	
ابداع	ebda? *innovation* n 4693	
ابر	æbr *cloud* n 2795	
ابراز	ebraz *expression* n 637	
ابراهیم	ebrahim *Abraham, Ebrahim* pn 1309	
ابراهیمی	ebrahimi *Ebrahimi, Abrahamic* pn 3957	
ابری	æbri *cloudy* adj,n 4147	
ابریشم	æbriʃæm *silk* n,pn 4025	
ابزار	æbzar *tool* adj,n 864	
ابلاغ	eblaɣ *notification* n 2606	
ابهام	ebham *ambiguity* n 1906	
ابومسلم	æbumoslem *Abu Muslim* pn 4898	
اتاق	otaɣ *room* n 1408	
اتحاد	ettehad *union, alliance* adj,n 1806	
اتحادیه	ettehadije *union* n 906	
اتخاذ	ettexaz *adoption* n 1225	
اتریش	otriʃ *Austria* pn 3905	
اتصال	ettesal *connection, joint* n 3892	
اتفاق	ettefaɣ *event* n 878	
اتفاق افتادن	ettefaɣ oftadæn *happen* v 765	
اتفاقاً	ettefaɣæn *by chance, in fact* adv 3590	
اتفاقی	ettefaɣi *accidental, occasional* adj,n 2046	
اتمام	etmam *completion* n 1531	
اتمی	ætomi *atomic* adj 2262	
اتهام	etteham *charge* n 1150	
اتوبوس	otobus *bus* n 2181	
اتومبیل	otomobil *car* n 2437	
اتکا	etteka *reliance* n 3185	
اثبات	esbat *proof* n 1712	
اثر	æsær *mark, effect* n 173	
اثر گذاشتن	æsær gozaʃtæn *impress, affect* v 4638	
اثرگذار	æsærgozar *impressive* adj,n 4530	
اجاره	edʒare *rent* n 3631	
اجازه	edʒaze *permit* n 882	
اجازه خواستن	edʒaze xastæn *ask permission* v 4651	

اجازه دادن	edʒaze dadæn *permit* v 838	
اجبار	edʒbar *compulsion* n 4860	
اجباری	edʒbari *mandatory* adj,n 2873	
اجتماع	edʒtema? *community* n 2121	
اجتماعی	edʒtema?i *social* adj 335	
اجتناب	edʒtenab *avoidance* n 3124	
اجرا	edʒra *implementation* n 185	
اجرا کردن	edʒra kærdæn *execute, perform* v 1891	
اجرایی	edʒraji *executive* adj 954	
اجلاس	edʒlas *session* n 1156	
اجماع	edʒma? *consensus* n 3912	
احترام	ehteram *respect* n 619	
احتساب	ehtesab *calculation* n 4842	
احتمال	ehtemal *probability* n 596	
احتمالاً	ehtemalæn *probably* adv 1676	
احتمالی	ehtemali *probable* adj 1418	
احتیاج	ehtiadʒ *need* n 2799	
احتیاط	ehtijat *caution* n 3649	
احداث	ehdas *construction* n 1709	
احساس	ehsas *feeling* adj,n 547	
احساس کردن	ehsas kærdæn *feel* v 1561	
احسان	ehsan *charity, Ehsan* n,pn 3296	
احضار	ehzar *summons* n 3110	
احقاق	ehɣaɣ *rectifying* n 4786	
احمد	æhmæd *Ahmad* pn 862	
احیا	ehja *revival* n 1592	
اختراع	extera? *invention* n 3485	
اختصاص	extesas *allocation* n 767	
اختصاصی	extesasi *special* adj 2142	
اختلاس	extelas *embezzlement* n 4471	
اختلاف	extelaf *difference* n 623	
اختلال	extelal *disruption* n 2442	
اختیار	extijar *authority* n 247	
اخذ	æxz *obtaining* n 1871	
اخراج	exradʒ *dismissal* n 2249	
اخلاق	æxlaɣ *morality* n 1371	
اخلاقی	æxlaɣi *moral, ethical* adj 1390	
اخلال	exlal *disruption* n 4124	
اخیر	æxir *recent* adj 267	
اخیراً	æxiræn *recently* adv 1111	
ادا	æda *coquettish, payment* n 2242	
اداره	edare *office* n 484	
اداری	edari *administrative* adj 1480	
ادامه	edame *continuation* n 329	
ادامه دادن	edame dadæn *continue* v 395	
ادب	ædæb *politeness* n 1569	
ادبی	ædæbi *literary* adj 1699	
ادبیات	ædæbijjat *literature* n 1349	
ادعا	edde?a *claim* adj,n 652	
ادعا کردن	edde?a kærdæn *claim* v 2626	
ادغام	edɣam *integration, merger* n 3772	
ادیب	ædib *literary scholar* adj,n,pn 4231	
اذعان	ez?an *admission* n 4001	

اسکی   eski *ski* n 4825

اسیر   æsir *captive* adj,n 2752

اشاره   eʃare *indication* n 156

اشتباه   eʃtebah *mistake* adj,adv,n 817

اشتباه کردن   eʃtebah kærdæn *make a mistake* v 4507

اشتراک   eʃterak *participation, subscription, commonality* n 3944

اشتغال   eʃteɣal *occupation* n 1164

اشتیاق   eʃtijaɣ *eagerness* n 3532

اشراف   æʃraf, eʃraf *noblemen, being in high position* n 3265

اشرف   æʃræf *nobler, noblest, Ashraf* adj,pn 3694

اشغال   eʃɣal *occupation* n 2130

اشغالگر   eʃɣalgær *occupier, occupying* adj,n 3937

اشغالی   eʃɣali *occupied* adj 3613

اشک   æʃk *tear* n,pn 3082

اشکال   eʃkal *difficulty* n 1265

اصابت   esabæt *hitting* n 3931

اصالت   esalæt *authenticity, originality, gentility* n 4028

اصرار   esrar *insistence* n 1884

اصطلاح   estelah *expression* n 1297

اصغر   æsɣær *Asghar* pn 3046

اصفهان   esfæhan *Esfahan* pn 1076

اصفهانی   esfæhani *Esfahani* adj,pn 3322

اصل   æsl *principle* n 292

اصلاً   æslæn *originally, by no means* adv 1355

اصلاح   eslah *correction* n 431

اصلاح کردن   eslah kærdæn *reform, correct* v 3443

اصلی   æsli *main* adj 186

اصولاً   osulæn *in principle* adv 3260

اصولی   osul *principled, systematic* adj,n 2709

اصیل   æsil *noble* adj 2802

اضافه   ezafe *addition* adj 964

اضافی   ezafi *additional* adj 2916

اضطراب   ezterab *anxiety* n 3802

اضطراری   ezterari *forced, emergency* adj 4129

اطاعت   etaʔæt *obedience* n 4920

اطرافیان   ætrafijan *entourage* n 4312

اطلاع   ettelaʔ *information* adj,n 209

اطلاع رسانی   etelaʔræsani *information technology* n 4900

اطلاعیه   etelaʔijje *announcement* n 3069

اطلاق   etlaɣ *calling a name* n 4685

اطمینان   etminan *confidence* n 1302

اظهار   ezhar *statement* n 726

اظهار داشتن   ezhar daʃtæn *express, declare* v 1534

اظهارنظر   ezharnæzær *comment* n 4721

اعتبار   eʔtebar *credit, validity* n 811

اعتباری   eʔtebari *credit* adj,n 2448

اعتراض   eʔteraz *protest* n 1298

اعتراض کردن   eʔteraz kærdæn *protest, object* v 4311

اعتراف   eʔteraf *confession* n 2013

اعتراف کردن   eʔteraf kærdæn *confess* v 2688

اعتصاب   eʔtesab *strike* n 3513

اعتقاد   eʔteɣad *belief* adj,n 616

اعتلا   eʔtela *raising, exaltation* n 4412

اعتماد   eʔtemad *trust* n 972

اعتمادی   eʔtemadi *Etemadi* n,pn 4574

اعتیاد   eʔtijad *addiction* n 3387

اعدام   eʔdam *execution* n 1345

اعزام   eʔzam *dispatch* n 1410

اعزامی   eʔzami *dispatched* adj 2944

اعطا   eʔta *giving* n 1933

اعظم   æʔzæm *greater, greatest* adj 2685

اعلا   æʔla *superior* adj,pn 3696

اعلام   eʔlam *announcement* n 208

اعلام کردن   eʔlam kærdæn *announce* v 713

اعلامیه   eʔlamijje *announcement* n 3769

اعم   æʔæm *more common* adj 2174

اغلب   æɣlæb *often, frequently* adv,pron,q 1333

افت   oft *drop* n 2313

افتادن   oftadæn *fall* adj,v 850

افتتاح   eftetah *opening* n 1547

افتتاحیه   eftetahijje *inaugural* n 4571

افتخار   eftexar *honor* n 889

افتخاری   eftexari *honorary* adj,n 2710

افراط   efrat *excess* n 3695

افراطی   efrati *extremist* adj,n 2230

افزار   æfzar *tool* n 4043

افزایش   æfzajeʃ *increase* n 226

افزایش یافتن   æfzajeʃ jaftæn *increase* v 1198

افزودن   æfzudæn *add* v 277

افزوده   æfzude *added* adj 1257

افزون   æfzun *exceeding* adj 1938

افسانه   æfsane *legend* n,pn 3208

افسر   æfsær *officer, crown* n 2398

افسردگی   æfsordegi *depression* n 3793

افشا   efʃa *disclosure* adj,n,pn 3153

افشار   æfʃar *Afshar* pn 4768

افغان   æfɣan *Afghan* adj,n,pn 2093

افغانستان   æfɣanestan *Afghanistan* pn 433

افغانی   æfɣani *Afghan* adj,pn 3388

افق   ofoɣ *horizon* n,pn 1889

افکندن   æfkændæn *throw* adj,n,v 2451

اقامت   eɣamæt *stay* n 2399

اقامه   eɣame *setting up, holding* n 3212

اقبال   eɣbal *good luck, Eghbal* n,pn 2772

اقتدار   eɣtedar *power* n 1914

اقتصاد   eɣtesad *economy* n 537

اقتصادی   eɣtesadi *economic* adj 149

اقتضا   eɣteza *exigency, necessity* n 4840

اقدام   eɣdam *action* n 225

اقصا   æɣsa *farther* adj,n 3815

اقلیت   æɣællijæt *minority* n 2675

اقلیم   eɣlim *climate* n 3780

اقیانوس   oɣjanus *ocean* n 2883

اقیانوسیه   oɣjanusije *Oceania* pn 4932

اگر   æɡær *if* conj 77

اگرچه	ægærtʃe *although* conj 1168		انتخاب کردن	entexab kærdæn *elect, choose* v 498
الان	ælan *now* adv 1335		انتخابات	entexabat *elections* n 337
البته	ælbætte *of course* adv,conj 125		انتخاباتی	entexabati *electoral* adj,n 1683
البرز	ælborz *Alborz* pn 3331		انتخابیه	entexabije *electoral* adj,n 4239
الجزایر	ældʒæzajer *Algeria* pn 3242		انتشار	enteʃar *publication* n 1065
الجزیره	ældʒæzire *Al Jazeera* n,pn 3831		انتصاب	entesab *appointment* n 3720
الزام	elzam *necessity, requirement* n 4618		انتظار	entezar *waiting* n 363
الف	ælef *alef* n,pn 2484		انتظار داشتن	entezar daʃtæn *expect* v 1411
القا	elɣa *suggestion, induction* n 4019		انتظامی	entezami *security* adj 1754
القاعده	ælɣaede *Al Qaeda* pn 3027		انتقاد	enteɣad *criticism* n 827
الگو	olgu *pattern* n 1178		انتقادی	enteɣadi *critical* adj,n 2914
الله	ællah *Allah* pn 1052		انتقال	enteɣal *transfer* n 477
المپیاد	olæmpijad *Olympics* n 4098		انتقال دادن	enteɣal dadæn *transfer* v 4880
المپیک	olæmpik *olympic, olympics* n,pn 1701		انتقالی	enteɣali *transferred* adj 3881
الهام	elham *inspiration* n,pn 3500		انتقام	enteɣam *revenge* n 3336
الهی	elahi *divine* adj,pn 1582		انتها	enteha *end* n 1645
الکترونیک	elektronik *electronics* adj,n 2784		انجام	ændʒam *performance* n 206
الکترونیکی	elektroniki *electronic* adj 2505		انجام دادن	ændʒam dadæn *accomplish* v 169
الکتریکی	elektriki *electric* adj 4931		انجام شدن	ændʒam ʃodæn *be done* v 462
الکساندر	æleksandr *Alexander* pn 3742		انجامیدن	ændʒamidæn *end* adj,v 2034
اما	æmma *but* conj 31		انجمن	ændʒomæn *association* n 1115
امارت	emaræt *emirate* n,pn 1863		انحراف	enheraf *deviation* n 2700
امام	emam *imam* n,pn 460		انحصار	enhesar *monopoly* n 2969
امامت	emamæt *imamship* n 4562		انحصاری	enhesari *exclusive, monopoly* adj,n 4803
امامی	emami *imam, Emami* adj,pn 4781		انحلال	enhelal *liquidation* n 3229
امانت	æmanæt *honesty, consignment* n 4541		انداختن	ændaxtæn *throw* n,v 1030
امپراتوری	emperaturi *empire* n 3236		اندازه	ændaze *size* n 879
امت	ommæt *Ummah* n 2723		اندام	ændam *organ, figure* n 3303
امتحان	emtehan *test* n 3112		اندونزی	ændonezi *Indonesia* pn 3104
امتیاز	emtijaz *point, privilege* adj,n 804		اندوه	ænduh *grief* n 4895
امداد	emdad *help* n 3107		اندک	ændæk *little* adj,adv,n,q 1137
امر	æmr *affair* n 76		اندیشمند	ændiʃmænd *thinker* adj,n 1977
امروز	emruz *today* adv 201		اندیشه	ændiʃe *thought* n 300
امروزه	emruze *nowadays* adv 1684		اندیشیدن	ændiʃidæn *think* n,v 1738
امروزی	emruzi *modern, contemporary* adj 2830		انرژی	enerʒi *energy* n 783
امسال	emsal *this year* adv 656		انزلی	ænzæli *Anzali* pn 3687
امشب	emʃæb *tonight* adv 2643		انزوا	enzeva *isolation* n 3380
امضا	emzaʔ *signature* n 1053		انس	ons *friendship, intimacy* n 3570
امن	æmn *safe* adj 2637		انسان	ensan *human* n 304
امنیت	æmnijæt *security* n 404		انسانی	ensani *human* adj,n 341
امنیتی	æmnijjæti *security* adj 1005		انسانیت	ensanijjæt *humanity* n 4101
امکان	emkan *possibility* n 361		انسجام	ensedʒam *cohesion* n 2892
امکان‌پذیر	emkanpæzir *possible* adj 4085		انشا	enʃa *composition* n 3566
امید	omid *hope* n 402		انصاری	ænsari *Ansari* pn 3385
امیدوار	omidvar *hopeful* adj,v 1085		انصاف	ensaf *equity* n 3538
امیدوار بودن	omidvar budæn *be hopeful* v 1525		انضباط	enzebat *discipline* n 3939
امیدواری	omidvari *hopefulness* n 2163		انعقاد	enʔeɣad *coagulation, conclusion* n 4966
امیدی	omidi *Omidi* n,pn 4122		انعکاس	enʔekas *reflection* n 2878
امیر	æmir *emir* n,pn 1301		انفجار	enfedʒar *explosion* n 1127
امین	æmin *honest, Amin* adj,pn 2271		انفرادی	enferadi *individual, solitary* adj,n 3243
امینی	æmini *Amini* pn 4151		انقلاب	enɣelab *revolution* n 348
انبار	ænbar *storehouse* n 3343		انقلابی	enɣelabi *revolutionary* adj,n 1827
انبوه	ænbuh *crowded, thick* adj,n 2947		انگار	engar *as if* adv,conj 2926
انتخاب	entexab *selection, choice* adj,n 253		انگشت	ængoʃt *finger* n 3162

انگلستان	engelestan *England* pn 1130		ایشان	iʃan *they* pron 424
انگلیس	engelis *England, Britain* pn 611		ایفا	ifa *play* n 1357
انگلیسی	engelisi *English* adj,n,pn 478		ایلام	ilam *Ilam* pn 3024
انگیزه	æŋgize *motivation* n 1319		ایمان	iman *faith* n 1585
انکار	enkar *denial* n 2010		ایمنی	imæni *safety* adj,n 2215
اهانت	ehanæt *insult* n 3728		این	in *this* pron 6
اهتمام	ehtemam *endeavor* n 4237		اینگونه	ingune *this kind of* adv,pron 1671
اهدا	ehda *offering* n 2678		اینترنت	internet *internet* n,pn 1532
اهرم	æhrom *lever* n,pn 4170		اینترنتی	interneti *internet* adj 2951
اهل	æhl *native* n 770		اینجا	indʒa *here* adv,n 821
اهل بیت	æhle bejt *Mohammad's family* n 3658		اینجابودن	indʒabudæn *be here* v 3160
اهمیت	ahæmmijjæt *importance* n 299		اینچنین	inʧenin *such* adv,pron 4740
اهواز	æhvaz *Ahvaz* pn 3088		اینطور	intur *this way* adv 4168
او	u *he, she* pron 54		اینک	inæk *now* adv 1581
اوباما	obama *Obama* pn 3461		اینکه	inke *that* conj 2362
اوپک	opek *OPEC* pn 3019		ایوان	ejvan *portico* n,pn 4299
اوج	owdʒ *altitude, highest point* n 748		با	ba *with* prep 8
اورانیوم	uranijom *uranium* n 4909		باب	bab *gate, chapter* n 1462
اول	ævvæl *first* adj,n 20		بابا	baba *dad* n 2300
اولویت	owlævvijæt *priority* n 977		بابت	babæt *matter, for* n,prep 2143
اولیه	ævvælijje *primary, original* adj 991		بابل، بابل	babel, babol *Babylon/Babel, Babol* pn 4953
اولاً	ævvælæn *first* adv,conj,n 2445		بابک	babæk *Babak* pn 3934
اوکراین	okrajn *Ukraine* pn 3237		باخت	baxt *losing, loss, lost* n,v 3888
اکبر	ækbær *greater, Akbar* pn 1279		باختری	baxtæri *western, Bactrian* adj 3597
اکبری	ækbæri *Akbari* pn 3994		باختن	baxtæn *lose* n,v 3071
اکتبر	oktobr *October* n 2908		باد	bad *wind, may (it) be* n,v 1350
اکتشاف	ekteʃaf *exploration* n 3632		بادی	badi *wind, air* adj,n 4182
اکتفا	ektefa *contenting oneself, finding sufficient* n 4628		بار	bar *load, turn* adv,n 96
			باران	baran *rain* n 1642
اکثر	æksær *most* q 1157		باراک	barak *Barack, Barak* pn 3448
اکثراً	æksæræn *mostly* adv 4797		باردار	bardar *pregnant, loaded* adj 4729
اکثریت	æksærijjæt *majority* n,q 1624		بارز	barez *distinct, prominent* adj,pn 2536
اکرم	ækræm *dearer* adj,pn 4261		بارسلونا	barselona *Barcelona* pn 4134
اکنون	æknun *now* adv 298		بارش	bareʃ *precipitation* n 2660
ایالت	ejalæt *state* n 1004		بارندگی	barændegi *precipitation* n 2472
ایالتی	ejalæti *provincial, state* adj,n 4355		باره	bare *subject* n 1059
ایتالیا	italija *Italy* pn 1000		باز	baz *open, again* adj,adv 514
ایتالیایی	italijaji *Italian* adj,n 2199		باز شدن	baz ʃodæn *open* v 2995
ایثار	isar *altruism, sacrifice* n 4193		باز کردن	baz kærdæn *open* v 2515
ایجاب	idʒab *obligation* n 4120		بازار	bazar *market* n 365
ایجاد	idʒad *creation* n 145		بازاری	bazari *businessman* adj,n 3368
ایجاد کردن	idʒad kærdæn *create* v 1028		بازاریابی	bazarjabi *marketing* n 4719
ایدز	ejdz *AIDS* n 3681		بازبینی	bazbini *inspection, review* n 4566
ایده	ide *idea* n 2113		بازتاب	baztab *reflection* adj,n 2325
ایراد	irad *objection* n 2290		بازجویی	bazdʒuji *interrogation* n 4201
ایران	iran *Iran* pn 43		بازداشت	bazdaʃt *arrest* n 1700
ایرانی	irani *Iranian* adj,n 233		بازداشت شدن	bazdaʃt ʃodæn *be arrested* v 3090
ایرلند	irlænd *Ireland* pn 4282		بازده	bazdeh *yield* n 4388
ایرنا	irna *IRNA* pn 1795		بازدهی	bazdehi *result, productivity, efficiency* n 4508
ایستادگی	istadegi *resistance* n 4374			
ایستادن	istadæn *stand* n,pn,v 1223		بازدید	bazdid *visit* n 1148
ایستاده	istade *standing* adj 2844		بازرس	bazres *inspector* n 2881
ایستگاه	istgah *station* n 1885		بازرسی	bazresi *inspection* n 2390
ایسنا	isna *ISNA* pn 3092		بازرگان	bazærgan *merchant* n,pn 2933

بازرگانی	bazærgani *commerce* adj,n 1866		بایستن	bajestæn *must* v 19
بازسازی	bazsazi *reconstruction* n 1231		بجای	bedʒaje *instead of* prep 4005
بازگرداندن	bazgærdandæn *repatriate* adj,n 3823		بجز	bedʒoz *except* conj 4999
بازگشایی	bazgoʃaji *reopening* n 4064		بچه	bætʃʃe *child* n 1116
بازگشت	bazgæʃt *return, returned* n,v 884		بحث	bæhs *discussion* n 174
بازگشتن	bazgæʃtæn *return* n,v 2625		بحث کردن	bæhs kærdæn *discuss* v 4637
بازگشته	bazgæʃte *returned* adj 4830		بحران	bohran *crisis* n 909
بازگو	bazgu *retelling* n 4866		بحرانی	bohrani *critical* adj,n 2757
بازمانده	bazmande *survivor* adj,n 3416		بحرین	bæhrejn *Bahrain* pn 2555
بازنشستگی	bazneʃæstegi *retirement* n 3575		بخار	boxar *steam* n 4372
بازنشسته	bazneʃæste *retired* adj,n 3290		بخاطر	bexater *due to* prep 3108
بازنگری	baznegæri *reappraisal* n 2875		بخت	bæxt *luck* n 3438
بازهم	bazhæm *again* adv 4737		بختیاری	bæxtijari *Bakhtiari* adj,pn 3854
بازو	bazu *arm* n 4585		بخش	bæxʃ *section, part* n,q 72
بازی	bazi *game, play* n 285		بخشش	bæxʃeʃ *donating, pardon* n 4533
بازی کردن	bazi kærdæn *play* v 1255		بخشیدن	bæxʃidæn *forgive, give* adj,n,v 714
بازیافتن	bazjaftæn *recycle, recover* adj,n,v 4681		بخصوص	bexosus *especially* adv,conj 1465
بازیگر	bazigær *actor* n 1895		بخیر	bexejr *good* adv 4194
بازیگری	bazigæri *acting* n 4745		بد	bæd *bad* adj,adv,n 1184
بازیکن	bazikon *player* n 830		بدل	bædæl *imitation* n 2680
باستان	bastan *ancient* adj,n 2517		بدن	bædæn *body* n 945
باستانی	bastani *ancient* adj,pn 2702		بدنه	bædæne *body, frame* n 4049
باشگاه	baʃgah *club* n 920		بدنی	bædæni *physical* adj 2843
باشکوه	baʃokuh *magnificent* adj 4209		بدهکار	bedehkar *debtor, indebted* adj,n 4050
باطل	batel *null, void* adj,n 3564		بدهی	bedehi *debt* n,v 1964
باعث	baʔes *cause* n 250		بدو	bædv *beginning* n 4284
باعث شدن	baes ʃodæn *cause* v 881		بدون	bedune *without* prep 81
باغ	baɣ *garden* n 1605		بدی	bædi *evil* adj,n 2745
بافت	baft *context, texture, tissue* n 2146		بدین	bedin *to this, this much* adv 948
بافتن	baftæn *weave* adj,n,v 4327		بدیهی	bædihi *evident, obvious* adj 3089
باقری	baɣeri *Bagheri* pn 3556		بر	bær *on* n,prep 21
باقی	baɣi *remaining* adj,n,pn 833		برآمدن	bæramædæn *rise* n,v 4321
باقی ماندن	baɣi mandæn *remain* v 1602		برآورد	bæravord *estimate* n 3549
باقیمانده	baɣimande *remainder* adj,n 2936		برابر	bærabær *equal, opposite* adj,n 227
بال	bal *wing* n,pn 3164		برابری	bærabæri *equality* n 2164
بالا	bala *top, high* adj,adv,n,prep 101		برادر	bæradær *brother* n 1263
بالا بردن	bala bordæn *put up, raise* v 2522		برادری	beradæri *brotherhood, fraternity* n 5000
بالا رفتن	bala ræftæn *go up* v 2065		برانگیخته	bærængixte *stimulated, excited* adj, n,v 3351
بالاخره	belʔæxære *finally* adv,conj 1424		برای	bæraje *for* prep 10
بالغ	baleɣ *adult, mature* adj 1821		برپا	bærpa *up, established* adj 1959
بالقوه	belɣovve *potential, potentially* adj,adv 3717		برپایی	bærpaji *erection, setting up* n 2257
بالندگی	balændegi *growth, exuberance* n 4398		برتر	bærtær *superior* adj 1315
بام	bam *roof* n 4448		برتری	bærtæri *superiority, advantage* n 1811
بامداد	bamdad *morning* n 2796		برج	bordʒ *tower* n 2316
باند	band *band* n 2183		برجا	bærdʒa *stable, fixed* adj 4086
بانو	banu *lady* n 1419		برجسته	bærdʒeste *outstanding* adj 986
بانک	bank *bank* n 473		برچیدن	bærtʃidæn *pack up, remove* adj,n 3456
بانکداری	bankdari *banking* n 4611		برخاستن	bærxastæn *get/rise up* adj,n,v 3310
بانکی	banki *banking* adj 1662		برخورد	bærxord *collision* n 641
بانی	bani *sponsor, builder* n 4232		برخورد کردن	bærxord kærdæn *meet, collide* v 2713
باور	bavær *belief* n,v 787		برخوردار	bærxordar *in possession of* adj,v 1637
باور کردن	bavær kærdæn *believe* v 3403		برخوردار بودن	bærxordar budæn *be in possession* v 822
باکو	baku *Baku* pn 4605		برخورداری	bærxordari *having, enjoying* n 2528
بایرن	bajern *Bayern* n,pn 4340			

برخی	bærxi *some* pron,q 141	بسا	bæsa *many* adv 4907
برداشت	bærdaʃt *harvest, withdrawal, understanding, removed* n,v 851	بست	bæst *clip, sanctuary, closed* pn,v 3332
		بستر	bestær *bed* n 1625
برداشتن	bærdaʃtæn *pick up, remove* adj,n,v 585	بستری	bestæri *admitted, confined to bed* adj, n 3070
بردن	bordæn *take* n,v 147		
برده	bærde, borde *slave, carried* adj,v 1055	بستگی	bæstegi *dependence* n 2404
بررسی	bærresi *check* n 224	بستگی داشتن	bæstegi daʃtæn *depend* v 3492
بررسی کردن	bærræsi kærdæn *examine* v 2127	بستن	bæstæn *close* n,pn,v 1361
برزیل	berezil *Brazil* pn 1957	بسته	bæste *package* adj,n 702
برزیلی	brezili *Brazilian* adj 4449	بسزا	beseza *appropriate, well-deserved, considerable* adj 4485
برشمردن	bærʃomordæn *enumerate* n,v 2499		
برطرف	bærtæræf *eliminated* adj 2169	بسط	bæst *extension* n 4884
برعکس	bærʔæks *vice versa* adj,adv,conj 3465	بسنده	bæsænde *sufficient, content* adj 3240
برف	bærf *snow* n 2135	بسکتبال	bæsketbal *basketball* n 2549
برق	bærɣ *electricity, lightning* n 506	بسیار	besjar *very* adj,adv,q 51
برقرار	bærɣærar *established* adj,n 1363	بسیج	bæsidʒ *mobilization, Basij* n 2253
برقراری	bærɣærari *establishing* n 1466	بسیجی	bæsidʒi *member of Basij* adj,n 4339
برقی	bærɣi *electric* adj,n,pn 2324	بشار	bæʃar *Bashar* pn 4800
برگ	bærg *leaf* n 2322	بشر	bæʃær *human* n 1404
برگرداندن	bærgærdandæn *return* adj,n,v 4078	بشری	bæʃæri *human* adj,n 1859
برگرفته	bærgerefte *taken up, adapted* adj,n 3546	بشریت	bæʃærijjæt *humanity* n 2736
برگزار	bærgozar *held* adj 287	بشکه	boʃke *barrel* n 1996
برگزاری	bærgozari *holding* n 572	بعد	bæʔd *then, after* adj,conj,n 118
برگزیدن	bærgozidæn *pick* n,v 4661	بعداً	bæʔdæn *later, then* adv,conj 2989
برگزیده	bærgozide *choice, elite* adj,n 1741	بعدازظهر	bæʔdæzzohr *afternoon* adv,n 3967
برگشت	bærgæʃt *return, returned* n,v 1978	بعدی	bæʔdi *next* adj,n 732
برگشتن	bærgæʃtæn *return* adj,v 1823	بعضی	bæʔzi *some* n,pron,q 563
برگه	bærge *index card, clue, dried fruit* n 4370	بعید	bæʔid *remote, unlikely* adj 1949
برلین	berlin *Berlin* pn 2793	بغداد	bæɣdad *Baghdad* pn 1834
برملا	bærmæla *exposed* adj 4483	بقا	bæɣa *survival* n 3086
برنامه	bærname *program* n 71	بقیه	bæɣijje *rest, remainder, balance* n, pron 1258
برنامه‌ریزی	bærnamerizi *planning* n 1488		
برنج	berendʒ *rice, brass* n 2426	بلا	bæla, bela *disaster, without* n,prep,pn 4791
برنده	bærænde *winner* adj,n 1396	بلافاصله	belafasele *immediately* adv 1955
برنز	boronz *bronze* adj,n 3115	بلژیک	belʒik *Belgium* pn 2870
برهان	borhan *proof, logic* n 4000	بلغارستان	bolɣarestan *Bulgaria* pn 4612
بروز	boruz *appearance* n 825	بلند	bolænd *long, high* adj 1094
برون	borun *outside* adj,adv,n,prep 3276	بلند شدن	bolænd ʃodæn *rise, grow* v 3732
بروکسل	bruksel *Brussels* pn 4631	بلندپایه	bolændpaje *high-ranking* adj 3951
برکت	bærekæt *blessing* n 2687	بلندی	bolændi *height* adj,n 2566
برکنار	bærkenar *removed* adj 3759	بله	bæle *yes* n 1636
برکناری	bærkenari *dismissal* n 4342	بلوچستان	bæluʧestan *Baluchestan* pn 3042
بریتانیا	beritanja *Britain* pn 2712	بلوغ	boluɣ *puberty, maturity* n 4922
بریده	boride *cut, clipping* adj,v 4992	بلوک	boluk, belok *district, block* n 3319
بزرگ	bozorg *large* adj 38	بلکه	bælke *but* conj 291
بزرگ شدن	bozorg ʃodæn *grow up* v 3248	بلیت	belit *ticket* n 4409
بزرگداشت	bozorgdaʃt *ceremony* n 2578	بم	bæm *bass, deep, Bam* adj,pn 4419
بزرگراه	bozorgrah *expressway, highway* n 3827	بمب	bomb *bomb* n 2222
بزرگسال	bozorgsal *adult* adj,n 2869	بمباران	bombaran *bombardment* n 3454
بزرگوار	bozorgvar *generous, honorable* adj,n 3373	بنا	bæna *building* n 627
بزرگی	bozorgi *magnitude* adj,n 170	بنا بودن	bæna budæn *be supposed to* v 3122
بزودی	bezudi *soon* adv 2355	بنابر	bænabær *according to* prep 2571
بس	bæs *enough* adj,adv 3129	بنابراین	bænabærin *therefore* conj 866

بند baend *string, paragraph* n 591

بندر baendær *port* n 1439

بندری baendæri *port* adj,n 4779

بنده baende *slave* n,pron,pn 1484

بنزین benzin *gasoline* n 2403

بنگاه bongah *establishment* n 2254

بنی bæni *sons, Bani* n,pn 4180

بنیاد bonjad *foundation* n 1985

بنیادی bonjadi *fundamental* adj 2506

بنیادین bonjadin *fundamental, basic* adj 4278

بنیان bonjan *structure* n 2541

بنیانگذار bonjangozar *founder* n,pn 3361

به be *to* prep 4

به ثمر رساندن be sæmær resandæn *bear fruit* v 3536

به رسمیت شناختن be ræsmijjæt ʃenaxtæn *officially recognize* v 3193

بهکارگیری bekargiri *utilization, hiring, employment* n 4427

بها bæha *price, cost, value* n 1860

بهادار bæhadar *valuable* adj 3830

بهار bæhar *spring* n,pn 584

بهاری bæhari *spring* adj,pn 3294

بهانه bæhane *excuse* n 1440

بهایی bæhaji *Bahai* n,pn 4711

بهبود behbud *improvement* n 745

بهبودی behbudi *improvement, gaining in health* n,pn 3408

بهتر behtær *better* adj,adv 89

بهداشت behdaʃt *hygiene* n 1239

بهداشتی behdaʃti *hygienic* adj 2080

بهرام bæhram *Bahram* pn 4004

بهره bæhre *portion, interest* n 1073

بهرهبرداری bæhrebærdari *exploitation, operation* n 1674

بهرهگیری bæhregiri *utilization* n 3358

بهرهوری bæhreværi *productivity* n 3641

بهروز behruz *Behruz* pn 4469

بهزاد behzad *Behzad* pn 4902

بهزیستی behzisti *social welfare* adj,n 4334

بهسازی behsazi *improving living conditions* n 4927

بهشت beheʃt *heaven* n,pn 2599

بهشتی beheʃti *heavenly, Beheshti* adj,pn 3609

بهمن bæhmæn *avalanche, Bahman* n,pn 1391

بهینه behine *optimum* adj 3008

بو bu *smell* n,pn 2510

بودجه buddʒe *budget* n 766

بودن budæn *be* v 2

بورس burs *stock exchange, scholarship* n 1196

بوستان bustan *orchard* n,pn 3647

بوسنی bosni *Bosnia, Bosnian* pn 4096

بوش buʃ *Bush* pn 2475

بوشهر buʃehr *Bushehr* pn 2631

بومی bumi *native* adj,n 1800

بویراحمد bojeræhmæd *Boyer Ahmad* pn 4986

بکارگیری bekargiri *utilization, application, employment* n 3545

بیتوجهی bitævædʒohi *inattentiveness* n 4215

بیسابقه bisabeʃe *unprecedented* adj 4130

بینظیر binæzir *unique, unparalleled* adj,pn 4643

بیابان bijaban *desert* n,pn 3580

بیات bæjat *stale* adj,n,pn 4991

بیان bæjan *expression* n 390

بیان کردن bæjan kærdæn *state, express* v 2022

بیانگر bæjangær *expressive, indicative* adj,n 1647

بیانیه bæjanijje *statement* n 1112

بیت bejt *distich, house* n 1921

بیچاره biʃare *helpless* adj,n 4799

بیدار bidar *awake* adj 4546

بیداری bidari *being awake* n 2913

بیروت bejrut *Beirut* pn 2952

بیرون birun *outside* adv,n 1159

بیرون آمدن birun amædæn *emerge* v 3412

بیرونی biruni *external* adj,n,pn 2491

بیژن biʒæn *Bijan* pn 4703

بیست bist *twenty* n 593

بیستم bistom *twentieth* adj,n 1757

بیش biʃ *more* adj,adv,q 28

بیگانه bigane *foreign, alien* adj,n 1686

بیل bil *shovel* pn 3409

بیم bim *fear* n 3007

بیمار bimar *sick, patient* adj,n 1139

بیمارستان bimarestan *hospital* n 1095

بیمارستانی bimarestani *hospital* adj,n 4071

بیماری bimari *illness* n 603

بیمه bime *insurance* n 1383

بین bejn *between* n,prep 64

بین الملل bejnolmelæl *international* adj 3018

بینالمللی bejnolmelæli *international* adj 576

بینش bineʃ *insight* n 3015

بیننده binænde *viewer* n 1918

بینی bini *nose* n,v 2525

بیهوده bihude *futile* adj,adv 3347

بیکار bikar *unemployed* adj,n 2508

بیکاری bikari *unemployment* n 1986

پا pa *foot, leg* n 628

پاپ pap *Pope* adj,n,pn 3786

پاداش padaʃ *reward, bonus* n 3987

پادشاه padʃah *king* n 2018

پادشاهی padʃahi *kingdom, reign* n 2811

پادگان padegan *garrison, barracks, base* n 4068

پارچه parʃe *cloth, fabric* n 2691

پارس pars *bark, Pars* n,pn 2075

پارسال parsal *last year* adv 3711

پارسی parsi *Parsi, Persian* adj,n,pn 4488

پارلمان parleman *parliament* n 2079

پارلمانی parlemani *parliamentary* adj 2413

پاره	pare *torn, part* adj,n,q 2278		پرتو	pærtow *ray* n 2998
پارک	park *park* n 1735		پرچم	pærtʃæm *flag* n 2785
پاریس	paris *Paris* pn 1567		پرداخت	pærdaxt *payment, paid* n,v 439
پاس	pas *pass* n,pn 2105		پرداختن	pærdaxtæn *pay, engage in* adj,n,v 211
پاسخ	pasox *reply* n 423		پرده	pærde *curtain* n 1306
پاسخ دادن	pasox dadæn *reply* v 1291		پررنگ	porræng *conspicuous, prominent* adj,adv 4596
پاسخگو	pasoxgu *answerable* adj,n 2000			
پاسخگویی	pasoxguʔi *responding* n 3328		پرسپولیس	perspolis *Persepolis* pn 2647
پاسدار	pasdar *guard* adj,n 2658		پرستار	pæræstar *nurse* n,pn 4233
پاشیدن	paʃidæn *scatter, sprinkle* adj,n,v 4833		پرسش	porseʃ *question* n 1066
پافشاری	pafeʃari *insistence, persistence* n 3667		پرسنل	personel *personnel* n 3964
پالایش	palajeʃ *refining* n 4395		پرسیدن	porsidæn *ask* v 1463
پالایشگاه	palajeʃgah *refinery* n 3659		پرش	pæreʃ *jump* n 3321
پانزده	panzdæh *fifteen* n 2381		پرشور	porʃur *passionate* adj 4918
پانزدهم	panzdæhom *fifteenth* adj,n 3834		پرنده	pærænde *bird* n 1952
پانصد	pansæd *five hundred* n 2653		پرهیز	pærhiz *avoidance* n 2258
پاک	pak *pure* adj 1742		پرواز	pærvaz *flight* adj,n,pn 634
پاکسازی	paksazi *purging, purification* n 4117		پروانه	pærvane *butterfly* n,pn 3050
پاکستان	pakestan *Pakistan* pn 845		پروردگار	pærværdegar *Creator* n,pn 4694
پاکستانی	pakestani *Pakistani* adj 3285		پرورش	pærværeʃ *training, education, breeding* n 1273
پاکی	paki *cleanliness, purity* adj,n 3972			
پایان	pajan *end* n 163		پروژه	poroʒe *project* n 675
پایانه	pajane *terminal* n 4835		پروسه	prose *process* n 4715
پایانی	pajani *final* adj,n 1618		پروفسور	porofosor *professor* n 3704
پایبند	pajbænd *fettered, loyal* adj 3918		پرونده	pærvænde *file* n 759
پایبندی	pajbændi *adherence, compliance* n 4489		پرویز	pærviz *Parviz* pn 2585
پایتخت	pajtæxt *capital* n 1146		پروین	pærvin *Parvin* pn 4640
پایدار	pajdar *stable* adj 1437		پری	pæri, pori *fairy/Pari, fullness* n,pn 4980
پایداری	pajdari *endurance, resistance* adj,n 3105		پریدن	pæridæn *jump, fly, evaporate* n,v 4633
پایگاه	pajgah *base, site* n 1272		پزشک	pezeʃk *doctor* n 1129
پایه	paje *base* adj,n 610		پزشکی	pezeʃki *medical* adj,n 847
پاییز	pajiz *autumn* n 3389		پژوهش	pæʒuheʃ *research* n 1720
پایین	pajin *bottom, down* adj,adv,n 790		پژوهشگر	pæʒuheʃgær *researcher* adj,n 1793
پایینی	paʔini *downstairs, lower* adj 4968		پژوهشی	pæʒuheʃi *research* adj,n 2353
پتانسیل	potansijel *potential* n 3738		پس	pæs *then* adj,conj,n 25
پتروشیمی	petroʃimi *petrochemistry* n 2110		پس گرفتن	pæs gereftæn *take back, withdraw* v 4116
پختن	poxtæn *cook* n,v 4936		پست	post *post* adj,n 831
پخش	pæxʃ *distribution, broadcasting* n 794		پسته	peste *pistachio* n 4760
پدر	pedær *father* n 883		پستی	posti *postal* adj,n 4080
پدید	pædid *visible* adj,n 2486		پسر	pesær *son* adj,n 1064
پدیدار	pædidar *visible* adj,n 4307		پسندیدن	pæsændidæn *approve* n 1989
پدیده	pædide *phenomenon* n 1173		پسندیده	pæsændide *admirable, approved* adj,v 4812
پذیرا	pæzira *welcoming* adj 3611		پشت	poʃt *back* n,prep 958
پذیرایی	pæziraji *reception, entertainment* n 4653		پشتوانه	poʃtvane *backing* n 2615
پذیرش	pæzireʃ *reception, admission* n 839		پشتیبانی	poʃtibani *support* n 1658
پذیرفتن	pæziroftæn *accept* v 689		پل	pol *bridge* n,pn 1492
پذیرفته	pæzirofte *accepted, admitted* adj,v 1747		پلاستیکی	pelastiki *plastic* adj 4189
پر	pær, por *feather, full* adj,n 885		پلاک	pelak *license plate, plaque* n 4855
پر کردن	por kærdæn *fill* v 3325		پله	pelle *step* n 2953
پراکنده	pærakænde *dispersed* adj 2305		پلید	pælid *dirty, evil* adj,n 4993
پرتاب	pærtab *throw* n 2965		پلیس	polis *police* n 598
پرتاب کردن	pærtab ʃodæn *be thrown, launched* v 3989		پلیسی	polisi *police* adj,n 4701
پرتغال	porteɣal *Portugal* pn 3278		پنالتی	penalti *penalty* n 3614

تأمین   tæʔmin *security* n 357

تأکید   tæʔkid *emphasis* n 314

تأکید داشتن   tæʔkid daʃtæn *emphasize* v 2248

تأکید کردن   tæʔkid kærdæn *emphasize* v 1491

تأیید   tæʔjid *confirmation* n 1027

تا   tɑ *until* prep 15

تاب   tɑb *endurance* n 4477

تابستان   tɑbestɑn *summer* n 1672

تابستانی   tɑbestɑni *summer* adj 3171

تابع   tɑbeʔ *citizen, follower* adj,n 2575

تابعیت   tɑbeʔijjæt *citizenship* n 3928

تابلو   tɑblo *panel, sign* n 1736

تابیدن   tɑbidæn *shine, twist* adj,v 4769

تاج   tɑdʒ *crown* n 3909

تاجر   tɑdʒer *merchant* n,pn 3365

تاجیک   tɑdʒik *Tajik* adj,pn 4087

تاجیکستان   tɑdʒikestɑn *Tajikistan* pn 2331

تار   tɑr *dim, string, lute* adj,n 3760

تاریخ   tɑrix *history* n 332

تاریخچه   tɑrixtʃe *short history* n 4375

تاریخی   tɑrixi *historical* adj 589

تاریک   tɑrik *dark* adj 3424

تاریکی   tɑriki *darkness* adj,n 3730

تازگی   tɑzegi *novelty, freshness, recently* n 2624

تازه   tɑze *fresh* adj,adv 455

تالاب   tɑlɑb *pond, wetlands* n 4250

تالار   tɑlɑr *hall* n 1855

تام   tɑm *full, Tom* adj,pn 4845

تانک   tɑnk *tank* n 3269

تاکتیک   tɑktik *tactic* n 3543

تاکتیکی   tɑktiki *tactical* adj 4504

تاکسی   tɑksi *taxi* n 3521

تاکنون   tɑknun *yet* adv 497

تایلند   tɑjlænd *Thailand* pn 2481

تایمز   tɑjmz *Times* pn 2792

تایوان   tɑjvɑn *Taiwan* pn 3130

تب   tæb *fever* n 3512

تبادل   tæbɑdol *exchange* n 1429

تبار   tæbɑr *lineage* n 4360

تبدیل   tæbdil *conversion* n 803

تبدیل شدن   tæbdil ʃodæn *convert* v 922

تبدیل کردن   tæbdil kærdæn *convert* v 2638

تبریز   tæbriz *Tabriz* pn 1286

تبریزی   tæbrizi *Tabrizi* adj,pn 4062

تبریک   tæbrik *congratulations* n 2415

تبصره   tæbsere *note, clause* n 3715

تبع   tæbæʔ *follower, following* n 3895

تبعه   tæbæʔe *citizen* n 1727

تبعیت   tæbæʔijjæt *following* n 3477

تبعید   tæbʔid *exile* n 2644

تبعیض   tæbʔiz *discrimination* n 2077

تبلیغ   tæbliɣ *propaganda, advertising* n 1063

تبلیغاتی   tæbliɣati *publicity, promotional* adj,n 1956

تبیین   tæbjin *explanation* n 2205

تپه   tæppe *hill* n 3450

تثبیت   tæsbit *stabilizing* n 2649

تجارت   tedʒɑræt *trade* n 854

تجاری   tedʒɑri *commercial* adj 999

تجاوز   tædʒɑvoz *aggression* n 2096

تجدید   tædʒdid *renewal* n 1568

تجربه   tædʒrobe *experience* n 528

تجربه کردن   tædʒrobe kærdæn *experience* v 2188

تجربی   tædʒrobi *experimental* adj 4461

تجزیه   tædʒzije *analysis, breakdown* n 2583

تجلی   tædʒælli *manifestation* n 4298

تجلیل   tædʒlil *honoring* n 2470

تجمع   tædʒæmmoʔ *gathering* n 2373

تجهیز   tædʒhiz *equipping* n 2468

تجهیزات   tædʒhizat *equipment* n 1186

تحت   tæht *under* n,prep 246

تحرک   tæhærrok *movement* n 1847

تحریر   tæhrir *writing* n 3316

تحریف   tæhrif *distortion, falsification* n 4012

تحریم   tæhrim *sanction* n 1723

تحریک   tæhrik *stimulation* n 2006

تحسین   tæhsin *praise* n 2669

تحصیل   tæhsil *study* n 1318

تحصیل کردن   tæhsil kærdæn *study* v 4509

تحصیلی   tæhsili *school* adj 1983

تحقق   tæhæɣɣoɣ *realization* n 650

تحقیر   tæhɣir *contempt* n 3458

تحقیق   tæhɣiɣ *research* n 479

تحقیقاتی   tæhɣiɣati *research* adj,n 1321

تحقیقی   tæɣiɣi *research* adj,n 2753

تحلیل   tæhlil *analysis* n 1070

تحلیل کردن   tæhlil kærdæn *analyze* v 4420

تحلیلگر   tæhlilgær *analyst* n 3078

تحلیلی   tæhlili *analytic, analytical* adj,n 3101

تحمل   tæhæmmol *tolerance* n 1161

تحمل کردن   tæhæmmol kærdæn *tolerate* v 3132

تحمیل   tæhmil *imposition* n 2178

تحمیل کردن   tæhmil kærdæn *impose* v 3146

تحمیلی   tæhmili *imposed, forced* adj,n 4453

تحول   tæhævvol *evolution, development* n 532

تحویل   tæhvil *delivery, submission* n 1057

تحویل دادن   tæhvil dɑdæn *deliver, hand over* v 3605

تحکیم   tæhkim *consolidation, strengthening* n 2721

تخت   tæxt *throne, bed, flat* n 2343

تختی   tæxti *Takhti* pn 4294

تخریب   tæxrib *destruction* n 1374

تخریبی   tæxribi *destructive* adj 4908

تخصص   tæxæssos *specialization, specialty* n 2521

تخصصی   tæxæssosi *specialized* adj 1277

تخصیص   tæxsis *allocation* n 3489

تخفیف   tæxfif *discount* n 2941

تخلف   tæxællof *violation* n 1737

تعبیر   tæʔbir *interpretation* n 2197

تعبیری   tæʔbiri *interpretive* n 4512

تعجب   tæʔædʒdʒob *surprise* n 3258

تعداد   teʔdad *number* n,q 221

تعدیل   tæʔdil *modification* n 3326

تعرض   tæʔærroz *offensive, aggression* n 4021

تعرفه   tæʔrefe *tariff* n 4243

تعریف   tæʔrif *definition, description* n 829

تعریف کردن   tæʔrif kærdæn *define, describe* v 2411

تعصب   tæʔæssob *prejudice* n 4851

تعطیل   tæʔtil *holiday* adj,n 1759

تعطیل شدن   tæʔtil ʃodæn *shut down* v 2695

تعطیلی   tæʔtili *vacation, closure* n 2798

تعقیب   tæʔɣib *chase* n 1870

تعقیب کردن   tæʔɣib kærdæn *pursue* v 3996

تعلق   tæʔælloɣ *attachment, belonging* n 4249

تعلق داشتن   tæʔælloɣ daʃtæn *belong* v 3514

تعلق گرفتن   tæʔælloɣ gereftæn *be given to, go to* v 4958

تعلیق   tæʔliɣ *suspension* n 3619

تعلیم   tæʔlim *teaching* n 2504

تعمیر   tæʔmir *repair* n 3196

تعمیق   tæʔmiɣ *fathoming, deepening* n 4128

تعهد   tæʔæhhod *commitment* n 1340

تعویض   tæʔviz *replacing* n 4091

تعویق   tæʔviɣ *delay, postponement* n 3345

تعیین   tæʔin *determination* n 597

تعیین کردن   tæʔin kærdæn *determine, appoint* v 1960

تعیین‌کننده   tæʔinkonænde *decisive* adj 4915

تغذیه   tæɣzije *feeding, nutrition* n 2592

تغییر   tæɣjir *change* n 220

تغییر دادن   tæɣjir dadæn *change* v 1293

تغییر کردن   tæɣjir kærdæn *change* v 2023

تفاهم   tæfahom *understanding* adj,n 1526

تفاوت   tæfavot *difference* n 1007

تفرقه   tæfreɣe *discord* n 4555

تفریحی   tæfrihi *recreational* adj 4369

تفسیر   tæfsir *commentary* n 1971

تفکر   tæfækkor *thinking* n 1584

تفکیک   tæfkik *separation* n 3664

تقابل   tæɣabol *confronting* n 3151

تقاضا   tæɣaza *demand* n 1226

تقدیر   tæɣdir *destiny, appreciation* n 1450

تقدیم   tæɣdim *present* n 1994

تقریباً   tæɣribæn *approximately* adv 777

تقسیم   tæɣsim *division* n 1368

تقسیم کردن   tæɣsim kærdæn *divide, distribute* v 3211

تقلید   tæɣlid *imitation* adj,n 2962

تقویت   tæɣvijæt *reinforcement* n 595

تقویم   tæɣvim *calendar* n 2642

تقی   tæɣi *Taghi* pn 3083

تل   tæll, tel *hill/pile, headband* n,pn 4691

تلاش   tælaʃ *effort* n 325

تلاش کردن   tælaʃ kærdæn *make effort* v 1219

تلخ   tælx *bitter* adj 2250

تلخی   tælxi *bitterness* adj,n 4262

تلف   tælæf *waste, casualty* n 1966

تلفن   telefon *telephone* n 1082

تلفنی   telefoni *telephone* adj 1908

تلفیق   tælfiɣ *combination* n 4428

تلقی   tælæɣɣi *attitude, point of view* n 2741

تلقی شدن   tælæɣɣi ʃodæn *be considered* v 2822

تلقی کردن   tælæɣɣi kærdæn *consider* v 3767

تلگراف   telegraf *telegraph* n 4065

تلویزیون   televizijon *television* n 893

تلویزیونی   televizijoni *television* adj 1467

تماس   tæmas *contact* n 1089

تماشا   tæmaʃa *watching* n 2729

تماشا کردن   tæmaʃa kærdæn *watch, view* v 3853

تماشاگر   tæmaʃagær *spectator* n 1798

تمام   tæmam *whole, all* adj,q 65

تمام شدن   tæmam ʃodæn *finish* v 1726

تمامیت   tæmamijjæt *integrity* n 4642

تمایز   tæmajoz *distinction* n 4396

تمایل   tæmajol *tendency* n 1586

تمایل داشتن   tæmajol daʃtæn *tend to, gravitate to* v 3299

تمجید   tæmdʒid *praise* n 3813

تمدن   tæmæddon *civilization* n 1498

تمدنی   tæmæddoni *civilization* adj,n 3654

تمدید   tæmdid *extension* n 3221

تمرکز   tæmærkoz *centralization, concentration* n 2676

تمرین   tæmrin *practice* n 1017

تمهید   tæmhid *scheme, maneuver* n,pn 4962

تمیز   tæmiz *clean* adj,adv 4588

تن   tæn, ton *body, ton* n 155

تناسب   tænasob *proportion* n 3064

تناقض   tænaɣoz *contradiction* n 2901

تند   tond *fast* adj,adv 3225

تندرو   tondrow *fast, extremist* adj,n 4026

تندیس   tændis *statue* n 4924

تنزل   tænæzzol *decline, decrease* n 4704

تنش   tæneʃ *tension* n 1791

تنظیم   tænzim *regulation, adjustment* n 1106

تنفر   tænæffor *aversion, hatred* n 4146

تنگ   tæng *narrow, tight* adj,n,pn 3079

تنگنا   tængna *bottleneck, difficulty* n 4622

تنگه   tænge *straits, channel* n,pn 4354

تنها   tænha *only* adj,adv 57

تنهایی   tænhaji *loneliness* n 2153

تنوع   tænævvoʔ *diversity* n 2033

تنیس   tenis *tennis* n 3740

ته   tæh *bottom, end* n 3510

تهاجم   tæhadʒom *aggression* n 3120

تهاجمی   tæhadʒomi *aggressive* adj,n 4454

تهدید   tæhdid *threat* n 927

تهران   tehran *Tehran* pn 140

تهرانی   tehrani *Tehrani* adj,pn 3540

تهیه   tæhijje *preparation* n 602

تو	to, tu *you, in* n,prep,pron 381		تکذیب	tækzib *denial, contradiction* n 3706
توأم	tow?æm *linked* adj 3471		تکرار	tekrɑr *repeating* n 701
توازن	tævɑzon *balance* n 2980		تکرار کردن	tekrɑr kærdæn *repeat* v 3764
توافق	tævɑfoɣ *agreement* adj,n 1014		تکراری	tekrɑri *repetitious* adj 2907
توافقنامه	tævɑfoɣname *written agreement* n 3447		تکلیف	tæklif *task* adj,n 1511
توان	tævɑn *ability* n 638		تکمیل	tækmil *completion* n 1369
توانا	tævɑnɑ *able, mighty* adj,pn 3978		تکمیل کردن	tækmil kærdæn *complete* v 4649
توانایی	tævɑnɑji *ability* n 1035		تکمیلی	tækmili *supplementary, complementary* adj 4937
توانستن	tævɑnestæn *be able* n,v 23			
توانمند	tævɑnmænd *capable* adj 3838		تکنولوژی	teknoloʒi *technology* n 2081
توانمندی	tævɑnmændi *strength* n 2440		تکنیک	teknik *technique* n 3656
توپ	tup *ball, cannon* n 1616		تکه	tekke *piece* n 3849
توجه	tævædʒdʒoh *attention* n 75		تکیه	tekje *reliance, stress* n 1890
توجه کردن	tævædʒdʒoh kærdæn *pay attention* v 1122		تیپ	tip *brigade, type* n 4848
توجیه	towdʒih *explanation, justification* n 1448		تیتر	titr *headline* n 4739
توجیه کردن	towdʒih kærdæn *justify* v 4077		تیر	tir *arrow, Tir* n,pn 1287
توده	tude *mass, Tudeh* n 2286		تیراندازی	tirændɑzi *shooting* n 3478
تور	tur *net, tour* n 3677		تیرماه	tirmɑh *Tir* n 3980
تورم	tæværrom *inflation* n 2805		تیره	tire *dark, family, dash* adj,n 2469
توزیع	towziʔ *distribution* n 1299		تیز	tiz *sharp, fart* adj 4874
توزیع شدن	towziʔ ʃodæn *be distributed* v 3847		تیم	tim *team* n 121
توسط	tævæssot *by* prep 295		ثابت	sɑbet *fixed* adj,n 1261
توسعه	towseʔe *expansion, development* n 204		ثابت کردن	sɑbet kærdæn *prove* v 2029
توسعه دادن	towseʔe dɑdæn *expand, develop* v 4188		ثانیاً	sɑnijæn *secondly* adv,conj,n 3971
توسل	tævæssol *resorting* n 3626		ثانیه	sɑnije *second* n 2095
توصیف	towsif *description* adj,n 1392		ثبات	sobɑt, sæbbɑt *stability, clerk* n 1475
توصیف کردن	towsif kærdæn *describe* v 2462		ثبت	sæbt *registration* n 935
توصیه	towsije *recommendation* n 1389		ثبتنام	sæbtenɑm *enrollment* n 3856
توصیه کردن	towsije kærdæn *recommend* v 2473		ثروت	særvæt *wealth* n 1238
توضیح	towzih *explanation* n 1284		ثروتمند	servætmænd *wealthy* adj,n 1802
توضیح دادن	towzih dɑdæn *explain* v 2366		ثمر	sæmær *fruit, result* n 3093
توطئه	towteʔe *conspiracy* n 3245		ثمره	sæmære *fruit, offspring* n,pn 4984
توفیق	towfiɣ *success* n,pn 2773		جا	dʒɑ *place* n 166
توقع	tævæɣɣoʔ *expectation* n 2471		جا گذاشتن	dʒɑgozɑʃtæn *leave behind* v 2196
توقف	tævæɣɣof *stop* n 1565		جا گرفتن	dʒɑ gereftæn *reserve, hold* v 1529
توقیف	towɣif *arrest, sequestration* n 2627		جابجایی	dʒɑbedʒɑji *movement* n 3076
تولد	tævællod *birth* n 1482		جاده	dʒɑdde *road* n 814
تولید	towlid *production* n 286		جاذبه	dʒɑzebe *attraction* n 3533
تولید شدن	towlid ʃodæn *be produced* v 1907		جاری	dʒɑri *flowing, current, sister-in-law* adj 943
تولید کردن	towlid kærdæn *produce* v 2309		جاسوسی	dʒɑsusi *espionage* adj,n 2737
تولیدکننده	towlidkonænde *producer* adj,n 1992		جالب	dʒɑleb *interesting, attractive* adj 962
تولیدی	towlidi *manufactured, manufacturing* adj 1456		جام	dʒɑm *cup* n 688
			جامع	dʒɑmeʔ *comprehensive* adj,pn 1294
توماس	tomɑs *Thomas* pn 4387		جامعه	dʒɑmeʔe *society* n 171
تومان	tumɑn *toman* n 763		جامه	dʒɑme *clothes* n 3463
تونس	tunes *Tunisia, Tunis* pn 3309		جان	dʒɑn *life* n,pn 633
توهم	tævæhhom *hallucination, fantasy* n 4654		جانب	dʒɑneb *side, behalf* n 2303
توهین	towhin *insult* n 2747		جانباز	dʒɑnbɑz *disabled war veteran* adj,n 3496
توکل	tævækkol *trust* n,pn 4889		جانبه	dʒɑnebe *-lateral* adj 2646
توکیو	tokjo *Tokyo* pn 2317		جانبی	dʒɑnebi *lateral, side* adj,n 4139
تک	tæk, tok *single/attack, tip* adj,n 1690		جانشین	dʒɑneʃin *successor, substitute* n 2053
تکامل	tækɑmol *evolution* n 3148		جانشینی	dʒɑneʃini *succession, substitution* n 4040
تکان	tækɑn *shake, shock* n 4520		جانور	dʒɑnevær *animal* n 4858
تکثیر	tæksir *multiplication, reproduction* n 4672		جانی	dʒɑni *sincere, criminal* adj,n 2401

جایزه   dʒajeze *award* n 1385

جایگاه   dʒajgah *position* n 615

جایگزین   dʒajgozin *replacement* adj,n 1483

جبران   dʒobran *compensation* n 1617

جبهه   dʒebhe *front* n 1409

جدا   dʒoda *separate* adj 1237

جدا شدن   dʒoda ʃodæn *be separated* v 2518

جدا کردن   dʒoda kærdæn *separate* v 3800

جداگانه   dʒodagane *separately* adj,adv 2145

جدال   dʒedal *conflict* n 3884

جدایی   dʒodaji *separation* n 1353

جدول   dʒædvæl *table* n 1251

جدی   dʒeddi *serious* adj 307

جدیت   dʒeddijæt *seriousness* n 2176

جدید   dʒædid *new* adj 108

جذاب   dʒæzzab *attractive* adj 2726

جذابیت   dʒæzzabijjæt *attractiveness, charm* n 3865

جنب   dʒæzb *absorption* n 1087

جرئت   dʒorʔæt *daring, courage* n 4577

جراح   dʒærrah *surgeon* adj,n 4599

جراحت   dʒerahæt *wound* n 4853

جراحی   dʒærrahi *surgery* adj,n 1941

جرج   dʒordʒ *George* pn 3725

جرگه   dʒærge *circle, jirga* n 4921

جرم   dʒorm, dʒerm *crime, substance* n 1384

جریان   dʒæræjan *flow* n 324

جریمه   dʒærime *fine* n 1619

جز   dʒoz *except* conj 454

جزء   dʒozʔ *part, detail, ingredient* adj,n 3382

جزئی   dʒozʔi *slight* adj,n 2866

جزئیات   dʒozʔijjat *details* n 2526

جزو   dʒozv *part, particle* n 1535

جزیره   dʒæzire *island* n 1362

جستجو   dʒostedʒu *search* n 1352

جستن   dʒæstæn, dʒostæn *jump, search* adj,n, v 2044

جسد   dʒæsæd *corpse* n 2117

جسم   dʒesm *body* n 3100

جسمانی   dʒesmani *corporeal, physical* adj 3177

جسمی   dʒesmi *physical* adj,n 2610

جشن   dʒæʃn *celebration* n 1373

جشنواره   dʒæʃnvare *festival* n 924

جعفر   dʒæʔfær *Jafar* pn 3423

جعفری   dʒæʔfæri *parsley, Jafari* adj,n,pn 2648

جعل   dʒæʔl *forgery* n 4709

جعلی   dʒæʔli *forged* adj 4066

جغرافیا   dʒoɣrafija *geography* n 3908

جغرافیایی   dʒoɣrafjaji *geographical* adj 2201

جلالی   dʒælali *Jalali* n,pn 2057

جلب   dʒælb *attraction* n 842

جلد   dʒeld, dʒæld *volume, quick* n 2066

جلسه   dʒælæse *meeting* n 374

جلو   dʒelow *forward* adj,adv,n,prep 1199

جلوگیری   dʒelowgiri *prevention* n 644

جلوگیری کردن   dʒelowgiri kærdæn *prevent* v 2358

جلوه   dʒelve *revealing* n 1464

جم   dʒæm, dʒom *Jamshid/Jam, motion/wag* n,pn 4757

جماعت   dʒæmaʔæt *assembly* n 3314

جمال   dʒæmal *beauty, Jamal* n,pn 3475

جمشید   dʒæmʃid *Jamshid* pn 4440

جمع   dʒæmʔ *total, addition* n 349

جمع شدن   dʒæmʔ ʃodæn *gather* v 2598

جمع کردن   dʒæmʔ kærdæn *collect* v 4102

جمع‌آوری   dʒæmʔaværi *collection* n 4524

جمعه   dʒomʔe *Friday* n 552

جمعی   dʒæmʔi *collective* adj,n,q 835

جمعیت   dʒæmʔijjæt *population* adj,n 359

جمله   dʒomle *sentence, total* n 91

جمهور   dʒomhur *republic* n 785

جمهوری   dʒomhuri *republic* n 219

جمهوری‌اسلامی   dʒomhurije eslami *Islamic Republic* pn 1962

جمهوریخواه   dʒomhurixah *republican* adj,n 3752

جناب   dʒenab *excellency* n 1610

جنابعالی   dʒænabeali *your excellency* pron 4540

جناح   dʒenah *faction* n 2498

جنازه   dʒenaze *corpse* n 4302

جنایت   dʒenajæt *crime* n 1725

جنایتکار   dʒenajætkar *criminal* adj,n 4547

جنایی   dʒenaji *criminal* adj 4749

جنبش   dʒombeʃ *movement* n 1557

جنبه   dʒæmbe *aspect* n 1739

جنتی   dʒænnæti *Jannati* pn 4879

جنجال   dʒændʒal *tumult* n 2100

جنجالی   dʒændʒali *tumultuous* adj 4173

جنس   dʒens *gender, merchandise* n 2148

جنسی   dʒensi *sexual* adj,n 2895

جنگ   dʒæng *war* n 263

جنگل   dʒængæl *forest, jungle* n 1925

جنگلی   dʒængæli *forest* adj 4297

جنگنده   dʒængænde *warrior* adj,n 4421

جنگی   dʒængi *military* adj,n 1695

جنگیدن   dʒængidæn *fight* adj,n,v 4755

جنوب   dʒonub *south* n 601

جنوبی   dʒonubi *southern* adj 824

جنین   dʒænin *fetus* n 4162

جهاد   dʒæhad *jihad* n 1176

جهان   dʒæhan *world* n 104

جهانگرد   dʒæhangærd *tourist, explorer* adj,n,pn 4954

جهانگردی   dʒæhangærdi *tourism* n 4959

جهانی   dʒæhani *global* adj 203

جهت   dʒæhæt *direction, reason* n,prep 184

جهش   dʒæheʃ *jumping, mutation* n 4385

جو   dʒu, dʒow, dʒævv *stream, barley, atmosphere* n,pn 1518

جواب   dʒævab *answer* n 1995

جواب دادن   dʒævab dadæn *reply* v 3363

جواد   dʒævad *Javad* pn 1728

جوار	dʒævar *proximity* n 4789		چهارده	tʃæhardæh *fourteen* n 3603
جواز	dʒævaz *license* n 3843		چهاردهم	tʃæhardæhom *fourteenth* adj,n 3735
جوان	dʒævan *young* adj,n 122		چهارشنبه	tʃæharʃæmbe *Wednesday* n 1200
جوانی	dʒævani *youth* adj,n 1845		چهارصد	tʃæharsæd *four hundred* n 2964
جواهر	dʒævaher *jewel* n,pn 2920		چهارم	tʃæharom *fourth* adj,n 443
جور	dʒur *sort* adj,n,pn 2342		چهره	tʃehre *face* n 587
جورج	dʒordʒ *George* pn 4933		چهل	tʃehel *forty* n 1322
جولای	dʒulaj *July* n 4515		چهلم	tʃehelom *fortieth* adj,n 3974
جوی	dʒuj, dʒævvi *brook, atmospheric* adj,n 2812		چوب	tʃub *wood* n 2871
جویا	dʒuja *searching* adj,pn 2715		چوبی	tʃubi *wooden* adj,n 4022
جی	dʒi, dʒej *g, j* pn 2760		چون	tʃun *like, because* adv,conj 157
جیب	dʒejb, dʒib *collar/sine, pocket* n 3998		چک	tʃek *check, Czech* n,pn 2699
جیمز	dʒejmz *James* pn 4910		چیدن	tʃidæn *pick, pluck, set* adj,n,v 4203
چاپ	tʃap *print* n 408		چیز	tʃiz *thing* n 328
چاپ کردن	tʃap kærdæn *print* v 4459		چین	tʃin *China* pn 458
چادر	tʃador *tent, chador* n 4682		چینی	tʃini *Chinese* adj,n 1105
چارچوب	tʃartʃub *framework* n 1149		حائز	haez *possessing, holding, eligible* adj 4148
چاره	tʃare *remedy* n 2244		حاج	hadʒ *Haji* n 1926
چاقو	tʃaɣu *knife* n 4686		حاجی	hadʒi *Hajji* n,pn 3359
چاقی	tʃaɣi *obesity* n 4092		حادثه	hadese *accident, incident* n 447
چالش	tʃaleʃ *challenge* n 1603		حاشیه	hæʃije *margin* n 1339
چاه	tʃah *well* n 2320		حاصل	hasel *result* adj,n 877
چای	tʃaj *tea* n 2527		حاضر	hazer *present, ready* adj 158
چپ	tʃæp *left* adj,n 1837		حافظ	hafez *keeper, Hafez* n,pn 1615
چتر	tʃætr *umbrella, parachute* n 4973		حافظه	hafeze *memory* n 2900
چرا	tʃera, tʃæra *why, grazing* adv 386		حال	hal *condition, state* n 113
چراغ	tʃeraɣ *light* n 2607		حالا	hala *now* adv 760
چراکه	tʃerake *because* conj 3841		حالت	halæt *condition* n,pn 639
چربی	tʃærbi *fat* n 3633		حامد	hamed *Hamed* pn 3880
چرخ	tʃærx *wheel, turn* n 3457		حامل	hamel *carrier* adj,n 2359
چرخش	tʃærxeʃ *turn, rotation* n 4744		حامی	hami *protector* adj,n 2391
چرخه	tʃærxe *reel, cycle* n 4747		حاوی	havi *containing* adj 2603
چرخیدن	tʃærxidæn *turn* v 4766		حاکم	hakem *ruler* adj,n 420
چشم	tʃæʃm, tʃeʃm *eye* n 590		حاکمیت	hakemijjæt *rule* n 1107
چشم‌انداز	tʃeʃmændaz *perspective* n 3249		حاکی	haki *indicative* adj,v 1523
چشمگیر	tʃeʃmgir *impressive* adj 1515		حاکی بودن	haki budæn *indicate* v 4063
چشمه	tʃeʃme *spring* n 3643		حبس	hæbs *prison* n 2192
چطور	tʃetowr *how* adv 2587		حبیب	hæbib *friend, lover, Habib* n,pn 4418
چقدر	tʃeɣædr *how much* adv 1936		حتماً	hætmæn *certainly* adv 1939
چگونگی	tʃegunegi *position, nature* n 1576		حتی	hætta *even* adv,conj 160
چگونه	tʃegune *how* adv 818		حج	hædʒdʒ *Hajj* n 2855
چلسی	tʃelsi *Chelsea* pn 4967		حجاب	hedʒab *veil* n 4211
چمن	tʃæmæn *grass, lawn* n 4608		حجت	hodʒdʒæt *reasoning, proof* n,pn 2957
چنان	tʃenan *such* adv,n,pron 1444		حجم	hædʒm *volume* n 1163
چنانچه	tʃenantʃe *if* conj 1868		حد	hædd *limit* n 401
چنانکه	tʃenanke *as* conj 2765		حداقل	hæddeæɣæl *at least, minimum* adv,n,q 694
چند	tʃænd *several* n 67		حداکثر	hæddæksær *maximum* adv,n,q 2024
چندان	tʃændan *so many, so* adv 1153		حدود	hodud *limits, range* n,q 144
چندانی	tʃændani *quantitative, so much* adj 2657		حدوداً	hodudæn *approximately* adv,q 4153
چندین	tʃændin *several* n 631		حدیث	hædis *hadith* n 3006
چنین	tʃenin *such* adv,pron 191		حذف	hæzf *elimination* n 1940
چه	tʃe *what* adv,conj,n,pron,v 110		حذف شدن	hæzf ʃodæn *be eliminated* v 2803
چهار	tʃæhar *four* n 438		حذف کردن	hæzf kærdæn *eliminate, delete* v 4356
چهارچوب	tʃæhartʃub *frame, framework* n 33/4		حذفی	hæzfi *elimination, playoff* adj 3628

حراج	hæradʒ *sale* n 4869		حمید	hæmid *Hamid* pn 2114
حرارت	hærɑræt *heat* n 3789		حوالی	hævɑli *vicinity* n 3537
حراست	hærɑsæt *protection* n 4514		حوزه	howze *district, domain* n 385
حرام	hærɑm *forbidden* adj 4319		حوصله	howsele *patience* n 4626
حرف	hærf *letter, talk* n 868		حول	howl *power, area, around* n 4027
حرف زدن	hærf zædæn *speak* v 2120		حومه	hume *outskirts* n,pn 3113
حرفه	herfe *profession* n 3494		حکایت	hekɑjæt *story* n 1329
حرفهای	herfeji *professional* adj 2293		حکم	hokm *order, sentence* adj,n 679
حرم	hæræm *sanctuary* n 2236		حکمت	hekmæt *philosophy, wisdom* n,pn 2742
حرمت	hormæt *sanctity* n 3333		حکومت	hokumæt *government* n 538
حرکت	hærekæt *motion, movement* adj,n 136		حکومتی	hokumæti *governmental* adj,n 1522
حرکت کردن	hærekæt kærdæn *move, set off* v 1378		حکیم	hækim *wise person* adj,n 3155
حریف	hærif *opponent* n 1382		حیات	hæjɑt *life* n 1360
حریم	hærim *confines* n 2513		حیاتی	hæjɑti *vital* adj,n 2032
حزب	hezb *party* n 412		حیاط	hæjɑt *yard* n 3914
حزبی	hezbi *party* adj,n 3128		حیث	hejs *respect* n 4052
حس	hess *sense, feeling* n 2212		حیثیت	hejsijjæt *prestige* n 4944
حساب	hesɑb *account* n 718		حیدری	hejdæri *Heidari* pn 4149
حساب کردن	hesɑb kærdæn *calculate, compute* v 4625		حیرت	hejræt *amazement* n 4175
حسابی	hesɑbi *proper* adj,adv,n,pn 4732		حیطه	hite *domain* n 4616
حساس	hæssɑs *sensitive* adj 1331		حین	hin *time* n 2837
حساسیت	hæssɑsijjæt *sensitivity* adj,n 2247		حیوان	hejvɑn *animal* n 1927
حسب	hæsb *quantity, agreement* n 3226		خاتمه	xɑteme *conclusion* n 2273
حسن	hæsæn, hosn *Hasan, virtue* n,pn 278		خاتمی	xɑtæmi *Khatami* pn 1499
حسنی	hosni, hæsæni *Hosni, Hasani* n,pn 4186		خارج	xɑredʒ *external* n 268
حسی	hessi *sensory* adj 4624		خارج شدن	xɑredʒ ʃodæn *leave* v 369
حسین	hosejn *Hossein* pn 834		خارجه	xɑredʒe *foreign* adj 561
حسینی	hosejni *Hosseini* pn 1606		خارجی	xɑredʒi *foreign* adj 198
حسینیه	hosejnijje *assembly hall* n 3618		خاص	xɑss *specific* adj,n 342
حضرت	hæzræt *holiness* n 626		خاصیت	xɑsijjæt *property* n 3033
حضور	hozur *presence* n 151		خاطر	xɑter *mind, sake* n 259
حفاری	hæffɑri *excavation* n 3084		خاطرنشان	xɑterneʃɑn *reminder* n 1280
حفاظت	hefɑzæt *protection* n 1858		خاطره	xɑtere *memory* n 1804
حفظ	hefz *preservation* n 442		خالص	xɑles *pure* adj 3014
حفظ کردن	hefz kærdæn *protect, memorize* v 1563		خالق	xɑleɣ *creator* n 3426
حق	hæɣ *right* n 172		خالی	xɑli *empty* adj 1740
حقوق	hoɣuɣ *rights, salary* n 371		خام	xɑm *raw* adj 2449
حقوقبشر	hoɣuɣbæʃær *human rights* n 3726		خامنهای	xɑmeneji *Khamenei* pn 4283
حقوقی	hoɣuɣi *legal* adj,n 1379		خاموش	xɑmuʃ *silent, extinguished* adj 4432
حقیقت	hæɣiɣæt *truth* n,pn 356		خان	xɑn *Khan* n 2122
حقیقی	hæɣiɣi *real* adj,pn 1540		خاندان	xɑndɑn *clan* n 3317
حل	hæll *solution* n 543		خانگی	xɑnegi *homemade, domestic, interior* adj 2620
حل شدن	hæl ʃodæn *dissolve, be solved* v 1808			
حل کردن	hæl kærdæn *solve* v 1813		خانم	xɑnom *lady, Mrs.* n 870
حلقه	hælɣe *ring* n 1817		خانه	xɑne *house* n 358
حماس	hæmɑs *Hamas* pn 3170		خانوادگی	xɑnevɑdegi *familial* adj,n 2285
حماسه	hæmɑse *epic* n 2779		خانواده	xɑnevɑde *family* n 282
حماسی	hæmɑsi *epic* adj 4288		خانوار	xɑnevɑr *household* n 2323
حمام	hæmmɑm *bath, bathroom* n 3562		خاور	xɑvær *east* n,pn 4100
حمایت	hemɑjæt *protection* n 327		خاورمیانه	xɑværemijɑne *Middle East* pn 1590
حمل	hæml *shipping* n 1118		خاک	xɑk *soil, dust* n 551
حمله	hæmle *attack* n 534		خاکی	xɑki *earthen, terrestrial* adj 2560
حمله کردن	hæmle kærdæn *attack* v 2612		خب	xob *well* adv 2327

خبر	xæbær *news* n 232		خطا	xæta *error* n 2371
خبر دادن	xæbær dadæn *inform* v 1479		خطاب	xetab *address* n 1648
خبر داشتن	xæbær daʃtæn *know, be aware* v 4961		خطبه	xotbe *sermon, homily* n 4460
خبرگان	xebregan *experts* n 2663		خطر	xætær *risk* n 485
خبرگزاری	xæbærgozari *news agency* n 1179		خطرناک	xætærnak *dangerous* adj 1091
خبرنگار	xæbærnegar *reporter* n 629		خطه	xette *territory, country* n 4938
خبری	xæbæri *news* adj,n 744		خطیر	xætir *important, dangerous* adj 4684
ختم	xætm *completing* n 3535		خلاصه	xolase *summary* adj,n 2177
خدا	xoda *God* n,pn 546		خلاف	xælaf *contrary* adj,conj,n 676
خداحافظی	xodahafezi *saying goodbye* n 4035		خلاق	xællaɣ *creative* adj 4368
خداوند	xodavænd *god* pn 1088		خلاقیت	xælaɣijæt *creativity* n 2724
خدایی	xodaji *divine* adj,pn,v 4324		خلال	xelal *interval, pick* n 3723
خدشه	xædʃe *scratch, blemish* n 4268		خلبان	xælæban *pilot* n 4417
خدمت	xedmæt *service* adj,n 231		خلع	xælʔ *deposing* n 2924
خراب	xærab *broken, demolished* adj 3644		خلق	xælɣ, xolɣ *creation/people, temper* n 1504
خرابی	xærabi *destruction* n 2751		خلل	xelæl *crack, defect* n 4928
خرازی	xærrazi *haberdashery* pn 4876		خلوت	xælvæt *seclusion, privacy* adj,n 4518
خراسان	xorasan *Khorasan* pn 2008		خلیج	xælidʒ *gulf* n 2060
خرج	xærdʒ *expense* n 2329		خلیج‌فارس	xalidʒefars *Persian Gulf* pn 4815
خرد	xeræd, xord *wisdom, small* adj,n 2368		خلیفه	xælife *caliph* n,pn 2893
خرداد	xordad *Khordad* n 1760		خلیل	xælil *Khalil* pn 3085
خرده	xorde *bit* adj,n 4397		خم	xæm, xom *bend, jar* adj,n 4301
خرسندی	xorsændi *satisfaction, contentment* n 3651		خمینی	xomejni *Khomeini* pn 1655
خرم	xorræm *green, lush* adj,pn 4217		خنثی	xonsa *neutral, neuter* adj 3172
خرمشهر	xorræmʃæhr *Khorramshahr* pn 4609		خنده	xænde *laughter* n 3736
خروج	xorudʒ *exit* n 1447		خندیدن	xændidæn *laugh* v 3234
خروجی	xorudʒi *exit, output* adj,n 3346		خواب	xab *sleep, dream* n 1822
خرید	xærid *purchase, bought* n,v 855		خوابیدن	xabidæn *sleep* n,v 3782
خریدار	xæridar *buyer* n 3547		خواجه	xadʒe *eunuch, master* n,pn 3665
خریداری	xæridari *purchasing* n 2847		خوار	xar *contemptible* adj,pn 4883
خریداری کردن	xæridari kærdæn *purchase* v 4095		خواست	xast *wish, wanted* n,v 469
خریدن	xæridæn *buy* n,v 2600		خواستار	xastar *applicant, desirous* n 895
خزانه	xæzane *treasury* n 3876		خواستار شدن	xastar ʃodæn *demand* v 3959
خزر	xæzær *Caspian* pn 2806		خواستن	xastæn *want* v 14
خسارت	xesaræt *damage* n 1600		خواسته	xaste *demand* adj,adv,n 802
خستگی	xæstegi *fatigue* n 3414		خواندن	xandæn *read* adj,n,v 280
خسته	xæste *tired* adj 4253		خواننده	xanænde *reader, singer* n 2239
خسته شدن	xæste ʃodæn *become tired* v 4772		خواهان	xahan *plaintiff, desirous* adj,n 1501
خسرو	xosrow *Khosrow* pn 3327		خواهر	xahær *sister* n 2430
خشم	xæʃm *anger* n 2211		خواهش	xaheʃ *request* n 4997
خشمگین	xæʃmgin *angry* adj 3965		خواهش کردن	xaheʃ kærdæn *request* v 4794
خشن	xæʃen *rough* adj 2556		خوب	xub *good* adj,adv 510
خشونت	xoʃunæt *violence* n 955		خوبی	xubi *goodness* adj,adv,n 445
خشک	xoʃk *dry* adj 2479		خود	xod *self* pron 11
خشکسالی	xoʃksali *drought* n 3032		خودداری	xoddari *self-control* n 2226
خشکی	xoʃki *dryness, dry land* adj,n 3775		خودداری کردن	xoddari kærdæn *refrain* v 2335
خصوص	xosus *concern, regard* n 504		خودرو	xodrow *car* adj,n 993
خصوصاً	xosusæn *especially* adv,conj 2074		خودروساز	xodrowsaz *auto worker/maker* n 4846
خصوصی	xosusi *private* adj 693		خودروسازی	xodrowsazi *automobile manufacturing* n 4434
خصوصیت	xosusijjæt *characteristic* n 2686			
خصومت	xosumæt *enmity, animosity* n 4590		خودگردان	xodgærdan *autonomous* adj 3138
خط	xætt *line* adj,n 237		خودکشی	xodkoʃi *suicide* n 2266
خط لوله	xætelule *pipeline* n 2540		خودکفایی	xodkæfaji *self-sufficiency* n 4990

خودی xodi *insider* adj,n 1881

خوراک xorak *food* n 3329

خوردن xordæn *eat* adj,n,v 686

خورشید xorʃid *sun* pn 1537

خورشیدی xorʃidi *solar* adj,n,pn 3574

خوزستان xuzestan *Khuzestan* pn 1880

خوش xoʃ *good* adj,adv 1673

خوش آمدن xoʃ amædan *welcome* v 3199

خوشایند xoʃajænd *pleasant, pleasure* adj,n 4864

خوشبختانه xoʃbæxtane *fortunately* adv 1998

خوشحال xoʃhal *happy* adj,v 2393

خوشحالی xoʃhali *happiness, joy* n 4020

خوشنویسی xoʃnevisi *calligraphy* n 3848

خوشی xoʃi *joy* adj,n 3897

خون xun *blood* n 566

خونریزی xunrizi *bleeding, bloodshed* n 3949

خونی xuni *blood* adj,n 2858

خونین xunin *bloody* adj 3523

خوی xuj, xoj *habit/temperament, sweat/Khoy* n,pn 4886

خویش xiʃ *self* pron 1109

خیابان xijaban *street* n 796

خیابانی xijabani *street* adj,n,pn 3473

خیال xijal *imagination* n 3035

خیام xæjjam *Khayyam* pn 4832

خیانت xijanæt *treachery* n 3682

خیر xejr, xæjjer *good/no, generous* adj,adv, n 1182

خیره xire *dazzled, staring* adj,adv 4511

خیریه xejrijje *charitable* adj 4106

خیز xiz *rise, leap, swelling* n,pn,v 4828

خیلی xejli *very* adv,q 387

داخل daxel *inside* n,prep 210

داخلی daxeli *internal* adj 320

دادستان dadestan *public prosecutor* n 3942

دادگاه dadgah *court* n 735

دادگستری dadgostæri *justice* n 2679

دادن dadæn *give* n,v 42

داده dade *given, datum* adj,v 50

دارا dara *having* adj 525

دارایی daraji *property* n 1366

دارنده darænde *possessor* adj,n 3531

دارو daru *drug* n 1019

دارویی daruji *pharmaceutical* adj,n 2333

داریوش darjuʃ *Darius* pn 3676

داستان dastan *story* n 869

داستانی dastani *fictional* adj,n 3293

داشتن daʃtæn *have* v 16

داشته daʃte *had, possession* adj,v 48

داغ daɣ *hot* adj,n 2978

دال dal, dall *letter dal, indicative* adj,n 4265

دام dam *trap, livestock* n 2193

داماد damad *groom, son-in-law* n,pn 4480

دامن damæn *skirt* n 3955

دامن زدن damæn zædæn *add fuel* v 3301

دامنه damæne *range, slope* n 1820

دامی dami *livestock* adj,n 4287

دانستن danestæn *know* v 87

دانسته daneste *knowledge, knew* adj,v 1912

دانش daneʃ *knowledge* n 780

دانش‌آموز daneʃamuz *student* n 2982

دانشجو daneʃdʒu *student* n 521

دانشجویی daneʃdʒuji *university student* adj 2204

دانشگاه daneʃgah *university* n 312

دانشگاهی daneʃgahi *academic, university* adj,n 1543

دانشمند daneʃmænd *scientist* adj,n 947

دانشکده daneʃkæde *college, faculty* n 1769

دانمارک danmark *Denmark* pn 4032

دانه dane *seed, grain* n 3749

داور davær *referee* n 2031

داوری daværi *judgment, arbitration, refereeing* n 2586

داوطلب davtælæb *volunteer, applicant* adj,n 2068

داوود davud *Davood* pn 3227

دایر dajer *functioning* adj 2584

دایره dajere *circle* n 2416

دایم dajem *permanent* adj,adv 3280

دایمی dajemi *permanent* adj 3179

دایی daji *maternal uncle* n,pn 3396

دبیر dæbir *secretary* n 1446

دبیرخانه dæbirxane *secretariat* n 4030

دبیرستان dæbirestan *high school* n 3313

دبیرکل dæbirekol *secretary general* n 2124

دچار dotʃar *afflicted with* adj 857

دخالت dexalæt *interference* n 1612

دخالت کردن dexalæt kærdæn *interfere* v 4443

دختر doxtær *girl, daughter* adj,n 859

در dær *in* prep 7

در حال dærhal *in the process of* conj 143

در زدن dær zædæn *knock* v 4056

درآمد dæramæd *income* n,v 657

درآمدن dæramædæn *emerge* adj,v 1679

درآوردن dæraværdæn *extract, produce* adj,n,v 2389

دراز deraz *long* adj 2764

دربار dærbar *royal court, palace* n 4183

درباره dærbare *about* prep 228

دربند dærbænd *Darband, captive* adj,pn 3943

درج dærdʒ *insertion, incorporation* n 3241

درجه dærædʒe *degree* n 1097

درحالیکه dærhalike *while, as* conj 4476

درخت deræxt *tree* n 1496

درخشان deræxʃan *brilliant* adj 2718

درخشش deræxʃeʃ *brilliance* n 4135

درخشیدن deræxʃidæn *shine* adj,n,v 4818

درخواست dærxast *request* n 756

درخواست کردن dærxast kærdæn *request* v 4687

درد	dærd *pain* n 1572		دستمزد	dæstmozd *wages* n 3182
دردسر	dærdesær *trouble* n 4934		دسته	dæste *bunch* n 573
دردناک	dærdnak *painful* adj 4246		دستور	dæstur *order, instruction* n 430
درس	dærs *lesson* n 1236		دستور دادن	dæstur dadæn *order* v 4281
درست	dorost *right, correct* adj,adv 1001		دستورالعمل	dæsturolʔæmæl *instructions* n 3357
درست بودن	dorost budæn *be right* v 1455		دستی	dæsti *manual, handmade, tame* adj, n 1812
درست کردن	dorost kærdæn *correct, prepare* v 4016			
درستی	dorosti *correctness, truth* adj,n 1654		دستیابی	dæstjabi *access, achieving* n 1270
درسی	dærsi *instructional* adj,n 2433		دستیار	dæstjar *assistant* n 2993
درصد	dærsæd *percent* adj,n 159		دشت	dæʃt *plain* n 2838
درگذشت	dærgozæʃt *death, died* n,v 2235		دشمن	doʃmæn *enemy* n 789
درگذشتن	dærgozæʃtæn *die* v 4580		دشمنی	doʃmæni *hostility* n 2890
درگذشته	dærgozæʃte *deceased* adj,n 4923		دشوار	doʃvar *difficult* adj 1407
درگیر	dærgir *involved* adj 1555		دشواری	doʃvari *difficulty* adj,n 2245
درگیر شدن	dærgir ʃodæn *engage* v 4114		دعا	doʔa *prayer* n 3111
درگیری	dærgiri *involvement, engagement* n 1247		دعوا	dæʔva *quarrel* n 3963
درمان	dærman *treatment* n 840		دعوت	dæʔvæt *invitation* n 697
درمانی	dærmani *therapeutic* adj 1562		دغدغه	dæɣdæɣe *fear, anxiety* n 2899
دره	dærre *valley* n 3295		دفاع	defaʔ *defense* n 302
درهم	derhæm, dærhæm *dirham, mixed* adj,n,pn 4841		دفاعی	defaʔi *defensive* adj 2132
			دفتر	dæftær *office* n 380
دروازه	dærvaze *gate,goal* n 1102		دفترچه	dæftærtʃe *notebook* n 4499
درواقع	dærvaɣeʔ *indeed* adv,conj 3017		دفع	dæfʔ *repelling, fend off* n 3991
درود	dorud *greeting* n,pn,v 4751		دفعه	dæfʔe *time* n 3774
دروغ	doruɣ *lie* adj,n 2664		دفن	dæfn *burial* n 4371
درون	dærun *inside* n,prep 950		دقت	deɣɣæt *accuracy* n 1305
درونی	dæruni *inner* adj 2259		دقیق	dæɣiɣ *exact* adj,pn 793
درک	dærk, dæræk *perception, hell* n 1274		دقیقاً	dæɣiɣæn *exactly* adv 1851
درک کردن	dærk kærdæn *comprehend* v 2186		دقیقه	dæɣiɣe *minute* n 388
دری	dæri *Dari* adj,n,pn 4158		دگرگون	degærgun *changed* adj 4441
دریا	dærja *sea* n 625		دگرگونی	degærguni *transformation* n 3809
دریاچه	dærjatʃe *lake* n 2512		دل	del *heart* n 910
دریافت	dærjaft *receipt, perception* n 565		دلار	dolar *dollar* n 330
دریافت کردن	dærjaft kærdæn *receive* v 1559		دلاری	dolari *dollar* adj,n 3081
دریافتن	dærjaftæn *perceive, receive* adj,v 2243		دلخواه	delxah *desired, ideal* adj,n 3948
دریافتی	dærjafti *received, receipt* adj 4088		دلسوز	delsuz *compassionate* adj,n 4531
دریایی	dærjaji *maritime* adj,n 1380		دلیل	dælil *reason* n 127
دریچه	dæritʃe *window, valve, vent* n 4813		دم	dæm, dom *breath/near, tail* n,prep 2758
دریغ	deriɣ *regret, pity* adv,n 4061		دما	dæma *temperature* n 2496
دزد	dozd *thief* n 3684		دمشق	dæmæʃɣ *Damascus* pn 3137
دزدی	dozdi *theft, burglary* adj,n 4679		دموکرات	demokrat *democrat* adj,n 3266
دسامبر	desambr *December* n 3175		دموکراتیک	demokratik *democratic* adj 2841
دست	dæst *hand* n 66		دموکراسی	demokrasi *democracy* n 2147
دست دادن	dæst dadæn *shake hands, lose* v 217		دمکراسی	demokrasi *democracy* n 4925
دستاندرکار	dæstændærkar *involved* n 4636		دنبال	dombal *follow* n 252
دستاورد	dæstaværd *achievement* n 1398		دنبال کردن	donbal kærdæn *look for* v 1657
دستخوش	dæstxoʃ *gratuity, prone, subject to* adj, n 4829		دنباله	dombale *continuation* n 4521
			دندان	dændan *tooth* n 2891
دسترس	dæstres *access* n 2574		دنیا	donja *world* n 197
دسترسی	dæstresi *accessibility* n 1414		ده	dæh, deh *ten, town* n 481
دستگاه	dæstgah *machine, system* n 464		دهان	dæhan *mouth* n 2635
دستگیر	dæstgir *arrested* adj 965		دهم	dæhom *tenth* adj,n,v 1386
دستگیری	dæstgiri *capturing, assist* n 1987		دهنده	dæhænde *donor, -giving* n 2558

دهه	dæhe decade n 499
دهکده	dehkæde village n 4138
دو	do, dow two, running n 39
دوازده	dævazdæh twelve n 2076
دوازدهم	dævazdæhom twelfth adj,n 3394
دوام	dævam durability n 3986
دوبار	dobar twice adv 4563
دوباره	dobare again adj,adv 813
دوجانبه	dodʒanebe bilateral adj 2594
دوچرخه	dotʃærxe bicycle n 3699
دوحه	dowhe Doha pn 4788
دوختن	duxtæn sew adj,n,v 3873
دود	dud smoke n 3882
دور	dowr, dur period, far adj,n 283
دوران	dowran, dæværan period, circulation n 407
دوربین	durbin camera adj,n 1785
دوره	dowre period n 132
دوری	duri, dowri distance, plate n 1770
دوست	dust friend n 496
دوست داشتن	dust daʃtæn like v 1634
دوستانه	dustane friendly adj 1924
دوستدار	dustdar devotee adj,n,pn 4415
دوستی	dusti friendship n 1051
دوش	duʃ shoulder, shower adv,n 2198
دوشنبه	doʃæmbe Monday n,pn 1262
دوگانه	dogane double adj 3766
دولت	dowlæt government n 90
دولتمرد	dowlætmærd statesman, official n 3048
دولتی	dowlæti governmental adj,n 470
دوم	dovvom second adj,n 126
دوهزار	dohezar two thousand n 3970
دویدن	dævidæn run adj,n,v 3283
دویست	devist two hundred n 2026
دکتر	doktor doctor n 375
دکترا	doktora doctorate n 1748
دی	dej Dey n,pn 1743
دیابت	dijabet diabetes n 4072
دیار	dijar land n 3661
دیپلمات	diplomat diplomat n 3601
دیپلماتیک	diplomatik diplomatic adj 3298
دیپلماسی	diplomasi diplomacy n 2182
دیجیتال	didʒital digital adj 3927
دیدار	didar visit n 308
دیدگاه	didgah point of view n 653
دیدن	didæn see n,v 202
دیدنی	didæni worth watching, spectacular adj 3582
دیده	dide eye, seen adj,n 290
دیر	dir, dejr late, monastery adj,adv,n,pn 2086
دیروز	diruz yesterday adv 940
دیرین	dirin old, ancient adj 4950
دیرینه	dirine old adj,n 2733
دیسک	disk disk n 4698
دیشب	diʃæb last night adv 3976

دیگر	digær other adj,adv,conj,pron 29
دین	din religion n 360
دینی	dini religious adj 466
دیوار	divar wall n 1566
دیوان	divan court, book of poetry adj,n 1170
دیوانه	divane crazy adj,n 4790
دیوید	devid David pn 2450
دیکتاتوری	diktatori dictatorship, dictatorial adj,n 4054
ذات	zat essence n 3820
ذاتی	zati inherent, intrinsic adj 4197
ذخیره	zæxire supply n 1096
ذره	zærre particle n 3062
ذهن	zehn mind n 1113
ذهنی	zehni mental adj 2424
ذهنیت	zehnijæt mentality n 4859
ذوب	zowb fusion, melting adj,n 3596
ذوق	zowɣ good taste, enthusiasm n 3818
ذکر	zekr, zækær mention, penis n 1377
ذکر کردن	zekr kærdæn mention, cite v 4885
ذیربط	ziræbt relevant adj 4403
ذیل	zejl appendix, following, below adj,n 3350
رأس	ræʔs head, top n,pn 1766
رآکتور	reaktor reactor n 4981
رأی	ræʔj vote n 354
رویا	roʔja dream n,pn 3031
رئیس	ræʔis head n 88
رئیس‌جمهور	ræʔisdʒomhur president n 2227
رابرت	rabert Robert pn 2788
رابط	rabet intermediary, connector adj,n 4773
رابطه	rabete relation n 105
راجع	radʒeʔ referring prep 2152
راحت	rahæt comfort, comfortable adj,adv 2591
راحتی	rahæti comfort adj,n 2073
راحل	rahel deceased adj 4899
راد	rad rad, Rad, rod pn 4353
رادیو	radijo radio n 1098
رادیویی	radijoji radio adj 3452
راز	raz secret, mystery n,pn 2546
رازی	razi Razi n,pn 3219
راست	rast right adj,adv,n 1758
راستا	rasta direction n 1040
راستی	rasti indeed, truth adj,adv,n 3198
راستین	rastin true adj 4741
راسخ	rasex firm adj,pn 4306
راضی	razi satisfied adj 4213
راضی بودن	razi budæn be satisfied v 3623
راندن	randæn drive adj,n,pn,v 2103
رانده	rande driven, expelled adj,v 4274
رانندگی	ranændegi driving n 2263
راننده	ranænde driver n 1646
راه	rah way, road n 47
راه افتادن	rah oftadæn set out v 3788
راه انداختن	rah ændaxtæn operate, launch v 1560
راه رفتن	rah ræftæn walk v 4560

راه‌اندازی	rahændazi *making operational* n 3879		رشوه	reʃve *bribery* n 4696
راه‌حل	rahehæll *solution* n 3220		رشید	ræʃid *well grown, Rashid* adj,pn 4677
راهبرد	rahbord *strategy* n 3095		رضا	reza *Reza* n,pn 1026
راهبردی	rahbordi *strategic* adj,n 3304		رضایت	rezajæt *satisfaction* n 983
راهپیمایی	rahpejmaji *march, rally* n 3584		رضایی	rezaji *Rezai* pn 2834
راهنما	rahnæma *guide* adj,n 2767		رضوی	ræzævi *Razavi* adj,pn 3435
راهنمایی	rahnæmaji *guidance* adj,n 2304		رعایت	reʔajæt *observance* n 1165
راهکار	rahkar *strategy, solution* adj,n 1426		رغبت	reɣbæt *desire, inclination* n,pn 4971
راهی	rahi *bound for, a path* adj,n 782		رغم	ræɣm *spite* n 2959
رایانه	rajane *computer* n 3202		رفاه	refah *welfare, comfort* n 2350
رایانه‌ای	rajaneji *computer* adj 3372		رفاهی	refahi *welfare, leisure* adj 3862
رایج	rajedʒ *current* adj 2672		رفتار	ræftar *behavior* n 642
رایزنی	rajzæni *consultation* n 3338		رفتار کردن	ræftar kærdæn *behave* v 4291
رایگان	rajegan *free* adj 3191		رفتاری	ræftari *behavioral* adj,n 2617
ربطی	ræbti *linking, connecting* adj,n 4641		رفتن	ræftæn *go* adj,n,v 128
ربع	robʔ *quarter* n 4523		رفسنجانی	ræfsændʒani *Rafsanjani* pn 4161
ربودن	robudæn *steal* adj,n,v 1744		رفع	ræfʔ *removing* n 1058
رتبه	rotbe *rank* n 1922		رفیق	ræfiɣ *pal* adj,n,pn 4593
رجب	rædʒæb *Rajab* n,pn 4839		رقابت	reɣabæt *competition* n 533
رجوع	rodʒuʔ *reference* n 4856		رقابتی	reɣabæti *competitive* adj,n 2888
رحم	ræhm, ræhem *compassion, womb* n 4190		رقم	ræɣæm *digit, number* adj,n,pn 580
رحمت	ræhmæt *compassion* n,pn 2956		رقیب	ræɣib *competitor* adj,n 1308
رحیم	ræhim *merciful, Rahim* pn 3822		رم	rom *Rome* pn 2580
رحیمی	ræhimi *Rahimi* pn 4254		رمان	roman *novel* n 2863
رخ	rox *face* n 531		رمز	ræmz *code* n 2582
رخداد	roxdad *happening* n 3733		رمضان	ræmezan *Ramadan* n,pn 1970
رد	rædd *refusal, trail* adj,n 757		رنج	rændʒ *pain* n 1234
رد کردن	ræd kærdæn *reject* v 2047		رنگ	ræng *color* n 951
رده	ræde *category* n 1524		رنگی	rængi *colored* adj,n 2720
ردیف	rædif *row* n 1704		رنگین	rængin *colored* adj 4289
رزمنده	ræzmænde *warrior* adj,n 3569		رها	ræha *loose, free* adj 4079
رزمی	ræzmi *combat* adj 4090		رها شدن	ræha ʃodæn *be freed* v 4381
رژیم	reʒim *regime* n 747		رها کردن	ræha kærdæn *free, let go* v 2746
رسالت	resalæt *mission* n,pn 2922		رهایی	ræhaji *release* n 2397
رساله	resale *letter, treatise* n 4975		رهبر	ræhbær *leader* n 524
رساندن	resandæn *deliver* adj,n,v 192		رهبری	ræhbæri *leadership* n 666
رسانه	resane *medium* n 600		رهگذر	ræhgozær *passerby* n 4258
رسانه‌ای	resaneʔi *media* adj,n 2906		رو	ru *on, face* n,prep 82
رستم	rostæm *Rostam* pn 4817		رو آوردن	ru avordæn *turn* v 1664
رستوران	restoran *restaurant* n 3630		رو شدن	ru ʃodæn *be exposed, bold* v 3941
رسم	ræsm *custom* n 3472		رو کردن	ru kærdæn *turn to, look at* v 4607
رسماً	ræsmæn *officially* adv 2268		رواج	rævadʒ *currency, circulation* n 3023
رسمی	ræsmi *official* adj 471		روال	ræval *procedure* n 4376
رسمیت	ræsmijjæt *state of being official/formal* n 3425		روان	rævan *smooth* adj,n 1984
رسوایی	rosvaji *disgrace, scandal* n 4716		روانشناسی	rævanʃenasi *psychology* n 4037
رسوب	rosub *sedimentation, sediment* n 4972		روانه	rævane *bound for* adj 4097
رسول	ræsul *messenger* n,pn 2439		روانی	rævani *fluency, psychotic* adj 1438
رسیدگی	residegi *investigation* n 988		روایت	revajæt *narrative* n 2107
رسیدن	residæn *arrive* adj,n,v 24		روبرو	ruberu *opposite* adj,adv,n,prep,v 792
رشت	ræʃt *Rasht* pn 3482		روبرو شدن	ruberu ʃodæn *meet* v 1575
رشته	reʃte *field, noodle* n 373		روح	ruh *spirit* n 1580
رشد	roʃd *growth* n 251		روحانی	rowhani *cleric, Rowhani* adj,n,pn 1853
رشد کردن	roʃd kærdæn *grow* v 4391		روحانیت	rowhanijæt *clergy* n 4400
			روحی	ruhi *spiritual, mental* adj,n,pn 2372

روحیه	ruhijje *mood, morale* n 1454	زبانی	zæbani *verbal, lingual* adj,n 2972
رود	rud *river* n,v 1160	زحمت	zæhmæt *trouble* n 2503
رودخانه	rudxane *river* n 1848	زخم	zæxm *wound* n 3366
روز	ruz *day* n 30	زخمی	zæxmi *wounded* adj,n 1901
روزافزون	ruzæfzun *ever-increasing* adj 3021	زدن	zædæn *strike, beat* adj,n,prep,v 310
روزانه	ruzane *daily* adj,adv 1296	زرد	zærd *yellow* adj,n 3061
روزگار	ruzegar *times* n 1886	زرین	zærrin *golden* adj 4602
روزمره	ruzmærre *routine* adj 3264	زشت	zeʃt *ugly* adj 4680
روزنامه	ruzname *newspaper* n 256	زلزله	zelzele *earthquake* n 2446
روزنامه‌نگار	ruznamenegar *journalist* n 3604	زمان	zæman *time* n 83
روزه	ruze *fast* adj,n 1622	زمانه	zæmane *era, age* n 3598
روزی	ruzi *someday, daily bread* n 1093	زمانی	zæmani *chronological* adj,n 396
روس	rus *Russian* adj,n,pn 2218	زمره	zomre *group* n 4150
روستا	rusta *village* n 665	زمستان	zemestan *winter* n 2123
روستایی	rustaji *villager, rural* adj,n 1138	زمستانی	zemestani *winter* adj 4597
روسی	rusi *Russian* adj 1420	زمین	zæmin *ground, earth* n,pn 243
روسیه	rusije *Russia* pn 568	زمینه	zæmine *background, field* n 117
روش	ræveʃ *method* n 403	زمینی	zæmini *land, earthling* adj,n 837
روشن	rowʃæn *bright, turned on* adj 544	زن	zæn *woman, wife* adj,n 214
روشنایی	rowʃænaji *brightness* n 3983	زنجان	zændʒan *Zanjan* pn 2618
روشنفکر	rowʃænfekr *intellectual* adj,n 3176	زنجیره	zændʒire *chain* n 4363
روشنگری	rowʃængæri *enlightenment* n 3335	زند	zænd *radius, ulna, Zand* pn,v 3311
روشنی	rowʃæni *light* adj,n 1011	زندان	zendan *prison* n 733
روغن	rowɣæn *oil* n 2611	زندانی	zendani *prisoner* adj,n 1218
رومانی	romani *Romania* pn 4121	زندگی	zendegi *life* n 190
روند	rævænd *process* n 418	زندگی کردن	zendegi kærdæn *live* v 832
رونق	rownæɣ *boom* n 1402	زنده	zende *live* adj 932
رویارویی	rujaruji *confrontation* n 2696	زنگ	zæng *bell, ring* n 3615
رویتر	rujter *Reuters* pn 4210	زنگ زدن	zæng zædæn *ring* v 3753
رویداد	rujdad *event* n 1564	زننده	zænænde *repulsive, player* adj,n 4473
رویه	rævijje *method* n 3119	زهرا	zæhra *Zahra* pn 2650
رویکرد	rujkærd *approach* n 1693	زوج	zowdʒ *pair, couple* adj,n 3777
رکن	rokn *pillar, foot* n 2677	زود	zud *soon* adj,adv 1520
رکود	rokud *stagnation, recession* n 2825	زودی	zudi *soon* n 1988
رکورد	rekord *record* n 2500	زور	zur *force* n 2619
ری	rej *Rey* pn 3657	زیاد	zijad *a lot* adj,adv 446
ریاست	rijasæt *presidency* n 523	زیادی	zijadi *excessive* adj 183
ریاض	rijaz *Riyadh* pn 4247	زیارت	zijaræt *pilgrimage* n 2220
ریاضی	rijazi *mathematical* adj,n,pn 2337	زیان	zijan *loss, harm* n 1902
ریاضیات	rijazijjat *mathematics* n 3761	زیبا	ziba *beautiful* adj 875
ریال	rijal *rial* n 989	زیبایی	zibaji *beauty* adj,n 1123
ریالی	rijali *Rial-based* adj 3985	زیر	zir *under* adj,n,prep 296
ریختن	rixtæn *pour* adj,n,v 1513	زیرا	zira *because* conj 558
ریز	riz *tiny* adj 3889	زیربنا	zirbæna *infrastructure* n 4055
ریزش	rizeʃ *spilling, precipitation* n 4218	زیربنایی	zirbænaji *infrastructural* adj,n 3548
ریسک	risk *risk* n 3091	زیرزمینی	zirzæmini *underground* adj 4621
ریشه	riʃe *root* n 704	زیرساخت	zirsaxt *infrastructure* n 3768
زائر	zaʔer *pilgrim* pn 4603	زیروبمی	zirobæmi *pitch* adj,n 4754
زادگاه	zadgah *birthplace* n 3534	زیست	zist *life* n 3194
زانو	zanu *knee, bend* n 3946	زیست‌محیطی	zistmohiti *environmental* adj 4495
زاویه	zavije *angle* n 2064	زیستن	zistæn *live* adj,n,v 4665
زباله	zobale *garbage* n,pn 3098	زیستی	zisti *life, vital, biological* adj 3583
زبان	zæban *language, tongue* n 383	زین	zin *saddle, from this* conj,n 4987

سرتیپ	særtip *brigadier general* n 4195	سفید	sefid *white* adj 1597
سرچشمه	særtʃeʃme *source* n 2874	سفیر	sæfir *ambassador* n 1240
سرخ	sorx *red* adj,n 2223	سقف	sæɣf *ceiling, roof* n 1550
سرد	særd *cold* adj 1406	سقوط	soɣut *fall* n 1266
سردار	særdɑr *commander, general* n,pn 1327	سگ	sæg *dog* n 3405
سرزمین	særzæmin *land* n 683	سلاح	selah *weapon* n 946
سرشار	særʃɑr *abundant* adj 2414	سلام	sælam *hello, greeting* n 1514
سرشماری	særʃomɑri *census* n 4315	سلامت	sælɑmæt *health* adj,n 1181
سرشناس	særʃenɑs *well-known* adj 3770	سلامتی	sælɑmæti *health* n,pn 1828
سرطان	særætɑn *cancer* n 2003	سلب	sælb *divesting* n 2547
سرطانی	særætɑni *cancerous, cancer* adj 4310	سلسله	selsele *chain* n 2810
سرعت	sorʔæt *speed* adj,n 575	سلطان	soltɑn *sultan, king* n,pn 3011
سرقت	serɣæt *theft* n 2705	سلطانی	soltɑni *royal* adj,n,pn 4998
سرگردان	særgærdɑn *wandering, vagrant* adj 4678	سلطنت	sæltænæt *monarchy* n 3872
سرگرم	særgærm *amused, busy* adj 3550	سلطنتی	sæltænæti *royal* adj,n 4123
سرما	særmɑ *cold* n 2490	سلطه	solte *domination* n 2670
سرمایه	særmɑje *capital* n 706	سلمان	sælmɑn *Salman, Solomon* pn 4730
سرمایه‌داری	særmɑjedɑri *capitalism, capitalist* n 4115	سلول	sellul *cell* n 1762
سرمایه‌گذار	særmɑjegozɑr *investor* adj,n 3806	سلیقه	sæliɣe *taste* n 2938
سرمایه‌گذاری	særmɑjegozɑri *investment* n 917	سلیمان	solejmɑn *Soleiman, Solomon* pn 2988
سرمربی	særmoræbbi *head coach* n 3025	سمت	sæmt, semæt *side, position* n 260
سرنشین	særneʃin *passenger* n 2656	سمنان	semnɑn *Semnan* pn 4076
سرنگونی	særneguni *overthrow* n 4305	سمینار	seminɑr *seminar* n 3765
سرنوشت	særneveʃt *fate* n 710	سن	senn *age* n 678
سره	sære *pure* adj,n 4836	سنا	senɑ *senate* n,pn 3281
سرهنگ	særhæng *colonel* n 3390	سناتور	senɑtor *senator* n 4939
سرو	særv, serv *cypress, serve* n 4332	سناریو	senɑrijo *scenario, screenplay* n 4059
سرود	sorud *song, sang* n,pn,v 3743	سنت	sonnæt *tradition* n 912
سروده	sorude *sung, poem* adj,n,v 4045	سنتی	sonæti *traditional* adj 1132
سرور	sorur, særvær, server *joy, leader, server* n,pn 4069	سنجش	sændʒeʃ *measurement* n 2102
سروش	soruʃ *angel* n,pn 3139	سنجیدن	sændʒidæn *measure* n,v 4647
سرویس	servis *service* n 1809	سند	sænæd *document* n,pn 772
سرکوب	særkub *suppression* n 3004	سنگ	sæng *rock* n 1326
سری	seri, særi *series, a head* adj,n 1400	سنگاپور	sængɑpur *Singapore* pn 4331
سریال	serijɑl *series* n 2826	سنگی	sængi *rocky* adj,n 3181
سریع	særiʔ *fast* adj,adv 586	سنگین	sængin *heavy* adj 483
سست	sost *weak* adj 4784	سنگینی	sængini *weight* adj,n 1717
سطح	sæth *level* n 334	سنی	sonni, senni *Sunni, age* adj,n 1171
سطحی	sæthi *superficial* adj,n 3284	سه	se *three* n 142
سطر	sætr *line* n 4406	سه‌شنبه	seʃæmbe *Tuesday* n 2098
سعادت	sæʔadæt *happiness* n,pn 2786	سهامدار	sæhɑmdɑr *shareholder* n 4362
سعدی	sæʔdi *Sa'di* pn 3099	سهل	sæhl *easy* adj,n,pn 4897
سعودی	sæʔudi *Saudi* adj 1953	سهم	sæhm *share, lot* n 709
سعی	sæʔj *try* n 436	سهمیه	sæhmijje *quota, share* n 3253
سعی کردن	sæʔj kærdæn *try* v 941	سهیم	sæhim *involved, shareholder* adj 4565
سعید	sæʔid *Said* adj,pn 1217	سو	su *side* n 94
سعیدی	sæʔidi *Saidi* pn 4275	سواد	sævɑd *literacy* n,pn 3432
سفارت	sefɑræt *embassy* n 2005	سوار	sævɑr *rider* adj,n 2561
سفارتخانه	sefɑrætxɑne *embassy* n 3578	سواری	sævɑri *riding* adj,n 2750
سفارش	sefɑreʃ *order* adj,n 2864	سوخت	suxt *fuel, burned* n,v 1056
سفر	sæfær *travel* n 344	سوختن	suxtæn *burn* adj,n,v 2564
سفر کردن	sæfær kærdæn *travel* v 1753	سود	sud *profit* n 925
سفره	sofre *tablecloth* n 4167	سودان	sudɑn *Sudan* pn 3552
		سوره	sure *sura* n 3673

سوری	suri *Syrian* adj,n,pn 3453	شام	ʃam *dinner* n,pn 3460
سوریه	surije *Syria* pn 856	شامل	ʃamel *included* adj 664
سوز	suz *burning, pain* n 2889	شانزده	ʃanzdæh *sixteen* n 4008
سوزان	suzan *burning* adj,pn 4985	شانزدهم	ʃanzdæhom *sixteenth* adj,n 3511
سوژه	suʒe *subject* n 3973	شانس	ʃans *good luck* n 2370
سوسیالیست	sosijalist *socialist* adj,n 4780	شانگهای	ʃanghaj *Shanghai* pn 4241
سوق دادن	sowɣ dadæn *guide, drive* v 3990	شانه	ʃane *comb, shoulder* n 3639
سوگند	sowgænd *oath* n 4292	شاه	ʃah *king, shah* n,pn 1074
سوم	sevvom *third* adj,n 230	شاهد	ʃahed *witness* adj,n 400
سومالی	somali *Somalia* adj,pn 4431	شاهد بودن	ʃahed budæn *witness* v 2520
سکته	sekte *stoppage, stroke* n 4451	شاهزاده	ʃahzade *prince* n,pn 4125
سکه	sekke *coin* n 1556	شاهنامه	ʃahname *Shahname* pn 4650
سکو	sækku *platform* n 3263	شاهی	ʃahi *kingship, royal* adj,n,pn 4660
سکوت	sokut *silence* n 1558	شاهین	ʃahin *falcon, Shahin* n 3439
سکونت	sokunæt *residence* n 3371	شاکی	ʃaki *plaintiff* adj,n 3721
سی	si *thirty* n,pn 769	شایان	ʃajan *worthy* adj,n 2849
سیا	sija *CIA* pn 2716	شایستگی	ʃajestegi *merit* n 4112
سیار	sæjjar *mobile* adj,pn 4630	شایستن	ʃajæstæn *be possible* adv 494
سیاره	sæjjare *planet* n 4252	شایسته	ʃajeste *worthy* adj 1937
سیاست	sijasæt *policy, politics* n 223	شایع	ʃaje? *widespread* adj 3467
سیاستگذاری	sijasætgozari *policy making* n 4545	شایعه	ʃaje?e *rumor* n 2945
سیاستمدار	sijasætmædar *politician* adj,n 2070	شب	ʃæb *night* n 417
سیاسی	sijasi *political* adj 103	شبانه	ʃæbane *nightly* adj,adv 2443
سیاه	sijah *black* adj 1595	شباهت	ʃæbahæt *similarity* n 2856
سیاوش	sijavæʃ *Siavash* pn 4994	شبه	ʃebh, ʃæbe *quasi, night* adj,n,pn 2823
سیب	sib *apple* n 4538	شبهه	ʃobhe *doubt* n 4494
سید	sejjed *descendant of prophet* n 691	شبکه	ʃæbæke *network* n 409
سیر	sir, sejr *garlic/full, travel* adj,n,pn 1203	شبیه	ʃæbih *similar* adj 1451
سیزده	sizdæh *thirteen* n 3433	شتاب	ʃetab *haste* n 2279
سیزدهم	sizdæhom *thirteenth* adj,n 2809	شجاع	ʃodʒa? *brave, courageous* adj,pn 4015
سیستان	sistan *Sistan* pn 2835	شجاعت	ʃodʒa?æt *courage* n,pn 3719
سیستم	sistem *system* n 465	شخص	ʃæxs *person* n 800
سیصد	sisæd *three hundred* n 1660	شخصأ	ʃæxsæn *personally* adv 3204
سیطره	sejtære *control, predominance* n 4503	شخصی	ʃæxsi *personal* adj,n 1078
سیگار	sigar *cigarette* n 2983	شخصیت	ʃæxsijjæt *personality* adj,n 681
سیل	sejl *flood* n 2385	شدت	ʃeddæt *intensity* adv,n 370
سیلاب	sejlab *flood waters* n 4914	شدن	ʃodæn *become* adj,v 9
سیم	sim *wire* n 2436	شدید	ʃædid *severe* adj 488
سیما	sima *face* n 1509	شدیدأ	ʃædidæn *severely* adv 4502
سیمان	siman *cement* n 2968	شر	ʃærr *evil* adj,n 4645
سینا	sina *Sina* pn 2604	شرح	ʃærh *explaining* n 1626
سینما	sinema *cinema* n 1099	شرط	ʃært *condition* n 106
سینمایی	sinemaji *cinematic* adj 2326	شرعی	ʃær?i *religiously correct* adj 3527
سینه	sine *breast* n 1872	شرف	ʃæræf *honor* n,pn 3625
شاخ	ʃax *horn, branch* n 4394	شرق	ʃærɣ *east* n 806
شاخص	ʃaxes *index* adj,n 1204	شرقی	ʃærɣi *eastern* adj 1041
شاخه	ʃaxe *branch* n 1777	شروع	ʃoru? *start* n 437
شاد	ʃad *happy* adj,pn 2570	شروع شدن	ʃoru? kærdæn *begin* v 1276
شادابی	ʃadabi *freshness* adj,n 4629	شروع کردن	ʃoru? kærdæn *begin* v 2118
شادمانی	ʃadmani *rejoicing* n 3508	شرکت	ʃerkæt *company* n 138
شادی	ʃadi *joy* n,pn 2030	شرکت داشتن	ʃerkæt daʃtæn *participate, attend* v 2534
شاعر	ʃa?er *poet* n 971	شرکت کردن	ʃerkæt kærdæn *participate* v 1348
شاغل	ʃaɣel *employed* adj,n 3933	شرکت‌کننده	ʃerkætkonænde *participant* adj,n 3010
شاگرد	ʃagerd *student* n 2319	شریعت	ʃæri?æt *sharia* n 3136

شریعتی	ʃæriʔæti *Shariati* n,pn 4024	شهروند	ʃæhrvænd *citizen* n 936
شریف	ʃærif *honorable* adj,pn 1443	شهروندی	ʃæhrvændi *citizenship* adj,n 4172
شریک	ʃærik *partner* adj,n 2027	شهرک	ʃæhræk *town* n 1768
شستن	ʃostæn *wash* adj,n,v 3470	شهری	ʃæhri *urban* adj,n 1037
شش	ʃeʃ, ʃoʃ *six, lung* n 740	شهریار	ʃæhrijar *monarch* n,pn 3883
ششصد	ʃeʃsæd *six hundred* n 3616	شهریور	ʃæhrivær *Shahrivar* n 1974
ششم	ʃeʃom *sixth* adj 1197	شهریورماه	ʃæhriværmah *Shahrivar* n 4576
شصت	ʃæst *sixty* n 1786	شهید	ʃæhid *martyr* adj,n 399
شطرنج	ʃætrændʒ *chess* n 4389	شوخی	ʃuxi *joke* n 4854
شعار	ʃeʔar *slogan* n 1436	شور	ʃur, ʃowr *salty/passion, deliberation* adj,n,pn 1365
شعاع	ʃoʔaʔ *ray, beam* n,pn 4887		
شعبه	ʃoʔbe *branch* n,pn 1731	شورا	ʃura *council* n 124
شعر	ʃeʔr *poetry* adj,n 617	شورش	ʃureʃ *rebellion* n,pn 2961
شعله	ʃoʔle *flame* n,pn 4320	شورشی	ʃureʃi *rebel* adj,n,pn 3379
شغل	ʃoɣl *job* n 1767	شوروی	ʃowrævi *Soviet* pn 1946
شغلی	ʃoɣli *job related* adj,n 1898	شوق	ʃowɣ *eagerness* n 2859
شفاف	ʃæffaf *transparent* adj 2004	شوم	ʃum *ominous* adj,v 2727
شفافیت	ʃæffafijjæt *transparency* n 4539	شوهر	ʃowhær *husband* n 2296
شگفت	ʃegeft *amazing* adj,n 4777	شوک	ʃok *shock* n 4736
شگفتی	ʃegefti *surprise* adj,n 3192	شک	ʃækk *doubt* n,pn 1110
شل	ʃæl, ʃol, ʃel *lame, loose, Shell* adj,pn 4905	شکار	ʃekar *hunting* n 2973
شلیک	ʃellik *firing* n 3167	شکاف	ʃekaf *crack, gap* n 1948
شما	ʃoma *you* pron 148	شکایت	ʃekajæt *complaint* n 1320
شمار	ʃomar *number* n,q 535	شکایت کردن	ʃekajæt kærdæn *complain* v 3476
شمارش	ʃomareʃ *counting* n 2363	شکر	ʃekær, ʃokr *sugar, thanks* n 2551
شماره	ʃomare *number* n 957	شکست	ʃekæst *defeat, failure, break* n 1006
شمال	ʃomal *north* n 582	شکست خوردن	ʃekæst xordæn *be defeated* v 1220
شمالی	ʃomali *northern* adj 926	شکست دادن	ʃekæst dadæn *defeat* v 2306
شمردن	ʃemordæn *count* adj,n,v 2661	شکستن	ʃekæstæn *break* adj,n,v 1080
شمس	ʃæms *sun, Shams* pn 4226	شکل	ʃekl *shape* adj,n 195
شمسی	ʃæmsi *solar* adj,pn 2159	شکل‌گیری	ʃeklgiri *formation* n 2840
شمشیر	ʃæmʃir *sword* n 4435	شکم	ʃekæm *stomach* n 4365
شن	ʃen *gravel* n 4212	شکنجه	ʃekændʒe *torture* n 2409
شنا	ʃena *swim* n 2595	شکننده	ʃekænænde *fragile* adj,n 3911
شناخت	ʃenaxt *recognition, knowledge, knew* n, v 1252	شکوفایی	ʃokufaji *flowering* n 2377
		شکوه	ʃokuh, ʃekve *splendor, complaint* n 2287
شناختن	ʃenaxtæn *know, recognize* adj,n,v 705	شکیبایی	ʃækibaji *patience, fortitude* n 4529
شناخته	ʃenaxte *known* adj 828	شی	ʃeʔ *thing* n 2318
شناس	ʃenas *acquaintance, -ologist* n 4377	شیخ	ʃejx *sheikh* n,pn 677
شناسایی	ʃenasaʔi *identification* n 1103	شیر	ʃir *milk, lion* n 1593
شناسایی کردن	ʃenasaji kærdæn *identify* v 2511	شیراز	ʃiraz *Shiraz* pn 1412
شناسنامه	ʃenasname *identity card* n 3344	شیرازی	ʃirazi *Shirazi* adj,pn 2478
شناور	ʃenavær *floating* adj,n 3716	شیری	ʃiri *milk, dairy* adj,n,pn 4776
شنبه	ʃæmbe *Saturday* n 476	شیرین	ʃirin *sweet* adj,pn 1521
شنونده	ʃenævænde *listener* n 4154	شیرینی	ʃirini *sweet, pastry* adj,n 3417
شنیدن	ʃenidæn *hear* n,v 1233	شیشه	ʃiʃe *glass, bottle* n 2514
شنیده	ʃenide *heard* adj 2704	شیشه‌ای	ʃiʃeʔi *glass* adj,n 4964
شهادت	ʃæhadæt *evidence, martyrdom* n 1530	شیطان	ʃejtan *Satan, naughty* n,pn 4023
شهر	ʃæhr *city* n 40	شیعه	ʃiʔe *Shiite* adj,n 894
شهرت	ʃohræt *renown* n 2423	شیعی	ʃiʔi *Shiite* adj 4187
شهردار	ʃæhrdar *mayor* n 2662	شیفته	ʃifte *infatuated, fascinated* adj,n 4670
شهرداری	ʃæhrdari *municipality* n 1194	شیمی	ʃimi *chemistry* n 4405
شهرسازی	ʃæhrsazi *urban development* n 2116	شیمیایی	ʃimijaji *chemical* adj 2195
شهرستان	ʃæhrestan *county* n 1152	شیوع	ʃojuʔ *outbreak* n 3150

طریق	tæriɣ *way* n 265	
طفل	tefl *child* n 3858	
طلا	tæla *gold* adj,n 938	
طلاق	tælaɣ *divorce* n 3693	
طلایی	tælaji *golden* adj,pn 2011	
طلب	tælæb *demand, desire, -seeker* n 1469	
طلبه	tælæbe *seminary student* n 3117	
طلبیدن	tælæbidæn *call, ask, require* n,v 1849	
طنز	tænz *satire* adj,n 3812	
طور	towr *manner* n 80	
طوفان	tufan *storm* n 2234	
طول	tul *length* n 440	
طول کشیدن	tul keʃidæn *last long* v 3268	
طولانی	tulani *long* adj 435	
طی	tej *during* n,prep 258	
طی کردن	tej kærdæn *journey* v 3134	
طیف	tejf *spectrum* n 3397	
ظاهر	zaher *appearance* n 1816	
ظاهر شدن	zaher ʃodæn *appear* v 2853	
ظاهراً	zaheræn *apparently* adv 1893	
ظاهری	zaheri *apparent, superficial* adj,n 3339	
ظرف	zærf *container, vessel* n 1068	
ظرفیت	zærfijæt *capacity* n 667	
ظریف	zærif *delicate* adj,pn 3001	
ظلم	zolm *oppression* n 2507	
ظهر	zohr, zæhr *noon, back* n 2477	
ظهور	zohur *appearance* n 2089	
عادت	adæt *habit* n 2605	
عادل	adel *just* adj,pn 4103	
عادلانه	adelane *justly* adj,adv 2315	
عادی	adi *normal* adj 905	
عارضه	areze *incident* n 2282	
عارف	aref *Sufi, conoisseur* adj,n,pn 2958	
عاری	ari *bereft, free* adj 3846	
عازم	azem *bound for* adj 2150	
عاشق	aʃeɣ *lover* adj,n 2640	
عاشورا	aʃura *Ashura* n 3287	
عاطفی	atefi *emotional* adj 3898	
عالم	alem, alæm *learned, world* n 848	
عالی	ali *high* adj 731	
عام	am *common* adj,n 2790	
عامل	amel *agent, factor* adj,n 261	
عامه	amme *public* n,q 4204	
عبادت	ebadæt *worship* n 3666	
عبارت	ebaræt *phrase, expression* n,v 968	
عباس	æbbas *Abbas* pn 730	
عباسی	æbbasi *Abbasi, Abbasid* adj,pn 2380	
عبدالله	æbdollah *Abdollah* pn 1417	
عبرت	ebræt *lesson, example* n 4543	
عبور	obur *passing* n 690	
عثمانی	osmani *Ottoman* adj,n,pn 3891	
عجیب	ædʒib *strange* adj 2050	
عدالت	edalæt *justice* adj,n 916	
عدد	ædæd *number* n 1665	

عدم	ædæm *lack* n 764	
عده	edde *number* n,q 716	
عذرخواهی	ozrxahi *apology* n 4349	
عراق	eraɣ *Iraq* pn 518	
عراقی	eraɣi *Iraqi* adj,n,pn 2261	
عرب	æræb *Arab* adj,n,pn 942	
عربستان	æræbestan *Arabia* pn 1188	
عربی	æræbi *Arabic* adj,n 1032	
عرصه	ærse *area* n 451	
عرض	ærz *width, saying* n 994	
عرضه	ærze, orze *presenting/offering, capability* n 1193	
عرضه کردن	ærze kærdæn *present, offer, supply* v 3557	
عرفات	æræfat *Arafat* pn 4220	
عرفان	erfan *Sufism, mysticism* n 3945	
عرفانی	erfani *Sufist, mystic* adj 4759	
عرق	æræɣ, erɣ *sweat, blood vessel* n 3920	
عروس	ærus *bride, daugher-in-law* n 4429	
عروسی	ærusi *marriage, wedding* n 4033	
عروقی	oruɣi *vascular* adj 4863	
عزاداری	æzadari *mourning* n 4849	
عزت	ezzæt *esteem* n 1613	
عزم	æzm *resolve* n 1503	
عزیز	æziz *dear* adj,n,pn 1050	
عزیزی	æzizi *Azizi, dear* adj,pn 2872	
عزیمت	æzimæt *departure* n 4564	
عشق	eʃɣ *love* n 1253	
عشیره	æʃire *nomadic tribe* n 2818	
عصب	æsæb *nerve* n 3207	
عصبانی	æsæbani *angry* adj 4814	
عصبانیت	æsæbanijæt *anger* n 4752	
عصبی	æsæbi *nervous* adj 2781	
عصر	æsr *afternoon, age* n 511	
عضو	ozv *member* n 153	
عضویت	ozvijæt *membership* n 1330	
عظمت	æzæmæt *majesty* n 3126	
عظیم	æzim *great* adj 1243	
عظیمی	æzimi *greatness, Azimi* adj,pn 2485	
عفو	æfv *pardon* n 4452	
عقب	æɣæb *back* adj,adv,n 1401	
عقد	æɣd *(marriage) contract* n 3244	
عقل	æɣl *reason* n 2056	
عقیده	æɣide *belief* n 1020	
علاقمند	ælaɣemænd *interested* adj,n 1571	
علاقه	ælaɣe *interest* n 1222	
علاقه داشتن	ælaɣe daʃtæn *be interested* v 3992	
علامت	ælamæt *mark* n 1677	
علامه	ællame *erudite, Allameh* n,pn 3271	
علاوه	ælave *addition* n 781	
علت	ellæt *reason* n 319	
علم	elm *science* n 362	
علمی	elmi *scientific* adj 333	
علمیه	elmijje *scientific* adj 4446	
علنی	ælæni *open, public* adj 1919	

علی	æli *Ali* pn 109		غربی	ɣærbi *western* adj 630
علی‌رغم	ælaræɣm *despite* conj 2361		غرض	ɣæræz *motive, grudge* n 4433
علیرضا	ælireza *Alireza* pn 1929		غرفه	ɣorfe *booth* n 4196
علیزاده	ælizade *Alizadeh* pn 4810		غرق	ɣærɣ *drowning, sinking* adj,n 2915
علیه	ælejh *against* n,prep 635		غروب	ɣorub *sunset* n 4343
علیه السلام	ælejhessælam *peace be upon him* expression 4359		غرور	ɣorur *pride, vanity* n 4978
عمارت	emaræt *building* n 4668		غریب	ɣærib *strange* adj,n,pn 3637
عمان	omman *Oman* pn 3429		غزل	ɣæzæl *ghazal* n 4373
عمداً	omdætæn *chiefly* adv 1854		غزه	ɣæze *Gaza* pn 3166
عمده	omde *main* adj 996		غفلت	ɣeflæt *neglect* n 3739
عمر	omr *life* n,pn 1018		غلبه	ɣælæbe *triumph* n 2516
عمران	omran *construction* n,pn 3541		غلط	ɣælæt *mistake* adj,n 2379
عمرانی	omrani *development* adj 2168		غم	ɣæm *sorrow, grief* n 3223
عمق	omɣ *depth* n 2190		غنا	ɣæna *wealth, Ghana* n,pn 4386
عمل	æmæl *action* n 189		غنی	ɣæni *rich* adj 1551
عمل کردن	æmæl kærdæn *act, perform* v 614		غیبت	ɣejbæt *absence* n 3798
عملاً	æmælæn *practically* adv,conj 1397		غیر	ɣejr *other* n 281
عملکرد	æmælkærd *operation* n 703		غیردولتی	ɣejrdowlæti *non-governmental* adj 4945
عملی	æmæli *practical* adj,n 959		غیرقانونی	ɣejrɣanuni *illegal* adj 2206
عملیات	æmælijat *campaign* n 553		غیرنظامی	ɣejrnezami *civilian* adj,n 3810
عملیاتی	æmælijjati *operational* adj,n 2652		غیره	ɣejre *other* adj,n 2694
عمو	æmu *paternal uncle* n 4136		فاتح	fateh *victorious* adj,n,pn 2949
عموم	omum *public, whole* n,q 1711		فاجعه	fadʒeʔe *disaster* n 1631
عموماً	omumæn *generally* adv 3356		فارس	fars *Fars* pn 815
عمومی	omumi *public* adj 306		فارسی	farsi *Persian* adj,n 981
عمیق	æmiɣ *deep* adj 1043		فارغ	fareɣ *free* adj 2851
عنان	enan/ænan *rein, Annan* pn 3935		فاز	faz *phase* n 2659
عنایت	enajæt *favor* n 3255		فاسد	fased *rotten, corrupt* adj 3593
عنصر	onsor *element* n 1338		فاش	faʃ *frank, reveal* adj 2714
عنوان	onvan *title* n 62		فاصله	fasele *distance* n 536
عهد	æhd *promise, treaty* n 3518		فاضلاب	fazelab *sewage* n 4525
عهده	ohde *responsibility* n,prep 557		فاطمه	fateme *Fateme* pn 3040
عواقب	ævaɣeb *consequences* n 2666		فاقد	faɣed *lacking* adj,prep 2563
عوام	ævam *common people* n 4119		فاکتور	faktor *invoice, factor* n 3274
عوض	ævæz *change* n 2119		فایده	fajede *benefit* n 3999
عکاس	ækkas *photographer* adj,n 3559		فتح	fæth *victory* n 1694
عکاسی	ækasi *photography* n 4259		فتنه	fetne *sedition* n 3158
عکس	æks *picture* adj,n 742		فتوا	fætva *fatwa* n 4960
عیار	æjar *purity, Ayyar* n 2911		فجر	fædʒr *dawn* n,pn 3065
عیب	ejb *fault* n 4457		فدا	feda *sacrifice* adj,n 4031
عید	ejd *holiday* n 2817		فداکاری	fædakari *selfless devotion* n 4316
عیسی	isa *Jesus* pn 4105		فدراسیون	fedrasijon *federation* n 1140
عین	ejn *same, original, eye* n 660		فدرال	fedral *federal* adj 2189
عینک	ejnæk *glasses* n,pn 4787		فرآورده	færaværde *product* n 2314
عینی	ejni *objective* adj 2269		فرا	færa *beyond* adj,adv,prep 1343
غارت	ɣaræt *looting* n 3189		فرا گرفتن	færa gereftæn *surround, learn* v 3750
غافل	ɣafel *negligent, unaware* adj 2804		فراخوان	færaxan *invitation, summons* n 4916
غالب	ɣaleb *prevailing* adj,n,q 3499		فراخواندن	færaxandæn *invite, summon* adj,v 3899
غالباً	ɣalebæn *frequently* adv 3938		فرار	færar *escape* n 931
غبار	ɣobar *dust, haze* n 3002		فرار کردن	færar kærdæn *escape* v 4224
غذا	ɣæza *food* n 1275		فراری	færari *fugitive* adj,n 2299
غذایی	ɣæzaji *food* adj 1838		فراز	færaz *top* n 1630
غرب	ɣærb *west* n,pn 541		فراغت	faraɣæt *leisure* n 4264
			فراگیر	færagir *comprehensive* adj,n 2438

فراگیری   færagiri *comprehensiveness, learning* n 4337

فراموش   færamuʃ *forgotten* adj,n 2160

فراموش کردن   færamuʃ kærdæn *forget* v 2703

فراموشی   færamuʃi *oblivion, amnesia* n 3576

فرانسه   færanse *France, French* pn 389

فرانسوی   færansævi *French* adj,n 952

فراهم   færahæm *available* n 640

فراهم کردن   færahæm kærdæn *assemble* v 1310

فراوان   færavan *abundant* adj,adv 724

فراوانی   færavani *abundance* adj,n 1325

فراکسیون   fraksijon *parliamentary group* n 3979

فرایند   færajænd *process* n 1381

فرد   færd *individual* n 120

فردا   færda *tomorrow* adv,n 1216

فردوسی   ferdowsi *Ferdowsi* pn 3036

فردی   færdi *individual* adj,n 858

فرزانه   færzane *learned, wise* adj,n,pn 4639

فرزند   færzænd *child* n 527

فرستادن   ferestadæn *send* n,v 1666

فرستاده   ferestade *sent, messenger* adj,n 1856

فرسوده   færsude *worn out* adj 4309

فرش   færʃ, forʃ *carpet, silt* n 1638

فرشته   fereʃte *angel* n,pn 3968

فرصت   forsæt *opportunity* n 311

فرض   færz *assumption* n 1935

فرضی   færzi *hypothetical* adj 4808

فرضیه   færzijje *hypothesis* n 3874

فرعی   fær?i *secondary* adj 3792

فرق   færɣ *difference* n 2052

فرقه   ferɣe *sect* n 4410

فرم   form *form* n 2568

فرمان   færman *command* n 1421

فرماندار   færmandar *governor* n 3586

فرمانداری   færmandari *governorship* n 3698

فرمانده   færmande *commander* n 911

فرماندهی   færmandehi *command* n 1651

فرمایش   færmajeʃ *command* n 4942

فرمودن   færmudæn *order* v 967

فرمول   formul *formula* n 3984

فرنگی   færængi *European, Western* adj 3401

فرهاد   færhad *Farhad* pn 2814

فرهنگ   færhæng *culture* n 346

فرهنگسرا   færhængsæra *cultural center* n 4007

فرهنگی   færhængi *cultural, educational* adj 368

فرو   foru *down* adj,prep 3757

فروپاشی   forupaʃi *collapse* n 2756

فروختن   foruxtæn *sell* adj,v 1818

فرود   forud *landing* n 2655

فرودگاه   forudgah *airport* n 1264

فروردین   færværdin *Farvardin* pn 2918

فروش   foruʃ *sale* n 599

فروشگاه   foruʃgah *shop* n 3436

فروشنده   foruʃænde *salesperson, vendor* n 4550

فروشی   foruʃi *for sale* adj,v 4127

فروند   færvænd *counter for ships and planes* n 3468

فریاد   færjad *shout* n 3096

فریب   færib *deception* n 2140

فریدون   ferejdun, færidun *Fereydun* pn 4484

فزاینده   fæzajænde *increasing* adj 2766

فساد   fesad *corruption* n 1850

فشار   feʃar *pressure* n 429

فشرده   feʃorde *pressed, concise* adj,n 2791

فصل   fæsl *season, chapter* n 414

فصلی   fæsli *seasonal* adj 4731

فضا   fæza *space* n 377

فضایی   fæzaji *space* adj,n 1761

فضل   fæzl *excellence, erudition* n,pn 4272

فعال   fæ?al *active* adj,n 579

فعالیت   fæ?alijæt *activity* n 154

فعل   fe?l *verb* n 4821

فعلاً   fe?læn *at present* adv 2429

فعلی   fe?li *present* adj 1084

فقدان   feɣdan *loss, lack* n 3415

فقر   fæɣr *poverty* n 975

فقره   fæɣære *vertebra, case, incidence* n 3683

فقط   fæɣæt *only* adv 318

فقه   feɣh *Islamic law* n 3525

فقید   fæɣid *deceased* adj 4317

فقیر   fæɣir *poor* adj,n 1038

فقیه   fæɣih *Islamic jurist* adj,n 2028

فلان   folan *so and so, such and such* adj,n,pron 4094

فلج   fælædʒ *crippled* adj,n 3246

فلز   felez *metal* n 2771

فلزی   felezzi *metal* adj 3867

فلسطین   felestin *Palestine* pn 1135

فلسطینی   felestini *Palestinian* adj,n 1354

فلسفه   fælsæfe *philosophy* n 1517

فلسفی   fælsæfi *philosophical* adj 2971

فلفل   felfel *pepper* n 4383

فلوریدا   florida *Florida* pn 4450

فن   fæn *technique* n,pn 1621

فناوری   fænaværi *technology* n 1888

فنی   fænni *technical* adj 992

فهرست   fehrest *list* n 1536

فهم   fæhm *understanding* n 2731

فهمیدن   fæhmidæn *understand* v 1782

فوت   fowt, fut *death, blow* n 2396

فوتبال   futbal *soccer* n 490

فوتسال   futsal *indoor soccer* n 4141

فوراً   fowræn *immediately* adv 4492

فوری   fowri *immediate* adj,adv 2237

فوریت   fow?rijjæt *urgency* n 4057

فوریه   fevrije *February* n 3958

قطعاً   qæt?æn *certainly* adv 1552

قطعنامه   yæt?name *resolution* n 2588

قطعه   yæt?e *piece* n 1071

قطعی   yæt?i *definite* adj 1732

قلب   yælb *heart* n 1341

قلبی   yælbi *cordial, heart* adj 1875

قلعه   yæl?e *castle* n 2537

قلم   yælæm *pen* n 1201

قلمداد   yælæmdad *considered* adj,n 3049

قلمرو   yælæmrow *realm* n 3620

قله   yolle *peak* n 3431

قم   yom *Qom* pn 1528

قمری   yæmæri, yomri *lunar, turtle dove* adj 2162

قند   yænd *lump sugar* n 3037

قهرمان   yæhreman *champion* adj,n 1162

قهرمانی   yæhremani *heroism, championship* adj,n 923

قهوه   yæhve *coffee* n 4952

قوت   yovvæt, yut *strength, nourishment* n 1461

قول   yowl *promise, saying* n 997

قوم   yowm *people* n 2007

قومی   yowmi *ethnic* adj,n 2880

قوه   yovve *strength* n 874

قوی   yævi *strong* adj 1183

قیاس   yijas *analogy, comparison* n 4269

قیام   yijam *rising* n 2641

قید   yejd *restriction* n 3127

قیمت   yejmæt *price* n 530

قیمتی   yejmæti *costly, expensive* adj,n 3161

گارد   gard *guard* n 4542

گاردین   gardijen *Guardian* pn 3751

گاز   gaz *gas* n 728

گازی   gazi *gas* adj 3376

گام   gam *step* n 545

گاه   gah *time, sometimes* adv,n 707

گاو   gav *cow, bull, ox* n 4238

گذاشتن   gozaʃtæn *put, leave* adj,v 194

گذراندن   gozærandæn *spend time, pass* adj,n,pn, v 1706

گذرگاه   gozærgah *crossing point, passageway* n 4896

گذرنامه   gozærname *passport* n 4658

گذشتن   gozæʃtæn *pass* n,v 257

گذشته   gozæʃte *past* adj,n 78

گرامی   gerami *esteemed* adj 2975

گرامی داشتن   gerami daʃtæn *honor* v 4673

گرامیداشت   geramidaʃt *honoring* n 3870

گران   geran *expensive* adj 1841

گرانبها   geranbæha *precious* adj 3149

گرانی   gerani *expensive, high prices* adj,n 4070

گرایش   gerajeʃ *tendency* n 1627

گراییدن   gerajidæn *tend, incline* v 2819

گربه   gorbe *cat* n 4888

گرجستان   gordʒestan *Georgia* pn 3437

گرچه   gærtʃe *although* conj 1814

گرد   gærd, gerd, gord *powder/dust, round, champion* adj,n 1399

گردان   gærdan, gordan *turning, battalion* n 3231

گرداندن   gærdandæn *rotate, manage* v 4623

گردش   gærdeʃ *circulation* n 2090

گردشگر   gærdeʃgær *tourist* n 3353

گردشگری   gærdeʃgæri *tourism* n 2386

گردن   gærdæn *neck* n 2544

گردهمایی   gerdehæmaji *conference* n 3483

گردیدن   gærdidæn *turn* adj,v 604

گرسنگی   gorosnegi *hunger* n 2502

گرفتار   gereftar *caught, occupied* adj 2216

گرفتار شدن   gereftar ʃodæn *get caught* v 4191

گرفتاری   gereftari *captivity, trouble, involvement* n 2948

گرفتن   gereftæn *take* adj,n,v 34

گرگان   gorgan *Gorgan* pn 3519

گرم   gærm, geræm *hot, gram* adj,n 1177

گرما   gærma *heat* n 1909

گرمی   gærmi *warmth* adj,n,pn 3746

گره   gereh *knot, problem* n 2824

گرو   gerow *pledge, pawn, mortgage* n 2697

گروه   goruh *group* adj,n,q 70

گرویدن   gerævidæn *adopt a belief* v 4438

گریبان   geriban *collar* n 3781

گریختن   gorixtæn *flee* adj,v 3209

گریز   goriz *escaping* n 2984

گریه   gerje *cry* n 4171

گریه کردن   gerje kærdæn *weep, cry* v 4970

گزارش   gozareʃ *report* n 215

گزارش دادن   gozareʃ dadæn *report* v 2435

گزارش شدن   gozareʃ ʃodæn *be reported* v 2850

گزارشی   gozareʃi *reporting* n 1415

گزیده   gozide *chosen, selected, excerpt* adj,n 4826

گزینش   gozineʃ *selection* n 4857

گزینه   gozine *choice* n 1932

گستردگی   gostærdegi *span* n 4178

گسترده   gostærde *widespread* adj 812

گسترش   gostæreʃ *spread* n 542

گسترش دادن   gostæreʃ dadæn *expand* v 3747

گستره   gostære *expanse* n 3900

گشایش   goʃajeʃ *opening, relief* n 2058

گشتن   gæʃtæn *turn* n,v 658

گشودن   goʃudæn *open* n,v 2378

گشوده   goʃude *opened, open* adj 4382

گفتگو   goftogu *conversation* n 254

گفتار   goftar *speech* n 3565

گفتمان   gofteman *discourse, dialogue* n 3362

گفتن   goftæn *say* v 37

گفتنی   goftæni *mentionable* adj 1574

گفته   gofte *saying* adj,n 213

مال   mal *property* n 1591

مالزی   malezi *Malaysia* pn 2529

مالک   malek *owner* n,pn 2963

مالکیت   malekijjæt *possession* n 2455

مالی   mali *financial* adj 453

مالیات   malijat *tax, taxes* n 1425

مالیاتی   malijati *tax* adj 2674

مامان   maman *mom* n 3724

ماندگار   mandegar *lasting* adj 2367

ماندن   mandæn *stay* n,v 505

مانده   mande *stale, leftover, balance, remained* adj,v 915

مانع   mane? *obstacle* adj,n 413

مانند   manænd *like* adv,n 297

مانور   manovr *maneuver* n 3755

ماه   mah *month, moon* n 79

ماهانه   mahane *monthly* adj,adv,n 3674

ماهر   maher *skillful* adj 4656

ماهه   mahe *month* n 1915

ماهواره   mahvare *satellite* n 2602

ماهی   mahi *fish, a month* n 1434

ماهیت   mahijjæt *nature, essence* n 1923

مایع   maje? *liquid* adj,n 3369

مایل   majel *willing* adj,n,v 1453

مایه   maje *source, cause, yeast* n 1487

مبادا   mæbada *lest* adv 4707

مبادرت   mobaderæt *undertaking* n 3238

مبادله   mobadele *exchange* n 1807

مبارز   mobarez *fighter* adj,n 2078

مبارزه   mobareze *struggle* n 507

مبارک   mobaræk *blessed* adj,pn 1703

مبتلا   mobtæla *suffering from* adj,n 2868

مبتنی   mobtæni *based* adj 1570

مبدأ   mæbdæ? *origin* n 3689

مبدل   mobæddæl *transformed* adj,n 3690

مبلغ   mæblæɣ, mobælleɣ *amount, missionary* n 1510

مبنا   mæbna *base, basis* n 1104

مبنی   mæbni *based* adj 956

مبهم   mobhæm *ambiguous* adj 3610

متأثر   motæ?æsser *saddened, affected by* adj 3558

متأسفانه   mote?æssefane *unfortunately* adv 717

متجاوز   motædʒavez *aggressor, exceeding* adj, n 4326

متحد   mottæhed *united, ally* adj,n 1337

متحده   mottæhede *united* adj 2203

متحمل   motæhæmmel *suffering* adj 3522

متخصص   motexæsses *expert, specialist* adj,n 978

متخلف   motæxællef *offender* adj,n 3748

متداول   motædavel *in common use* adj 4378

متر   metr *meter* n 620

مترجم   motærdʒem *translator* n 3481

مترو   metro *metro* n 3384

متری   metri *metric, meter* n 2251

متشکر   motæʃækker *thankful, grateful* v 3916

متشکل   motæʃækkel *consisting of* adj 2312

متصل   mottæsel *connected* adj 3118

متضاد   motæzadd *opposite* adj 4522

متعادل   motæ?adel *moderate* adj 4333

متعارف   motæ?aref *common* adj 4809

متعال   motæ?al *exalted, almighty* adj 3434

متعدد   motæ?ædded *numerous* adj 768

متعلق   mottæ?ælleɣ *belonging* adj 1632

متعهد   motæ?æhhed *obliged, committed* adj 2180

متغیر   motæɣæjjer *variable* adj,n 4234

متفاوت   motæfavet *different* adj 820

متفکر   motæfækker *thinker, thoughtful* adj,n 3845

متقابل   motæɣabel *reciprocal* adj 2017

متقاضی   motæɣazi *applicant* adj,n 2126

متقاعد   motæɣa?ed *convinced* adj 4006

متمادی   motæmadi *protracted, long* adj 3602

متمایز   motæmajez *distinct* adj 4692

متمرکز   motæmærkez *concentrated* adj 2524

متن   mætn *text* n 1143

متناسب   motænaseb *elegant* adj 2055

متنوع   motænævve? *varied* adj 2614

متهم   mottæhæm *accused* adj,n 647

متوالی   motævali *successive* adj 3824

متوجه   motevædʒdʒeh *conscious* adj,n 966

متوجه شدن   motevædʒdʒeh ʃodæn *notice* v 2277

متوسط   motevæsset *average* adj,n 1500

متوسطه   motevæssete *middle, secondary (school)* adj,n 4573

متوسل   motevæssel *seeking help* adj 2831

متوقف   motevæɣɣef *stopped* adj 2208

متوقف شدن   motevæɣɣef ʃodæn *stop* v 2533

متوقف کردن   motevæɣɣef kærdæn *stop* v 3486

متولد   motevælled *born* adj,n 3349

متولد شدن   motevælled ʃodæn *be born* v 2719

متولی   motevælli *custodian, administrator* n, pn 3868

متکی   mottæki *dependent on* adj 2156

مثابه   mæsabe *similar* n 4871

مثال   mesal *example* n 1307

مثبت   mosbæt *positive* adj 673

مثل   mesl, mæsæl *like, proverb* adv,n 570

مثلاً   mæsælæn *for example* adv,conj 1047

مثنوی   mæsnævi *Masnavi* n,pn 4500

مجارستان   mædʒarestan *Hungary* pn 3924

مجاز   modʒaz, mædʒaz *allowed, metaphor* adj 1979

مجازات   modʒazat *punishment* n 1328

مجازی   mædʒazi *virtual, metaphorical* adj 4870

مجال   mædʒal *opportunity* n 3917

مجاهد   modʒahed *holy warrior* adj,n,pn 3142

مجاور   modʒaver *adjacent, neighboring* adj,n 4384

مجبور   mædʒbur *forced* adj 741

مدل	model *model* n 1702	مرکب	mærkæb, morækkæb *horse, compound/ink* adj,n 4179
مدنی	mædæni *civic, civil* adj 1752		
مدیترانه	mediterane *Mediterranean* pn 3005	مرکز	mærkæz *center* n 207
مدیر	modir *manager, director* adj,n 708	مرکزی	mærkæzi *central* adj 338
مدیرعامل	modire amel *managing director* n 2291	مریم	mærjæm *Maryam* pn 3022
مدیرکل	modirekol *director general* n 3159	مزار	mæzar *shrine, tomb* n 4901
مدیریت	modirijjæt *management* adj,n 715	مزبور	mæzbur *aforesaid* adj 3503
مدینه	mædine *Medina* pn 4364	مزرعه	mæzræʔe *farm* n 3103
مدیون	mædjun *indebted* adj 3305	مزیت	mæzijjæt *advantage* n 1687
مذاکرات	mozakerat *negotiations* n 960	مس	mes, mæss *copper, touching* n 2905
مذاکره	mozakere *negotiation* n 1221	مسئله	mæsʔæle *problem* n,pn 74
مذهب	mæzhæb *religion* n 2067	مسئول	mæsʔul *responsible* adj,n 240
مذهبی	mæzhæbi *religious* adj 896	مسئولیت	mæsʔulijjæt *responsibility* n 687
مذکور	mæzkur *mentioned* adj 1897	مسابقه	mosabeye *competition* n 384
مراجع	mæradʒe, moradʒe *references, visitor* n 2407	مساحت	mæsahæt *surface area* n 2917
		مساعد	mosaʔed *favorable* adj 3869
مراجعه	moradʒeʔe *reference* n 1133	مساعدت	mosaʔedæt *assistance* n 4439
مراد	morad *desire, Morad* n,pn 3520	مسافت	mæsafæt *distance* n 3072
مرادی	moradi *Moradi* pn 3341	مسافر	mosafer *traveler, passenger* n 873
مراسم	mærasem *ceremony* n 564	مسافربری	mosaferbæri *passenger (service)* adj,n 4229
مراقب	morayeb *minder, attentive* adj,n 2821	مسافرت	mosaferæt *travel* n 2394
مراقبت	morayebæt *supervision* n 2154	مسافرتی	mosaferæti *travel* adj,n 4943
مربع	moræbbæʔ *square* adj,n 3837	مسالمت	mosalemæt *conciliation, non-violence* n 4823
مربوط	mærbut *related* adj 489		
مربوط بودن	mærbut budæn *be relevant* v 3487	مساوی	mosavi *equal, tie* adj 2463
مربوطه	mærbute *relevant* adj 2532	مستبد	mostæbed *despotic* adj,n 4867
مربی	moræbbi *coach* n 1282	مستحکم	mostæhkæm *fortified* adj 3430
مرتب	morættæb *orderly, arranged* adj,adv 3259	مستعد	mostæʔedd *talented* adj 4235
مرتبط	mortæbet *linked* adj 1794	مستقر	mostæyærr *established* adj 1643
مرتبه	mærtæbe *time, floor* n 1314	مستقل	mostæyell *independent* adj 1144
مرتضی	morteza *Morteza* pn 3195	مستقیم	mostæyim *direct* adj 449
مرتع	mærtæʔ *pasture* n 4553	مستقیماً	mostæyimæn *directly* adv 2867
مرتفع	mortæfæʔ, mortæfe ʔ *removed, elevated* adj 4404	مستلزم	mostælzem *requiring* adj,n 3762
		مستمر	mostæmærr *continuous* adj 2302
مرتکب	mortækeb *perpetrator* adj 1878	مستند	mostænæd *documentary* adj,n 2109
مرتکب شدن	mortækeb ʃodæn *commit* v 3878	مسجد	mæsdʒed *mosque* n 788
مرجع	mærdʒæʔ *authority* adj,n 2739	مسدود	mæsdud *obstructed* adj 4108
مرحله	mærhæle *stage* n 271	مسعود	mæsʔud *Masoud* pn 2241
مرحوم	mærhum *deceased* n 2155	مسلح	mosællæh *armed* adj 1375
مرد	mærd *man* n 459	مسلحانه	mosællæhane *armed* adj 3034
مرداد	mordad *Mordad* n 2365	مسلط	mosællæt *dominant* adj 2461
مردم	mærdom *people* n 56	مسلم	moslem, mosællæm *Muslim, certain* adj,n,pn 1241
مردمی	mærdomi *popular* adj,n 1232		
مردن	mordæn *die* n,pn,v 2369	مسلماً	mosællæmæn *certainly* adv 2492
مرده	morde *dead, lifeless* adj,n 3395	مسلمان	mosælman *Muslim* adj,n 684
مردود	mærdud *rejected, failed* adj 4516	مسن	mosenn *elderly* adj 4892
مردی	mærdi *virility* n 1861	مسکن	mæskæn, mosækken *housing, sedative* n 1190
مرز	mærz *border* n 550		
مرزی	mærzi *border* adj 1831	مسکو	mosko *Moscow* pn 1783
مرغ	mory *fowl* n 2557	مسکونی	mæskuni *residential* adj 1899
مرگ	mærg *death* n 393	مسی	mesi *copper* adj 3966
مرگبار	mærgbar *deadly* adj 4472	مسیحی	mæsihi *Christian* adj,n 1633
مرمت	mæræmmæt *restoration* n 4314	مسیر	mæsir *route* n 426
مرور	morur *review* adj,n 1573	مشابه	moʃabeh *similar* adj 980

مشاركت moʃarekæt *partnership* n 577

مشاهده moʃahede *observation* n 734

مشاور moʃaver *consultant* adj,n 1542

مشاوره moʃavere *consultation* n 3239

مشت moʃt *fist* n,q 4160

مشتاق moʃtaɣ *eager* adj,n,pn 4192

مشترک moʃtæræk, moʃtærek *common, subscriber* adj 444

مشتری moʃtæri *customer, Jupiter* n,pn 1892

مشتمل moʃtæmel *containing* adj 4717

مشخص moʃæxxæs *specified* adj 345

مشخصه moʃæxxæse *characteristic* adj,n 2554

مشرف moʃærræf, moʃref *honored, near/overlooking* adj,n,pn 2877

مشروط mæʃrut *conditional* adj 3851

مشروطه mæʃrute *constitutional* adj,n 3188

مشروع mæʃruʔ *permissible* adj,n 1920

مشغله mæʃɣæle *occupation* n 2374

مشغول mæʃɣul *busy* adj 876

مشغول بودن mæʃɣul budæn *be busy* v 2940

مشمول mæʃmul *included, subject to, draftee* adj, n 2542

مشهد mæʃhæd *Mashhad* pn 1589

مشهود mæʃhud *evident* adj 3860

مشهور mæʃhur *famous* adj 1449

مشورت mæʃveræt *consultation* n 1950

مشکل moʃkel *problem* adj,n 85

مشکوک mæʃkuk *doubtful, suspicious* adj 2063

مشی mæʃʃ *gait, manner* n 4875

مصاحبه mosahebe *interview* n 1416

مصادف mosadef *coinciding, meeting* adj 3506

مصاف mæsaf *battle* n 2976

مصداق mesdaɣ *proof, typical specimen* adj,n 4527

مصر mesr *Egypt* pn 1119

مصرف mæsræf *consumption* n 517

مصرف شدن mæsræf ʃodæn *be consumed* v 3585

مصرف کردن mæsræf kærdæn *consume* v 2668

مصرف‌کننده mæsræfkonænde *consumer* adj,n 3932

مصرفی mæsræfi *consumer* adj 3587

مصری mesri *Egyptian* adj,n,pn 2778

مصطفی mostæfa *Mostafa* pn 2161

مصلحت mæslæhæt *expediency* n 1993

مصمم mosæmmæm *determined* adj 2264

مصنوعی mæsnuʔi *artificial* adj 3828

مصوب mosævvæb *ratified, approved* adj 3981

مصوبه mosævvæbe *legislation* n 1649

مصونیت mæsunijjæt *immunity* n 4770

مصیبت mosibæt *tragedy* n 4551

مضاعف mozaʔæf *double* adj 3484

مضمون mæzmun *theme* n 2601

مطابق motabeɣ *corresponding* adj 2104

مطالبه motalebe *demanding payment* n 2170

مطالعه motaleʔe *study* adj,n 886

مطالعه کردن motaleʔe kærdæn *read, study* v 4586

مطبوعات mætbuat *press* n 1476

مطبوعاتی mætbuʔati *press* adj,n 2572

مطرح mætræh *talked about, much discussed* adj 340

مطرح کردن mætræh kærdæn *propose* v 1044

مطلب mætlæb *subject* n 655

مطلع mætlæʔ, mottæleʔ *rising place, well-informed/witness* adj,n 2902

مطلق motlæɣ *absolute* adj 2467

مطلوب mætlub *desirable, desired* adj 1527

مطمئن motmæʔen *sure* adj 1604

مطهر motæhhær *pure, holy* adj,pn 3653

مظلوم mæzlum *oppressed* adj,n 3383

مظنون mæznun *suspect* adj,n 4208

مظهر mæzhær *manifestation, symbol* n 4131

معادل moʔadel *equivalent* adj 1771

معادله moʔadele *equation* n 3778

معاصر moaʔser *contemporary* adj 1460

معاف moʔaf *exempt* adj 3640

معافیت moʔafijjæt *exemption* n 3662

معالجه moʔaledʒe *medical treatment* n 4436

معامله moʔamele *transaction* adj,n 1228

معاهده moʔahede *treaty* n 4174

معاون moʔaven *assistant* n 503

معاونت moʔavenæt *directorate* n 2530

معاویه moʔavije *Muawiyah* pn 4225

معاینه moʔajene *examination* n 3713

معبر mæʔbær, moʔæbber *thoroughfare, dream interpreter* n 4046

معتاد moʔtad *addicted* adj,n 4257

معتبر moʔtæbær *reliable, valid* adj 1457

معترض moʔtærez *objector, protestor* adj,n 3097

معتقد moʔtæɣed *believing* adj,v 441

معجزه moʔdʒeze *miracle* n 4390

معدن mæʔdæn *mine* n 872

معدنی mæʔdæni *mineral* adj 2846

معدود mæʔdud *few* adj,n,q 2763

معرض mæʔræz *exhibition hall, place of exposure* n 1601

معرفت mæʔrefæt *knowledge* n 2807

معرفی moærrefi *introduction* n 555

معرفی شدن moʔærrefi ʃodæn *be introduced* v 1495

معرفی کردن moʔærrefi kærdæn *introduce* v 736

معروف mæʔruf *famous* adj,n 1072

معصوم mæʔsum *innocent* adj,n 4617

معصومه mæʔsume *Masume* pn 4137

معضل moʔzæl *difficulty* n 2388

معطوف mæʔtuf *inclined, focused* adj 3551

معظم moʔæzæm *supreme* adj 1334

معقول mæʔɣul *reasonable* adj,n 3393

معلم moʔællem *teacher* n 1269

معلول mæʔlul *disabled, effect* adj,n 3277

معلوم mæʔlum *clear* adj 1945

معلوم شدن mæʔlum ʃodæn *become known* v 3106

معمار   meʔmɑr *architect* n 3624

معماری   meʔmɑri *architecture* n 1776

معمول   mæʔmul *usual* adj 1151

معمولاً   mæʔmulæn *usually* adv 1230

معمولی   mæʔmuli *ordinary* adj 2091

معنا   mæʔnɑ *meaning* adj,n 352

معنوی   mæʔnævi *spiritual* adj 1842

معنویت   mæʔnævijjæt *spirituality* n 4526

معکوس   mæʔkus *reversed* adj 3700

معیار   meʔjɑr *standard* adj,n 1852

معیشتی   mæʔiʃæti *subsistence* adj 4535

معین   moʔæjjæn, moʔin *determined, assistant* adj,pn 1721

مغازه   mæɣɑze *shop* n 3502

مغایر   moɣɑjer *contrary* adj 3669

مغرب   mæɣreb *west, Maghreb, Morocco* n, pn 2794

مغز   mæɣz *brain* n 1650

مغزی   mæɣzi *cerebral* adj 3840

مغلوب   mæɣlub *defeated* adj 2351

مفاخر   mæfɑxer *sources of pride* n 4655

مفاد   mofɑd *substance* n 2943

مفاسد   mæfɑsed *evils, corruption* n 4620

مفصل   mæfsɑl, mofæssæl *joint, lengthy* adj,n 3509

مفصلی   mæfsæli *joint, articular* adj 4720

مفهوم   mæfhum *concept* n 1271

مفهومی   mæfhumi *conceptual* adj,n 4142

مفید   mofid *useful* adj 1594

مفیدی   mofidi *Mofidi, useful* adj,pn 4718

مقابل   moɣɑbel *opposite* adj,n,prep 343

مقابله   moɣɑbele *confronting* n 1114

مقاله   mæɣɑle *article* n 457

مقام   mæɣɑm *rank, official* n 182

مقاوم   moɣɑvem *resistant* adj 4073

مقاومت   moɣɑvemæt *resistance* n 1067

مقایسه   moɣɑjese *comparison* n 836

مقایسه کردن   moɣɑjese kærdæn *compare* v 3493

مقبره   mæɣbære *tomb* n 4724

مقتدر   moɣtæder *powerful, strong* adj 4988

مقدار   meɣdɑr *amount* adv,n,q 995

مقدس   moɣæddæs *holy* adj,n 1205

مقدم   moɣæddæm, mæɣdæm *having priority, arrival* adj,n,pn 2408

مقدمه   moɣæddæme *introduction* adj,n 567

مقر   mæɣærr, moɣerr *headquarters, confessing* n 2848

مقرر   moɣærrær *arranged* adj 2045

مقررات   moɣærrærɑt *regulations* n 1661

مقصد   mæɣsæd *destination* n 1705

مقصر   moɣæsser *guilty* adj,n 3451

مقصود   mæɣsud *purpose* n 3936

مقطع   moɣættæʔ, mæɣtæʔ *broken, section* adj, n 1324

مقطعی   mæɣtæʔi *sectional, improvised* adj,n 4276

مقوله   mæɣule *category, topic* n 2276

مقیاس   meɣjɑs *scale* n 3954

مقیم   moɣim *resident* adj 2238

مگاواتی   megɑvɑti *megawatt* adj,n,pn 4753

مگر   mægær *by chance* adv,conj 1775

ملا   mollɑ, mælæʔ *mullah, assembly* n 4133

ملاحظه   molɑheze *observation* n 723

ملاقات   molɑɣɑt *meeting* n 1185

ملاک   melɑk, mællɑk *criterion, landowner* n 3591

ملایم   molɑjem *gentle* adj 4723

ملت   mellæt *nation* n 244

ملحق   molhæɣ *joined* adj 3906

ملزم   molzæm *obliged, bound* adj 4118

ملموس   mælmus *tangible* adj 4594

ملک   mælæk, mælek, melk *angel, king, estate* n,pn 1680

ملکه   mæleke *queen* n 4979

ملکی   melki, mæleki *real estate, Maleki* adj,n,pn 4690

ملی   melli *national* adj 123

ملی شدن   melli ʃodæn *be nationalized* v 4519

ملیت   mellijjæt *nationality* n 3306

ممانعت   momɑneʔæt *prevention* n 2887

ممتاز   momtɑz *super, top* adj 2997

مملو   mæmlovv *full* adj 3474

مملکت   mæmlekæt *country* n 2330

ممنوع   mæmnuʔ *forbidden* adj 2021

ممنوعیت   mæmnuʔijjæt *prohibition* n 3300

ممکن   momken *possible* adj 167

ممیز   momæjjez *auditor, decimal point, censor* adj,n,pn 4559

من   mæn *I* pron 102

مناسب   monɑseb *appropriate* adj 416

مناسبت   monɑsebæt *suitability, relevance to occasion* n 898

منافق   monɑfeɣ *hypocritical, hypocrite* adj,n 3894

مناقشه   monɑɣeʃe *dispute* n 2609

منبع   mænbæʔ *source* n 236

منتخب   montæxæb *chosen, elected* adj,n 2138

منتشر   montæʃer *published* adj 1175

منتشر کردن   montæʃer kærdæn *publish* v 2903

منتظر   montæzer *waiting, expectant* adj 1667

منتفی   montæfi *no longer probable, canceled* adj 4965

منتقد   montæɣed *critic* adj,n 2689

منتقل   montæɣel *transferred* adj 1206

منتقل کردن   montæɣel kærdæn *transfer, transmit* v 2955

منتها   montæhɑ *extremity, but* adv,conj,n 3790

منتهی   montæhi, montæhɑ *ending, but* adj, conj 2307

منجر   mondʒær *leading to* adj 750

منحرف   monhæref *deviant* adj 3528

منحصر   monhæser *limited* adj 1942

منحل   monhæll *dissolved* adj 4847

میان	mijan *between* n,prep 45	
میانگین	mijangin *average* n 2569	
میانه	mijane *middle* adj,n,pn 1810	
میثاق	misaɣ *promise, convention* n 4266	
میدان	mejdan *plaza, square, field* n 367	
میر	mir *emir, Mir* n,pn 2338	
میراث	miras *heritage* n 1958	
میرزا	mirza *scribe, Mirza* n,pn 2112	
میز	miz *table* n 2565	
میزان	mizan *rate* n 245	
میزبان	mizban *host* adj,n 2166	
میزبانی	mizbani *hospitality* n 3464	
میسر	mojæssær *possible* adj 2474	
میل	mejl, mil *desire, rod/mile* n 2272	
میلاد	milad *birth* n 2051	
میلادی	miladi *A.D.* adj 897	
میلان	milan *Milan* pn 3066	
میلیارد	miljard *billion* n 425	
میلیون	miljun *million* n 222	
مین	min *mine* n 4481	
میهمان	mihman *guest* n 2682	
میهن	mihæn *homeland* n 2292	
میوه	mive *fruit* n 1869	
ناامنی	naæmni *insecurity* n 3116	
ناامید	naomid *hopeless* adj,adv,n 3418	
ناامیدی	naomidi *hopelessness* n 3402	
ناب	nab *pure* adj 2340	
نابرابری	nabærabæri *inequality* n 4572	
نابسامانی	nabesamani *chaos* n 4219	
نابود	nabud *destroyed* adj 3455	
نابود شدن	nabud ʃodæn *be destroyed* v 4407	
نابود کردن	nabud kærdæn *destroy* v 3152	
نابودی	nabudi *destruction* n 1516	
ناپدید	napædid *vanished* adj 2412	
ناتمام	natæmam *incomplete* adj 4358	
ناتو	nato *NATO* pn 1836	
ناتوان	natævan *unable* adj 3016	
ناتوانی	natævani *inability* n 2754	
ناجا	nadʒa *Iranian police* pn 4792	
ناچار	natʃar *compelled* adj,adv,n,v 3020	
ناچیز	natʃiz *worthless* adj 3297	
ناحیه	nahije *area* n 1549	
ناخالص	naxales *impure* adj 3030	
ناخواسته	naxaste *unwanted* adj,adv 4222	
نادر	nader *rare, Nader* adj,pn 2987	
نادرست	nadorost *incorrect* adj 2630	
نادیده گرفتن	nadide gereftæn *overlook* v 1623	
ناراحتی	narahæti *discomfort* n 3292	
ناراضی	narazi *dissatisfied* adj,n 1990	
نارسایی	naræsaji *inadequacy, insufficiency, failure* n 4873	
نارضایتی	narezajæti *dissatisfaction* n 3364	
نازل	nazel *low, humble, sent down* adj 4036	

ناشر	naʃer *publisher* n 2466
ناشناخته	naʃenaxte *unknown* adj 4047
ناشناس	naʃenas *unidentified* adj,n 2919
ناشی	naʃi *resulting* adj 791
ناصر	naser *Nasser* pn 2489
ناظر	nazer *observer* adj,n 1756
ناقص	naɣes *defective* adj 3375
ناگزیر	nagozir *inevitable* adj,adv 2985
ناگهان	nagæhan *suddenly* adv,conj 3187
ناگهانی	nagæhani *sudden* adj 3561
ناگوار	nagovar *unpleasant* adj 4568
نام	nam *name* adj,n 130
نامدار	namdar *famous* adj,n 3581
نامزد	namzæd *candidate* n 891
نامزدی	namzædi *engagement, nomination* n 4044
نامشروع	namæʃruʔ *unlawful* adj 3960
نامطلوب	namætlub *undesirable* adj 4587
نامعلوم	namæʔlum *unknown* adj 4329
نامگذاری	namgozari *giving a name* n 3044
نامناسب	namonaseb *inappropriate* adj 3340
نامه	name *letter* n 303
نامیدن	namidæn *name* adj,v 1681
نان	nan *bread* n 1640
ناو	nav *naval vessel, drain* n 3029
ناکام	nakam *frustrated* adj 3709
ناکامی	nakami *frustration* n 2387
نایب	najeb *deputy* n 2634
نبرد	næbærd *battle, didn't carry* n,v 1599
نبی	næbi *prophet* adj,n,pn 4039
نتانیاهو	netanjahu *Netanyahu* pn 4782
نتیجه	nætidʒe *result* n 92
نثر	næsr *prose* n 4725
نجات	nedʒat *rescue* n 727
نجف	nædʒæf *Najaf* pn 2743
نجفی	nædʒæfi *Najafi* pn 4601
نحو	nahv *manner, syntax* n 2493
نحوه	næhve *method* n 1668
نحوی	næhvi *syntactic, grammarian* adj, n 2348
نخبه	noxbe *elite* adj,n 2020
نخست	noxost *first* adj,adv,n 248
نخست‌وزیر	noxostvæzir *prime minister* n 1826
نرخ	nerx *rate* n 737
نرخ تورم	nerxetæværom *inflation rate* n 4820
نرگس	nærges *narcissus* n,pn 4350
نرم	nærm, norm *soft, norm* adj 1764
نرم‌افزار	nærmæfzar *software* n 4067
نزاع	nezaʔ *quarrel* n 4113
نزدیک	næzdik *close* adj,n 61
نزدیکی	næzdiki *proximity* adj,n 982
نزول	nozul *fall, descent* n 4767
نژاد	neʒad *race* n 1877
نژادی	neʒadi *racial* adj 3784
نسبت	nesbæt *relation* n 196

نوپا	nowpɑ *newly established, toddler* adj 4811	هدف	hædæf *goal, target* n 168
نوجوان	nowdʒævɑn *teenager* adj,n 1316	هدفمند	hædæfmænd *targeted, purposeful* adj 4399
نوجوانی	nowdʒævɑni *adolescence* adj,n 3866	هدیه	hedje *gift* n 2134
نود	nævæd *ninety* n 1947	هر	hær *each* q 26
نور	nur *light* n 1209	هرات	hærɑt, herɑt *Herat* pn 3554
نوروز	nowruz *Nowruz* n,pn 3068	هراس	hærɑs *fear* n 3729
نوروزی	nowruzi *Nowruz* adj,pn 3491	هراسیدن	hærɑsidæn *fear* n,v 4852
نوری	nuri *light* adj,n,pn 1824	هرچند	hærtʃænd *however* adv,conj 865
نوزاد	nowzɑd *newborn* n 3446	هرچه	hærtʃe *whatever* adv 695
نوزده	nuzdæh *nineteen* n 4793	هرگاه	hærgɑh *whenever* adv 4534
نوزدهم	nuzdæhom *nineteenth* adj,n 2827	هرگز	hærgez *never* adv 1154
نوسازی	nowsɑzi *renovating* n 2854	هرمزگان	hormozgɑn *Hormozgan* pn 4581
نوسان	nævæsɑn *fluctuation* n 2780	هرکس	hærkæs *anyone, everyone* pron 3026
نوشتن	neveʃtæn *write* adj,n,v 315	هزار	hezɑr *thousand* n 150
نوشته	neveʃte *writing* adj,n 522	هزاره	hezɑre *millennium, Hazara* n 3028
نوشیدن	nuʃidæn *drink* n,v 4361	هزینه	hæzine *cost* n 472
نوع	now? *type* n 181	هزینه کردن	hæzine kærdæn *expend* v 4831
نوید	nævid *good news, Navid* n,pn 4244	هسته	hæste *nucleus, core* n 1805
نویسندگی	nevisændegi *writing* n 4344	هستهای	hæsteji *nuclear* adj 2789
نویسنده	nevisænde *writer* n 852	هشت	hæʃt *eight* n 1079
نوین	novin *new* adj 1281	هشتاد	hæʃtɑd *eighty* n 1682
نکته	nokte *point* n 643	هشتصد	hæʃt sæd *eight hundred* n 3950
نی	nej *straw, flute* n 3817	هشتم	hæʃtom *eighth* adj,n 1554
نیاز	nijɑz *need* n 239	هشدار	hoʃdɑr *warning* n 1473
نیاز داشتن	nijɑz dɑʃtæn *need* v 1312	هفت	hæft *seven* n 853
نیازمند	nijɑzmænd *needy, in need* adj,n 1029	هفتاد	hæftɑd *seventy* n 1685
نیازی	nijɑzi *needy, Niazi* n,pn 2384	هفتصد	hæftsæd *seven hundred* n 3808
نیت	nijjæt *intent* n 1734	هفتگی	hæftegi *weekly* adj,adv,n 3232
نیجریه	nidʒerije *Nigeria* pn 4600	هفتم	hæftom *seventh* adj,n 1009
نیرو	niru *power, force* n 152	هفته	hæfte *week* n 269
نیروگاه	nirugɑh *power station* n 2289	هفتهنامه	hæftenɑme *weekly publication* n 4891
نیرومند	nirumænd *powerful* adj,pn 4595	هفده	hevdæh *seventeen* n 4425
نیز	niz *also* conj 44	هفدهم	hevdæhom *seventeenth* adj,n 3230
نیل	nil, nejl *indigo/Nile, attainment* n,pn 3833	هلند	holænd *Holland* pn 2460
نیم	nim *half* n,q 755	هلندی	holændi *Dutch* adj,n,pn 4632
نیما	nimɑ *Nima* pn 4176	هم	hæm *both, also* conj,pron 36
نیمه	nime *half* n 581	هماکنون	hæmæknun *just now* adv 3324
نیویورک	nijujork *New York* pn 1394	همان	hæmɑn *that very* pron 272
نیک	nik *good* adj,adv,n,pn 3184	همانا	hæmɑnɑ *indeed* adv 4669
نیکو	niku *good, fair, well* adj,adv,pn 4579	همانطور	hæmɑntur *as, just as* conj 2684
نیکی	niki *goodness, good deed* n,pn 3622	همانند	hæmɑnænd *similar* adv,n 1507
هادی	hɑdi *conductor, Hadi* n,pn 2265	هماهنگ	hæmɑhæng *harmonious* adj 2175
هاشم	hɑʃem *Hashem* pn 4666	هماهنگی	hæmɑhængi *harmony, coordination* n 1290
هاشمی	hɑʃemi *Hashemi* pn 2295	همایش	hæmɑjeʃ *conference* n 1008
هاله	hɑle *halo, aura* n,pn 4157	همایون	homɑjun *Homayun* pn 4592
هامبورگ	hɑmburg *Hamburg* pn 4877	همبستگی	hæmbæstegi *solidarity* n 2072
هتل	hotel *hotel* n 3206	همت	hemmæt *ambition, magnanimity* n 2012
هجده	hedʒdæh *eighteen* n 4497	همتا	hæmtɑ *peer* n 2970
هجدهم	hedʒdæhom *eighteenth* adj,n 3516	همجوار	hæmdʒævɑr *neighboring* adj 3756
هجری	hedʒri *A.H.* adj 1351	همچنان	hæmtʃenɑn *thus* adv 663
هجوم	hodʒum *attack* n 2613	همچنانکه	hæmtʃenɑnke *as* conj 4676
هخامنشی	hæxɑmæneʃi *Achaemenian* adj,pn 4528	همچنین	hæmtʃenin *so, also* conj 164
هدایت	hedɑjæt *guidance* n,pn 771	همچون	hæmtʃun *like* adv 659
هدایت کردن	hedɑjæt kærdæn *guide* v 4270	همدان	hæmedɑn *Hamadan* pn 2094

ورا	væra *beyond* n,prep,pron 4496		ویروس	virus *virus* n 3224
ورزش	værzeʃ *sport* n 961		ویژگی	viʒegi *characteristic* n 892
ورزشگاه	værzeʃgah *stadium* n 1787		ویژه	viʒe *special* adj,adv,conj 205
ورزشکار	værzeʃkar *athlete* adj,n 1722		ویلیام	viljam *William* pn 4348
ورزشی	værzeʃi *athletic* adj 880		وین	vijen *Vienna* conj,pn 2897
ورزیدن	værzidæn *exercise* n,pn,v 2228		کابل	kabol, kabl *Kabul, cable* n,pn 2157
ورشکستگی	værʃekæstegi *bankruptcy* n 4868		کابینه	kabine *cabinet* n 1963
ورق	væræɣ *sheet* n 1477		کاپیتان	kapitan *captain* n 4627
ورود	vorud *entry* n 632		کاخ	kax *palace* n 2375
ورودی	vorudi *entrance, input* adj,n 1900		کادر	kadr *cadre* n 2782
وزارت	vezaræt *ministry* n 289		کار	kar *work* n 27
وزارتخانه	vezaærætxane *ministry* n 2200		کار کردن	kar kærdæn *work* v 841
وزش	væzeʃ *blowing* n 4303		کارآمد	karamæd *skillful, proficient* adj 4614
وزن	væzn *weight* n 762		کارایی	karaji *efficiency* n 3370
وزنه	væzne *weight* n 3988		کاربر	karbær *labor intensive, user* n 3156
وزیر	væzir *minister* n 133		کاربرد	karbord *application, use* adj,n 1779
وزیری	væziri *ministerial, Vaziri* n,pn 3318		کاربردی	karbordi *applied, functional* adj,n 3422
وسط	væsæt *middle* n 1857		کاربری	karbæri *function, use* n 4893
وسعت	vosʔæt *extent* n 2275		کارت	kart *card* n 1086
وسیع	væsiʔ *large* adj 1370		کارخانه	karxane *factory* n 900
وسیله	væsile *means, instrument* n 807		کاردانی	kardani *professional skill, 2-year degree* adj,n 4951
وصف	væsf *description* n 4392			
وصل	væsl *union, joining* n 3832		کارشناس	karʃenas *expert* n 661
وصول	vosul *collection* n 4401		کارشناسی	karʃenasi *expertise, bachelor's degree* adj,n 2097
وضع	væzʔ *situation, condition* n 463			
وضعیت	væzʔijjæt *situation* n 322		کارفرما	karfærma ʿemployer* n 3919
وضوح	vozuh *clarity* adj,n 3940		کارگاه	kargah *workshop* n 2509
وطن	vætæn *homeland* adj,n,pn 3291		کارگر	kargær *worker* n 1015
وظیفه	væzife *duty* n 578		کارگردان	kargærdan *director* n 2671
وعده	væʔde *promise* n 1049		کارگردانی	kargærdani *direction* n 3302
وفا	væfa *loyalty* n 4989		کارگری	kargæri *labor, workers* adj,n 3495
وفادار	væfadar *faithful, loyal* adj 3131		کارگزار	kargozar *agent* adj,n 3921
وفاداری	væfadari *loyalty* n 1689		کارمند	karmænd *employee* n 1347
وفاق	vefaɣ *harmony* n 4589		کارنامه	karname *report card* n 2548
وقت	væɣt *time* n 410		کاروان	karevan *caravan* n 2354
وقتی	væɣti *when* conj,n 411		کارکرد	karkærd *performance, mileage* n 2979
وقف	væɣf *religious endowment, devotion* n 4200		کارکنان	karkonan *employees* n 1332
وقفه	væɣfe *pause* n 4646		کاری	kari *active, working* adj,n 392
وقوع	voɣuʔ *occurrence* n 1169		کاریکاتور	karikatur *caricature, cartoon* n 4912
وگرنه	vægærne *otherwise* conj 4734		کاستن	kastæn *reduce* adj,n,v 2410
ولادیمیر	veladimir *Vladimir* pn 4041		کاستی	kasti *decrease, shortcoming* n 4285
ولایت	velajæt *province* n 1641		کاسه	kase *bowl* n 4957
ولایتی	velajæti *provincial* adj,n,pn 4956		کاش	kaʃ *I wish* adv 4468
ولسوالی	volosvali *Afghan county* n 4486		کاشان	kaʃan *Kashan* pn 2946
ولی	væli *but* conj 131		کاشانی	kaʃani *Kashani* adj,pn 3859
ولیعهد	væliʔæhd *crown prince* n 4806		کاشتن	kaʃtæn *plant* n,v 3758
وکالت	vekalæt *lawyering, power of attorney* n 4552		کاشی	kaʃi *Kashani, tile* n,pn 2960
وکیل	vækil *attorney* n,pn 1300		کاظم	kazem *Kazem* pn 1746
وی	vej *he, she* pron 116		کاظمی	kazemi *Kazemi* pn 4700
ویتامین	vitamin *vitamin* n 3799		کاغذ	kaɣæz *paper* n 2910
ویتنام	vijetnam *Vietnam* pn 3250		کافی	kafi *sufficient* adj 492
ویران	viran *ruined* adj 3930		کالا	kala *goods* n 721
ویرانی	virani *destruction* n 4144		کالیفرنیا	kalifornija *California* pn 3688

کام	kam *palate, goal, com* n 3579		کشتیرانی	keʃtirani *shipping* n 4267
کامپیوتر	kampjuter *computer* n 3279		کشف	kæʃf *discovery* n 921
کامران	kamran *Kamran* pn 4974		کشمکش	keʃmækeʃ *conflict* n 3257
کامل	kamel *complete* adj 234		کشور	keʃvær *country* n 33
کامل شدن	kamel ʃodæn *be completed, perfected* v 4862		کشوری	keʃværi *state* adj,n 1039
			کشیدن	keʃidæn *pull, draw* conj,n,v 786
کاملاً	kamelæn *completely* adv 212		کشیده	keʃide *tall, slap* adj 1147
کامیون	kamjon *truck* n 2382		کف	kæf *bottom, palm, foam* n 2816
کانادا	kanada *Canada* pn 1801		کفایت	kefajæt *adequacy* n 3592
کانادایی	kanadaji *Canadian* adj 4475		کفش	kæfʃ *shoe* n 3844
کانال	kanal *channel, canal* n 2149		کل	kol *whole, total* n,q 366
کاندیدا	kandida *candidate* n 3233		کلاً	kollæn *totally* adv 4207
کانون	kanun *focus, association* n 1652		کلاس	kelas *class* n 1010
کاهش	kaheʃ *decrease* n 266		کلاسیک	kelasik *classic* adj 3205
کاهیدن	kahidæn *decline* v 4758		کلام	kælam *speech* n 1579
کاوش	kavoʃ *excavation* n 4416		کلامی	kælami *verbal* adj,n 4583
کبیر	kæbir *great, adult* adj,pn 3821		کلان	kælan *big, macro-* adj 1710
کتاب	ketab *book* n 200		کلانتری	kælantæri *police station* n,pn 4976
کتابخانه	ketabxane *library* n 2141		کلاه	kolah *hat* n 4256
کتابی	ketabi *bookish, flat* adj,n 2231		کلمبیا	kolombija *Colombia* pn 3407
کتبی	kætbi *written* adj 4081		کلمه	kælæme *word* n 1422
کتیبه	kætibe *inscription* n 4198		کلی	kolli *total, general* adj 355
کثیر	kæsir *numerous, abundant* adj,n,pn 4996		کلیات	kollijjat *generalities, general works* n 3323
کجا	kodʒa *where* adv,n,v 1545		کلید	kelid *key, switch* n 2347
کد	kædd, kod *toil, code* n 3381		کلیدی	kelidi *key* adj,n 2224
کدام	kodam *which* n 682		کلیسا	kelisa *church* n 2444
کرامت	kæramæt *generosity, dignity* n 3627		کلینتون	kelinton *Clinton* pn 2392
کرانه	kerane *shore* n 3710		کلیه	kolje, kollije *kidney, all* n,q 1083
کربلا	kærbæla *Karbala* pn 3060		کم	kæm *low, little* adj,adv,n,q 60
کرج	kæradʒ *Karaj* pn 3055		کمال	kæmal *perfection* n,pn 1538
کرد	kærd, kord *did, Kurd* v 18		کماکان	kæmakan *as before, still* adv 3903
کردستان	kordestan *Kurdistan* pn 2376		کمبود	kæmbud *shortage* n 1229
کردن	kærdæn *do* adj,n,v 17		کمپانی	kompani *company* n 4083
کرزی	kærzæj *Karzai* pn 3047		کمر	kæmær *waist* n 4140
کرسی	korsi *seat* n 1864		کمربند	kæmærbænd *belt* n,pn 4290
کرمان	kerman *Kerman* pn 1911		کمرنگ	kæmræng *pale* adj 2912
کرمانشاه	kermanʃah *Kermanshah* pn 2628		کمونیست	komonist *communist* adj,n 3125
کره	kære, kore, korre *butter, Korea/globe, foal* n,pn 1675		کمونیستی	komonisti *communist* adj 4824
			کمک	komæk *help* n 293
کره‌جنوبی	korejedʒonubi *South Korea* pn 4230		کمک گرفتن	komæk gereftæn *get help* v 3563
کروبی	kærrubi *Karroubi* pn 3925		کمک کردن	komæk kærdæn *help* v 861
کریم	kærim *generous, great* adj,pn 1867		کمکی	komæki *auxiliary* adj,n 1862
کریمی	kærimi *Karimi* pn 2845		کمیته	komite *committee* n 711
کس	kæs *person* n 146		کمیسیون	komisijon *commission* n 801
کسب	kæsb *acquisition, business* n 519		کمین	kæmin *ambush* n 4107
کسری	kæsri, kæsra *deficit, Kasra* n,pn 3075		کنار	kenar *beside* n,prep 353
کشاندن	keʃandæn *drag, pull* adj,n,v 752		کنار گذاشتن	kenar gozaʃtæn *put away* v 2681
کشاورز	keʃaværz *farmer* n,pn 2084		کناره	kenare *edge, bank* n 3956
کشاورزی	keʃaværzi *agriculture* adj,n 826		کناره‌گیری	kenaregiri *resignation* n 4199
کشتار	koʃtar *killing* n 2432		کنترل	kontrol *control* n 495
کشتن	koʃtæn *kill* n,v 903		کند	konæd, kond *does, slow* v 49
کشته	koʃte, keʃte *killed, cultivated* adj,n 819		کندی	kondi, kenedi *slowness, Kennedy* n,pn 3852
کشتی	keʃti, koʃti *ship, wrestling* n 823		کنسرت	konsert *concert* n 3577

كنفدراسيون konfederasijon confederation n 4109

كنفرانس konferans conference n 699

كنگره kongere congress n 1303

كننده konænde doer n 738

كنوانسيون konvansijon convention n 3855

كنون konun now adv,n 3413

كنونى konuni present adj 761

كنكور konkur entrance exam n 4819

كه ke which conj 5

كهن kohæn old adj 2419

كهنه kohne old adj 2981

كوبا kuba Cuba pn 3524

كوبيدن kubidæn pound, grind n,v 3039

كوتاه kutah short adj 364

كوتاهى kutahi brevity, negligence adj,n 1598

كوچ kutʃ migration n 4688

كوچه kutʃe lane n 2364

كوچك kutʃæk small adj 432

كوچكى kutʃæki smallness adj,n 2061

كود kud fertilizer, manure n 3861

كودتا kudeta coup d'état n 2101

كودك kudæk child n 467

كودكى kudæki childhood n 1999

كور kur blind adj,n 3342

كوره kure furnace n 3745

كوشش kuʃeʃ effort n 1844

كوشيدن kuʃidæn attempt v 1506

كوفى kufi Kufic, Kofi adj,pn 3352

كوه kuh mountain n 1678

كوهستان kuhestan highland, mountain country n 3977

كوهستانى kuhestani mountainous adj 4074

كوهى kuhi mountain adj,n,pn 4762

كوى kuj quarter, alley, street n 3427

كويت kovejt Kuwait pn 1967

كوير kævir salt desert n 4796

كى kej, ki when, who adv 1931

كيست kist who is, cyst v 4038

كيسه kise bag n 4156

كيش kiʃ faith, Kish n,pn 2708

كيف kif, kejf bag, intoxication n,pn 3678

كيفرى kejfæri penal, criminal adj,n 4807

كيفى kejfi, kifi qualitative, portable adj 2128

كيفيت kejfijjæt quality n 953

كيلو kilo kilo, kilogram n 1749

كيلوگرم kilogræm kilogram n 1393

كيلومتر kilometr kilometer n 1022

كيلومترى kilometri kilometer adj,n 2167

كينه kine grudge n 3744

كيهان kejhan universe n,pn 4906

يا ja or conj 41

ياد jad memory n 583

ياد گرفتن jad gereftæn learn v 3275

ياد كردن jad kærdæn remember v 2722

يادآور jadavær reminder, memento, reminiscent adj 3354

يادآورى jadaværi reminder n 4051

يادداشت jaddæʃt note n 1882

يادگار jadegar souvenir n 1494

يادگيرى jadgiri learning n 2884

يار jar sweetheart, friend, partner n 1259

يارانه jarane subsidy n 2820

يارى jari help n 1533

يازده jazdæh eleven n 2165

يازدهم jazdæhom eleventh adj,n 2232

ياس jas, jæʔs jasmine, despair n 3705

يافتن jaftæn find n,v 99

يافته jafte found, finding adj,v 279

يخ jæx ice n 3560

يخچال jæxtʃal refrigerator n 4544

يزد jæzd Yazd pn 2787

يزدى jæzdi Yazdi adj,pn 4532

يعنى jæʔni namely, meaning adv,conj 95

يقين jæyin certain n 3796

يقيناً jæyinæn certainly adv,conj 4634

يگان jegan detachment n,pn 4882

يگانه jegane unique, sole adj,pn 4491

يمن jæmæn, jomn Yemen, auspiciousness pn 2623

ين jen yen n 4948

يهود jæhud Jewry pn 4774

يهودى jæhudi Jew, Jewish adj,n,pn 1846

يورش joreʃ attack n 4110

يورو juro Euro n,pn 1982

يوسف jusof, jusef Joseph pn 2441

يوسفى jusefi Yusefi pn 4456

يوم jowm day n 1235

يونان junan Greece pn 1614

يونانى junani Greek adj,n,pn 2616

يونسكو junesko UNESCO pn 3307

يك jek one n,pron 12

يكبار jekbar once adv 2862

يكباره jekbare all at once adj,adv 4615

يكپارچگى jekpartʃegi integrity n 4505

يكپارچه jekpartʃe whole, entirely adj,adv 3157

يكديگر jekdigær each other pron 674

يكسال jeksal one year adv,n 3783

يكسان jeksan similar adj,adv 2214

يكسانى jeksani identicality adj,n 3997

يكشنبه jekʃæmbe Sunday n 1433

يكصد jeksæd one hundred n 1930

يكم jekom first adj,n 2345

Part of speech index

Rank, **word family head**, pronunciation, *gloss*

Adjectives: 1551 words

9 شدن	ʃodæn *become*	
17 کردن	kærdæn *do*	
20 اول	ævvæl *first*	
24 رسیدن	residæn *arrive*	
25 پس	pæs *then*	
28 بیش	biʃ *more*	
29 دیگر	digær *other*	
34 گرفتن	gereftæn *take*	
35 پیش	piʃ *before*	
38 بزرگ	bozorg *large*	
48 داشته	dɑʃte *had, possession*	
50 داده	dɑde *given, datum*	
51 بسیار	besjɑr *very*	
52 قبل	ɣæbl *before*	
57 تنها	tænhɑ *only*	
59 مهم	mohem *important*	
60 کم	kæm *low, little*	
61 نزدیک	næzdik *close*	
65 تمام	tæmɑm *whole, all*	
70 گروه	goruh *group*	
78 گذشته	gozæʃte *past*	
85 مشکل	moʃkel *problem*	
86 اسلامی	eslɑmi *Islamic*	
89 بهتر	behtær *better*	
93 آمدن	ɑmædæn *come*	
100 مختلف	moxtælef *different*	
101 بالا	bɑlɑ *top, high*	
103 سیاسی	sijɑsi *political*	
108 جدید	dʒædid *new*	
112 آوردن	ɑværdæn *bring*	
114 وارد	vɑred *enter*	
118 بعد	bæʔd *then, after*	
122 جوان	dʒævɑn *young*	
123 ملی	melli *national*	
126 دوم	dovvom *second*	
128 رفتن	ræftæn *go*	
130 نام	nɑm *name*	
136 حرکت	hærekæt *motion, movement*	
149 اقتصادی	eɣtesɑdi *economic*	
158 حاضر	hɑzer *present, ready*	
159 درصد	dærsæd *percent*	
167 ممکن	momken *possible*	
170 بزرگی	bozorgi *magnitude*	

175 ارزش	ærzeʃ *value*	
180 آینده	ɑjænde *future*	
183 زیادی	zijɑdi *excessive*	
186 اصلی	æsli *main*	
188 آخر	ɑxær *final*	
192 رساندن	resɑndæn *deliver*	
194 گذاشتن	gozɑʃtæn *put, leave*	
195 شکل	ʃekl *shape*	
198 خارجی	xɑredʒi *foreign*	
199 همراه	hæmrɑh *together*	
203 جهانی	dʒæhɑni *global*	
205 ویژه	viʒe *special*	
209 اطلاع	ettelɑʔ *information*	
211 پرداختن	pærdɑxtæn *pay, engage in*	
213 گفته	gofte *saying*	
214 زن	zæn *woman, wife*	
227 برابر	bærɑbær *equal, opposite*	
230 سوم	sevvom *third*	
231 خدمت	xedmæt *service*	
233 ایرانی	irɑni *Iranian*	
234 کامل	kɑmel *complete*	
235 آزاد	ɑzɑd *free*	
237 خط	xætt *line*	
240 مسئول	mæsʔul *responsible*	
248 نخست	noxost *first*	
253 انتخاب	entexɑb *selection, choice*	
255 موفق	movæffæɣ *successful*	
261 عامل	ɑmel *agent, factor*	
267 اخیر	æxir *recent*	
279 یافته	jɑfte *found, finding*	
280 خواندن	xɑndæn *read*	
283 دور	dowr, dur *period, far*	
287 برگزار	bærgozɑr *held*	
290 دیده	dide *eye, seen*	
294 قابل	ɣɑbel *capable*	
296 زیر	zir *under*	
305 نمودن	nemudæn *show, do*	
306 عمومی	omumi *public*	
307 جدی	dʒeddi *serious*	
310 زدن	zædæn *strike, beat*	
315 نوشتن	neveʃtæn *write*	
320 داخلی	dɑxeli *internal*	

326 لازم	lɑzem *necessary*	
333 علمی	elmi *scientific*	
335 اجتماعی	edʒtemɑʔi *social*	
338 مرکزی	mærkæzi *central*	
340 مطرح	mætræh *talked about, much discussed*	
341 انسانی	ensɑni *human*	
342 خاص	xɑss *specific*	
343 مقابل	moɣɑbel *opposite*	
345 مشخص	moʃæxxæs *specified*	
352 معنا	mæʔnɑ *meaning*	
355 کلی	kolli *total, general*	
359 جمعیت	dʒæmʔijjæt *population*	
364 کوتاه	kutɑh *short*	
368 فرهنگی	færhængi *cultural, educational*	
391 واحد	vɑhed *unit*	
392 کاری	kɑri *active, working*	
396 زمانی	zæmɑni *chronological*	
398 موافق	movɑfeɣ *agreeable*	
399 شهید	ʃæhid *martyr*	
400 شاهد	ʃɑhed *witness*	
413 مانع	mɑneʔ *obstacle*	
416 مناسب	monɑseb *appropriate*	
420 حاکم	hɑkem *ruler*	
421 آماده	ɑmɑde *ready*	
428 موجود	mowdʒud *available, creature*	
432 کوچک	kutʃæk *small*	
434 پیدا	pejdɑ *find*	
435 طولانی	tulɑni *long*	
441 معتقد	moʔtæɣed *believing*	
443 چهارم	tʃæhɑrom *fourth*	
444 مشترک	moʃtæræk, moʃtærek *common, subscriber*	
445 خوبی	xubi *goodness*	
446 زیاد	zijɑd *a lot*	
449 مستقیم	mostæɣim *direct*	
452 آمریکایی	amrikɑji *American*	
453 مالی	mɑli *financial*	
455 تازه	tɑze *fresh*	
456 ساخته	sɑxte *manufactured*	
461 واقعی	vɑɣeʔi *real*	
466 دینی	dini *religious*	
470 دولتی	dowlæti *governmental*	

471 رسمی	ræsmi *official*	
478 انگلیسی	engelisi *English*	
483 سنگین	sængin *heavy*	
486 نظامی	nezami *military*	
488 شدید	ʃædid *severe*	
489 مربوط	mærbut *related*	
491 واقع	vaɣeʔ *located*	
492 کافی	kafi *sufficient*	
509 نمونه	nemune *sample*	
510 خوب	xub *good*	
512 پنج	pændʒ *five*	
514 باز	baz *open*	
520 آمار	amar *statistics*	
522 نوشته	neveʃte *writing*	
525 دارا	dara *having*	
544 روشن	rowʃæn *bright, turned on*	
547 احساس	ehsas *feeling*	
549 قرارداد	ɣærardad *contract*	
561 خارجه	xaredʒe *foreign*	
567 مقدمه	moɣæddæme *introduction*	
571 سخت	sæxt *hard*	
575 سرعت	sorʔæt *speed*	
576 بین‌المللی	bejnolmelæli *international*	
579 فعال	fæʔal *active*	
580 رقم	ræɣæm *digit, number*	
585 برداشتن	bærdaʃtæn *pick up, remove*	
586 سریع	særiʔ *fast*	
589 تاریخی	tarixi *historical*	
592 مخالف	moxalef *opposed*	
604 گردیدن	gærdidæn *turn*	
605 صرف	særf, serf *spending/ consuming, pure*	
607 نمایش	næmajeʃ *exhibiting, display*	
608 اساسی	æsasi *basic*	
609 قبلی	ɣæbli *previous*	
610 پایه	paje *base*	
616 اعتقاد	eʔteɣad *belief*	
617 شعر	ʃeʔr *poetry*	
618 نو	now *new*	
624 محسوب	mæhsub *considered*	
630 غربی	ɣærbi *western*	
634 پرواز	pærvaz *flight*	
645 سابق	sabeɣ *former*	
646 گویا	guja *talking, clear, seems*	
647 متهم	mottæhæm *accused*	
651 قانونی	ɣanuni *legal*	
652 ادعا	eddeʔa *claim*	
664 شامل	ʃamel *included*	
668 نظارت	nezaræt *supervision*	
669 طبیعی	tæbiʔi *natural*	
671 صنعتی	sænʔæti *industrial*	
673 مثبت	mosbæt *positive*	
676 خلاف	xælaf *contrary*	
679 حکم	hokm *order, sentence*	
681 شخصیت	ʃæxsijjæt *personality*	
684 مسلمان	mosælman *Muslim*	
685 ساز	saz *instrument*	
686 خوردن	xordæn *eat*	
693 خصوصی	xosusi *private*	
696 وابسته	vabæste *dependent*	
698 ترک	tærk, tork *leave, Turk*	
702 بسته	bæste *package*	
705 شناختن	ʃenaxtæn *know, recognize*	
708 مدیر	modir *manager, director*	
714 بخشیدن	bæxʃidæn *forgive, give*	
715 مدیریت	modirijjæt *management*	
720 صورتی	suræti *pink, a form*	
724 فراوان	færavan *abundant*	
725 پیچیده	piʧide *complex*	
731 عالی	ali *high*	
732 بعدی	bæʔdi *next*	
741 مجبور	mædʒbur *forced*	
742 عکس	æks *picture*	
744 خبری	xæbæri *news*	
750 منجر	mondʒær *leading to*	
752 کشاندن	keʃandæn *drag, pull*	
757 رد	rædd *refusal, trail*	
761 کنونی	konuni *present*	
768 متعدد	motæʔædded *numerous*	
774 نشستن	neʃæstæn *sit*	
782 راهی	rahi *bound for, a path*	
790 پایین	pajin *bottom*	
791 ناشی	naʃi *resulting*	
792 روبرو	ruberu *opposite*	
793 دقیق	dæɣiɣ *exact*	
798 محقق	mohæɣɣeɣ, mohæɣɣæɣ *scholar, ascertained*	
799 ساکن	saken *resident*	
802 خواسته	xaste *demand*	
804 امتیاز	emtijaz *point, privilege*	
812 گسترده	gostærde *widespread*	
813 دوباره	dobare *again*	
817 اشتباه	eʃtebah *mistake*	
819 کشته	koʃte, keʃte *killed, cultivated*	
820 متفاوت	motæfavet *different*	
824 جنوبی	dʒonubi *southern*	
826 کشاورزی	keʃaværzi *agriculture*	
828 شناخته	ʃenaxte *known*	
831 پست	post *post*	
833 باقی	baɣi *remaining*	
835 جمعی	dʒæmʔi *collective*	
837 زمینی	zæmini *land, earthling*	
843 محروم	mæhrum *deprived, banned*	
846 قضایی	ɣæzaji *judiciary*	
847 پزشکی	pezeʃki *medical*	
849 آموزشی	amuzeʃi *educational*	
850 افتادن	oftadæn *fall*	
857 دچار	doʧar *afflicted with*	
858 فردی	færdi *individual*	
859 دختر	doxtær *girl, daughter*	
860 نهایی	nahaji *final*	
864 ابزار	æbzar *tool*	
871 قربانی	ɣorbani *victim, sacrifice*	
875 زیبا	ziba *beautiful*	
876 مشغول	mæʃɣul *busy*	
877 حاصل	hasel *result*	
880 ورزشی	værzeʃi *athletic*	
885 پر	pær, por *feather, full*	
886 مطالعه	motaleʔe *study*	
894 شیعه	ʃiʔe *Shiite*	
896 مذهبی	mæzhæbi *religious*	
897 میلادی	miladi *A.D.*	
899 محترم	mohtæræm *honorable*	
904 محلی	mæhælli *local*	
905 عادی	adi *normal*	
907 قدیمی	ɣædimi *old, old-fashioned*	
914 اروپایی	orupaji *European*	
915 مانده	mande *stale, leftover, balance*	
916 عدالت	edalæt *justice*	
923 قهرمانی	ɣæhremani *heroism, championship*	
926 شمالی	ʃomali *northern*	
928 ساده	sade *simple*	
929 قادر	ɣader *able*	
932 زنده	zende *live*	
934 سالم	salem *healthy*	
938 طلا	tæla *gold*	
939 هوایی	hævaji *aerial*	
942 عرب	æræb *Arab*	
943 جاری	dʒari *flowing, current, sister-in-law*	
947 دانشمند	daneʃmænd *scientist*	

1400 سری	seri, særi *series, a head*	1554 هشتم	hæʃtom *eighth*	1695 جنگی	dʒængi *military*
1401 عقب	æɣæb *back*	1555 درگیر	dærgir *involved*	1697 صادر	sader *issued, exported*
1403 سبز	sæbz *green*	1562 درمانی	dærmani *therapeutic*	1699 ادبی	ædæbi *literary*
1405 هنری	honæri *artistic*	1570 مبتنی	mobtæni *based*	1703 مبارک	mobaræk *blessed*
1406 سرد	særd *cold*	1571 علاقمند	ælaɣemænd *interested*	1706 گذراندن	gozærandæn *spend time, pass*
1407 دشوار	doʃvar *difficult*	1573 مرور	morur *review*	1710 کلان	kælan *big, macro-*
1418 احتمالی	ehtemali *probable*	1574 گفتنی	goftæni *mentionable*	1714 اردو	ordu *camp*
1420 روسی	rusi *Russian*	1578 پیوسته	pejvæste *connected, permanent*	1717 سنگینی	sangini *weight*
1423 منطقی	mænteɣi *logical*			1718 مخصوص	mæxsus *special*
1426 راهکار	rahkar *strategy, solution*	1582 الهی	elahi *divine*	1721 معین	moʔæjjæn, moʔin *determined, assistant*
		1583 منطقهای	mæntæɣeʔi *regional*		
1428 مادی	maddi *material*	1588 سازنده	sazænde *manufacturer, constructive*	1722 ورزشکار	værzeʃkar *athlete*
1437 پایدار	pajdar *stable*			1724 وادار	vadar *persuaded*
1438 روانی	rævani *fluency, psychotic*	1594 مفید	mofid *useful*	1732 قطعی	ɣætʔi *definite*
		1595 سیاه	sijah *black*	1740 خالی	xali *empty*
1443 شریف	ʃærif *honorable*	1597 سفید	sefid *white*	1741 برگزیده	bærgozide *choice, elite*
1449 مشهور	mæʃhur *famous*	1598 کوتاهی	kutahi *brevity, negligence*	1742 پاک	pak *pure*
1451 شبیه	ʃæbih *similar*			1744 ربودن	robudæn *steal*
1453 مایل	majel *willing*	1604 مطمئن	motmæʔen *sure*	1747 پذیرفته	pæzirofte *accepted, admitted*
1456 تولیدی	towlidi *manufactured, manufacturing*	1607 نماد	næmad *symbol*		
		1609 نقد	næɣd *cash, critique*	1751 محمدی	mohæmmædi *Mohammadi*
1457 معتبر	moʔtæbær *reliable, valid*	1618 پایانی	pajani *final*	1752 مدنی	mædæni *civic, civil*
		1622 روزه	ruze *fast*	1754 انتظامی	entezami *security*
1460 معاصر	moaʔser *contemporary*	1628 ارشد	ærʃæd *elder, senior*	1756 ناظر	nazer *observer*
1467 تلویزیونی	televizioni *television*	1632 متعلق	mottæʔælleɣ *belonging*	1757 بیستم	bistom *twentieth*
1480 اداری	edari *administrative*			1758 راست	rast *right*
1481 استاندارد	estandard *standard*	1633 مسیحی	mæsihi *Christian*	1759 تعطیل	tæʔtil *holiday*
1483 جایگزین	dʒajgozin *replacement*	1637 برخوردار	bærxordar *in possession of*	1761 فضایی	fæzaji *space*
1493 ارزشمند	ærzeʃmænd *valuable*	1639 آشنا	aʃna *familiar*	1764 نرم	nærm, norm *soft, norm*
1500 متوسط	motævæsset *average*	1643 مستقر	mostæɣærr *established*		
1501 خواهان	xahan *plaintiff, desirous*	1644 قاتل	ɣatel *killer*	1771 معادل	moʔadel *equivalent*
		1647 بیانگر	bæjangær *expressive, indicative*	1774 قضاییه	ɣæzaʔijje *judiciary*
1511 تکلیف	tæklif *task*			1779 کاربرد	karbord *application, use*
1512 گوناگون	gunagun *various*	1654 درستی	dorosti *correctness, truth*		
1513 ریختن	rixtæn *pour*			1785 دوربین	durbin *camera*
1515 چشمگیر	ʧeʃmgir *impressive*	1656 پولی	puli *monetary*	1792 نمایان	nemajan *apparent, visible*
1520 زود	zud *soon*	1662 بانکی	banki *banking*		
1521 شیرین	ʃirin *sweet*	1663 مخفی	mæxfi *hidden*	1793 پژوهشگر	pæʒuheʃgær *researcher*
1522 حکومتی	hokumæti *governmental*	1667 منتظر	montæzer *waiting, expectant*	1794 مرتبط	mortæbet *linked*
1523 حاکی	haki *indicative*	1673 خوش	xoʃ *good*	1796 آباد	abad *place*
1526 تفاهم	tæfahom *understanding*	1679 درآمدن	dæramædæn *emerge*	1800 بومی	bumi *native*
1527 مطلوب	mætlub *desirable, desired*	1681 نامیدن	namidæn *name*	1802 ثروتمند	servætmænd *wealthy*
		1683 انتخاباتی	entexabati *electoral*	1806 اتحاد	ettehad *union, alliance*
1539 سبک	sæbk, sæbok *style, light*	1686 بیگانه	bigane *foreign, alien*		
		1688 مهندسی	mohændesi *engineering*	1810 میانه	mijane *middle*
1540 حقیقی	hæɣiɣi *real*			1812 دستی	dæsti *manual, handmade, tame*
1542 مشاور	moʃaver *consultant*	1690 تک	tæk, tok *single/attack, tip*		
1543 دانشگاهی	daneʃgahi *academic, university*			1818 فروختن	foruxtæn *sell*
1551 غنی	ɣæni *rich*	1692 آسان	asan *easy*	1821 بالغ	baleɣ *adult, mature*

2224 کلیدی	kelidi *key*	
2230 افراطی	efrati *extremist*	
2231 کتابی	ketabi *bookish, flask*	
2232 یازدهم	jazdæhom *eleventh*	
2237 فوری	fowri *immediate*	
2238 مقیم	moyim *resident*	
2243 دریافتن	dærjaftæn *perceive, receive*	
2245 دشواری	doʃvari *difficulty*	
2247 حساسیت	hæssasijjæt *sensitivity*	
2250 تلخ	tælx *bitter*	
2255 پوشاندن	puʃandæn *dress*	
2259 درونی	dæruni *inner*	
2260 فیلسوف	filsuf *philosopher*	
2261 عراقی	erayi *Iraqi*	
2262 اتمی	ætomi *atomic*	
2264 مصمم	mosæmmæm *determined*	
2269 عینی	ejni *objective*	
2270 پیرو	pejrow *follower*	
2271 امین	æmin *honest, Amin*	
2278 پاره	pare *torn, part*	
2280 مجهز	modʒæhhæz *well-equipped*	
2285 خانوادگی	xanevadegi *familial*	
2293 حرفه‌ای	herfeji *professional*	
2294 صدد	sædæd *intention*	
2297 مکرر	mokærrær *repeated*	
2299 فراری	færari *fugitive*	
2302 مستمر	mostæmærr *continuous*	
2304 راهنمایی	rahnæmaji *guidance*	
2305 پراکنده	pærakænde *dispersed*	
2307 منتهی	montæhi, montæha *ending, but*	
2308 ابتدایی	ebtedaji *elementary*	
2311 اسرائیلی	esraʔili *Israeli*	
2312 متشکل	motæʃækkel *consisting of*	
2315 عادلانه	adelane *justly*	
2324 برقی	bæryi *electric*	
2325 بازتاب	baztab *reflection*	
2326 سینمایی	sinemaji *cinematic*	
2328 همگانی	hæmegani *public, general*	
2333 دارویی	daruji *pharmaceutical*	
2336 آسمانی	asemani *heavenly*	
2337 ریاضی	rijazi *mathematical*	
2340 ناب	nab *pure*	
2342 جور	dʒur *sort*	
2345 یکم	jekom *first*	
2348 نحوی	nahvi *syntactic, grammarian*	

2351 مغلوب	mæylub *defeated*	
2353 پژوهشی	pæʒuheʃi *research*	
2356 هوادار	hævadar *supporter*	
2359 حامل	hamel *carrier*	
2367 ماندگار	mandegar *lasting*	
2368 خرد	xeræd, xord *wisdom, small*	
2372 روحی	ruhi *spiritual, mental*	
2379 غلط	yælæt *mistake*	
2380 عباسی	æbbasi *Abbasi, Abbasid*	
2383 صادق	sadey *truthful*	
2389 درآوردن	dæraværdæn *extract, produce*	
2391 حامی	hami *protector*	
2393 خوشحال	xoʃhal *happy*	
2395 محض	mæhz *pure*	
2400 نقره	noyre *silver*	
2401 جانی	dʒani *sincere, criminal*	
2408 مقدم	moyæddæm, mæydæm *having priority, arrival*	
2410 کاستن	kastæn *reduce*	
2412 ناپدید	napædid *vanished*	
2413 پارلمانی	parlemani *parliamentary*	
2414 سرشار	særʃar *abundant*	
2419 کهن	kohæn *old*	
2424 ذهنی	zehni *mental*	
2427 ترکیبی	tærkibi *synthetic, compound, hybrid*	
2433 درسی	dærsi *instructional*	
2438 فراگیر	færagir *comprehensive*	
2443 شبانه	ʃæbane *nightly*	
2448 اعتباری	eʔtebari *credit*	
2449 خام	xam *raw*	
2451 افکندن	æfkændæn *throw*	
2454 واحدی	vahedi *modular, Vahedi*	
2459 محبوب	mæhbub *popular, beloved*	
2461 مسلط	mosællæt *dominant*	
2463 مساوی	mosavi *equal, tie*	
2467 مطلق	motlæy *absolute*	
2469 تیره	tire *dark, family, dash*	
2474 میسر	mojæssær *possible*	
2478 شیرازی	ʃirazi *Shirazi*	
2479 خشک	xoʃk *dry*	
2480 استوار	ostovar *stable*	
2485 عظیمی	æzimi *greatness, Azimi*	
2486 پدید	pædid *visible*	

2491 بیرونی	biruni *external*	
2494 قاطع	yateʔ *decisive*	
2505 الکترونیکی	elektroniki *electronic*	
2506 بنیادی	bonjadi *fundamental*	
2508 بیکار	bikar *unemployed*	
2517 باستان	bastan *ancient*	
2524 متمرکز	motæmærkez *concentrated*	
2532 مربوطه	mærbute *relevant*	
2536 بارز	barez *distinct, prominent*	
2539 پنهان	penhan *hidden*	
2542 مشمول	mæʃmul *included, subject to, draftee*	
2550 نگریستن	negæristæn *look*	
2552 تعاونی	tæʔavoni *cooperative*	
2553 آشکار	aʃkar *evident*	
2554 مشخصه	moʃæxxæse *characteristic*	
2556 خشن	xæʃen *rough*	
2559 نهاده	næhade *resource, input*	
2560 خاکی	xaki *earthen, terrestrial*	
2561 سوار	sævar *rider*	
2563 فاقد	fayed *lacking*	
2564 سوختن	suxtæn *burn*	
2566 بلندی	bolændi *height*	
2567 موظف	movæzzæf *duty-bound*	
2570 شاد	ʃad *happy*	
2572 مطبوعاتی	mætbuʔati *press*	
2575 تابع	tabeʔ *citizen, follower*	
2584 دایر	dajer *functioning*	
2589 محکم	mohkæm *solid*	
2591 راحت	rahæt *comfort, comfortable*	
2594 دوجانبه	dodʒanebe *bilateral*	
2603 حاوی	havi *containing*	
2610 جسمی	dʒesmi *physical*	
2614 متنوع	motænævveʔ *varied*	
2616 یونانی	junani *Greek*	
2617 رفتاری	ræftari *behavioral*	
2620 خانگی	xanegi *homemade, domestic, interior*	
2630 نادرست	nadorost *incorrect*	
2632 فیزیکی	fiziki *physical*	
2637 امن	æmn *safe*	
2639 پیر	pir *old*	
2640 عاشق	aʃey *lover*	
2646 جانبه	dʒanebe *-lateral*	
2648 جعفری	dʒæʔfæri *parsley, Jafari*	
2652 عملیاتی	æmælijjati *operational*	

3034 مسلحانه	mosællæhane *armed*	
3049 قلمداد	yælæmdad *considered*	
3056 استدلال	estedlal *reasoning*	
3057 مکانی	mækani *local*	
3061 زرد	zærd *yellow*	
3067 وارداتی	varedati *imported*	
3070 بستری	bestæri *admitted, confined to bed*	
3073 پیشرو	piʃrow *progressive*	
3074 گیاهی	gijahi *herbal, vegetable*	
3079 تنگ	tæng *narrow, tight*	
3081 دلاری	dolari *dollar*	
3089 بدیهی	bædihi *evident, obvious*	
3097 معترض	moʔtærez *objector, protestor*	
3101 تحلیلی	tahlili *analytic, analytical*	
3102 مکمل	mokæmmel *complementary, supplementary*	
3105 پایداری	pajdari *endurance, resistance*	
3115 برنز	bronz *bronze*	
3118 متصل	mottæsel *connected*	
3125 کمونیست	komunist *communist*	
3128 حزبی	hezbi *party*	
3129 بس	bæs *enough*	
3131 وفادار	væfadar *faithful, loyal*	
3138 خودگردان	xodgærdan *autonomous*	
3140 محفوظ	mæhfuz *protected*	
3142 مجاهد	modʒahed *holy warrior*	
3144 مهمان	mehman *guest*	
3147 ترکی	torki *Turkish*	
3149 گرانبها	geranbæha *precious*	
3153 افشا	efʃa *disclosure*	
3155 حکیم	hækim *wise person*	
3157 یکپارچه	jekpartʃe *whole*	
3161 قیمتی	γejmæti *costly, expensive*	
3163 منصوب	mænsub *appointed*	
3165 وحشتناک	væhʃætnak *terrible*	
3169 وحشی	væhʃi *wild*	
3171 تابستانی	tabestani *summer*	
3172 خنثی	xonsa *neutral, neuter*	
3176 روشنفکر	rowʃænfekr *intellectual*	
3177 جسمانی	dʒesmani *corporeal, physical*	

3178 آرامی	arami *tranquility, Aramaic*	
3179 دایمی	dajemi *permanent*	
3180 پناهنده	pænahænde *refugee*	
3181 سنگی	sæŋgi *rocky*	
3183 استانی	ostani *provincial*	
3184 نیک	nik *good*	
3188 مشروطه	mæʃrute *constitutional*	
3190 صهیونیست	sæhjunist *Zionist*	
3191 رایگان	rajegan *free*	
3192 شگفتی	ʃegefti *surprise*	
3197 نهادینه	næhadine *institutionalized*	
3198 راستی	rasti *indeed, truth*	
3205 کلاسیک	kelasik *classic*	
3209 گریختن	gorixtæn *flee*	
3210 مخرب	moxærreb *destructive*	
3215 آفریقایی	afriγaji *African*	
3216 پوشیده	puʃide *covered, clothed*	
3222 ترانزیت	tranzit *transit*	
3225 تند	tond *fast*	
3228 مجرم	modʒrem *guilty, criminal*	
3230 هفدهم	hevdæhom *seventeenth*	
3232 هفتگی	hæftegi *weekly*	
3240 بسنده	bæsænde *sufficient, content*	
3243 انفرادی	enferadi *individual, solitary*	
3246 فلج	fælædʒ *crippled*	
3247 مهربان	mehræban *kind, gentle*	
3251 لازمه	lazeme *requisite, precondition*	
3256 محیطی	mohiti *environmental*	
3259 مرتب	morættæb *orderly, arranged*	
3264 روزمره	ruzmærre *routine*	
3266 دموکرات	demokrat *democrat*	
3276 برون	borun *outside*	
3277 معلول	mæʔlul *disabled, effect*	
3280 دایم	dajem *permanent*	
3283 دویدن	dævidæn *run*	
3284 سطحی	sæthi *superficial*	
3285 پاکستانی	pakestani *Pakistani*	
3286 هموار	hæmvar *flat, smooth, paved*	
3290 بازنشسته	bazneʃæste *retired*	
3291 وطن	vætæn *homeland*	

3293 داستانی	dastani *fictional*	
3294 بهاری	bæhari *spring*	
3297 ناچیز	natʃiz *worthless*	
3298 دیپلماتیک	diplomatik *diplomatic*	
3304 راهبردی	rahbordi *strategic*	
3305 مدیون	mædjun *indebted*	
3310 برخاستن	bærxastæn *get/rise up*	
3315 صنفی	senfi *guild, trade*	
3322 اصفهانی	esfæhani *Esfahani*	
3339 ظاهری	zaheri *apparent, superficial*	
3340 نامناسب	namonaseb *inappropriate*	
3342 کور	kur *blind*	
3346 خروجی	xorudʒi *exit, output*	
3347 بیهوده	bihude *futile*	
3348 صمیمی	sæmimi *intimate*	
3349 متولد	motævælled *born*	
3350 ذیل	zejl *appendix, following, below*	
3351 برانگیخته	bærængixte *stimulated, excited*	
3352 کوفی	kufi *Kufic, Kofi*	
3354 یادآور	jadavær *reminder, memento, reminiscent*	
3355 ارزنده	ærzænde *valuable*	
3367 مداوم	modavem *continuous*	
3368 بازاری	bazari *businessman*	
3369 مایع	majeʔ *liquid*	
3372 رایانه‌ای	rajaneji *computer*	
3373 بزرگوار	bozorgvar *generous, honorable*	
3375 ناقص	naγes *defective*	
3376 گازی	gazi *gas*	
3378 پنهانی	penhani *secret*	
3379 شورشی	ʃureʃi *rebel*	
3382 جزء	dʒozʔ *part, detail, ingredient*	
3383 مظلوم	mæzlum *oppressed*	
3386 تدارکاتی	tædarokati *logistical, supply*	
3388 افغانی	æfγani *Afghan*	
3391 هوشمند	huʃmænd *clever*	
3392 گیرنده	girænde *recipient, receiver*	
3393 معقول	mæʔγul *reasonable*	
3394 دوازدهم	dævazdæhom *twelfth*	
3395 مرده	morde *dead, lifeless*	
3401 فرنگی	færæŋgi *European, Western*	
3410 سالیانه	salijane *annually*	

3795 نمایشگاهی næmajeʃgahi exhibition

3803 واجد شرایط vadʒede ʃærajæt eligible, qualified

3805 تربیتی tærtibi disciplinary, systematic, ordinal

3806 سرمایهگذار særmajegozar investor

3807 مکتوب mæktub written, letter

3810 غیرنظامی ɣejrnezami civilian

3812 طنز tænz satire

3814 پیمودن pejmudæn measure, traverse

3815 اقصا æɣsa farther

3819 تروریست terorist terrorist

3821 کبیر kæbir great, adult

3823 بازگرداندن bazgærdandæn repatriate

3824 متوالی motævali successive

3828 مصنوعی mæsnuʔi artificial

3829 موشکی muʃæki missile

3830 بهادار bæhadar valuable

3834 پانزدهم panzdæhom fifteenth

3837 مربع moræbbæʔ square

3838 توانمند tævanmænd capable

3840 مغزی mæɣzi cerebral

3842 آتی ati upcoming

3845 متفکر motæfækker thinker, thoughtful

3846 عاری ari bereft, free

3851 مشروط mæʃrut conditional

3854 بختیاری bæxtijari Bakhtiari

3857 نهفته næhofte hidden

3859 کاشانی kaʃani Kashani

3860 مشهود mæʃhud evident

3862 رفاهی refahi welfare, leisure

3866 نوجوانی nowdʒævani adolescence

3867 فلزی felezzi metal

3869 مساعد mosaʔed favorable

3873 دوختن duxtæn sew

3881 انتقالی enteɣali transferred

3886 قاچاقچی ɣatʃaɣtʃi smuggler

3887 ساختگی saxtegi forged

3889 ریز riz tiny

3891 عثمانی osmani Ottoman

3894 منافق monafeɣ hypocritical, hypocrite

3897 خوشی xoʃi joy

3898 عاطفی atefi emotional

3899 فراخواندن færaxandæn invite, summon

3902 نهادی næhadi institutional

3906 ملحق molhæɣ joined

3907 منکر monker, monkær denying, detestable/vice

3911 شکننده ʃekænænde fragile

3918 پایبند pajbænd fettered, loyal

3921 کارگزار kargozar agent

3922 ماشینی maʃini mechanical

3926 قطبی ɣotbi polar

3927 دیجیتال didʒital digital

3930 ویران viran ruined

3932 مصرفکننده mæsræfkonænde consumer

3933 شاغل ʃaɣel employed

3937 اشغالگر eʃɣalgær occupier, occupying

3940 وضوح vozuh clarity

3943 دربند dærbænd Darband, captive

3948 دلخواه delxah desired, ideal

3951 بلندپایه bolændpaje high-ranking

3952 منصفانه monsefane just, fair

3953 موکول mowkul depending, postpone

3960 نامشروع namæʃruʔ unlawful

3961 آلوده alude polluted

3962 آسانی asani ease

3965 خشمگین xæʃmgin angry

3966 مسی mesi copper

3969 منسجم monsædʒem coherent

3972 پاکی paki cleanliness, purity

3974 چهلم tʃehelom fortieth

3978 توانا tævana able, mighty

3981 مصوب mosævvæb ratified, approved

3985 ریالی rijali Rial-based

3995 مؤسس moʔæsses founder

3997 یکسانی jeksani identicality

4006 متقاعد motæɣaʔed convinced

4015 شجاع ʃodʒaʔ brave, courageous

4017 وخیم væxim serious

4018 تسلیحاتی tæslihati armament

4022 چوبی tʃubi wooden

4026 تندرو tondrow fast, extremist

4031 فدا feda sacrifice

4036 نازل nazel low, humble, sent down

4039 نبی næbi prophet

4045 سروده sorude sung, poem

4047 ناشناخته naʃenaxte unknown

4050 بدهکار bedehkar debtor, indebted

4054 دیکتاتوری diktatori dictatorship, dictatorial

4058 همگام hæmgam marching together

4060 واجب vadʒeb necessary

4062 تبریزی tæbrizi Tabrizi

4066 جعلی dʒæʔli forged

4070 گرانی gerani expensive, high prices

4071 بیمارستانی bimarestani hospital

4073 مقاوم moɣavem resistant

4074 کوهستانی kuhestani mountainous

4078 برگرداندن bærgærdandæn return

4079 رها ræha loose, free

4080 پستی posti postal

4081 کتبی kætbi written

4085 امکانپذیر emkanpæzir possible

4086 برجا bærdʒa stable, fixed

4087 تاجیک tadʒik Tajik

4088 دریافتی dærjafti received, receipt

4090 رزمی ræzmi combat

4093 صعودی soʔudi ascending, upward

4094 فلان folan so and so, such and such

4097 روانه rævane bound for

4103 عادل adel just

4104 نواختن nævaxtæn play

4106 خیریه xejrijje charitable

4108 مسدود mæsdud obstructed

4118 ملزم molzæm obliged, bound

4123 سلطنتی sæltænæti royal

4126 تطبیق tætbiɣ comparison

4127 فروشی foruʃi for sale

4129 اضطراری ezterari forced, emergency

4130 بیسابقه bisabeɣe unprecedented

4139 جانبی dʒanebi lateral, side

4142 مفهومی mæfhumi conceptual

4143 ترکمن torkæmæn Turkmen

4147 ابری æbri cloudy

4148 حائز haez possessing, holding, eligible

4568 ناگوار	nagovar *unpleasant*	4684 خطیر	xætir *important,*	4803 انحصاری	enhesari *exclusive,*
4570 مکلف	mokællæf *obliged*		*dangerous*		*monopoly*
4573 متوسطه	motævæssete *middle,*	4689 پیشگام	piʃgam *pioneer*	4807 کیفری	kejfæri *penal,*
	secondary (school)	4690 ملکی	melki, mæleki *real*		*criminal*
4579 نیکو	niku *good, fair*		*estate, Maleki*	4808 فرضی	færzi *hypothetical*
4582 پیگیر	pejgir *persistent*	4692 متمایز	motæmajez *distinct*	4809 متعارف	motæʔaref *common*
4583 کلامی	kælami *verbal*	4695 ساقط	saɤet *fallen,*	4811 نوپا	nowpa *newly*
4587 نامطلوب	namætlub		*miscarried, lapsed*		*established, toddler*
	undesirable	4697 آمیختن	amixtæn *mix*	4812 پسندیده	pæsændide
4588 تمیز	tæmiz *clean*	4701 پلیسی	polisi *police*		*admirable*
4591 مختص	moxtæss *special*	4705 صدم	sædom *hundredth*	4814 عصبانی	æsæbani *angry*
4593 رفیق	ræfiɤ *pal*	4708 پیشتاز	piʃtaz *pioneer, front-*	4816 ارجمند	ærdʒomænd *valuable*
4594 ملموس	mælmus *tangible*		*running*	4818 درخشیدن	deræxʃidæn *shine*
4595 نیرومند	nirumænd *powerful*	4713 مهربانی	mehræbani *kindness*	4824 کمونیستی	komunisti *communist*
4596 پررنگ	porræng *conspicuous,*	4717 مشتمل	moʃtæmel *containing*	4826 گزیده	gozide *chosen,*
	prominent	4718 مفیدی	mofidi *Mofidi, useful*		*selected, excerpt*
4597 زمستانی	zemestani *winter*	4720 مفصلی	mæfsæli *joint,*	4827 موجی	mowdʒi *wavy, shell-*
4599 جراح	dʒærrah *surgeon*		*articular*		*shocked*
4602 زرین	zærrin *golden*	4722 قرآنی	ɤorʔani *Koranic*	4829 دستخوش	dæstxoʃ *gratuity,*
4604 موقتی	movæɤɤæti	4723 ملایم	molajem *gentle*		*prone, subject to*
	temporary	4726 مجزا	modʒæzza *separate*	4830 بازگشته	bazgæʃte *returned*
4613 منزوی	monzævi *reclusive*	4729 باردار	bardar *pregnant,*	4833 پاشیدن	paʃidæn *scatter,*
4614 کارآمد	karamæd *skillful,*		*loaded*		*sprinkle*
	proficient	4731 فصلی	fæsli *seasonal*	4834 پوستی	pusti *(made of) skin,*
4615 یکباره	jekbare *all at once*	4732 حسابی	hesabi *proper*		*fur*
4617 معصوم	mæʔsum *innocent*	4733 پهلوان	pæhlævan *champion,*	4836 سره	sære *pure*
4621 زیرزمینی	zirzæmini		*hero*	4841 درهم	derhæm, dærhæm
	underground	4741 راستین	rastin *true*		*dirham, mixed*
4624 حسی	hessi *sensory*	4749 جنایی	dʒenaji *criminal*	4845 تام	tam *full, Tom*
4629 شادابی	ʃadabi *freshness*	4750 مجریه	modʒrije *executive*	4847 منحل	monhæll *dissolved*
4630 سیار	sæjjar *mobile*	4753 مگاواتی	megavati *megawatt*	4850 لبنانی	lobnani *Lebanese*
4632 هلندی	holændi *Dutch*	4754 زیرومبی	zirobæmi *pitch*	4863 عروقی	oruɤi *vascular*
4639 فرزانه	færzane *learned,*	4755 جنگیدن	dʒængidæn *fight*	4864 خوشایند	xoʃajænd *pleasant,*
	wise	4756 محبوس	mæhbus *imprisoned*		*pleasure*
4641 ربطی	ræbti *linking,*	4759 عرفانی	erfani *Sufist, mystic*	4867 مستبد	mostæbed *despotic*
	connecting	4762 کوهی	kuhi *mountain*	4870 مجازی	mædʒazi *virtual,*
4643 بینظیر	binæzir *unique,*	4763 تشریفاتی	tæʃrifati *ceremonial*		*metaphorical*
	unparalleled	4765 ترانزیتی	tranziti *transit*	4874 تیز	tiz *sharp, fart*
4644 ساکت	saket *silent,*	4769 تابیدن	tabidæn *shine, twist*	4878 مندرج	mondæredʒ *inserted,*
	extinguished	4773 رابط	rabet *intermediary,*		*printed*
4645 شر	ʃærr *evil*		*connector*	4881 پیمانی	pejmani *contractual*
4656 ماهر	maher *skillful*	4776 شیری	ʃiri *milk, dairy*	4883 خوار	xar *contemptible*
4660 شاهی	ʃahi *kingship, royal*	4777 شگفت	ʃegeft *amazing*	4892 مسن	mosenn *elderly*
4665 زیستن	zistæn *live*	4779 بندری	bændæri *port*	4897 سهل	sæhl *easy*
4670 شیفته	ʃifte *infatuated,*	4780 سوسیالیست	sosialist *socialist*	4899 راحل	rahel *deceased*
	fascinated	4781 امامی	emami *imam,*	4904 استعماری	esteʔmari *colonial*
4677 رشید	ræʃid *well grown,*		*Emami*	4905 شل	ʃæl, ʃol, ʃel *lame,*
	Rashid	4784 سست	sost *weak*		*loose, Shell*
4678 سرگردان	særgærdan *wandering,*	4785 ژنتیکی	ʒenetiki *genetic*	4908 تخریبی	tæxribi *destructive*
	vagrant	4790 دیوانه	divane *crazy*	4915 تعیینکننده	tæʔjinkonænde
4679 دزدی	dozdi *theft, burglary*	4795 مؤلف	moʔallef *author,*		*decisive*
4680 زشت	zeʃt *ugly*		*compiler*	4917 منوط	mænut *dependent*
4681 بازیافتن	bazjaftæn *recycle,*	4798 ارضی	ærzi *territorial, land*	4918 پرشور	porʃur *passionate*
	recover	4799 بیچاره	biʧare *helpless*	4919 استواری	ostovari *stability*

درگذشته	4923	dærgozæʃte deceased	امروز	201	emruz today	چندان	1153	ʧændan so many, so
الکتریکی	4931	elektriki electric	کاملاً	212	kamelæn completely	هرگز	1154	hærgez never
گمراه	4935	gomrah misled	هنوز	218	hænuz still, yet	بیرون	1159	birun outside
تکمیلی	4937	takmili supplementary, complementary	نخست	248	noxost first	خیر	1182	xejr no
			مانند	297	manænd like	بد	1184	bæd bad
آموخته	4940	amuxte learned, accustomed	اکنون	298	æknun now	جلو	1199	dʒelow forward
آهسته	4941	aheste slow, slowly	فقط	318	fæɣæt only	فردا	1216	færda tomorrow
مسافرتی	4943	mosaferæti travel	آیا	323	aja whether	معمولاً	1230	mæʔmulæn usually
غیردولتی	4945	ɣejrdowlæti non-governmental	چرا	386	ʧera why	واقعاً	1285	vaɣeʔæn really
آفت	4949	afæt calamity, blight	خیلی	387	xejli very	روزانه	1296	ruzane daily
دیرین	4950	dirin old, ancient	زیاد	446	zijad a lot	آرام	1311	aram peaceful
کاردانی	4951	kardani professional skill, 2-year degree	تازه	455	taze fresh	اغلب	1333	æɣlæb often, frequently
			ابتدا	468	ebteda beginning	الان	1335	ælan now
جهانگرد	4954	dʒæhangærd tourist, explorer	تاکنون	497	taknun yet	فرا	1343	færa beyond
ولایتی	4956	velajæti provincial	خوب	510	xub good	اصلاً	1355	æslæn originally, by no means
لفظی	4963	læfzi verbal	همیشه	513	hæmiʃe always			
شیشه‌ای	4964	ʃiʃeʔi glass	باز	514	baz again	عملاً	1397	æmælæn practically
منتفی	4965	montæfi no longer probable, canceled	همواره	540	hæmvare always	عقب	1401	æɣæb back
			سرانجام	554	særændʒam finally	آره	1413	are yes
پایینی	4968	paʔini downstairs, lower	سخت	571	sæxt hard	بالاخره	1424	belʔæxære finally
سوزان	4985	suzan burning	سریع	586	særiʔ fast	چنان	1444	ʧonæn such
مقتدر	4988	moɣtæder powerful, strong	گویا	646	guja seems	بخصوص	1465	bexosus especially
			امسال	656	emsal this year	زود	1520	zud soon
بیات	4991	bæjat stale	همچنان	663	hæmʧenan thus	کجا	1545	kodʒa where
بریده	4992	boride cut, clipping	حداقل	694	hæddeæɣæl at least, minimum	قطعاً	1552	qætʔæn certainly
پلید	4993	pælid dirty, evil	هرچه	695	hærʧe whatever	پیوسته	1578	pejvæste connected, permanent
کثیر	4996	kæsir numerous, abundant	گاه	707	gah sometimes			
			متأسفانه	717	moteʔæssefane unfortunately	اینک	1581	inæk now
سلطانی	4998	soltani royal				اینگونه	1671	ingune this kind of
			فراوان	724	færavan abundant	خوش	1673	xoʃ good
Adverbs: 219 words			حالا	760	hala now	احتمالاً	1676	ehtemalæn probably
			آنجا	775	andʒa there	امروزه	1684	emruze nowadays
بیش	28	biʃ more	تقریباً	777	tæqribæn approximately	راست	1758	rast right
دیگر	29	digær other				مگر	1775	mægær by chance
بسیار	51	besjar very	پایین	790	pajin down	اساساً	1830	æsasæn basically
تنها	57	tænha only	روبرو	792	ruberu opposite	دقیقاً	1851	dæɣiɣæn exactly
کم	60	kæm low, little	دوباره	813	dobare again	عمداً	1854	omdætæn chiefly
بهتر	89	behtær better	چگونه	818	ʧegune how	ظاهراً	1893	zaheræn apparently
یعنی	95	jæʔni namely, meaning	اینجا	821	indʒa here	مجدداً	1910	modʒæddædæn once again
بار	96	bar load, turn	هرچند	865	hærʧænd however			
بالا	101	bala top, high	دیروز	940	diruz yesterday	کی	1931	kej, ki when, who
چه	110	ʧe what	بدین	948	bedin to this, this much	چقدر	1936	ʧeɣædr how much
البته	125	ælbætte of course				حتماً	1939	hætmæn certainly
چون	157	ʧun like, because	مقدار	995	meɣdar amount	هیچگاه	1954	hiʧgah never
حتی	160	hætta even	درست	1001	dorost right, correct	بلافاصله	1955	belafasele immediately
نه	178	næ no	قبلاً	1016	qæblæn before			
آخر	188	axær final	همزمان	1033	hæmzæman simultaneously	خوشبختانه	1998	xoʃbæxtane fortunately
چنین	191	ʧenin such				حداکثر	2024	hæddæksær maximum
			مثلاً	1047	mæsælæn for example	صریح	2043	særih explicit
			سالانه	1092	salane annual	خصوصاً	2074	xosusæn especially
			اخیراً	1111	æxiræn recently	دیر	2086	dir, dejr late, monastery
			اندک	1137	ændæk little			

2133	صرفاً	serfæn *merely, purely*	3276	برون	borun *outside*	4563	دوبار
2145	جداگانه	dʒodagane *separately*	3280	دایم	dajem *permanent*	4579	نیکو

2133 صرفاً serfæn *merely, purely*
2145 جداگانه dʒodagane *separately*
2198 دوش duʃ *shoulder, shower*
2214 یکسان jeksan *similar*
2237 فوری fowri *immediate*
2268 رسماً ræsmæn *officially*
2284 نسبتاً nesbætæn *relatively*
2297 مکرر mokærrær *repeated*
2301 مخصوصاً mæxsusæn *especially*
2315 عادلانه adelane *justly*
2327 خب xob *well*
2355 بزودی bezudi *soon*
2429 فعلاً fe?læn *at present*
2443 شبانه ʃæbane *nightly*
2445 اوّلاً ævvælæn *first*
2492 مسلماً mosællæmæn *certainly*
2576 پیشتر piʃtær *before, further*
2587 چطور tʃetowr *how*
2589 محکم mohkæm *solid*
2591 راحت rahæt *comfort, comfortable*
2643 امشب emʃæb *tonight*
2673 نهایتاً næhajætæn *eventually*
2728 طبیعتاً tæbi?ætæn *naturally*
2738 آنقدر anqædr *so much*
2776 آهان ahan *yes*
2800 همیشگی hæmiʃegi *perpetual*
2836 پیاده pijade *pedestrian, on foot*
2862 یکبار jekbar *once*
2867 مستقیماً mostæqimæn *directly*
2926 انگار engar *as if*
2985 ناگزیر nagozir *inevitable*
2989 بعداً bæ?dæn *later, then*
2999 ارزان ærzan *cheap*
3013 فوق‌العاده fowqol?ade *extraordinary*
3017 درواقع dærvaqe? *indeed*
3020 ناچار natʃar *compelled*
3051 قدری qædri *a little, slight*
3129 بس bæs *enough*
3157 یکپارچه jekpartʃe *entirely*
3187 ناگهان nagæhan *suddenly*
3198 راستی rasti *indeed, truth*
3200 آنگاه angah *then*
3204 شخصاً ʃæxsæn *personally*
3225 تند tond *fast*
3232 هفتگی hæftegi *weekly*
3235 قایم qajem *firm, hidden*
3259 مرتب morættæb *orderly, arranged*
3260 اصولاً osulæn *in principle*

3276 برون borun *outside*
3280 دایم dajem *permanent*
3324 هماکنون hæmæknun *just now*
3347 بیهوده bihude *futile*
3356 عموماً omumæn *generally*
3378 پنهانی penhani *secret*
3410 سالیانه salijane *annually*
3411 آشکارا aʃkara *explicitly*
3413 کنون konun *now*
3418 ناامید naomid *hopeless*
3441 قرص qors *tablet*
3465 برعکس bær?æks *vice versa*
3572 صمیمانه sæmimane *sincerely*
3590 اتفاقاً ettefaqæn *by chance, in fact*
3674 ماهانه mahane *monthly*
3711 پارسال parsal *last year*
3717 بالقوه belqovve *potential, potentially*
3734 هیچگونه hitʃgune *no way*
3783 یکسال jeksal *one year*
3790 منتها montæha *extremity, but*
3903 کماکان kæmakan *as before, still*
3938 غالباً γalebæn *frequently*
3952 منصفانه monsefane *just, fair*
3967 بعدازظهر bæ?dæzzohr *afternoon*
3971 ثانیاً sanijæn *secondly*
3976 دیشب diʃæb *last night*
4061 دریغ deriγ *regret, pity*
4089 ضمناً zemnæn *incidentally*
4153 حدوداً hodudæn *approximately*
4168 اینطور intur *this way*
4194 بخیر bexejr *good*
4207 کلاً kollæn *totally*
4222 ناخواسته naxaste *unwanted*
4227 هی hej *hey, continuously, keep*
4228 صادقانه sadeqane *truthful, truthfully*
4263 طبعاً tæb?æn *naturally*
4273 مدام modam *continuous*
4366 قاطعانه qate?ane *decisive, decisively*
4468 کاش kaʃ *I wish*
4470 وای vaj *oh, alas*
4478 مجموعاً mædʒmu?æn *altogether*
4492 فوراً fowræn *immediately*
4502 شدیداً ʃædidæn *severely*
4511 خیره xire *dazzled, staring*
4534 هرگاه hærgah *whenever*

4563 دوبار dobar *twice*
4579 نیکو niku *well*
4588 تمیز tæmiz *clean*
4615 یکباره jekbare *all at once*
4634 یقیناً jæqinæn *certainly*
4652 لااقل la?æqæl *at least*
4669 همانا hæmana *indeed*
4707 مبادا mæbada *lest*
4732 حسابی hesabi *proper*
4737 بازهم bazhæm *again*
4740 اینچنین intʃenin *such*
4748 پیشاپیش piʃapiʃ *in advance*
4797 اکثراً æksæræn *mostly*
4907 بسا bæsa *many*
4941 آهسته aheste *slow, slowly*

Conjunctions: 66 words

1 و vav, væ *and*
5 که ke *which*
25 پس pæs *then*
29 دیگر digær *other*
31 اما æmma *but*
36 هم hæm *both, also*
41 یا ja *or*
44 نیز niz *also*
77 اگر ægær *if*
95 یعنی jæ?ni *namely, meaning*
110 چه tʃe *what*
118 بعد bæ?d *then, after*
125 البته ælbætte *of course*
131 ولی væli *but*
143 در حال dærhal *in the process of*
157 چون tʃun *like, because*
160 حتی hætta *even*
164 همچنین hæmtʃenin *so, also*
178 نه næ *not, neither, nor*
188 آخر axær *final*
291 بلکه bælke *but*
411 وقتی væqti *when*
454 جز dʒoz *except*
554 سرانجام særændʒam *finally*
558 زیرا zira *because*
676 خلاف xælaf *contrary*
754 سپس sepæs *then*
865 هرچند hærtʃænd *however*
866 بنابراین bænabærin *therefore*
1047 مثلاً mæsælæn *for example*
1060 آنکه anke *that which*
1168 اگرچه ægærtʃe *although*
1256 لذا leza *therefore*

1397 عملاً æmælæn *practically*	35 پیش piʃ *before*	119 سازمان sɑzmɑn *organization*
1424 بالاخره belʔæxære *finally*	39 دو do, dow *two, running*	120 فرد færd *individual*
1465 بخصوص bexosus *especially*	40 شهر ʃæhr *city*	121 تیم tim *team*
1775 مگر mægær *by chance*	42 دادن dɑdæn *give*	122 جوان dʒævɑn *young*
1814 گرچه gærʧe *although*	45 میان mijɑn *between*	124 شورا ʃurɑ *council*
1868 چنانچه ʧenɑnʧe *if*	46 صورت suræt *face*	126 دوم dovvom *second*
2074 خصوصاً xosusæn *especially*	47 راه rɑh *way, road*	127 دلیل dælil *reason*
2307 منتهی montæhi, montæha *ending, but*	52 قبل qæbl *before*	128 رفتن ræftæn *go*
2361 علیرغم ælɑræym *despite*	53 مدت moddæt *term, period*	129 نقش næqʃ *role*
2362 اینکه inke *that*	55 نظر næzær *opinion*	130 نام nɑm *name*
2445 اولاً ævvælɑn *first*	56 مردم mærdom *people*	132 دوره dowre *period*
2673 نهایتاً næhɑjætæn *eventually*	59 مهم mohem *important*	133 وزیر væzir *minister*
2684 همانطور hæmɑntur *as, just as*	60 کم kæm *low, little*	134 استفاده estefɑde *use*
2765 چنانکه ʧenɑnke *as*	61 نزدیک næzdik *close*	135 آقا ɑqɑ *mister*
2926 انگار engɑr *as if*	62 عنوان onvɑn *title*	136 حرکت hærekæt *motion, movement*
2989 بعداً bæʔdæn *later, then*	63 مورد mowred *case*	138 شرکت ʃerkæt *company*
3017 درواقع dærvɑqeʔ *indeed*	64 بین bejn *between*	139 طرح tærh *design*
3187 ناگهان nɑgæhɑn *suddenly*	66 دست dæst *hand*	142 سه se *three*
3200 آنگاه ɑngɑh *then*	67 چند ʧænd *several*	144 حدود hodud *limits, range*
3419 والا vɑlɑ, vɑʔellɑ *eminent, otherwise*	68 قرار qærɑr *agreement*	145 ایجاد idʒɑd *creation*
3465 برعکس bærʔæks *vice versa*	70 گروه goruh *group*	146 کس kæs *person*
3787 همینطور hæmintowr *also, likewise*	71 برنامه bærnɑme *program*	147 بردن bordæn *take*
3790 منتها montæhɑ *extremity, but*	72 بخش bæxʃ *section, part*	150 هزار hezɑr *thousand*
3841 چراکه ʧerɑke *because*	73 وجود vodʒud *existence*	151 حضور hozur *presence*
3971 ثانیاً sɑnijæn *secondly*	74 مسئله mæsʔæle *problem*	152 نیرو niru *power, force*
4089 ضمناً zemnæn *incidentally*	75 توجه tævædʒdʒoh *attention*	153 عضو ozv *member*
4413 لیکن likæn *but*	76 امر æmr *affair*	154 فعالیت fæʔɑlijæt *activity*
4476 درحالیکه dærhɑlike *while, as*	78 گذشته gozæʃte *past*	155 تن tæn, ton *body, ton*
4634 یقیناً jæqinæn *certainly*	79 ماه mɑh *month, moon*	156 اشاره eʃɑre *indication*
4652 لااقل lɑʔæqæl *at least*	80 طور towr *manner*	159 درصد dærsæd *percent*
4676 همچنانکه hæmʧenɑnke *as*	82 رو ru *on, face*	163 پایان pɑjɑn *end*
4734 وگرنه vægærne *otherwise*	83 زمان zæmɑn *time*	165 قانون qɑnun *law*
4999 بجز bedʒoz *except*	85 مشکل moʃkel *problem*	166 جا dʒa *place*

Nouns: 3416 words

12 یک jek *one*	88 رئیس ræʔis *head*	168 هدف hædæf *goal, target*
13 آن ɑn *that*	90 دولت dowlæt *government*	170 بزرگی bozorgi *magnitude*
17 کردن kærdæn *do*	91 جمله dʒomle *sentence, total*	171 جامعه dʒɑmeʔe *society*
20 اول ævvæl *first*	92 نتیجه nætidʒe *result*	172 حق hæq *right*
21 بر bær *on*	94 سو su *side*	173 اثر æsær *mark, effect*
22 سال sɑl *year*	96 بار bɑr *load, turn*	174 بحث bæhs *discussion*
23 توانستن tævɑnestæn *be able*	97 منطقه mæntæqe *region*	175 ارزش ærzeʃ *value*
24 رسیدن residæn *arrive*	98 نفر næfær *person*	176 موضوع mowzuʔ *subject, topic*
25 پس pæs *then*	99 یافتن jɑftæn *find*	177 طرف tæræf *side*
27 کار kɑr *work*	101 بالا bɑlɑ *top, high*	178 نه næ, noh *no, nine*
30 روز ruz *day*	104 جهان dʒæhɑn *world*	179 آب ɑb *water*
33 کشور keʃvær *country*	105 رابطه rɑbete *relation*	180 آینده ɑjænde *future*
34 گرفتن gereftæn *take*	106 شرط ʃært *condition*	181 نوع nowʔ *type*
	110 چه ʧe *what*	182 مقام mæqɑm *rank, official*
	111 اساس æsɑs *basis*	184 جهت dʒæhæt *direction, reason*
	112 آوردن ɑværdæn *bring*	185 اجرا edʒrɑ *implementation*
	113 حال hɑl *condition, state*	187 مجلس mædʒles *parliament*
	114 وارد vɑred *enter*	188 آخر ɑxær *final*
	117 زمینه zæmine *background, field*	189 عمل æmæl *action*
	118 بعد bæʔd *then, after*	

190 زندگی zendegi *life*	250 باعث baʔes *cause*	310 زدن zædæn *strike, beat*
192 رساندن resandæn *deliver*	251 رشد roʃd *growth*	311 فرصت forsæt *opportunity*
193 نظام nezam *system*	252 دنبال dombal *follow*	312 دانشگاه daneʃgah *university*
195 شکل ʃekl *shape*	253 انتخاب entexab *selection,*	314 تأکید tæʔkid *emphasis*
196 نسبت nesbæt *relation*	*choice*	315 نوشتن neveʃtæn *write*
197 دنیا donja *world*	254 گفتگو goftogu *conversation*	316 ساختن saxtæn *build*
199 همراه hæmrah *together*	256 روزنامه ruzname *newspaper*	317 ترتیب tærtib *order*
200 کتاب ketab *book*	257 گذشتن gozæʃtæn *pass*	319 علت ellæt *reason*
202 دیدن didæn *see*	258 طی tej *during*	321 آزادی azadi *freedom*
204 توسعه towseʔe *expansion,*	259 خاطر xater *mind, sake*	322 وضعیت væzʔijjæt *situation*
development	260 سمت sæmt, semæt *side,*	324 جریان dʒæræjan *flow*
206 انجام ændʒam *performance*	*position*	325 تلاش tælaʃ *effort*
207 مرکز mærkæz *center*	261 عامل amel *agent, factor*	327 حمایت hemajæt *protection*
208 اعلام eʔlam *announcement*	262 تأثیر tæʔsir *impression,*	328 چیز tʃiz *thing*
209 اطلاع ettelaʔ *information*	*effect*	329 ادامه edame *continuation*
210 داخل daxel *inside*	263 جنگ dʒæng *war*	330 دلار dolar *dollar*
211 پرداختن pærdaxtæn *pay,*	264 ساخت saxt *construction,*	332 تاریخ tarix *history*
engage in	*structure*	334 سطح sæth *level*
213 گفته gofte *saying*	265 طریق tæriɣ *way*	336 استاد ostad *professor*
214 زن zæn *woman, wife*	266 کاهش kaheʃ *decrease*	337 انتخابات entexabat *elections*
215 گزارش gozareʃ *report*	268 خارج xaredʒ *external*	339 تصویر tæsvir *image*
216 سر sær, serr *head, secret*	269 هفته hæfte *week*	341 انسانی ensani *human*
219 جمهوری dʒomhuri *republic*	270 آغاز aɣaz *beginning*	342 خاص xass *specific*
220 تغییر tæɣjir *change*	271 مرحله mærhæle *stage*	343 مقابل moɣabel *opposite*
221 تعداد teʔdad *number*	273 صنعت sænʔæt *industry*	344 سفر sæfær *travel*
222 میلیون miljun *million*	274 تشکیل tæʃkil *formation*	346 فرهنگ færhæng *culture*
223 سیاست sijasæt *policy, politics*	275 همکاری hæmkari *collaboration*	348 انقلاب enɣelab *revolution*
224 بررسی bærresi *check*	276 اسلام eslam *Islam*	349 جمع dʒæmʔ *total, addition*
225 اقدام eɣdam *action*	278 حسن hæsæn, hosn *Hasan,*	350 پیشنهاد piʃnehad *proposal*
226 افزایش æfzajeʃ *increase*	*virtue*	351 ماده made, madde *female,*
227 برابر bærabær *equal,*	280 خواندن xandæn *read*	*matter*
opposite	281 غیر ɣejr *other*	352 معنا mæʔna *meaning*
229 گونه gune *type, species,*	282 خانواده xanevade *family*	353 کنار kenar *beside*
cheek	283 دور dowr, dur *period, far*	354 رأی ræʔj *vote*
230 سوم sevvom *third*	284 نقطه noɣte *point*	356 حقیقت hæɣiɣæt *truth*
231 خدمت xedmæt *service*	285 بازی bazi *game, play*	357 تأمین tæʔmin *security*
232 خبر xæbær *news*	286 تولید towlid *production*	358 خانه xane *house*
233 ایرانی irani *Iranian*	289 وزارت vezaræt *ministry*	359 جمعیت dʒæmʔijjæt *population*
236 منبع mænbæʔ *source*	290 دیده dide *eye, seen*	360 دین din *religion*
237 خط xætt *line*	292 اصل æsl *principle*	361 امکان emkan *possibility*
238 قدرت ɣodræt *power*	293 کمک komæk *help*	362 علم elm *science*
239 نیاز nijaz *need*	296 زیر zir *under*	363 انتظار entezar *waiting*
240 مسئول mæsʔul *responsible*	297 مانند manænd *like*	365 بازار bazar *market*
241 نماینده næmajænde	299 اهمیت ahæmmijjæt	366 کل kol *whole, total*
representative	*importance*	367 میدان mejdan *plaza, square,*
242 ساعت saʔæt *hour, time*	300 اندیشه ændiʃe *thought*	*field*
243 زمین zæmin *ground*	301 استان ostan *province*	370 شدت ʃeddæt *intensity*
244 ملت mellæt *nation*	302 دفاع defaʔ *defense*	371 حقوق hoɣuɣ *rights, salary*
245 میزان mizan *rate*	303 نامه name *letter*	372 گل gol, gel *flower/goal,*
246 تحت tæht *under*	304 انسان ensan *human*	*mud*
247 اختیار extijar *authority*	305 نمودن nemudæn *show, do*	373 رشته reʃte *field, noodle*
248 نخست noxost *first*	308 دیدار didar *visit*	374 جلسه dʒælæse *meeting*
249 ارائه eraʔe *presentation*	309 سایر sajer *other*	375 دکتر doktor *doctor*

560 صحنه	sæhne *stage, scene*	
562 صدا	seda *sound*	
563 بعضی	bæ?zi *some*	
564 مراسم	mærasem *ceremony*	
565 دریافت	dærjaft *receipt, perception*	
566 خون	xun *blood*	
567 مقدمه	moɣæddæme *introduction*	
569 استقلال	esteɣlal *independence*	
570 مثل	mesl, mæsæl *like, proverb*	
572 برگزاری	bærgozari *holding*	
573 دسته	dæste *bunch*	
574 آتش	atæʃ *fire*	
575 سرعت	sor?æt *speed*	
577 مشارکت	moʃarekæt *partnership*	
578 وظیفه	væzife *duty*	
579 فعال	fæ?al *active*	
580 رقم	ræɣæm *digit, number*	
581 نیمه	nime *half*	
582 شمال	ʃomal *north*	
583 یاد	jad *memory*	
584 بهار	bæhar *spring*	
585 برداشتن	bærdaʃtæn *pick up, remove*	
587 چهره	tʃehre *face*	
588 محصول	mæhsul *product*	
590 چشم	tʃæʃm, tʃeʃm *eye*	
591 بند	bænd *string, paragraph*	
592 مخالف	moxalef *opposed*	
593 بیست	bist *twenty*	
595 تقویت	tæɣvijæt *reinforcement*	
596 احتمال	ehtemal *probability*	
597 تعیین	tæ?jin *determination*	
598 پلیس	polis *police*	
599 فروش	foruʃ *sale*	
600 رسانه	resane *medium*	
601 جنوب	dʒonub *south*	
602 تهیه	tæhijje *preparation*	
603 بیماری	bimari *illness*	
605 صرف	særf, serf *spending/ consuming, pure*	
606 مجموعه	mædʒmu?e *collection*	
607 نمایش	næmajeʃ *exhibiting, display*	
610 پایه	paje *base*	
612 موقعیت	mowɣe?ijjæt *situation, position*	

613 مهر	mehr, mohr *sun/Mehr/ affection, seal*	
615 جایگاه	dʒajgah *position*	
616 اعتقاد	e?teɣad *belief*	
617 شعر	ʃe?r *poetry*	
619 احترام	ehteram *respect*	
620 متر	metr *meter*	
622 پیروزی	piruzi *victory*	
623 اختلاف	extelaf *difference*	
625 دریا	dærja *sea*	
626 حضرت	hæzræt *holiness*	
627 بنا	bæna *building*	
628 پا	pa *foot, leg*	
629 خبرنگار	xæbærnegar *reporter*	
631 چندین	tʃændin *several*	
632 ورود	vorud *entry*	
633 جان	dʒan *life*	
634 پرواز	pærvaz *flight*	
635 علیه	ælejh *against*	
636 پیشرفت	piʃræft *progress*	
637 ابراز	ebraz *expression*	
638 توان	tævan *ability*	
639 حالت	halæt *condition*	
640 فراهم	færahæm *available*	
641 برخورد	bærxord *collision*	
642 رفتار	ræftar *behavior*	
643 نکته	nokte *point*	
644 جلوگیری	dʒelowgiri *prevention*	
647 متهم	mottæhæm *accused*	
648 تأسیس	tæ?sis *establishing, foundation*	
650 تحقق	tæhæɣɣoɣ *realization*	
651 قانونی	ɣanuni *legal*	
652 ادعا	edde?a *claim*	
653 دیدگاه	didgah *point of view*	
654 مکان	mækan *place*	
655 مطلب	mætlæb *subject*	
657 درآمد	dæramæd *income*	
658 گشتن	gæʃtæn *turn*	
660 عین	ejn *same, original, eye*	
661 کارشناس	karʃenas *expert*	
662 هنر	honær *art*	
665 روستا	rusta *village*	
666 رهبری	ræhbæri *leadership*	
667 ظرفیت	zærfijæt *capacity*	
668 نظارت	nezaræt *supervision*	
672 هنگام	hengam *time*	
675 پروژه	poroʒe *project*	
676 خلاف	xælaf *contrary*	
677 شیخ	ʃejx *sheikh*	
678 سن	senn *age*	
679 حکم	hokm *order, sentence*	

680 تصویب	tæsvib *approval*	
681 شخصیت	ʃæxsijjæt *personality*	
682 کدام	kodam *which*	
683 سرزمین	særzæmin *land*	
684 مسلمان	mosælman *Muslim*	
685 ساز	saz *instrument*	
686 خوردن	xordæn *eat*	
687 مسئولیت	mæs?ulijjæt *responsibility*	
688 جام	dʒam *cup*	
690 عبور	obur *passing*	
691 سید	sejjed *descendant of prophet*	
692 پیام	pæjam *message*	
694 حداقل	hæddeæɣæl *at least, minimum*	
696 وابسته	vabæste *dependent*	
697 دعوت	dæ?væt *invitation*	
698 ترک	tærk, tork *leave, Turk*	
699 کنفرانس	konferans *conference*	
700 نمایشگاه	næmajeʃgah *exhibition*	
701 تکرار	tekrar *repeating*	
702 بسته	bæste *package*	
703 عملکرد	æmælkærd *operation*	
704 ریشه	riʃe *root*	
705 شناختن	ʃenaxtæn *know, recognize*	
706 سرمایه	særmaje *capital*	
707 گاه	gah *time*	
708 مدیر	modir *manager, director*	
709 سهم	sæhm *share, lot*	
710 سرنوشت	særneveʃt *fate*	
711 کمیته	komite *committee*	
714 بخشیدن	bæxʃidæn *forgive, give*	
715 مدیریت	modirijjæt *management*	
716 عده	edde *number*	
718 حساب	hesab *account*	
720 صورتی	suræti *pink, a form*	
721 کالا	kala *goods*	
722 طبق	tebɣ, tæbæɣ *according to, tray*	
723 ملاحظه	molaheze *observation*	
726 اظهار	ezhar *statement*	
727 نجات	nedʒat *rescue*	
728 گاز	gaz *gas*	
729 شیوه	ʃive *method*	
732 بعدی	bæ?di *next*	
733 زندان	zendan *prison*	
734 مشاهده	moʃahede *observation*	

735 دادگاه dadgah *court*
737 نرخ nerx *rate*
738 كننده konænde *doer*
739 ضرورت zæruræt *necessity*
740 شش ʃeʃ, ʃoʃ *six, lung*
742 عكس æks *picture*
743 ترديد tærdid *hesitation, doubt*
744 خبرى xæbæri *news*
745 بهبود behbud *improvement*
746 نشانه neʃane *sign*
747 رژيم reʒim *regime*
748 اوج owdʒ *altitude, highest point*
749 منفعت mænfæʔæt *profit, gain*
751 نهاد næhad *institution*
752 كشاندن keʃandæn *drag, pull*
753 سابقه sabeʝe *precedent*
755 نيم nim *half*
756 درخواست dærxast *request*
757 رد rædd *refusal, trail*
758 منزل mænzel *house*
759 پرونده pærvænde *file*
762 وزن væzn *weight*
763 تومان tuman *toman*
764 عدم ædæm *lack*
766 بودجه buddʒe *budget*
767 اختصاص extesas *allocation*
769 سى si *thirty*
770 اهل æhl *native*
771 هدايت hedajæt *guidance*
772 سند sænæd *document*
773 صد sæd *hundred*
774 نشستن neʃæstæn *sit*
775 آنجا andʒa *there*
776 تسليم tæslim *surrender*
779 طراحى tærrahi *design*
780 دانش daneʃ *knowledge*
781 علاوه ælave *addition*
782 راهى rahi *bound for, a path*
783 انرژى enerʒi *energy*
784 قالب ʝaleb, bar *model*
785 جمهور dʒomhur *republic*
786 كشيدن keʃidæn *pull, draw*
787 باور bavær *belief*
788 مسجد mæsdʒed *mosque*
789 دشمن doʃmæn *enemy*
790 پايين pajin *bottom*
792 روبرو ruberu *opposite*
794 پخش pæxʃ *distribution, broadcasting*
796 خيابان xijaban *street*

797 ساختمان saxteman *building*
798 محقق mohæɣɣeɣ, mohæɣɣæɣ *scholar, ascertained*
799 ساكن saken *resident*
800 شخص ʃæxs *person*
801 كميسيون komisijon *commission*
802 خواسته xaste *demand*
803 تبديل tæbdil *conversion*
804 امتياز emtijaz *point, privilege*
805 لحاظ læhaz *perspective*
806 شرق ʃærɣ *east*
807 وسيله væsile *means, instrument*
808 نسل næsl *generation*
809 قسمت ɣesmæt *section*
810 سراسر særasær *throughout*
811 اعتبار eʔtebar *credit, validity*
814 جاده dʒadde *road*
816 سالگى salegi *years old*
817 اشتباه eʃtebah *mistake*
819 كشته koʃte, keʃte *killed, cultivated*
821 اينجا indʒa *here*
823 كشتى keʃti, koʃti *ship, wrestling*
825 بروز boruz *appearance*
826 كشاورزى keʃaværzi *agriculture*
827 انتقاد enteɣad *criticism*
829 تعريف tæʔrif *definition, description*
830 بازيكن bazikon *player*
831 پست post *post*
833 باقى baɣi *remaining*
835 جمعى dʒæmʔi *collective*
836 مقايسه moɣajese *comparison*
837 زمينى zæmini *land, earthling*
839 پذيرش pæzireʃ *reception, admission*
840 درمان dærman *treatment*
842 جلب dʒælb *attraction*
843 محروم mæhrum *deprived, banned*
844 صادرات saderat *exports*
847 پزشكى pezeʃki *medical*
848 عالم alem, alæm *learned, world*
851 برداشت bærdaʃt *harvest, withdrawal, understanding*
852 نويسنده nevisænde *writer*
853 هفت hæft *seven*

854 تجارت tedʒaræt *trade*
855 خريد xarid *purchase*
858 فردى færdi *individual*
859 دختر doxtær *girl, daughter*
863 ارسال ersal *sending*
864 ابزار æbzar *tool*
868 حرف hærf *letter, talk*
869 داستان dastan *story*
870 خانم xanom *lady, Mrs.*
871 قربانى ɣorbani *victim, sacrifice*
872 معدن mæʔdæn *mine*
873 مسافر mosafer *traveler, passenger*
874 قوه ɣovve *strength*
877 حاصل hasel *result*
878 اتفاق ettefaɣ *event*
879 اندازه ændaze *size*
882 اجازه edʒaze *permit*
883 پدر pedær *father*
884 بازگشت bazgæʃt *return*
885 پر pær, por *feather, full*
886 مطالعه motaleʔe *study*
887 ارتش ærteʃ *army*
888 ضعف zæʔf *weakness*
889 افتخار eftexar *honor*
890 آمادگى amadegi *readiness, preschool*
891 نامزد namzæd *candidate*
892 ويژگى viʒegi *characteristic*
893 تلويزيون televizijun *television*
894 شيعه ʃiʔe *Shiite*
895 خواستار xastar *applicant, desirous*
898 مناسبت monasebæt *suitability, relevance to occasion*
900 كارخانه karxane *factory*
901 موافقت movafeɣæt *agreement*
902 مجموع mædʒmuʔ *total*
903 كشتن koʃtæn *kill*
904 محلى mæhælli *local*
906 اتحاديه ettehadije *union*
908 وحدت væhdæt *unity*
909 بحران bohran *crisis*
910 دل del *heart*
911 فرمانده færmande *commander*
912 سنت sonnæt *tradition*
916 عدالت edalæt *justice*
917 سرمايه‌گذارى særmajegozari *investment*
918 صبح sobh *morning*
919 سخنرانى soxænrani *speech*

920 باشگاه	baʃgah *club*	
921 كشف	kæʃf *discovery*	
923 قهرمانى	yæhremani *heroism, championship*	
924 جشنواره	dʒæʃnvare *festival*	
925 سود	sud *profit*	
927 تهديد	tæhdid *threat*	
930 مادر	madær *mother*	
931 فرار	færar *escape*	
933 قتل	yætl *killing, murder*	
935 ثبت	sæbt *registration*	
936 شهروند	ʃæhrvænd *citizen*	
937 صلح	solh *peace*	
938 طلا	tæla *gold*	
942 عرب	æræb *Arab*	
944 هويت	hovijjæt *identity*	
945 بدن	bædæn *body*	
946 سلاح	selah *weapon*	
947 دانشمند	daneʃmænd *scientist*	
950 درون	dærun *inside*	
951 رنگ	ræng *color*	
952 فرانسوى	færansævi *French*	
953 كيفيت	kejfijjæt *quality*	
955 خشونت	xoʃunæt *violence*	
957 شماره	ʃomare *number*	
958 پشت	poʃt *back*	
959 عملى	æmæli *practical*	
960 مذاكرات	mozakerat *negotiations*	
961 ورزش	værzeʃ *sport*	
963 موضع	mowzeʔ *position*	
966 متوجه	motevædʒdʒeh *conscious*	
968 عبارت	ebaræt *phrase, expression*	
969 ارزيابى	ærzjabi *assessment*	
970 تصور	tæsævvor *imagination*	
971 شاعر	ʃaʔer *poet*	
972 اعتماد	eʔtemad *trust*	
973 آرامش	arameʃ *tranquility*	
974 نفع	næfʔ *profit, benefit*	
975 فقر	fæyr *poverty*	
976 همكار	hæmkar *colleague*	
977 اولويت	owlævvijæt *priority*	
978 متخصص	motæxæsses *expert, specialist*	
979 صندوق	sænduy *fund, box*	
981 فارسى	farsi *Persian*	
982 نزديكى	næzdiki *proximity*	
983 رضايت	rezajæt *satisfaction*	
984 نگرانى	negærani *anxiety*	
987 قرن	yærn *century*	
988 رسيدگى	residegi *investigation*	

989 ريال	rijal *rial*	
993 خودرو	xodrow *car*	
994 عرض	ærz *width, saying*	
995 مقدار	meydar *amount*	
997 قول	yowl *promise, saying*	
998 سپرده	seporde *entrusted, deposit*	
1002 قطع	yætʔ *cut*	
1003 مأمور	mæʔmur *agent, officer*	
1004 ايالت	ejalæt *state*	
1006 شكست	ʃekæst *defeat, failure, break*	
1007 تفاوت	tæfavot *difference*	
1008 همايش	hæmajeʃ *conference*	
1009 هفتم	hæftom *seventh*	
1010 كلاس	kelas *class*	
1011 روشنى	rowʃæni *light*	
1012 وجه	vædʒh *manner*	
1013 ساختار	saxtar *structure*	
1014 توافق	tævafoy *agreement*	
1015 كارگر	kargær *worker*	
1017 تمرين	tæmrin *practice*	
1018 عمر	omr *life*	
1019 دارو	daru *drug*	
1020 عقيده	æyide *belief*	
1021 آهن	ahæn *iron*	
1022 كيلومتر	kilometr *kilometer*	
1023 محور	mehvær *axis*	
1024 ارتقا	erteya *promotion, upgrade*	
1025 استقبال	esteybal *welcome*	
1026 رضا	reza *Reza*	
1027 تأييد	tæʔjid *confirmation*	
1029 نيازمند	nijazmænd *needy, in need*	
1030 انداختن	ændaxtæn *throw*	
1032 عربى	æræbi *Arabic*	
1034 پنجم	pændʒom *fifth*	
1035 توانايى	tævanaji *ability*	
1036 صفر	sefr *zero*	
1037 شهرى	ʃæhri *urban*	
1038 فقير	fæyir *poor*	
1039 كشورى	keʃværi *state*	
1040 راستا	rasta *direction*	
1042 فكرى	fekri *mental, intellectual*	
1045 پوشش	puʃeʃ *cover*	
1046 سخنگو	soxængu *spokesperson*	
1049 وعده	væʔde *promise*	
1050 عزيز	æziz *dear*	
1051 دوستى	dusti *friendship*	

1053 امضا	emzaʔ *signature*	
1054 ماست	mast *yogurt*	
1056 سوخت	suxt *fuel*	
1057 تحويل	tæhvil *delivery, submission*	
1058 رفع	ræfʔ *removing*	
1059 باره	bare *subject*	
1063 تبليغ	tæbliy *propaganda, advertising*	
1064 پسر	pesær *son*	
1065 انتشار	enteʃar *publication*	
1066 پرسش	porseʃ *question*	
1067 مقاومت	moyavemæt *resistance*	
1068 ظرف	zærf *container, vessel*	
1069 قبول	yæbul *accepting*	
1070 تحليل	tæhlil *analysis*	
1071 قطعه	yætʔe *piece*	
1072 معروف	mæʔruf *famous*	
1073 بهره	bæhre *portion, interest*	
1074 شاه	ʃah *king, shah*	
1075 ضد	zedd *against*	
1077 هواپيما	hævapejma *airplane*	
1078 شخصى	ʃæxsi *personal*	
1079 هشت	hæʃt *eight*	
1080 شكستن	ʃekæstæn *break*	
1082 تلفن	telefon *telephone*	
1083 كليه	kolje, kollijje *kidney, all*	
1086 كارت	kart *card*	
1087 جذب	dʒæzb *absorption*	
1089 تماس	tæmas *contact*	
1090 مجمع	mædʒmæʔ *assembly, convention*	
1093 روزى	ruzi *someday, daily bread*	
1095 بيمارستان	bimarestan *hospital*	
1096 ذخيره	zæxire *supply*	
1097 درجه	dærædʒe *degree*	
1098 راديو	radijo *radio*	
1099 سينما	sinema *cinema*	
1100 پيش‌بينى	piʃbini *prediction*	
1102 دروازه	dærvaze *gate, goal*	
1103 شناسايى	ʃenasaʔi *identification*	
1104 مبنا	mæbna *base, basis*	
1105 چينى	tʃini *Chinese*	
1106 تنظيم	tænzim *regulation, adjustment*	
1107 حاكميت	hakemijjæt *rule*	
1108 نهايت	næhajæt *extremity, end*	
1110 شك	ʃækk *doubt*	

1287 تیر	tir *arrow, Tir*	
1289 مجله	mædzælle *magazine*	
1290 هماهنگی	hæmahængi *harmony, coordination*	
1295 صحبت	sohbæt *talk*	
1297 اصطلاح	estelah *expression*	
1298 اعتراض	eʔteraz *protest*	
1299 توزیع	towziʔ *distribution*	
1300 وکیل	vækil *attorney*	
1301 امیر	æmir *emir*	
1302 اطمینان	etminan *confidence*	
1303 کنگره	kongere *congress*	
1304 پیگیری	pejgiri *follow-through*	
1305 دقت	deɣɣæt *accuracy*	
1306 پرده	pærde *curtain*	
1307 مثال	mesal *example*	
1308 رقیب	ræɣib *competitor*	
1313 نظیر	næzir *equal*	
1314 مرتبه	mærtæbe *time, floor*	
1316 نوجوان	nowdzævan *teenager*	
1317 محله	mæhælle *district*	
1318 تحصیل	tæhsil *study*	
1319 انگیزه	ængize *motivation*	
1320 شکایت	ʃekajæt *complaint*	
1321 تحقیقاتی	tæhɣiɣati *research*	
1322 چهل	tʃehel *forty*	
1323 مدعی	moddæʔi *plaintiff*	
1324 مقطع	moɣættæʔ, mæɣtæʔ *broken, section*	
1325 فراوانی	færavani *abundance*	
1326 سنگ	sæng *rock*	
1327 سردار	særdar *commander, general*	
1328 مجازات	modzazat *punishment*	
1329 حکایت	hekajæt *story*	
1330 عضویت	ozvijæt *membership*	
1332 کارکنان	karkonan *employees*	
1336 قابلیت	ɣabelijjæt *capability*	
1337 متحد	mottæhed *united, ally*	
1338 عنصر	onsor *element*	
1339 حاشیه	hæʃije *margin*	
1340 تعهد	tæʔæhhod *commitment*	
1341 قلب	ɣælb *heart*	
1342 آدم	adæm *person*	
1344 قشر	ɣeʃr *bark, stratum*	
1345 اعدام	eʔdam *execution*	
1346 سایه	saje *shadow*	
1347 کارمند	karmænd *employee*	
1349 ادبیات	ædæbijjat *literature*	
1350 باد	bad *wind*	
1352 جستجو	dzostedzu *search*	
1353 جدایی	dzodaji *separation*	

1354 فلسطینی	felestini *Palestinian*	
1356 تدبیر	tædbir *measure, plan*	
1357 ایفا	ifa *play*	
1359 مهاجر	mohadzer *immigrant*	
1360 حیات	hæjat *life*	
1361 بستن	bæstæn *close*	
1362 جزیره	dzæzire *island*	
1363 برقرار	bæryærar *established*	
1364 قطر	ɣotr, ɣætær *diagonal/ diameter, Qatar*	
1365 شور	ʃur, ʃowr *salty/ passion, deliberation*	
1366 دارایی	daraji *property*	
1367 مهاجرت	mohadzeræt *emigration, immigration*	
1368 تقسیم	tæɣsim *division*	
1369 تکمیل	tækmil *completion*	
1371 اخلاق	æxlaɣ *morality*	
1373 جشن	dzæʃn *celebration*	
1374 تخریب	tæxrib *destruction*	
1376 محفل	mæhʔfel *social circle*	
1377 ذکر	zekr, zækær *mention, penis*	
1379 حقوقی	hoɣuɣi *legal*	
1380 دریایی	dærjaji *maritime*	
1381 فرایند	færajænd *process*	
1382 حریف	hærif *opponent*	
1383 بیمه	bime *insurance*	
1384 جرم	dzorm, dzerm *crime, substance*	
1385 جایزه	dzajeze *award*	
1386 دهم	dæhom *tenth*	
1387 همسایه	hæmsaje *neighbor*	
1388 صف	sæff *queue*	
1389 توصیه	towsije *recommendation*	
1391 بهمن	bæhmæn *avalanche, Bahman*	
1392 توصیف	towsif *description*	
1393 کیلوگرم	kilogræm *kilogram*	
1396 برنده	bærænde *winner*	
1398 دستاورد	dæstaværd *achievement*	
1399 گرد	gærd, gerd, gord *powder/dust, round, champion*	
1400 سری	seri, særi *series, a head*	
1401 عقب	æɣæb *back*	
1402 رونق	rownæɣ *boom*	
1403 سبز	sæbz *green*	
1404 بشر	bæʃær *human*	

1408 اتاق	otaɣ *room*	
1409 جبهه	dzebhe *front*	
1410 اعزام	eʔzam *dispatch*	
1414 دسترسی	dæstresi *accessibility*	
1415 گزارشی	gozareʃi *reporting*	
1416 مصاحبه	mosahebe *interview*	
1419 بانو	banu *lady*	
1421 فرمان	færman *command*	
1422 کلمه	kælæme *word*	
1423 منطقی	mænteɣi *logical*	
1425 مالیات	malijat *tax, taxes*	
1426 راهکار	rahkar *strategy, solution*	
1429 تبادل	tæbadol *exchange*	
1432 نفوذ	nofuz *influence*	
1433 یکشنبه	jekʃæmbe *Sunday*	
1434 ماهی	mahi *fish, a month*	
1435 ستاره	setare *star*	
1436 شعار	ʃeʔar *slogan*	
1439 بندر	bændær *port*	
1440 بهانه	bæhane *excuse*	
1441 واسطه	vasete *mediator*	
1442 منطق	mænteɣ *logic*	
1444 چنان	tʃonæn *such*	
1446 دبیر	dæbir *secretary*	
1447 خروج	xorudz *exit*	
1448 توجیه	towdzih *explanation, justification*	
1450 تقدیر	tæɣdir *destiny, appreciation*	
1452 ماشین	maʃin *machine, car*	
1453 مایل	majel *willing*	
1454 روحیه	ruhijje *mood, morale*	
1458 تربیت	tærbijæt *training, upbringing*	
1459 ستاد	setad *headquarters*	
1461 قوت	ɣovvæt, ɣut *strength, nourishment*	
1462 باب	bab *gate, chapter*	
1464 جلوه	dzelve *revealing*	
1466 برقراری	bæryærari *establishing*	
1469 طلب	tælæb *demand, desire, -seeker*	
1470 محاکمه	mohakeme *trial*	
1471 استقرار	esteɣrar *positioning, settlement*	
1472 نظریه	næzærijje *theory*	
1473 هشدار	hoʃdar *warning*	
1474 سالن	salon *hall*	
1475 ثبات	sobat, sæbbat *stability, clerk*	
1476 مطبوعات	mætbuat *press*	

1670 تشخیص tæʃxis distinguishing, diagnosis	1729 لایحه lajehe bill	1797 وابستگی vabæstegi dependence
1672 تابستان tabestan summer	1730 والیبال valibal volleyball	1798 تماشاگر tæmaʃagær spectator
1674 بهرهبرداری bæhrebærdari exploitation, operation	1731 شعبه ʃoʔbe branch	1799 نماینده næmajændeje مجلس mædʒles member of parliament
1675 کره kære, kore, korre butter, Korea/earth, foal	1733 پیرامون piramun perimeter	
	1734 نیت nijjæt intent	1800 بومی bumi native
1677 علامت ælamæt mark	1735 پارک park park	1802 ثروتمند servætmænd wealthy
1678 کوه kuh mountain	1736 تابلو tablo panel, sign	1803 ترسیم tærsim drawing, tracing
1680 ملک mælæk, mælek, melk angel, king, estate	1737 تخلف tæxællof violation	
	1738 اندیشیدن ændiʃidæn think	1804 خاطره xatere memory
1682 هشتاد hæftad eighty	1739 جنبه dʒæmbe aspect	1805 هسته hæste nucleus, core
1683 انتخاباتی entexabati electoral	1741 برگزیده bærgozide choice, elite	1806 اتحاد ettehad union, alliance
1685 هفتاد hæftad seventy	1743 دی dej Dey	
1686 بیگانه bigane foreign, alien	1744 ربودن robudæn steal	1807 مبادله mobadele exchange
1687 مزیت mæzijjæt advantage	1745 مخاطب moxatæb viewer, reader	1809 سرویس servis service
1688 مهندسی mohændesi engineering		1810 میانه mijane middle
1689 وفاداری væfadari loyalty	1748 دکترا doktora doctorate	1811 برتری bærtæri superiority, advantage
1690 تک tæk, tok single/attack, tip	1749 کیلو kilo kilo, kilogram	
	1750 نوار nævar tape	1812 دستی dæsti manual, handmade, tame
1691 ترس tærs fear	1755 تشریح tæʃrih dissection, anatomy	1815 مهار mæhar control
1693 رویکرد rujkærd approach	1756 ناظر nazer observer	1816 ظاهر zaher appearance
1694 فتح fæth victory	1757 بیستم bistom twentieth	1817 حلقه hælye ring
1695 جنگی dʒængi military	1758 راست rast right	1819 گلوله golule bullet
1696 قاره yare continent	1759 تعطیل tæʔtil holiday	1820 دامنه damæne range, slope
1697 صادر sader issued, exported	1760 خرداد xordad Khordad	1822 خواب xab sleep, dream
1698 ترور teror assassination	1761 فضایی fæzaji space	1824 نوری nuri light
1700 بازداشت bazdaʃt arrest	1762 سلول sellul cell	1825 مهندس mohændes engineer
1701 المپیک olæmpik olympic, olympics	1763 آسمان asman heaven	1826 نخستوزیر noxostvæzir prime minister
1702 مدل model model	1765 ضرب zærb multiplication, assault	
1704 ردیف rædif row	1766 رأس ræʔs head, top	1827 انقلابی enyelabi revolutionary
1705 مقصد mæysæd destination	1767 شغل ʃoyl job	1828 سلامتی sælamæti health
1706 گذراندن gozærandæn spend time, pass	1768 شهرک ʃæhræk town	1829 گوشه guʃe corner
	1769 دانشکده daneʃkæde college, faculty	1832 لیگ lig league
1707 واردات varedat imports		1833 محیطزیست mohitezist environment
1708 تسهیلات tæshilat facilities, amenities	1770 دوری duri, dowri distance, plate	
	1773 طبیعت tæbiʔæt nature	1837 چپ tʃæp left
1709 احداث ehdas construction	1774 قضائیه yæzaʔijje judiciary	1839 سد sædd dam, block
1711 عموم omum public, whole	1776 معماری meʔmari architecture	1840 لیست list list
1712 اثبات esbat proof	1777 شاخه ʃaxe branch	1843 ترجمه tærdʒome translation
1713 استراتژی estrateʒi strategy	1779 کاربرد karbord application, use	1844 کوشش kuʃeʃ effort
1714 اردو ordu camp		1845 جوانی dʒævani youth
1715 گوش guʃ ear	1780 ازدواج ezdevadʒ marriage	1846 یهودی jæhudi Jew, Jewish
1716 استراحت esterahæt rest	1784 ارز ærz foreign currency	1847 تحرک tæhærrok movement
1717 سنگینی sangini weight	1785 دوربین durbin camera	1848 رودخانه rudxane river
1720 پژوهش pæʒuheʃ research	1786 شصت ʃæst sixty	1849 طلبیدن tælæbidæn call, ask, require
1722 ورزشکار værzeʃkar athlete	1787 ورزشگاه værzeʃgah stadium	
1723 تحریم tæhrim sanction	1788 قبال yebal opposite, facing	1850 فساد fesad corruption
1725 جنایت dʒenajæt crime	1789 وام vam loan	1852 معیار meʔjar standard
1727 تبعه tæbæʔe citizen	1790 تظاهرات tæzahorat protests	1853 روحانی rowhani cleric, Rowhani
	1791 تنش tæneʃ tension	
	1793 پژوهشگر pæʒuheʃgær researcher	1855 تالار talar hall

2051 میلاد milad *birth*

2052 فرق færγ *difference*

2053 جانشین dʒaneʃin *successor, substitute*

2056 عقل æγl *reason*

2057 جلالی dʒælali *Jalali*

2058 گشایش goʃajeʃ *opening, relief*

2059 پوست pust *skin*

2060 خلیج xælidʒ *gulf*

2061 کوچکی kutʃæki *smallness*

2062 آگاه agah *aware*

2064 زاویه zavije *angle*

2066 جلد dʒeld, dʒæld *volume, quick*

2067 مذهب mæzhæb *religion*

2068 داوطلب davtælæb *volunteer, applicant*

2069 ارتفاع ertefaʔ *altitude, height*

2070 سیاستمدار sijasætmædar *politician*

2072 همبستگی hæmbæstegi *solidarity*

2073 راحتی rahæti *comfort*

2075 پارس pars *bark, Pars*

2076 دوازده dævazdæh *twelve*

2077 تبعیض tæbʔiz *discrimination*

2078 مبارز mobarez *fighter*

2079 پارلمان parleman *parliament*

2081 تکنولوژی teknoloʒi *technology*

2082 آزمون azmun *test*

2084 کشاورز keʃaværz *farmer*

2086 دیر dir, dejr *late, monastery*

2088 لطف lotf *kindness*

2089 ظهور zohur *appearance*

2090 گردش gærdeʃ *circulation*

2092 آبی abi *blue*

2093 افغان æfγan *Afghan*

2095 ثانیه sanije *second*

2096 تجاوز tædʒavoz *aggression*

2097 کارشناسی karʃenasi *expertise, bachelor's degree*

2098 سه‌شنبه seʃæmbe *Tuesday*

2099 وحشت væhʃæt *panic*

2100 جنجال dʒændʒal *tumult*

2101 کودتا kudeta *coup d'état*

2102 سنجش sændʒeʃ *measurement*

2103 راندن randæn *drive*

2105 پاس pas *pass*

2106 ترویج tærvidʒ *promotion*

2107 روایت revajæt *narrative*

2109 مستند mostænæd *documentary*

2110 پتروشیمی petroʃimi *petrochemistry*

2111 واگذاری vagozari *settlement, transferring*

2112 میرزا mirza *scribe, Mirza*

2113 ایده ide *idea*

2115 آرزو arezu *wish*

2116 شهرسازی ʃæhrsazi *urban development*

2117 جسد dʒæsæd *corpse*

2119 عوض ævæz *change*

2121 اجتماع edʒtemaʔ *community*

2122 خان xan *Khan*

2123 زمستان zemestan *winter*

2124 دبیرکل dæbirekol *secretary general*

2125 هندی hendi *Indian, Hindi*

2126 متقاضی motæγazi *applicant*

2130 اشغال eʃγal *occupation*

2131 نشانی neʃani *address*

2134 هدیه hedje *gift*

2135 برف bærf *snow*

2137 ابتکار ebtekar *initiative, innovation*

2138 منتخب montæxæb *chosen, elected*

2139 پیروی pejrævi *obedience, following*

2140 فریب færib *deception*

2141 کتابخانه ketabxane *library*

2143 بابت babæt *matter, for*

2146 بافت baft *context, texture, tissue*

2147 دموکراسی demokrasi *democracy*

2148 جنس dʒens *gender, merchandise*

2149 کانال kanal *channel, canal*

2151 مدافع modafeʔ *defender*

2153 تنهایی tænhaji *loneliness*

2154 مراقبت moraγebæt *supervision*

2155 مرحوم mærhum *deceased*

2157 کابل kabol, kabl *Kabul, cable*

2158 موتور motor *engine, motorcycle*

2160 فراموش færamuʃ *forgotten*

2163 امیدواری omidvari *hopefulness*

2164 برابری bærabæri *equality*

2165 یازده jazdæh *eleven*

2166 میزبان mizban *host*

2167 کیلومتری kilometri *kilometer*

2170 مطالبه motalebe *demanding payment*

2171 تضعیف tæzʔif *weakening*

2176 جدیت dʒeddijæt *seriousness*

2177 خلاصه xolase *summary*

2178 تحمیل tæhmil *imposition*

2179 قدم γædæm *step*

2181 اتوبوس otobus *bus*

2182 دیپلماسی diplomasi *diplomacy*

2183 باند band *band*

2184 مهارت mæharæt *skill*

2185 نقض næγz *violation*

2187 تعامل tæʔamol *interaction*

2190 عمق omγ *depth*

2191 تصمیم‌گیری tæsmimgiri *decision making*

2192 حبس hæbs *prison*

2193 دام dam *trap, livestock*

2194 پیامبر pæjambær *prophet*

2197 تعبیر tæʔbir *interpretation*

2198 دوش duʃ *shoulder, shower*

2199 ایتالیایی italijaji *Italian*

2200 وزارتخانه vezarætxane *ministry*

2202 محاسبه mohasebe *calculation*

2205 تبیین tæbjin *explanation*

2210 تشویق tæʃviγ *encouragement*

2211 خشم xæʃm *anger*

2212 حس hess *sense, feeling*

2213 قضاوت γæzavæt *judgment*

2215 ایمنی imæni *safety*

2217 پیشنهادی piʃnehadi *proposed*

2218 روس rus *Russian*

2219 نشر næʃr *publishing*

2220 زیارت zijaræt *pilgrimage*

2222 بمب bomb *bomb*

2223 سرخ sorx *red*

2224 کلیدی kelidi *key*

2225 سامان saman *orderliness*

2226 خودداری xoddari *self-control*

2227 رئیس‌جمهور ræʔisdʒomhur *president*

2228 ورزیدن værzidæn *exercise*

2229 تدارک tædarok *provision, preparation*

2230 افراطی efrati *extremist*

2231 کتابی ketabi *bookish, flask*

2232 یازدهم jazdæhom *eleventh*

2233 پناه pænah *shelter*

2234 طوفان tufan *storm*

2235 درگذشت dærgozæʃt *death*

2236 حرم hæræm *sanctuary*

2239 خواننده xanænde *reader, singer*

2240 سپتامبر septambr *September*

2242 ادا æda *coquettish, payment*

2244 چاره tʃare *remedy*

2245 دشواری doʃvari *difficulty*

2444 كليسا	kelisa church	2514 شيشه	ʃiʃe glass, bottle	2582 رمز	ræmz code
2445 اوّلاً	ævvælæn first	2516 غلبه	yælæbe triumph	2583 تجزيه	tædʒzije analysis,
2446 زلزله	zelzele earthquake	2517 باستان	bastan ancient		breakdown
2448 اعتبارى	eʔtebari credit	2519 گمرک	gomrok customs	2586 داورى	daværi judgment,
2451 افکندن	æfkændæn throw	2521 تخصص	tæxæssos		arbitration, refereeing
2452 نعمت	neʔmæt gift, blessing		specialization,	2588 قطعنامه	yætʔname resolution
2453 صلاحيت	sælahijjæt		specialty	2590 اسفند	esfænd Esfand
	competence	2523 مد	mædd, mod high tide,	2592 تغذيه	tæyzije feeding,
2454 واحدى	vahedi modular,		fashion		nutrition
	Vahedi	2525 بينى	bini nose	2593 پيکر	pejkær body
2455 مالکيت	malekijjæt possession	2526 جزئيات	dʒozʔijjat details	2595 شنا	ʃena swim
2456 پيدايش	pejdajeʃ genesis	2527 چاى	tʃaj tea	2596 آدمى	adæmi human being
2457 منع	mænʔ forbidding	2528 برخوردارى	bærxordari having,	2597 گواهى	govahi certificate
2458 تساوى	tæsavi equality, tie		enjoying	2599 بهشت	beheʃt heaven
2459 محبوب	mæhbub popular,	2530 معاونت	moʔavenæt	2600 خريدن	xæridæn buy
	beloved		directorate	2601 مضمون	mæzmun theme
2464 نهصد	nohsæd nine hundred	2535 گياه	gijah plant	2602 ماهواره	mahvare satellite
2465 نما	næma front, shot	2537 قلعه	yælʔe castle	2605 عادت	adæt habit
2466 ناشر	naʃer publisher	2538 نشاط	neʃat joy	2606 ابلاغ	eblay notification
2468 تجهيز	tædʒhiz equipping	2541 بنيان	bonjan structure	2607 چراغ	tʃeray light
2469 تيره	tire dark, family, dash	2542 مشمول	mæʃmul included,	2608 لايه	laje layer
2470 تجليل	tædʒlil honoring		subject to, draftee	2609 مناقشه	monayeʃe dispute
2471 توقع	tævæyyoʔ expectation	2543 نهادن	næhadæn put, place	2610 جسمى	dʒesmi physical
2472 بارندگى	barændegi	2544 گردن	gærdæn neck	2611 روغن	rowyæn oil
	precipitation	2545 پيشينه	piʃine background	2613 هجوم	hodʒum attack
2476 تضمين	tæzmin assurance	2546 راز	raz secret, mystery	2615 پشتوانه	poʃtvane backing
2477 ظهر	zohr, zæhr noon,	2547 سلب	sælb divesting	2616 يونانى	junani Greek
	back	2548 کارنامه	karname report card	2617 رفتارى	ræftari behavioral
2482 تخليه	tæxlije evacuation,	2549 بسکتبال	bæsketbal basketball	2619 زور	zur force
	discharge	2550 نگريستن	negæristæn look	2624 تازگى	tazegi novelty,
2484 الف	ælef alef	2551 شکر	ʃekær, ʃokr sugar,		freshness, recently
2486 پديد	pædid visible		thanks	2625 بازگشتن	bazgæʃtæn return
2487 استخدام	estexdam employment	2552 تعاونى	tæʔavoni cooperative	2627 توقيف	towyif arrest,
2490 سرما	særma cold	2554 مشخصه	moʃæxxæse		sequestration
2491 بيرونى	biruni external		characteristic	2629 پيکان	pejkan arrow, Paykan
2493 نحو	nahv manner, syntax	2557 مرغ	mory fowl	2634 نايب	najeb deputy
2496 دما	dæma temperature	2558 دهنده	dæhænde donor,	2635 دهان	dæhan mouth
2497 والدين	valedejn parents		-giving	2639 پير	pir old
2498 جناح	dʒenah faction	2561 سوار	sævar rider	2640 عاشق	aʃey lover
2499 برشمردن	bærʃomordæn	2562 سالگرد	salgærd anniversary	2641 قيام	yijam rising
	enumerate	2564 سوختن	suxtæn burn	2642 تقويم	tæyvim calendar
2500 رکورد	rekord record	2565 ميز	miz table	2644 تبعيد	tæbʔid exile
2501 ارديبهشت	ordibeheʃt	2566 بلندى	bolændi height	2645 صبا	sæba zephyr
	Ordibehesht	2568 فرم	form form	2648 جعفرى	dʒæʔfæri parsley,
2502 گرسنگى	gorosnegi hunger	2569 ميانگين	mijangin average		Jafari
2503 زحمت	zæhmæt trouble	2572 مطبوعاتى	mætbuʔati press	2649 تثبيت	tæsbit stabilizing
2504 تعليم	tæʔlim teaching	2573 تأسف	tæʔæssof regret	2651 منظر	mænzær perspective
2507 ظلم	zolm oppression	2574 دسترس	dæstres access	2652 عملياتى	æmælijjati operational
2508 بيکار	bikar unemployed	2575 تابع	tabeʔ citizen, follower	2653 پانصد	pansæd five hundred
2509 کارگاه	kargah workshop	2578 بزرگداشت	bozorgdaʃt ceremony	2655 فرود	forud landing
2510 بو	bu smell	2579 صفت	sefæt adjective,	2656 سرنشين	særneʃin passenger
2512 درياچه	dærjatʃe lake		quality	2658 پاسدار	pasdar guard
2513 حريم	hærim confines	2581 مو	mu, mow hair, vine	2659 فاز	faz phase

2857 آینه	ajene *mirror*	2908 اکتبر	oktobr *October*	2968 سیمان	siman *cement*
2858 خونی	xuni *blood*	2909 مخابرات	moxaberat	2969 انحصار	enhesar *monopoly*
2859 شوق	ʃowy *eagerness*		*telecommunication*	2970 همتا	hæmta *peer*
2861 هموطن	hæmvætæn	2910 کاغذ	kayæz *paper*	2972 زبانی	zæbani *verbal, lingual*
	compatriot	2911 عیار	æjar *purity, Ayyar*	2973 شکار	ʃekar *hunting*
2863 رمان	roman *novel*	2913 بیداری	bidari *being awake*	2974 محوطه	mohævvæte
2864 سفارش	sefareʃ *order*	2914 انتقادی	enteyadi *critical*		*enclosure, campus*
2866 جزئی	dʒozʔi *slight*	2915 غرق	yæry *drowning,*	2976 مصاف	mæsaf *battle*
2868 مبتلا	mobtæla *suffering*		*sinking*	2977 سرانه	særane *per capita*
	from	2917 مساحت	mæsahæt *surface*	2978 داغ	day *hot*
2869 بزرگسال	bozorgsal *adult*		*area*	2979 کارکرد	karkærd *performance,*
2871 چوب	tʃub *wood*	2918 فروردین	færværdin *Farvardin*		*mileage*
2873 اجباری	edʒbari *mandatory*	2919 ناشناس	naʃenas *unidentified*	2980 توازن	tævazon *balance*
2874 سرچشمه	særtʃeʃme *source*	2920 جواهر	dʒævaher *jewel*	2982 دانش‌آموز	daneʃamuz *student*
2875 بازنگری	baznegæri	2922 رسالت	resalæt *mission*	2983 سیگار	sigar *cigarette*
	reappraisal	2924 خلع	xælʔ *deposing*	2984 گریز	goriz *escaping*
2877 مشرف	moʃærræf, moʃref	2925 نوآوری	nowaværi *innovation*	2986 نگارش	negareʃ *authorship,*
	honored, near/	2929 گلی	geli, goli *muddy, red*		*writing*
	overlooking	2930 تعالی	tæʔali, tæʔala	2990 آهنگ	ahæng *tune*
2878 انعکاس	enʔekas *reflection*		*elevation, exalted*	2991 استخوان	ostoxan *bone*
2879 محوری	mehværi *pivotal*	2931 پیکار	pejkar *battle*	2992 صادرکننده	saderkonænde
2880 قومی	yowmi *ethnic*	2933 بازرگان	bazærgan *merchant*		*exporter*
2881 بازرس	bazres *inspector*	2934 صحت	sehhæt *health,*	2993 دستیار	dæstjar *assistant*
2882 لیتر	liter *liter*		*correctness*	2994 لذت	lezzæt *pleasure*
2883 اقیانوس	oyjanus *ocean*	2936 باقیمانده	bayimande *remainder*	2996 واداشتن	vadaʃtæn *persuade,*
2884 یادگیری	jadgiri *learning*	2937 ساختاری	saxtari *structural*		*force*
2885 محرم	mæhræm, mohærræm	2938 سلیقه	sæliye *taste*	2998 پرتو	pærtow *ray*
	close relative/	2941 تخفیف	tæxfif *discount*	3000 سایپا	sajpa *Saipa*
	confidant, Moharram	2942 ائتلاف	eʔtelaf *coalition*	3002 غبار	yobar *dust, haze*
2887 ممانعت	momaneʔæt	2943 مفاد	mofad *substance*	3003 آبادانی	abadani *development*
	prevention	2945 شایعه	ʃajeʔe *rumor*	3004 سرکوب	særkub *suppression*
2888 رقابتی	reyabæti *competitive*	2947 انبوه	æmbuh *crowded,*	3006 حدیث	hædis *hadith*
2889 سوز	suz *burning, pain*		*thick*	3007 بیم	bim *fear*
2890 دشمنی	doʃmæni *hostility*	2948 گرفتاری	gereftari *captivity,*	3009 اردوگاه	ordugah *camp*
2891 دندان	dændan *tooth*		*trouble, involvement*	3010 شرکت‌کننده	ʃerkætkonænde
2892 انسجام	ensedʒam *cohesion*	2949 فاتح	fateh *victorious*		*participant*
2893 خلیفه	xælife *caliph*	2950 مارس	mars *March*	3011 سلطان	soltan *sultan, king*
2894 ترسیدن	tærsidæn *fear*	2953 پله	pelle *step*	3012 هواپیمایی	hævapejmaji *aviation,*
2895 جنسی	dʒensi *sexual*	2954 گناه	gonah *sin*		*airline*
2896 لوازم	lævazem *equipment*	2956 رحمت	ræhmæt *compassion*	3015 بینش	bineʃ *insight*
2898 لوله	lule *pipe, tube*	2957 حجت	hodʒdʒæt *reasoning,*	3020 ناچار	natʃar *compelled*
2899 دغدغه	dæydæye *fear,*		*proof*	3023 رواج	rævadʒ *currency,*
	anxiety	2958 عارف	aref *Sufi, conoisseur*		*circulation*
2900 حافظه	hafeze *memory*	2959 رغم	ræym *spite*	3025 سرمربی	særmoræbi *head*
2901 تناقض	tænayoz *contradiction*	2960 کاشی	kaʃi *Kashani, tile*		*coach*
2902 مطلع	mætlæʔ, mottæleʔ	2961 شورش	ʃureʃ *rebellion*	3028 هزاره	hezare *millennium,*
	rising place, well-	2962 تقلید	tæylid *imitation*		*Hazara*
	informed/witness	2963 مالک	malek *owner*	3029 ناو	nav *naval vessel,*
2904 مورخ	moværræx, moværrex	2964 چهارصد	tʃæharsæd *four*		*drain*
	dated, historian		*hundred*	3031 رویا	roʔja *dream*
2905 مس	mes, mæss *copper,*	2965 پرتاب	pærtab *throw*	3032 خشکسالی	xoʃksali *drought*
	touching	2966 سادگی	sadegi *simplicity*	3033 خاصیت	xasijæt *property*
2906 رسانه‌ای	resaneʔi *media*	2967 استمرار	estemrar *continuity*	3035 خیال	xijal *imagination*

3229 انحلال enhelal *liquidation*	3291 وطن vætæn *homeland*	3357 دستورالعمل dæsturolʔæmæl
3230 هفدهم hevdæhom *seventeenth*	3292 ناراحتی narahæti *discomfort*	*instructions*
	3293 داستانی dastani *fictional*	3358 بهرهگیری bæhregiri *utilization*
3231 گردان gærdan, gordan *turning, battalion*	3295 دره dærre *valley*	3359 حاجی hadʒi *Hajji*
	3296 احسان ehsan *charity, Ehsan*	3360 گوشی guʃi *receiver,*
3232 هفتگی hæftegi *weekly*	3300 ممنوعیت mæmnuʔijjæt	*headphones, phone*
3233 کاندیدا kandida *candidate*	*prohibition*	3361 بنیانگذار bonjangozar *founder*
3235 قایم ɣajem *firm, hidden*	3302 کارگردانی kargærdani *direction*	3362 گفتمان gofteman *discourse,*
3236 امپراتوری emperaturi *empire*	3303 اندام ændam *organ, figure*	*dialogue*
3238 مبادرت mobaderæt *undertaking*	3304 راهبردی rahbordi *strategic*	3364 نارضایتی narezajæti *dissatisfaction*
	3306 ملیت mellijjæt *nationality*	
3239 مشاوره moʃavere *consultation*	3308 هوش huʃ *intelligence*	3365 تاجر tadʒer *merchant*
	3310 برخاستن bærxastæn *get/rise up*	3366 زخم zæxm *wound*
3241 درج dærdʒ *insertion, incorporation*	3312 مه mæh, meh, me *moon, fog, May*	3368 بازاری bazari *businessman*
		3369 مایع majeʔ *liquid*
3243 انفرادی enferadi *individual, solitary*	3313 دبیرستان dæbirestan *high school*	3370 کارایی karaji *efficiency*
		3371 سکونت sokunæt *residence*
3244 عقد æɣd *(marriage) contract*	3314 جماعت dʒæmaʔæt *assembly*	3373 بزرگوار bozorgvar *generous, honorable*
	3316 تحریر tæhrir *writing*	
3245 توطئه towteʔe *conspiracy*	3317 خاندان xandan *clan*	3374 چهارچوب tʃæhartʃub *frame, framework*
3246 فلج fælædʒ *crippled*	3318 وزیری væziri *ministerial, Vaziri*	
3249 چشمانداز tʃeʃmændaz *perspective*		3377 صدمه sædme *injury*
	3319 بلوک boluk, belok *district, block*	3378 پنهانی penhani *secret*
3251 لازمه lazeme *requisite, precondition*		3379 شورشی ʃureʃi *rebel*
	3320 آنکارا ankara *Ankara*	3380 انزوا enzeva *isolation*
3253 سهمیه sahmijje *quota, share*	3321 پرش pæreʃ *jump*	3381 کد kædd, kod *toil, code*
3254 ارگان organ *organ*	3323 کلیات kollijat *generalities, general works*	3382 جزء dʒozʔ *part, detail, ingredient*
3255 عنایت enajæt *favor*		
3256 محیطی mohiti *environmental*	3326 تعدیل tæʔdil *modification*	3383 مظلوم mæzlum *oppressed*
3257 کشمکش keʃmækeʃ *conflict*	3328 پاسخگویی pasoxguʔi *responding*	3384 مترو metro *metro*
3258 تعجب tæʔædʒdʒob *surprise*	3329 خوراک xorak *food*	3387 اعتیاد eʔtiad *addiction*
3262 ت te *letter te*	3330 پنجره pændʒere *window*	3388 افغانی æfɣani *Afghan*
3263 سکو sækku *platform*	3333 حرمت hormæt *sanctity*	3389 پاییز pajiz *autumn*
3265 اشراف æʃraf, eʃraf *noblemen, being in high position*	3334 نفرت nefræt *hatred*	3390 سرهنگ særhæng *colonel*
	3335 روشنگری rowʃængæri *enlightenment*	3392 گیرنده girænde *recipient, receiver*
3266 دموکرات demokrat *democrat*		
3269 تانک tank *tank*	3336 انتقام enteɣam *revenge*	3393 معقول mæʔɣul *reasonable*
3270 پویایی pujaji *dynamism*	3337 نفی næfj *negation*	3394 دوازدهم dævazdæhom *twelfth*
3271 علامه ællame *erudite, Allameh*	3338 رایزنی rajzæni *consultation*	3395 مرده morde *dead, lifeless*
	3339 ظاهری zaheri *apparent, superficial*	3396 دایی daji *maternal uncle*
3272 ستایش setajeʃ *praise*		3397 طیف tejf *spectrum*
3274 فاکتور faktor *invoice, factor*	3342 کور kur *blind*	3398 پیچیدگی piʃidegi *twist, complexity*
3276 برون borun *outside*	3343 انبار ænbar *storehouse*	
3277 معلول mæʔlul *disabled, effect*	3344 شناسنامه ʃenasname *identity card*	3400 هیجان hæjædʒan *excitement, emotion*
3279 کامپیوتر kampjuter *computer*	3345 تعویق tæʔviɣ *delay, postponement*	3402 ناامیدی naomidi *hopelessness*
3281 سنا sena *senate*	3346 خروجی xorudʒi *exit, output*	3405 سگ sæg *dog*
3282 هیاهو hæjahu *tumult*	3349 متولد motævælled *born*	3406 سازش sazeʃ *reconciliation, compromise*
3283 دویدن dævidæn *run*	3350 ذیل zejl *appendix, following, below*	
3284 سطحی sæthi *superficial*		3408 بهبودی behbudi *improvement, gaining in health*
3287 عاشورا aʃura *Ashura*	3351 برانگیخته bærængixte *stimulated, excited*	
3288 استبداد estebdad *tyranny*		3410 سالیانه salijane *annually*
3289 سپاهان sepahan *Sepahan*	3353 گردشگر gærdeʃgær *tourist*	3413 کنون konun *now*
3290 بازنشسته bazneʃæste *retired*		

3608 تأليف	tæʔlif *compilation*	
3612 ارمغان	ærmæɣan *souvenir*	
3614 پنالتى	penalti *penalty*	
3615 زنگ	zæng *bell, ring*	
3616 ششصد	ʃeʃsæd *six hundred*	
3618 حسينيه	hosejnijje *assembly hall*	
3619 تعليق	tæʔliɣ *suspension*	
3620 قلمرو	ɣælæmrow *realm*	
3622 نيكى	niki *goodness, good deed*	
3624 معمار	meʔmar *architect*	
3625 شرف	ʃæræf *honor*	
3626 توسل	tævæssol *resorting*	
3627 كرامت	kæramæt *generosity, dignity*	
3629 گنبد	gombæd *dome*	
3630 رستوران	restoran *restaurant*	
3631 اجاره	edʒare *rent*	
3632 اكتشاف	ekteʃaf *exploration*	
3633 چربى	tʃærbi *fat*	
3634 مؤمن	moʔmen *devout*	
3637 غريب	ɣærib *strange*	
3638 منشى	monʃi *secretary*	
3639 شانه	ʃane *comb, shoulder*	
3641 بهرورى	bahreværi *productivity*	
3642 صنف	senf *guild, trade*	
3643 چشمه	tʃeʃme *spring*	
3646 محال	mohal *impossible*	
3647 بوستان	bustan *orchard*	
3648 استعمار	esteʔmar *colonialism*	
3649 احتياط	ehtijat *caution*	
3651 خرسندى	xorsændi *satisfaction, contentment*	
3652 تظاهركننده	tæzahor konænde *protester*	
3654 تمدنى	tamaddoni *civilization*	
3655 پيشروى	piʃrævi *progress*	
3656 تكنيك	teknik *technique*	
3658 اهل بيت	æhle bejt *household*	
3659 پالايشگاه	palajeʃgah *refinery*	
3660 گور	gur *tomb*	
3661 ديار	dijar *land*	
3662 معافيت	moʔafijjæt *exemption*	
3664 تفكيك	tæfkik *separation*	
3665 خواجه	xadʒe *eunuch, master*	
3666 عبادت	ebadæt *worship*	
3667 پافشارى	pafeʃari *insistence, persistence*	
3670 موش	muʃ *mouse, rat*	
3671 صحرا	sæhra *fields, desert*	
3672 قبيله	ɣæbile *tribe*	
3673 سوره	sure *sura*	

3674 ماهانه	mahane *monthly*	
3675 آزار	azar *torture, torment*	
3677 تور	tur *net, tour*	
3678 كيف	kif, kejf *bag, intoxication*	
3679 ليبرال	liberal *liberal*	
3681 ايدز	ejdz *AIDS*	
3682 خيانت	xijanæt *treachery*	
3683 فقره	fæɣære *vertebra, case, incidence*	
3684 دزد	dozd *thief*	
3685 تزيين	tæzjin *decoration*	
3686 ضريب	zærib *factor, ratio, index*	
3689 مبدأ	mæbdæʔ *origin*	
3690 مبدل	mobæddæl *transformed*	
3691 مادرى	madæri *maternal*	
3692 تذكر	tæzækkor *reminder, notice*	
3693 طلاق	tælaɣ *divorce*	
3695 افراط	efrat *excess*	
3698 فرماندارى	færmandari *governorship*	
3699 دوچرخه	dotʃærxe *bicycle*	
3701 ترياك	tærjak *opium*	
3702 سرتاسر	særtasær *throughout*	
3704 پروفسور	profesor *professor*	
3705 ياس	jas, jæʔs *jasmine, despair*	
3706 تكذيب	tækzib *denial, contradiction*	
3708 ارمنى	ærmæni *Armenian*	
3710 كرانه	kerane *shore*	
3712 نشانگر	neʃangær *marker*	
3713 معاينه	moʔajene *examination*	
3715 تبصره	tæbsere *note, clause*	
3716 شناور	ʃenavær *floating*	
3718 تسليحات	taslihat *armaments*	
3719 شجاعت	ʃodʒaʔæt *courage*	
3720 انتصاب	entesab *appointment*	
3721 شاكى	ʃaki *plaintiff*	
3723 خلال	xelal *interval, pick*	
3724 مامان	maman *mom*	
3726 حقوق‌بشر	hoɣuɣebæʃær *human rights*	
3727 آژانس	aʒans *agency*	
3728 اهانت	ehanæt *insult*	
3729 هراس	hæras *fear*	
3730 تاريكى	tariki *darkness*	
3731 محضر	mæhzær *notary public, presence*	

3733 رخداد	roxdad *happening*	
3735 چهاردهم	tʃæhardæhom *fourteenth*	
3736 خنده	xænde *laughter*	
3737 مجسمه	modʒæssæme *statue*	
3738 پتانسيل	potansijel *potential*	
3739 غفلت	ɣeflæt *neglect*	
3740 تنيس	tenis *tennis*	
3743 سرود	sorud *song*	
3744 كينه	kine *grudge*	
3745 كوره	kure *furnace*	
3746 گرمى	gærmi *warmth*	
3748 متخلف	motæxællef *offender*	
3749 دانه	dane *seed, grain*	
3752 جمهوريخواه	dʒomhurixah *republican*	
3754 تزريق	tæzriɣ *injection*	
3755 مانور	manovr *maneuver*	
3758 كاشتن	kaʃtæn *plant*	
3760 تار	tar *dim, string, lute*	
3761 رياضيات	rijazijjat *mathematics*	
3762 مستلزم	mostælzem *requiring*	
3763 موضعى	mowzeʔi *local*	
3765 سمينار	seminar *seminar*	
3768 زيرساخت	zirsaxt *infrastructure*	
3769 اعلاميه	eʔlamijje *announcement*	
3771 آيين	ajin *religion, ceremony, ritual*	
3772 ادغام	edɣam *integration, merger*	
3773 ستم	setæm *cruelty*	
3774 دفعه	dæfʔe *time*	
3775 خشكى	xoʃki *dryness, dry land*	
3777 زوج	zowdʒ *pair, couple*	
3778 معادله	moʔadele *equation*	
3780 اقليم	eɣlim *climate*	
3781 گريبان	geriban *collar*	
3782 خوابيدن	xabidæn *sleep*	
3783 يكسال	jeksal *one year*	
3785 گوناگونى	gunaguni *diversity, variety*	
3786 پاپ	pap *Pope*	
3789 حرارت	hæraræt *heat*	
3790 منتها	montæha *extremity, but*	
3791 قسم	ɣæsæm, ɣesm *oath, sort*	
3793 افسردگى	æfsordegi *depression*	
3795 نمايشگاهى	næmajeʃgahi *exhibition*	
3796 يقين	jæɣin *certain*	

فرمول 3984 formul *formula*

دوام 3986 dævam *durability*

پاداش 3987 padaʃ *reward, bonus*

وزنه 3988 væzne *weight*

دفع 3991 dæfʔ *repelling, fend off*

مؤسس 3995 moʔæsses *founder*

یکسانی 3997 jeksani *identicality*

جیب 3998 dʒejb, dʒib *collar/sine, pocket*

فایده 3999 fajede *benefit*

برهان 4000 borhan *proof, logic*

اذعان 4001 ezʔan *admission*

لوح 4003 lowh *tablet, disk*

فرهنگسرا 4007 færhængsæra *cultural center*

شانزده 4008 ʃanzdæh *sixteen*

پوند 4009 pond *pound*

ترمیم 4011 tærmim *repair, restore*

تحریف 4012 tæhrif *distortion, falsification*

اسکان 4013 eskan *resettlement*

لیسانس 4014 lisans *bachelor's degree*

القا 4019 elɣa *suggestion, induction*

خوشحالی 4020 xoʃhali *happiness, joy*

تعرض 4021 tæʔærroz *offensive, aggression*

چوبی 4022 tʃubi *wooden*

شیطان 4023 ʃejtan *Satan, naughty*

شریعتی 4024 ʃæriʔæti *Shariati*

ابریشم 4025 æbriʃæm *silk*

تندرو 4026 tondrow *fast, extremist*

حول 4027 howl *power, area, around*

اصالت 4028 esalæt *authenticity, originality, gentility*

مابقی 4029 mabæɣi *remainder*

دبیرخانه 4030 dæbirxane *secretariat*

فدا 4031 feda *sacrifice*

عروسی 4033 ærusi *marriage, wedding*

همسایگی 4034 hæmsajegi *neighborhood, proximity*

خداحافظی 4035 xodahafezi *saying goodbye*

روانشناسی 4037 rævanʃenasi *psychology*

نبی 4039 næbi *prophet*

جانشینی 4040 dʒaneʃini *succession, substitution*

افزار 4043 æfzar *tool*

نامزدی 4044 namzædi *engagement, nomination*

سروده 4045 sorude *sung, poem*

معبر 4046 mæʔbær, moʔæbber *thoroughfare, dream interpreter*

تراکم 4048 tærakom *compression, density*

بدنه 4049 bædæne *body, frame*

بدهکار 4050 bedehkar *debtor, indebted*

یادآوری 4051 jadaværi *reminder*

حیث 4052 hejs *respect*

صفا 4053 sæfa *purity*

دیکتاتوری 4054 diktatori *dictatorship, dictatorial*

زیربنا 4055 zirbæna *infrastructure*

فوریت 4057 fowʔrijjæt *urgency*

سناریو 4059 senarijo *scenario, screenplay*

دریغ 4061 deriɣ *regret, pity*

بازگشایی 4064 bazgoʃaji *reopening*

تلگراف 4065 telegraf *telegraph*

نرم‌افزار 4067 nærmafzar *software*

پادگان 4068 padegan *garrison, barracks, base*

سرور 4069 sorur, særvær, server *joy, leader, server*

گرانی 4070 gerani *expensive, high prices*

بیمارستانی 4071 bimarestani *hospital*

دیابت 4072 dijabet *diabetes*

فیلمنامه 4075 filmname *screenplay*

برگرداندن 4078 bærgærdandæn *return*

پستی 4080 posti *postal*

کمپانی 4083 kompani *company*

پیک 4084 pejk, pik *courier, spades*

تعویض 4091 tæʔviz *replacing*

چاقی 4092 tʃaɣi *obesity*

فلان 4094 folan *so and so, such and such*

المپیاد 4098 olæmpijad *Olympics*

موازات 4099 movazat *parallel*

خاور 4100 xavær *east*

انسانیت 4101 ensanijjæt *humanity*

نواختن 4104 nævaxtæn *play*

کمین 4107 kæmin *ambush*

کنفدراسیون 4109 konfederasijon *confederation*

یورش 4110 joreʃ *attack*

تراکتورسازی 4111 traktorsazi *tractor manufacturing*

شایستگی 4112 ʃajestegi *merit*

نزاع 4113 nezaʔ *quarrel*

سرمایه‌داری 4115 særmajedari *capitalism, capitalist*

پاکسازی 4117 paksazi *purging, purification*

عوام 4119 ævam *common people*

ایجاب 4120 idʒab *obligation*

امیدی 4122 omidi *Omidi*

سلطنتی 4123 sæltænæti *royal*

اخلال 4124 exlal *disruption*

شاهزاده 4125 ʃahzade *prince*

تطبیق 4126 tætbiɣ *comparison*

تعمیق 4128 tæʔmiɣ *fathoming, deepening*

مظهر 4131 mæzhær *manifestation, symbol*

فیلمساز 4132 filmsaz *filmmaker*

ملا 4133 molla, mælæʔ *mullah, assembly*

درخشش 4135 deræxʃeʃ *brilliance*

عمو 4136 æmu *paternal uncle*

دهکده 4138 dehkæde *village*

جانبی 4139 dʒanebi *lateral, side*

کمر 4140 kæmær *waist*

فوتسال 4141 futsal *indoor soccer*

مفهومی 4142 mæfhumi *conceptual*

ترکمن 4143 torkæmæn *Turkmen*

ویرانی 4144 virani *destruction*

محموله 4145 mæhmule *shipment*

تنفر 4146 tænæffor *aversion, hatred*

ابری 4147 æbri *cloudy*

زمره 4150 zomre *group*

همزیستی 4152 hæmzisti *coexistence*

شنونده 4154 ʃenævænde *listener*

کیسه 4156 kise *bag*

هاله 4157 hale *halo, aura*

دری 4158 dæri *Dari*

ضمانت 4159 zemanæt *guarantee*

مشت 4160 moʃt *fist*

جنین 4162 dʒænin *fetus*

همفکری 4165 hæmfekri *exchanging ideas*

سفره 4167 sofre *tablecloth*

اهرم 4170 æhrom *lever*

گریه 4171 gerje *cry*

شهروندی 4172 ʃæhrvændi *citizenship*

معاهده 4174 moʔahede *treaty*

حیرت 4175 hejræt *amazement*

سبزی 4177 sæbzi *greens*

4371 دفن   dæfn *burial*

4372 بخار   boxar *steam*

4373 غزل   yæzæl *ghazal*

4374 ایستادگی   istadegi *resistance*

4375 تاریخچه   tarixtʃe *short history*

4376 روال   ræval *procedure*

4377 شناس   ʃenas *acquaintance, -ologist*

4380 اسمی   esmi *nominal*

4383 فلفل   felfel *pepper*

4384 مجاور   modʒaver *adjacent, neighboring*

4385 جهش   dʒæheʃ *jumping, mutation*

4386 غنا   yæna *wealth, Ghana*

4388 بازده   bazdeh *yield*

4389 شطرنج   ʃætrændʒ *chess*

4390 معجزه   moʔdʒeze *miracle*

4392 وصف   væsf *description*

4394 شاخ   ʃax *horn, branch*

4395 پالایش   palajeʃ *refining*

4396 تمایز   tæmajoz *distinction*

4397 خرده   xorde *bit*

4398 بالندگی   balændegi *growth, exuberance*

4400 روحانیت   rowhanijæt *clergy*

4401 وصول   vosul *collection*

4402 استانداری   ostandari *governor generalship*

4405 شیمی   ʃimi *chemistry*

4406 سطر   sætr *line*

4408 قانون‌اساسی   yanune æsasasi *constitution*

4409 بلیت   belit *ticket*

4410 فرقه   ferye *sect*

4412 اعتلا   eʔtela *raising, exaltation*

4415 دوستدار   dustdar *devotee*

4416 کاوش   kavoʃ *excavation*

4417 خلبان   xælæban *pilot*

4418 حبیب   hæbib *friend, lover, Habib*

4421 جنگنده   dʒængænde *warrior*

4422 تشریفات   tæʃrifat *formalities*

4423 سازه   saze *factor, structure*

4424 سرا   særa *house*

4425 هفده   hevdæh *seventeen*

4427 به‌کارگیری   bekargiri *utilization, hiring, employment*

4428 تلفیق   tælfiy *combination*

4429 عروس   ærus *bride, daugher-in-law*

4430 مدد   mædæd *help*

4433 غرض   yæræz *motive, grudge*

4434 خودروسازی   xodrowsazi *automobile manufacturing*

4435 شمشیر   ʃæmʃir *sword*

4436 معالجه   moʔaledʒe *medical treatment*

4439 مساعدت   mosaʔedæt *assistance*

4447 استخر   estæxr *pool*

4448 بام   bam *roof*

4451 سکته   sekte *stoppage, stroke*

4452 عفو   æfv *pardon*

4453 تحمیلی   tæhmili *imposed, forced*

4454 تهاجمی   tæhadʒomi *aggressive*

4457 عیب   ejb *fault*

4458 صنعتگر   sænʔætgær *artisan*

4460 خطبه   xotbe *sermon, homily*

4463 استقامت   esteyamæt *resistance*

4467 قزاق   yæzzay *Cossack, Kazakh*

4471 اختلاس   extelas *embezzlement*

4473 زننده   zænænde *repulsive, player*

4477 تاب   tab *endurance*

4478 مجموعاً   mædʒmuʔæn *altogether*

4479 پیچ   piʧ *bend, vine*

4480 داماد   damad *groom, son-in-law*

4481 مین   min *mine*

4482 سانسور   sansur *censorship*

4486 ولسوالی   volosvali *Afghan county*

4488 پارسی   parsi *Parsi, Persian*

4489 پایبندی   pajbændi *adherence, compliance*

4490 مار   mar *snake*

4493 گله   gælle, gele *flock/herd, complaint*

4494 شبهه   ʃobhe *doubt*

4496 ورا   væra *beyond*

4497 هجده   hedʒdæh *eighteen*

4498 قربان   yorban *sacrifice*

4499 دفترچه   dæftærʧe *notebook*

4500 مثنوی   mæsnævi *Masnavi*

4501 اسارت   esaræt *captivity*

4503 سیطره   sejtære *control, predominance*

4504 تاکتیکی   taktiki *tactical*

4505 یکپارچگی   jekparʧegi *integrity*

4506 موجودیت   mowdʒudijjæt *existence, presence, integrity*

4508 بازدهی   bazdehi *result, productivity, efficiency*

4510 آرامگاه   aramgah *grave*

4512 تعبیری   tæʔbiri *interpretive*

4513 گنجاندن   gondʒandæn *pack, include*

4514 حراست   hærasæt *protection*

4515 جولای   dʒulaj *July*

4518 خلوت   xælvæt *seclusion, privacy*

4520 تکان   tækan *shake, shock*

4521 دنباله   dombale *continuation*

4523 ربع   robʔ *quarter*

4524 جمع‌آوری   dʒæmʔaværi *collection*

4525 فاضلاب   fazelab *sewage*

4526 معنویت   mæʔnævijjæt *spirituality*

4527 مصداق   mesday *proof, typical specimen*

4529 شکیبایی   ʃækibaji *patience, fortitude*

4530 اثرگذار   æsærgozar *impressive*

4531 دلسوز   delsuz *compassionate*

4533 بخشش   bæxʃeʃ *donating, pardon*

4536 نظاره   nezare *observation*

4538 سیب   sib *apple*

4539 شفافیت   ʃæffafijjæt *transparency*

4541 امانت   æmanæt *honesty, consignment*

4542 گارد   gard *guard*

4543 عبرت   ebræt *lesson, example*

4544 یخچال   jæxʧal *refrigerator*

4545 سیاست‌گذاری   sijasætgozari *policy making*

4547 جنایتکار   dʒenajætkar *criminal*

4548 گوسفند   gusfænd *sheep*

4549 صرفه   særfe *profit, advantage*

4550 فروشنده   foruʃænde *salesperson, vendor*

4551 مصیبت   mosibæt *tragedy*

4552 وکالت   vekalæt *lawyering, power of attorney*

4553 مرتع   mærtæʔ *pasture*

4555 تفرقه   tæfreye *discord*

4556 پیرمرد   pirmærd *old man*

4557 آزاده   azade *free, liberated*

4558 قایق   yajey *boat, canoe*

4559 ممیز   momæjjez *auditor, decimal point, censor*

4787 عینک	ejnæk *glasses*	4848 تیپ	tip *brigade, type*	4912 کاریکاتور	karikatur *caricature,*
4789 جوار	dʒævar *proximity*	4849 عزاداری	æzadari *mourning*		*cartoon*
4790 دیوانه	divane *crazy*	4850 لبنانی	lobnani *Lebanese*	4913 صداوسیما	sedavæsima *radio and*
4791 بلا	bæla *disaster*	4851 تعصب	tæʔæssob *prejudice*		*television*
4793 نوزده	nuzdæh *nineteen*	4852 هراسیدن	hærasidæn *fear*	4914 سیلاب	sejlab *flood waters*
4795 مؤلف	moʔallef *author,*	4853 جراحت	dʒerahæt *wound*	4916 فراخوان	færaxan *invitation,*
	compiler	4854 شوخی	ʃuxi *joke*		*summons*
4796 کویر	kævir *salt desert*	4855 پلاک	pelak *license plate,*	4919 استواری	ostovari *stability*
4799 بیچاره	bitʃare *helpless*		*plaque*	4920 اطاعت	etaʔæt *obedience*
4801 تعارض	tæʔaroz *antagonism,*	4856 رجوع	rodʒuʔ *reference*	4921 جرگه	dʒærge *circle, jirga*
	opposition	4857 گزینش	gozineʃ *selection*	4922 بلوغ	boluɣ *puberty,*
4803 انحصاری	enhesari *exclusive,*	4858 جانور	dʒanevær *animal*		*maturity*
	monopoly	4859 ذهنیت	zehnijæt *mentality*	4923 درگذشته	dærgozæʃte *deceased*
4804 ماسه	mase *sand*	4860 اجبار	edʒbar *compulsion*	4924 تندیس	tændis *statue*
4805 مخاطره	moxatere *peril*	4864 خوشایند	xoʃajænd *pleasant,*	4925 دمکراسی	demokrasi *democracy*
4806 ولیعهد	væliʔæhd *crown*		*pleasure*	4926 سانتیمتر	santimetr *centimeter*
	prince	4865 سرایت	serajæt *contagion,*	4927 بهسازی	behsazi *improving*
4807 کیفری	kejfæri *penal, criminal*		*transmission*		*living conditions*
4813 دریچه	dæritʃe *window, valve,*	4866 بازگو	bazgu *retelling*	4928 خلل	xelæl *crack, defect*
	vent	4867 مستبد	mostæbed *despotic*	4929 هندبال	hændbal *handball*
4818 درخشیدن	deræxʃidæn *shine*	4868 ورشکستگی	værʃekæstegi	4930 ارگ	ærg, org *citadel,*
4819 کنکور	konkur *entrance exam*		*bankruptcy*		*organ*
4820 نرخ تورم	nerxetæværom	4869 حراج	hæradʒ *sale*	4934 دردسر	dardesær *trouble,*
	inflation rate	4871 مثابه	mæsabe *similar*		*headache*
4821 فعل	feʔl *verb*	4872 قالی	ɣali *carpet, rug*	4936 پختن	poxtæn *cook*
4822 نشیب	næʃib *descent*	4873 نارسایی	naræsaji *inadequacy,*	4938 خطه	xette *territory, country*
4823 مسالمت	mosalemæt		*insufficiency, failure*	4939 سناتور	senator *senator*
	conciliation,	4875 مشی	mæʃj *gait, manner*	4940 آموخته	amuxte *learned,*
	non-violence	4881 پیمانی	pejmani *contractual*		*accustomed*
4825 اسکی	eski *ski*	4882 یگان	jegan *detachment*	4942 فرمایش	færmajeʃ *command*
4826 گزیده	gozide *chosen,*	4884 بسط	bæst *extension*	4943 مسافرتی	mosaferæti *travel*
	selected, excerpt	4886 خوی	xuj, xoj *habit/*	4944 حیثیت	hejsijjæt *prestige*
4827 موجی	mowdʒi *wavy,*		*temperament, sweat/*	4947 آفرینش	afærineʃ *creation*
	shell-shocked		*Khoy*	4948 ین	jen *yen*
4828 خیز	xiz *rise, leap,*	4887 شعاع	ʃoʔaʔ *ray, beam*	4949 آفت	afæt *calamity, blight*
	swelling	4888 گربه	gorbe *cat*	4951 کاردانی	kardani *professional*
4829 دستخوش	dæstxoʃ *gratuity,*	4889 توکل	tævækkol *trust*		*skill, 2-year degree*
	prone, subject to	4891 هفتهنامه	hæftename *weekly*	4952 قهوه	ɣæhve *coffee*
4833 پاشیدن	paʃidæn *scatter,*		*publication*	4954 جهانگرد	dʒæhangærd *tourist,*
	sprinkle	4893 کاربری	karbæri *function, use*		*explorer*
4835 پایانه	pajane *terminal*	4894 لطمه	lætme *injury*	4955 لفظ	læfz *word*
4836 سره	sære *pure*	4895 اندوه	ænduh *grief*	4956 ولایتی	velajæti *provincial*
4837 نگه	negæh *hold, look*	4896 گذرگاه	gozærgah *crossing*	4957 کاسه	kase *bowl*
4838 پوشاک	puʃak *clothing*		*point, passageway*	4959 جهانگردی	dʒæhangærdi *tourism*
4839 رجب	rædʒæb *Rajab*	4897 سهل	sæhl *easy*	4960 فتوا	fætva *fatwa*
4840 اقتضا	eɣteza *exigency,*	4900 اطلاعرسانی	etelaʔræsani	4962 تمهید	tæmhid *scheme,*
	necessity		*information*		*maneuver*
4841 درهم	derhæm, dærhæm		*technology*	4963 لفظی	læfzi *verbal*
	dirham, mixed	4901 مزار	mæzar *shrine, tomb*	4964 شیشهای	ʃiʃeʔi *glass*
4842 احتساب	ehtesab *calculation*	4903 استعمال	esteʔmal *utilization*	4966 انعقاد	enʔeɣad *coagulation,*
4843 پیشه	piʃe *craft, profession*	4906 کیهان	kejhan *universe*		*conclusion*
4844 آری	ari *yes*	4909 اورانیوم	uranijom *uranium*	4969 ننه	næne *mom*
4846 خودروساز	xodrowsaz *auto*	4911 سحر	sæhær, sehr *dawn,*	4971 رغبت	reɣbæt *desire,*
	worker/maker		*magic*		*inclination*

4972 رسوب	rosub *sedimentation, sediment*	
4973 چتر	tʃætr *umbrella, parachute*	
4975 رساله	resale *letter, treatise*	
4976 کلانتری	kælantæri *police station*	
4977 سارق	sareɣ *thief*	
4978 غرور	ɣorur *pride, vanity*	
4979 ملکه	mæleke *queen*	
4980 پری	pæri, pori *fairy/Pari, fullness*	
4981 رآکتور	reaktor *reactor*	
4982 طبل	tæbl *drum*	
4983 ترابری	tærabæri *transportation*	
4984 ثمره	sæmære *fruit, offspring*	
4987 زین	zin *saddle, from this*	
4989 وفا	væfa *loyalty*	
4990 خودکفایی	xodkæfaji *self-sufficiency*	
4991 بیات	bæjat *stale*	
4993 پلید	pælid *dirty, evil*	
4996 کثیر	kæsir *numerous, abundant*	
4997 خواهش	xaheʃ *request*	
4998 سلطانی	soltani *royal*	
5000 برادری	beradæri *brotherhood, fraternity*	

Prepositions: 42 words

3 از	æz *from*	
4 به	be *to*	
7 در	dær *in*	
8 با	ba *with*	
10 برای	bæraje *for*	
15 تا	ta *until*	
21 بر	bær *on*	
45 میان	mijan *between*	
64 بین	bejn *between*	
81 بدون	bedune *without*	
82 رو	ru *on, face*	
101 بالا	bala *top, high*	
184 جهت	dʒæhæt *direction, reason*	
210 داخل	daxel *inside*	
228 درباره	dærbare *about*	
246 تحت	tæht *under*	
258 طی	tej *during*	
295 توسط	tævæssot *by*	
296 زیر	zir *under*	
343 مقابل	moɣabel *opposite*	

353 کنار	kenar *beside*	
381 تو	tu *in*	
559 ضمن	zemn *inside, while*	
635 علیه	ælejh *against*	
792 روبرو	ruberu *opposite*	
950 درون	dærun *inside*	
958 پشت	poʃt *back*	
1199 جلو	dʒelow *forward*	
1343 فرا	færa *beyond*	
1733 پیرامون	piramun *perimeter*	
2143 بابت	babæt *matter, for*	
2152 راجع	radʒe? *referring*	
2395 محض	mæhze *for, for the sake of*	
2563 فاقد	faɣed *lacking*	
2571 بنابر	bænabær *according to*	
2758 دم	dæm, dom *breath/near, tail*	
3108 بخاطر	bexater *due to*	
3276 برون	borun *outside*	
3757 فرو	foru *down*	
4005 بجای	bedʒaje *instead of*	
4496 ورا	væra *beyond*	
4791 بلا	bela *without*	

Pronouns: 27 words

6 این	in *this*	
11 خود	xod *self*	
13 آن	an *that*	
32 ما	ma *we*	
54 او	u *he, she*	
58 همه	hæme *every*	
69 همین	hæmin *the same, this very*	
102 من	mæn *I*	
110 چه	tʃe *what*	
116 وی	vej *he, she*	
141 برخی	bærxi *some*	
148 شما	ʃoma *you*	
272 همان	hæman *that very*	
381 تو	to, tu *you, in*	
424 ایشان	iʃan *they*	
516 آنچه	antʃe *that which*	
563 بعضی	bæ?zi *some*	
674 یکدیگر	jekdigær *each other*	
1109 خویش	xiʃ *self*	
1258 بقیه	bæɣijje *rest*	
1484 بنده	bænde *slave*	
2136 همگی	hæmegi *all*	
2577 همدیگر	hæmdigær *each other*	
3026 هرکس	hærkæs *anyone, everyone*	
4155 هیچکس	hitʃkæs *nobody*	

Proper nouns: 586 words

13 آن	an *Anne*	
43 ایران	iran *Iran*	
107 آمریکا	amrika *America*	
109 علی	æli *Ali*	
135 آقا	aɣa *Mister*	
140 تهران	tehran *Tehran*	
161 محمد	mohæmmæd *Mohammad*	
243 زمین	zæmin *Earth*	
278 حسن	hæsæn *Hasan*	
356 حقیقت	hæɣiɣæt *Haghighat*	
389 فرانسه	færanse *France, French*	
433 افغانستان	æfɣanestan *Afghanistan*	
450 اروپا	orupa *Europe*	
458 چین	tʃin *China*	
478 انگلیسی	engelisi *English*	
486 نظامی	nezami *Nezami*	
518 عراق	eraɣ *Iraq*	
529 آسیا	asija *Asia*	
541 غرب	ɣærb *west*	
546 خدا	xoda *God*	
568 روسیه	rusije *Russia*	
569 استقلال	esteɣlal *Esteghlal F.C.*	
584 بهار	bæhar *Bahar*	
594 آلمان	alman *Germany*	
611 انگلیس	engelis *England, Britain*	
621 ترکیه	torkije *Turkey*	
622 پیروزی	piruzi *Piruzi*	
633 جان	dʒan *John*	
634 پرواز	pærvaz *Parvaz*	
677 شیخ	ʃejx *Sheikh*	
712 هند	hend *India*	
730 عباس	æbbas *Abbas*	
771 هدایت	hedajæt *Hedayat*	
793 دقیق	dæɣiɣ *Daghigh*	
795 محمود	mæhmud *Mahmoud*	
798 محقق	mohæɣɣeɣ *Mohaghegh*	
815 فارس	fars *Fars*	
833 باقی	baɣi *Baghi*	
834 حسین	hosejn *Hossein*	

845 پاکستان	pakestan Pakistan	1443 شریف	ʃærif Sharif	1957 برزیل	brezil Brazil
856 سوریه	surije Syria	1445 آذربایجان	azærbajdʒan Azerbaijan	1962 جمهوریاسلامی	dʒomhurije eslami Islamic Republic
862 احمد	æhmæd Ahmad				
867 ژاپن	ʒapon Japan	1492 پل	pol Paul	1967 کویت	kovejt Kuwait
871 قربانی	ɣorbani Ghorbani	1497 استرالیا	ostralija Australia	1970 رمضان	ræmezan Ramadan
913 اسرائیل	esraʔil Israel	1499 خاتمی	xatæmi Khatami	1982 یورو	juro Euro
942 عرب	æræb Arab	1518 جو	dʒow Joe	2001 ترکمنستان	torkmenestan Turkmenestan
1000 ایتالیا	italja Italy	1521 شیرین	ʃirin Shirin		
1018 عمر	omr Omar	1528 قم	ɣom Qom	2008 خراسان	xorasan Khorasan
1026 رضا	reza Reza	1537 خورشید	xorʃid Khorshid	2011 طلایی	tælaji Talai
1031 واشنگتن	vaʃængton Washington	1538 کمال	kæmal Kamal	2030 شادی	ʃadi Shadi
		1540 حقیقی	hæɣiɣi Haghighi	2057 جلالی	dʒælali Jalali
1042 فکری	fekri Fekri	1548 طالبان	taleban Taliban	2075 پارس	pars Pars
1050 عزیز	æziz Aziz	1567 پاریس	paris Paris	2084 کشاورز	keʃaværz Keshavarz
1052 الله	ællah Allah	1582 الهی	elahi Elahi		
1062 لندن	lændæn London	1589 مشهد	mæʃhæd Mashhad	2085 منصور	mænsur Mansour
1074 شاه	ʃah Shah	1590 خاورمیانه	xaværemijane Middle East	2093 افغان	æfɣan Afghan
1076 اصفهان	esfæhan Esfahan			2094 همدان	hæmedan Hamadan
1088 خداوند	xodavænd God	1596 پیمان	pejman Peyman		
1119 مصر	mesr Egypt	1606 حسینی	hosejni Hosseini	2105 پاس	pas Pas
1125 لبنان	lobnan Lebanon	1611 قرآن	ɣorʔan Koran	2108 اردن	ordon Jordan
1130 انگلستان	engelestan England	1614 یونان	junan Greece	2112 میرزا	mirza Mirza
		1615 حافظ	hafez Hafez	2114 حمید	hæmid Hamid
1135 فلسطین	felestin Palestine	1655 خمینی	xomejni Khomeini	2129 موسی	musa Musa, Moses
1188 عربستان	æræbestan Arabia	1675 کره	kore Korea		
1191 مهدی	mehdi Mehdi	1680 ملک	mælek Malek	2137 ابتکار	ebtekar Ebtekar
1217 سعید	sæʔid Said	1701 المپیک	olæmpik Olympics	2157 کابل	kabol Kabul
1241 مسلم	moslem Muslim	1703 مبارک	mobaræk Mobarak	2159 شمسی	ʃæmsi Shamsi
1262 دوشنبه	doʃæmbe Dushanbe	1721 معین	moʔin Moin	2161 مصطفی	mostæfa Mostafa
		1728 جواد	dʒævad Javad	2194 پیامبر	pæjambær Prophet
1278 صدر	sædr Sadr	1743 دی	dej Dey	2218 روس	rus Russian
1279 اکبر	ækbær Akbar	1746 کاظم	kazem Kazem	2221 مجید	mædʒid Majid
1286 تبریز	tæbriz Tabriz	1751 محمدی	mohæmmædi Mohammadi	2241 مسعود	mæsʔud Masoud
1287 تیر	tir Tir			2261 عراقی	eraɣi Iraqi
1288 قریب	ɣærib Gharib	1772 اسماعیل	esmaʔil Ishmael, Esmail	2265 هادی	hadi Hadi
1300 وکیل	vækil Vakil			2271 امین	æmin Amin
1301 امیر	æmir Emir	1783 مسکو	mosko Moscow	2295 هاشمی	haʃemi Hashemi
1309 ابراهیم	ebrahim Abraham, Ebrahim	1795 ایرنا	irna IRNA	2298 گلستان	golestan Golestan
		1801 کانادا	kanada Canada	2317 توکیو	tokjo Tokyo
1311 آرام	aram Aram	1824 نوری	nuri Nuri	2324 برقی	bærɣi Barghi
1327 سردار	særdar Commander, General	1834 بغداد	bæɣdad Baghdad	2331 تاجیکستان	tadʒikestan Tajikistan
		1836 ناتو	nato NATO		
		1846 یهودی	jæhudi Jew	2337 ریاضی	rijazi Riazi
1342 آدم	adæm Adam	1853 روحانی	rowhani Rowhani	2338 میر	mir Mir
1359 مهاجر	mohadʒer Mohajer	1867 کریم	kærim Karim	2341 آبادی	abadi Abadi
1364 قطر	ɣætær Qatar	1873 محسن	mohsen Mohsen	2344 گیلان	gilan Gilan
1391 بهمن	bæhmæn Bahman	1880 خوزستان	xuzestan Khuzestan	2376 کردستان	kordestan Kurdistan
1394 نیویورک	nijujork New York				
1412 شیراز	ʃiraz Shiraz	1892 مشتری	moʃtæri Jupiter	2380 عباسی	æbbasi Abbasi, Abbasid
1417 عبدالله	æbdollah Abdollah	1911 کرمان	kerman Kerman		
1430 اسپانیا	espanja Spain	1929 علیرضا	ælireza Alireza	2383 صادق	sadeɣ Sadegh
1431 افریقا	afriɣa Africa	1934 پهلوی	pæhlævi Pahlavi	2384 نیازی	nijazi Niazi
1435 ستاره	setare Setareh	1946 شوروی	ʃowrævi Soviet	2392 کلینتون	kelinton Clinton

3294	بهاری	bæhari Bahari	3637	غریب	yærib Gharib
3296	احسان	ehsan Ehsan	3647	بوستان	bustan Bustan
3307	یونسکو	junesko UNESCO	3657	ری	rej Rey
3309	تونس	tunes Tunisia, Tunis	3660	گور	gur Gur
3311	زند	zænd Zand	3665	خواجه	xadʒe Master
3318	وزیری	væziri Vaziri	3676	داریوش	darjuʃ Darius
3320	آنکارا	ankara Ankara	3680	ژنو	ʒenev Geneva
3322	اصفهانی	esfæhani Esfahani	3687	انزلی	ænzæli Anzali
3327	خسرو	xosrow Khosrow	3688	کالیفرنیا	kalifornija California
3331	البرز	ælborz Alborz	3694	اشرف	æʃræf Ashraf
3341	مرادی	moradi Moradi	3707	ساری	sari Sari
3348	صمیمی	sæmimi Samimi	3719	شجاعت	ʃodʒaʔæt Shojaat
3352	کوفی	kufi Kufic, Kofi	3725	جرج	dʒordʒ George
3359	حاجی	hadʒi Hajji	3742	الکساندر	æleksandr Alexander
3365	تاجر	tadʒer Tajer	3751	گاردین	gardijen Guardian
3385	انصاری	ansari Ansari	3786	پاپ	pap Pope
3396	دایی	daji maternal uncle	3811	هندوستان	hendustan India
3404	لهستان	læhestan Poland	3821	کبیر	kæbir Kabir
3407	کلمبیا	kolombija Colombia	3822	رحیم	ræhim Rahim
3408	بهبودی	behbudi Behbudi	3831	الجزیره	ældʒæzire Al Jazeera
3409	بیل	bil Bill	3833	نیل	nil Nile
3423	جعفر	dʒæʔfær Jafar	3852	کندی	kenedi Kennedy
3429	عمان	omman Oman	3854	بختیاری	bæxtijari Bakhtiari
3435	رضوی	ræzævi Razavi	3859	کاشانی	kaʃani Kashani
3437	گرجستان	gordʒestan Georgia	3863	شیکاگو	ʃikago Chicago
3439	شاهین	ʃahin Shahin	3868	متولی	motevælli Motavalli
3440	پویا	puja Puya	3880	حامد	hamed Hamed
3444	فیلیپین	filipin Philippines	3883	شهریار	ʃæhrijar Shahriar
3445	لاتین	latin Latin	3885	فیفا	fifa FIFA
3448	باراک	barak Barack, Barak	3891	عثمانی	osmani Ottoman
3453	سوری	suri Syrian	3905	اتریش	otriʃ Austria
3460	شام	ʃam Sham, Levant	3915	ترقی	tæræyyi Taraghi
3461	اوباما	obama Obama	3924	مجارستان	mædʒarestan Hungary
3475	جمال	dʒæmal Jamal	3925	کروبی	kærrubi Karroubi
3482	رشت	ræʃt Rasht	3934	بابک	babæk Babak
3490	مونیخ	munix Munich	3935	عنان	ænan Annan
3491	نوروزی	nowruzi Nowruz	3943	دربند	dærbænd Darband
3500	الهام	elham Elham	3957	ابراهیمی	ebrahimi Ebrahimi, Abrahamic
3519	گرگان	gorgan Gorgan	3968	فرشته	fereʃte Fereshteh
3520	مراد	morad Morad	3982	قاسم	yasem Ghasem
3524	کوبا	kuba Cuba	3993	مجیدی	mædʒidi Majidi
3526	صفوی	sæfævi Safavid	3994	اکبری	ækbæri Akbari
3540	تهرانی	tehrani Tehrani	4002	صادقی	sadeyi Sadeghi
3542	قاجار	yadʒar Qajar	4004	بهرام	bæhram Bahram
3552	سودان	sudan Sudan	4010	مهران	mehran Mehran
3554	هرات	hærat, herat Herat	4015	شجاع	ʃodʒaʔ Shoja
3556	باقری	bayeri Bagheri	4023	شیطان	ʃejtan Satan
3568	قاسمی	yasemi Ghasemi	4024	شریعتی	ʃæriʔæti Shariati
3574	خورشیدی	xorʃidi Khorshidi	4025	ابریشم	æbriʃæm Abrisham
3588	نصر	næsr Nasr	4032	دانمارک	danmark Denmark
3594	مارک	mark Mark			
3609	بهشتی	beheʃti Beheshti			
3622	نیکی	niki Nicki			

4041	ولادیمیر	veladimir Vladimir
4042	محمدعلی	mohæmmædæli Mohammad Ali
4062	تبریزی	tæbrizi Tabrizi
4076	سمنان	semnan Semnan
4082	مولوی	mowlævi Rumi
4087	تاجیک	tadʒik Tajik
4096	بوسنی	bosni Bosnia, Bosnian
4103	عادل	adel Adel
4105	عیسی	isa Jesus
4121	رومانی	romani Romania
4122	امیدی	omidi Omidi
4134	بارسلونا	barselona Barcelona
4137	معصومه	mæʔsume Masume
4143	ترکمن	torkæmæn Turkmen
4149	حیدری	hejdæri Heidari
4151	امینی	æmini Amini
4157	هاله	hale Haleh
4158	دری	dæri Dari
4161	رفسنجانی	ræfsændʒani Rafsanjani
4163	اراک	ærak Arak
4169	طباطبایی	tæbatæbaji Tabatabai
4176	نیما	nima Nima
4180	بنی	bæni Bani
4186	حسنی	hosni Hosni
4210	رویتر	rujter Reuters
4217	خرم	xorræm Khorram
4220	عرفات	æræfat Arafat
4225	معاویه	moʔavije Muawiyah
4226	شمس	ʃæms Shams
4230	کرهجنوبی	korejdʒonubi South Korea
4241	شانگهای	ʃanghaj Shanghai
4242	وحید	væhid Vahid
4244	نوید	nævid Navid
4247	ریاض	rijaz Riyadh
4251	اسکار	oskar Oscar
4254	رحیمی	ræhimi Rahimi
4261	اکرم	ækræm dearer
4272	فضل	fæzl Fazl
4275	سعیدی	sæʔidi Saidi
4282	ایرلند	irlænd Ireland
4283	خامنهای	xameneji Khamenei
4294	تختی	tæxti Takhti
4299	ایوان	ivan Ivan
4306	راسخ	rasex Rasekh
4320	شعله	ʃoʔle Sholeh
4325	لاله	lale Laleh

Quantifiers: 38 words

716	عده	edde *number*	211	پرداختن	pærdaxtæn *pay, engage in*	822	برخوردار بودن	bærxordar budæn *be in possession*
755	نیم	nim *half*	217	دست دادن	dæst dadæn *shake hands, lose*	832	زندگی کردن	zendegi kærdæn *live*
810	سراسر	særasær *throughout*	257	گذشتن	gozæʃtæn *pass*	838	اجازه دادن	edʒaze dadæn *permit*
835	جمعی	dʒæmʔi *collective*	277	افزودن	æfzudæn *add*	841	کار کردن	kar kærdæn *work*
995	مقدار	meɣdar *amount*	280	خواندن	xandæn *read*	850	افتادن	oftadæn *fall*
1083	کلیه	kolje, kollijje *kidney, all*	288	پیدا کردن	pejda kærdæn *find*	861	کمک کردن	komæk kærdæn *help*
1137	اندک	ændæk *little*	305	نمودن	nemudæn *show, do*	881	باعث شدن	baes ʃodæn *cause*
1157	اکثر	æksær *most*	310	زدن	zædæn *strike, beat*	903	کشتن	koʃtæn *kill*
1333	اغلب	æɣlæb *often, frequently*	313	قرار دادن	ɣærar dadæn *put, place*	922	تبدیل شدن	tæbdil ʃodæn *convert*
1624	اکثریت	æksærijjæt *majority*	315	نوشتن	neveʃtæn *write*	941	سعی کردن	sæʔj kærdæn *try*
1711	عموم	omum *public, whole*	316	ساختن	saxtæn *build*	967	فرمودن	færmudæn *order*
2024	حداکثر	hæddæksær *maximum*	331	قرار داشتن	ɣærar daʃtæn *be located*	990	تصمیم گرفتن	tæsmim gereftæn *decide*
2136	همگی	hæmegi *all*	347	استفاده کردن	estefade kærdæn *use*	1028	ایجاد کردن	idʒad kærdæn *create*
2278	پاره	pare *torn, part*	369	خارج شدن	xaredʒ ʃodæn *leave*	1030	انداختن	ændaxtæn *throw*
2763	معدود	mæʔdud *few*	395	ادامه دادن	edame dadæn *continue*	1044	مطرح کردن	mætræh kærdæn *propose*
3051	قدری	ɣædri *a little, slight*	405	قرار بودن	ɣærar budæn *be supposed to*	1080	شکستن	ʃekæstæn *break*
3499	غالب	ɣaleb *prevailing*	462	انجام شدن	ændʒam ʃodæn *be done*	1081	تشکیل دادن	tæʃkil dadæn *form*
3702	سرتاسر	særtasær *throughout*	498	انتخاب کردن	entexab kærdæn *elect, choose*	1122	توجه کردن	tævædʒdʒoh kærdæn *pay attention*
4153	حدوداً	hodudæn *approximately*	505	ماندن	mandæn *stay*	1131	گفته شدن	gofte ʃodæn *be said*
4160	مشت	moʃt *fist*	585	برداشتن	bærdaʃtæn *pick up, remove*	1198	افزایش یافتن	æfzajeʃ jaftæn *increase*
4204	عامه	amme *public*	604	گردیدن	gærdidæn *turn*	1219	تلاش کردن	tælaʃ kærdæn *make effort*

Verbs: 392 words

2	بودن	budæn *be*	614	عمل کردن	æmæl kærdæn *act, perform*	1220	شکست خوردن	ʃekæst xordæn *be defeated*
9	شدن	ʃodæn *become*	649	سال بودن	sal budæn *be years since*	1223	ایستادن	istadæn *stand*
14	خواستن	xastæn *want*	658	گشتن	gæʃtæn *turn*	1233	شنیدن	ʃenidæn *hear*
16	داشتن	daʃtæn *have*	670	آغاز شدن	aɣaz ʃodæn *begin*	1242	پیوستن	pejvæstæn *join*
17	کردن	kærdæn *do*	686	خوردن	xordæn *eat*	1244	آغاز کردن	aɣaz kærdæn *begin*
19	بایستن	bajestæn *must*	689	پذیرفتن	pæziroftæn *accept*	1255	بازی کردن	bazi kærdæn *play*
23	توانستن	tævanestæn *be able*	705	شناختن	ʃenaxtæn *know, recognize*	1276	شروع کردن	ʃoruʔ kærdæn *begin*
24	رسیدن	residæn *arrive*	713	اعلام کردن	eʔlam kærdæn *announce*	1291	پاسخ دادن	pasox dadæn *reply*
34	گرفتن	gereftæn *take*	714	بخشیدن	bæxʃidæn *forgive, give*	1293	تغییر دادن	tæɣjir dadæn *change*
37	گفتن	goftæn *say*	719	فکر کردن	fekr kærdæn *think*	1310	فراهم کردن	færahæm kærdæn *assemble*
42	دادن	dadæn *give*	736	معرفی کردن	moʔærrefi kærdæn *introduce*	1312	نیاز داشتن	nijaz daʃtæn *need*
87	دانستن	danestæn *know*	752	کشاندن	keʃandæn *drag, pull*	1348	شرکت کردن	ʃerkæt kærdæn *participate*
93	آمدن	amædæn *come*	765	اتفاق افتادن	ettefaɣ oftadæn *happen*	1358	ترک کردن	tærk kærdæn *leave, abandon*
99	یافتن	jaftæn *find*	774	نشستن	neʃæstæn *sit*	1361	بستن	bæstæn *close*
112	آوردن	aværdæn *bring*	778	وارد شدن	vared ʃodæn *enter*	1378	حرکت کردن	hærekæt kærdæn *move, set off*
115	نشان دادن	neʃan dadæn *show*	786	کشیدن	keʃidæn *pull, draw*	1411	انتظار داشتن	entezar daʃtæn *expect*
128	رفتن	ræftæn *go*				1427	صحبت کردن	sohbæt kærdæn *talk*
137	قرار گرفتن	ɣærar gereftæn *be located*				1455	درست بودن	dorost budæn *be right*
147	بردن	bordæn *take*				1463	پرسیدن	porsidæn *ask*
162	وجود داشتن	vodʒud daʃtæn *exist*				1468	قصد داشتن	ɣæsd daʃtæn *intend*
169	انجام دادن	ændʒam dadæn *accomplish*						
192	رساندن	resandæn *deliver*						
194	گذاشتن	gozaʃtæn *put, leave*						
202	دیدن	didæn *see*						

خبر دادن 1479 xæbær dadæn *inform*

وارد کردن 1490 vared kærdæn *import, enter*

تأکید کردن 1491 tæʔkid kærdæn *emphasize*

معرفی شدن 1495 moʔærrefi ʃodæn *be introduced*

استفاده شدن 1505 estefade ʃodæn *be used*

کوشیدن 1506 kuʃidæn *attempt*

ریختن 1513 rixtæn *pour*

مواجه شدن 1519 movadʒeh ʃodæn *be confronted*

امیدوار بودن 1525 omidvar budæn *be hopeful*

جا گرفتن 1529 dʒa gereftæn *reserve, hold*

اظهار داشتن 1534 ezhar daʃtæn *express, declare*

دریافت کردن 1559 dærjaft kærdæn *receive*

راه انداختن 1560 rah ændaxtæn *operate, launch*

احساس کردن 1561 ehsas kærdæn *feel*

حفظ کردن 1563 hefz kærdæn *protect, memorize*

روبرو شدن 1575 ruberu ʃodæn *meet*

آموختن 1587 amuxtæn *learn, teach*

باقی ماندن 1602 baɣi mandæn *remain*

نادیده گرفتن 1623 nadide gereftæn *overlook*

سخن گفتن 1629 soxæn goftæn *speak, talk*

دوست داشتن 1634 dust daʃtæn *like*

دنبال کردن 1657 donbal kærdæn *look for*

رو آوردن 1664 ru avordæn *turn*

فرستادن 1666 ferestadæn *send*

درآمدن 1679 dæramædæn *emerge*

نامیدن 1681 namidæn *name*

گذراندن 1706 gozærandæn *spend time, pass*

نگاه کردن 1719 negah kærdæn *look*

تمام شدن 1726 tæmam ʃodæn *finish*

اندیشیدن 1738 ændiʃidæn *think*

ربودن 1744 robudæn *steal*

سفر کردن 1753 sæfær kærdæn *travel*

مواجه بودن 1778 movadʒe budæn *confront*

واقع شدن 1781 vaɣeʔ ʃodæn *happen, be located*

فهمیدن 1782 fæhmidæn *understand*

حل شدن 1808 hæl ʃodæn *dissolve, be solved*

حل کردن 1813 hæl kærdæn *solve*

فروختن 1818 foruxtæn *sell*

برگشتن 1823 bærgæʃtæn *return*

صادر شدن 1835 sader ʃodæn *be exported, issued*

طلبیدن 1849 tælæbidæn *call, ask, require*

آشنا شدن 1883 aʃna ʃodæn *be familiar, acquainted*

اجرا کردن 1891 edʒra kærdæn *execute, perform*

تولید شدن 1907 towlid ʃodæn *be produced*

تعیین کردن 1960 tæʔjin kærdæan *determine, appoint*

آزاد شدن 2016 azad ʃodæn *be freed*

بیان کردن 2022 bæjan kærdæn *state, express*

تغییر کردن 2023 tæɣjir kærdæn *change*

ثابت کردن 2029 sabet kærdæn *prove*

انجامیدن 2034 ændʒamidæn *end*

پوشیدن 2041 puʃidæn *wear*

جستن 2044 dʒæstæn, dʒostæn *jump, search*

رد کردن 2047 ræd kærdæn *reject*

سپردن 2049 sepordæn *deposit, entrust*

صادر کردن 2054 sader kærdæn *export, issue*

بالا رفتن 2065 bala ræftæn *go up*

راندن 2103 randæn *drive*

شروع کردن 2118 ʃoruʔ kærdæn *begin*

حرف زدن 2120 hærf zædæn *speak*

بررسی کردن 2127 bærræsi kærdæn *examine*

درک کردن 2186 dærk kærdæn *comprehend*

تجربه کردن 2188 tædʒrobe kærdæn *experience*

جا گذاشتن 2196 dʒagozaʃtæn *leave behind*

تأثیر گذاشتن 2207 tæʔsir gozaʃtæn *leave impression*

ورزیدن 2228 værzidæn *exercise*

دریافتن 2243 dærjaftæn *perceive, receive*

تأکید داشتن 2248 tæʔkid daʃtæn *emphasize*

پوشاندن 2255 puʃandæn *dress*

متوجه شدن 2277 motævædʒdʒeh ʃodæn *notice*

تصور کردن 2288 tæsavvor kærdæn *imagine*

شکست دادن 2306 ʃekæst dadæn *defeat*

تولید کردن 2309 towlid kærdæn *produce*

خودداری کردن 2335 xoddari kærdæn *refrain*

جلوگیری کردن 2358 dʒelowgiri kærdæn *prevent*

توضیح دادن 2366 towzih dadæn *explain*

مردن 2369 mordæn *die*

گشودن 2378 goʃudæn *open*

درآوردن 2389 dæraværdæn *extract, produce*

کاستن 2410 kastæn *reduce*

تعریف کردن 2411 tæʔrif kærdæn *define, describe*

گزارش دادن 2435 gozareʃ dadæn *report*

استقبال کردن 2447 esteɣbal kærdæn *welcome*

افکندن 2451 æfkændæn *throw*

توصیف کردن 2462 towsif kærdæn *describe*

توصیه کردن 2473 towsije kærdæn *recommend*

ترجیح دادن 2483 tærdʒih dadæn *prefer*

نگه داشتن 2488 negæh daʃtæn *keep*

برشمردن 2499 bærʃomordæn *enumerate*

شناسایی کردن 2511 ʃenasaji kærdæn *identify*

باز کردن 2515 baz kærdæn *open*

جدا شدن 2518 dʒoda ʃodæn *be separated*

شاهد بودن 2520 ʃahed budæn *witness*

بالا بردن 2522 bala bordæn *put up, raise*

سال داشتن 2531 sal daʃtæn *be years old*

متوقف شدن 2533 motævæɣɣef ʃodæn *stop*

شرکت داشتن 2534 ʃerkæt daʃtæn *participate, attend*

نهادن 2543 næhadæn *put, place*

نگریستن 2550 negæristæn *look*

سوختن 2564 suxtæn *burn*

جمع شدن 2598 dʒæmʔ ʃodæn *gather*

خریدن 2600 xæridæn *buy*

2612	حمله کردن	hæmle kærdæn attack	3106	معلوم شدن	mæʔlum ʃodæn become known	3493	مقایسه کردن	moɣajese kærdæn compare

2612 حمله کردن hæmle kærdæn *attack*

2625 بازگشتن bazgæʃtæn *return*

2626 ادعا کردن eddeʔa kærdæn *claim*

2633 قبول داشتن ɣæbul daʃtæn *accept*

2638 تبدیل کردن tæbdil kærdæn *convert*

2661 شمردن ʃemordæn *count*

2668 مصرف کردن mæsræf kærdæn *consume*

2681 کنار گذاشتن kenar gozaʃtæn *put away*

2688 اعتراف کردن eʔteraf kærdæn *confess*

2690 نشاندن neʃandæn *seat*

2695 تعطیل شدن tæʔtil ʃodæn *shut down*

2703 فراموش کردن færamuʃ kærdæn *forget*

2713 برخورد کردن bærxord kærdæn *meet, collide*

2719 متولد شدن motævælled ʃodæn *be born*

2722 یاد کردن jad kærdæn *remember*

2746 رها کردن ræha kærdæn *free, let go*

2801 ساله بودن sale budæn *be years old*

2803 حذف شدن hazf ʃodæn *be eliminated*

2819 گراییدن gerajidæn *tend, incline*

2822 تلقی شدن tælæɣɣi ʃodæn *be considered*

2850 گزارش شدن gozareʃ ʃodæn *be reported*

2853 ظاهر شدن zaher ʃodæn *appear*

2894 ترسیدن tærsidæn *fear*

2903 منتشر کردن montæʃer kærdæn *publish*

2939 قطع شدن ɣætʔ ʃodæn *be cut off, terminated*

2940 مشغول بودن mæʃɣul budæn *be busy*

2955 منتقل کردن montæɣel kærdæn *transfer, transmit*

2995 باز شدن baz ʃodæn *open*

2996 واداشتن vadaʃtæn *persuade, force*

3039 کوبیدن kubidæn *pound, grind*

3071 باختن baxtæn *lose*

3090 بازداشت شدن bazdaʃt ʃodæn *be arrested*

3106 معلوم شدن mæʔlum ʃodæn *become known*

3122 بنا بودن bæna budæn *be supposed to*

3132 تحمل کردن tæhæmmol kærdæn *tolerate*

3134 طی کردن tej kærdæn *journey*

3146 تحمیل کردن tæhmil kærdæn *impose*

3152 نابود کردن nabud kærdæn *destroy*

3160 اینجابودن indʒabudæn *be here*

3174 تشخیص دادن tæʃxis dadæn *distinguish, diagnose*

3193 رسمیت شناختن ræsmijjæt ʃenaxtæn *officially recognize*

3199 خوش آمدن xoʃ amædan *welcome*

3209 گریختن gorixtæn *flee*

3211 تقسیم کردن tæɣsim kærdæn *divide, distribute*

3217 پی بردن pej bordæn *discover, find out*

3234 خندیدن xændidæn *laugh*

3248 بزرگ شدن bozorg ʃodæn *grow up*

3261 آسیب دیدن asib didæn *be injured*

3268 طول کشیدن tul keʃidæn *last long*

3273 قبول کردن ɣæbul kærdæn *accept*

3275 یاد گرفتن jad gereftæn *learn*

3283 دویدن dævidæn *run*

3299 تمایل داشتن tæmajol daʃtæn *tend to, gravitate to*

3301 دامن زدن damæn zædæn *add fuel*

3310 برخاستن bærxastæn *get/rise up*

3325 پر کردن por kærdæn *fill*

3363 جواب دادن dʒævab dadæn *reply*

3399 تشکر کردن tæʃækkor kærdæn *thank*

3403 باور کردن bavær kærdæn *believe*

3412 بیرون آمدن birun amædæn *emerge*

3443 اصلاح کردن eslah kærdæn *reform, correct*

3470 شستن ʃostæn *wash*

3476 شکایت کردن ʃekajæt kærdæn *complain*

3486 متوقف کردن motævæɣɣef kærdæn *stop*

3487 مربوط بودن mærbut budæn *be relevant*

3492 بستگی داشتن bæstegi daʃtæn *depend*

3493 مقایسه کردن moɣajese kærdæn *compare*

3514 تعلق داشتن tæʔæloɣ daʃtæn *belong*

3515 پنداشتن pendaʃtæn *suppose*

3536 ثمر رساندن sæmær resandæn *bear fruit*

3557 عرضه کردن arze kærdæn *present, offer, supply*

3563 کمک گرفتن komæk gereftæn *get help*

3585 مصرف شدن mæsræf ʃodæn *be consumed*

3605 تحویل دادن tæhvil dadæn *deliver, hand over*

3623 راضی بودن razi budæn *be satisfied*

3645 آگاه بودن agah budæn *be aware*

3650 قائل بودن ɣael budæn *believe, profess*

3714 سؤال کردن soʔal kærdæn *ask*

3722 گمان کردن goman kærdæn *suppose*

3732 بلند شدن bolænd ʃodæn *rise, grow*

3747 گسترش دادن gostæreʃ dadæn *expand*

3750 فرا گرفتن færagereftæn *surround, learn*

3753 زنگ زدن zæng zædæn *ring*

3758 کاشتن kaʃtæn *plant*

3764 تکرار کردن tekrar kærdæn *repeat*

3767 تلقی کردن tælæɣɣi kærdæn *consider*

3779 قطع کردن ɣætʔ kærdæn *cut*

3782 خوابیدن xabidæn *sleep*

3788 راه افتادن rah oftadæn *set out*

3794 ارتباط داشتن ertebat daʃtæn *be in contact*

3800 جدا کردن dʒoda kærdæn *separate*

3804 تشویق کردن tæʃviɣ kærdæn *encourage*

3814 پیمودن pejmudæn *measure, traverse*

3847 توزیع شدن towziʔ ʃodæn *be distributed*

3853 تماشا کردن tæmaʃa kærdæn *watch, view*

3864 طراحی کردن tærrahi kærdæn *design*

3873 دوختن duxtæn *sew*

3878 مرتکب شدن mortækeb ʃodæn *commit*

3899	فراخواندن	færaxandæn *invite, summon*	4356	حذف کردن	hæzf kærdæn *eliminate, delete*	4647	سنجیدن	sændʒidæn *measure*

3899 فراخواندن færaxandæn *invite, summon*

3941 رو شدن ru ʃodæn *be exposed, bold*

3959 خواستار شدن xastar ʃodæn *demand*

3989 پرتاب شدن pærtab ʃodæn *be thrown, launched*

3990 سوق دادن sowɣ dadæn *guide, drive*

3992 علاقه داشتن ælaɣe daʃtæn *be interested*

3996 تعقیب کردن tæʔɣib kærdæn *pursue*

4016 درست کردن dorost kærdæn *correct, prepare*

4056 در زدن dær zædæn *knock*

4063 حاکی بودن haki budæn *indicate*

4077 توجیه کردن towdʒih kærdæn *justify*

4078 برگرداندن bærgærdandæn *return*

4095 خریداری کردن xæridari kærdæn *purchase*

4102 جمع کردن dʒæmʔ kærdæn *collect*

4104 نواختن nævaxtæn *play*

4114 درگیر شدن dærgir ʃodæn *engage*

4116 پس گرفتن pæs gereftæn *take back, withdraw*

4166 صرف کردن særf kærdæn *spend time, consume, conjugate*

4188 توسعه دادن towseʔe dadæn *expand, develop*

4191 گرفتار شدن gereftar ʃodæn *get caught*

4203 چیدن ʃidæn *pick, pluck, set*

4224 فرار کردن færar kærdæn *escape*

4270 هدایت کردن hedajæt kærdæn *guide*

4281 دستور دادن dæstur dadæn *order*

4291 رفتار کردن ræftar kærdæn *behave*

4293 واگذار کردن vagozar kærdæn *hand over*

4296 آسیب رساندن asib resandæn *cause injury*

4311 اعتراض کردن eʔteraz kærdæn *protest, object*

4321 برآمدن bæramædæn *rise*

4327 بافتن baftæn *weave*

4336 سپری کردن sepæri kærdæn *spend time*

4347 پی گرفتن pej gereftæn *follow up*

4356 حذف کردن hæzf kærdæn *eliminate, delete*

4361 نوشیدن nuʃidæn *drink*

4379 پیاده کردن pijade kærdæn *take apart, unload, execute*

4381 رها شدن ræha ʃodæn *be freed*

4391 رشد کردن roʃd kærdæn *grow*

4407 نابود شدن nabud ʃodæn *be destroyed*

4420 تحلیل کردن tæhlil kærdæn *analyze*

4426 ازدواج کردن ezdevadʒ kærdæn *marry*

4438 گرویدن gerævidæn *adopt a belief*

4443 دخالت کردن dexalæt kærdæn *interfere*

4459 چاپ کردن ʃap kærdæn *print*

4464 گوش دادن guʃ dadæn *listen*

4466 لازم داشتن lazem daʃtæn *need*

4474 تضمین کردن tæzmin kærdæn *guarantee*

4507 اشتباه کردن eʃtebah kærdæn *make a mistake*

4509 تحصیل کردن tæhsil kærdæn *study*

4513 گنجاندن gondʒandæn *pack, include*

4519 ملی شدن melli ʃodæn *be nationalized*

4537 گل زدن gol zædæn *score a goal*

4560 راه رفتن rah ræftæn *walk*

4580 درگذشتن dærgozæʃtæn *die*

4584 آگاه شدن agah ʃodæn *be informed*

4586 مطالعه کردن motaleʔe kærdæn *read, study*

4607 رو کردن ru kærdæn *turn to, look at*

4623 گرداندن gærdandæn *rotate, manage*

4625 حساب کردن hesab kærdæn *calculate, compute*

4633 پریدن pæridæn *jump, fly, evaporate*

4637 بحث کردن bæhs kærdæn *discuss*

4638 اثر گذاشتن æsær gozaʃtæn *impress, affect*

4647 سنجیدن sændʒidæn *measure*

4648 ترجمه شدن tærdʒome ʃodæn *be translated*

4649 تکمیل کردن tækmil kærdæn *complete*

4651 اجازه خواستن edʒaze xastæn *ask permission*

4661 برگزیدن bærgozidæn *pick*

4665 زیستن zistæn *live*

4673 گرامی داشتن gerami daʃtæn *honor*

4681 بازیافتن bazjaftæn *recycle, recover*

4687 درخواست کردن dærxast kærdæn *request*

4697 آمیختن amixtæn *mix*

4755 جنگیدن dʒængidæn *fight*

4758 کاهیدن kahidæn *decline*

4766 چرخیدن ʃærxidæn *turn*

4769 تابیدن tabidæn *shine, twist*

4771 صرف شدن særf ʃodæn *be spent, consumed, conjugated*

4772 خسته شدن xæste ʃodæn *become tired*

4794 خواهش کردن xaheʃ kærdæn *request*

4802 پیچیدن piʃidæn *twist*

4818 درخشیدن deræxʃidæn *shine*

4831 هزینه کردن hæzine kærdæn *expend*

4833 پاشیدن paʃidæn *scatter, sprinkle*

4852 هراسیدن hærasidæn *fear*

4862 کامل شدن kamel ʃodæn *be completed, perfected*

4880 انتقال دادن enteɣal dadæn *transfer*

4885 ذکر کردن zekr kærdæn *mention, cite*

4890 پنهان کردن penhan kærdæn *hide*

4936 پختن poxtæn *cook*

4958 تعلق گرفتن tæʔælloɣ gereftæn *be given to, go to*

4961 خبر داشتن xæbær daʃtæn *know, be aware*

4970 گریه کردن gerje kærdæn *weep, cry*

Taylor & Francis eBooks

Helping you to choose the right eBooks for your Library

Add Routledge titles to your library's digital collection today. Taylor and Francis ebooks contains over 50,000 titles in the Humanities, Social Sciences, Behavioural Sciences, Built Environment and Law.

Choose from a range of subject packages or create your own!

Benefits for you

» Free MARC records
» COUNTER-compliant usage statistics
» Flexible purchase and pricing options
» All titles DRM-free.

Benefits for your user

» Off-site, anytime access via Athens or referring URL
» Print or copy pages or chapters
» Full content search
» Bookmark, highlight and annotate text
» Access to thousands of pages of quality research at the click of a button.

REQUEST YOUR FREE INSTITUTIONAL TRIAL TODAY

Free Trials Available
We offer free trials to qualifying academic, corporate and government customers.

eCollections – Choose from over 30 subject eCollections, including:

Archaeology	Language Learning
Architecture	Law
Asian Studies	Literature
Business & Management	Media & Communication
Classical Studies	Middle East Studies
Construction	Music
Creative & Media Arts	Philosophy
Criminology & Criminal Justice	Planning
Economics	Politics
Education	Psychology & Mental Health
Energy	Religion
Engineering	Security
English Language & Linguistics	Social Work
Environment & Sustainability	Sociology
Geography	Sport
Health Studies	Theatre & Performance
History	Tourism, Hospitality & Events

For more information, pricing enquiries or to order a free trial, please contact your local sales team:
www.tandfebooks.com/page/sales

Routledge
Taylor & Francis Group

The home of
Routledge books

www.tandfebooks.com